Catalyst 2.0

The Brief McGraw-Hill Handbook Online Learning Center
(www.mhhe.com/bmhh) provides full coverage of writing,
researching, and editing, featuring diagnostic quizzes that
help students assess their knowledge of usage, grammar,
and mechanics. A list of print and online resources in 30
disciplines provides a starting point for student research
projects.

The site features all the resources of *Catalyst 2.0,* the
online tool for writing, research, and editing.

Catalyst
To access premium *Catalyst* content, please use the
following code:
G8JR-Y97-TTEH-9487-THW4

Catalyst 2.0 features interactive tutorials on document design and visual rhetoric, guides for avoiding plagiarism and
evaluating sources, electronic writing tutors for composing
a range of essays, and more than 4,500 exercises with feedback in grammar, usage, and punctuation.

Visit www.mhhe.com/bmhh to access a wealth of online
writing resources.

D0024824

The Brief McGraw-Hill Handbook

Elaine P. Maimon
Governors State University

Janice H. Peritz
The City University of New York, Queens College

Kathleen Blake Yancey
Florida State University

McGraw-Hill Higher Education

Boston   Burr Ridge, IL   Dubuque, IA   New York   San Francisco   St. Louis
Bangkok   Bogotá   Caracas   Kuala Lumpur   Lisbon   London   Madrid   Mexico City
Milan   Montreal   New Delhi   Santiago   Seoul   Singapore   Sydney   Taipei   Toronto

The **McGraw·Hill** Companies

McGraw-Hill
Higher Education

Published by McGraw-Hill, an imprint of The McGraw-Hill Companies, Inc., 1221 Avenue of the Americas, New York, NY 10020. Copyright © 2010. All rights reserved. No part of this publication may be reproduced or distributed in any form or by an means, or stored in a database or retrieval system, without the prior written consent of The McGraw-Hill Companies, Inc., including but not limited to, in any network or other electronic storage or transmission, or broadcast for distance learning.

This book is printed on acid-free paper.

2 3 4 5 6 7 8 9 0 DOC DOC 0 9

ISBN: 978-0-07-738920-8
MHID: 0-07-738920-4

Editor-in-Chief: *Michael Ryan*
Publisher: *David S. Patterson*
Senior Sponsoring Editor:
   Christopher Bennem
Executive Marketing Manager:
   Allison Jones
Director of Development:
   Dawn Groundwater
Development Editor: *Anne Kemper*
Editorial Coordinator:
   Jesse Hassenger
Project Manager: *Catherine Morris*

Manuscript Editor: *Thomas Briggs*
Design Manager: *Cassandra Chu*
Interior and Cover Designer:
   Maureen McCutcheon
Art Editor: *Robin Mouat*
Photo Research: *Sonia Brown*
Production Supervisor:
   Richard DeVitto
Composition: *9/11 New Century
   Schoolbook by Thompson Type*
Printing: *PMS 072, 45# Pub Matte
   Plus, R.R. Donnelley & Sons*

Cover images: (*from left to right*) *Frank Lloyd Wright Foundation, Scottsdale, AZ/Artist Rights Society (ARS), NY; Mike Nevros/Folio Inc.; Philadelphia Museum of Art/Corbis;* © *Corbis*

Credits: The credits section for this book begins on page C-1 and is considered an extension of the copyright page.

Library of Congress Control Number: 2007042475

The Internet addresses listed in the text were accurate at the time of publication. The inclusion of a Web site does not indicate an endorsement by the authors or McGraw-Hill, and McGraw-Hill does not guarantee the accuracy of the information presented at these sites.

www.mhhe.com

Preface for Students and Tutorials

The Brief McGraw-Hill Handbook will help you improve your writing in all areas of your life, whether you are taking a composition class or applying for a job. It offers help with writing across the curriculum, including developing a topic, working with print and online sources, and mastering tricky grammar rules. It also includes chapters on community service writing, business writing, multimedia presentations, and help for multilingual writers.

The first part, "Writing and Designing Papers," focuses on the writing process, from defining a topic to incorporating visuals, revising, and creating a portfolio. Part 2, "Writing in College and Beyond College," provides advice for common writing assignments, oral presentations, Web site creation, business letters, and service learning projects. Part 3, "Researching," offers a complete guide to finding and evaluating sources while avoiding plagiarism. Parts 4 and 5 present the MLA and APA documentation systems. The next three sections cover the details of usage and grammar conventions, as well as sentence punctuation, mechanics, and spelling. Part 9 provides a quick review of grammar basics. Take the online diagnostic tests on clarity, grammar, and correctness to see which topics you need to review most (see pages 299, 364, 446, and 514 for links).

We've designed this handbook for your ease of use as a quick reference. Read on to learn how to find the information you need.

Brief Contents

The Brief Contents inside the front cover lists the topics covered in this handbook. If you need help preparing a list of works cited in MLA style, you can scan the contents and find Part 4 (MLA Documentation

Style), Chapter 22 (MLA Style: List of Works Cited). You can look up the page number or use the shaded tabs on the pages to flip to "22."

Detailed Contents

For a more specific question, use the detailed contents inside the back cover. Maybe you want to find out when to use *who* vs. *whom*. If you know both are pronouns, you can find Chapter 46 (Problems with Pronouns), section d. Look up the section by page number, or find section 46d with the tabs on the pages.

Index

If you don't know that *who* and *whom* are pronouns, you can look in the index and find *who, whom*. The index will point you to pages 415–16. Use the index to find specific subjects quickly (such as blogs, pp. 135–36).

Glossary of Usage

The Glossary of Usage defines words or phrases that are commonly confused or misused (*farther* vs. *further, different than* vs. *different from*).

Documentation Directories and Flowcharts

Find out how to cite a source in MLA or APA format by using the directories or the foldout charts at the beginning of Parts 4 or 5. For proper in-text citation of a government publication in MLA style, look up "Government publication" in the directory at the beginning of Chapter 21. You will be directed to the appropriate section and page. Alternately, you can look at the flowchart and answer a series of questions.

Resources for Multilingual Students

If English is not your first language, look for the following helpful sections and features:

- Chapter 48, "Special Editing Topics for Multilingual Writers": This chapter covers a broad range of topics.
- Quick Reference for Multilingual Writers: This handy pullout card at the back of the book includes common trouble spots for multilingual writers.

- ESL Index: When you look up a term or phrase in this index, it will direct you to spots throughout the text that focus on the concerns of multilingual writers.
- "For Multilingual Students" boxes throughout the text: These boxes offer advice on culture, learning in college, writing, research, and grammar.

Features at a Glance

The sample pages to the right shows the key features of each page of the text.
Chapter number and title
Reference to *Catalyst 2.0*
Example with handwritten correction
Main heading with chapter number and section letter
Thumb tab
Exercises
Outcomes box
URL for online diagnostic quiz

The features shown on page ix will help you find the advice you need:

- The **chapter number and title** give the topic of the chapter.
- The **running head** gives the topic covered on the page.
- The **marginal reference to *Catalyst 2.0*** provides the URL for *Catalyst 2.0* and a path to follow for more information and practice exercises on the topic.
- The **main heading** includes the chapter number and section letter as well as the title of the section.
- **Examples,** many of them with hand corrections, illustrate typical errors and how to correct them.
- **Shaded thumb tabs,** each containing the number and letter of the last section on the page, and an abbreviation or symbol for that section, help you find the topic you are looking for.
- **Exercises** test your understanding of the material with a range of activities. Answers to the first three questions of each set (boldface numerals) appear in the back of the book.
- **Outcomes** listed on the back of each part title page describe the skills that section of the book supports.
- **Links** at the beginnings of Parts 6–9 direct you to online quizzes that evaluate your knowledge of editing for clarity, grammar, sentence punctuation, and mechanics and spelling.

Go Online! (www.mhhe.com/bmhh)

Throughout the text, boxes on the sides of the pages will direct you online for more information and exercises. Use the product code in the front of the book to log on. You'll find the following features:

(continued on p. x)

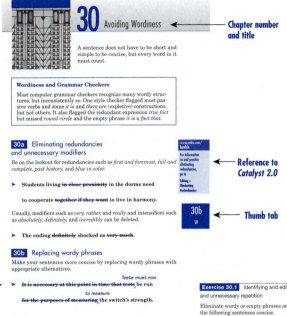

Chapter number and title →

30 Avoiding Wordiness

A sentence does not have to be short and simple to be concise, but every word in it must count.

Wordiness and Grammar Checkers

Most computer grammar checkers recognize many wordy structures, but inconsistently so. One style checker flagged most passive verbs and some *it is* and *there are* (expletive) constructions, but not others. It also flagged the redundant expression *true fact* but missed *round circle* and the empty phrase *it is a fact that*.

Main heading with chapter number and section letter →

30a Eliminating redundancies and unnecessary modifiers

Be on the lookout for redundancies such as *first and foremost, full and complete, past history,* and *blue in color.*

www.mhhe.com/bmhh
For information on and practice eliminating redundancies, go to
Editing >
Eliminating Redundancies

Reference to Catalyst 2.0 ←

➤ Students living ~~in close proximity~~ in the dorms need

to cooperate ~~together if they want~~ to live in harmony.

Usually, modifiers such as *very, rather,* and *really* and intensifiers such as *absolutely, definitely,* and *incredibly* can be deleted.

30b
w

Thumb tab ←

➤ The ending ~~definitely~~ shocked us ~~very much.~~

30b Replacing wordy phrases

Make your sentences more concise by replacing wordy phrases with appropriate alternatives.

Example with handwritten correction →

➤ ~~It is necessary at this point in time that tests~~ be run

Tests must now

~~for the purposes of measuring~~ the switch's strength.

to measure

Exercises →

Exercise 30.1 Identifying and editing wordy or empty phrases and unnecessary repetition

Eliminate wordy or empty phrases and unnecessary repetition to make the following sentences concise.

EXAMPLE

~~The truth is that the time of the~~ rainy season in Hawaii is

The

from ~~the month of~~ November to ~~the month of~~ March.

1. Charlotte Perkins Gilman was first and foremost known as a woman who was a champion of women's rights.
2. She was born on the date July 3, 1860, in the city of Hartford, which is in the state of Connecticut.
3. Gilman's "The Yellow Wallpaper," a novella about the holy matrimony of marriage and a state of madness, still speaks to contemporary readers in this present day and age.
4. The leading female heroine in Gilman's story is diagnosed by her physician husband as having an illness that is mental in origin.
5. Gilman wrote and published her book *Women and Economics* in the year 1898 and then published her book *Concerning Children* in the year 1900.

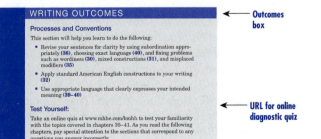

WRITING OUTCOMES

Processes and Conventions

This section will help you learn to do the following:

- Revise your sentences for clarity by using subordination appropriately (**36**), choosing exact language (**40**), and fixing problems such as wordiness (**30**), mixed constructions (**31**), and misplaced modifiers (**35**)
- Apply standard American English constructions to your writing (**32**)
- Use appropriate language that clearly expresses your intended meaning (**39–40**)

Test Yourself:

Take an online quiz at www.mhhe.com/bmhh to test your familiarity with the topics covered in chapters 30–41. As you read the following chapters, pay special attention to the sections that correspond to any questions you answer incorrectly.

Outcomes box ←

URL for online diagnostic quiz ←

- Interactive tutorials on document design and visual rhetoric
- Guides for avoiding plagiarism and evaluating sources
- Electronic writing tutors for composing informative, interpretive, and argumentative papers
- *Bibliomaker* software for the MLA, APA, Chicago, and CSE styles of documentation
- Over 4,500 exercises with feedback in grammar, usage, and punctuation
- "Test Yourself" diagnostic quizzes in editing for clarity, grammar, sentence punctuation, and mechanics and spelling
- Discipline-specific resources from the library and Internet
- Answers to all exercises in the book

Tutorials

Before you begin using this book, take a moment to complete the following tutorials. They will give you practice navigating through *The Brief McGraw-Hill Handbook* via the Brief Contents, Contents, Index, Glossary of Usage, and MLA directory or documentation flowchart. Answers appear at the back of the book.

Tutorial A: Brief Contents and Contents

Joe Green is a first-year college student writing a paper about plagiarism in college. As he writes, he wonders whether the following sentences are correct. Using the Brief Contents in the front of this book or the expanded Contents in the back, find the section of the book with the answer, and correct the sentence if necessary. List the section of the book that contains the answer.

1. Student's today face many pressures that can lead to plagiarism. [Should it be *Student's, Students,* or *Students'*?]
2. If a student paraphrases another writer's work too closely without giving the source, they have plagiarized. [Is *they* the correct pronoun to use here?]
3. Although many students do not realize it. They can plagiarize by using their own words in another writer's sentence structure. [Are these complete and correct sentences?]

4. Colleges deal with plagiarism in different ways, some expel students caught plagiarizing. Others give warnings first. [Are these complete and correct sentences?]

5. The Internet have made a variety of sources available to students. [Does the subject of this sentence agree with the verb?]

6. Students often copy source material from the Internet, but then they may confuse it with their own notes. [Is the comma in this sentence used correctly?]

7. Plagiarism-detection software be helpful to teachers. [Is there a complete verb in this sentence?]

Tutorial B: Index

Maria Hernandez is peer-reviewing the first draft of Joe's paper. She has questions about each of the following sentences. Using the index at the back of the book, find the information needed and edit the sentences appropriately.

1. The reason some students plagiarize is because they feel pressured to keep a high GPA. [Does *is because* go with *the reason*?]

2. Of the students accused of plagiarism at our school this year, none have been expelled. [Does *none* agree with *have* or *has*?]

3. In our honor code, it says students must report others who plagiarize. [Is *it* used correctly here?]

4. A student who lets other students turn in his/her work for a paper is guilty of plagiarism. [Is the use of *his/her* acceptable?]

5. A teacher once accused my friend and I of copying material from Wikipedia. [Should it be *my friend and I* or *my friend and me*?]

6. Turning in someone else's writing as your own is no different than any other type of cheating. [Is *different from* or *different than* correct?]

7. Many students do not understand plagiarism because our society excepts many forms of borrowing, such as music samples and Web site mashups. [Is *excepts* the correct word to use here?]

Tutorial C: Glossary of Usage

Joe is revising his paper based on Maria's peer review. He wants to add the following sentences. Using the Glossary of Usage, check to see if the italicized words are used correctly and fix any incorrect usage.

1. The *amount* of prominent authors accused of plagiarism has increased recently.
2. Instructors must ensure that *everyone* of their students knows how to use sources appropriately.
3. Schools should *adapt* a program of educational seminars about integrating and documenting sources.
4. Students who *flaunt* school policy by failing to document sources must be *censured*.
5. Even when unintentional, plagiarism has a negative *affect* on the academic community.
6. When writing research papers, students have to *site* their sources.

Tutorial D: MLA Documentation Directory and Flowchart

Joe is preparing the list of works cited for his paper. For each of the following sources, create an entry in MLA style using the flowchart at the beginning of Chapter 21 (p. 214) or the directory at the beginning of Chapter 22 (pp. 224–26). Arrange the entries into an appropriately formatted list of works cited.

1. A book by Ann Lathrop and Kathleen Foss titled *Student Cheating and Plagiarism in the Internet Era: A Wake-Up Call*. The book was published by Libraries Unlimited in Englewood, Colorado, in 2000.
2. An article in the online magazine *Slate* by Ann Hulbert titled "How Kaavya Got Packaged and Got into Trouble." The article was published on April 27, 2006, at http://www.slate.com/id/2140683/. Joe found this article on March 15, 2007.
3. A posting to the blog *The Wired Campus* by Brock Read titled "Are Professors to Blame for Plagiarism?" The posting was published on October 18, 2006, at http://chronicle.com/wiredcampus/index.php?id=1644. Joe read this article on March 5, 2007.

Tutorial E: Contents and Index

1. Joe wants to know what typeface and point size he should use for his paper. Where can he find this information in *The Brief McGraw-Hill Handbook*? What are the answers?

2. Joe plans to use a visual to show the increase in the reported instances of plagiarism at his school over the last three years. Would a pie chart, flowchart, or line graph illustrate this most effectively? Which section of this book should he consult?

3. Joe's professor has asked him to convert his paper into a hypertext essay. What are the two types of links a hypertext essay can contain? Which section of this book should he consult?

4. What is the best way for Joe to find library books on the topic of his paper? Which section of this book should he consult to find the answer?

5. Joe has found a Web site advocating use of a particular type of anti-plagiarism software, which is also sold on that site. The site's URL ends in ".com." Should Joe incorporate information from this site into his paper? Which section of this book should he consult to help him decide?

Preface for Instructors

When writing this book, we kept the needs of our students in mind. Today's college students don't just write papers; they create multimedia presentations. They don't just do research; they sift through a mountain of online information. They don't just read print texts; they analyze visual information of all kinds. They don't just come to class; they participate in an online learning community. *The Brief McGraw-Hill Handbook* helps meet their requirements with extensive coverage of visuals, treatment of online research and documentation, and integrated online resources.

Presenting the comprehensive instruction of *The New McGraw-Hill Handbook* in a streamlined package, *The Brief McGraw-Hill Handbook* provides students an essential, economical tool for writing in college and beyond. Students from all backgrounds will find it easy to navigate. This resource covers writing and designing papers, common assignments, business and community writing, research documentation, and plagiarism, as well as usage, grammar, mechanics, and style. Throughout the book and in a special chapter, non-native speakers of standard American English will find targeted tips and help.

In addition to covering the above topics, *The Brief McGraw-Hill Handbook* addresses the outcomes set by the Council of Writing Program Administrators in the WPA Outcomes Statement for First-Year Composition (see box for details). Each section of the book teaches multiple aspects of the skills described in the WPA Outcomes Statement. Writing Outcomes boxes at the beginning of each part highlight the ways in which that section contributes to these learning goals.

WPA Outcomes Statement for First-Year Composition

This statement was adopted by the Council of Writing Program Administrators (WPA), April 2000. For further information about the development of the Outcomes Statement, please see http://comppile.tamucc.edu/WPAoutcomes/continue.html.

For further information about the Council of Writing Program Administrators, please see http://www.wpacouncil.org. A version of this statement was published in *WPA: Writing Program Administration* 23.1/2 (fall/winter 1999): 59–66.

Introduction

This statement describes the common knowledge, skills, and attitudes sought by first-year composition programs in American postsecondary education. To some extent, we seek to regularize what can be expected to be taught in first-year composition; to this end the document is not merely a compilation or summary of what currently takes place. Rather, the following statement articulates what composition teachers nationwide have learned from practice, research, and theory. This document intentionally defines only "outcomes," or types of results, and not "standards," or precise levels of achievement. The setting of standards should be left to specific institutions or specific groups of institutions.

Learning to write is a complex process, both individual and social, that takes place over time with continued practice and informed guidance. Therefore, it is important that teachers, administrators, and a concerned public do not imagine that these outcomes can be taught in reduced or simple ways. Helping students demonstrate these outcomes requires expert understanding of how students actually learn to write. For this reason we expect the primary audience for this document to be well-prepared college writing teachers and college writing program administrators. In some places, we have chosen to write in their professional language. Among such readers, terms such as "rhetorical" and "genre" convey a rich meaning that is not easily simplified. While we have also aimed at writing a document that the general public can understand, in limited cases we have aimed first at communicating effectively with expert writing teachers and writing program administrators.

These statements describe only what we expect to find at the end of first-year composition, at most schools a required general education course or sequence of courses. As writers move beyond first-year composition, their writing abilities do not merely improve. Rather, students' abilities not only diversify along disciplinary and professional lines but also move into whole new levels where expected outcomes expand, multiply, and diverge. For this reason, each statement of outcomes for first-year composition is followed by suggestions for further work that builds on these outcomes.

Rhetorical Knowledge
By the end of first year composition, students should

- Focus on a purpose
- Respond to the needs of different audiences
- Respond appropriately to different kinds of rhetorical situations
- Use conventions of format and structure appropriate to the rhetorical situation
- Adopt appropriate voice, tone, and level of formality
- Understand how genres shape reading and writing
- Write in several genres

Faculty in all programs and departments can build on this preparation by helping students learn

- The main features of writing in their fields
- The main uses of writing in their fields
- The expectations of readers in their fields

Critical Thinking, Reading, and Writing
By the end of first year composition, students should

- Use writing and reading for inquiry, learning, thinking, and communicating
- Understand a writing assignment as a series of tasks, including finding, evaluating, analyzing, and synthesizing appropriate primary and secondary sources
- Integrate their own ideas with those of others
- Understand the relationships among language, knowledge, and power

Faculty in all programs and departments can build on this preparation by helping students learn

- The uses of writing as a critical thinking method
- The interactions among critical thinking, critical reading, and writing
- The relationships among language, knowledge, and power in their fields

Processes

By the end of first year composition, students should

- Be aware that it usually takes multiple drafts to create and complete a successful text
- Develop flexible strategies for generating, revising, editing, and proofreading
- Understand writing as an open process that permits writers to use later invention and re-thinking to revise their work
- Understand the collaborative and social aspects of writing processes
- Learn to critique their own and others' works
- Learn to balance the advantages of relying on others with the responsibility of doing their part
- Use a variety of technologies to address a range of audiences

Faculty in all programs and departments can build on this preparation by helping students learn

- To build final results in stages
- To review work-in-progress in collaborative peer groups for purposes other than editing
- To save extensive editing for later parts of the writing process
- To apply the technologies commonly used to research and communicate within their fields

Knowledge of Conventions

By the end of first year composition, students should

- Learn common formats for different kinds of texts
- Develop knowledge of genre conventions ranging from structure and paragraphing to tone and mechanics
- Practice appropriate means of documenting their work
- Control such surface features as syntax, grammar, punctuation, and spelling

Faculty in all programs and departments can build on this preparation by helping students learn

- The conventions of usage, specialized vocabulary, format, and documentation in their fields
- Strategies through which better control of conventions can be achieved [http://www.wpacouncil.org/positions/outcomes.html, accessed 9/28/2007]

To meet these requirements, we present a student-centered text, designed as a resource for achieving excellence in writing and learning in the ever-changing digital environment that students confront in college. *The Brief McGraw-Hill Handbook* responds to this environment in a number of ways.

Learning

- **A unique focus on outcomes**

  Not only does the text help students develop their rhetorical knowledge, critical-thinking skills, understanding of the writing process, and knowledge of conventions, it also provides boxes on each part-opening page to indicate to instructors how the material in that section of the book supports these writing outcomes. All of the goals from the WPA Outcomes Statement appear as terms in the index.

- **Exercises to reinforce learning**

  Most of the chapters contain a variety of exercises so students can practice the skills they are learning. Answers to the first three questions (numbers boldfaced) in each set appear in the back of the book, while answers to remaining items appear in the online Instructor's Manual. In Parts 6–9, the part-opening page contains a Web link to a special diagnostic test to help students identify their areas of weakness.

- **Emphasis on critical thinking and effective writing**

  Thinking critically and writing logically are underlying expectations across the curriculum. For this reason, the handbook begins with a chapter on critical thinking, reading, and writing. Reading text and visuals critically leads to writing critically and presenting persuasive arguments.

- **User-friendly navigation**

  Like *A Writer's Resource*, this book features a brief table of contents on the inside front cover and an expanded contents on the inside back cover. The index is designed for ease of use.

Students who do not know grammatical terminology still can tell whether to use *who* or *whom* in a given situation by looking up *who, whom.* A tutorial section in the front of the book helps students learn to use the Contents, Index, and Glossary of Usage, so they can use the book on their own as a resource.

Writing

- **Guidelines for college writing assignments and real-world writing**

  Part 2, "Writing in College and beyond College," gives students step-by-step advice on writing informative, interpretive, and argumentative essays, as well as help with essay exams, personal essays, oral presentations, and multimedia assignments (such as hypertext essays, Web sites, and blogs). Five complete student papers appear throughout as models. Since writing skills developed in college support success beyond college, we include guidelines for producing résumés as well as business letters, memos, and e-mails. A sample résumé, cover letter, and business e-mail illustrate these sections. In addition, a section on service learning opportunities offers a model brochure and newsletter.

- **Strong, integrated coverage of visual rhetoric**

  All of the chapters in Part 1, "Writing and Designing Papers," include extensive coverage of visual rhetoric. Chapters 2–4 provide advice on the selection and appropriate use of photos, charts, and graphs in papers. Chapter 1, on critical reading, thinking, and writing, integrates a discussion of the critical analysis of images with its discussion of the critical analysis of written texts. A separate chapter (Chapter 5) provides guidelines for using design to enhance written communication.

- **Real student writing**

  The Brief McGraw-Hill Handbook offers five full student papers, including samples of informative, interpretive, and argumentative writing as well as full MLA- and APA-formatted papers. We also have used student examples in the editing sections to illustrate the concerns students are most likely to have.

- **Boxes that offer support for today's diverse student population of writers**

The boxes in *The Brief McGraw-Hill Handbook* supplement the text discussion with important information and helpful advice.

Writing Outcomes: Appearing on the opening page of Parts 1–9, these boxes describe how each part of the book helps students and instructors meet the outcomes set by the Writing Program Administrators for first-year composition.

Identify and Edit: These boxes appear in key style, grammar, and punctuation chapters. They give students strategies for identifying their most serious sentence problems and are especially useful for quick reference.

Learning in College: Featured throughout the text, these boxed tips offer students information and strategies that will help them become better learners and writers.

Charting the Territory: These boxes present relevant information on such topics as interpretive assignments in different disciplines, giving students a sense of how requirements and conventions vary across the curriculum.

TextConnex: Offering advice on using electronic resources and composing on a computer, as well as lists of useful Web sites, the TextConnex boxes help today's hyperconnected students take full advantage of the technology that is available to them.

Writing after College: These boxes alert students to a variety of related writing situations beyond college.

Boxes for Multilingual Students: These boxes offer advice on learning in college, writing, and research.

Researching

- **Support for conducting research, evaluating sources, and avoiding plagiarism**

To assist students with research in the library, on the Internet, and in the field, we provide guidance on posing research questions, conducting keyword searches in the library and on the Web, and critically evaluating print and electronic sources. We also teach how to take notes on and summarize and synthesize material without plagiarizing. A list of specific resources for research assignments in thirty disciplines appears on the companion Web site.

- **Extensive documentation guides including flowcharts**

  Parts 4 (Chapters 21–25) and 5 (Chapters 26–29) include comprehensive coverage of the MLA and APA documentation styles, including detailed treatment of electronic sources. The MLA material reflects the *MLA Handbook for Writers of Research Papers, Seventhxxi Edition* (New York: MLA, 2009). Each part contains multiple examples and a complete model student paper. Foldout, decision tree-like diagrams in each section help students identify what kind of source they are dealing with and where to find the model they are looking for.

- **Visual guides for documenting sources**

  To show busy students where to find the information they need to cite their sources properly, the foldout sections in Parts 4 and 5 feature facsimile pages from books, periodicals, and Web sites that illustrate where students can find the author's name, the date of publication, and so on.

Editing

- **Grammar in the context of editing**

  The book's structure helps students organize their editing and proofreading by beginning with issues of clarity (Part 6, Chapters 30–41), moving to grammar conventions (Part 7, Chapters 42–48), and ending with the surface concerns of mechanics, punctuation, and spelling (Part 8, Chapters 49–60). A review of grammar basics appears at the end of the book (Part 9, Chapters 61–64). The Glossary of Usage (Chapter 41) lists commonly misused terms, such as *farther* and *further.*

- **Strong support for multilingual writers**

  Chapter 48 includes the grammatical topics that cause the most difficulty for non-native speakers of standard American English. The chapter also teaches multilingual students how to use writing to deal with their unique challenges. In addition, boxes with tips for multilingual writers appear throughout the text. A separate index for multilingual writers follows the main index, and the pullout Quick Reference for Multilingual Writers is easy for students to carry with them for grammar review on the go.

Technology

- **Advice on using technology**

  We provide specific, practical suggestions for using online resources to collaborate with peer reviewers and to revise; a chapter on designing documents and preparing print and online
  portfolios in Part 1 (Chapter 5); advice for writing scannable
  résumés as well as designing Web sites, producing blogs, and
  using presentation software for oral presentations in Part 2;
  help in researching and citing electronic sources in Parts 3–5;
  and TextConnex boxes with advice on technology and useful
  links throughout the text.

Supplements for *The Brief McGraw-Hill Handbook*

**Partners in Teaching: Faculty Development Web site for
Rhetoric and Composition
(www.mhhe.com/englishcommunity)**
McGraw-Hill is proud to partner with many of the top names in the field
to build a *community of teachers helping teachers. Partners in Teaching*
features up-to-date scholarly discourse, practical teaching advice, and
community support for new and experienced instructors. The site features two main parts:

- **The Teaching Comp Blog and Discussion Board**

  Moderated by Chris Anson, The Teaching Comp Blog and Discussion Board is the next stage of the successful Partners in Teaching Listserv for Composition. Join in the new topics each month
  to discuss the latest trends, strategies, and issues in composition.

- **Teaching Topic Modules**

  Created by experts, The Teaching Topics Modules explore key
  concerns in composition today. Each module contains a wealth of
  information on the topic—from an introductory Background, extensive Bibliography, practical Teaching Strategies, to helpful
  Video Mentors—in addition to downloadable resources for teaching including Handouts, PowerPoint Presentations, and Video
  Lecture Launchers. Combining the latest academic research with
  practical teaching tools, the modules provide incredible resources
  for individual instructors, graduate student programs, and professional development seminars.

Catalyst 2.0: A Tool for Writing and Research (www.mhhe.com/bmhh)

Throughout *The Brief McGraw-Hill Handbook*, Web references in the margin let students know where they can find additional resources on the text's comprehensive Web site. Access to the site—which is powered by *Catalyst 2.0*, the premier online resource for writing, research, and editing—is free with every copy of *The Brief McGraw-Hill Handbook*. The site includes the following resources for students:

- Interactive tutorials on document design and visual rhetoric
- Guides for avoiding plagiarism and evaluating sources
- Electronic writing tutors for composing informative, interpretive, and argumentative papers
- Over 4,500 exercises with feedback in grammar, usage, and punctuation
- "Test Yourself" diagnostic quizzes in editing for clarity, grammar, sentence punctuation, and mechanics and spelling
- Discipline-specific resources from the library and Internet
- Answers to all exercises in the book

Catalyst 2.0 also offers instructors a state-of-the-art course management and peer review system that allows users to do the following:

- Embed comments and links contextually alongside reviewed papers
- Create and select from lists of "favorite" comments
- Drag and drop editing abbreviations and symbols that link to *Catalyst* grammar coverage into papers
- Create and comment on multiple drafts among groups of student reviewers
- Use instructor-created review questions to respond to drafts

Instructor's Manual (available online in printable format) (www.mhhe.com/bmhh)
Deborah Coxwell Teague, Florida State University, and Dan Melzer, California State University, Sacramento

This guide contains classroom activities, suggested readings, answers to all exercises, and more.

The New McGraw-Hill Exercise Book (ISBN 0-07-326032-0)
**Santi Buscemi, Middlesex College, and Susan Popham,
University of Memphis**
Featuring numerous sentence- and paragraph-level editing exercises
as well as exercises in research, documentation, and the writing pro-
cess, this workbook can be used for any composition course.

The McGraw-Hill Exercise Book for Multilingual Writers
(ISBN 0-07-326030-4)
Maggie Sokolik, University of California, Berkeley
This workbook features numerous sentence- and paragraph-level
editing exercises tailored specifically for multilingual students.

The McGraw-Hill Writer's Journal (ISBN 0-07-326031-2)
Lynée Gaillet, Georgia State University
This elegant, spiral-bound journal for students includes quotes on
writing from famous authors as well as advice and tips on writing
and the writing process.

Dictionary and Vocabulary Resources

Merriam-Webster's Collegiate Dictionary, **Eleventh Edition**
(ISBN 978-0-877-79808-8)
The new edition of America's best-selling dictionary merges print,
CD-ROM, and online formats to deliver unprecedented accessibility
and flexibility. Fully revised content features more than 225,000
clear and precise definitions and more than 10,000 new words and
meanings. Includes an easy-to-install Windows/Macintosh CD-ROM
and a free one-year subscription to the dictionary's Web site.

The Merriam-Webster Dictionary **(paperback)**
(ISBN 978-0-877-79930-6)
This completely revised new edition of the best-selling dictionary of all
time covers the core vocabulary of everyday life. With over 75,000 definitions, pronunciations, word origins, and synonym lists, and more than
7,000 usage examples, special reference sections, and tables, the new
edition is an exceptional resource for every student.

The Merriam-Webster Thesaurus **(paperback)**
(ISBN 978-0-877-79637-4)
The new edition of this classic thesaurus features over 150,000 synonyms, antonyms, related and contrasted words, idioms, usage examples, and brief definitions describing shared meanings.

Alphabetically organized for ease of use, this best-selling guide is an excellent resource for students.

Merriam-Webster's Notebook Dictionary (ISBN 978-0-8777-9650-3)

This handy, quick-reference word resource is conveniently designed for three-ring binders. Concise, easy-to-understand definitions and pronunciations for 40,000 widely used words, combined with a brief punctuation guide, make this an excellent resource for students.

Merriam-Webster's Notebook Thesaurus (ISBN 978-0-8777-9671-8)

Conveniently designed for three-ring binders, this quick-reference compendium provides synonyms, related words, and antonyms for over 100,000 words. Special sections include prefixes and suffixes, often-confused words, and word roots.

Merriam-Webster's Dictionary and Thesaurus (ISBN 978-0-8777-9851-4)

This incredible new addition to the Merriam-Webster family features two essential references in one handy volume. Over 60,000 alphabetical dictionary entries integrated with more than 13,000 thesaurus entries, extensive synonym lists, and clear and concise word guidance with abundant example phrases make this an indispensable resource for every student.

Merriam-Webster's Vocabulary Builder (ISBN 978-0-877-79910-8)

Introducing 3,000 words and including quizzes to test progress, this excellent resource will help students improve their vocabulary skills.

Merriam-Webster's Dictionary of Basic English (ISBN 978-0-8777-9605-3)

Over 33,000 entries offer concise, easy-to-understand definitions. More than 10,000 word use examples and over 400 black-and-white illustrations as well as word histories, abbreviations, and proper names make this a great resource for multilingual students.

Acknowledgments

When we wrote *The Brief McGraw-Hill Handbook,* we started with the premise that it takes a campus to teach a writer. It is also the case that it takes a community to write a handbook. This text has been a major collaborative effort for all three of us. And over the years, that ever-widening circle of collaboration has included reviewers, editors, librarians, faculty colleagues, and family members.

Let us start close to home. Mort Maimon did line editing, checked sources, and brought to this project his years of insight and experience as a writer and as a secondary and postsecondary English teacher. Gillian Maimon, a first-grade teacher, a Ph.D. candidate, and a writing workshop leader, and Alan Maimon, a journalist who is expert in using every resource available to writers, inspired and encouraged their mother in this project. Elaine also drew inspiration from her young granddaughters, Dasia and Madison Stewart and Annabelle Elaine Maimon, who already show promise of becoming writers. Rudy Peritz and Lynne Haney reviewed drafts of a number of chapters, bringing to our cross-curricular mix the pedagogical and writerly perspectives of, respectively, a law professor and a sociologist. Jess Peritz, a recent college graduate, was consulted on numerous occasions for her expert advice on making examples both up-to-date and understandable. David, Genevieve, and Matthew Yancey—whose combined writing experience includes the fields of biology, psychology, medicine, computer engineering, mathematics, industrial engineering, and information technology—helped with examples as well as with their understanding of writing both inside and outside of the academy.

At Arizona State University West, Beverly Buddee, executive assistant to the provost, worried with us over this project for many years. Our deepest gratitude goes to Lisa Kammerlocher and Dennis Isbell for the guidelines on critically evaluating Web resources in Chapter 16, as well as to Sharon Wilson. Thanks, too, go to C. J. Jeney and Cheryl Warren for providing assistance. ASU West professors Thomas McGovern and Martin Meznar shared assignments and student papers with us. During work on this book, Denise Burger, and Christine Tullius in the Chancellor's Office at the University of Alaska Anchorage showed admirable support and patience. As the work on the handbook came to a close, Elaine was inspired by her move to the presidency of Governors State University, an institution dedicated to access for college learners of all ages.

At Queens College, several colleagues in the English department not only shared their reflections on teaching and writing, but also gave us valuable classroom materials to use as we saw fit. Our thanks go to Fred Buell, Nancy Comley, Ann Davison, Hugh English, Sue Goldhaber, Marci Goodman, Eric Lehman, Norman Lewis, Charles Molesworth, and Amy Tucker. We are especially grateful to the multitalented Steve Kruger and to the pedagogically gifted Stuart Cochran, who helped us with writing samples and class tests. The Queens College librarians also gave us various kinds of help with the researching and documentation chapters, and we thank them, especially Sharon Bonk, Alexandra DeLuise, Izabella Taler, and Manny Sanudo.

At Queens, faculty from across the curriculum sent us material to consider for the book and, in some cases, also filled out questionnaires about their own practices as researchers and writers; our thanks go to David Baker, Linda Edwards, Ray Erickson, Peg Franco, Vivian Gruder, Marty Hanlon, Elaine Klein, Michael Krasner, Joel Lidov, Jacqueline Newman, Barbara Sandler, Dean Savage, and John Troynaski. We would also like to thank countless other faculty and administrative colleagues at ASU West, at Queens College, at the University of Alaska Anchorage, and at Governors State University whose commitment to learner-centered education informs this text.

We are also grateful to the following faculty from other institutions who contributed valuable materials and advice: Jane Collins, Joan Dupre, Jane Hathaway, Beth Stickney, Jan Tecklin, Christine Timm, Stan Walker, Scott Zaluda, Diane Zannoni, and Richard Zeikowitz.

We want to give special thanks to the students whose papers we include in full: Joseph Smulowitz, Rajeev Bector, Nick Buglione, Esther Hoffman, and Audrey Galeano. We also want to acknowledge the following students who allowed us to use substantial excerpts from their work: Diane Chen, Jennifer Koehler, Ilona Bouzoukashvili, Wilma Ferrarella, Jacob Grossman, and Umawattie Roopnarian. Our thanks also go to Judy Williamson and Trent Batson for contributing their expertise on writing and computers as well as for sharing what they learned from the Epiphany Project. We also thank Rich Rice of Texas Tech for reviewing the technology coverage and for suggesting the image interpretation assignment in Chapter 11, as well as Dene Grigar of Texas Woman's University, Donna Reiss of Tidewater Community College, Cheryl Ball of Utah State University, and Elizabeth Nist of Anoka-Ramsey Community College for their advice on technology and for suggestions in the chapter on multimedia assignments. We are grateful to Harvey Wiener and the late Richard Marius for their permission to draw on their explanations of grammatical points in the *McGraw-Hill Handbook*. We also appreciate the work of Andras Tapolcai and Charlotte Smith of Adirondack Community College, who collected many of the examples used in the documentation chapters, and of Maria Zlateva,

Boston University, our ESL consultant. Thanks also go to librarians Debora Person, University of Wyoming, and Ronelle K. H. Thompson, Augustana College, who provided us with helpful comments on Part 3, "Researching." Our colleague Don McQuade has inspired us, advised us, and encouraged us throughout the years of this project.

Within the McGraw-Hill organization, many wonderful people have been our true teammates. Tim Julet believed in this project initially and signed us on to what has become a major life commitment. From 1999, Lisa Moore, first as executive editor for the composition list, then as publisher for English, and now as publisher for art, humanities, and literature, has creatively, expertly, and tirelessly led the group of development editors and in-house experts who have helped us find the appropriate form to bring our insights as composition teachers to the widest possible group of students. We have learned a great deal from Lisa. Thanks also to Christopher Bennem, who had the unenviable job of filling Lisa's shoes as sponsoring editor. This book has benefited enormously from three extraordinary editors: Anne Kemper, development editor; Carla Samodulski, senior development editor; and David Chodoff, senior development editor. All were true collaborators; as the chapters on editing show, the book has benefited enormously from their care and intelligence. Other editorial kudos go out to Margaret Manos, Molly Meneely, and Betty Chen for their tireless work on this project, as well to Paul Banks and Alex Rohrs, without whom there would be no *Catalyst 2.0*. Catherine Morris, project manager, monitored every detail of production; Cassandra Chu, senior designer, supervised every aspect of the striking text design and cover; and Robin Mouat, art editor, was responsible for the stunning visuals that appear throughout the book. Tami Wederbrand, marketing manager and Ray Kelley, Paula Radosevich, Byron Hopkins, Audra Bussey, and Brian Gore, field publishers, have worked tirelessly and enthusiastically to market *The Brief McGraw-Hill Handbook*. Jeff Brick provided valuable promotional support for the project. We also appreciate the hands-on attention of McGraw-Hill senior executives Mike Ryan, editor-in-chief of the Humanities, Social Science, and Languages group; and Steve Debow, president of the Humanities, Social Science, and Languages group.

Finally, many, many thanks go to the reviewers who read various versions of this text, generously shared their perceptions, and had confidence in us as we shaped this book to address the needs of their students. We wish to thank the following instructors:

David Beach, George Mason University; Evelyn Beck, Piedmont Technical College; Monica Bosson, Community College of San Francisco;

Polly Buckingham, Eastern Washington University; Mary Cassidy, South Carolina State University; Peter Caster, University of South Carolina Upstate; Gilman Chandler, Lyndon State College; Brenda Davenport, University of South Carolina Upstate; John Delgado, Community College of San Francisco; Michael Donnelly, University of Tampa; Doug Downs, Utah Valley State College; Taylor Emery; Austin Peay State University; Lauren Faulkenberry, Western Carolina University; Alyce Frankenhoff, Cincinnati State and Technical Community College; Maurice Gandy, University of South Alabama—Mobile; Audley Hall, Northwest Arkansas Community College; Beth Huber, Western Carolina University; Barbara Jaffe, El Camino College; Robert Jakubovic, Cincinnati State Technical and Community College; Alex Johns, Gainesville State College; Joseph Justice, South Plains College; Glenn Klopfestein, Passaic County Community College; Belinda Kremer, Long Island University—C.W. Post Campus; Jill Lahnstein, Cape Fear Community College; Jennifer Lee, University of Pittsburgh—Pittsburgh; Nathan Leslie, North Virginia Community College—Loudoun Campus; Andrea Luna, Lyndon State College; Joyce Malek, University of Cincinnati; Denice Martone, New York University; Kathleen Mayberry, Lehigh Carbon Community College; Rebecca Millan, South Texas College; Jamie Moore, Scottsdale Community College; Samuel Prestridge, Gainesville State College; Chuck Ramshaw, Santa Ana College; James Rawlins, Sussex County Community College; Peggy Richards, University of Akron; John Ritz, University of Pittsburgh—Johnstown; Al Romano, Ramapo College of New Jersey; Emmanuel Sigauke, Cosumnes River College; Rebecca Steward, Eastern Washington University; Connie Wasem, Spokane Falls Community College; Gayle Williamson, Cuyahoga Community College.

Elaine P. Maimon
Janice H. Peritz
Kathleen Blake Yancey

About the Authors

Elaine P. Maimon is President of Governors State University in the south suburbs of Chicago, where she is also Professor of English. Previously, she was Chancellor of the University of Alaska Anchorage, Provost (Chief Executive Campus Officer) at Arizona State University West, and Vice President of Arizona State University as a whole. In the 1970s, she initiated and then directed the Beaver College writing-across-the-curriculum program, one of the first WAC programs in the nation. A founding Executive Board member of
the National Council of Writing Program Administrators (WPA), she has directed national institutes to improve the teaching of writing and to disseminate the principles of writing across the curriculum. With a PhD in English from the University of Pennsylvania, where she later helped to create the Writing across the University (WATU) program, she has also taught and served as an academic administrator at Haverford College, Brown University, and Queens College.

Janice Haney Peritz is an Associate Professor of English who has taught college writing for more than thirty years, first at Stanford University, where she received her PhD in 1978, and then at the University of Texas at Austin; Beaver College; and Queens College, City University of New York. From 1989 to 2002, she directed the Composition Program at Queens College, where in 1996 she also initiated the college's writing-across-the-curriculum program and the English Department's involvement with the Epiphany
Project and cyber-composition. She also worked with a group of CUNY colleagues to develop The Write Site, an online learning center, and more recently directed the CUNY Honors College at Queens College for three years. Currently, she is back in the English Department doing what she loves most: full-time classroom teaching of writing, literature, and culture.

Kathleen Blake Yancey is the Kellogg W. Hunt Professor of English and Director of the Graduate Program in Rhetoric and Composition at Florida State University. Past President of the Council of Writing Program Administrators (WPA) and past Chair of the Conference on College Composition and Communication (CCCC), she is President-Elect of the National Council of Teachers of English (NCTE). In addition, she codirects the Inter/National Coalition on Electronic Portfolio Research. She has directed several institutes focused  on electronic portfolios and on service learning and reflection, and with her colleagues in English education, she is working on developing a program in new literacies. Previously, she taught at UNC Charlotte and at Clemson University, where she directed the Pearce Center for Professional Communication and created the Class of 1941 Studio for Student Communication, both of which are dedicated to supporting communication across the curriculum.

INTRODUCTION Writing to Learn

College is a place for exploration. During your studies, you will travel through many courses, participating in numerous conversations—oral and written—about nature, society, and culture. As you navigate your college experience, use this book as your map and guide:

- **As a map:** This text will help you understand the different approaches to knowledge you may encounter as you move from course to course and see how your studies relate to the larger world of learning.

- **As a guide:** This text will help you write everything from notes to exams to research papers—the record of your participation in the culture of your campus.

1a Studying a range of academic disciplines

www.mhhe.com/
bmhh
For discipline-
related
resources, go to
Learning > Links
across the
Curriculum

Each department in your college represents a specialized field of academic study, or area of inquiry, called a **discipline.** Each discipline has its own history, terminology, and concerns. Sociology, for example, is concerned with the conditions, patterns, and problems of people in groups and societies. Sociologists collect, analyze, and interpret data about groups and societies; they also debate the data's reliability and the credibility of various ways to interpret the data. These debates occur in journals, books, conferences, and classrooms—sites where knowledge is produced and communicated.

Each discipline is composed of diverse communities or social groups. For example, all economists do not see and say things in the same way. Although they belong to the same discipline—the discipline of economics—economists identify with various groups within their discipline based on their approaches to economic theory.

Your college curriculum is likely to include distribution requirements that will expose you to a range of disciplines. You may be asked to take one or two courses in the humanities (the disciplines of literature, music, and philosophy, for example), the social sciences (sociology, economics, and psychology, for example), and the natural sciences (physics, biology, and chemistry, for example). When you write in each discipline—taking notes, writing papers, answering essay exam questions—you will deepen your understanding of how knowledge is constructed. In doing so, you will join the academic conversation. You will also learn to see and think about the world from different vantage points.

CHARTING the TERRITORY

Getting the Most from a Course

When you take a course, your purpose is not just to amass information about this or that topic. Your purpose is also to understand the kinds of questions people who work in the discipline ask.

- In an art history class, you might ask how a work relates to an artist's life and times.
- In a math class, you might ask what the practical applications of a particular concept are.
- In a sociology class, you might ask how race or gender relate to income.

www.mhhe.com/
bmhh

For activities to
help strengthen
your active
reading skills,
go to

**Learning > Writing
to Learn Exercises**

1b Using writing as a tool for learning

One important goal of this handbook is to help you research and write your papers. As you go from course to course, however, remember that writing itself is a great aid to learning. Travelers often keep journals and write letters, e-mails, and blogs to record what they have seen, heard, and done; to react to their experiences; and to reflect on the meaning of it all. Think of how a simple shopping list aids your memory once you get to the store or how taking minutes in a meeting focuses your attention. Writing helps you remember, understand, and create.

- **Writing aids memory.** From taking class notes to jotting down ideas for later development, writing ensures that you will be able to retrieve important information. Many students find it useful to use an informal outline for lecture notes (*see Figure I.1*) and then go back and fill in details after class. Also write down ideas inspired by your course work—in any form or order—so that you won't forget them. These ideas can be seeds for research projects or some other critical inquiry.

- **Writing sharpens observations.** When you record what you see, hear, taste, smell, and feel, you increase the powers of your senses. Write down each place where a flute is heard in a piece of music, and you will hear the instrument more clearly. Note the smells during a chemistry experiment, and you will detect changes caused by reactions more readily.

- **Writing clarifies thought.** "How do I know what I think until I see what I say?" The writer E. M. Forster's oft-quoted question reminds us that we frequently write our way into a topic. Carefully reading your own early drafts helps you pinpoint what you

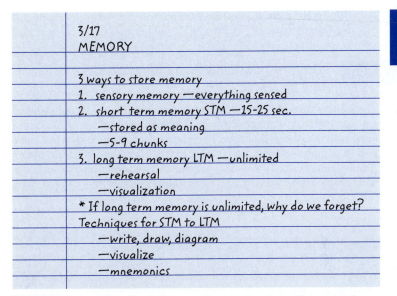

FIGURE I.1 An outline for lecture notes. Jotting down the main ideas of a lecture and the questions they raise helps you become a more active listener.

really want to say. Often, the last paragraph of a first draft becomes the first paragraph of the next one.

- **Writing uncovers connections.** Maybe a character in a short story reminds you of your next-door neighbor, or an image in a poem makes you feel sad. What is it about your next-door neighbor that is similar to the fictional character? What is it about the image that evokes memories of loss? If you write down answers to these questions, you will learn more about the short story and the poem, and possibly more about yourself.

- **Writing improves reading.** When you read, taking notes on the main ideas and drafting a brief summary of the writer's points sharpens your reading skills and helps you retain what you have read. Writing a personal reaction to the reading enhances your understanding.

- **Writing strengthens argument.** In the academic disciplines, an **argument** is not a fiery disagreement but rather a path of reasoning to a position. When you write an argument, you work out the connections between your ideas—sometimes uncovering flaws that force you to rethink your position, and other times finding new connections that make your position even stronger. Writing also requires you to consider your audience and the objections they might raise.

www.mhhe.com/
bmhh

For help with
college survival
techniques,
go to

**Learning > Study
Skills Tutor**

1c Taking responsibility for reading, writing, and research

The college academic community assumes that you are an independent learner, capable of managing your workload without supervision. For most courses, the syllabus will be your primary guide to what is expected of you, serving as a contract between you and your instructor. The syllabus will tell you what reading you need to do before each class, when tests are scheduled, and when papers or stages of papers (topic

---

Tips LEARNING in COLLEGE

Whether academic pursuits are a struggle or come easily to you, whether you are fresh out of high school or are returning to school many years after high school graduation, college is a challenge. Here are a few hints and strategies to help you succeed.

- **Make the most of your time by setting clear priorities.** Deal with surprises by saying "no," getting away from it all, taking control of phone and e-mail interruptions, and leaving slack in your schedule to accommodate the unexpected.

- **Evaluate the information you gather.** Consider how authoritative the source is, whether the author has any potential biases, how recent the information is, and whether anything important is missing from the research. In college, critical thinking is essential.

- **Take good notes.** The central feature of good note taking is listening and distilling important information—not writing down everything that is said.

- **Build reading and listening skills.** When you read, identify the main ideas, prioritize them, think critically about the arguments, and explain the writer's ideas to someone else. Listen actively: focus on what is being said, pay attention to nonverbal messages, listen for what is not being said, and take notes.

- **Improve your memory.** Rehearsal is the key strategy in remembering information. Repeat the information, summarize it, associate it with other memories, and above all, think about it when you first come across it.

Source: Based on Robert S. Feldman, *P.O.W.E.R. Learning: Strategies for Success in College and Life,* 2nd ed. (New York: McGraw-Hill, 2003).

and research plan, draft, final paper) are due. Use the syllabus to map out your weekly schedule for reading, research, and writing. (*For tips on how to schedule a research paper, see Chapter 13, p. 157.*)

If you are collaborating on a project, it is essential to schedule a series of meetings well in advance to avoid calendar conflicts. It is just as important, however, to plan time for your solo projects away from all distractions. You will be much more efficient if you work in shorter blocks of concentrated time than if you let your reading and writing drag on for interruption-filled hours.

Id Recognizing that writing improves with practice

Composition courses will help you learn to write at the college level, but your development as a writer does not end there. Writing in all your courses will enable you to mature as a writer while preparing you for more writing after college.

Birds Wild life & Habitat

I like to do first drafts at night, when I'm tired, and then do the surgical work in the morning when I'm sharp.

—ALEX HALEY

Writing and Designing Papers

1 Writing and Designing Papers

WRITING OUTCOMES

Processes

This section will help you learn to do the following:

- Understand and engage in the writing process, from prewriting strategies **(2b)** through drafting **(3)** as well as revision and editing **(4)**

- Review the work of classmates and receive response to your own writing **(4a)**

- Use technology to aid in drafting **(3a)**, revising **(4b, 4j)**, and visually designing documents **(5b)**

Writers get intellectually involved. They recognize that meanings and values are made, not found, so they take what they read, see, and hear critically. They pose pertinent questions, note significant features, and examine the credibility of various kinds of texts.

Advances in technology have made it easier than ever to obtain information in a variety of ways. It is essential to be able to "read" critically not just written texts but visuals, sounds, and spoken texts as well. We use the word *text,* then, to refer to works that readers, viewers, or listeners invest with meaning and that can be critically analyzed.

1a Reading critically

1. Preview

Critical reading begins with **previewing**—a quick review of the author, publication information, title, headings, visuals, and key sentences or paragraphs.

Previewing written texts Whenever possible, ask questions about the following:

- **Author:** Who wrote this piece? What are the writer's credentials? Who is the writer's employer? What is the writer's occupation? Age? What are his or her interests and values?

- **Purpose:** What do the title and first and last paragraphs tell you about the purpose of this piece? Do the headings and visuals provide clues to its purpose? What might have motivated the author to write it? Is the main purpose to inform, to interpret, to argue, to entertain, or is it something else?

- **Audience:** Who is the author trying to inform or persuade? Is the author addressing you or readers like you?

- **Content:** What does the title tell you about the piece? Does the first paragraph include the main point? What do the headings tell you about the gist of the piece? Does the conclusion say what the author has focused on?

- **Context:** Is the publication date current? Does the date matter? What kind of publication is it? Where and by whom was it published? If it has been published electronically, was it posted by the author? By an organization with a special interest?

www.mhhe.com/ bmhh

For help with evaluating sources, go to

Research > CARS Source Evaluation Tutor

FIGURE 1.1 ACLU advertisement. The text superimposed on this photograph reads: "I AM NOT AN AMERICAN WHO BELIEVES WE SHOULD ALL HAVE THE SAME OPINIONS. I AM AN AMERICAN who believes that our right to have lively discussion and thorough investigation are the things that make our country great. I AM AN ACLU MEMBER because free speech is the foundation of freedom. Keep America SAFE & FREE. SIGN ON AT: WWW.ACLU.ORG."

Previewing visuals You can use most of the previewing questions for written texts to preview visuals. You should also ask some additional questions, however. For example, suppose you were asked to preview the advertisement shown in Figure 1.1. Here are some preview questions you might ask:

- In what context does the visual appear?
- Does the visual consist of a single image, or is it part of a series of images?
- Is it a representation of a real event, person, or thing, or is it fictional?
- What does the visual depict?
- Is the visual accompanied by audio or printed text?

2. Reading and recording initial impressions

Read the selection for its literal meaning. Identify the main topic and the main point the writer makes about the topic. Read the work in one sitting if possible. Note difficult passages to come back to as well as ideas that grab your attention. Record your initial impressions:

1a
crit

- If the text or image is an argument, what opinion is being expressed? Were you persuaded by the argument?
- Did you have an emotional response to the text or image? Were you surprised, amused, or angered by anything in it?
- What was your initial sense of the writer or speaker?
- What key ideas did you take away from the work?

Exercise 1.1   Preview and first reading of an essay

Find an article that interests you in a newspaper or magazine, preview it using the questions on page 4, then read through it in one sitting and record your initial impressions using the questions above.

Exercise 1.2   First reading of a visual

Spend some time looking at the image and text for the ACLU ad in Figure 1.1. Record your responses to the following questions:

1. Did you have an emotional response to the ad?
2. What opinion, if any, did you have of the spokesperson (the actor Kristin Davis, from the television series *Sex and the City*) before you read the ad? What opinion do you have of her now?
3. What opinion, if any, did you have of the ACLU before you read the ad? Has your opinion changed in any way as a result of the ad?
4. What key ideas does the ad present?

3. Using annotation and summary to analyze a text

Once you understand the literal or surface meaning of a text, dig deeper by analyzing and interpreting it.

Using annotation and summary   **Annotation** combines reading with analysis. To annotate a text, read through it slowly and carefully while asking yourself the *who, what, how,* and *why* questions. As you read, underline or make separate notes about words, phrases, and sentences that strike you as significant or puzzling, and write down questions and observations.

SAMPLE ANNOTATED PASSAGE   *Opens with a story about his childhood*

Establishes his author-ity —he's experienced multi-culturalism

Both my parents were immigrants from Russia. In my neighborhood, Yiddish was a first and second language. I grew up in the depths of the Great Depression. There were weeks when my father came home with $5 or less. My mother walked blocks to save a few cents on food.

I went to public school. Some of my friends were sent to the yeshiva—an Orthodox Jewish religious school—but my parents, having experienced the vicious, pervasive anti-Semitism in the Old Country, wanted me to learn what America was all about.

Supreme Court. Does he assume they would inspire everyone?

At Boston Latin School and Northeastern University—a working-class college—I took classes that taught a great deal about the fundamental rights and liberties that had to be fought for during this still "unfinished American revolution," as Thurgood Marshall called it. These were required courses, and inspired my lifelong involvement in civil rights and civil liberties.

—NAT HENTOFF, "Misguided Multiculturalism"

A **summary** conveys the basic content of a text. When you summarize, your goal is to communicate the text's main points in your own words. A summary of an essay or article is typically about one paragraph in length. Although writing a summary requires simplification, be careful to avoid misrepresenting a writer's points by oversimplifying them.

Here are some suggestions for approaching the task:

- **Write down the text's main point.** Compose a sentence that identifies the text, the writer, the approach (reports, explores, analyzes, argues), and the key point the writer makes about the topic.

- **Divide the text into sections.** To develop the main point, writers move from one subtopic to another or from the statement of an idea to the reasons, evidence, and examples that support it. If you own the text, annotate it to indicate where sections begin and end.

- **In one or two sentences, sum up what each of the text's sections says.** When you summarize, you in effect compose your own topic sentence for each major section of the text. If you own the text, highlight key sentences in each section to help focus your summary.

- **Combine your sentence stating the writer's main point with the sentences summarizing each of the text's major sections.** Now you have a summary of your source. (*For specific examples of summaries, see Chapter 19, pp. 202–3.*)

Questioning the text   Analysis and interpretation require a critical understanding of the *who, what, how,* and *why* of a text:

- **What is the writer's *stance*, or attitude toward the subject?** Does the writer appear to be objective, or does she or he seem to have personal feelings about the subject?

- **What is the writer's *voice?*** Is it like that of a reasonable judge, an enthusiastic preacher, or a reassuring friend?
- **What assumptions does the writer seem to be making about the audience?** Does the writer assume that the reader agrees with him or her, or does the writer try to build agreement? Does the writer seem to choose examples and evidence with a certain audience in mind?
- **What is the writer's primary purpose?** Is it to present findings, offer an objective analysis, or argue for a particular action or opinion?
- **How does the writer develop ideas?** Does the writer define key terms? Include supporting facts? Tell relevant stories? Provide logical reasons?
- **Does the text appeal to emotions?** Does the writer use words, phrases, clichés, images, or examples that are emotionally charged?
- **Is the text fair?** Does the writer consider opposing ideas, arguments, or evidence? Does he or she deal with them fairly?
- **Is the evidence strong?** Does the writer provide sufficient evidence for his or her position?
- **Is the text effective?** Have your beliefs on this subject been changed by the text?

Visuals, too, can be subjected to critical analysis, as the comments a reader made on the ACLU ad indicate (*see Figure 1.2*).

4. Synthesizing your observations in a critical-response paper

To **synthesize** means to bring together, to make something out of different parts. In the last stage of critical reading, you pull your summary, analysis, and interpretation together into a coherent whole.

Exercise 1.3   Analyzing and summarizing a visual

Add to the annotated analysis of the ACLU ad in Figure 1.2, focusing on the text as well as the photograph. Summarize the content and message of the ad. Using this summary and analysis, write a critical response to the ACLU ad.

1b   Thinking critically

Critical thinkers never simply gather information and present it without question. They inquire about what they see, hear, and read. They evaluate a text's argument in order to figure out its strengths and weaknesses.

Davis is projecting a serious image, and she's dressed very plainly. She looks directly at the camera, directly at the viewer.

She seems to be in a dangerous place, a tunnel entrance with a car whizzing by, at night on a slippery road—but she is unafraid. Does her statement require bravery?

Davis's character "Charlotte" is associated with New York City, and this seems to be a NYC scene. Is there a 9/11 connection?

Black and white—like photojournalism—"real," "serious."

Why are these words emphasized?

FIGURE 1.2 Sample annotations on the ACLU ad.

1. Recognizing an argument

An **argument** means a path of reasoning aimed at persuading people to accept or reject an assertion. The assertion must be arguable: it must be on an issue about which reasonable people can disagree. For example, the assertion that women should be allowed to try out for all college sports teams is arguable.

2. Analyzing and evaluating an argument

There are a number of ways to analyze an argument and evaluate its effectiveness. Two common methods are (1) to concentrate on the type of reasoning the writer is using and (2) to question the logical relation of a writer's claims, grounds, and warrants, using the Toulmin method.

Types of reasoning   When writers use inductive reasoning to make an argument, they do not prove that the argument is true; instead, they convince reasonable people that it is probable by presenting evidence (facts and statistics, anecdotes, and expert opinion). When writers use **deductive reasoning,** they are making the claim that a conclusion follows necessarily from a set of assertions, or premises—in other words, that if the premises are true, the conclusion must be true.

For example, a journalism student writing for the school paper might make the following assertion:

> As Saturday's game shows, the Buckeyes are on their way to winning the Big Ten title.

If the student is reasoning inductively, she will present a number of facts—her evidence—that support her claim but do not prove it conclusively:

FACT 1   With three games remaining, the Buckeyes have a two-game lead over the second-place Badgers.

FACT 2   The Buckeyes' final three opponents have a combined record of 10 wins and 17 losses.

FACT 3   The Badgers lost their two star players to season-ending injuries last week.

FACT 4   The Buckeyes' last three games will be played at home, where they are undefeated this season.

A reader would evaluate this student's argument by judging the quality of her evidence, using the criteria listed in the "Tips" box.

Tips   LEARNING in COLLEGE

Assessing Evidence in an Inductive Argument

- **Is it accurate?** Make sure that any facts presented as evidence are correct.
- **Is it relevant?** Check to see if the evidence is clearly connected to the point being made.
- **Is it representative?** Make sure that the writer's conclusion is supported by evidence gathered from a sample that accurately reflects the larger population (for example, it has the same proportion of men and women, older and younger people, and so on). If the writer is using an example, make sure that the example is typical and not a unique situation.
- **Is it sufficient?** Evaluate whether there is enough evidence to satisfy questioning readers.

Inductive reasoning is a feature of the **scientific method.** Scientists gather data from experiments, surveys, and careful observations to formulate hypotheses—arguments—that explain the data. Then they test their hypotheses by collecting additional information.

Now suppose the journalism student is using deductive reasoning in an article about great baseball teams; in that case, the truth of her conclusion will depend on the truth of her premises:

PREMISE | Any baseball team that wins the World Series more than twenty-five times in a hundred years is one of the greatest teams in history.

PREMISE | The New York Yankees have won the World Series more than twenty-five times in the past hundred years.

CONCLUSION | The New York Yankees are one of the greatest baseball teams in history.

This is a deductive argument: if its premises are true, its conclusion must be true. To challenge the argument, a reader has to evaluate the premises. Do you think, for example, that the number of World Series wins is a proper measure of a team's greatness? If not, then you could claim that the first premise is false and does not support the conclusion.

The Toulmin method   Philosopher Stephen Toulmin's analysis of arguments is based on claims (assertions about a topic), grounds (reasons and evidence), and warrants (assumptions or principles that link the grounds to the claims).

Consider the following sentence from an argument by a student:

The death penalty should be abolished because innocent people could be executed.

This example, like all logical arguments, has three facets:

■ **The argument makes a claim.** A **claim** is the same thing as a point or a thesis: it is an assertion about a topic. A strong claim responds to an issue of real interest to an audience in clear, precise terms. It also allows for some uncertainty by including qualifying words such as *might* or *possibly*. A weak claim is merely a statement of fact or a statement that few would argue with. Personal feelings are not debatable and thus are not an appropriate claim for an argument.

WEAK CLAIMS | The death penalty is highly controversial.

The death penalty makes me sick.

■ **The argument presents grounds for the claim.** Here, **grounds** consist of the reasons and evidence (facts and statistics, anecdotes, and expert opinion) that support the claim. A strong argument relies on evidence that is varied, relevant to the claim, and sufficient to support the claim. As grounds for the claim in the example, the student would present anecdotes and statistics related to innocent people being executed. The following box should help you assess the evidence supporting a claim.

TYPES of EVIDENCE for CLAIMS

■ **Facts and statistics:** Facts and statistics can be convincing support for a claim. Be aware, however, that people on different sides of an issue can interpret the same facts and statistics differently or can cite different facts and statistics to support their point.

■ **Anecdotes:** An anecdote is a brief story used as an illustration to support a claim. Stories appeal to the emotions as well as to the intellect and can be very effective in making an argument. Be especially careful to check anecdotes for logical fallacies (*see pp. 12–13*).

■ **Expert opinion:** The views of authorities in a given field can also be powerful support for a claim. Check that the expert cited has proper credentials to comment on the issue.

■ **The argument depends on assumptions that link the grounds to the claim.** When you analyze an argument, be aware of the unstated assumptions, or **warrants,** that underlie both the claim and the grounds that support it. The warrants underlying the example argument against the death penalty include the idea that it is not possible to be completely sure of a person's guilt.

As you read the writings of others and as you write yourself, look for unstated assumptions. What does the reader have to assume—take for granted—to accept the evidence in support of the claim? In particular, hidden assumptions sometimes show **bias**—positive or negative inclinations that can manipulate unwary readers.

3. Recognizing common logical fallacies
In their enthusiasm to make a point, writers sometimes commit errors called fallacies, or mistakes in logic. Use the box on pages 12–13 to help you identify fallacies when you read and avoid them when you write.

COMMON LOGICAL FALLACIES

- **Non sequitur:** A conclusion that does not logically follow from the evidence presented or one that is based on irrelevant evidence: "Students who default on their student loans have no sense of responsibility." [*Students who default on loans could be faced with high medical bills or prolonged unemployment.*]

- **False cause:** An argument that falsely assumes that because one thing happens after another, the first event was a cause of the second event. Also known as *post hoc:* "I drank green tea and my headache went away: therefore, green tea makes headaches go away." [*How do we know that the headache didn't go away for another reason?*]

- **False analogy:** A comparison in which a surface similarity masks a significant difference: "Governments and businesses both work within a budget to accomplish their goals. Just as business must focus on the bottom line, so should government." [*Is the goal of government to make a profit? Or does government have other, more important goals?*]

- **Red herring:** An argument that diverts attention from the true issue by concentrating on something irrelevant: "Hemingway's book *Death in the Afternoon* is not successful because it glorifies the brutal sport of bullfighting." [*Why can't a book about a brutal sport be successful? The statement is irrelevant.*]

- **Begging the question:** A form of circular reasoning that assumes the truth of a questionable opinion: "The president's poor relationship with the military has weakened the armed forces." [*Does the president really have a poor relationship with the military?*]

- **Hasty generalization:** A conclusion based on inadequate evidence: "Temperatures across the United States last year exceeded the fifty-year average by two degrees, thus proving that global warming is a reality." [*Is this evidence enough to prove this very broad conclusion?*]

- **Bandwagon:** An argument that depends on going along with the crowd, on the false assumption that truth can be determined by a popularity contest: "Everybody knows that Toni Morrison is preoccupied with the theme of death in her novels." [*How do we know that "everybody" agrees with this statement?*]

- **Ad hominem:** A personal attack on someone who disagrees with you rather than on the person's argument: "The district attorney is a lazy political hack, so naturally she opposes streamlining the court system." [*Even if the district attorney usually supports her party's position, does that make her wrong about this issue?*]

- **Circular reasoning:** An argument that restates the point rather than supporting it with reasonable evidence: "The wealthy should pay more taxes because taxes should be higher for people with higher incomes." [*Why should wealthy people pay more taxes? The rest of the statement doesn't answer this question; it just restates the position.*]

- **Either/or fallacy:** The idea that a complicated issue can be resolved by resorting to one of only two options when in reality there are additional choices: "Either the state legislature will raise taxes or our state's economy will falter." [*Are there really only two possibilities?*]

Exercise 1.4   Analyzing and summarizing an article

Reread the article you selected for Exercise 1.1, analyzing it with annotations or in separate notes. Now summarize the article. What claims does it make and how does it support them?

Exercise 1.5   Recognizing warrants

For each of the following claims, identify one or more underlying warrants (assumptions).

1. College students should have fewer required courses and more electives, because they should have more control over their own education.
2. The drinking age should be lowered to eighteen because that is the legal age for voting and serving in the military.
3. The United States should intervene in areas of the world where humanitarian crises exist because we are the strongest country in the world and should set an example for other nations.
4. To reduce the rate of global warming, the government should offer tax credits to consumers who buy hybrid cars.
5. The new sports arena should not be built because it will reduce the amount of parkland in the community.

1c   Writing critically

In college, you will gain practice in addressing issues that are important in the larger community. Selecting a topic that you care about will give you the energy to think matters through and to make cogent arguments. Of course, you will have to go beyond your personal feelings about an issue to make the most convincing case. You will also have to empathize with potential readers who may disagree with you about something that is important to you. (*For more help with writing arguments, see Chapter 8, pp. 101–11.*)

1. Finding a topic worth writing about

Arguments occur in the context of debate and usually concern one or more of the following questions:

- What is true?
- What is good?
- What is to be done?

Your purpose in presenting your position to others is not to win but to take part in the discussion about the issue. As you present your argument, keep in mind that reasonable people can see things differently. Acknowledge and respect the views of others. Negotiating differences should become part of your purpose.

2. Making a strong claim

Advancing a strong, debatable thesis on a topic of interest to the discipline or to the public is key to writing a successful argument. Keep in mind, however, that writing itself is a tool for thinking through your position on an issue. As you think, write, and learn about your topic, you will develop, clarify, and sometimes entirely change your views.

Your personal feelings are not open to debate and so cannot serve as the thesis for an argument. If you write, "I feel that life in the ghetto is dangerous," there is nothing to debate because you are saying something about yourself rather than about the ghetto. But when William Julius Wilson writes, in his article "When Work Disappears," that "joblessness in the ghetto is not a result of welfare dependency," he is making a debatable claim on an issue of real concern. (*For more on theses, see Chapter 2, pp. 23–26.*)

3. Supporting and developing your claim with evidence

The intelligent selection and careful documentation of evidence—facts and statistics, anecdotes, and expert opinion—will determine whether you make a credible case. (*The box on p. 11 describes three types of evidence writers use to support their claims.*)

- **Facts and statistics:** In the article "When Work Disappears," Wilson argues that joblessness prevails in so many inner-city neighborhoods because jobs have disappeared from the ghetto. Wilson supports this claim with the following facts:

In the neighborhood of Woodlawn, on the South Side of Chicago, there were more than 800 commercial and industrial establishments in 1950. Today, it is estimated that only 100 are left.

- **Anecdotes:** In his article, Wilson uses quotations from long-term residents in several urban ghettos in Chicago. These residents contrast life in their neighborhoods today to local employment opportunities in the 1950s.

- **Expert opinion:** Wilson cites a former secretary of labor to support the claim that educational reform is part of the solution to the problem of joblessness:

  Ray Marshall, former secretary of labor, points out that Japan and Germany have developed policies designed to increase the number of workers with "higher-order thinking skills."

In well-written arguments, reasoning often relies on research. As you find and read a variety of sources, you will figure out your claim and gather the evidence you need to support it. You will also want to demonstrate your credibility to readers by properly quoting and documenting the information you have gathered from your sources. (*See the guidelines for documenting sources in Parts 4 and 5.*)

4. Appealing to your audience

You display the quality of your thought, character, and feelings—what the ancient Greeks called **logos, ethos,** and **pathos**—by the way you argue for what you believe.

Giving reasons and supplying evidence for your position and arguing responsibly by avoiding fallacies establish your logos. (*For more on fallacies, see pp. 12–13.*) You also need to show that you are sincere (ethos) and that you care about your readers' feelings (pathos). For example, you might refer to a quality or belief you share with others, even those who disagree with you. Establishing common ground in this way will make readers more open to your argument.

5. Considering opposing viewpoints

Don't ignore **counterarguments**—claims that challenge or refute your thesis. Instead, look for ways to refute or accommodate them. For example, you might present at least one counterargument and then refute it by presenting evidence that shows why it is open to question. You can often accommodate a counterargument by qualifying your thesis with words such as *likely, usually, most,* or *some.* These kinds of qualifications often appear in the conclusion of an argument, where it is appropriate to include a more subtle version of the thesis.

6. Checking for errors in your logic

Checking the logic of your own writing is probably the greatest challenge to your ability to read critically. It is essential to step outside yourself and assess your argument objectively for errors in reasoning. (*Use the chart of Common Logical Fallacies on pp. 12–13 to test your reasoning.*) Of course, peer review is one of the best tools for developing critical thinking and writing skills. (*For advice on peer review, see Chapter 4, pp. 53–54.*)

| **Exercise 1.6** | Taking a position on an issue from an article |

Using the summary and critical response that you prepared in Exercise 1.3, take a position on an issue from the article you selected for Exercise 1.1.

2 Planning and Shaping

The advice in this chapter will help you determine the kind of writing a particular assignment requires and get you started on a first draft.

2a Learning how to approach assignments

1. Writing about a question

Whether you choose your topic or it is assigned, most topics must be narrowed. To arrive at a manageable topic, it helps to try to write about a question. The particular course you are taking defines a range of questions that are appropriate within a given discipline. Here are examples of the way your course would help define the questions you might ask if, for example, you were writing about Thomas Jefferson:

- **U.S. history:** How did Jefferson's ownership of slaves affect his public stance on slavery?

- **Political science:** To what extent did Jefferson's conflict with the courts redefine the balance of power among the three branches of government?

- **Education:** Given his beliefs about the relationship between democracy and public education, what would Jefferson think about contemporary proposals for a school voucher system?

Exercise 2.1   Exploring your writing process

Write a brief narrative about your own experiences as a writer. The following questions will help you get started:

1. How were you taught to write in school? Were you encouraged to explore ideas and use your imagination, or was the focus primarily on writing correct sentences? Did you struggle with writing assignments, or did they come easily to you? Have you ever written for pleasure, not just in response to a school assignment? What is your earliest memory as a writer?

2. Describe the writing process you use for academic papers. Does your writing process vary according to the assignment? If so, how?

---

2. Asking questions about your audience

Who makes up your audience? In college, instructors are usually your primary readers, of course, but they represent a larger group of readers who have an interest or a stake in your topic. An education professor reads and evaluates a paper as a representative of other students in the course, experts in educational policy, school board members, public school principals, and parents of school-age children, among others. Here are some questions to answer about your audience:

- What are the demographics of your audience? What is the education level, social status, occupation, gender, and ethnicity of a typical audience member?

- What common assumptions and differences of opinion do these readers bring to the issue?

- What images do they have, what ideas do they hold, and what actions do they support?

- What is your goal in writing for this audience? Do you want to intensify, clarify, complicate, or change one or more of their assumptions and opinions?

3. Being clear about your purpose

What kind of assignment are you doing? Are you expected to inform, interpret, or argue?

- **Informing:** writing to transmit knowledge. Terms like *classify, illustrate, report,* and *survey* are often associated with the task of informing.

- **Interpreting:** writing to produce understanding. Terms like *analyze, compare, explain,* and *reflect* are more likely to appear when the purpose is interpreting.

- **Arguing:** writing to assert and negotiate matters of public debate. Terms like *agree, assess, defend,* and *refute* go with the task of arguing.

4. Selecting the appropriate genre

Genre simply means kind of writing. Poems, stories, and plays are genres of literature, with clear differences in the way they look and sound. Different genres of writing predominate in different disciplines.

Sometimes an assignment will specify the kind of work, or genre, you are being asked to produce. For example, you may be asked to write a report (an informative genre), a comparative analysis (an interpretive genre), or a critique (an argumentative genre).

Understanding the genre that is called for is very important in fulfilling an assignment. If you are supposed to write a description of a snake for a field guide, you will not be successful if you write a poem—even a very good poem—about a snake.

5. Using appropriate language

Understanding genre helps you make decisions about language. For a description of a snake in a field guide, you would use highly specific terms to differentiate one type of snake from another. A poem would incorporate striking images, vivid words and phrases that evoke the senses, and other forms of literary language.

6. Choosing an appropriate voice

We hear voices when we read, and we create voices when we write. The following two passages both deal with the death of a sportswriter named Steve Schoenfeld. Read both passages aloud, and listen to the different voices:

> Tobin originally planned his news conference for Wednesday but postponed it out of respect for Valley sports journalist Steve Schoenfeld, who was killed Tuesday night in a hit-and-run accident in downtown Tempe.
>
> —LEE SHAPPELL, *Arizona Republic*

> Steve Schoenfeld probably would find it amusing that the NFL plans to honor him with a moment of silence in press boxes before

games on Sunday and Monday. He was hardly ever quiet in the press box or anywhere else.

—MARK ARMIJO AND KENT SOMERS, *Arizona Republic*

The first passage is written in an even tone that emphasizes factual reporting. The second passage is written in a poignant style that movingly celebrates the sportswriter's life.

Different writing situations and assignments allow you to try out different voices. As a college student, you will usually want to inspire trust by sounding informed, reasonable, and fair. Your **stance**—where you stand in relation to your audience and your subject—is seldom that of an expert. Instead, you are writing as an educated person who is sharing what you have learned and what you think about it.

Readers tend to appreciate an even tone of voice, a style that values the middle ground and avoids the extremes of the impersonal or the intimate, the stuffy or the casual.

2b Exploring your ideas

You usually explore ideas when you are getting started on a project, but exploration also helps when you are feeling stuck. The following strategies will help you brainstorm and come up with ideas at any stage. You can do much of your exploratory writing in a **journal,** which is simply a place to record your thoughts on a regular basis. Your class notes constitute a type of academic journal, as do the notes you take on your reading and research.

As you explore, turn off your internal critic and generate as much material as possible.

1. Freewriting

When you feel blocked or unsure about what you think, try **freewriting.** Just write whatever occurs to you about a topic. If nothing comes to mind, then write "nothing comes to mind" until something else occurs to you. The trick is to keep pushing forward without stopping. Do not worry about spelling, punctuation, or grammar rules as you write. Usually, you will discover some implicit point in your seemingly random writing. You might then try doing some **focused freewriting,** in which you begin with a point or a specific question. The following is a student's freewriting on the topic of work:

> I want to talk about the difference between a job and work—between a job and a career. If you don't get paid, is it work? If it is, what's the difference between work and play? There are some things I would only do for money—like work as a waiter. But there are other things I would do even if I weren't paid—garden or ride my bike or play with kids.

www.mhhe.com/
bmhh

For more on strategies for exploring your ideas, go to

**Writing >
Paragraph/Essay
Development >
Prewriting**

The trick is to find a career that would allow me to get paid for doing those things.

2. Listing

The key to brainstorming is to turn off your internal editor and just jot things down. Start with a topic and list the words, phrases, images, and ideas that come to mind. Later, you can review this list, underline one or more key terms, add or delete items, and look for patterns and connections. You can then zero in on the areas of most interest, add new ideas, and arrange the items into main points and subpoints. Here is a list a student produced on the topic of work:

Work—what is it?
Skilled/unskilled
Most jobs today in service industries
Work and retirement
My dad's retired, but has he stopped working?
If you never want to retire, is your job still considered work?
Jobs I have had: babysitter, camp counselor, salesclerk, office worker—I'd be happy to retire from those, especially the salesclerk job
Standing all day
Do this, do that
Punch the clock
Do it over again and again
Difference between work and career

3. Clustering

Clustering, sometimes called **mapping,** is a brainstorming technique that generates categories and connections from the beginning. To make an idea cluster, do the following:

- Write your topic in the center of a piece of paper, and circle it.
- Surround the topic with subtopics that interest you. Circle each, and draw a line from it to the center circle.
- Brainstorm more ideas, connecting each one to a subtopic already on the sheet or making it into a new subtopic.

Working as a group, the students in a composition course produced the cluster in Figure 2.1 on the topic of "Work in the U.S. today."

4. Questioning

The journalist's five *w*'s and an *h* (*who? what? where? when? why?* and *how?*) can help you find specific ideas and details. For example, a stu-

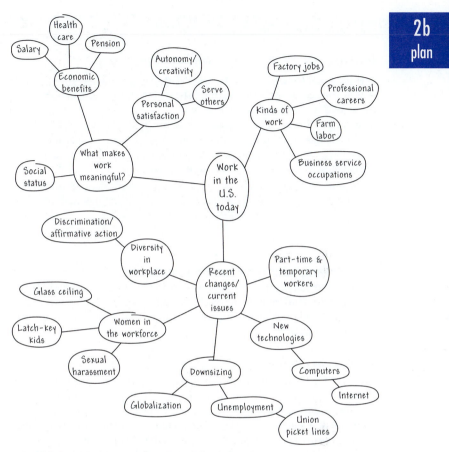

FIGURE 2.1 A cluster on the topic of work.

dent group assigned to research and write a paper about some aspect of work came up with the following questions:

- In terms of age, gender, and ethnicity, who is working in the new cyberspace infotainment industry?
- What are the working conditions, benefits, and job security of those employed in the current U.S. service economy?
- Where are all the manufacturing jobs these days?
- When is it best for people to retire from jobs?
- Why are so many U.S. businesses "downsizing"?
- How do people prepare themselves for career changes?

CHARTING the TERRITORY

Different Questions Lead to Different Answers

Always consider what questions make the most sense in the context of the course you are taking. Scholars in different disciplines pose questions related to their fields.

- **Sociology:** A sociologist might ask questions about the ways management and workers interact in the high-tech workplace.
- **History:** A historian might ask how women's roles in the workplace have—or have not—changed since 1960.
- **Economics:** An economist might wonder what effect, if any, the North American Free Trade Agreement (NAFTA) has had on factory layoffs and closings in the United States.

5. Reviewing your notes and annotations

Review your notes and annotations on your reading or research. If you are writing about something you have observed, review any notes or sketches you made. These immediate comments and reactions are one of your best sources for ideas.

6. Keeping a journal or notebook

You may find it helpful to go beyond note taking and start recording ideas and questions connected to your classes or your exploratory writing. For example, you might write about connections between your personal life and your academic subjects, connections among your subjects, or ideas touched on in class that you would like to know more about. Jotting down one or two thoughts at the end of class and exploring those ideas at greater length later in the day will help you build a store of essay ideas.

> My economics textbook says that moving jobs to companies overseas ultimately does more good than harm to the economy, but how can that be? When the electronics factory closed, it devastated my town.

Exercise 2.2	Keeping an academic journal

Start a print or electronic journal, and write in it daily for two weeks. Using your course work as a springboard, record anything that comes to mind, including personal reactions and memories. At the end of two weeks, reread your journal and write about the journal-keeping experience. Does your journal contain any ideas or information that might be useful for the papers you are writing? Has the journal helped you gain any insight into your courses or your life as a student?

7. Browsing in the library or surfing the Net

Your college library is filled with ideas—and it can be a great inspiration when you need to come up with your own. Browse the bookshelves containing texts that relate to a topic of interest. Exploring a subject on the Web is the electronic equivalent of browsing in the library. Type keywords related to your topic into a search engine such as Google, and visit several sites on the list that results. (*See Chapter 14, pp. 166–68.*)

8. Exchanging ideas

Writing is a social activity. Most authors thank family members, editors, librarians, and colleagues for help on work in progress. Talking about your writing with classmates, friends, and family can also be a source of ideas.

Online tools offer another way for you to collaborate with others. Discuss your assignments by exchanging e-mail and instant messages. You also might create a blog (Web log) where you and others can post ideas, drafts, and peer reviews. If your class has a course Web site, you might also exchange ideas in chat rooms.

Writing e-mail   When you work on papers with classmates, you can use e-mail in the following ways:

- To check out your understanding of the assignment
- To try out various topics
- To ask each other questions about ideas
- To share freewriting, listing, and other exploratory writing
- To respond to each other's ideas

Chatting about ideas   You can also use online chat rooms as well as other virtual spaces to share ideas. Your instructor may include **chat** activities, in which you go into virtual rooms to work on assignments in small groups or visit and interact with classes at other colleges. In the exchange shown in Figure 2.2, for example, two students share ideas about volunteerism.

www.mhhe.com/
bmhh

For more help
with developing
a thesis, go to

Writing >
Paragraph/Essay
Development >
Thesis/Central
Idea

2c   Developing a working thesis

The **thesis** is the central idea of your paper. It needs to communicate a specific point about your topic and suit the purpose of the assignment. As you explore your topic, ideas for your thesis will begin to

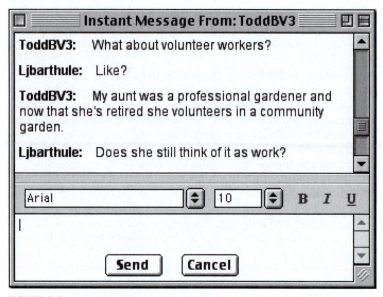

FIGURE 2.2 An online discussion. Chatting online with classmates allows you to test ideas, as in this exchange.

emerge. You can focus these ideas by drafting a preliminary or working **thesis statement,** which can be one or more sentences long. As you draft and revise your paper, you may change your thesis several times to make it stronger.

A good way to develop a thesis is to begin with the answer to a question posed by your assignment. For example, an assignment in a political science class might ask you to defend or critique "Healthy Inequality," an article by George Will on the increasing gap between rich and poor in the United States. The question your thesis must answer is, "Is George Will's position that inequality is healthy correct?"

All strong theses are suitable, specific, and significant. (*For more on strong theses, see Chapter 1, p. 14.*)

1. Making sure your thesis is suitable

A suitable thesis fits the paper's main purpose. All theses make an assertion, but while a thesis for an argument will take a clear position on an issue or recommend an action, a thesis for an informative or interpretive paper will often preview the paper's content or express the writer's insight into the topic. All of the following theses are on the same topic, but each is for a paper with a different purpose:

THESIS TO INFORM

In terms of income and wealth, the gap between rich and poor has increased substantially during the past decade.

THESIS TO INTERPRET

The economic ideas George Will expresses in "Healthy Inequality" are politically conservative.

THESIS TO ARGUE

George Will is wrong about economic inequality being good for the United States.

2. Making sure your thesis is specific

Vague theses usually lead to weak, unfocused papers. Watch out in particular for thesis statements that simply announce your topic, state an obvious fact about it, or offer a general observation:

ANNOUNCEMENT

I will discuss the article "Healthy Inequality" by George Will. [*What is the writer's point about the article?*]

STATEMENT OF FACT

The article "Healthy Inequality" by George Will is about the gap between rich and poor. [*This thesis gives us information about the article, but it does not make a specific point about it.*]

GENERAL OBSERVATION

George Will's article "Healthy Inequality" is interesting. [*While this thesis makes a point about the article, the point could apply to many articles. What makes this article worth reading?*]

By contrast, a specific thesis signals a focused, well-developed paper.

SPECIFIC

George Will's argument that economic inequality is healthy for the United States should not be accepted. His interpretation of the recent increase in income inequality is questionable. His reasoning about history is flawed. Above all, his idea of what is healthy is too narrow.

In this example, the thesis expresses the writer's particular point—there are three reasons to reject Will's argument. It also forecasts the structure of the whole paper, providing readers with a sense of direction.

> **Note:** A thesis statement can be longer than one sentence (if necessary) to provide a framework for your main idea. All of the sentences taken together, though, should build to one specific, significant point that fits the purpose of your assignment. (Some instructors may prefer that you limit your thesis statements to one sentence.)

3. Making sure your thesis is significant

A topic that makes a difference to you is much more likely to make a difference to your readers. When you are looking for possible theses, be sure to challenge yourself to develop one that you care about.

Exercise 2.3 Evaluating thesis statements

Evaluate the thesis statements that accompany each of the following assignments. If the thesis statement is inappropriate or weak, explain why and suggest how it could be stronger.

1. *Assignment:* For a social ethics course, find an essay by a philosopher on a contemporary social issue, and argue either for or against the writer's position.
   Thesis: In "Active and Passive Euthanasia," James Rachels argues against the standard view that voluntary euthanasia is always wrong.

2. *Assignment:* For an economics course, find an essay on the gap between rich and poor in the United States, and argue either for or against the writer's position.
   Thesis: George Will's argument that economic inequality is healthy for the United States depends on two false analogies.

3. *Assignment:* For a nutrition course, report on recent research on an herbal supplement.
   Thesis: Although several researchers believe that echinacea supplements may help reduce the duration of a cold, all agree that the quality and the content of these supplements vary widely.

4. Assignment: For a literature course, analyze the significance of setting in a short story.
   Thesis: William Faulkner's "A Rose for Emily" is set in the fictional town of Jefferson, Mississippi, a once-elegant town that is in decline.

5. Assignment: For a history course, describe the factors that led to the fall of the Achaemenid Empire.
   Thesis: Governments that attempt to build far-flung empires will suffer the same fate as the Achaemenids.

2d Planning a structure that suits your assignment

2d
plan

Every paper needs the following components:

- A beginning, or **introduction,** that hooks readers and usually states the thesis
- A middle, or **body,** that develops the main idea in a series of paragraphs—each making a point supported by specific details
- An ending, or **conclusion,** that gives readers a sense of completion, often by offering a final comment on the thesis

It is not essential to have an outline before you start drafting; indeed, some writers prefer to discover how to connect and develop their ideas as they compose. However, an outline of your first draft can help you spot organizational problems or places where the support for your thesis is weak.

1. Preparing an informal plan

A **scratch outline** is a simple list of points, without the levels of subordination found in more complex outlines. Scratch outlines are useful for briefer papers. Here is a scratch outline for a paper on an exhibit of photographs by Sebastião Salgado:

www.mhhe.com/
bmhh

For more on
outlines, go to

**Writing >
Paragraph/Essay
Development >
Outlines**

- Photojournalism should be factual and informative, but it can be beautiful and artful too, as Salgado's *Migrations* exhibit illustrates.
- The exhibit overall—powerful pictures of people uprooted, taken in 39 countries over 7 years. Salgado documents a global crisis; over 100 million displaced due to war, resource depletion, overpopulation, natural disasters, extreme poverty.

Tips LEARNING in COLLEGE

Using Presentation Software as a Writing Process Tool

Presentation software slides provide a useful tool for exploring and organizing your ideas prior to drafting. The slides also give you another way to get feedback from peer reviewers and others, using the following process:

- Well before a paper is due, create a very brief, three- to five-slide presentation—with visuals if appropriate—that previews the key points you intend to make in the paper.
- Present the preview to an audience—friends, classmates, perhaps even your instructor—and ask for suggestions for improvement.

- Specific picture—"Orphanage"—describe subjects, framing, lighting, emotions it evokes.
- Salgado on the purpose of his photographs. Quote.

A **do/say plan** is a more detailed type of informal outline. To come up with such a plan, review your notes and other relevant material. Then write down your working thesis, and list what you will say for each of the following "do" categories: introduce, support and develop, and conclude. Here is an example:

Thesis: George Will is wrong about economic inequality being good for the United States.

1. **Introduce** the issue and my focus.

   - Use two examples to contrast rich and poor: "approximately 17,000 Americans declared more than $1 million of annual income on their 1985 tax returns" (Mantsios 196). Between 1979 and 1992, there was a 15% decrease in the manufacturing workforce, and in 1993, Sears eliminated 50,000 merchandising jobs (Rifkin 2).

   - Say that the issue is how to evaluate increasing economic inequality, and introduce Will's article "Healthy Inequality." Summarize Will's argument.

   - Give Will credit for raising the issue, but then state the thesis: he's wrong about more inequality being good for the United States.

2. **Support and develop** the thesis that Will's argument is wrong.

   - Point out that Will relies on the economic interpretations of Greenwood and Yorukoglu. They see a decline ("modest") in labor productivity beginning in 1974. But Rifkin says "manufacturing productivity is soaring"—up 35%.

   - Point out one thing Will and Rifkin agree on: the computer revolution is affecting economy/jobs. But Will thinks effects are like "economic turbulence" caused in 1770 by the steam engine and in 1840 by electricity.

   - Show that these analogies aren't convincing—too many differences. Use Aronowitz on "jobless future" and Rifkin for support.

   - Say that Will makes fun of those who "decr[y] . . . injustice," people like Rifkin and Aronowitz. Will thinks inequality motivates people to learn new skills so they can compete. A skilled workforce makes society better/healthier.

■ Will's idea of a healthy society is narrow—an economic idea only. And who will pay to train unemployed workers?

3. **Conclude** that Will doesn't ask or answer such key questions because he denies that there is any problem. Earlier, he says, "Suffering is good." Where would he draw the line? Maybe quote from Max Weber?

2d

plan

In outlining his plan, this student has already begun drafting because as he works on the outline, he gets a clearer sense of what he thinks is wrong with Will's argument.

2. Preparing a formal outline

A **formal outline** classifies and divides the information you have gathered, showing main points, supporting ideas, and specific details by organizing them into levels of subordination.

www.mhhe.com/
bmhh

For help with outlining, go to

Writing >
Outlining Tutor

A **topic outline** uses single words or phrases; a **sentence outline** states every idea in a sentence. Because the process of division always results in at least two parts, in a formal outline, every I must have a II; every A, a B; and so on. Also, items placed at the same level must be of the same kind; for example, if I is London, then II can be New York City but not the Bronx or Wall Street. Items at the same level should also be grammatically parallel; if A is "Choosing screen icons," then B can be "Creating away messages" but not "Away messages."

Here is a formal sentence outline for a paper on Salgado's *Migrations* exhibit:

Thesis: Like a photojournalist, Salgado brings us images of newsworthy events, but he goes beyond objective reporting, imparting his compassion for refugees and migrants to the viewer.

I. The images in *Migrations,* an exhibit of his work, suggest that Salgado does more then simply point and shoot.

II. Salgado's photograph "Orphanage attached to the hospital at Kibumba, Number One Camp, Goma Zaire" illustrates the power of his work.

  A. The photograph depicts three infants who are victims of the war in Rwanda.

    1. The label indicates that there are 4,000 orphans in the camp and 100,000 orphans overall.

    2. The numbers are abstractions that the photo makes real.

  B. Salgado's use of black and white gives the photo a documentary feel, but he also uses contrasts of light and dark to create a dramatic image of the babies.

    1. The vertical black-and-white stripes of the blanket direct viewers' eyes to the infants' faces and hands.

   2. The whites of their eyes stand out against the dark-
      ness of the blankets.
   3. The camera's lens focuses sharply on the babies'
      faces, highlighting their expressions.
      a. The baby on the left has a heart-wrenching look.
      b. The baby in the center has a startled look.
      c. The baby on the right has a glazed and sunken
         look and is near death.
   C. The vantage point of this photograph is one of a parent
      standing directly over his or her child.
   1. The infants seem to belong to the viewer.
   2. The photo is framed so that the babies take up the
      entire space, consuming the viewer with their inno-
      cence and vulnerability.
III. Salgado uses his artistic skill to get viewers to look closely
     at painful subjects, illustrating a big, complex topic with
     a collection of intimate, intensely moving images.

Exercise 2.4   Reflecting on your own work: outlining

Try making an outline in response to one of your current assignments.
Freewrite about your experience with outlining. Were you able to generate an outline before you started drafting paragraphs? If so, did you
stick with your outline, or did you deviate from it? What kind of outline are you most comfortable with? If you were not able to create an
outline before you started drafting, why not?

2e   Using visuals

Visuals such as tables, charts, and graphs provide clarity. Effective visuals are used for a specific purpose, and each type of visual illustrates
some kinds of material better than others. For example, compare the
table on page 31 and the line graph on page 32. Both present similar
types of data, but do both have the same effect? Does one strike you
as clearer or more powerful than the other?

Caution: Because the inclusion of visual elements in papers is
more accepted in some fields than in others, you may want to
ask your instructor for advice before planning to include visuals
in your paper.

1. Tables

Tables organize data for readers. Consider this example taken from the Web site of the Environmental Protection Agency:

TABLE 1

U.S. Emissions of Criteria Pollutants, 1989–1996
(million metric tons of gas)

SOURCE	1989	1990	1991	1992	1993	1994	1995	1996
Carbon monoxide	93.5	91.3	88.3	85.3	85.4	89.6	83.5	**NA**
Nitrogen oxides	21.1	20.9	20.6	20.7	21.1	21.5	19.7	**NA**
Nonmethane VOCs	21.7	21.4	20.8	20.3	20.5	21.1	20.7	**NA**

NA = not available.
Note: Data in this table are revised from the data contained in the previous EIA report, *Emissions of Greenhouse Gases in the United States 1995,* DOE/EIA-0573(95) (Washington, DC, October 1996).
SOURCE: U.S. Environmental Protection Agency, Office of Air Quality Planning and Standards, *National Air Pollutant Emission Trends,* 1900–1995, EPA-454/R-96-007 (Research Triangle Park, NC, October 1996), pp. A-5, A-9, and A-16.

It would be more difficult to compare the numbers for different years if the data were presented in paragraph form, and because the measurements include decimals, it would also be difficult to place them precisely on a graph. A table is ideal for displaying this type of precise data.

TEXTCONNEX

Preparing Tables

You can usually create and edit tables using your word-processing software. If you use Microsoft Word, for example, you can size columns proportionally to avoid distorting their contents and make them fit your text. Under the "Table" pulldown menu, select "Insert," then click on "Table." You will see a dialogue box. Choose "Autofit to content" instead of "Fixed column width." As you create the table, the borders will automatically increase. You can also create tables using database, spreadsheet, presentation, and Web site construction software.

2. Bar graphs

Bar graphs show relationships and highlight comparisons between two or more variables, such as the cost of tuition and fees at different public universities. Bar graphs allow readers to see relative sizes quickly, as in Figure 2.3.

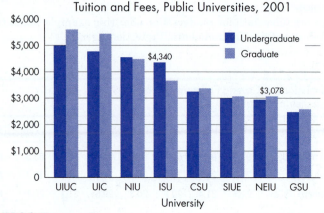

FIGURE 2.3 **Bar graph.**

3. Pie charts

Pie charts are useful for showing differences between parts in relation to a whole, as long as the differences are significant and there are not too many parts. The segments of a pie chart should add up to 100% of something, such as the sources of water contamination shown in Figure 2.4.

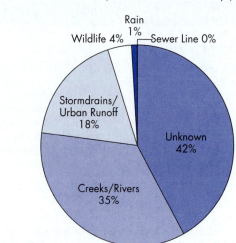

FIGURE 2.4 **Pie chart.**

4. Line graphs

Line graphs or charts are used to show changes over time, such as the changes shown in Figure 2.5—three sources of nitrous oxide emissions over a sixteen-year period.

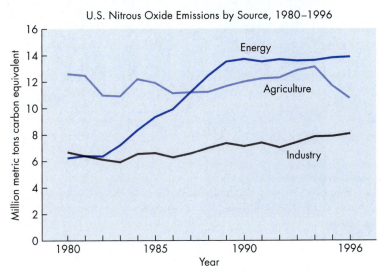

U.S. Nitrous Oxide Emissions by Source, 1980–1996

FIGURE 2.5 Line graph.

5. Photographs and illustrations

Photographs and illustrations can reinforce a point you are making in your text in ways that words cannot, showing readers what your subject actually looks like or how it has been affected or changed.

When you use photographs or illustrations, always credit your source, and be aware that most photographs and illustrations are protected by copyright. If you plan to use a photograph as part of a Web page, for example, you will usually need to obtain permission from the copyright holder.

6. Diagrams

Used to show processes or structures visually, diagrams include such visuals as time lines, organization charts, and decision trees. The diagram in Figure 2.6 shows the factors involved in the decision to commit a burglary.

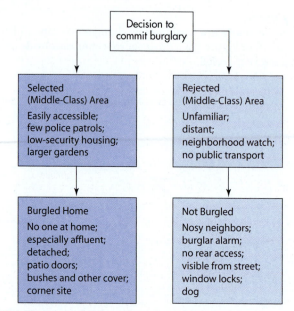

FIGURE 2.6 Event model for a burglary.

Exercise 2.5 Using visuals

For each of the following kinds of information, decide which type of visual would be most effective. (You do not need to prepare the visual itself.)

1. For an education paper, show the percentage of teaching time per week devoted to math, language arts, science, social studies, world languages, art, music, and physical education using a

   _____.

2. For a business paper, compare the gross domestic product for ten leading industrial countries using a _____.

3. For a criminal justice paper, compare the incidence of three different types of crime in one precinct during a three-month period using a _____.

4. For a health paper, chart the number of new cases of AIDS in North America and Africa over a ten-year period in order to show which continent has had the greater increase, using a

   _____.

3 Drafting

Think of drafting as an attempt to discover a beginning, a middle, and an end for what you have to say, but remember that a draft is preliminary. Avoid putting pressure on yourself to make it perfect.

3a   Using online tools for drafting

The following tips will make this process go smoothly:

www.mhhe.com/
bmhh

For more on
drafting, go to

**Writing >
Paragraph/Essay
Development >
Drafting and
Revising**

- **Save your work.** Always protect your creativity and hard-won drafts from power surges and other mishaps. Save often, and make backups.

Tips   LEARNING in COLLEGE

Avoiding Writer's Block

While it is important to allot time for generating and organizing your ideas, do not put off writing the first draft. If you find it difficult to get started, consider these tips.

- **Resist the temptation to be a perfectionist.** The poet William Stafford said, "There's no such thing as writer's block for writers whose standards are low enough." Reserve your high standards for the revising and editing stages. For your first draft, do not worry about getting the right word, the stylish phrase, or even the correct spelling.
- **Take it "bird by bird."** Writer Anne Lamott counsels students to break down writing assignments into manageable units and then make a commitment to finishing each unit in one session. She passes along her father's advice to her brother, who had procrastinated on a report about birds and was paralyzed by the enormity of the project: "Bird by bird, buddy. Just take it bird by bird."
- **Start anywhere.** If you are stuck on the beginning, pick a section where you have a clearer sense of what you want to say. You can go back later and work out the transitions. Writers often compose the introduction after drafting a complete text.
- **Generate more ideas.** If you hit a section where you are drawing a blank, you may need to do more reading, research, or brainstorming. Be careful, though, not to use reading and research as a stalling tactic.

- **Label revised drafts with different file names.** Use a different file name for each successive version of your paper. For example, you might save drafts of a paper on work as Work1, Work2, Work3, and so on.

- **Print hard copies early and often.** If you save and print the original, you can feel free to experiment.

Tips LEARNING in COLLEGE

Using Hypertext as a Writing Process Tool

If you are writing and submitting assignments electronically, a variety of links in your essays can help you during the writing process. For example, you might include a link to additional research, or to a source that refutes an argument, or to interesting information that is not directly relevant to the primary subject. These links can help you refer to supplemental material without undermining the coherence of the text. If a reader of an early draft—an instructor or classmate—thinks the linked material should be in the essay itself, you can include it in the next draft.

---

www.mhhe.com/
bmhh

For more on
developing
paragraphs,
go to

**Writing >
Paragraph
Patterns**

3b Developing ideas and using visuals

The following strategies can help you develop the ideas that support your thesis into a complete draft. Depending on the purpose of your paper, you may use a few of these strategies throughout or a mix of all of them.

Photographs and other kinds of visuals can also serve as rhetorical strategies. As with paragraphs, you can use a mix of visuals in a paper. Keep in mind, though, that any visuals you use should always serve the overall purpose of your work.

www.mhhe.com/
bmhh

For help with the
use of illustration,
go to

**Writing >
Writing Tutors >
Exemplification**

1. Illustration

No matter what your purpose and point may be, to appeal to readers, you have to show as well as tell. Detailed examples and well-chosen visuals (*see Figure 3.1*) can make abstractions more concrete and generalizations more specific, as the following paragraph shows:

As Rubin explains, "for much of the Accord era, the ideal-typical family . . . was composed of a 'stay-at-home-mom,' a working father, and dependent children. He earned wages; she cooked, cleaned, cared for the home, managed the family's social life, and nurtured the family members" (97). Just such an arrangement characterized my grandmother's married life. My

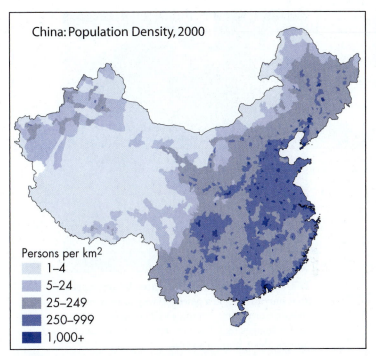

3b
draft

China: Population Density, 2000

Persons per km²
1–4
5–24
25–249
250–999
1,000+

FIGURE 3.1 Visuals that illustrate. This map illustrates the population densities in various regions of China in the year 2000.

grandmother, who had four children, stayed at home with them, while her husband went off to work as a safety engineer. Sadly, when he died, she was left with nothing. She needed to support herself, yet had no work experience, no credit, and little education. But even though society frowned on her for seeking employment, my grandmother eventually found a clerical position—a low-level job with few perks.

—JENNIFER KOEHLER, "Women's Work in the United States: The 1950s and 1990s"

Caution: Although any image you choose to include in your paper will be illustrative, images should not function merely as decoration. Ask yourself if each image you are considering truly adds information to your paper.

FIGURE 3.2 Visuals that narrate. Using images that narrate can be a powerful way to reinforce a message or portray events you discuss in your paper. Images like this one help tell one of many stories about the war in Iraq.

www.mhhe.com/
bmhh

For help with the use of narration, go to

Writing > Writing Tutors > Narration

2. Narration

When you narrate, you tell a story. (*See Figure 3.2 above for an example of a narrative visual.*) The following paragraph comes from a personal essay on the goods that result from "a lifetime of production":

> My dad changed too. He had come to that job feeling—as I do now—that everything was still possible. He'd served his time in the Air Force during the Korean War. Then, while my mother worked as a secretary to support them, he earned a college degree courtesy of the GI Bill. After graduation, my father painted houses for a season until he was offered a position scheduling the production of corrugated board. He took it, though he has told me that he never planned to stay. It was not something he envisioned as his life's work. I try to imagine what it is like suddenly to look up from a stack of orders and discover that the job you started one December day has watched you age.
>
> —MICHELLE M. DUCHARME, "A Lifetime of Production"

Notice that Ducharme begins with two sentences that state the topic and point of her narration. Then, using the past tense, she recounts in chronological sequence some key events that led to her father's taking a job in the box manufacturing business.

FIGURE 3.3 Visuals that describe. Although it may seem obvious that images can serve a descriptive purpose, you should pay careful attention to the effect a particular image will have on your paper. This photograph of Kurt Cobain, for example, could add dimension to a portrayal of the musician as a talented but conflicted artist.

3. Description

To make an object, person, or activity vivid for your readers, describe it in concrete, specific words that appeal to the senses of sight, sound, taste, smell, and touch. (*See Figure 3.3 for an example of a descriptive visual.*) In the following paragraph, Diane Chen describes her impression of a photograph:

> The vertical black-and-white stripes of the blanket direct our eyes to the infants' faces and hands, which are framed by a horizontal white stripe. The whites of their eyes in particular stand out against the darkness created by the shell of the blankets. The camera's lens also seems to be in sharper focus on the faces than on the blankets, again focusing our attention on the babies' expressions.
>
> —DIANE CHEN, "The Caring Eye of Sebastião Salgado,"
> student paper

www.mhhe.com/
bmhh

For help with
the use of
classification,
go to

Writing >
Writing Tutors >
Classification

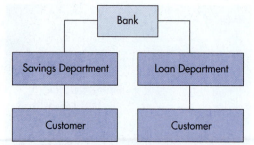

FIGURE 3.4 Visuals that classify or divide.
An image can help you make the categories
in or parts of complex systems or organizations easier to understand. The image shown
here, for example, helps readers comprehend
the structure of a business.

4. Classification

Classification is a useful way of grouping individual entities into identifiable categories. (*See Figure 3.4.*) Classifying often appears with its
complement—**division,** or breaking a whole entity into its parts.

In the following passage, Robert Reich first classifies future work
into two broad categories: complex services and person-to-person services. Then, in the next paragraph, he develops the idea of complex
services in more detail, in part by dividing that category into more specific—and familiar—categories like engineering and advertising.

> [M]ost of America's traditional, routinized manufacturing jobs
> will disappear. So will routinized service jobs that can be done
> from remote locations, like keypunching of data transmitted by
> satellite. Instead, you will be engaged in one of two broad cate-
> gories of work: either complex services, some of which will be
> sold to the rest of the world to pay for whatever Americans want
> to buy from the rest of the world, or person-to-person services,
> which foreigners can't provide for us because (apart from new
> immigrants and illegal aliens) they aren't here to provide them.
>
> Complex services involve the manipulation of data and ab-
> stract symbols. Included in this category are insurance, engi-
> neering, law, finance, computer programming, and advertising.
> Such activities now account for almost 25 percent of our GNP,
> up from 13 percent in 1950. They have already surpassed manu-
> facturing (down to about 20 percent of GNP).
>
> —ROBERT REICH, "The Future of Work"

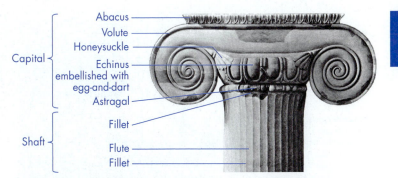

3b
draft

FIGURE 3.5 Visuals that define. Visuals can be extremely effective when used to support a written definition or to identify parts of a whole. This image uses labels and leader lines to identify the characteristics of an Ionic column.

5. Definition

Define any concepts that readers might need to understand to follow your ideas. (*See Figure 3.5 above for an example of a visual that defines.*) Interpretations and arguments often depend on one or two key ideas that cannot be quickly and easily defined. In the following example, John Berger defines "image," a key idea in his televised lectures on the way we see things:

> An image is a sight which has been recreated or reproduced. It is an appearance, or a set of appearances, which has been detached from the place and time in which it first made its appearance and preserved—for a few moments or centuries. Every image embodies a way of seeing. Even a photograph. For photographs are not, as is often assumed, a mechanical record. Every time we look at a photograph, we are aware, however slightly, of the photographer selecting that sight from an infinity of other possible sights. This is true even in the most casual family snapshot. The photographer's way of seeing is reflected in his choice of subject.
>
> —JOHN BERGER, *Ways of Seeing*

www.mhhe.com/
bmhh

For help with the use of definition, go to

**Writing >
Writing Tutors >
Definition**

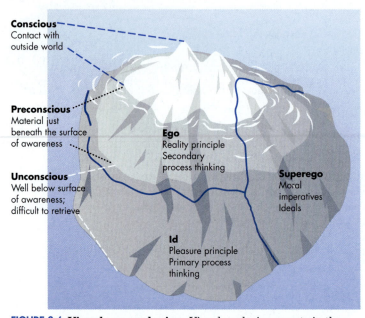

Conscious
Contact with
outside world

Preconscious
Material just
beneath the surface
of awareness

Unconscious
Well below surface
of awareness;
difficult to retrieve

Ego
Reality principle
Secondary
process thinking

Superego
Moral
imperatives
Ideals

Id
Pleasure principle
Primary process
thinking

FIGURE 3.6 **Visuals as analogies.** Visual analogies operate in the same way as written analogies. This figure uses the image of an iceberg to illustrate Freud's theory of the unconscious. The portion of the iceberg below the surface of the water represents the preconscious and unconscious mind.

6. Analogy

An **analogy** compares topics that at first glance seem quite different. (*See Figure 3.6.*) A well-chosen analogy can make new or technical information appear more commonplace and understandable:

> The human eye provides a good starting point for learning how a camera works. The lens of the eye is like the *lens* of the camera. In both instruments the lens focuses an image of the surroundings on a *light-sensitive surface*—the *retina* of the eye and the *film* in the camera. In both, the light-sensitive material is protected within a light-tight container—the *eyeball* of the eye and the *body* of the camera. Both eye and camera have a mechanism for shutting off light passing through the lens to the interior of the container—the *lid* of the eye and the *shutter* of the camera. In both, the size of the lens opening, or *aperture,* is regulated by an *iris diaphragm.*

—MARVIN ROSEN, *Introduction to Photography*

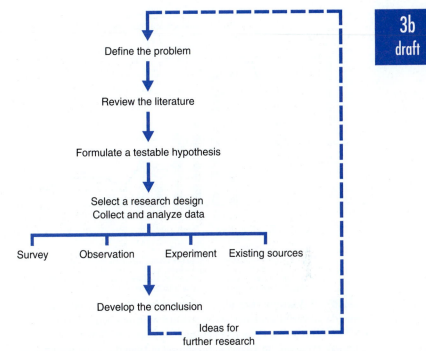

FIGURE 3.7 Visuals that show a process. Flow charts and diagrams are especially useful when illustrating a process. This one shows the scientific method used in disciplines throughout the sciences and social sciences.

7. Process

When you need to explain how to do something or show readers how something is done, you use process analysis (*see Figure 3.7*), explaining each step in the process in chronological order, as in the following example:

> To end our Hawan ritual of thanks, *aarti* is performed. First, my mother lights a piece of camphor in a metal plate called a *taree*. Holding the taree with her right hand, she moves the fire in a circular, clockwise movement in front of the altar. Next, she stands in front of my father and again moves the fiery *taree* in a circular, clockwise direction. After touching his feet and receiving his blessing, she attends to each of us children in turn, moving the fire in a clockwise direction before kissing us, one by one. When she is done, my father performs his *aarti* in a similar way and then my sister and I do ours. When everyone is done, we say some prayers and sit down.
>
> —U. ROOPNARIAN, "A Family Ritual," student paper

www.mhhe.com/
bmhh

For help with describing a process, go to

Writing > Writing Tutors > Process Analysis

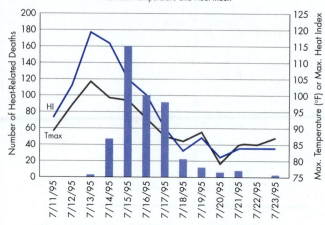

This graph tracks maximum temperature (Tmax), heat index (HI), and heat-related deaths in Chicago each day from July 11 to 23, 1995. The dark gray line shows maximum daily temperature, the blue line shows the heat index, and the bars indicate number of deaths for the day.

FIGURE 3.8 Visuals that show cause and effect. Visuals can provide powerful evidence when you are writing about causes and effects. Although graphs like this one may seem self-explanatory, you will still need to analyze and interpret them for your readers.

8. Cause and effect

You can use this strategy when you need to trace the causes of some event or situation, to describe its effects, or both. (*See Figure 3.8.*) In the following example, Rajeev Bector explains the reasons for a character's feelings and actions in a short story:

> Given the differences between Mrs. Chestny's and her son's values, as well as the oppressiveness of Mrs. Chestny's racist views, we can understand why Julian struggles to "teach" his mother "a lesson" (185) throughout the entire bus ride. Goffman would point out that "each individual is engaged in providing evidence to establish a definition of himself at the expense of what can remain for the other" (29). But in the end, neither character wins the contest. Julian's mother loses her sense of self when she is pushed down to the ground by a "colored woman" wearing a hat identical to hers (187). Faced with his mother's breakdown, Julian feels his own identity being overwhelmed by "the world of guilt and sorrow."
>
> —RAJEEV BECTOR, "The Character Contest in
> Flannery O'Connor's 'Everything That
> Rises Must Converge,'" student paper

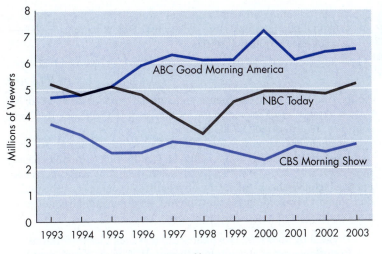

FIGURE 3.9 Visuals that compare and contrast. Graphs and charts are effective for comparing parallel sets of data. This line graph tracks the population of viewers for the three most popular morning shows over ten years.

9. Comparison and contrast

When you *compare,* you explore the similarities and differences among various items. When the term *compare* is used along with the term *contrast, compare* has a narrower meaning: "to spell out key similarities." *Contrast* always means "to itemize important differences." (*See Figure 3.9.*)

In the following example, the student writer uses a **subject-by-subject** pattern to contrast the ideas of two social commentators, Jeremy Rifkin and George Will:

> Rifkin and Will have different opinions about unemployment due to downsizing and the widening income gap between rich and poor. Rifkin sees both the decrease in employment and the increase in income disparity as evils that must be immediately dealt with lest society fall apart: "If no measures are taken to provide financial opportunities for millions of Americans in an era of diminishing jobs, then . . . violent crime is going to increase" (3). Will, on the other hand, seems to believe that both unemployment and income differences are necessary to the health of American society. Will writes, "A society that chafes against stratification derived from

www.mhhe.com/ bmhh

For help with the use of comparison and contrast, go to

Writing >
Writing Tutors >
Comparison/
Contrast

3b
draft

disparities of talents will be a society that discourages individual talents" (92). Apparently, the society that Rifkin wants is just the kind of society that Will rejects.

—JACOB GROSSMAN, "Dark Comes before Dawn,"
student paper

Notice that Grossman comments on Rifkin first and then turns to his second subject, Will. To ensure paragraph unity, he begins with a topic sentence that mentions both subjects.

In the following paragraph, the student writer organizes her comparison **point by point** rather than subject by subject. Instead of saying everything about Smith's picture before commenting on the AP photo, she moves back and forth between the two images as she makes and supports two points: (1) that the images differ in figure and scene and (2) that they are similar in theme.

Divided by an ocean, two photographers took pictures that at first glance seem absolutely different. W. Eugene Smith's well-known *Tomoko in the Bath* and the less well-known AP photo *A Paratrooper Works to Save the Life of a Buddy* portray distinctively different settings and people. Smith brings us into a darkened room where a Japanese woman is lovingly bathing her malformed child, while the AP staff photographer captures two soldiers on the battlefield, one intently performing CPR on his wounded friend. But even though the two images seem as different as women and men, peace and war, or life and death, both pictures figure something similar: a time of suffering. It is the early 1970s—a time when the hopes and dreams that modernity promoted are being exposed as deadly to human beings. Perhaps that is why the bodies in both pictures seem humbled. Grief pulls you down onto your knees. Terror impels you to crawl along the ground.

—ILONA BOUZOUKASHVILI, "On Reading Photographs,"
student paper

Exercise 3.1   Developing ideas

Experiment with the development strategies just discussed—narration, description, classification, definition, illustration, comparison and contrast, analogy, process, and cause and effect—in a paper you are currently drafting. Are some strategies inappropriate to your assignment? Have you combined any of the strategies in a single paragraph?

3c Writing focused, clearly organized paragraphs

Paragraphs break the text into blocks for your readers, allowing them to see how your essay builds step by step and providing a rhythm for their reading. Introductory and concluding paragraphs have special functions in a piece of writing, but all paragraphs should have a single, clear focus and a clear organization.

1. Focusing on one main point or example

In a strong paragraph, the sentences form a unit that explores one main point or elaborates on one main example. When you are drafting, start a new paragraph when you introduce a new reason in support of your thesis, a new step in a process, or a new element in an analysis. As you draft, if you bear in mind that each paragraph develops a main point or example, then ideas will flow and revising will be easier.

In the following example, the paragraph focuses on a theory that the writer will refer to later in his essay. The main idea is highlighted:

> Current thinking on the topic of loss and mourning rests on foundations constructed by the British psychiatrist John Bowlby. Using examples from animal and human behavior, Bowlby (1977) posited "attachment theory" as a means of understanding the powerful bonds between humans and the disruption that comes when the bonds are jeopardized or destroyed. The bonds are formed because of a need for security and safety, are developed early in life, are long enduring, and are directed toward a few special individuals. In normal maturation, the child becomes ever more independent, moving away from the figure of attachment, and returning periodically for safety and security. If the bonds are threatened, the individual will try to restore them through crying, clinging, or other types of coercion; if they are destroyed, withdrawal, apathy, and despair will follow.
>
> —JONATHAN FAST, "After Columbine: How People Mourn Sudden Death"

Details of attachment theory are developed in the rest of the paragraph.

2. Signaling the main idea of your paragraph with a topic sentence

A topic sentence can be a helpful starting point as you draft a paragraph. In the following paragraph, the topic sentence (highlighted) provides the writer with a launching point for a series of details:

The topic sentence announces that the paragraph will focus on a certain kind of evidence.

The excavation also revealed dramatic evidence for the commemorative rituals that took place after the burial. Four cattle had been decapitated and their skulls symbolically placed in a ditch enclosing the burial pit. In the soil above the skulls archaeologists found the butchered bones of at least 250 slaughtered cattle, evidence for a huge ceremonial feast. Clearly this was an expensive way to commemorate a leader. Indeed, the huge quantity of meat suggests that the entire tribe may have gathered at the grave to take part in a ritual feast. Perhaps this was one way the bonds between scattered communities were strengthened.

—DAMIAN ROBINSON, "Riding into the Afterlife"

Sometimes the sentences in a paragraph will lead to a unifying conclusion, as in the highlighted part of this example:

Table 1 presents the 15 mechanisms for gaining prestige that were reported for girls and for boys. There were few differences in the avenues to prestige between those in public and private high schools, particularly for girls. Avenues to prestige for girls that focus on their physical attributes, such as attractiveness, popularity with boys, clothes, sexual activity, and participation in sports, were more prominent in public schools than in private schools. In private schools the avenues more indicative of personality attributes, such as general sociability, having a good reputation/virginity, and participating in school clubs/government and cheerleading, were more prominent. Contrary to what parents may expect, avenues considered to be more negative, such as partying and being class clown, appeared more prevalent in private schools than in public schools. However, only clothes remained a significantly more important route to prestige for girls in public schools compared to girls in private schools once controls were introduced for region, size of community, year of graduation, and gender of respondent. Thus, taken together, type of high school had little effect on the ways in which girls accrued prestige in high school.

—J. JILL SUITOR, REBECCA POWERS, AND RACHEL BROWN, "Avenues to Prestige among Adolescents"

If a topic sentence would simply state the obvious, it can be omitted. In the following example, it is not necessary to state that the paragraph is about Igor Stravinsky's preprofessional life:

Stravinsky was born in Russia, near St. Petersburg, grew up in a musical atmosphere, and studied with Nikolai Rimsky-Korsakov. He had his first important opportunity in 1909, when the great impresario Sergei Diaghilev heard his music.

—ROGER KAMIEN, *Music: An Appreciation*

Exercise 3.2   Paragraph unity

Underline the topic sentences in the following paragraphs. If there is no topic sentence, state the main idea.

1. Based on the results of this study, it appears that a substantial amount of bullying by both students and teachers may be occurring in college. Over 60% of the students reported having observed a student being bullied by another student, and over 44% had seen a teacher bully a student. More than 6% of the students reported having been bullied by another student occasionally or very frequently, and almost 5% reported being bullied by a teacher occasionally or very frequently, while over 5% of the students stated that they bullied students occasionally or very frequently.

    —MARK CHAPELL ET AL., "Bullying in College
    by Students and Teachers"

2. ARS [the Agricultural Research Service] launched the first area-wide IPM [Integrated Pest Management] attacks against the codling moth, a pest in apple and pear orchards, on 7,700 acres in the Pacific Northwest. Other programs include a major assault against the corn rootworm on over 40,000 acres in the Corn Belt, fruit flies in the Hawaiian Islands, and leafy spurge in the Northern Plains area. In 2001, an areawide IPM project began for fire ants in Florida, Mississippi, Oklahoma, South Carolina, and Texas on pastures using natural enemies, microbial pesticides, and attracticides.

    —ROBERT FAUST, "Integrated Pest Management
    Programs Strive to Solve
    Agricultural Problems"

3. As far as the starting point of investigating the Dao of the universe is concerned, Feng and Kant have something in common. Contrary to advocates of positivism, Feng, like Kant, does not reject the discussion of ontological problems. However, he has not endeavored to construct an ontological system outside the human knowing process. As mentioned earlier, his theory of wisdom can be characterized as a theory about the nature of human beings and the Dao of the universe. However, the main content of the theory is how to know the world and know oneself. It is by no means accidental that the first volume of his Trilogy on Wisdom, which set the guidelines for the whole work, is titled Knowing the World and Knowing the Self. Therefore, in Feng's eyes, the theory of the Dao of the universe, although an ontological problem, is essentially a question of knowing the world.

    —YANG GUORONG, "Transforming
    Knowledge into Wisdom"

www.mhhe.com/
bmhh

For more on
paragraphs,
go to

Writing >
**Paragraph
Patterns**

3. Writing paragraphs that have a clear organization

The sentences in your final draft need to be clearly related to one another. As you are drafting, make connections among your ideas and information as a way of moving your writing forward. The strategies covered in section 3b are ways of developing your ideas. Another way to make your ideas work together is to use one of the common organizational schemes for paragraphs:

- **Chronological organization:** The sentences in a paragraph with a chronological organization describe a series of events, steps, or observations as they occur in time: this happened, then that, and so on.

- **Spatial organization:** The sentences in a paragraph with a spatial organization present details as they appear to a viewer: from top to bottom, outside to inside, east to west, and so on.

- **General-to-specific organization:** As we have seen, paragraphs often start with a general topic sentence that states the main idea and then proceed with specifics that elaborate on that idea. The general topic sentence can include a question that the paragraph then answers or a problem that the paragraph goes on to solve.

- **Specific-to-general organization:** The general topic sentence can come at the end of the paragraph, with the specific details leading up to that general conclusion (*see the paragraph from "Avenues to Prestige among Adolescents," p. 48*). This organization is especially effective when you are preparing readers for a revelation.

Exercise 3.3   Paragraph organization

Go back to the paragraphs in Exercise 3.2 and identify the organizational strategy used in each one.

---

www.mhhe.com/
bmhh

For more on
introductions and
conclusions, go to

Writing >
**Paragraph/Essay
Development**

4. Drafting introductions and conclusions

As you begin your first draft, you may want to skip over the introduction and focus on the body of your paper. After your paper has taken shape, you can go back and sketch out the main ideas for your introduction.

The best way to get readers' attention is to show why the topic matters. The opening of your paper should encourage readers to share your view of its importance. Here are some opening strategies:

- Tell a brief story related to the issue your thesis raises.
- Begin with a relevant, attention-getting quotation.

- Begin with a paraphrase of a commonly held view that you immediately question.
- State a working hypothesis.
- Define a key term, but avoid the tired opener that begins, "According to the dictionary . . ."
- Pose an important question.

For informative reports, arguments, and other types of papers, your opening paragraph or paragraphs will include a thesis statement, usually at the beginning or near the end of the introduction. If your purpose is analytic, however, you may instead choose to build up to your thesis. For some types of writing, such as narratives, an explicitly stated thesis may not be needed if the main idea is clear without it.

Just as the opening makes a first impression and motivates readers to continue reading, the closing makes a final impression and motivates readers to think further. Your conclusion should remind readers of your paper's significance and satisfy those who might be asking, "So what?" Here are some common strategies for concluding a paper:

- Refer to the story or quotation you used in your introduction.
- Answer the question you posed in your introduction.
- Summarize your main point.
- Call for some action on your readers' part.
- Present a powerful image or forceful example.
- Suggest some implications for the future.

3d Integrating visuals

If you decide to use a table, chart, diagram, or photograph in your paper, keep this general advice in mind:

- **Number tables and other figures** consecutively throughout your paper, and label them appropriately: Table 1, Table 2, and so on. Do not abbreviate *Table*. *Figure* may be abbreviated as *Fig.*

- **Refer to the visual element in your text** before it appears, placing the visual as close as possible to the text in which you state why you are including it. If your project contains complex tables or many other visuals, however, you may want to group them in an appendix. Always refer to a visual by its label—for example, "See Figure 1."

- **Give each visual a title and caption** that clearly explains what the visual shows. A visual with its caption should be clear without the discussion in the text, and the discussion of the visual in the text should be clear without the visual itself.

■ **Include explanatory notes below the visuals.** If you want to explain a specific element within the visual, use a superscript letter (not a number) both after the specific element and before the note. The explanation should appear directly beneath the graphic, not at the foot of the page or at the end of your paper.

■ **Credit sources for visuals.** If you use a visual element from a source, you need to credit the source. Unless you have specific guidelines to follow, you can use the word *Source,* followed by a colon and complete documentation of the source, including the author, title, publication information, and page number if applicable.

Note: The Modern Language Association (MLA) and the American Psychological Association (APA) provide guidelines for figure captions and crediting sources of visuals that differ from the preceding guidelines. (*See Chapter 24: MLA Style: Paper Format, p. 250, and Chapter 28: APA Style: Paper Format, p. 286.*)

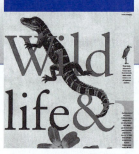

4 Revising and Editing

In the **revising** stage of the writing process, you review the whole paper, adding, deleting, and moving text as necessary. After you are satisfied with the substance of your paper, **editing** begins. When you edit, you polish sentences so that you say what you want to say as effectively as possible.

4a Getting comments from readers

Asking actual readers to comment on your draft is the best way to get fresh perspectives on your writing.

1. Using peer review

Peer review involves reading and critiquing your classmates' work while they review yours. Most readers want to be helpful. Help your readers help you by giving them information and asking them specific questions. When you share a draft with readers, give them answers to the following questions:

- **What is your assignment?** Readers need to understand the context for your paper—especially your intended purpose and audience.

- **How close is the project to being finished?** Your answer lets readers know where you are in the writing process and how best to assist you in taking the next step.

- **What steps do you plan to take to complete the project?** If readers know your plans, they can either question the direction you are taking or give you more specific advice, such as the titles of additional sources you might consult.

- **What kind of feedback do you need?** Let your readers know what you are looking for. Do you want readers to summarize your main points so you can determine if you have communicated them clearly? Do you want a response to the logic of your argument or the development of your thesis?

Tips LEARNING in COLLEGE

Re-Visioning Your Paper

Revising is a process of "re-visioning"—of looking at your work through the eyes of your audience. Here are some tips for getting a fresh perspective on your paper:

- **Get feedback from other readers.** Candid, respectful feedback can help you discover the strong and weak areas of your paper. See section 4a for advice on making use of readers' reactions to your drafts.

- **Let your draft "cool."** Try to schedule a break between drafting and revising. A good night's sleep, a movie break, or some physical exercise will help you view your paper more objectively.

- **Read your paper aloud.** Some people find that reading aloud helps them "hear" their paper the way their audience will.

- **Use revising and editing checklists.** The checklists on pages 57, 67, and 70 will assist you in evaluating your paper systematically.

Tips

WRITING in COLLEGE

Guidelines for Giving Feedback

- **Focus on strengths as well as weaknesses.** Writers need to know what parts of their paper are strongest so they can retain those sections when they revise and use them as models as they work to improve weaker sections. At the same time, do not withhold constructive criticism, or you will deprive the writer of an opportunity to improve the paper.
- **Be specific.** Give examples to back up your general reactions.
- **Be constructive.** Phrase negative reactions in a way that will help the writer see a solution. Instead of saying that an example is a bad choice, explain that you did not understand how the example was connected to the main point, and suggest a way to make the connection clearer.
- **Ask questions.** Jot down any questions that occur to you while reading. Ask for clarification or note an objection that readers of the final version might make.

Guidelines for Receiving Feedback

- **Resist any tendency to be defensive.** Keep in mind that readers are discussing your paper, not you, and their feedback offers a way for you to see your paper differently. Be respectful of their time and effort.
- **Ask for more feedback if you need it.** Some readers may be hesitant to share all of their reactions, and you may need to do some coaxing.
- **Try not to be frustrated by conflicting comments.** When you have two or more readers, you may receive differing—and sometimes contradictory—views on your work. Examine points of conflict and rethink the parts of your paper that caused them.

Reading other writers' drafts will help you view your own work more objectively, and comments from readers will help you see your own writing as others see it. In addition, the approaches that you see your classmates taking to the assignment will give you ideas for new directions in your own writing.

2. Responding to readers

Consider and evaluate your readers' suggestions, but remember that you are under no obligation to do what they say. Sometimes you will receive contradictory advice: one reader may like a particular sentence

4b
edit

Tips for Multilingual Writers: *Peer Review*

As a multilingual writer, you will find peer editing helpful in many ways. It will challenge you to look at your writing with a critical eye and to present your ideas to a diverse audience. It also will show you that many errors you make are quite common; it will help you improve your ability to detect mistakes and decide which ones to correct first.

that a second reader suggests you eliminate. Is there common ground? Yes. Both readers stopped at that sentence. Ask yourself why—and whether you want readers to pause there.

4b Using online tools for revising

www.mhhe.com/
bmhh

For help with
revising, go to
**Writing >
Paragraph/Essay
Development >
Drafting and
Revising**

It is always a good idea to print out a copy of your draft because the hard copy, unlike the computer screen, allows you to see your paper as a whole. Be sure to check for problems in content, structure, and style. Move paragraphs around, add details, and delete irrelevant sentences.

To work efficiently, become familiar with the revising and editing tools in your word-processing program.

- **Comments:** Many word-processing programs have a "Comments" feature that allows you to add marginal notes or notes that pop up when readers run the cursor over highlighted text, as shown in Figure 4.1. This feature is useful for giving feedback on someone else's draft. Some writers also use it to make notes to themselves.

- **Track changes:** The "Track Changes" feature allows you to edit a piece of writing while also maintaining the original text. Usually,

FIGURE 4.1 Using Microsoft Word's Comments feature.

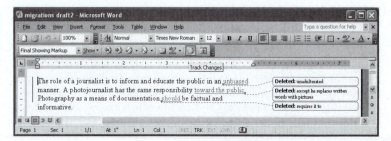

FIGURE 4.2 Showing revisions with Track Changes.

strike-through marks or marginal notes show what you have deleted or replaced, as shown in Figure 4.2. Because you can still see the original text, you can judge whether a change has improved the paper and whether any vital information has been lost. If you change your mind, you can restore the deleted text. When collaborating with another writer, you should keep the original text intact while suggesting changes. To do this, track changes onscreen only, or save the Track Changes version as a separate file.

4c Focusing on the purpose of your writing

As you reread your paper and decide how to revise it, base your decisions on the purpose of your paper. Is your primary purpose to inform, to interpret, or to argue?

Clarity about your purpose is especially important when an assignment calls for interpretation. A description is not the same as an interpretation. With this principle in mind, Diane Chen read over the first draft of her paper on the *Migrations* photography exhibit. Here is part of her description of the photograph she chose to discuss in detail:

FIRST DRAFT

The photograph is black and white, as are the others in the show. The faces of the babies are in sharp focus while the blanket is a bit defocused. Light, which is essential to photography, is disseminated from a single source coming from the upper left-hand corner of the picture. The light source is not too bright as to bathe the babies in light, but just bright enough to illuminate their faces, which have expressions of interest and puzzlement. Perhaps they are wondering who Salgado is or what is that strange contraption he is holding.

Keeping her purpose in mind, Chen realized that she needed to discuss the significance of her observations—to interpret and analyze the

CHECKLIST

Revising Your Draft for Content and Organization

☐ 1. **Purpose:** Is your purpose for writing clear? If not, how can you revise to make your purpose apparent?

☐ 2. **Audience:** Is your approach—including evidence and tone—appropriate for the intended readers?

☐ 3. **Thesis:** Is your thesis clear and specific, and do you introduce it early in your draft? (If not, do you have a good reason for withholding it or not stating it at all?)

☐ 4. **Order:** Are your key points arranged effectively? Would another order better support your thesis?

☐ 5. **Paragraphs:** Is each paragraph well developed, unified, and coherent?

☐ 6. **Visuals:** If you are using visuals, do they communicate what you intend them to, without resulting in unnecessary clutter?

details. She wanted to show her readers how the formal elements of the photograph functioned. Her revision makes this interpretation clearer:

REVISION

> The orphanage photograph is shot in black and white, as are the other images in the show, giving it a documentary feel that emphasizes the truth of the situation. But Salgado's choice of black-and-white photography is also an artistic decision. He uses the contrasts of light and dark to create a dramatic image of the three babies.
>
> The vertical black and white stripes of the blanket direct our eyes to the infants' faces and hands, which are framed by a horizontal white stripe . . .

4d Testing your thesis

Remember that a thesis makes an assertion about a topic. It links the *what* and the *why*. Is your thesis evident on the first page of your draft? Before readers get very far along, they expect an answer to the question "What is the point of all this?" If you do not find the point on the first page, its absence is a signal to revise, unless you are deliberately waiting until the end to share your thesis. (*For more on strong theses, see Chapter 2, pp. 23–26.*)

www.mhhe.com/
bmhh

For help with developing a strong thesis, go to

Writing > Paragraph/Essay Development > Thesis/Central Idea

Many writers start with a working thesis, which often evolves into a more specific, complex assertion as they develop their ideas. One of the key challenges of revising is to compose a clear statement of this revised thesis. When she drafted a paper on Germany's economic prospects, Jennifer Koehler stated her working thesis as follows:

WORKING THESIS

Germany is experiencing a great deal of change.

During the revision process, Koehler realized that her working thesis was too weak to serve as the thesis of her final draft. A weak thesis is predictable: readers read it, agree, and that's that. A strong thesis, on the other hand, stimulates thoughtful inquiry. Koehler's revised thesis provokes questions:

REVISED THESIS

With proper follow-through, Germany can become one of the world's primary sources of direct investment and maintain its status as one of the world's preeminent exporters.

Sometimes writers find that their ideas change altogether, and the working thesis needs to be completely revised.

Your thesis should evolve throughout the paper. Readers need to see a statement of the main idea on the first page, but they also expect a more complex or general statement near the end. After presenting evidence to support her revised thesis, Koehler concludes her paper by stating her thesis in a more general way:

If the government efforts continue, the economy will strengthen over the next decade, and Germany will reinforce its position as an integral nation in the global economy.

Exercise 4.1   Revising thesis statements

Examine some of your recent papers to see if the thesis is clearly stated. Is the thesis significant? Can you follow the development of this idea throughout the paper? Does the version of your thesis in the conclusion answer the "so what?" question?

4e   Reviewing the structure of your paper

Does the paper have a beginning, a middle, and an end, with bridges between those parts? When you revise, you can refine and even change this structure so that it supports what you want to say more effectively.

One way to review your structure is by outlining the first draft. (*For help with outlining, see Chapter 2, pp. 27–30.*) Try listing the key points of your draft in sentence form; whenever possible, use sentences that actually appear in the draft. This kind of point-by-point outlining will allow you to see the draft's logic (or lack thereof). Ask yourself if the key points are arranged effectively or if another arrangement would work better. The following structures are typical ways of organizing papers:

■ **Informative:** sets out the key parts of a topic.

■ **Exploratory:** begins with a question or problem and works step-by-step to discover an answer or a solution.

■ **Argumentative:** presents a set of linked reasons plus supporting evidence.

4f   Revising for paragraph development, paragraph unity, and coherence

As you revise, examine each paragraph, asking yourself what role it plays—or should play—in the paper as a whole. Keeping this role in mind, check the paragraph for development and unity. You should also check each paragraph for coherence—and consider whether all of the paragraphs together contribute to the paper as a whole.

1. Paragraph development

Does each paragraph provide enough detail? Paragraphs in academic papers are usually about a hundred words long. Although sometimes you will deliberately use a one- or two-sentence paragraph for emphasis, short paragraphs generally need to be developed more fully or combined with other paragraphs. Would more information make the point clearer? Should a term be defined? Do generalizations need to be supported with examples?

Note how this writer developed one of her paragraphs, adding details and examples to make her argument more effective:

FIRST DRAFT

A 1913 advertisement for Shredded Wheat illustrates Kellner's claim that advertisements sell self-images. The ad suggests that serving Shredded Wheat will give women the same sense of accomplishment as gaining the right to vote.

REVISION

According to Kellner, "advertising is as concerned with selling lifestyles and socially desirable identities . . . as with selling the products themselves" (193). A 1913 ad for Shredded Wheat shows how the selling of self-images works. At first glance, this ad seems to be promoting the women's suffrage movement. In big, bold letters, "Votes for Women" is emblazoned across the top of the ad. But a closer look reveals that the ad is for Shredded Wheat cereal. Holding a piece of the cereal in her hand, a woman stands behind a large bowlful of Shredded Wheat biscuits that is made to look like a voting box. The text claims that "every biscuit is a vote for health, happiness, and domestic freedom." Like the rest of the advertisement, this claim suggests that serving Shredded Wheat will give women the same sense of accomplishment as gaining the right to vote.

—HOLLY MUSETTI, "Targeting Women," student paper

2. Paragraph unity

www.mhhe.com/
bmhh

For more help with paragraph unity, go to

Writing >
Paragraph/Essay
Development >
Unity

A unified paragraph has a single, clear focus. To check for **unity,** identify the paragraph's topic sentence (*see pp. 47–50*). Everything in the paragraph should be clearly connected to the topic sentence.

Compare the first draft of the following paragraph with its revision, and note how the addition of a topic sentence (in bold in the revision) makes the paragraph more clearly focused and therefore easier for the writer to revise further. Note also that the writer deleted the underlined ideas because they did not directly relate to the paragraph's main point:

FIRST DRAFT

Germany is ranked first on worldwide production levels. Automobiles, aircraft, and electronic equipment are among Germany's most important products for export. As the standard of living of the citizens of what was formerly East Germany increases due to reunification, their purchasing power and productivity will increase. A major problem is that east Germany is not as productive or efficient as west Germany, and so it would be better if less money were invested in the east. Germany is involved in most global treaties that protect business interests, and intellectual property is well protected. A plus for potential ventures and production plans is its highly skilled workforce. Another factor that indicates that Germany will remain strong in the arena of productivity and trade is its physical location in the world. "Its terrain and geographical position have combined to make Germany an important crossroads for traffic between the North Sea, the Baltic, and the Mediterranean. International transportation routes pass through all of Germany," thus utilizing a comprehensive and efficient network of transportation, both on land and over water ("Germany," 1995, p. 185). Businesses can operate plants in Germany and have no difficulties transporting goods and services to other parts of the country. Generally, private enterprise, government, banks, and unions cooperate, making the country more amenable to negotiations for business entry or joint ventures.

REVISION

> **For many reasons, Germany is attractive both as a market for other nations and as a location for production.** As the standard of living of the citizens of what was formerly East Germany increases due to reunification, their purchasing power and productivity increase. Intellectual property is well protected, and Germany is involved in most global treaties that protect business interests. Germany's highly skilled workforce is another plus for potential ventures and production plans. Generally, private enterprise, government, banks, and unions cooperate, making the country amenable to negotiations for business entry or joint ventures. Germany also has an excellent physical location that makes it an "important crossroads for traffic between the North Sea, the Baltic, and the Mediterranean" ("Germany," 1995, p. 185). Equally important, a comprehensive and efficient transportation system allows businesses to operate plants in Germany and easily transport their goods and services to other parts of the country and the world.

> —JENNIFER KOEHLER, "Germany's Path to Continuing Prosperity," student paper

3. Coherence

A coherent paragraph flows smoothly, with an organization that is easy to follow and each sentence clearly related to the next. You can improve coherence both within and among the paragraphs in your draft by using repetition, pronouns, parallel structure, synonyms, and transitions.

www.mhhe.com/
bmhh

For more help with coherence, go to

Writing >
Paragraph/Essay
Development >
Coherence

■ Repeat key words to emphasize the main idea:

> A photograph displays a unique *moment*. To capture that *moment* . . .

■ Use pronouns and antecedents to form connections between sentences and avoid unnecessary repetition. In the following example, *it* refers back to *Germany* and connects the two sentences:

> *Germany* imports raw materials, energy sources, and food products. *It* exports a wide range of industrial products, including automobiles, aircraft, and machine tools.

■ Repeat sentence structures to emphasize connections:

> *Because the former West Germany* lived through a generation of prosperity, its people developed high expectations of material

comfort. *Because the former East Germany* lived through a generation of deprivation, its people developed disdain for material values.

- Use **synonyms**—words that are close in meaning to words or phrases that have preceded them:

  In the world of photography, critics *argue* for either a scientific or an artistic approach. This *controversy* . . .

- Use transitional words and phrases. One-word transitions and **transitional expressions** link one idea with another, showing the relationship between them (such as contrast, exception, and illustration). (*See the list of common transitional expressions in the box on p. 63.*) Compare the following two paragraphs, the first version without transitions and the second, revised version with transitions (in bold type) that connect one thought to another:

  FIRST DRAFT

  Glaser was in a position to powerfully affect Armstrong's career and his life. There is little evidence that the musician submitted to whatever his business manager wanted or demanded. Armstrong seemed to recognize that he gave Glaser whatever power the manager enjoyed over him. Armstrong could and did resist Glaser's control when he wanted to. That may be one reason why he liked and trusted Glaser as much as he did.

  REVISION

  Clearly, Glaser was in a position to affect Armstrong's career and his life powerfully. **However,** there is little evidence that the musician submitted to whatever his business manager wanted or demanded. **In fact,** Armstrong seemed to recognize that he gave Glaser whatever power the manager enjoyed over him. When he wanted to, Armstrong could and did resist Glaser's control, and that may be one reason why he liked and trusted Glaser as much as he did.

  —ESTHER HOFFMAN, "Louis Armstrong and Joe Glaser"

- Use repetition, pronouns, parallelism, transitions, and **transitional sentences,** which refer back to the previous paragraph and move your essay on to the next point, to show how paragraphs in an essay are related to one another:

TRANSITIONAL EXPRESSIONS

- **To show relationships in space:** above, adjacent to, against, alongside, around, at a distance from, at the . . . , below, beside, beyond, encircling, far off, forward, from the . . . , in front of, in the rear, inside, near the back, near the end, nearby, next to, on, over, surrounding, there, through the, to the left, to the right, up front

- **To show relationships in time:** afterward, at last, before, earlier, first, former, formerly, immediately, in the first place, in the interval, in the meantime, in the next place, in the last place, later on, meanwhile, next, now, often, once, previously, second, simultaneously, sometime later, subsequently, suddenly, then, third, today, tomorrow, until now, when, years ago, yesterday

- **To show something added to what has come before:** again, also, and, and then, besides, further, furthermore, in addition, last, likewise, moreover, next, too

- **To give examples that intensify points:** after all, as an example, certainly, clearly, for example, for instance, indeed, in fact, in truth, it is true, of course, specifically, that is

- **To show similarities:** alike, in the same way, like, likewise, resembling, similarly

- **To show contrasts:** after all, although, but, conversely, differ(s) from, difference, different, dissimilar, even though, granted, however, in contrast, in spite of, nevertheless, notwithstanding, on the contrary, on the other hand, otherwise, still, though, unlike, while this may be true, yet

- **To indicate cause and effect:** accordingly, as a result, because, consequently, hence, since, then, therefore, thus

- **To conclude or summarize:** finally, in brief, in conclusion, in other words, in short, in summary, that is, to summarize

---

The vertical black and white stripes of the blanket direct our eyes to the infants' faces and hands, which are framed by a horizontal white stripe. The whites of their eyes in particular stand out against the darkness created by the shell of the blankets. The camera's lens also seems to be in sharper focus on the faces than on the blankets, again focusing our attention on the babies' expressions.

Each baby has a different response to the camera. The baby on the left returns our gaze with a heart-wrenching look. . . .

Exercise 4.2 Revising paragraphs

Revise the paragraphs below to improve their unity, development, and coherence.

1. Vivaldi was famous and influential as a virtuoso violinist and composer. Vivaldi died in poverty, having lost popularity in the last years before his death. He had been acclaimed during his lifetime and forgotten for two hundred years after his death. Many composers suffer that fate. The baroque revival of the 1950s brought his music back to the public's attention.

2. People who want to adopt an exotic pet need to be aware of the consequences. Baby snakes and reptiles can seem fairly easy to manage. Adult snakes and reptiles can grow large. Many species of reptiles and snakes require carefully controlled environments. Lion and tiger cubs are playful and friendly. They can seem as harmless as kittens. Domestic cats can revert to a wild state quite easily. Big cats can escape. An escaped lion or tiger is a danger to itself and to others. Most exotic animals need professional care. This kind of care is available in zoos and wild-animal parks. The best environment for an exotic animal is the wild.

Exercise 4.3 Writing well-developed, coherent paragraphs

Using the strategies for paragraph development and coherence discussed in section 4f, write a paragraph for one of the following topic sentences. Working with two or more classmates, decide where your paragraph needs more details or improved coherence.

1. Awards shows on television often fail to recognize creativity and innovation.
2. Most people learn only those aspects of a computer program that they need to use every day.
3. First-year students who also work can have an easier time adjusting to the demands of college life than nonworking students.
4. E-mail messages that circulate widely can be broken down into several categories.

Exercise 4.4 Revising your paragraphs

Review the paragraphs you wrote in Exercise 4.3, and revise them using the strategies in this section.

4g Revising visuals

If you have used visuals in your paper, you should return to them during the revision stage to eliminate what scholar Edward Tufte calls **chartjunk,** or distracting visual elements. The following are Tufte's suggestions for editing visuals so that your readers will focus on your data rather than your "data containers":

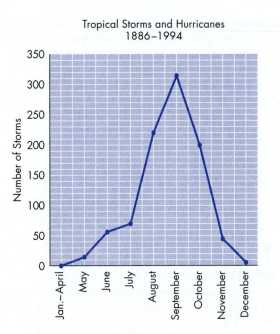

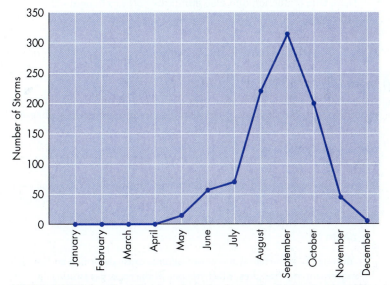

FIGURE 4.3 Misleading (top) and revised graph. In the graph at the top, the activity in the first part of the year is combined into one point on the axis, misleading readers. The chart at the bottom has been revised to correct this problem.

- **Eliminate grid lines or, if the lines are needed for clarity, lighten them.** Tables should not look like nets with every number enclosed. Vertical rules are needed only when space is extremely tight between columns.

- **Eliminate any unnecessary 3D renderings.** Cubes and shadows can distort the information in a visual. For most charts, including pie charts, a flat image makes it easier for readers to compare parts.

- **Label data clearly,** avoiding abbreviations and legends if possible. Make sure each visual has an informative title.

- **Use bright colors for emphasis,** to focus attention on the key data. For example, if you are including a map, use muted colors over large areas and save strong colors for areas you want to emphasize.

- **Avoid decorating your visual with distracting pictures.** Clip art and other decorative elements seldom make data more interesting or more substantial.

- **Look out for and correct distortions of the data.** In the first graph in Figure 4.3, each month gets its own point, except for January, February, March, and April. This creates a misleading impression of hurricane activity by month. The revision corrects this distortion and also eliminates other elements of chartjunk.

www.mhhe.com/
bmhh

For additional help
with editing, go to

Editing

4h   Editing sentences

When you are satisfied with the overall placement and development of your ideas, you can turn your attention to individual sentences, phrases, and words.

1. Editing for clarity

As you edit, concentrate on sentence style, aiming for clearly focused writing. You should condense and focus sentences that are wordy and lack a clear subject and vivid verb:

DRAFT

Although both vertebral and wrist fractures cause deformity and impair movement, hip fractures, which are one of the most devastating consequences of osteoporosis, significantly increase the risk of death, since 12%–30% of patients with a hip fracture die within one year after the fracture, while the mortality rate climbs to 40% for the first two years post fracture.

CHECKLIST

4h
edit

Editing Your Draft for Style and Grammar

To create a personalized editing checklist, fill in the boxes next to your trouble spots, as determined from your instructor's comments on your writing, as well as any diagnostic tests you have taken.

1. Clarity (*Part 6, Chapters 30–38, pp. 299–339*): Does every sentence communicate your meaning in a clear, direct style? Does your paper contain any of the following common causes of unclear sentences?

   ☐ Wordiness
   ☐ Missing words
   ☐ Mixed constructions
   ☐ Confusing shifts
   ☐ Faulty parallelism
   ☐ Misplaced and dangling modifiers
   ☐ Problem with coordination and subordination
   ☐ Other: _____

2. Word choice (*Part 6, Chapters 39–41, pp. 340–62*): Is your choice of words as precise as it could be? Have you avoided slang, biased language, clichés, and other inappropriate usages? Have you misused any commonly confused words (for example, *advice* vs. *advise*) or used any nonstandard expressions (for example, *could of*)?

3. Grammar conventions (*Part 7, Chapters 42–48, pp. 365–443*): Does your paper contain any of the common errors that may confuse or distract readers?

   ☐ Sentence fragments
   ☐ Comma splices
   ☐ Run-on sentences
   ☐ Subject-verb agreement problems
   ☐ Incorrect verb forms
   ☐ Inconsistent verb tenses
   ☐ Pronoun-antecedent agreement problems
   ☐ Incorrect pronoun forms
   ☐ Misused adjectives or adverbs
   ☐ Other: _____

If you are in the process of developing fluency in English, consult Chapter 48.

REVISED

Hip fractures are one of the most devastating consequences of osteo-porosis. Although vertebral and wrist fractures cause deformity and impair movement, hip fractures significantly increase the risk of death. Within one year after a hip fracture, 12%–20% of the injured die. The mortality rate climbs to 40% after two years.

More often than not, sentences beginning with *it is* or *there is* or *there are* (*it was* or *there was*)—called **expletive constructions**—are weak and indirect. Using a clear subject and a vivid verb usually makes such sentences more powerful:

DRAFT

There are stereotypes from the days of a divided Germany.

REVISED

Stereotypes formed in the days of a divided Germany persist.

2. Editing for word choice

As you review your draft, look for general terms that might need to be made more specific:

DRAFT

Foreign direct investment (FDI) in Germany will probably remain low because of several *factors*. [*Factors is a general word. To get specific, answer the question* "What *factors?"*]

REVISED

Foreign direct investment (FDI) in Germany will probably remain low because of *high labor costs, high taxation, and government regulation.*

Your search for more specific words can lead you to a dictionary and thesaurus, two essential tools for choosing precise words.

3. Editing for grammar conventions

Sometimes writers will construct a sentence or choose a word form that does not follow the rules of standard written English:

DRAFT

Photographs of illegal immigrants being captured by the U.S. border patrol, of emotional immigrants on the plane to their new country, and of villagers fleeing rebel gangs. [*This is a sentence fragment because it lacks a verb and omits the writer's point about these images.*]

TEXTCONNEX

When You Know More Than Grammar and Spell Checkers

Grammar and spell checkers can help you spot some errors, but they miss many others and may even flag a correct sentence. Consider the following example:

Thee neighbors puts there cats' outsider.

A spelling and grammar checker did not catch the five errors in the sentence. (Correct version: *The neighbors put their cats outside.*)

If you are aware of your program's deficiencies, then you can make some use of it as you edit your document. Be sure, however, to review your writing carefully yourself.

EDITED SENTENCE

Photographs of illegal immigrants being captured by the U.S. border patrol, of emotional immigrants on the plane to their new country, and of villagers fleeing rebel gangs exemplify the range of migration stories.

Exercise 4.5 Editing sentences

Type the following sentences into your word processor and activate the grammar and spell-checker feature. Copy the sentence suggested by the software, and then write your own edited version of the sentence.

1. Lighting affects are sense of the shape and texture of the objects depict.

2. A novelist's tells the truth even though he invent stories and characters.

3. There are the question of why bad things happen to good people, which story of Job illustrate.

4. A expensive marketing campaign is of little value if the product stinks.

5. Digestive enzymes melt down the nutrients in food so that the body is able to put in effect a utilization of those nutrients when the body needs energy to do things.

4i Proofreading carefully

Once you have revised your paper at the essay, paragraph, and sentence levels, it is time to give your work one last check to make sure that it is free of typos and other mechanical errors.

CHECKLIST

Proofreading

☐ 1. Have you included your name, the date, your professor's name, and the paper title? *(See Chapters 21–29 for the formats to use for MLA or APA style.)*

☐ 2. Are all words spelled correctly? Be sure to check the spelling of titles and headings. *(See Chapter 60, pp. 506–12.)*

☐ 3. Have you used the words you intended, or have you substituted words that sound like the ones you want but have a different spelling and meaning, such as *too* for *to, their* for *there,* or *it's* for *its*? *(See Chapter 41, pp. 353–62.)*

☐ 4. Are all proper names capitalized? Have you capitalized titles of works correctly and either italicized them or put them in quotation marks as required? *(See Chapter 55, pp. 490–94, and Chapter 58, pp. 500–03.)*

☐ 5. Have you punctuated your sentences correctly? *(See Part 9.)*

☐ 6. Are sources cited correctly? Is the works-cited or references list in the correct format? *(See Parts 4–5.)*

☐ 7. Have you checked anything you retyped—for example, quotations and tables—against the original?

Proofread a printout of your paper even if you are submitting an electronic version. A ruler placed under each line as you are proofing can make it easier to focus. Another proofreading technique is to start at the end of the paper and proofread your way backwards to the beginning, sentence by sentence.

4j   Using campus, Internet, and community resources

As you revise and edit your paper, you can call on a number of resources outside of the classroom for help.

1. Using the campus writing center

Tutors in the writing center can read and comment on drafts of your work. They can also help you find and correct problems with grammar and punctuation.

www.mhhe.com/ bmhh

For links to OWLs, go to

Writing > Writing Web Links

2. Using online writing labs (OWLs)

Most OWLs offer information about writing that you can access anytime, including lists of useful online resources. Some OWLs are staffed by tutors who support students working on specific writing assignments. OWLs with tutors can be useful in the following ways:

- You can submit a draft via e-mail for feedback. OWL tutors will return your work, often within forty-eight hours.

- You can post your paper in a public access space where you will receive feedback from more than just one or two readers.

- You can read papers online and learn how others are handling writing issues.

You can learn more about what OWLs have to offer by checking out the following Web sites:

- Purdue University's Online Writing Lab: <http://owl.english .purdue.edu>

- Writing Labs and Writing Centers on the Web (visit almost fifty OWLs): <http://owl.english.purdue.edu/internet/owls/ writing-labs.html>

- Washington State University's Online Writing Lab: <http://owl.wsu.edu>

3. Working with experts and instructors

In addition to sharing your work with peers in class, through e-mail, or in online environments, you can use e-mail to consult your instructor or other experts. Many students don't think to ask their instructor questions by e-mail.

Your instructor's comments on an early draft are especially valuable. He or she will raise questions and make suggestions, but remember, it is your responsibility to address the issues your instructor raises and to revise your work accordingly.

4k Learning from one student's revisions

In the following paragraphs from the second draft of Diane Chen's paper on an exhibit of photographs by Sebastião Salgado, you can see how she revised her draft to tighten the focus of her descriptive paragraphs and edited to improve clarity, word choice, and grammar.

The Caring Eye of Sebastião Salgado

Photographer Sebastiao Salgado spent seven years ~~of his life~~ traveling along migration routes to city slums and refugee camps, in order to document the lives of people uprooted from their homelands. A selection of his photographs can be seen in the exhibit, *"Migrations: Humanity in Transition."* Like a photojournalist, Salgado brings us images of newsworthy events, but he goes beyond objective reporting, imparting his compassion for refugees and migrants to the viewer.

M~~So m~~any of the photographs in Salgado's show are certain to ~~impress and~~ touch viewers ~~the viewer with their subject matter and sheer beauty~~. Whether capturing the millions of refugee tents in Africa that seem to stretch on for miles or the disheartened faces of ~~small~~ immigrant children, the images in *Migrations*~~Salgado brings an artistic element to his pictures that~~ suggests~~ he~~ that Salgado does so much more with his camera than ~~just~~ point and shoot.

Salgado's photograph of the most vulnerable of these refugees illustrates the power of his work. "Orphanage attached to the hospital at Kibumba, Number One Camp, Goma Zaire," (fig. 1) depicts three infants~~apparently newborn or several-month-old babies,~~ who are victims of the genocidal war in neighboring Rwanda. The label for the photograph reveals~~tells us~~ that there were 4,000 orphans at this camp and an estimated 100,000 Rwandan orphans overall. Those numbers are mind-numbing abstractions, but this picture is not.

5 Designing Academic Papers and Portfolios

One of your final writing tasks is to format your text so that readers can "see" your ideas clearly. In this chapter, our main focus is on designing academic papers.

In your writing course, as well as in other courses and in your professional life, you may be called on to compile a **portfolio**—a collection of your writings. This chapter offers guidelines for designing print and electronic portfolios that showcase your work effectively.

5a Considering audience and purpose

As you plan your document, consider your purpose as well as the needs of your audience. If you are writing an informative paper for a psychology class, your instructor will probably prefer that you follow the guidelines provided by the American Psychological Association (APA). However, interpretive papers for language and literature courses usually use the style recommended by the Modern Language Association (MLA). In any paper, however, your goal is to enhance the content of your text, not decorate it.

www.mhhe.com/
bmhh

For links to
information on
document and
Web design,
go to

**Writing > Writing
Web Links >
Annotated Links
on Design**

5b Using computer toolbars

The toolbars on your computer give you a range of options for editing, sharing, and, especially, designing your documents. A variety of toolbars are available in most widely used word-processing programs. For example, if you are using Microsoft Word, you can find them by looking at the pulldown menu under "View." In Figure 5.1, three toolbars are open: standard, drawing, and reviewing. The *standard* toolbar allows you to choose different typefaces; bold, italic, or underlined type; numbered or bulleted lists; and so on. The *drawing* toolbar allows you to insert boxes, drawings, and clip art into your text. The *reviewing* toolbar enables you to mark changes, add comments, and even send your document to a reader.

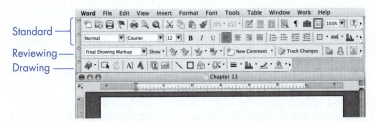

FIGURE 5.1 The standard, drawing, and reviewing toolbars in Microsoft Word.

73

Take some time to learn the different toolbars and formatting options available to you.

5c Thinking intentionally about design

For any document that you create, whether for an academic course or for a purpose and audience outside of college, you need to apply the same basic design principles:

- Organize information for readers.
- Use type style, lists, and other graphic elements to make your text readable and to emphasize key material.
- Format related design elements consistently.
- Include headings to organize long papers.
- Show restraint.
- Meet the needs of readers with disabilities.

A sample page from a student's report on a local food bank, which includes information that she gathered while serving as a volunteer, illustrates these principles. The content in the sample on page 76 is at a disadvantage because the author has not employed these principles. By contrast, the same material on page 77 is clearer and easier for readers to understand because of its design.

1. Organizing information for readers

You can organize information visually and topically by grouping related items, using boxes, indents, headings, spacing, and lists. For example, in this book, headings help to group information for readers, and bulleted and numbered lists such as the bulleted list in the "Tips" box on the next page present related points. These variations in text appearance help readers scan, locate information, and dive in when they need to know more about a topic.

You can also use **white space**—the areas of your document that do not contain type or graphics—to help organize information for your readers. Allowing generous margins and plenty of white space above headings and around other elements makes text easier to read.

You should also introduce any visuals within your text and position them so that they appear near—but never before—this text reference. Strive for a pleasing balance between visuals and other text elements; for example, don't try to cram too many visuals onto one page.

2. Using type style and lists for readability and emphasis

Typefaces are designs that have been established by printers for the letters in the alphabet, numbers, punctuation marks, and special

Tips for LEARNING in COLLEGE

The Basics: Margins, Spacing, Type, and Page Numbers

Here are a few basic guidelines for formatting academic papers:

- **First page:** In a paper that is no longer than five pages, you can usually place a header with your name, your professor's name, your course and section number, and the date on the first page, above the text. (*See the first page of Esther Hoffman's paper on p. 251.*) If your paper exceeds five pages, page 1 is often a title page. (*See the first page of Audrey Galeano's paper, which is in APA style, on p. 287.*)
- **Type:** Select a common typeface, or font, and choose an 11- or 12-point size.
- **Margins:** Use one-inch margins on all four sides of your text. Adequate margins make your paper easier to read and give your instructor room to write comments and suggestions.
- **Margin justification:** Line up, or justify, the lines of your document along the left margin but not along the right margin. Leaving a "ragged right" or uneven right margin, as in this box, enables you to avoid odd spacing between words.
- **Spacing:** Always double-space your paper unless you are instructed to do otherwise, and indent the first line of each paragraph five spaces. Use the ruler at the top of your screen to set this indent automatically. (Many business documents are single-spaced, with an extra line space between paragraphs, which are not indented.)
- **Page numbers:** Place page numbers in the upper or lower right-hand corner of the page. Some documentation styles require a header next to the page number. (*See Parts 4–5 for the requirements of the style you are following.*)

characters. **Fonts** are all of the variations available in a certain typeface and size (for example, 12-point Times New Roman is available in **bold** and *italics*). **Serif** typefaces have tiny lines (serifs) at the ends of letters such as *n* and *y;* **sans serif** typefaces do not have these lines. Standard serif typefaces such as the following are widely used for basic text because they are easy to read:

Times New Roman	Courier
Bookman Old Style	Palatino

For most academic papers, you should choose a standard, easy-to-read typeface and use an 11- or 12-point size. Sans serif typefaces such as

EXAMPLE OF A POORLY DESIGNED REPORT

Emphasis wrong: title of report not as prominent as heading within report.

Margins not wide enough, making page look crowded.

Bar chart not introduced in text, and does not have caption.

The Caring Express Food Bank

The Caring Express Food Bank serves a varied population of clients, including chronically homeless people, temporarily homeless people, recent immigrants, elderly people on fixed incomes, and people in need of temporary services.

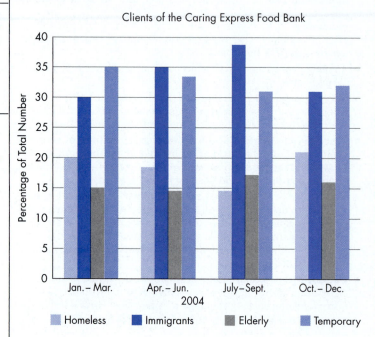

Clients of the Caring Express Food Bank

While the number of homeless, both temporary and permanent, that Caring Express assisted in 2004 decreased during the summer months, the number of immigrant workers increased. The percentage of elderly people and people in need of temporary services remained fairly stable throughout the year.

Description of procedure is dense, hard to follow.

Use of bold type and different typeface for no reason.

How Caring Express Helps Clients

When new clients come to Caring Express, a volunteer fills out a **form** with their **address** (if they have one), their **phone number,** their **income,** their **employment situation,** and the help they are receiving, if any, from the local department of human services. Clients who do not live in Maple Valley are referred to a food bank or outreach program in their area. Clients who qualify check off the food they need from a list, and then that food is packed and distributed to them.

EXAMPLE OF A BETTER DESIGN

The Caring Express Food Bank

The Caring Express Food Bank serves a varied population of clients, including chronically homeless people, temporarily homeless people, recent immigrants, elderly people on fixed incomes, and people in need of temporary services. As Figure 1 shows, while the number of homeless, both temporary and permanent, that Caring Express assisted in 2004 decreased during the summer months, the number of immigrant workers increased. The percentage of elderly people and people in need of temporary services remained fairly stable throughout the year.

Title centered and in larger type than text and heading.

Bar chart introduced and explained.

Wider margins and white space above and below figure make report easier to read.

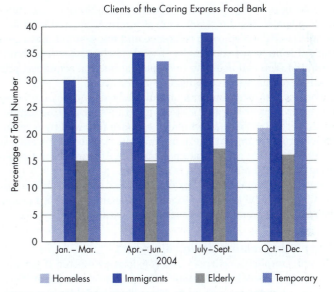

Figure 1. Percentage of clients in each group during 2004

Caption explains figure.

How Caring Express Helps Clients

When new clients come to Caring Express, the volunteers follow this procedure:

1. The volunteer fills out a form with the client's address (if he or she has one), phone number, income, and employment situation.
2. Clients who do not live in Maple Valley are referred to a food bank or outreach program in their area.
3. Clients who qualify check off the food they need from a list.
4. The food is packed and distributed to them.

Heading subordinate to title.

Procedure is explained in numbered list. Parallel structure is used for list entries.

the following are sometimes used for headings because they offer a pleasing contrast:

Arial

Verdana

Many typefaces available on your computer are known as **display fonts,** for example:

Curlz

𝔒𝔩𝔡 𝔈𝔫𝔤𝔩𝔦𝔰𝔥

These should be used rarely, if ever, in academic papers, on the screen, or in presentations. They can be used effectively in other kinds of documents, however, such as brochures, fliers, and posters.

You can emphasize a word or phrase in your text by selecting it and making it **bold,** *italicized,* or <u>underlined</u>. Numbered or bulleted lists help you cluster large amounts of information, making the information easier for readers to reference and understand. Because they stand out from your text visually, lists also help readers see that ideas are related. You can use lists to display steps in a sequence, present checklists, or suggest recommendations for action.

Format text as a numbered or bulleted list by choosing the option you want from your word-processing program's formatting commands. Introduce the list with a complete sentence followed by a colon, use parallel structure in your list items, and put a period at the end of each item if the entries are complete sentences. If they are not complete sentences, no end punctuation is necessary.

Putting information in a box emphasizes it and also makes it easier for readers to find if they need to refer to it again. Most word-processing programs offer several ways to enclose text within a border or box.

3. Formatting related design elements

In design, simplicity, contrast, and consistency matter. If you emphasize an item by putting it in italic or bold type or in color, or if you use a graphic element such as a box to set it off, consider repeating this effect for similar items so that your document has a unified look. Even a simple horizontal line can be a purposeful element in a long document when used consistently to help organize information.

4. Using headings to organize long papers

In short papers of one to two pages, headings can disrupt the text and are usually not necessary. In longer papers, though, they can help you organize complex information.

Effective headings are brief and descriptive. The headings in academic papers are usually in the form of phrases, although they might be in the form of questions or even imperative sentences. Make sure that your headings are consistent in grammatical structure as well as formatting:

PHRASES BEGINNING WITH *–ING* WORDS

Fielding Inquiries

Handling Complaints

NOUNS AND NOUN PHRASES

Customer Inquiries

Complaints

QUESTIONS

How Do I Field Inquiries?

How Do I Handle Complaints?

IMPERATIVE SENTENCES

Field Inquiries Efficiently

Handle Complaints Calmly and Politely

Headings at different levels can be in different forms. For example, the first-level headings in a book might be imperative sentences, while the second-level headings might begin with *–ing* words.

Place and highlight headings consistently throughout your paper. If you have not already done so, preparing a formal topic outline will help you decide what your main points and second-level points are and where headings should go. *(See Chapter 2, pp. 27–30.)* You might center all first-level headings, which correspond to the main points in your outline. If you have second-level headings—your supporting points—you might align them at the left margin and underline them. Third-level headings, if you have them, could be aligned at the left margin and set in plain type:

First-Level Heading

<u>Second-Level Heading</u>

Third-Level Heading

A heading should never appear at the very bottom of a page. If a heading falls in this position, move it to the top of the next page.

5. Using restraint

If you use too many graphics, headings, bullets, boxes, or other elements in a document, you risk making it as "noisy" as a loud radio.

Standard typefaces and fonts have become standard because they are easy on the eye. Variations from these standard fonts jar the eye. Bold or italic type, underlining, or any other graphic effect should not continue for more than one sentence at a time.

6. Meeting the needs of readers with disabilities

If you think that your audience may include the vision- or hearing-impaired, take a few simple principles into account:

- **Use a large, easily readable font.** The font should be 14 point or larger. Use a sans serif font such as Arial, as readers with poor vision find these fonts easier to read. (*See pp. 75–78.*) Set the entire document in bold. Make headings larger than the surrounding text (rather than relying on a change in font, bold, italics, or color to set them apart).

- **Use ample spacing between lines.** The American Council of the Blind recommends a line spacing of 1.5.

- **Use appropriate, high-contrast colors.** Black text on a white background is best. If you use color for text or visuals, put light material on a dark background and dark material on a light background. Use colors from different families (such as yellow on purple). Also, avoid red and green because color-blind readers may have trouble distinguishing them. Do not use glossy paper.

- **Include narrative descriptions of all visuals.** Describe each chart, map, photograph, or other visual in your paper. Indicate the key information and the point the visual makes. (This is a greater concern when writing for the Web; *see Chapter 11, p. 134.*)

- **If you include audio or video files in an electronic document, provide transcripts.** Also include narrative description of what is happening in the video.

For further information, consult the American Council of the Blind (http://acb.org/accessible-formats.html), Lighthouse International (http://www.lighthouse.org/print_leg.htm), and the American Printing House for the Blind (http://www.aph.org/edresearch/lpguide.htm).

5d Compiling a portfolio

When presenting their written work for final submission, students are often asked to collect it in a portfolio. Likewise, when applying for a position that calls for a great deal of writing, job candidates are often asked to provide a portfolio of their writing. Although most portfolios consist of a collection of papers in print form, many students create writing portfolios that are available electronically.

Portfolios, regardless of medium, share at least three common features:

- They are a *collection* of work.
- They offer a *selection*—or subset—of a larger body of work.
- Once assembled, they are introduced, narrated, or commented on by a document that offers the writer's *reflection* on her or his work.

As with any type of writing, portfolios serve a purpose and address an audience—to demonstrate your progress in a course for your instructor, for example, or to present your best work for a prospective employer.

When creating a print writing portfolio, you will usually need to complete the following five activities:

- Gather all your written work.
- Review your work and make appropriate selections.
- Arrange the selections deliberately.
- Include a reflective essay or letter.
- Polish your portfolio.

1. Gathering your writing

If you are preparing a portfolio for a writing course, you may need to provide your exploratory writing, notes, and comments from peer reviewers as well as all your drafts for one or more of the papers you include. Be sure that all of your materials have your name on them and that the copy of your final draft does not include errors.

2. Reviewing written work and making selections

Keep the purpose of the portfolio in mind as you review your work, as well as the criteria that will be used to evaluate it. If you are assembling a "showcase" portfolio, you will want to select only your very best work. If you are demonstrating your improvement as a writer, you will want to select papers that show your development and creativity.

If no criteria have been provided, consider the audience for the portfolio when deciding which selections will be most appropriate. Who will read it? What qualities will they be looking for as they read?

3. Arranging the selections deliberately

If you have not been told how to organize your portfolio, you can think of it as if it were a single text and decide on an arrangement that will best serve your purpose. Does it make sense to organize your work from weakest paper to strongest? From a less important paper to a more important one? How will you determine importance?

TEXTCONNEX

Preparing an Electronic Portfolio

For some courses or professional purposes, you will need to present your work in an electronic format. Here are some brief guidelines for preparing electronic portfolios:

- Use your opening screen to establish your purpose, appeal to your audience, provide links to help readers navigate your portfolio, and suggest who you are as a writer.
- Use links to help readers move within your portfolio. You can link to texts from your table of contents, from other texts, and from your reflective letter or essay.
- Consider using links to connect to related files that are external to the work in the portfolio but relevant to it, such as audio files and video clips.
- Before releasing it, make sure your portfolio works—both conceptually and structurally—by navigating all the way through it yourself.

Whatever arrangement you choose, you will need to explain your rationale for it in a letter to the reader, in a brief introduction, or in annotations in your table of contents.

4. Writing a reflective essay or letter

This is one of the most important pieces of writing in the portfolio. It may take the form of either an essay or a letter, depending on your purpose or the requirements you have been given. Common topics in the reflective text include the following:

- How you developed various papers
- Which papers you believe are particularly strong, and why
- What you learned as you worked on these assignments
- Who you are now as a writer

Once you have written, revised, and edited your reflective essay or letter, you should assemble all the components of your portfolio in a folder.

5. Polishing your portfolio

Although the steps in preparing a portfolio are listed in a sequence, many students find that, as they work through them, they need to backtrack to an earlier step. In the process of writing the reflective letter or essay, for example, you might discover a better way to arrange your work.

If you want a portfolio that presents you and your work in the best light, it is also wise to share it with classmates or colleagues before submitting it for a class grade, a writing requirement, or a job interview. As with any piece of writing, a portfolio will improve if it is revised on the basis of peer review.

The good news is that most students learn about themselves and their writing as they compile their portfolios and write reflections on their work. The process not only makes them better writers but also helps them learn how to demonstrate their strengths.

Auguste Rodin's sculpture The Thinker evokes the psychological complexity of human thought and suggests the spirit of critical inquiry common to all disciplines across the curriculum.

Anybody who is involved in working across

the disciplines is much more likely to have a

lively mind and a lively life.

—MARY FIELD BELENKY

Writing in
College and
beyond
College

WRITING OUTCOMES

Rhetorical Knowledge

This section will help you learn to do the following:

- Recognize that different writing situations require different approaches

- Adapt your writing to different purposes and audiences on the job and in the community **(12)**

- Use the appropriate format for each genre of writing, such as arguments **(8)**, interpretive analyses **(7)**, and informative reports **(6)**

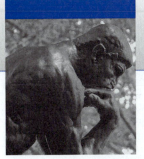

6 Informative Reports

Imagine what the world would be like if each person had to learn everything from scratch, by trial and error, with no recipes, no encyclopedias, no textbooks, no newspapers—nothing that recorded what others have learned. Fortunately, we have many sources of information to draw on, including informative reports.

6a Understanding the assignment

An **informative report** passes on what someone has learned about a topic or issue; it teaches. When your instructor assigns an informative report, he or she expects you to find out what is currently known about some specific topic and to present what you discover in a clear, unbiased way.

An informative report gives you a chance to do the following:

- Learn more about an issue that interests you.
- Make sense of what you have read, heard, and seen.
- Teach others what you have learned.

6b Approaching writing an informative report as a process

www.mhhe.com/
bmhh

For an interactive tutorial on writing informative reports, go to

Writing > Writing Tutors > Informative Reports

1. Selecting a topic that interests you

The major challenge in writing informative reports is engaging the reader's interest. Selecting a topic that interests you makes it more likely that your report will interest your readers.

Consider connecting what you are learning in one course with a topic you are studying in another course or with your personal experience. For example, one student, Joe Smulowitz, worked part-time for a stockbroker and wanted to make a career in that field. For his topic, he decided to investigate what online stock traders were doing and saying. (*Smulowitz's paper begins on p. 89.*)

2. Considering what your readers know about the topic

Assume that your readers have some familiarity with the topic but that most do not have clear, specific knowledge of it.

3. Developing an objective stance

A commitment to objectivity gives your report its authority. Present differing views fairly, and do not take sides in a debate.

www.mhhe.com/
bmhh

For more help
with developing
a thesis, go to

**Writing >
Paragraph/Essay
Development >
Thesis/Central
Idea**

4. Composing a thesis that summarizes your knowledge of the topic

An informative thesis typically states an accepted generalization or reports the results of the writer's study. Before you decide on a thesis, review the information you have collected. Compose a thesis statement that summarizes what the information in your paper shows. In his paper about online stock trading, Smulowitz's thesis is a generalization that he supports in the body of his paper with information he groups into categories:

> Besides honest investors with various levels of expertise, the Internet grants access to numerous investors who post false information in hopes of making a quick and sometimes large profit. . . . *The one hundred or so postings that I read can be divided into four categories.*

Notice how Smulowitz forecasts the body of his report. We expect to learn something about each of the four categories, and the report is structured to give us that information category by category.

5. Providing context in your introduction

Informative reports usually begin with a relatively simple introduction to the topic and a straightforward statement of the thesis. Provide some context or background, but get to your specific topic as quickly as possible and keep it in the foreground.

6. Organizing your report by classifying and dividing information

Clarity matters. Develop ideas in an organized way by classifying and dividing information into categories, subtopics, or the stages of a process.

www.mhhe.com/
bmhh

For more on
using patterns
of development,
go to

**Writing >
Paragraph
Patterns**

7. Illustrating key ideas with examples

Use specific examples to help readers understand your most important ideas. Examples make reports interesting as well as educational.

8. Defining specialized terms and spelling out unfamiliar abbreviations

Specialized terms will probably not be familiar to most readers. Explain these terms with a synonym (a word with the same meaning) or a brief definition—as we have just done. Spell out unfamiliar abbreviations like Computer-Mediated Communication (CMC) the first time you use them, putting the abbreviation in parentheses.

9. Concluding by answering "so what?"

Conclude with an image that suggests the information's value or sums it all up. The conclusion reminds readers of the topic stated in the introduction and answers the "so what?" question.

| **6c** | Student paper: Informative report |

In the informative paper that follows, Joe Smulowitz reports what he has learned about the people who are talking online about stocks. As you read his report, notice how Smulowitz provides a context for his topic, cites various sources (using the APA documentation style), categorizes the information, and illustrates his ideas with examples, all hallmarks of a clear, carefully developed report. The annotations in the margin of this paper point out specific aspects of the informative report.

> **Note:** For details on the proper formatting of a paper in APA style, see Chapter 28 and the sample paper that begins on page 287.

SAMPLE STUDENT INFORMATIVE REPORT

Chatting Online about Stocks

The Internet has produced a new kind of investor: the online stock market investor. Until a few years ago, a person who wanted to invest in the stock market had to hire a professional broker, who might charge $300 per trade as well as a substantial commission. Nowadays, an investor can buy and sell stocks over the Internet at costs ranging from only $7.95 to $25 per trade. As a result, more and more laypeople have become online traders—investors who use the Internet to buy and sell stocks. Of the 143 million Americans who are currently using the Internet, 39% use it to trade stocks online (National Telecommunications and Information Administration, 2002, chap. 3). *Silicon Investor,* a popular site for chatting about stocks, receives over 12,000 posts a day from online traders (Lucchetti, 1998).

Who are these online traders, and what are they talking about in investment-related chats? Besides honest investors with various levels

Margin annotations

6c
info

www.mhhe.com/
bmhh
For more information on conclusions, go to
Writing > Paragraph/Essay Development > Conclusions

www.mhhe.com/
bmhh
For another sample of informative writing, go to
Writing > Writing Samples > Informative Paper

Topic introduced.

Important term defined.

Source information summarized rather than quoted directly.

Thesis stated.

of expertise, the Internet grants access to numerous investors who post false information in hopes of making a quick and sometimes large profit. The Internet is rife with "hundreds of fraudulent and abusive investment schemes, including stock manipulations, pyramid scams, and Ponzi schemes" (Connecticut Department of Banking, 1998, p. 2). State securities agencies and other investment regulators are now looking into cases in which the price of shares in little-known stocks appears to have been manipulated through messages posted on Internet bulletin boards.

Direct quotation: page number included in citation.

Many investors find out about online fraud the hard way. Consider the case of Interlock Consolidated Enterprises, Inc. This Canadian company was reported to have landed a major contract to construct housing in the former USSR. When the company became the topic of online hype in early 1994, its stock jumped from 42 cents a share to $1.30 before falling back to 60 cents (Gardner & Gardner, 1994, "The Fairy Tale" section, para. 4). In this type of scam, known as "pump and dump," investors spread unusually positive news about a stock, then sell it when the price gets unrealistically high. This scam is nothing new to the investment world. In fact, pump-and-dump schemes began in the 1700s (Lucchetti, 1998). But now the schemers can reach hundreds of thousands of people with a single posting, and that kind of reach clearly makes a difference.

Unfamiliar term defined.

An example of what is going on in investment-related chats is the online talk about Chico's, a women's clothing company. *Silicon Investor* includes a chat room called "Miscellaneous," where in 1999 one could read a tip about Chico's: the company was about to release good news, which would raise the price of its stock (Vanier, 1999). A savvy investor would have found out more about Chico's from sources such as *Yahoo! Finance* or *Hoover's Online,* Internet-based business information databases. There investors would have found a history of Chico's; a summary of what Chico's produces; the company's location, phone number, number of employees, and names of top management; a list of the company's recent press releases; and most importantly,

Objective stance: "one" used instead of "I."

financial data, including stock price and performance over the past
year (Yahoo! Finance, 2004; Hoover's Online, 2004).

Having read some facts about Chico's, investors would have been
better prepared to understand e-mail messages about the company's
stock posted on the *Silicon Investor* bulletin board, messages that fell
into four categories. In the first category belonged postings with only
positive things to say about Chico's, such as, "CHS [Chico's ticker
name] is expected to add 30 stores this year. . . . They are expecting
to grow to over 700 stores in the near future" (mfpcpa, 1999). About
75% of the approximately 100 messages belonged to this positive-only
category and appeared to be posted by stockholders trying to spread
hype about Chico's so that the stock's price would rise. The few replies
to these messages expressed agreement.

In the second category belonged messages that came from
investors called "shorts" and "longs." When they think a security's price
is going to decrease, shorts borrow the security from a broker or dealer
and sell it on the market. The short investor profits if the price goes
down, because he or she can replace the borrowed security at a lower
cost. Longs, on the other hand, purchase a security because they think
its price will increase. The long investor profits if the price goes up,
because he or she can sell the security for more than it cost originally.
Because the shorts want the price to decrease and the longs want the
price to increase, these two kinds of stock traders often feud in online
discussions. For example, in the following exchange about Chico's
stock, a short's message titled "Out of Steam" provoked a reaction
titled "Stay LONG" from cag174, a long:

> She can't take it Captain. The stock can't hold its new highs.
> It keeps closing at the bottom of the range. Shorts will live.
> We will see 28 again. (Startrader 1975, 1999)
>
> $38 will come before $28. $43 at year end. (cag174, 1999)

There seemed to be more long investors than short investors on the
Chico's bulletin board. Whenever a short posted a negative message

6c
info

Information
about
Smulowitz's
classifications.

Categories
illustrated
with exam-
ples and
unfamiliar
terms
defined.

E-mail
messages
central to
paper, and
thus quoted
directly, not
summarized.

aimed at lowering the stock price, several longs retaliated, warning that the short was misleading investors.

In the third category were posts from sneaky investors. For example, the following post appeared to be written by a woman: "Don't know much about stocks, just love the clothes and so do my daughters—31, 35, and 43. Talked hubby into buying in when I read Streisand was buying lots of sweaters . . ." (Katy10121, 1999). Since Chico's is a woman's clothing store, investors are likely to be interested in what women think about the store. But the person who posted this message might not have been female. The poster's online profile listed the poster's sex as "male." This investor could be trying to take advantage of other investors by engaging in gender-bending.

The last category of messages comprised posts from owners of little known and lightly traded stocks called "penny stocks." Here is an example of such messages:

> CHS has given us a great ride, but now would be a good time to get off, while we're on top, and reinvest profits in a little soon-to-be-rediscovered gem, SNKI (Swank). Low volume right now, but check out the P/E and other stats. . . . (gravytrain2030, 1999)

The price of penny stocks such as SNKI ranges from $0.01 to $5 a share. Enthusiasm from seemingly in-the-know observers like gravytrain2030 can sometimes lead to significant increases in the stock price. For that reason, *Yahoo!* does not offer bulletin boards for such stocks. Nevertheless, people still post their messages on other bulletin boards, just as gravytrain2030 did on the Chico's board.

The Internet gives the average person the opportunity to invest in the stock market without going through a broker. All the information essential to investing is available to *anyone* with access to a computer. But hype, manipulation, and fraud are also on the Internet. Before buying any stock, investors should investigate it thoroughly. When they read what others say about a company, they should remember that if it sounds too good to be true, it probably isn't true.

Interpretation provided without bias.

Point and purpose restated in conclusion.

References

cag174. (1999, November 9). Stay LONG. Message posted to Chico's message board, archived at http://finance.yahoo.com/q /mb?s=CHS

Connecticut Department of Banking. (1998). *Investor bulletin: On-line investment schemes.* Hartford, CT: Connecticut Department of Banking.

Gardner, D., & Gardner, T. (1994). Buy Zeigletics! *The Fool's School.* Retrieved from http://www.fool.com/School/Zeigletics /ZFairyTale.htm

gravytrain2030. (1998, July 3). Sell CHCS, reinvest in SNKI. Message posted to Chico's message board, archived at http:// finance.yahoo.com/q/mb?s=CHS

Hoover's Online. (2004, December 6). *Chico's FAS Inc.* Retrieved December 6, 2004, from http://premium.hoovers.com /subscribe/co/factsheet.xhtml?ID=16010

Katy10121. (1999, June 24). Just love the clothes. Message posted to Chico's message board, archived at http://finance.yahoo.com /q/mb?s=CHS

Lucchetti, A. (1998, May 28). Some Web sites getting tough on stock chat. *The Wall Street Journal,* pp. C1, C12.

mfpcpa. (1999, February 23). Response to Mish's post. Message posted to Chico's message board, archived at http://finance.yahoo.com /q/mb?s=CHS

National Telecommunications and Information Administration. (2002, February). *A nation online: How Americans are expanding their use of the Internet.* (U.S. Department of Commerce Report). Retrieved from http://www.ntia.doc.gov/ntiahome/dn/html/anationonline2 .htm

Startrader 1975. (1999, November 5). Out of steam. Message posted to Chico's message board, archived at http://finance.yahoo.com /q/mb?s=CHS

References list follows APA style and begins on new page.

**6c
info**

Vanier, G. (1999, May 1). Time to buy Chico's. Message posted to Chico's message board, archived at http://www.siliconinvestor.com /stocktalk/subject.gsp?subjectid=20636

Yahoo! Finance. (2004, December 6). *Chico's FAS Inc.* Retrieved December 6, 2004, from http://finance.yahoo.com/q/pr?s=chs

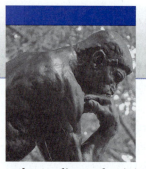

7 Interpretive Analyses and Writing about Literature

Interpretation involves figuring out a way of understanding a written document, literary work, cultural artifact, social situation, or natural event and presenting your understanding so that it is meaningful and convincing to readers.

7a Understanding the assignment

When an assignment asks you to compare, explain, analyze, or discuss something, you are expected to study that subject closely. An **interpretive analysis** moves beyond simple description and examines or compares particular items for a reason: to enhance your reader's understanding of people's conditions, actions, beliefs, or desires.

www.mhhe.com/ **bmhh**

For an interactive tutorial on writing interpretive analyses, go to

Writing > Writing Tutors > Interpretive Analysis

7b Approaching writing an interpretive analysis as a process

1. Discovering an aspect of the subject that is meaningful to you

Think about your own feelings and experiences while you read, listen, or observe. Connecting your own thoughts and experiences to what you are studying can help you develop fresh interpretations.

2. Developing a thoughtful stance

Think of yourself as an explorer. Be thoughtful, inquisitive, and open-minded. You are exploring the possible meaning of something. When you write your paper, invite your readers to join you on an intellectual journey, saying, in effect, "Come, think this through with me."

3. Using an intellectual framework

To interpret your subject effectively, use a relevant perspective or an intellectual framework. For example, the elements of a work of fiction, such as plot, character, and setting, are often used to analyze stories. Sigmund Freud's theory of conscious and unconscious forces in conflict might be applied to various subjects. In his analysis of Flannery O'Connor's story "Everything That Rises Must Converge," Rajeev Bector uses sociologist Erving Goffman's ideas about "character contests" to interpret the conflict between a son and his mother. (*Bector's analysis begins on p. 98.*)

> **7b**
> **lit**

No matter what framework you use, analysis often entails taking something apart and then putting it back together by figuring out how its parts contribute to a meaningful whole. Because the goal of analysis is to create a meaningful interpretation, you need to treat the whole as more than the sum of its parts and recognize that finding meaning is a complex problem with multiple solutions.

CHARTING the TERRITORY

Student Analyses across the Disciplines

Students are often called upon to write interpretive analyses such as the following:

- Rajeev Bector, a student in a literature course, asserts that Flannery O'Connor's story "Everything That Rises Must Converge" can be understood as a character contest.
- A student majoring in music outlines the emotional implications of the tempo and harmonic progression in Schubert's *Der Atlas.*
- A student in an economics course demonstrates that, according to an econometric model of nine variables, deregulation has not decreased the level of airline safety.

4. Listing, comparing, questioning, and classifying to discover your thesis

To figure out your thesis, explore separate aspects of your subject. Try one or more of the following strategies:

- Take notes about what you see or read, and if it helps, write a summary.

www.mhhe.com/
bmhh

For more help
with developing
a thesis, go to

Writing >
Paragraph/Essay
Development >
Thesis/Central
Idea

- Ask yourself questions about the subject you are analyzing, and write down any interesting answers. Imagine what kinds of questions your instructor or classmates might ask about the artifact, document, or performance.

- Name the class of things to which the item you are analyzing belongs (for example, memoirs), and then identify important parts or features of that class (for example, scene, point of view, helpers, and turning points).

5. Making your thesis focused and purposeful

To make a point about your subject, focus on one or two questions that are key to understanding it. Resist the temptation to describe everything you see. Consider this example of a focused, purposeful thesis:

> In O'Connor's short story, plot, setting, and characterization work together to reinforce the impression that racism is a complex and pervasive problem.

Although you want your point to be clear, you also want to make sure that your thesis anticipates the "so what?" question and sets up an interesting context for your interpretation. Unless you relate your specific thesis to some more general issue, idea, or problem, your interpretive analysis may seem pointless to readers.

www.mhhe.com/
bmhh

For more on
crafting intro-
ductions, go to

**Writing >
Paragraph/Essay
Development >
Introductions**

6. Introducing the general issue, a clear thesis or question, and relevant context

In interpretive analyses, an introduction needs to do the following:

- Identify the general issue, concept, or problem at stake. You can also present the intellectual framework that you are applying.

- Provide relevant background information.

- Name the specific item or items you will focus on.

- State the thesis you will support and develop or the main question(s) your analysis will answer.

Even though you may begin with a provocative statement or an example designed to capture your reader's attention, make sure that your introduction accomplishes its four purposes.

7. Planning your paper so that each point supports your thesis

After you pose a key question or state your thesis, you need to organize your points to answer the question or support your thesis. Readers must be able to follow your train of thought and see how each point is related to your thesis.

For example, if Bector had simply described the events in O'Connor's story or presented a random list of insights, his paper would not have shed any light on what the story means. Instead, Bector ends his introduction with a compelling question about one character's motives:

7c
lit

QUESTION But why would Julian want to hurt his mother, a woman who is already suffering from high blood pressure?

Bector answers this interpretive question in the body of his paper by pointing out and explaining three features of the character contest between mother and son.

8. Concluding by answering "so what?"
The conclusion of an interpretive analysis needs to answer the "so what?" question by saying why your thesis—as well as the analysis that supports and develops it—is relevant to the larger issue identified in the introduction. What does your interpretation reveal about that issue?

www.mhhe.com/
bmhh

For more information on conclusions, go to

Writing >
Paragraph/Essay
Development >
Conclusions

7c   Student paper: Interpretive analysis

In the following paper, Rajeev Bector uses Erving Goffman's ideas to analyze and interpret the actions of two characters in Flannery O'Connor's short story "Everything That Rises Must Converge." What provoked Bector's interpretation in the first place is this question: How can we understand the mean way Julian and his mother treat each other? As he helps us better understand Julian and his mother, Bector raises the larger issue of racism. To what extent does Bector's interpretive analysis of O'Connor's story also illuminate the workings of racism in our society?

> **Note:** For details on the proper formatting of a paper in MLA style, see Chapter 24 and the sample paper that begins on page 251.

CHARTING the TERRITORY

Ideas and Practices for Writing in the Humanities

■ **Base your analysis on the work itself.** Works of art affect each of us differently, and any interpretation has a subjective element. However, the possibility of different interpretations does not mean that any one interpretation is as valid as any other. Your reading of the work needs to be grounded in details from the work itself.

■ **Consider how the concepts you are learning in your course apply to the work you are analyzing.** If your course focuses on the formal elements of art, for example, you might look at how those elements function in the painting you have chosen. If your course focuses on the social context of a work, you might look at how it shares or subverts the belief system and worldview that was common in its time. Use your paper as an opportunity to see the humanities through different critical lenses.

■ **Use the present tense when writing about the work and the past tense when writing about its history.** Use the present tense to talk about the events that happen within a work: "In Aristophanes' plays, characters frequently *step* out of the scene and *address* the audience directly." Use the past tense, however, to relate historical information about the work or creator: "Kant *wrote* about science, history, criminal justice, and politics as well as philosophical ideas."

www.mhhe.com/
bmhh

For another sample
of interpretive
writing, go to

**Writing >
Writing Samples >
Interpretive Paper**

Key idea
that provides
intellectual
framework.

SAMPLE STUDENT ANALYSIS OF A SHORT STORY

The Character Contest in Flannery O'Connor's

"Everything That Rises Must Converge"

Sociologist Erving Goffman believes that every social interaction establishes our identity and preserves our image, honor, and credibility in the hearts and minds of others. Social interactions, he says, are in essence "character contests" that occur not only in games and sports but also in our everyday dealings with strangers, peers, friends, and even family members. Goffman defines character contests as "disputes [that] are sought out and indulged in (often with glee) as a means of establishing where one's boundaries are" (29). Just such a contest occurs in Flannery O'Connor's short story "Everything That Rises Must Converge."

As they travel from home to the Y, Julian and his mother, Mrs. Chestny, engage in a character contest, a dispute we must understand in order to figure out the story's theme. Julian is so frustrated with his mother that he virtually "declare[s] war on her," "allow[s] no glimmer of sympathy to show on his face," and "imagine[s] various unlikely ways by which he could teach her a lesson" (O'Connor 185, 186). But why would Julian want to hurt his mother, a woman who is already suffering from high blood pressure?

Julian's conflict with Mrs. Chestny results from pent-up hostility and tension. As Goffman explains, character contests are a way of living that often leaves a "residue": "Every day in many ways we can try to score points and every day we can be shot down" (29). For many years, Julian has had to live under his racist mother's authority, and every time he protested her racist views he was probably shot down because of his "radical ideas" and "lack of practical experience" (O'Connor 184). As a result, a residue of defeat and shame has accumulated that fuels a fire of rebellion against his mother. But even though Julian rebels against his mother's racist views, it doesn't mean that he isn't a racist himself. Julian doesn't realize that in his own way, he is as prejudiced as his mother. He makes it "a point" to sit next to blacks, in contrast to his mother, who purposely sits next to whites (182). They are two extremes, each biased, for if Julian were truly fair to all, he would not care whom he sat next to.

When we look at the situation from Mrs. Chestny's viewpoint, we realize that she must maintain her values and beliefs for two important reasons: to uphold her character as Julian's mother and to act out her prescribed role in society. Even if she finds Julian's arguments on race relations and integration valid and plausible, Mrs. Chestny must still refute them. If she didn't, she would lose face as Julian's mother—that image of herself as the one with authority. By preserving her self-image, Mrs. Chestny shows that she has what Goffman sees as key to "character": some quality that seems "essential and unchanging" (28).

7c
lit

Question posed.

Interpretation organized point by point—first point.

"We" indicates thoughtful stance, not Bector's personal feelings.

Second point.

Besides upholding her character as Julian's mother, Mrs. Chestny wants to preserve the honor and dignity of her family tradition. Like an actor performing before an audience, she must play the role prescribed for her—the role of a white supremacist. But her situation is hopeless, for the role she must play fails to acknowledge the racial realities that have transformed her world. According to Goffman, when a "situation" is "hopeless," a character "can gamely give everything . . . and then go down bravely, or proudly, or insolently, or gracefully or with an ironic smile on his lips" (32). For Mrs. Chestny, being game means trying to preserve her honor and dignity as she goes down to physical defeat in the face of hopeless odds.

Given the differences between Mrs. Chestny's and her son's values, as well as the oppressiveness of Mrs. Chestny's racist views, we can understand why Julian struggles to "teach" his mother "a lesson" (185) throughout the entire bus ride. Goffman would point out that "each individual is engaged in providing evidence to establish a definition of himself at the expense of what can remain for the other" (29). But in the end, neither character wins the contest. Julian's mother loses her sense of self when she is pushed down to the ground by a "colored woman" wearing a hat identical to hers (187). Faced with his mother's breakdown, Julian feels his own identity being overwhelmed by "the world of guilt and sorrow" (191).

—————————————[begin on new page]—————————————

Works Cited

Goffman, Erving. "Character Contests." *Text Book: An Introduction to Literary Language*. Ed. Robert Scholes, Nancy Comley, and Gregory Ulmer. New York: St. Martin's, 1988. 27–33. Print.

O'Connor, Flannery. "Everything That Rises Must Converge." *Fiction*. Ed. R. S. Gwynn. 2nd ed. New York: Addison, 1998. 179–91. Print.

Margin notes:

Third point.

Thesis.

Conclusion—main point about Julian and his mother related to larger issue of racism.

Works-cited list follows MLA style and begins on new page.

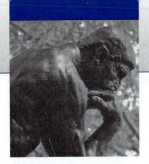

8 Arguments

Writing arguments is a way to form reasoned positions on debatable issues. Bearing in mind that reasonable people can see things differently, always strive to write well-informed, thoughtful arguments.

8a   Understanding the assignment

When you write an **argument paper,** you take part in a debate by stating and supporting your position on an issue. Written arguments appear in various forms, including critiques, reviews, and proposals.

- **Critiques:** Critiques address the question "What is true?" A critique fairly summarizes someone's position before either refuting or defending it. Refutations use one of two basic strategies: either exposing the reasoning of the position as inadequate or presenting evidence that contradicts the position. Defenses make use of three strategies: clarifying the author's reasoning, presenting new arguments to support the position, and showing that criticisms of the position are unconvincing.

- **Reviews:** Reviews address the question "What is good?" The writer evaluates an event, artifact, practice, or institution. Judgments in reviews should be principled; that is, they should be determined by reasonable criteria.

- **Proposals:** Proposals, sometimes called policy papers, address the question "What should be done?" They are designed to cause change. Readers are encouraged to see a situation in a specific way and to take action. Nicholas Buglione's argument about injuries to professional athletes (*see p. 106*) is an example of a proposal.

TEXTCONNEX

Blogs

While Weblogs or "blogs" can serve as personal online journals, they frequently function as vehicles for more public online debate and discussion. For example, many newspapers invite readers to use blogs to comment on the news of the day and to present dissenting opinions.

Remember that all blogs are more or less public, depending on the level of access they permit. Some are available to anyone searching the Web, while others can be accessed only by registered users of the Web site. (*For more on blogs, see Chapter 11, pp. 135–36.*)

www.mhhe.com/
bmhh

For an interactive
tutorial on writing
arguments, go to

Writing >
Writing Tutors >
Arguments

8b Approaching writing an argument as a process

Selecting a topic that you care about will give you the impetus to think matters through and make cogent arguments.

1. Figuring out what is at issue

Before you can take a position on a topic like air pollution or football injuries, you must figure out what is at issue. Ask questions about your topic. Are there indications that all is not as it should be? Have things always been this way, or have they changed for the worse? From what different perspectives—economic, social, political, cultural, medical, geographic—can problems like a wide receiver's recent knee injury or a quarterback's forced retirement be understood? Do people interested in the topic disagree about what is true, what is good, or what should be done?

Based on your answers to such questions, identify the issues your topic raises, and decide which of these issues you think is most important, interesting, and appropriate to write about.

2. Developing a reasonable stance that negotiates differences

You want your readers to respect your intelligence and trust your judgment. Conduct research to make yourself well informed. To enhance your thoughtfulness, find out what others have to say. Pay attention to the places where you disagree with other people's views, but also note what you have in common—interests, key questions, or underlying values.

Avoid language that may promote prejudice or fear. Misrepresentations of other people's ideas are out of place, as are personal attacks on character. Write arguments to open minds, not to slam doors shut.

Trying out different perspectives can also help you figure out where you stand on an issue. (*Also see the next section on stating your position.*) Make a list of the arguments for and against a specific position; then compare the lists and decide where you stand. Does one set of arguments seem stronger than the other? Do you want to change or qualify your initial position?

www.mhhe.com/
bmhh

For more help with
developing a
thesis, go to

Writing >
Paragraph/Essay
Development >
Thesis/Central
Idea

3. Composing a thesis that states your position

A strong, debatable thesis (a claim) on a topic of public interest is key to writing a successful argument. Without debate, there can be no argument and no reason to assert your position.

Personal feelings and accepted facts are not debatable and therefore cannot serve as an argument's thesis.

PERSONAL FEELING, NOT DEBATABLE THESIS

I feel that professional football players are treated poorly.

ACCEPTED FACT, NOT DEBATABLE THESIS

Many players in the NFL get injured.

DEBATABLE THESIS

Current NFL regulations are not sufficient to protect players from suffering the hardships caused by game-related injuries.

In proposals and policy papers, the thesis presents a solution in terms of the writer's definition of the problem. The logic behind a thesis for a proposal can be stated like this:

> Given these key variables and their underlying cause, one solution to the problem would be . . .

Because this kind of thesis is both complex and qualified, you will often need more than one sentence to state it clearly. You will also need numerous well-supported arguments to make it credible.

4. Supporting and developing your thesis

A strong, debatable thesis needs to be supported and developed with sound reasoning and carefully documented evidence. You can think of an argument as a dialogue between writer and readers. The writer states a debatable thesis, and one reader wonders, "Why do you believe that?" Another reader wants to know, "But what about this factor?" The writer needs to anticipate questions such as these and answer them by presenting claims (reasons) that are substantiated with evidence and by refuting opposing views.

Usually, a well-developed argument paper includes more than one type of claim and one kind of evidence. In addition to generalizations based on empirical data, it often includes authoritative claims based on the opinions of experts and ethical claims based on the application of principle. In his proposal about reducing injuries in professional football, Nicholas Buglione presents facts about the number of injuries in the previous and current seasons to establish the seriousness of the problem. He also includes quotations from an expert in football safety to explain the coach's role in promoting—or failing to promote—team safety (*see p. 108*). As you conduct research, note evidence—facts, examples, and expert testimony—that can be used to support each argument for or against your position.

In developing your argument, you should also pay attention to **counterarguments**—substantiated claims that do not support your position. Consider using one of the following strategies to take the most important counterarguments into account:

- Qualify your thesis in light of the counterargument by including a word such as *most, some, usually,* or *likely:* "Although many people—fans and nonfans alike—understand that football is a dangerous sport, few realize just how hard *some* NFL players have it."

■ Add to the thesis a statement of the conditions for or exceptions to your position: "The NFL pension plan is unfair to the players, except for those with more than five years in the league."

■ Choose one or two counterarguments and plan to refute their truth or their importance in your paper. Buglione, for example, refutes the counterargument that the NFL has a good pension plan for its players.

5. Creating an outline that includes a linked set of reasons

www.mhhe.com/
bmhh

For more help
with creating an
outline, go to

**Writing >
Paragraph/Essay
Development >
Outlines**

Begin drafting by writing down your thesis and outlining the way you will support and develop it. Your outline should include these parts:

■ An introduction to the topic and the debatable issue

■ A thesis stating your position on the issue

■ A point-by-point account of the reasons for your position, including the evidence (facts, examples, authorities) you will use to substantiate each major claim

■ A fair presentation and refutation of one or two key counter-arguments to your thesis

■ A response to the "so what?" question—why your argument matters

6. Emphasizing your commitment to dialogue in the introduction

www.mhhe.com/
bmhh

For more on
crafting intro-
ductions, go to

**Writing >
Paragraph/Essay
Development >
Introductions**

You want your readers to listen to what you have to say. When you present the topic and issue in your introduction, you should establish some kind of common ground or shared concern with them. In his essay on the NFL, Buglione begins with a vivid account of a football injury to awaken his readers' concern for injured athletes and make them receptive to his proposal about decreasing the number of injuries in professional football. If possible, return to that common ground at the end of your argument.

7. Concluding by restating your position and emphasizing its importance

After presenting your reasoning in detail, remind readers of your thesis. The version of your thesis that you present in your conclusion should be more complex and qualified than the version in your introduction. Readers may not agree with you, but they should know why the issue and your argument matter.

8. Reexamining your reasoning

After you have completed the first draft of your paper, take time to re-examine your reasoning. Answer the following questions:

- Have you given a sufficient number of reasons to support your thesis, or should you add one or two more?
- Have you made any mistakes in logic? (*See the list of common logical fallacies, pp. 13–14.*)
- Have you clearly and adequately developed each claim presented in support of your thesis? Is your supporting evidence sufficient? Have you quoted or paraphrased from sources accurately and documented them properly? (*For more on quoting, paraphrasing, and documenting sources, see Chapter 19, pp. 194–207, and Parts 4–5.*)

8c

arg

Tip for Multilingual Writers
Learning about Cultural Differences through Peer Review

In some cultures, writing direct and explicit arguments is discouraged, but not so in the United States. When you share your work with peers raised in the United States, you may learn that the way in which you have expressed certain ideas and values—the vocabulary or the style of presentation you have used—makes it difficult for them to understand and accept the point you are making. Ask your peers to suggest different words and approaches, and then decide if their suggestions would make your ideas more accessible to others. ▬▬▬▬

8c   Student paper: Argument

In the following position paper, Nicholas Buglione argues that the National Football League should do more to protect its players from the physical and economic hardships caused by game-related injuries. As you read Buglione's argument, notice how he tries to get readers to sympathize with the players and how he acknowledges what the league has already done to address the injury problem. Buglione asserts that more should be done in two areas: safety and pensions. How suitable, complex, and feasible do you think his solutions are?

> **Note:** For details on the proper formatting of a paper in MLA style, see Chapter 24 and the sample paper that begins on page 251.

SAMPLE STUDENT ARGUMENT

NFL:

Negligent Football League?

Lively open-
ing to hook
reader.

It's fourth down and short on the other team's thirty-five yard line. At this critical point in the game, all eyes are on you, the star running back. The ball is snapped from center into the quarterback's hands. You sprint up into the pocket, receive the hand-off, and race into the hole. At that instant, a rabid 245-pound linebacker drives his massive body into your legs. There is a crunch, followed by excruciating pain: your career in football is over.

Topic
introduced.

Injuries have been a fact of life in the National Football League (NFL) for many years. But in 1995, leg, knee, back, and head injuries piled up, and the NFL decided it was time to take action. Under the auspices of Commissioner Paul Tagliabue, league officials agreed on some basic safety guidelines to solve pro football's woes. These guidelines included the following: (1) making it illegal for players to lead with their heads when they tackle, thereby reducing helmet-to-body contact injuries; (2) allowing the quarterback to ground the ball intentionally in certain situations, thereby lessening the risk of his being injured by a lineman; (3) reducing the size of the helmet's facemask, thereby decreasing its potential as a weapon; and (4) levying a $10,000 to $20,000 fine on any player who hits another player after the play is over.

Issue
introduced.

The NFL expected that these regulations would reduce the number of injuries, but the situation got worse, not better. As an example, the 1996 season began with an unprecedented seven injuries to starting quarterbacks, all within the first week. As the season went on, more leg, rib, head, and shoulder injuries followed, and one quarterback, Chris Miller, was forced to retire after sustaining his fifth head injury in less than two seasons. The epidemic of injuries carried over into the 1997 season. Steve Young of the San Francisco 49ers suffered his third concussion in ten months, as shown in fig. 1, and wide receiver Jerry Rice missed much of the season because of a knee injury.

Issue
illustrated
with
photograph.

Fig. 1.   Jacksonville Jaguars linebacker Bryce Paup barrels down on
San Francisco 49ers quarterback Steve Young (holding the ball) and
tackle Jeremy Newberry in a 1999 game. Young suffered his third
concussion in ten months during the 1997 season. Mark Wallheiser/
Reuters/Corbis.

Injuries have an enormous impact on a player's life after football.
Retirees tell horror stories about the aftermath of injuries, which too
often turn simple, everyday acts like getting out of bed into backbreak-
ing work. Consider the case of Al Toon. Toon, a wide receiver for the
New York Jets, enjoyed a career filled with highlights. Unfortunately, his
career was also filled with concussions. After the ninth concussion, he
called it quits and tried to put the game behind him. Sadly, those nine
head injuries continue to punish Toon. On sunny days, he has to wear
dark sunglasses because bright light is too much for his damaged head
to handle. Even worse, Toon suffers from memory loss and chronic
migraine headaches. Fortunately, he has managed his finances well and
can afford to live comfortably with his wife and children. Many other

Issue ex-
plained with
anecdote.

retired players are not so fortunate. Those injured at an early age too often find themselves without a job, without a college degree, and witout physical health. Is it any wonder that a few turn to drugs and alcohol, become homeless, or end up in a morgue way before their time?

Thesis stated.

A significant problem exists in the NFL. Much more must be done to protect players. However, little progress will be made if the league tries to rectify the problem simply by passing rules and amendments to those rules. Such attempts fail to get at the root of the problem: a coaching tradition that emphasizes aggression over safety and a pension plan that fails to support all retired players adequately.

Causes of problem identified.

First point— supported by expert testimony.

Perhaps no one is more responsible for a player's physical welfare than the coach. Although it is true that coaches' need to win games can lead to aggressive methods, and players readily buy into those methods, a coach must balance this need to win with players' safety (SafeUSA, 2002). According to Carl Blyth, an expert on football safety, the head coach's "attitude and leadership" are the "most important" factors in creating this balance (94). Even though coaches should teach players to value safety, they seldom do so; instead, coaches often encourage feelings and behavior that compromise safety. Tommy Chaikin, a former lineman for South Carolina, has pointed out that his coaches encouraged aggressive feelings and behavior during practice. Fighting was not discouraged, and players were trained to fear being ridiculed for exhibiting any compassion (87).

Point also supported by anecdote.

Because a pugnacious team is more likely to win, it is understandable that coaches want to instill a fighting spirit in their players. What coaches fail to realize, however, is that the aggressive nature of their training programs increases the incidence and severity of injuries. To disregard a player's safety for the purposes of toughening him up is unethical (Lapchick). It is also foolish because ensuring that players stay healthy is in the best interests of the coach and team. According to Rick Reilly, when the Rams' quarterback Kurt Warner was sidelined in 2003 after two years of injuries to his head and shoulders, he was immediately relegated to being the backup for the other quarterback and saw very little play during

Refutes counter- argument that winning is more important than safety.

that season. If he had not been pushed so aggressively during those two years, he probably could have continued to play. Clearly, the coaches of the NFL do not have their players' safety in mind, and this situation must change. Their failure to teach players how to play football safely has made the NFL injury epidemic worse.

Injuries often continue to plague players even after they retire. When their football careers are finished, most players still need to work to support themselves and their families. However, as the sportswriter Bob Glauber reports, approximately 70% of today's players have not obtained a college degree (1: B6). Without a college degree, retired football players have little chance of securing white-collar jobs. The alternative, blue-collar work, is closed to many former players who suffer the lingering effects of injury. Glauber's survey of 1,425 former NFL players found that more than 50% are physically limited by previous injuries (2: A64). What compensation is there for these retired players, the ones who have essentially destroyed their bodies playing football for the league?

A pension would seem to be the answer. Though the NFL does have a pension plan, it is not adequate or fair. According to Glauber, the NFL's pension plan pays retired players with five or more years of NFL service $300 a month per year of service (4: A92). The minimum pension is, therefore, $1,500 a month. Although players with permanent injuries certainly deserve more, the bigger problem is that the pension plan applies only to players with five or more years of NFL service. Players injured within the first five years of their career receive no pension at all. What would Kurt Warner have done if he had not recovered from his injuries?

Why does the NFL treat its players so poorly? One reason may be that professional sports has become big business. In *The Political Economy of College Sports* (1986), Hart-Nibbrig and Cottingham coined the term "corporate athleticism" to describe the business-minded attitude that has taken over sports (1). Corporate athleticism means that sports organizations like the NFL are primarily concerned with increasing

8c

arg

Second point— supported by statistics.

Refutes counterargument that NFL pensions solve problem.

Third point— supported by expert testimony.

profits. Winning teams make a larger profit, so coaches try to increase the chance of winning by encouraging anger and aggression in their players. Moreover, it is not in the front office's financial interest to support disabled retirees. When players cease to be lucrative for the league's bottom line, the NFL can simply turn to a younger group of men, all of whom are eager to play pro football. The NFL can then exploit this new crop of players.

Exploitation can be resisted, especially by the Players Association—the collective bargaining unit of NFL players—even though some observers consider the association part of the problem (Zimmerman). To deal with the injury problem, the Players Association must take three important steps. First, it must make the rest of the sports world aware of the situation. Although many people—fans and nonfans alike—understand that football is a dangerous sport, few realize just how hard some NFL players have it. Second, the Players Association must pressure NFL coaches to monitor the physical well-being of their players closely and stress the value of staying healthy, not the ill-gotten gains of playing through injuries.

The Players Association must also work to ease the financial burden on injured retirees. It should demand that the NFL amend its pension plan so that coverage is extended to all players, regardless of how many years they played for the league. In the United States, workers injured on the job are eligible for compensation. Why should NFL players be treated differently just because they have been in the league less than five years? In addition, those players who serve five or more years in the NFL deserve more than $1,500 a month, especially if they suffer from debilitating injuries. Finally, young players should receive financial counseling to make them aware of just how short a football career can be. On average, an "NFL career last[s] only 3.6 years," and as Commissioner Paul Tagliabue admits, what follows that career is likely to be both "painful and tragic" for NFL players who have not been "well-advised and well-served" (Glauber 1: B6, B7).

Term—
Players
Associa-
tion—
defined.

Proposed
solution.

Works Cited

Blyth, Carl S. "Tackle Football." *Sports Safety*. Ed. Charles Peter
    Yost. Washington: American Association for Health, Physical
    Education, and Recreation, 1971. 93-96. Print.

Chaikin, Tommy. "The Nightmare of Steroids." *Sports Illustrated*
    Oct. 1988: 84-102. Print.

Glauber, Bob. "Life after Football." *New York Newsday* (four-pt.
    series) 12 Jan. 1997: B6+ (Pt. 1); 14 Jan. 1997: A64+ (Pt. 2);
    15 Jan. 1997: A66+ (Pt. 3); 16 Jan. 1997: A92+ (Pt. 4). Print.

Hart-Nibbrig, N., and Clement Cottingham. *The Political Economy of
    College Sports*. Lexington: Heath, 1986. Print.

Lapchick, R. E. "Dying for the Game." *Center for the Study of Sport
    in Society*. Northeastern U, 2004. Web. 4 April 2004.

Reilly, Rick. "Ram Shackled." *Sports Illustrated* 8 December 2003:
    104. Print.

"SafeUSA. Football Safety (American)." *SafeUSA*, N.p., 14 July
    2002. Web. 9 March 2003.

Zimmerman, Paul. "Union Job: Safety of Its Members Should Be
    Players' Association Top Priority." *Sports Illustrated*. Cable News
    Network, 1 October 2003. Web. 9 March 2004.

8c

arg

"Works
Cited" follows
MLA style
and begins
new page.

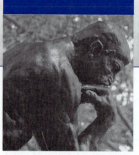

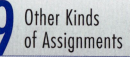

9 Other Kinds of Assignments

9a Personal essays

The **personal essay** is literary, like a poem, a play, or a story. It feels meaningful to readers and relevant to their lives. It speaks in a distinctive voice. It is both compelling and memorable.

1. Making connections between your experiences and those of your readers

When you write a personal essay, you are exploring your experiences, clarifying your values, and composing a public self. The focus, however, does not need to be on you. You might write a personal essay about a tree in autumn, an encounter with a stranger, or an athletic event. The real topic is how these objects and experiences have become meaningful to you.

When we read a personal essay, we expect to learn more than the details of the writer's experience; we expect to see the connections between that experience and our own.

TEXTCONNEX

Personal Writing and Social Networking Web Sites

Many people use the Web sites Facebook and MySpace for personal expression and autobiographical writing. Remember that these sites are networked so that anyone can read much of this information. Strangers, including prospective employers, often view people's profiles and make judgments.

2. Turning your essay into a conversation

Personal essayists usually use the first person (*I* and *we*) to create a sense that the writer and reader are engaged in the open-ended give-and-take of conversation. How you appear in this conversation—shy, belligerent, or friendly, for example—will be determined by the details you include in your essay as well as the connotations of the words you use. Consider how Meghan Daum represents herself in relation to both computer-literate and computer-phobic readers in the following excerpt from her personal essay "Virtual Love," which appeared in a 1997 issue of *The New Yorker:*

The kindness pouring forth from my computer screen was bizarrely exhilarating, and I logged off and thought about it for a few hours before writing back to express how flattered and "touched"—this was probably the first time I had ever used that word in earnest—I was by his message.

I am not what most people would call a computer person. I have no interest in chat rooms, news groups, or most Web sites. I derive a palpable thrill from sticking a letter in the United States mail.

Besides Daum's conversational stance, notice the emotional effect of her remark on the word *touched* and her choice of words connoting excitement: *pouring forth, exhilarating,* and *palpable thrill.*

3. Structuring your essay like a story

There are three common ways to narrate events and reflections:

- **Chronological sequence:** uses an order determined by clock time; what happened first is presented first, followed by what happened second, then third, and so on.

- **Emphatic sequence:** uses an order determined by the point you want to make; for emphasis, events and reflections are arranged either from least to most or most to least important.

- **Suspenseful sequence:** uses an order determined by the emotional effect the writer wants the essay to have on readers. To keep readers hanging, the essay may begin in the middle of things with a puzzling event, then flash back or go forward to clear things up. Some essays may even begin with the end and then flash back to recount how the writer came to that insight.

4. Letting details tell your story

It is in the details that the story takes shape. The details you emphasize, the words you choose, and the characters you create communicate the point of your essay. Often, it is not even necessary to state your thesis.

Consider, for example, the following passage by Gloria Ladson-Billings:

Mrs. Harris, my third-grade teacher, was quite a sharp dresser. She wore beautiful high-heeled shoes. Sometimes she switched to flats in the afternoon if her feet got tired, but every morning began with the click, click, click of her high heels as she greeted us up and down the rows. I wanted to dress the way Mrs. Harris did. I didn't want to wear old-lady comforters like Mrs. Benn's, and I certainly didn't want to wear worn-out loafers like those of my first-grade teacher, Miss Schwartz. I wanted to wear

> beautiful, shiny, high-heeled shoes like Mrs. Harris's. That was
> the way a teacher should look, I thought.
>
> —GLORIA LADSON-BILLINGS, *The Dreamkeepers:*
> *Successful Teachers of*
> *African-American Children*

Ladson-Billings uses details to make her idea of a good teacher come
alive for the reader. At one level—the literal—the "click, click, click"
refers to the sound of Mrs. Harris's shoes. At another level, it represents the glamorous teacher. And at the most figurative level, the
"click, click, click" evokes the kind of feminine power that the narrator both longs for and admires.

5. Connecting your experience to a larger issue

To demonstrate the significance of a personal essay to readers, writers
usually connect their individual experience to a larger issue. Here, for
example, are the closing lines of Daum's essay "Virtual Love":

> The world had proved to be too cluttered and too fast for us,
> too polluted to allow the thing we'd attempted through tech-
> nology ever to grow on the earth. PFSlider and I had joined
> the angry and exhausted living. Even if we met on the street,
> we wouldn't recognize each other, our particular version of in-
> timacy now obscured by the branches and bodies and falling
> debris that make up the physical world.

Notice how Daum relates the disappointment of her failed Internet
romance with "PFSlider" to a larger social issue: the general contrast between cyberspace and material realities. Her point, however, is surprising; most people do not think of cyberspace as more "intimate"—or
touching—than their everyday world of "branches and bodies."

9b Essay exams

When you take an essay exam, you are pressed for time and uninterested in thinking about how to approach test taking. If you spend some
of your study time thinking about what you are expected to do on these
tests, you may feel less stress the next time you take one.

1. Preparing with the course and your instructor in mind

Consider the specific course as your writing context and the course's
instructor as your audience:

- What questions or problems did your instructor explicitly or
  implicitly address?

- What frameworks did your instructor use to analyze topics?
- What key terms did your instructor repeatedly use during lectures and discussions?

2. Understanding your assignment

Essay exams are designed to test your knowledge, not just your memory. To study, create some essay questions that require you to do the following:

9b

- **Explain** what you have learned in a clear, well-organized way. (*See question 1 in the box below.*)
- **Connect** what you know about one topic with what you know about another topic. (*See question 2 in the box.*)
- **Apply** what you have learned to a new situation. (*See question 3 in the box.*)
- **Interpret** the causes, effects, meaning, value, or potential of something. (*See question 4 in the box.*)
- **Argue** for or against some controversial statement about what you have learned. (*See question 5 in the box.*)

CHARTING the TERRITORY

Essay Exam Questions across the Curriculum

During finals week, you may be asked to respond to essay questions like the following:

1. Discuss the power of the contemporary presidency as well as the limits of that power. [*from a political science course*]
2. Compare and contrast the treatment of labor supply decisions in the economic models proposed by Greg Lewis and Gary Becker. [*from an economics course*]
3. Describe the observations that would be made in an alpha-particle scattering experiment if (a) the nucleus of an atom were negatively charged and the protons occupied the empty space outside the nucleus and (b) the electrons were embedded in a positively charged sphere. [*from a chemistry course*]
4. Examine the uses of caesura and enjambment in the following poem, and analyze their effect on the poem's rhythm. [*from a literature course*]
5. In 1800, was Thomas Jefferson a "dangerous radical"? Define your key terms and support your position with evidence from specific events, documents, and so on. [*from an American history course*]

3. Planning your time

At the beginning of the exam, quickly look through the whole exam, and determine how much time you will spend on each part or question. You will want to move as quickly as possible through the questions with lower point values so that you can spend the bulk of your time responding to the questions that are worth the greatest number of points.

4. Responding to short-answer questions by showing the significance of the information

The most common type of short-answer question is the identification question: Who or what is X? In answering questions of this sort, present just enough information to show that you understand X's significance within the context of the course. For example, if you are asked to identify "Judith Loftus" on an American literature exam, don't just write, "character who knows Huckleberry Finn is a boy." Instead, craft one or two sentences that identify Loftus as a character Huckleberry Finn encounters while he is disguised as a girl; by telling Huck how she knows that he is not a girl, Loftus compels readers to think in complex ways about gender.

5. Being tactical in responding to essay questions

Keep in mind that essay questions usually ask you to do something specific. Begin by determining precisely what you are being asked to do. Before you write anything, read the question—all of it—and circle key words.

> Explain two ways in which Picasso's *Guernica* evokes war's terrifying destructiveness.

To answer this question, you need to focus on two of the painting's features, such as coloring and composition, not on Picasso's life.

6. Using the essay question to structure your response

Usually, you will be able to transform the question itself into the thesis of your answer. If you are asked to agree/disagree with the Federalists' characterization of Thomas Jefferson in the election of 1800, you might begin with the following thesis:

> In the election of 1800, the Federalists characterized Jefferson as a dangerous radical. Although Jefferson's ideas were radical for the times, they were not dangerous to the republic.

Take a minute or two to list evidence for each of your main points, and then write the essay.

7. Checking your work

Save a few minutes to read through your completed answer, looking for words you might have omitted or sentences that make no sense. Make corrections neatly.

SAMPLE ESSAY TEST RESPONSE

A student's response to an essay question in an art appreciation course appears below. Both the question and the student's notes are provided.

9b

QUESTION

Both of these buildings (Figure 1 and Figure 2) feature dome construction. Identify the buildings, and discuss the differences in the visual effects created by the different dome styles.

STUDENT'S NOTES

Fig 1: Pantheon. Plain outside—concrete, can barely see dome. Dramatic inside—dome opens up huge interior space. Oculus to sky: light, air, rain. Coffered ceiling.

Fig 2: Taj Mahal. Dramatic exterior—dome set high, marble, reflecting pool, exterior lines go up. Inside not meant to be visited.

STUDENT'S ANSWER

The Pantheon (Figure 1) and the Taj Mahal (Figure 2) are famous for their dome construction. The styles of the domes are dramatically different, however, resulting in dramatically different visual effects.

The Pantheon, which was built by the Romans as a temple to the gods, looks very plain on the exterior. The dome is barely visible from the

Answers identification question and states thesis.

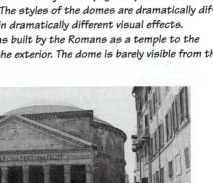

FIGURE 1

FIGURE 2

Key points
supported
by details.

Uses special-
ized terms
from course.

Sets up
comparison.

Key point
supported
by details.

Overall
comparison
as brief
conclusion.

*outside, and it is made of a dull grey concrete. Inside the building, how-
ever, the dome produces an amazing effect. It opens up a huge space
within the building, unobstructed by interior supports. The sides of the
dome are coffered, and those recessed rectangles both lessen the
weight of the dome and add to its visual beauty. Most dramatically,
the top of the dome is open to the sky, which allows sun or rain to
pour into the building. This opening is called the oculus, meaning "eye"
(to or of Heaven).*

*The Taj Mahal, which was built by a Muslim emperor of India as a
tomb for his wife, is the complete opposite of the Pantheon—dazzling
on the outside and plain on the inside. The large central dome is set up
high on the base so that it can be seen from far away. It is made of
white marble, which reflects light beautifully. The dome is surrounded by
other structures that frame it and draw attention to its exterior—a
long reflecting pond and four minarets. Arches and smaller domes on
the outside of the building repeat the large dome's shape. Because the
Taj Mahal's dome is tall and narrow, however, it does not produce the
kind of vast interior space of the shorter, squatter Pantheon dome.
Indeed, the inside of the Taj Mahal is not meant to be visited. Unlike the
Pantheon, the dome of the Taj Mahal is intended to be admired from
the outside.*

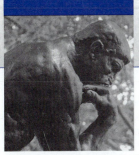

10 Oral Presentations

Preparing an oral presentation, like preparing a paper, is a process. You will need to consider your audience and purpose as you choose the focus and level of your topic. You will need to gather information, decide on the main idea of your presentation, think through the organization, and choose visuals that support your points.

10a Planning and shaping your presentation

1. Considering the interests, background knowledge, and attitudes of your audience

If your audience is composed of your classmates, you will have the advantage of knowing how much background knowledge they have and what their intellectual interests are. Do you want to intensify your audience's commitment to what they already think, provide new and clarifying information, provoke more analysis and understanding of the issue, or change what the audience believes about something?

If you are addressing an unfamiliar audience, ask the people who invited you to speak to fill you in on the audience's interests and expectations. It is also possible to make adjustments to your speech once you get in front of the actual audience, making your language more or less technical, for example, or offering additional examples to illustrate points.

2. Working within the time allotted to your presentation

Gauge how many words you speak per minute by reading a passage aloud at a conversational pace (about 120–150 words per minute is ideal). Be sure to time your presentation when you practice it.

10b Drafting your presentation

1. Making your opening interesting

A strong opening both sets the speaker at ease and gains the audience's confidence and attention. Try out several approaches to your introduction to see which gets the best reactions during rehearsal. Stories often make for an interesting beginning. Brief quotations, striking statistics, and surprising statements are also attention getters. Craft an introduction that lets your listeners know what they have to gain from your presentation—for example, new information or new perspectives on a subject of common interest.

**www.mhhe.com/
bmhh**

For more on crafting introductions, go to

**Writing >
Paragraph/Essay
Development >
Introductions**

2. Making the focus and organization of your presentation explicit

Select two or three ideas that you most want your audience to hear—and remember. Make these ideas the focus of your presentation, and let your audience know what to expect by previewing the content of your presentation—"I intend to make three points about fraternities on campus"—and then listing the three points.

The phrase "to make three points" signals a topical organization. Other common organizational patterns include chronological (*at first . . . later . . . in the end*), causal (*because of that . . . then this follows*), and problem-solution (*given the situation . . . then this set of proposals*). A question-answer format also works well, either as an overall strategy or as part of another organizational pattern.

3. Being direct

What your audience hears and remembers has as much to do with how you communicate your message as it does with what you say. Use a direct, simple style:

- Choose basic sentence structures.
- Repeat key terms.
- Pay attention to the rhythm of your speech.
- Don't be afraid to use the pronouns *I, you,* and *we*.

Notice how applying these principles transforms the following written sentence into a group of sentences appropriate for oral presentation:

WRITTEN

Although the claim that writing increases student learning has yet to be substantiated by either an ample body or an exemplary piece of empirical research, advocates of writing across the curriculum persist in pressing the claim.

ORAL

The more students write, the more they learn. So say advocates of writing across the curriculum. But what evidence do we have that writing improves learning? Do we have lots of empirical research or even one really good study? The answer is "Not yet."

4. Using visual aids

www.mhhe.com/
bmhh

For an interactive tutorial on using PowerPoint, go to

**Writing >
PowerPoint
Tutorial**

Slides, posters, objects, video clips, and music help make your focus explicit.

Presentation software such as PowerPoint can help you stay focused while you are speaking. The twelve PowerPoint slides in Figure 10.1 on pages 122–23 offer advice on how to design effective slides for a presentation. (*For more on using presentation software to incorporate multimedia elements into a presentation, see Chapter 11, pp. 127–29.*)

5. Concluding memorably

Try to make your ending truly memorable: return to that surprising opener, play with the words of your opening quotation, look at the initial image from another angle, or reflect on the story you have told. Make sure your listeners are aware that you are about to end your presentation, using such signal phrases as "in conclusion" or "let me end by saying," if necessary. Keep your conclusion short to hold the audience's attention.

10c
oral

www.mhhe.com/
bmhh

For more
information on
conclusions, go to

Writing >
Paragraph/Essay
Development >
Conclusions

10c Preparing for your presentation

1. Deciding whether to use notes or a written script

To be an effective speaker, you need to make eye contact with your listeners to monitor their responses and adjust your message accordingly. For most occasions, it is inappropriate to write out everything you want to say and then read it word for word. Write out only those parts of your presentation where precise wording counts, such as quotations.

Sometimes, however, the setting for your presentation may be so formal or the audience may be so large that a script feels necessary. In such instances, do the following:

- Triple-space the typescript of your text.
- Avoid carrying sentences over from one page to another.
- Mark your manuscript for pauses, emphasis, and the pronunciation of proper names.

2. Rehearsing, revising, and polishing

Whether you are using an outline or a script, practice your presentation aloud. Adjust transitions that don't quite work, points that need further development, and sections that go on too long. After you have settled on the content of your speech and can project it comfortably, focus on polishing the style of your delivery. Check that your posture is straight but relaxed, that your voice is loud and clear, and that you are making eye contact around the room. Time your final rehearsals, adding and cutting material as necessary.

3. Accepting nervousness as normal

The adrenaline surge you feel before a presentation can actually invest your talk with positive energy. Other people cannot always tell that you are nervous. Practice and revise your presentation until it flows smoothly, and make sure that you have a strong opener to get you through the first, most difficult moments of the speech.

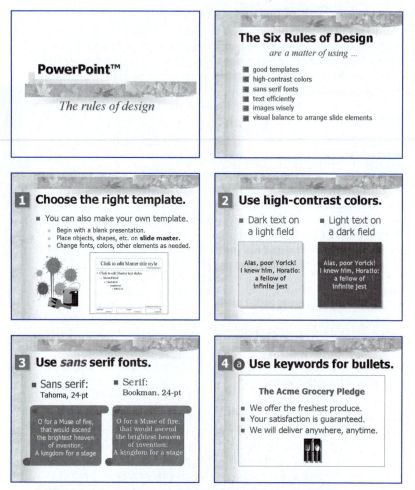

FIGURE 10.1 **Guidelines for preparing effective PowerPoint slides.**

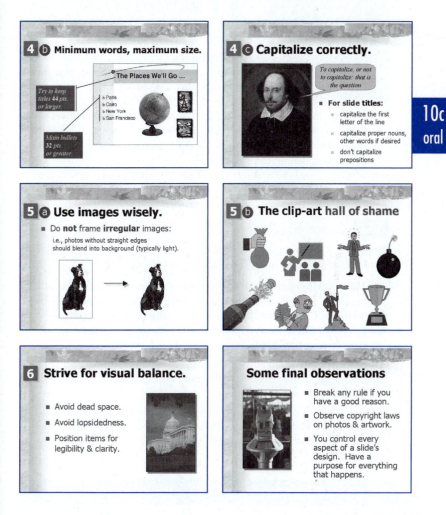

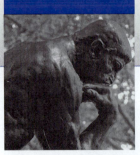

11 Multimedia Writing

Multimedia writing combines words with images, video, and audio into a single composition. The products of multimedia writing can be both dynamic and memorable. To be done well, they require considerable time and effort.

Like any form of writing, multimedia writing allows you to convey a message to a particular audience for a particular purpose—to inform, to interpret, or to persuade. A video or audio segment—like a photograph, map, or chart—must support this purpose in a way that is appropriate to the situation.

11a Learning about tools for creating multimedia texts

Multimedia writing can take a variety of forms and can be created with a variety of software tools. Here are a few options:

- Most word processors allow you to integrate still images and text into a single document, but many also make it possible to write text that permits readers, with the click of the mouse, to connect to various files—including audio, image, and video files (*see section 11b*).

- Most presentation software packages similarly allow you to accompany a presentation with audio and video files as well as still visuals (*see section 11c*).

- A variety of programs and Web-based tools allow you to create your own **Web pages** and **Web sites,** which can include a wide range of multimedia features (*see section 11d*).

TEXTCONNEX

Some Key Concepts in Multimedia Writing

- **File:** A computer file is a collection of information in computer-readable form. Text files store words, image files store pictures, audio files store sounds, and video files store video.
- **Link:** A link is a connection from one file to another, or to another place in the same file. You can link to files stored on your own computer or, through the Internet and World Wide Web, to files stored on other computers.
- **Hypertext:** Hypertext is text with links. (In a sense, the Web is one vast hypertext document with countless links to a nearly endless variety of files.)

■ You can create a **Weblog** (**blog** for short), on which, in addition to your written entries, you can post your own multimedia files and link to files on other blogs and Web sites (*see section 11e*).

11b Interpreting images

Texts that combine words and images are the most common form of multimedia writing. Two types of assignments you might be given are image analyses and imaginary stories.

1. Composing image analyses

You may be called on to analyze a single image such as a painting from a museum. In this case, your two tasks are to describe the picture as fully as possible, using adjectives, comparisons, and words that help readers look at the picture; and to analyze what the picture seems to be saying.

2. Imagining stories

Sometimes a writer tries to imagine the story behind an evocative photograph. Often, this is as much an expression of the writer as it is a statement about the photograph.

During the Great Depression of the 1930s, for example, the photographer Walker Evans and the writer James Agee traveled to Alabama to take pictures of poor farmers and sharecroppers. These pictures—such as the one in Figure 11.1—invite storytelling. One story this photograph might tell is of a hard-pressed farmer worried about his family and his unpayable debts. Or you might see this one farmer as a symbol of all the hardship brought on by the Depression. Remove him from his Depression-era context, however, and you might see a father suspiciously eyeing a young man bringing bad news about a family member. Is there anything in particular that ties this farmer to a specific time and place? What makes you think so?

11c Creating a hypertext essay

Multimedia hypertext essays are created by inserting links in the document that take readers to other files, including text, image, audio, and video files. (*See the "TextConnex" box on p. 124.*) Links can take several forms:

■ **Internal links** connect from one place in a document to another place in the same document or to other files stored on the writer's computer.

■ **External links** connect to Web sites on the Internet and any text, image, audio, or video files stored on them.

FIGURE 11.1 **A Walker Evans photograph.**

These links can either complement the essay's verbal claims or, like a good chart or graph, support the claims directly. However, unless your assignment includes specific directions to emphasize linked material as evidence, you should probably think of it as supplemental to your written claims.

Caution: When you revise your hypertext essay, be sure to check all links to make sure they are relevant and functioning correctly. Also, if your essay includes internal links to files on your computer, be sure to include those files with the file for the essay when you submit it to your instructor.

11d Creating multimedia presentations

Presentation software makes it possible to incorporate audio, video, and animation into a talk. Presentation software can also be used to create a multimedia composition that viewers can go through on their own.

1. Using presentation software for an oral presentation

Presentation slides that accompany a talk should identify major points and display information in a visually effective way. Remember that slides support your talk, but they do not replace it. Keep the amount of information on each slide to a minimum, and plan to show each slide for about one minute. (*For more on preparing and presenting slides for an oral presentation, see Chapter 10, pp. 120, 122–23.*)

2. Using presentation software to create an independent composition

With presentation software, you can also create compositions that run on their own or at the prompting of viewers. This capability is especially useful in distance-learning settings, in which students attend class and share information electronically.

3. Preparing a slide presentation

You should begin thinking about slides while you plan what you are going to say. As you decide on the words for the talk or composition, you will think of visuals that support your points, and as you work out the visuals, you are likely to see additional points you can make, and adjust your presentation accordingly. The following guidelines apply:

- **Decide on a slide format.** Before you create your slides, you need to establish their basic appearance. What background color will they have? What typeface or typefaces? What design elements such as borders and rules? If the templates provided by the software will not work in your situation, modify them or start from scratch, using the templates as a basis for comparison as you develop your design.

- **Incorporate visuals into your presentation.** Include visuals when appropriate. For example, to summarize quantitative information, you might use a chart or graph. Use only visuals that support your purpose. (*For more on choosing visuals, see Chapter 3, pp. 30–34.*)

- **Incorporate other multimedia elements.** Slides can also include audio files. You might record background information for each slide in an independent composition. Or, for a presentation

11d
media

www.mhhe.com/
bmhh

For an interactive
tutorial on using
PowerPoint, go to

Writing >
PowerPoint
Tutorial

www.mhhe.com/
bmhh

For more
on designing
documents, go to

Writing > Writing
Web Links >
Document and
Web Design

on music, you might insert audio files to show how a type of music has developed over time. Presentation slides can also include video files and **animation**—visuals that have moving parts or that change over time. An animated diagram of the process of cell division, for example, could help illustrate a presentation on cellular biology. (As you would for any other source, you need to provide documentation if you are using files that belong to others.)

■ **Incorporate hypertext links.** You might use an internal link within a slide sequence to jump to another slide that illustrates or explains a particular point or issue, enlivening the presentation and helping the audience remember the information. You can also create external links to files on the Web. The value of this kind of link is that it allows you to showcase resources for your audience. Be careful not to overload your presentation with external links, however, because they can undermine the coherence of a presentation. They can also take a long time to load; if possible, you should rehearse your presentation on-site, so that the external files are cached.

Caution: If you plan to make external links part of your presentation, make sure that you have a functioning Web browser on your computer and that a fast connection to the Internet is available where you will be giving the presentation.

---

4. Reviewing the presentation

Carefully review your slides to make sure they work together coherently:

■ **Check how the slides in your software's slide sorter window proceed one to the next.** Do you have an introductory slide? Do you need to include transitional effects, such as fades or animation, that reveal the content of a slide item by item? Some of these transitional effects permit audio—do you want that? Do you have a concluding slide? Are the slides consistent with the script of your talk? If the slides are intended as an independent document, do they include enough explanation and an adequate introduction and conclusion?

■ **Check the arrangement of your slides.** You might try printing them as paper handouts and spreading them out over a large surface or printing and cutting apart the handout version of the slides for sorting. You can then rearrange slides physically, if need be, and return to the computer to implement your changes.

■ **Check the slides to be sure they have a unified look.** Make sure, for example, that all the slides have the same background and that each uses the same typeface(s) in the same way.

11e Creating a Web site

11e
media

www.mhhe.com/
bmhh

For more on designing Web sites, go to

Writing > Writing Web Links > Document and Web Design

Thanks to Web editing software, it is now almost as easy to create a Web site and post it on the Internet as it is to write a paper using word-processing software. Web-based businesses like Yahoo! provide free server space for hosting sites and offer tools for creating Web pages. Many schools also make server space available for student Web sites.

A Web site, to be effective, must be well designed and serve a well-defined purpose for its audience. In creating a Web site, you will need to plan your site, draft content, select visuals, revise, and edit, just as you would for any kind of composition. However, each stage involves decisions and requirements that are unique to this medium; the following sections offer guidelines for making some of these decisions.

1. Planning a structure for your site

Like most paper documents, a Web site can have a linear structure, where one page leads to the next, and so on. Because of the hyperlinked nature of this medium, however, a site can also be organized in a hierarchy, or with a number of pages that connect to a central page, or hub, like the spokes of a wheel. The diagrams in Figure 11.2 illustrate these two possible structures.

To choose the structure that will work best for your site, consider how you expect visitors to use it. The structure of each site accommodates its users' needs.

2. Gathering content for your site

The content for a Web site will usually consist of written work along with links and graphics. Depending on your topic and purpose, you might also provide audio files, video files, and even animation.

There are some special requirements for written content that appears on a Web site:

■ Recognize that readers usually do not expect or want lengthy text explanations on the Web site. Instead, they want to find the link or button they are looking for quickly.

■ In general, create shorter paragraphs, and make sure the text for each page fits on that page. Avoid long passages that require readers to use the scroll bar.

■ Use links to connect your interests with those of others and to provide extra sources of information. Avoid using the command

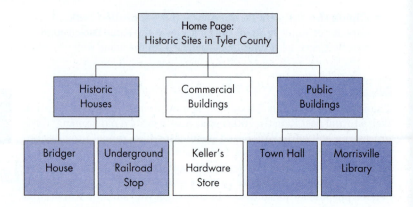

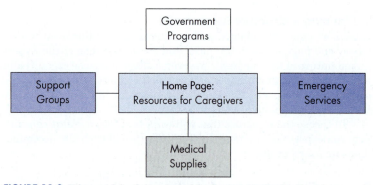

FIGURE 11.2 Hierarchical (top) and hub structure (bottom).

"Click here" on your Web site. Instead, make links part of your text. As with any evidence you use in your writing, your links should lead readers to content that is credible and relevant.

As you prepare your written text, you should also gather any graphics, photographs, and audio and video files that you plan to include. Whether or not an image is in the public domain, be sure to give proper credit for any material that you have not generated yourself and, if necessary, request permission for its use. (*See Chapter 18, pp. 189–194 for guidelines on what requires permission.*)

3. Designing Web pages to capture and hold interest

On effective Web sites, you will also find such easy-to-follow links as "what you'll find here," FAQs (frequently asked questions), or "list of those involved." In planning the structure and content of your site, keep your readers' convenience in mind.

4. Designing a readable site with a unified look

Because the Web is a visual medium, readers appreciate a site with a unified look. "Sets" or "themes" are readily available at free graphics

11e
media

TEXTCONNEX

Understanding Web Jargon

- **Browser:** software that allows you to access and view material on the Web. When you identify a site you want to see on the Web by typing in a URL (see below), your browser (*Mozilla Firefox* or *Microsoft Internet Explorer,* for example) tells a distant computer—a **server**—to send that site to you.

- **JPEG and GIF:** formats for photographs and other visuals that are recognized by browsers. Photographs that appear on a Web site should be saved in JPEG format (Joint Photographic Experts Group, pronounced *jay-peg*). The file extension is .jpg or .jpeg. Clip art should be saved as GIF files (Graphics Interchange Format, pronounced like *gift* without the *t*).

- **Home page:** the opening page of a Web site. A home page typically includes general information about the site as well as links to various parts of it.

- **HTML/XML:** hypertext markup language/extensible markup language. These languages tag or code text so that your browser can rebuild a document from the compressed files that are sent through the Internet. When your browser retrieves a page, you end up with an "original copy" of the document, usually in a matter of seconds. It is no longer necessary to learn HTML or XML to publish on the Web. Programs such as *FrontPage, PageMill,* and *Dreamweaver* now provide a WYSIWYG (What You See Is What You Get) interface for creating Web pages.

- **Protocol:** a set of rules controlling data exchange between computers. **HTTP** (hypertext transfer protocol) is a way of breaking down and then reconstructing a document when it is sent over the Internet.

- **URL:** uniform resource locator or Web address. When you type or paste a URL into your Web browser, you are sending a request through your browser to another computer, asking it to transfer data to your computer.

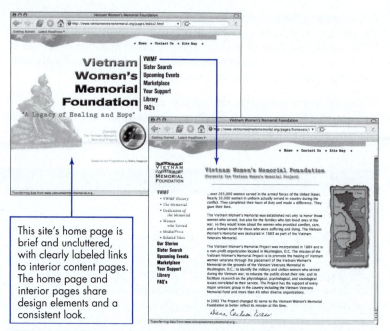

FIGURE 11.3 Home page and an interior page from the Web site of the Vietnam Women's Memorial Foundation.

sites offering banners, navigation buttons, and other design elements. You also can create your own images with a graphics program or scan your personal art and photographs. Design the Web site to complement your other pages, or your readers may lose track of where they are in the site—and lose their interest in staying.

- Consider including a site map—a Web page that serves as a table of contents for your entire site.

- Select elements such as buttons, signs, animations, sounds, and backgrounds with a consistent design.

- Use colors to provide adequate contrast, white space, and sans serif fonts to make text easy to read. Pages that are too busy are not visually compelling. (*For more on design, see Chapter 5, pp. 73–80.*)

- Avoid using overly wide lines of text; readers find them difficult to process.

The home page and interior page shown in Figure 11.3 illustrate some of these design considerations.

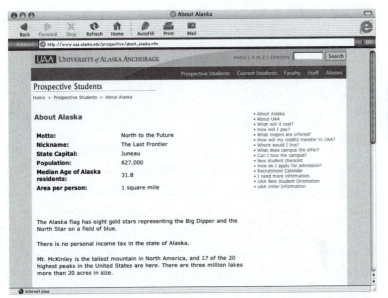

11e
media

FIGURE 11.4 A page from the Web site of the University of Alaska Anchorage. The navigation bar appears on every page of the site.

5. Designing a Web site that is easy to access and navigate

Since most Web sites are not linear, writers need to take special care to help their readers find their way to the areas of the site they want to visit. Here are some guidelines to help you accomplish this:

- **Identify your Web site on each page, and provide a link to the home page.** Remember that readers will not always enter your Web site through the home page. Give the title of the site on each page. Provide an easy-to-spot link to your home page as well.

- **Provide a navigation bar on each page.** A **navigation bar** can be a simple line of links that you copy and paste at the top or bottom of each page. For example, visitors can choose from five links in the navigation bar under the title on the University of Alaska Anchorage site (*see Figure 11.4*).

- **Use graphics that load quickly.** Limit the size of your images to no more than 40 kilobytes so that they will load faster.

- **Use graphics judiciously.** Your Web site should not depend on graphics alone to make its message clear and interesting. Graphics should be used to reinforce your message. The designers of the Library of Congress Web site (*see Figure 11.5*) use graphics to help visitors navigate the site.

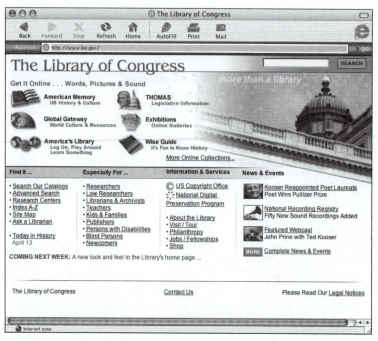

FIGURE 11.5 The home page of the Web site of the Library of Congress.

TextConnex

Web Resources for Site Design and Construction

- *www.teach.science's Surf and Master the Web: Writing Web Pages:* <http://www.science_house.org/workshops/web/writing.html>
- *Web Guide: Designing a Web Page:* <http://people.depauw.edu/djp/webguide/designwebpage.html>
- *WDVL: A Guide to Creating Web Sites with HTML, CGI, Java, JavaScript, Graphics:* <http://wdvl.com/Authoring>

- **Be aware of the needs of visitors with disabilities.** Provide alternate ways of accessing any visual or auditory information, such as descriptions of visual texts and transcriptions of audio files. (*See Chapter 5, p. 80.*)

Tip for Multilingual Writers
Designing a Web Site Collaboratively

If you are asked to create a Web site as part of a class assignment, try to make arrangements to work with a partner or a small group. The kind of interaction involved in writing the content and designing the site will provide you with beneficial language support. Periodically, you can invite peers to look over the writing you contribute and make suggestions. At the same time, you will be able to provide the project with the benefit of your unique multicultural viewpoint. ▬▬▬

11f
media

6. Using peer feedback to revise your Web site

When you publish on the Web, you offer your work to be read by anyone in the world. Make sure your site reflects favorably on your abilities.

11f Creating and interacting with Weblogs

Weblogs—called "blogs" for short—are simply Web sites that can be continuously updated. Some blogs are the exclusive creations of one writer; others provide a group of writers a space for sharing ideas and discussing each other's work. You can include images in a blog and link to other blogs and Web pages (*see Figure 11.6*).

To begin blogging, you will need to set up a blog site with a server such as www.blogger.com. You may at first want to confine yourself to a very specific purpose before launching into wide-ranging commentary. Remember that all blogs are more or less public, depending on how much access they allow. Don't post anything you would not want everybody to know about.

When you begin your blog, consider the following questions:

- What is your purpose?
- To whom will you give access? Will the blog be public, for all to see? Or will it be limited to specific viewers?
- Do you want to allow others to post on your blog?
- Do you want to set up a schedule of postings or a series of events that will cue you to post?
- Do you want to link to other blogs?

FIGURE 11.6 A personal blog. Musician Scott August's blog, hosted on blogger.com, contains posts about his music and travels.

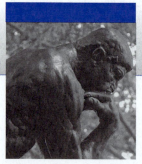

12 Writing beyond College

Writing is one way to connect your work, your other activities, and your studies. Your ability to research and write can be of great value to organizations that serve the community, such as homeless shelters, tutoring centers, and environmental groups. Strong writing skills will also help you to find a good job once you leave college and to advance in your chosen career.

12a   Addressing the community to effect change

When you are writing for a community group, consider these questions:

- What do community members talk about?
- How do they talk about these issues, and why?
- Who is an outsider (member of the community), and who is an insider (member of the organization)?
- How can you best write from the inside to the outside?

12b
comm

Your answers will help you shape your writing so that it reaches its intended audience and moves that audience to action.

Writing on behalf of a community organization almost always involves negotiation and collaboration. A community organization may revise your draft to fit its needs, and you will have to live with those revisions. In these situations, having a cooperative attitude is as important as having strong writing skills.

12b   Designing brochures, posters, and newsletters

www.mhhe.com/
bmhh

For interactive
help with design,
go to

Writing >
Visual Rhetoric

If you are participating in a service learning program or an internship, you may have opportunities to design brochures and newsletters for wide distribution, as well as posters to create awareness and promote events. Here are a few tips that will help you design effective brochures, and newsletters, whatever your audience and purpose may be:

- Before you begin, consider how readers will gain access to and review the brochure or newsletter. How will it be mailed or distributed?

- Sketch the design in pencil before you immerse yourself in the capacities of the computer.

- In making decisions about photographs, illustrations, type fonts, and the design in general, think about the overall image that should be conveyed about the organization sponsoring the brochure, poster, or newsletter.

- If the organization has a logo, include it; if not, suggest designing one. A **logo** is a small visual symbol, like the Nike "swoosh" or the distinctive font used for Coca-Cola.

- Create a template for the brochure, poster, or newsletter so that you can easily produce future editions. In word-processing and document design programs, a **template** is a blank document that includes all of the formatting and codes. When you use a template, you just "plug in" new content and visuals—the format and design are already done.

FIGURE 12.1 Example of an effective brochure.

Notice, for example, how the brochure for the PSFS Building in Philadelphia, Pennsylvania (*see Figure 12.1*) purposefully connects the history and importance of an architectural landmark with the prestige of the Loews Philadelphia Hotel, into which "the world's first Modernist skyscraper" has been renovated. The brochure has an informative and also a subtly persuasive purpose. Readers are meant to feel that by staying at this Loews they are participating in a great tradition. The front cover is divided in half, with a striking photo of the building on the left side and an account of its history on the right. The interior page places a photo of the bank above an image of hotel comfort. On both pages, quotations running vertically beside the photographs reinforce the building's architectural significance.

The newsletter from the Harvard Medical School titled "Women's Health Watch" (*see Figure 12.2*) has a simple, clear design. The designer keeps in mind the purpose and audience, which are explicitly stated in the title and the headline below the title. The shaded area on the right lists the topics that are covered on the interior pages so that readers can get to the information they need quickly and easily. The Web address is prominently displayed in blue so that readers can find further information. The lead article, "Does Excess Vitamin A Cause Hip Fracture?" is simply designed in two columns, with the headline in bold type, subheadings in blue, a readable typeface, and a graphic strategically placed to break up the text and add visual interest. In all of these ways, the design supports the Harvard Medical School's purpose of helping the general public get reliable information about the latest advances in medical research.

12c
job

12c Exploring internship possibilities

In an internship, writing and learning go together. Keep a journal to record and analyze your experiences, as well as a file of any writing you do on the job. Your final project for the internship credit may require that you analyze the file of writing you have produced.

Files of writing from internships, clippings of articles and editorials you have written for the school newspaper, writing you have done for a community organization—these and other documents demonstrate your ability to apply intellectual concepts to real-world demands. Organized into a portfolio (*see pp. 80–83*), this material displays your marketable skills. Your campus career resource center can help you assess your skills and determine what kind of internship would best suit your career goals. It may also help you compile a portfolio, keep it on file, and help you send it to potential employers or graduate schools.

H A R V A R D
Women's Health Watch

INFORMATION FOR ENLIGHTENED CHOICES FROM HARVARD MEDICAL SCHOOL

Does Excess Vitamin A Cause Hip Fracture?

Hip fracture is one of the most dreaded risks of aging. More than 350,000 hip fractures occur annually in the United States, mostly in women over 65. Half of these women never regain the ability to live independently. About 20% die within a year. Many others suffer chronic pain, anxiety, and depression. The consequences are so grim that many older women contacted in surveys on this subject say they'd rather die than suffer a hip fracture that would send them to a nursing home.

Current recommendations on reducing fracture risk advise women to exercise, make sure they get enough calcium and vitamin D, and, if necessary, take medications that help preserve bone strength. Some women also learn strategies for preventing falls or take classes such as tai chi to improve their balance. Now, a new study suggests that we should also pay attention to vitamin A. At high levels, this essential nutrient may actually increase our risk for hip fracture.

NEW STUDY FINDS LINK

Researchers at Harvard Medical School reported in the Jan. 2, 2002, *Journal of the American Medical Association* on the relationship between postmenopausal hip fracture and vitamin A intake. The data came from 72,337 women enrolled in the Nurses' Health Study. The women were divided into five groups according to their average daily consumption, over an 18-year period, of vitamin A from food and supplements.

Researchers then correlated vitamin A intake with hip fracture incidence. They found that women with the highest intake—3,000 micrograms (mcg) or more per day—had a 48% greater risk for hip fractures, compared to women with the lowest intake (1,250 mcg or less per day).

The increased risk was mainly due to *retinol*, a particular form of vitamin A. In fact, women consuming 2,000 mcg of retinol or more daily had a hip fracture risk almost *double* that of women whose daily intake was under 500 mcg. In contrast, consuming high levels of *beta-carotene*, also a source of vitamin A, had a negligible impact on hip fracture risk. Participants taking hormone replacement therapy (HRT) were somewhat protected from the effects of too much retinol.

ABOUT VITAMIN A

Vitamin A is important for vision, the immune system, and the growth of bone, hair, and skin cells. Retinol, also called "preformed vitamin A," is the active form of the vitamin. It occurs naturally in animal products such as eggs, whole milk, cheese, and liver. Other food sources of vitamin A are *carotenoids*, which are found in green leafy vegetables and in dark yellow or orange fruits and vegetables. The body can convert these plant compounds to retinol. Beta-carotene is the most plentiful carotenoid and it converts most efficiently. Even so, you need about 12 times as much beta-carotene as retinol to get the same amount of vitamin A.

Because vitamin A is lost in the process of removing fat, many fat-free dairy products are fortified with retinol. So are some margarines and ready-to-eat cereals. The vitamin A in supplements and multivitamins may come from retinol, beta-carotene, or both. Beta-carotene is preferable because it's also an antioxidant.

Although vitamin A deficiency is a leading cause of blindness in developing countries, it's not a major problem in the United States. The main concern here is excess vitamin A, which can produce birth defects, liver damage, and reduced bone mineral density (BMD).

15% of women age 50 will suffer a hip fracture before age 80.

Volume IX Number 7
March 2002

In Brief
HRT and Dry Eyes
page 3

❖

Mental Health
When Anxiety Is Overwhelming
pages 4–6

❖

Research Brief
The Genetics of Lactose Intolerance
page 6

❖

Massage
Massage Is More Than an Indulgence
page 7

❖

By the Way, Doctor
Should I Still Get Mammograms?
page 8

www.health.harvard.edu

FIGURE 12.2 Example of a well-designed newsletter.

12d Keeping an up-to-date résumé

A **résumé** is a brief summary of your education and your work experience that you send to prospective employers. Expect the person reviewing your résumé to give it no more than sixty seconds. Make that first impression count. Design a document that is easy to read, attractively formatted, and flawlessly edited.

Guidelines for writing a résumé

Always include the following *necessary* categories in a résumé:

12e
job

- Heading (name, address, phone number, e-mail address)
- Education (in reverse chronological order; do not include high school)
- Work experience (in reverse chronological order)
- References (often included on a separate sheet; for many situations, you can add the line "References available on request" instead)

Include the following *optional* categories in your résumé as appropriate:

- Honors and awards
- Internships
- Activities and service
- Special skills
- Objective

Sometimes career counselors recommend that you list a career objective under the heading of your résumé. If you do so, be sure you know what the prospective employer is looking for and tailor your objective.

Laura Amabisca organized the information in her résumé (*see p. 142*) by time and by categories. Within each category, she listed items from the most to least recent. This reverse chronological order gives appropriate emphasis to what she had just done and was doing when she prepared the résumé. Note that Laura's résumé contains no italic, bold, or other formatting, so it may be scanned or submitted electronically.

12e Applying for a job: Application letter and interview

A clear and concise **application letter** should always accompany a résumé. (*See Amabisca's application letter on p. 144.*) If the want ad you are answering does not include a name, call the organization and find out the name of the person responsible for your area of interest. If you are unable to identify an appropriate name, it is better to direct the letter to "Dear Director of Public Relations" than to "Dear Sir or Madam."

Here are some additional guidelines for applying for a job:

- **Tailor your letter.** A form letter accompanied by a generic résumé is not an effective way of getting a job interview. Before

Laura's entire résumé is just one page. A brief, well-organized résumé is more attractive to potential employers than a multipage, rambling résumé. Laura uses a simple font and no bold or italic type, ensuring that the résumé will be scannable.

Laura includes keywords (highlighted in blue here) that will be most likely to catch the eye of a potential employer. Laura knows that a position in public relations requires computer skills, communication skills, and experience working with diverse groups of people. Key words such as "sales," "bilingual," "HTML," and "public relations" are critical to her résumé.

LAURA AMABISCA
20650 North 58th Avenue, Apt. 15A
Glendale, AZ 85308
623-555-7310
lamabisca@peoplelink.com

OBJECTIVE
To obtain a position as public relations assistant at a nonprofit organization

EDUCATION
Arizona State University West, Phoenix
*Bachelor of Arts, History, Minor in Global Management (May 2007)
*Senior Thesis: Picturing the Hopi, 1920-1940: A Historical Analysis

Glendale Community College, Glendale, AZ (2003-2005)

EXPERIENCE
Public Relations Office, Arizona State University West (Summer 2006)
Intern
*Researched and reported on university external publications.
*Creator of original content for print and Web.
*Assisted in planning fundraising campaign and events.

Sears, Bell Road, Phoenix, AZ
Assistant Manager, Sporting Goods Department (2005–present)
*Supervised team of sales associates.
*Ensured quality customer service.

Sales Associate, Sporting Goods Department (2002-2005)
*Recommended products to meet customer needs.
*Processed sales and returns.

Stock Clerk, Sporting Goods Department (1999-2003)
*Received, sorted, and tracked incoming merchandise.
*Stocked shelves to ensure appropriate supply on sales floor.

SPECIAL SKILLS
Language: Bilingual: Spanish/English
Computer: Windows, Mac OS, MS Office, HTML

ACTIVITIES
America Reads (2006)
Tutor, Public-Relations Consultant
*Taught reading to first-grade students.
*Created brochure to recruit tutors.

Multicultural Festival, Arizona State University West (2006)
Student Coordinator
Organized festival of international performances, crafts, and community organizations.

Writing Center, Glendale State Community College (2004-2005)
Tutor
Met with peers to help them with writing assignments.

REFERENCES
Available upon request to Career Services, Arizona State University West

TextConnex

Electronic Résumé

Many employers now request résumés by e-mail and will electronically scan print résumés. Both of these innovations require you to take additional care with your résumé. (For more information and step-by-step advice on tailoring résumés for specific fields, see Monster.com <http://resume.monster.com/>.)

Before you apply for a job by e-mail, be sure that the employer accepts electronically submitted résumés. Also find out whether you should include the résumé in the body of an e-mail message or send it as an attached document. If the employer expects the résumé as an attached document, be sure to save it in a widely readable form such as rich text format (RTF) or ASCII. Use minimal formatting and no colors, unusual fonts, or other decorative flourishes. Many companies enter résumés into searchable databases, and unusual formatting or special characters can create problems. Be aware, too, that many companies have secure firewalls around their servers that screen out all attachments or attachments that include certain words. You can configure your e-mail program to send you an automatic reply when your e-mail has been successfully transmitted.

Because employers use certain specific keywords to search scanned or electronically submitted résumés, you will want to be sure to include those words in your résumé. The résumé section of Monster.com contains industry-specific advice on appropriate words. Use keywords from the job description whenever possible.

12e
job

writing an application letter or preparing a résumé, you need to have a sense of exactly what the employer is looking for. You can then tailor your documents to those requirements.

- **Use business style.** Use the block form shown on page 144. Type your address at the top of the page, with each line starting at the left margin; place the date at the left margin two lines above the recipient's name and address; use a colon (:) after the greeting; double-space between single-spaced paragraphs; use a traditional closing (*Sincerely, Sincerely yours, Yours truly*); and make sure that the inside address and the address on the envelope match exactly.

- **Be professional.** Your letter should be crisp and to the point. Avoid personal details, and be direct and objective in presenting your qualifications. Your tone toward and approach to the prospective employer should be courteous but dignified. Your résumé should contain only educational and work-related information. It is better not to include personal information (such as ethnicity, age, or marital status).

20650 North 58th Avenue, Apt. 15A
Glendale, AZ 85308
August 17, 2008

Ms. Jaclyn Abel
Director of Public Relations
Heard Museum
2301 North Central Avenue
Phoenix, AZ 85004

Dear Ms. Abel:

I am writing to apply for the position of Public Relations Assistant that you recently advertised in the *Arizona Republic*. I believe that my experience and qualifications fit well with your needs at the Heard, a museum that I have visited and loved all my life.

As the enclosed résumé indicates, I have experience in the public relations field. While at Arizona State University West, I worked as an intern in the Public Relations Office, where I was responsible for analyzing and reporting on the image projected by the university's external publications. I also had a hand in creating the brochure for the University-College Center and participated in planning ASU West's "Dream Big" campaign. In addition I assisted in organizing an opening convocation attended by 800 people. This work in the not-for-profit sector has prepared me well for employment at the Heard.

My undergraduate major in American history has also helped me understand the rich heritage of Native Americans. In my senior thesis, which received the Westmarc Writing Award, I studied the history of the relationship between the Hopis and the Anglo population as reflected in photographs taken from 1920 to 1940. Although my thesis focuses on a specific tribe, I have been interested for many years in Native-American culture and have often made use of resources in the Heard. I think that I would do a superior job of presenting the Heard as the premier museum of Native American culture.

Confidential reference letters are available from ASU West Career Services. I sincerely hope that we will have an opportunity to talk further about the Heard Museum and its outstanding cultural contributions to the Phoenix metropolitan area. Please contact me at 623-555-7310.

Sincerely,

Laura Amabisca

Laura Amabisca

Enc.

Laura writes to a specific person and uses the correct salutation (Mr., Ms., Dr., etc.). Never use only a first name in an application letter, even if you are writing to an acquaintance.

Laura briefly sums up her work experience. This information is also available on her résumé, but she makes evident in her cover letter why she is applying for the job. Without this explanation, a potential employer might not even look at her résumé.

Laura mentions her familiarity with the museum to which she is applying. This demonstrates her genuine interest in joining the organization.

- **Limit your letter to three or four paragraphs.** Focus clearly and concisely on what the employer needs to know. In the first paragraph, identify the position you are applying for, mention how you heard about it, and briefly state that you are qualified. In the following one or two paragraphs, explain your qualifications, elaborating on the most pertinent items in your résumé. Because Amabisca was applying for a public relations job at a museum of Native American culture, she chose to highlight her internship and her thesis. In another application letter, however, this time for a management position at American Express, she made different choices. In that letter, she emphasized her work experience at Sears, including the fact that she had moved up in the organization through positions of increasing responsibility.

- **State your expectation for future contact.** Conclude with a one- or two-sentence paragraph informing the reader that you are anticipating a follow-up to your letter.

- **Use *Enc.* if you are enclosing additional materials.** Decide whether it is appropriate to enclose supporting materials other than your résumé, such as samples of your writing. Amabisca decided to do so because she was applying for her ideal job and had highly relevant materials to send. If you have been instructed to send a cover letter and résumé by e-mail as attachments, include the word "Attachments" after your e-mail "signature."

- **Be on time.** Time is of the essence when you send in application materials and when you arrive at the interview. A last-minute application or a late appearance at an interview can count heavily against you.

- **Bring your materials to the interview.** Bring an additional copy of your résumé and cover letter to refer to during your interview.

- **Send a thank-you note.** After an interview, send a thank-you note or e-mail that reiterates your interest in the position.

Tip for Multilingual Writers
Applying for a Job

Before applying for an internship or a job in the United States, be sure that you have the appropriate visa or work permits. American employers are required by law to confirm such documentation before they can hire anyone. (American citizens must prove their citizenship as well.) For more information, visit your campus international student center and the campus career resource center. ▬▬▬

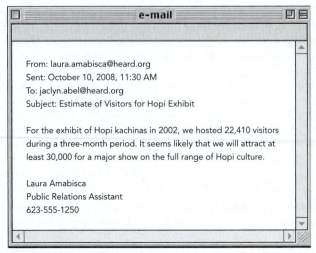

From: laura.amabisca@heard.org
Sent: October 10, 2008, 11:30 AM
To: jaclyn.abel@heard.org
Subject: Estimate of Visitors for Hopi Exhibit

For the exhibit of Hopi kachinas in 2002, we hosted 22,410 visitors during a three-month period. It seems likely that we will attract at least 30,000 for a major show on the full range of Hopi culture.

Laura Amabisca
Public Relations Assistant
623-555-1250

FIGURE 12.3 Sample workplace e-mail.

12f Applying college writing to writing on the job

Once you get a job, writing is a way to establish and maintain lines of communication with your colleagues and other contacts. When you write in the workplace, you should imagine a reader who is pressed for time and wants you to get to the point immediately.

1. Writing e-mail and memos in the workplace

In the workplace, you will do much of your writing online, in the form of e-mail. Most e-mail programs set up messages in memo format, with "To," "From," "Date," and "Subject" lines, as in Figure 12.3.

E-mail in the workplace requires a more formal style than the e-mail you send to family and friends. In an e-mail for a business occasion—communication with colleagues, a request for information, or a thank-you note after an interview—you should observe the same care with organization, spelling, and tone that you would in a business letter. More specifically:

- Use the subject line to cue the reader as to the intent of the e-mail. When replying to messages, replace subject lines that do not clearly reflect the topic.

- Maintain a courteous tone. Use joking, informality, and sarcasm cautiously, as they can cause the recipient to misunderstand your intent.

- Make sentences short and to the point.

TEXTCONNEX

12f
job

E-mail in the Workplace

Anything you write using a company's or an organization's computers is considered company property. If you want to gossip with a coworker, do so over a cup of coffee. If you want to e-mail your best friend about your personal life, do so from your home computer. The following guidelines will help you use e-mail wisely:

- When you are replying to an e-mail that has been sent to several people (the term *cc* means "carbon copy"), determine whether your response needs to go to all of the original recipients or just to the original sender. Avoid cluttering other people's in boxes.

- File your e-mail as carefully as you would paper documents. Create separate folders in your e-mail program for each client, project, or coworker.

- While it may be acceptable for you to browse news and shopping sites during your breaks and lunchtime, do not visit any sites while in the workplace that would embarrass you if a colleague or your supervisor suddenly looked over your shoulder.

To: Sonia Gonzalez, Grace Kim, Jonathan Jones
From: Jennifer Richer, Design Team Manager
Date: March 3, 2008
Re: Meeting on Monday

Please plan to attend a meeting on Monday at 9:00 a.m. in Room 401. At that time, we'll review our progress on the library project as well as outline future activities to ensure the following:

- Client satisfaction
- Maintenance of the current schedule
- Operation within budget constraints

In addition, we will discuss assignments related to other upcoming projects, such as the renovation of the gymnasium and science lab. Please bring design ideas and be prepared to brainstorm. Thanks.

Copy: Michael Garcia, Director, Worldwide Design

- Use standard punctuation and capitalization.
- Close with your name and contact information. (*See the box on p. 147 and the example on p. 146.*)

Business memos are used for communication with others within an organization. Like business e-mails, they are concise and formal. Memos may establish meetings, summarize information, or make announcements. (*See the example on p. 147.*) They generally contain the following elements and characteristics:

- A header at the top that identifies author, recipient, date, and subject
- Block paragraphs that are single-spaced within the paragraph and double-spaced between paragraphs
- Bulleted lists and other design elements (such as headers) to set off sections of longer memos
- A section at the bottom that indicates other members of the organization who have received copies of the memo
- A professional tone

Whether you are writing an e-mail message or a conventional memo, you need to consider not only what your workplace document says but also how it looks. Various strategies can make your document easier to read. For example, presenting your information as a numbered or bulleted list surrounded by white space aids readability and allows you to highlight important points and to emphasize crucial ideas.

www.mhhe.com/
bmhh

For help with
PowerPoint, go to

**Writing >
PowerPoint
Tutorial**

2. Writing in other business genres

Conventional forms increase readability because readers have built-in expectations for the genre and therefore know what to look for. Besides the memo, there are a number of common business genres:

- **Business letters:** Use business letters to communicate formally with people outside an organization. Typically, letters in business format have single-spaced block paragraphs with double spacing between the paragraphs. (*See the example on p. 144.*)

- **Business reports and proposals:** Like college research papers, business reports and proposals can be used to inform, analyze, and interpret. An abstract, sometimes called an **executive summary,** is almost always required, as are tables and graphs. (*For more on these visual elements, see Chapter 2, pp. 30–34.*)

- **Evaluations and recommendations:** You might need to evaluate a person, or you might be called on to evaluate a product or a procedure and recommend whether the company should buy or

TEXTCONNEX

Writing Connections

- *Job Central* <http://jobstar.org/tools/resume/samples.cfm>: This site provides samples of resumes for many different situations, as well as sample cover letters.
- *Career Collection: Write a Résumé* <http://college.library.wisc.edu/collections/career/careerresume.html>: This site provides help with preparing cover letters and writing resumes.

12f
job

use it. Always support your account of both strengths and weaknesses with specific illustrations or examples.

- **Presentations:** In many professions, information is presented in ways both formal and informal to groups of people. You might suddenly be asked to offer an opinion in a group meeting; or you might be given a week to prepare a formal presentation, with visuals, on an ongoing project. (*For more information on oral presentations, see Chapter 10, pp. 119–123. To learn more about PowerPoint and other presentation tools, see pp. 122–123.*)

Astronomers have used telescopes for centuries to research the mysteries of the night sky. This picture of Saturn was taken by the Hubble Space Telescope from its orbit around the Earth.

PART

3

For all knowledge and wonder (which is

the seed of knowledge) is an impression

of pleasure in itself.

—FRANCIS BACON

Researching

3 Researching

WRITING OUTCOMES

Critical Thinking, Reading, and Writing

This section will help you learn to do the following:

- Understand the steps in a research writing assignment **(13)**
- Locate and assess print and online sources **(14)**
- Integrate the words and ideas from sources with your own writing without plagiarizing **(19)**

13 Understanding Research

Doing research in the twenty-first century includes the library but is not limited to it. The Internet now provides rapid, direct access to an abundance of information unimaginable to earlier generations of students. The results of Internet searches, however, can sometimes provide an overwhelming flood of sources, many of them of questionable legitimacy.

The goal of the research section of this book is to help you learn to navigate today's research landscape skillfully, manage the information you discover within it, and use that information to write research papers.

13a
res

13a Understanding primary and secondary research

Primary research means working in a laboratory, in the field, or with an archive of raw data, original documents, and authentic artifacts to make firsthand discoveries. **Secondary research** means looking to see what other people have learned and written.

Knowing how to identify facts, interpretations, and evaluations is key to good secondary research:

- **Facts** are objective. Like your body weight, facts can be measured, observed, or independently verified in some way.
- **Interpretations** spell out the implications of facts. Are you as thin as you are because of your genes or because you exercise every day? The answer to this question is an interpretation.
- **Evaluations** are debatable judgments about a set of facts or a situation. The assertion that "one can never be too rich or too thin" is an evaluation.

Once you are up-to-date on the facts, interpretations, and evaluations in a particular area, you will be able to design a research project that adds your *perspective* on the sources you found and read:

- Given all that you have learned about the topic, what strikes you as important or interesting?
- What patterns do you see, or what connections can you make between one person's work and another's?
- Where is the research going, and what problems still need to be explored?

153

CHARTING the TERRITORY

Classic and Current Sources

Classic sources are well-known and respected older works that made such an important contribution to a discipline or a particular area of research that contemporary researchers use them as touchstones for further research in that area. In many fields, sources published within the past five years are considered current.

13b Recognizing the connection between research and college writing

In many ways, research informs all college writing. But some assignments require more rigorous and systematic research than others. **Research project** assignments offer you a chance to find and read both classic and current material on a specific issue.

A research paper constitutes your contribution to the ongoing academic conversation about a specific issue.

13c Choosing an interesting research question

Choosing an interesting topic will help you make the results of your inquiry meaningful—to yourself and your readers.

1. Choosing a question with personal significance

Get personally involved in your work. Begin with the wording of the assignment, analyzing the project's required scope, purpose, and audience (*see Chapter 2, pp. 16–19*). Then browse through the course texts and your class notes, looking for a match between your interests and topics, issues, or problems in the subject area.

www.mhhe.com/
bmhh

For more on
narrowing your
topic, go to

Writing >
Paragraph/Essay
Development >
Thesis/Central
Idea

2. Making your question specific

The more specific your question, the more your research will have direction and focus. To make a question more specific, ask about the *who, what, why, when, where,* and *how* of a topic.

After you have compiled a list of possible research questions, choose one that is relatively specific or rewrite a broad one to make it more specific and answerable. For example, a student could rewrite the following broad question to make it answerable:

TOO BROAD   How has globalization affected the Amazon River Basin?

CHARTING the TERRITORY

Typical Lines of Inquiry in Different Disciplines

Research topics and questions differ from one discipline to another, as the following examples show:

- **History:** How did India's experience of British imperialism affect its response to globalization?
- **Marketing:** How do corporations develop strategies for marketing their products to an international consumer audience?
- **Political science:** Why did many European nations agree to unite, creating a common currency and an essentially "borderless" state of Europe (the European Union, or EU)?
- **Anthropology:** What is the impact of globalization on the world's indigenous cultures?

13c

res

| ANSWERABLE | How has large-scale agriculture in the Amazon Basin affected the region's indigenous peoples? |

3. Finding a challenging question

To be interesting, a research question must be challenging. If it can be answered with a yes or no, a dictionary-like definition, or a textbook presentation of information, you should choose another question or rework it to make it more challenging.

| NOT CHALLENGING | Has economic globalization contributed to the destruction of the Amazon rain forest? |
| CHALLENGING | How can agricultural interests and indigenous peoples in the Amazon region work together to preserve the environment while creating a sustainable economy? |

Exercise 13.1   Creating answerable, challenging questions

For each of the following broad topics, create at least three answerable, challenging questions.

1. Internet access is becoming as important as literacy in determining the livelihood of a nation's people.
2. Genetically modified organisms (GMOs) and biotechnology are controversial approaches to addressing the world's food problems.
3. The problem of terrorism requires a multilateral solution.

---

4. Speculating about answers

Sometimes it can be useful to develop a **hypothesis**—an answer to your research question—to work with during the research process. Keep an open mind as you work, and be aware of the assumptions embedded in your hypothesis or research question. Consider, for example, the following:

> **HYPOTHESIS**   The global demand for agricultural products will destroy the Amazon rain forest.

This hypothesis assumes that destructive farming practices in the Amazon region are the only possible response to global demand. But assumptions are always open to question. Researchers must be willing to adjust their ideas as they learn more about a topic.

13d   Understanding the research assignment

Although your audience will most likely include only your instructor and perhaps your classmates, thinking critically about their needs and expectations will help you to plan a research strategy and create a schedule for writing your paper.

Consider the following questions about your audience:

- What do they already know about your topic? How much background information and context will you need to provide? (Your research should include **facts.**)

- Is your topic controversial or challenging? How should you accommodate and acknowledge different perspectives and viewpoints? (Your research should include **interpretations,** and you will need to be careful to balance interpretations that might be opposed to each other.)

- Will you expect the audience to take action based on the results of your research? (Your research should include **evaluations,** carefully supported by facts and interpretations, that demonstrate clearly why readers should adopt a course of action or point of view.)

Your purpose for writing a research paper depends on both the specifics of the assignment as set by your instructor and your own engagement with, and interest in, your topic. Your purpose might be **informative**—to educate your audience about an unfamiliar subject or point of view. Your purpose might be **interpretive**—to reveal the meaning or significance of a work of art, a historical document, a literary work, or a scientific study. Your purpose might be **argumentative**—to convince your audience, with logic and evidence, to accept your point of view on a controversial issue or to act on the information in your paper.

Tips LEARNING in COLLEGE

Scheduling Your Research Project

Task	Date

Phase I: Five days

- Complete general plan for research. _____
- Decide on topic and research question. _____
- Consult reference works and reference librarians. _____
- Make list of relevant keywords for online searching (*see Chapter 14, p. 161*). _____
- Compile **working bibliography** (*see Chapter 19, p. 194*). _____
- Sample some items in bibliography _____
- Make arrangements for primary research (if necessary). _____

Phase II: Twelve days

- Locate, read, and evaluate selected sources. _____
- Take notes. _____
- Cross-check notes with working bibliography. _____
- Conduct primary research (if necessary). _____
- Confer with instructor or Writing Center (optional). _____
- Outline or plan organization of paper. _____

Phase III: Ten days

- Write first draft, deciding which primary and secondary source materials to include. _____
- Have peer review (optional but strongly recommended). _____
- Revise draft. _____
- Confer with instructor or Writing Center (optional). _____
- Do final revision and editing. _____
- Create Works Cited or References page. _____

Due date _____

13e
res

13e Creating a research plan

Take some time at the beginning to outline a research plan. A detailed schedule helps you set priorities and meet your deadlines. The box on this page outlines the steps in a research project and can be used as a starting point.

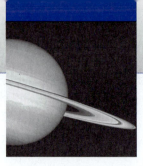

14 Finding and Managing Print and Online Sources

The amount of information available in the library and on the Internet is vast, so a search for useful sources entails three activities:

- Collecting keywords from reference works
- Using library databases
- Finding material in the library and on the Web

www.mhhe.com/
bmhh

For more
information
and links, go to

**Research > Using
the Library**

14a Using the library in person and online

Librarians know what is available at your library and how to get material from other libraries. They can also show you how to access the library's computerized book catalog, periodical databases, and electronic resources or how to use the Internet to find information relevant to your project. Your library's Web site may also have links to important reference works available on the Internet, as shown in Figure 14.1.

Help sheets, found at most college libraries, list the location of both general and discipline-specific periodicals and noncirculating reference books, along with information about special databases, indexes, and sources of information on the Internet.

Exercise 14.1 Finding information at your library

Choose anyone born between 1900 and 1950 whose life and accomplishments interest you. You could select a politician, a film director, a rock star, a Nobel Prize–winning economist—*anyone*. At your library, find at least one of each of the following resources with information about or relevant to this person:

- A directory of biographies
- An article in a pre-1990 newspaper
- An article in a scholarly journal
- An audio or video recording, a photograph, or a work of art
- A printout of the search results of your library's electronic catalog
- An obituary (if your subject has died)
- A list of your subject's accomplishments, including, for example, prizes received, books published, albums released, or movies made

---

14b Consulting various kinds of sources

Consult more than one source and more than one kind of source. These are some of the kinds of sources available to you:

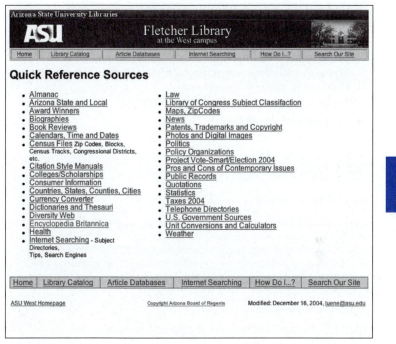

FIGURE 14.1 A page from the Web site of Arizona State University West. The Web page provides links to a variety of Web-based reference sources.

- **General reference works**
  Encyclopedias, annuals, almanacs
  Computer databases, bibliographies, abstracts
- **Specialized reference works**
  Discipline-specific encyclopedias, almanacs, and dictionaries
- **Books and electronic texts**
- **Periodical articles**
  In newspapers
  In magazines
  In scholarly and technical journals
  On the World Wide Web
- **Web sites**
- **Blogs**
- **News groups, ListServs, e-mail, virtual communities (MUDs and MOOs)**

14b
res

- **Pamphlets, government documents, census data**
- **Primary sources**
  Original documents like literary works, art objects, performances, manuscripts, letters, and personal journals
  Museum collections; maps; photo, film, sound, and music archives
  Field notes, surveys, interviews
  Results of observation and lab experiments
- **Specialized databases**

Tips LEARNING in COLLEGE

Popular or Scholarly?

Reading a Wikipedia entry may help you get started on your research, but to be taken seriously in academia, you will need to go further and consult scholarly sources. In fact, some instructors do not consider Wikipedia as a credible source. The audience and purpose of a source, especially a publication, determines whether it should be considered *scholarly* or *popular*.

Popular sources:

- Are widely available on newsstands and in retail stores
- Accept advertising for a wide range of consumer goods
- Are themselves widely advertised (in the case of books)
- Are printed on magazine paper with a color cover
- Are published by a commercial publishing house or media company (such as Time Warner)
- Include a wide range of topics in each issue, from international affairs to popular entertainment
- If online, have a URL that likely ends in .com

Scholarly sources:

- Are found generally in libraries, not on newsstands
- Include articles with extensive citations and bibliographies
- Are **refereed,** which means that each article has been reviewed, commented on, and accepted for publication by other scholars in the field
- List article titles and authors on the cover
- Include articles mostly by authors who are affiliated with a college, a museum, or some other scholarly institution
- Are published by a scholarly or nonprofit organization, often in association with a university press
- Focus on discipline-specific topics
- If online, have a URL that likely ends in .edu or .org

Tips LEARNING in COLLEGE

Refining Keyword Searches

Although search engines vary, the following guidelines should work for many of the search engines you will use:

- **Group words together.** Put quotation marks or parentheses around the phrase you are looking for—for example, "Dixieland Jazz."
- **Use Boolean operators.**

  AND (+) Use AND or + when you need sites with both of two or more words: Armstrong + Glaser.

  OR   Use OR when you want sites with either of two or more terms: jazz OR "musical improvisation".

  NOT   Use NOT in front of words that you do not want to appear together in your results: Armstrong NOT Neil.

- **Use a "wildcard."** For more results, combine part of a keyword with an asterisk (*) used as a wildcard: music* (for "music," "musician," "musical," and so forth).
- **Search the fields.** Some search engines permit you to search within fields, such as the title field of Web pages or the author field of a library catalog. Thus, TITLE + "Louis Armstrong" will give you all pages that have "Louis Armstrong" in their title.

14c
res

14c Understanding keywords and keyword searches

Most online research—whether in your library's catalog, in a specialized database, or on the Web—requires an understanding of **keyword searches.** In this context, a **keyword** is a term (or terms) you enter into a **search engine** (searching software) to find sources that have information you need.

To hone in on your subject, adjust your initial search term. The "Tips" box describes a variety of techniques for doing so that work in most search engines. Many search engines also have an advanced search feature that can help with the refining process.

Exercise 14.2 Finding information online

Look at the sample research topics listed in the "Charting the Territory" box on page 155, and conduct a keyword search for each on at least three search engines. Experiment with the phrasing of each keyword search, and compare your results with those of your classmates.

EXAMPLE   **What is the impact of globalization on the world's indigenous cultures?**

"indigenous culture" AND globalization

www.mhhe.com/
bmhh

For disciplinary
resources to begin
your search, go to

Research >
Discipline Specific
Resources

14d Using printed and online reference works

Reference works provide an overview of a subject area and typically are less up to date than the specialized knowledge found in academic journals and scholarly books. There is nothing wrong with starting your research by consulting a general encyclopedia, but for college research, you need to explore your topic in more scholarly sources. Often, the list of references at the end of an encyclopedia article can lead you to useful sources.

TEXTCONNEX

Wikipedia

The online encyclopedia Wikipedia offers information on almost any subject, and it can be a good starting place for research. However, you should evaluate its content critically and use other sources to verify information you find there. Volunteers (who may or may not be experts) write Wikipedia's articles, and any user may edit any existing article. While the site has some mechanisms to help it maintain the accuracy of its information, you should not rely on it alone.

Reference books do not circulate, so plan to take notes or make photocopies of the pages you may need to consult later. Many college libraries subscribe to services that provide access to online encyclopedias. Check your college library's home page for appropriate links.

Here is a list of some other kinds of reference materials available in print, on the Internet, or both:

ALMANACS	*Almanac of American Politics* *Information Please Almanac* *World Almanac*
BIBLIOGRAPHIES	*Bibliographic Index* *Bibliography of Asian Studies* *MLA International Bibliography*
BIOGRAPHIES	*African American Biographical Database* *American Men and Women of Science* *Dictionary of American Biography*

> Dictionary of Literary Biography:
>   Chicano Writers
> Dictionary of National Biography
> Webster's New Biographical Dictionary
> Who's Who

DICTIONARIES
> American Heritage Dictionary of the
>   English Language
> Concise Oxford Dictionary of Literary Terms
> Dictionary of American History
> Dictionary of Philosophy
> Dictionary of the Social Sciences
> Oxford English Dictionary (OED)

14e
res

Tip for Multilingual Writers
Researching a Full Range of Sources

Your mastery of a language other than English can sometimes give you access to important sources that would be beyond the reach of your monolingual classmates. You should not limit yourself to sources in your first language, however. Even if you find researching in English challenging, it is important to broaden the scope of your search as soon as you can to include a range of print and Internet resources written in English.

14e Using print indexes and online databases

1. Periodicals

Newspapers, magazines, and scholarly journals that are published at regular intervals are classified as **periodicals.** Scholarly and technical journals, written by experts and based on up-to-date research, are more reliable than articles in popular newspapers and magazines. Ask your instructor or librarian which periodicals are considered important in the discipline you are studying.

2. Indexes and databases

Articles published in periodicals are cataloged in general and specialized **indexes.** Indexes are available on subscription-only **databases** and as print volumes. If you are searching for articles that are more than twenty years old, use print indexes, which can be found in the reference section of your library. Print indexes can be searched by author, subject, or title. Electronic databases can also be searched by date and keyword and will provide you with a list of articles that meet your search criteria.

The "Tips" box on page 164 lists common formats for database information. The "TextConnex" box on pages 166–67 lists some of the

Tips | LEARNING in COLLEGE

Formats for Database Information

When searching a database, you will encounter both abstracts and full articles, and full-text articles may be available in either .pdf or .html format.

- **Abstract:** An abstract is a brief summary of a full-text article. Abstracts appear at the beginning of articles in some scholarly journals and are used in databases to summarize complete articles. (Do not mistake an abstract for the full-text source.)
- **Full text:** When an article is listed as "full text," the database provides you with a link to the complete text. Full-text articles accessed through databases do not always include accompanying photographs or other illustrations, however.
- **PDF** and **HTML:** Articles in databases and other online sources may be in either PDF or HTML format (or both). Documents in HTML (hypertext markup language) have been formatted to read as Web pages. Documents in PDF (portable document format) appear as a facsimile of the original pages. To read a PDF document, you need to have a program like *Adobe Acrobat Reader* installed on your computer.

major online databases, and the screen shots in Figure 14.2 illustrate a search on one of them, ProQuest. You can find databases on your school library's Web site. Note that different databases serve different disciplines. Take care to choose a database that includes relevant content for your assignment.

www.mhhe.com/
bmhh

For more information and links, go to

Research > Using the Internet

14f Using search engines and subject directories to find Internet sources

To find information that has been published in Web pages, you will need to use an Internet search engine. Because each search engine searches the Web in its own way, you will probably use more than one. (*See the box on p. 169 for a list of popular Internet search engines.*) To learn how a search engine can best serve your needs, look for a link labeled "search help," "about us," or something similar in any search engine you use.

Some Internet search engines provide for specialized searches—for images, for example. Google offers a service called "Google Scholar" that locates only scholarly sources in response to a search term. At this point, it offers incomplete information, and you should not rely on it alone.

Many Internet search engines also include sponsored links—links that a commercial enterprise has paid to have appear in response to specific search terms. These are usually clearly identified.

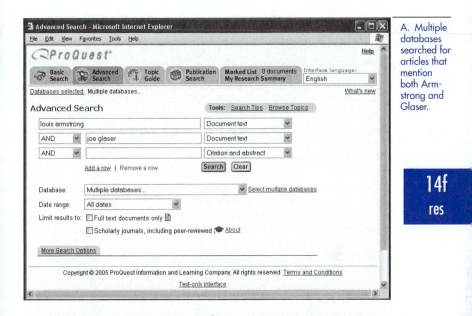

A. Multiple databases searched for articles that mention both Armstrong and Glaser.

14f
res

B. Entries include title, author, name of journal, viewing options (e.g., abstract).

FIGURE 14.2 ProQuest's Advanced Search page (A) and partial results of search (B).

TEXTCONNEX

Some Online Databases

- **ABC-CLIO:** This service offers access to two history-related databases: *America: History and Life* and *Historical Abstracts.*
- **EBSCOhost:** The Academic Search Premier Service provides full-text coverage for more than 8,000 scholarly publications and indexes articles in all academic subject areas.
- **ERIC:** This database lists publications in the area of education.
- **Factiva:** This database offers access to the Dow Jones and Reuters news agencies, including newspapers, magazines, journals, newsletters, and Web sites.
- **General Science Index:** This index is general rather than specialized. It lists articles by biologists, chemists, and other scientists.
- **GDCS:** Updated monthly, the Government Documents Catalog Service (GDCS) contains records of all publications printed by the United States Government Printing Office since 1976.
- **GPO Access:** This service of the U.S. Government Printing Office provides free electronic access to government documents.
- **Humanities Index:** This index lists articles from journals in language and literature, history, philosophy, and similar areas.
- **InfoTrac Web:** This Web-based service searches bibliographic and other databases such as the *General Reference Center Gold, General Business File ASAP,* and *Health Reference Center.*
- **JSTOR:** This archive provides full-text access to journals in the humanities, social sciences, and natural sciences.
- **LexisNexis Academic:** Updated daily, this online service provides full-text access to around 6,000 newspapers, professional publications, legal references, and congressional sources.
- **MLA Bibliography:** Covering 1963 to the present, the *MLA Bibliography* indexes journals, dissertations, and serials published worldwide in the fields of modern languages, literature, literary criticism, linguistics, and folklore.

Internet keyword searches need to be carefully worded to provide relevant results. For example, a search of Google using the keywords *louis armstrong* yields a list of more than 3.8 *million* Web sites, a staggering number of links, or **hits.**

Refining the search by putting quotes around *louis armstrong* and including the term *jazz* (which will find all sites with the words *louis* and *armstrong* together and also the word *jazz*) reduces the num-

- *New York Times Index:* This index lists major articles published by the *Times* since 1913.
- *Newspaper Abstracts:* This database provides an index to fifty national and regional newspapers.
- *PAIS International:* Produced by the Public Affairs Information Service, this database indexes literature on public policy, social policy, and the social sciences from 1972 to the present.
- *Periodical Abstracts:* This database indexes more than 2,000 general and academic journals covering business, current affairs, economics, literature, religion, psychology, and women's studies from 1987 to the present.
- *ProQuest:* This database provides access to dissertations; newspapers and journals; information on sources in business, general reference, the social sciences, and humanities; and historical sources dating back to the nineteenth century.
- *PsycInfo:* Sponsored by the American Psychological Association (APA), this database indexes and abstracts books, scholarly articles, technical reports, and dissertations in psychology and related disciplines.
- *PubMed:* The National Library of Medicine publishes this database, which indexes and abstracts 15 million journal articles in biomedicine and provides links to related databases.
- *Sociological Abstracts:* This database indexes and abstracts articles from more than 2,600 journals, as well as books, conference papers, and dissertations.
- *Social Science Index:* This index lists articles from such fields as economics, psychology, political science, and sociology.
- *WorldCat:* This is a catalog of books and other resources available in libraries worldwide.

14f

res

ber of hits to a still unmanageable 942,000. Altering the keywords to make them even more specific narrows the results significantly, as shown in Figure 14.3.

Like most search engines, Google has an Advanced Search option. This allows you to search for exact phrases, to exclude pages containing a specific term, to search only for pages in a certain language, and to refine searches in many other ways.

www.mhhe.com/bmhh

For a variety of search engines, go to

Research > Additional Links on Research

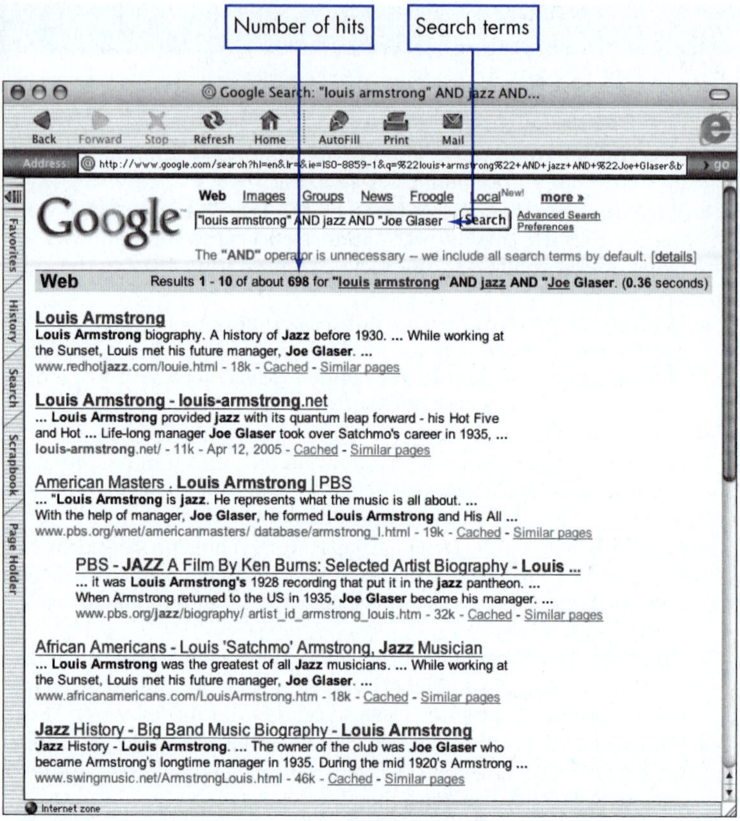

FIGURE 14.3 A narrowed search. Refining a search for Louis Armstrong by adding Joe Glaser (Armstrong's long-time manager) reduces the number of hits from over 3.8 million to an almost manageable 698. (Note that AND could have been omitted in this search—with no effect on the results—because Google treats terms by default as if they were joined by AND.)

In addition to keyword searches, many Internet search engines offer a **subject directory**—a listing of broad categories. Clicking on a category brings you to a more specific array of choices. Clicking through this hierarchy of choices eventually brings you to a list of sites related to a specific topic.

Just as with online databases and print indexes, some Web sites provide content-specific subject directories designed for research in a particular field. These sites are often reviewed or screened and are excellent starting points for academic research.

TextConnex

Popular Internet Search Engines

General search engines: These sites allow for both category and keyword searches.

- *AltaVista* <http://www.altavista.com>
- *Google* <http://www.google.com>
- *HotBot* <http://www.hotbot.com>
- *Vivisimo* <http://vivisimo.com>
- *WebCrawler* <http://www.webcrawler.com>
- *Yahoo!* <http://www.yahoo.com>

Meta search engines: These sites search several different search engines at once.

- *Dogpile* <http://www.dogpile.com>
- *Internet Public Library* <http://www.ipl.org>
- *Ixquick* <http://www.ixquick.com>
- *Librarian's Index to the Internet* <http://lii.org>
- *Library of Congress* <http://loc.gov>
- *MetaCrawler* <http://www.metacrawler.com>

Mediated search engines: These sites have been assembled and reviewed by people who sometimes provide annotations and commentary about topic areas and specific sites.

- *About.com* <http://www.about.com>
- *Looksmart* <http://search.looksmart.com>

14g
res

14g Using your library's online catalog or card catalog to find books

Books in most libraries are shelved by **call numbers** based on the Library of Congress classification system. In this system, books on the same topic have similar call numbers and are shelved together. You will need the call number to locate the actual book on the library's shelves.

You can conduct a keyword search of most online library catalogs by author, by title, or by subject. The results of a keyword search of a library's online catalog will provide a list composed mostly of books. In the examples in Figures 14.4 and 14.5 of a search of the City University of New York library's online catalog, notice that under the column "Format" other kinds of media that match a keyword subject search are also listed; you can alter the terms of a search to restrict the formats to a specific medium.

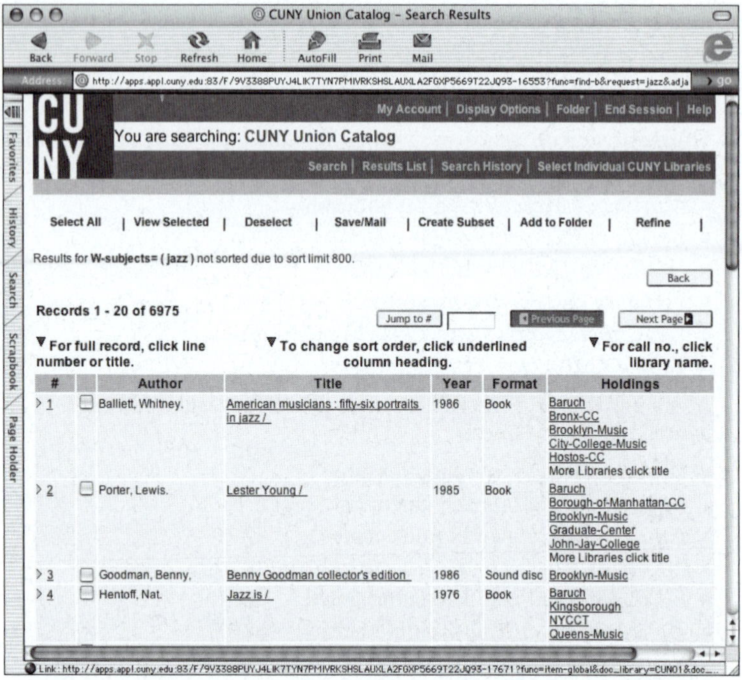

FIGURE 14.4 Initial search using the keyword *jazz*. Using the word *jazz* as a keyword in a subject search produces an unmanageable 6,975 sources. The "Holdings" column indicates which libraries in the CUNY system have the book. Clicking on a library name gives the book's call number at that library.

As with any keyword search, whether you get what you really need—a manageable number of relevant sources—depends on your choice of keywords. If your search terms are too broad, you will get too many hits; if they are too narrow, you will get few or none.

14h Taking advantage of printed and online government documents

The U.S. government publishes an enormous amount of information and research every year, most of which is available online. The *Monthly Catalog of U.S. Government Publications* and the *U.S. Government Periodicals Index* are both available as online databases. The Government Printing Office's own Web site, *GPO Access* <http://www.gpoaccess.gov/>, is an excellent resource for identifying what federal

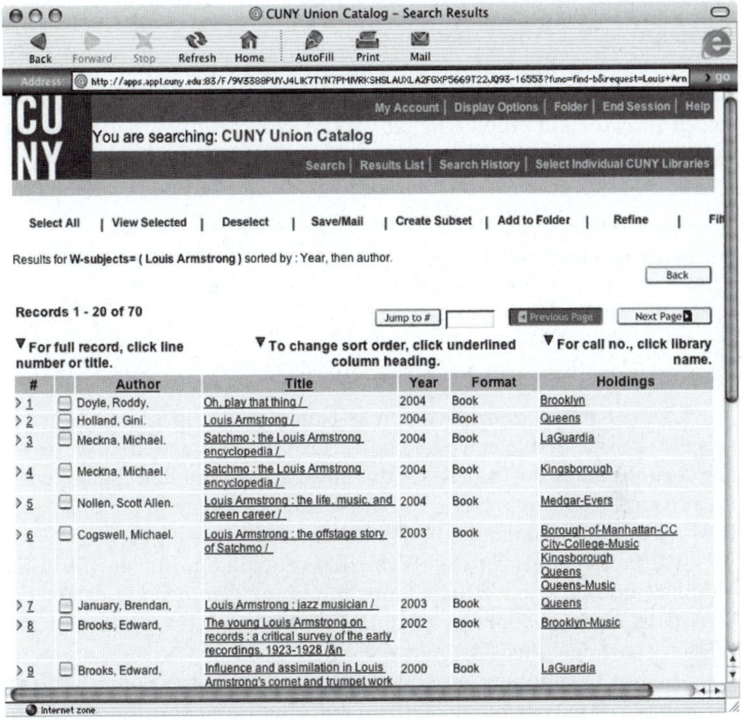

FIGURE 14.5 Second search with a narrower keyword. A keyword search using the term *Louis Armstrong* produces seventy results, a manageable number.

government publications are available and where to find them. Other online government resources include the following:

- *FedWorld Information Network* (maintained by the National Technical Information Service) <http://www.fedworld.gov/>
- *FirstGov* (the U.S. government's "Official Web Portal") <http://firstgov.gov/>
- *The National Institutes of Health* <http://www.nih.gov>
- *U.S. Census Bureau* <http://www.census.gov>

14i   Exploring online communication

The Internet provides access to communities with common interests and varying levels of expertise on different subjects. Discussion lists (electronic mailing lists), Usenet news groups, and Weblogs (blogs) are the most common communities.

Discussion lists (electronic mailing lists) are networked e-mail conversations on particular topics. Lists can be open (anyone can join) or closed (only certain people can join). If the list is open, you can subscribe by sending a message.

> **Caution:** The level of expertise among the people who partici-pate in online forums, and the scholarly seriousness of the forums themselves, varies widely.

Usenet news groups may exist on topics relevant to your re-search. Unlike lists, however, news groups are posted to a **news server**—a computer that hosts the news group and distributes post-ings to participating servers. You must subscribe to read postings, and they are not automatically distributed by e-mail.

Interactively structured Web sites provide another medium for online communication. **Blogs,** for example (*see Chapter 11*), can be de-signed to allow readers to post their own comments and queries. **Wikis,** sites designed for online collaboration, go further, allowing people both to comment on and modify one another's contributions.

Chat rooms permit one form of **synchronous communication,** which involves various types of real-time electronic exchanges be-tween individuals. Chat rooms are usually organized by topic, so the people who use a room are likely to share an interest in its topic. **In-stant messaging (IM)** is another medium for real-time communica-tion, but it involves only people who have agreed to form a group. Other, less common formats for synchronous communication include multiuser dimensions and object-oriented multiuser dimensions (MUDs and MOOs), both of which are used for collaborative projects and for role-playing simulations.

For a list of discipline-specific resources, go online to www .mhhe.com/bmhh.

15 Finding and Creating Effective Visuals

Visuals are often included as support for a writer's thesis, sometimes to enhance an argument and other times to make the writer's own argument. A relief organization, for example, might post a series of compelling visuals on its Web site to persuade potential donors to contribute money following a catastrophic event. In some writing situations, you will be able to prepare or provide your own visuals. You may, for example, create bar graphs from data that you collected. In other situations, however, you may decide to create a visual from data that you found in a source or to search in your library or on the Internet for a visual to use.

www.mhhe.com/
bmhh

For resources to begin your search, go to

Research > Discipline Specific Resources

15a Finding quantitative data and displaying it visually

Research writing often requires reference to quantitative information, and quantitative information often has more impact when it is displayed visually in a chart, graph, or map. (*For examples of graphs and charts, and a discussion of what situations to use them in, see Chapter 2, pp. 30–34.*)

> **Caution:** Whether you are using data from a source to create an image or incorporating an image created by someone else into your paper, you must give credit to the source of the data or image, just as you do when you paraphrase or quote the work of others. Furthermore, if you plan to publish a visual you selected from a source on a Web site or in another medium, you must obtain permission to use it from the copyright holder. If the copyright holder refuses permission, you must remove the image.

1. Finding existing graphs, charts, and maps

As you search for print and online sources, take notes on useful graphs, charts, or maps that you can incorporate (with proper acknowledgment) into your paper. If your source is available in print only, you may be able to use a scanner to capture and digitize it.

www.mhhe.com/
bmhh

For an interactive tutorial, go to

Writing > Visual Rhetoric

2. Creating visuals from quantitative data

Sometimes you may find data presented in writing or in tables that would be more effective as a chart or graph. Using the graphics tool available in spreadsheet or other software, you can create your own visual.

173

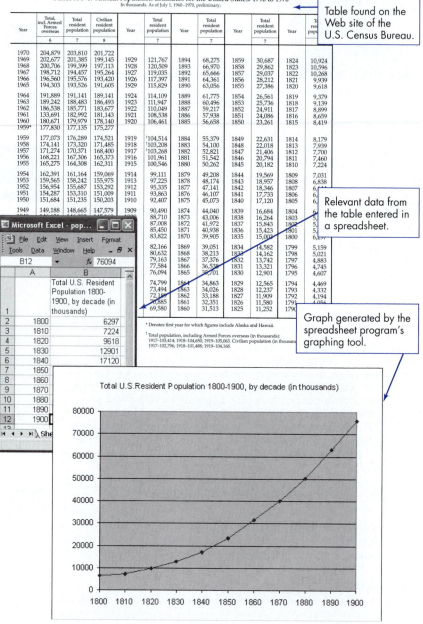

Series A 6–8. Annual Population Estimates for the United States: 1790 to 1970
In thousands. As of July 1, 1960–1970, preliminary;

Table found on the Web site of the U.S. Census Bureau.

Relevant data from the table entered in a spreadsheet.

Graph generated by the spreadsheet program's graphing tool.

* Denotes first year for which figures include Alaska and Hawaii.

[1] Total population, including Armed Forces overseas (in thousands):
1917–103,414; 1918–104,650; 1919–105,063. Civilian population (in thousands):
1917–102,796; 1918–101,488; 1919–104,168.

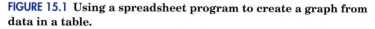

FIGURE 15.1 Using a spreadsheet program to create a graph from data in a table.

For example, suppose you are writing about population trends in the United States in the nineteenth century and want to illustrate the country's population growth in that period with a line graph, using U.S. Census Bureau data, which is in the public domain. Most census data, however, appears in tables like the one shown in Figure 15.1. If you transfer the data you need from a table like this to a spreadsheet program like *Microsoft Excel,* you can use it to create graphs that you can insert into a paper, as in Figure 15.1.

3. Displaying the right data

Make sure that you display data in a way that is consistent with your purpose and that what you display does not deceptively leave out information that could undermine your claims. Consider, for example, two maps of the paths of hurricanes in 2004 (*see Figures 15.2 and 15.3*). The first, Figure 15.2, shows the position of Hurricane Jeanne on September 23, 2004, and its predicted path for the next five days. The figure incorporates quantitative data such as the storm's predicted wind speed. The purpose of the map is to help the people in its path understand the risk they face from the storm.

15a
visual

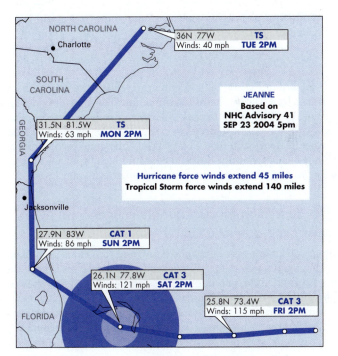

FIGURE 15.2 An accurate display of hurricane data.

FIGURE 15.3 **A display of hurricane data that could be used deceptively.**

The map in Figure 15.3 is comparative, showing the paths of two hurricanes that were active at the same time. This map does not provide information about the intensity of either storm, making them appear equal. Were the intent to deceive—to support the erroneous claim, say, that coastal Texas suffered as badly from Hurricane Ivan as did coastal Alabama—this seeming equivalence would be a problem. Always consider what a visual leaves out as well as what it displays.

15b Searching for appropriate images in online and print sources

Photographs, pictures of artwork, drawings, diagrams, and maps can provide visual support for many kinds of papers. As with the display of quantitative data, you might *choose* an image from another source, or you might *create one.* If you were doing a report comparing the way different corporations are organized, for example, you might use organizational charts that appear in corporate reports. Alternatively, you might use your word processor's drawing feature to create your own or-

---

Tips | **LEARNING in COLLEGE**

Deciding When to Use an Image in Your Paper

Regardless of the kind or number of images you use, there are several questions you will want to consider as you look for them:

- How many images do you need?
- Where will each image appear in the text?
- What contribution will each image make to the text?
- What contribution do the images taken as a whole make to the text?
- Does the audience have enough background information to interpret each image in the way you intend?
- If not, is there additional information that should be included in the text or in a caption?
- If no additional information is needed, does the image none-theless need a caption?
- Have you reviewed your own text (and perhaps asked a friend to review it as well) to see how well the image is "working"—in terms of appropriateness, location, and context?

15b
visual

---

ganizational charts based on information you find in the corporate reports. When using an image from another source, be sure to cite it correctly. If the image will appear on a public Web site, consult the copyright holder for permission.

The following are three sources of images that you can draw on:

- **Online image collections and subscription databases:** Several libraries and other archives maintain collections of images online. See the "TextConnex" box on page 178 for the URLs of image collections. Your library may also subscribe to an image database such as the Associated Press *AP Multimedia Archive.*

- **Images on the Internet:** Many search engines have the ability to search the Web for images alone. You can conduct an image search on Google, for example, by clicking on the "images" option, entering the key term, and then clicking on "search."

- **Images scanned from a book or journal:** You can use a scanner to scan some images from books and journals into a paper, but as always, only if you are sure your use is within fair-use guidelines. Also, be sure to credit the source.

Caution: The results of Internet image searches, like those of any Internet search, need to be carefully evaluated for relevance and reliability. (*See Chapter 16, pp.184–85.*) Make sure you have proper source information for any images you use.

TEXTCONNEX

Some Online Image Collections

- *Art Institute of Chicago* (selected works from the museum's collection) <http://www.artic.edu/aic/index.html>
- *The Library of Congress* <http://www.loc.gov/>
- *National Archives Digital Classroom* (documents and photographs from American history) <http://www.archives.gov/digital_classroom/index.html>
- *National Aeronautics and Space Administration* (images and multimedia features on space exploration) <http://www.nasa.gov/vision/universe/features/index.html>
- *National Park Service Digital Image Archive* (thousands of public domain photographs of U.S. national parks) <http://photo.itc.nps.gov/storage/images/index.html>
- *New York Public Library* <www.nypl.org/digital/>
- *Schomburg Center for Research in Black Culture* <www.nypl.org/research/sc/sc.html>
- *VRoma: A Virtual Community for Teaching and Learning Classics* (images and other resources related to ancient Rome) <http://www.vroma.org/>

16 Evaluating Sources

New technologies may grant fast access to a tremendous variety of sources, but they cannot by themselves help you decide which of those sources to use for your research. It is up to you to evaluate each potential source to determine whether it is both *relevant* and *reliable*. A source is relevant if it pertains to your research topic. A source is reliable if it provides trustworthy information.

Evaluating sources requires you to think critically and make judgments about which sources will be useful for answering your research question. This process helps you manage your research and focus your time on those sources that deserve close scrutiny.

16a Questioning print sources

Just because something is in print does not make it relevant or true. Here are some questions to ask about any source you are considering:

Relevance

- **Do the source's title and subtitle indicate that it addresses your specific research question?**
- **What is the publication date?** Is the material up-to-date, classic, or historically pertinent?
- **Does the table of contents indicate that the source covers useful information?**
- **If the source is a book, does it have an index?**
- **If the source is an article, does it have an abstract at the beginning or a summary at the end?**
- **Does the work contain headings?** Skim the headings to see if they indicate that the source covers useful information.

Reliability

- **What information can you find about the writer's credentials?**
- **Who is the publisher?** University presses and academic publishers are considered more scholarly than the popular press.
- **Does the work include a bibliography of works consulted or cited?** Trustworthy writers cite a variety of sources and document their citations properly.
- **Is the work balanced in tone, or does the writer appear biased?**

TEXTCONNEX

Evaluating Sources

- **Primary or secondary? Popular or scholarly?**
  <http://www.sport.ussa.edu/library/primary.htm>: discusses the difference between primary and secondary research sources, as well as the difference between popular and scholarly sources
- **Evaluating sources of information**
  <http://owl.english.purdue.edu/handouts/research/:r_evalsource .html>: from the Purdue Online Writing Lab; provides guidelines for evaluating print and online sources

16b Questioning Internet sources

The Internet offers new ways to research and requires new methods of assuring that the information presented is credible. For students, the library has been the conventional site of researching for at least the past hundred years. Most of the material in the library has been evaluated to some extent for credibility. Editors and publishers have reviewed the content of books, magazines, journals, and newspapers. However, some presses and publications are more reputable than others. Subscription databases generally compile articles that originally appeared in print, and librarians try to purchase the most reliable databases. While you can have some confidence that most of the material you find in the library is credible, you must evaluate all sources for bias and relevance to your paper.

In contrast, anyone can create a Web site that looks attractive but contains nonsense. So, while information on the Web may be valuable, you have to decide if you can trust it before using it as evidence in your paper. Here are some questions to ask when determining whether online information is reliable:

- Who is hosting the site? Is the site hosted by a university or by a government agency (like the National Science Foundation or the National Endowment for the Humanities)? In general, sites hosted by institutions with scholarly credentials are trustworthy.

- Who is speaking on the site? A nationally recognized biologist is likely to be more credible on biological topics than a graduate student in biology.

- What links does the site provide? If it is networked to sites with obviously biased or inaccurate content, you must question the credibility of the original site.

■ Is the information on the site supported with documentation from scholarly or otherwise reliable sources? Reliable sources of information might include government reports, for example.

Consider the following factors as well:

■ **Authority and credibility:** Are the author and producer of the Web site identifiable? Is there any indication that the author has relevant expertise on the subject? Look for information about the individual or organization sponsoring the site. The following extensions in the Web address, or uniform resource locator (URL), can help you determine the type of site (which often tells you something about its purpose):

16b
eval

.com	commercial (business)	**.edu** educational	**.mil** military
.org	nonprofit organization	**.gov** U.S. government	**.net** network

A tilde (~) followed by a name in a URL usually means the site is a personal home page not affiliated with any organization.

■ **Audience and purpose:** Does the appearance of the site and the tone of any written material suggest an audience? A site's purpose also influences the way it presents information and the reliability of that information. Is the site's main purpose to promote a cause, raise money, advertise a product or service, provide factual information, present research results, provide news, share personal information, or offer entertainment?

■ **Objectivity and bias:** Look carefully at the purpose and tone of the text. Clues that indicate a lack of reasonableness include an intemperate tone, broad claims, exaggerated statements of significance, conflicts of interest, no recognition of opposing views, and strident attacks on opposing views. Particularly when evaluating blogs and online newsgroup postings, compare any data and claims with those of other types of sources.

■ **Relevance and timeliness:** In what ways does the information from an online source specifically support (or refute) your thesis or topic? Do the site's intended audience and purpose include an academic audience? Does the site indicate how recently it has been updated, and are most of the included links still working?

Consider the example of a student researching sources for a paper comparing the experience of Northern and Southern women living in rural communities during the Civil War. Notice how in Figure 16.1 the home page establishes the Web site's authority and credibility, identifies its audience and purpose, and suggests its objectivity and relevance to

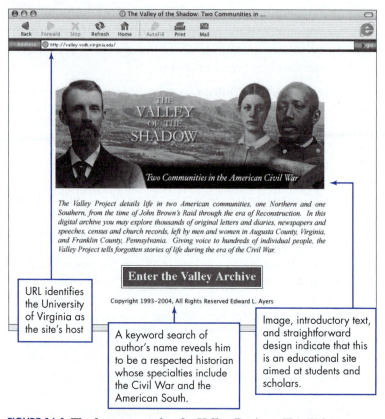

URL identifies the University of Virginia as the site's host

A keyword search of author's name reveals him to be a respected historian whose specialties include the Civil War and the American South.

Image, introductory text, and straightforward design indicate that this is an educational site aimed at students and scholars.

FIGURE 16.1 The home page for the Valley Project. This Web site provides a collection of primary-source documents related to two communities in the years before, during, and after the American Civil War.

the student's topic. This site contains archival resources such as diaries, newspapers, and church records from a community in Pennsylvania and one in Virginia during the Civil War era.

Now look at Figure 16.2 on page 183. Like the previous site, this one is organized based on geography. The home page contains links with the names of six states and Washington, D.C., leading to pages that discuss Civil War events within each region. Both Northern and Southern states appear. While the identity of its creator is unclear, scrolling down to the bottom of the home page and clicking on the publisher's name indicates this company also publishes popular Civil War

Links to podcasts, books, and events suggest that the site is aimed at a general audience.

URL ending in .com indicates site is for-profit or sponsored by business.

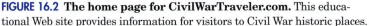

Information on state battlefields and museums indicates site's purpose: to facilitate tourism.

FIGURE 16.2 The home page for CivilWarTraveler.com. This educational Web site provides information for visitors to Civil War historic places.

books and magazines. The more sophisticated design and prominently advertised podcasts, books, and event calendar also suggest a general, rather than a primarily scholarly audience. (*See the box on p. 160.*) The .com domain name and the link to advertising rates suggest that this site is a for-profit business.

The paragraphs at the bottom of the screen, along with the site's title, indicate its purpose. It provides information and historical background for visitors to Civil War battlefields, museums, and parks. This information is likely to be accurate. However, the site is not a good source for this particular paper because it includes little related to the experiences of women. If the student's topic related to geography or specific military engagements, the site might provide a jumping-off point for further research. (*For more help evaluating Web sites, see the TextConnex box on pp. 184–85.*)

16c   Evaluating a source's arguments

As you read the sources you have selected, you should continue to assess their reliability. Look for arguments that are qualified, supported with evidence, and well documented. Avoid sources that appeal mostly to emotions or promote one-sided agendas. A fair-minded researcher needs to read and evaluate sources on both sides of issues.

Exercise 16.1   Evaluating Web sites

Working alone or in groups, choose one of the following topics:

1. The cost of prescription drugs in the United States
2. Drilling for oil in the Arctic National Wildlife Refuge
3. The reintroduction of wolves in Yellowstone National Park
4. The legalization of marijuana
5. Global warming
6. Second Amendment rights and gun control

For your topic, find at least three Web sites that clearly demonstrate at least one of the following characteristics:

Bias	Conflict of interest
Objectivity	Timeliness
Authority	Quality control (or lack thereof)
Fallacy	Obvious audience and purpose

TEXTCONNEX

Using the CARS Checklist to Evaluate Web Sites

A Web site that is Credible, Accurate, Reasonable, and Supported (CARS) should meet the following criteria:

Credibility

- The source is trustworthy; you would consider a print version to be authoritative (for example, an online edition of a major newspaper or news magazine).
- The argument and use of evidence are clear and logical.
- The author's or sponsor's credentials are available.
- Quality control is evident (for example, spelling and grammar are correct, and links are functional).
- The source is a known or respected authority; it has organizational support (such as a university, a research institution, or a major news publication).

Be prepared to share example Web pages with your class (either print them out or use a projection screen) and to point out how they demonstrate the characteristics you have identified.

TEXTCONNEX

- The source appears at or near the top of a Google search (Google.com ranks sites according to their popularity; sites near the top of a list of "hits" are the most frequently accessed by people looking for the same information you seek).

Accuracy

- The site is updated frequently, if not daily (and includes "last updated" information).
- The site provides evidence for its assertions.
- The site is detailed; text appears in full paragraphs.
- The site is comprehensive, including archives, links, and additional resources. A search feature and table of contents or tabs allow you to quickly find the information you need.
- The site's purpose includes completeness and accuracy.

Reasonableness

- The site is fair, balanced, and objective.
- The site makes its purpose clear. (Is it selling something? Prompting site visitors to sign a petition? Promoting a new film?)
- The site contains no conflict of interest.
- The site does not include fallacies or a slanted tone. (*For more on fallacies, see Chapter 1, pp. 12–13.*)

Support

- The site lists scholarly or otherwise reliable sources for its information, providing links where available.
- The site clarifies which content it is responsible for and which links are created by unrelated authors or sponsors.
- The site provides contact information for its authors and/or sponsors.
- If the site is an academic resource, it follows the conventions of a specific citation style (MLA, APA, or another accepted style).

Often, research involves more than finding answers to questions in books and other print and online resources (**secondary research**). When you conduct **primary research**—looking up old maps, consulting census records, polling community members about a current issue—you participate in the discovery of knowledge.

17a Adhering to ethical principles

In the archive, field, or lab, you are working directly with something precious and immediate: an original record, a group of people, or special materials. An ethical researcher shows respect for materials, experimental subjects, fellow researchers, and readers.

Here are some guidelines for ethical research:

- Handle original documents and materials with great care, always leaving sources and data available for other researchers.
- Accurately report your sources and results.
- Follow proper procedures when working with human participants.

Research with human participants should also adhere to the following basic principles:

- **Confidentiality:** People who fill out surveys, participate in focus groups, or respond to interviews should be assured that their names will not be used without their permission.
- **Informed consent:** Before participating in an experiment, participants must sign a statement affirming that they understand the general purpose of the research.
- **Minimal risk:** Participants in experiments should not incur any risks greater than they do in everyday life.
- **Protection of vulnerable groups:** Researchers must be held strictly accountable for research done with the physically disabled, prisoners, people who are mentally incompetent, minors, the elderly, and pregnant women.

17b Preparing yourself for archival research

Archives are found in libraries, museums, other institutions and private collections, and on video- and audiotape. Your own attic may contain family archives—letters, diaries, and photographs that could have value to a researcher. Some archival collections are accessible through audio- and videotape as well as the Internet; others you must visit in person. The more you know about your area of study, the more likely you will be to see the significance of an item in an archival collection.

Archives generally require that you call or e-mail to arrange a time for your visit, and some are restricted. If you find an archive on the Internet that you would like to visit, phone or e-mail well in advance to find out if you will need references, a letter of introduction, or other qualifying papers. Archives also generally require you to present a photo ID and to leave personal items in a locker or at a coat check, have strict policies about photocopying or otherwise reproducing materials, and rarely if ever allow anything to leave the premises. The more you know about the archive's policies and procedures before you visit, the more productive your visit will be.

17c

17c Planning your field research carefully

Field research involves recording observations, conducting interviews, or administering surveys.

1. Observing and writing field notes

When you use direct observation, keep careful records in order to retain the information you gather. Whenever you can, count or measure, and take down word for word what is said. Use frequency counts—the number of occurrences of specific, narrowly defined instances of behavior. If you are observing a classroom, for example, you might count the number of teacher-directed questions asked by several children.

2. Conducting interviews

To be useful as research tools, interviews require systematic preparation and implementation:

- Identify appropriate people for your interviews.
- Do background research, and plan your questions.
- Take careful notes, and if possible, tape-record the interview. (Be sure to obtain your subject's permission if you use audiotape or videotape.)
- Follow up on vague responses with questions that get at specific information.
- Politely probe inconsistencies and contradictions.
- Write thank-you notes to interviewees, and later send them copies of your report.

3. Taking surveys

Conducted either orally or in writing, **surveys** are made up of structured questions. Written surveys are called **questionnaires.** The following suggestions will help you prepare informal surveys:

- Define your purpose.
- Write clear directions and questions. For example, if you are asking multiple-choice questions, make sure that you cover all possible options and that your options do not overlap.
- Make sure that your questions do not suggest a preference for one answer over another.
- Make the survey brief and easy to complete.

17d   Keeping a notebook when doing lab research

To provide a complete and accurate account of your laboratory work, keep careful records in a notebook. The following guidelines will help you take accurate notes on your research:

- Record immediate, on-the-spot, accurate notes on what happens in the lab. Write down as much detail as possible. Measure precisely; do not estimate. Identify major pieces of apparatus, unusual chemicals, and laboratory animals in detail. Use drawings, when appropriate, to illustrate complicated equipment setups.
- Follow a basic format. Present your results in a format that allows you to communicate all the major features of an experiment. The five basic sections that must be included are title, purpose, materials and methods, results, and conclusions.
- Write in complete sentences, even if you are filling in answers to questions in a lab manual. Resist the temptation to use shorthand to record your notes. Later, the complete sentences will provide a clear record of your procedures and results. Highlight cause-effect relationships in your sentences by using the following transitions: *then, next, consequently, because,* and *therefore.*
- When necessary, revise and correct your laboratory notebook in visible ways. If you make a mistake in recording laboratory results, correct it as clearly as possible, either by erasing or by crossing out and rewriting on the original sheet. If you make an uncorrectable mistake in your notebook, simply fold the sheet lengthwise and mark *omit* on the face side. Unanticipated results often occur in the lab, and you may find yourself jotting down notes on a convenient piece of scrap paper. Attach these notes to your notebook.

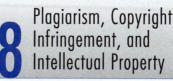

18 Plagiarism, Copyright Infringement, and Intellectual Property

Researchers who fail to acknowledge their sources—either intentionally or unintentionally—commit **plagiarism.** Buying a term paper from an online paper mill or "borrowing" a friend's completed assignment are obvious forms of plagiarism. But plagiarism also involves paraphrasing or summarizing material without properly citing its source.

18a Understanding how plagiarism relates to copyright and intellectual property

Plagiarism is theft of property—in this case, intellectual property—that belongs to someone else, the copyright holder. **Copyright** is the legal right to control the reproduction of any original work—a piece of writing, a musical composition, a play, a movie, a computer program, a photograph, a work of art. A copyrighted work is the **intellectual property** of the copyright holder, whether that entity is a publisher, a record company, an entertainment conglomerate, or the individual creator of the work. Here is some additional information on these legal concepts:

- **Copyright:** A copyrighted text cannot be reprinted (in print or online) without the written permission of the copyright holder. The copyright protects the right of authors and publishers to make money from their productions.

- **Fair use:** The concept of **fair use** protects most academic use of copyrighted sources. Under this provision of copyright law, you can legally quote a brief passage from a copyrighted text without infringing on copyright. To avoid plagiarism, you must identify the passage as a quotation and cite it properly. Always ask permission of the author in the case of blog entries and newsgroup postings.

- **Intellectual property:** In addition to works protected by copyright, intellectual property includes patented inventions, trademarks, industrial designs, and similar intellectual creations that are protected by other laws.

18b Avoiding plagiarism

Students under the pressure of a deadline can sometimes make poor choices. Inadvertent plagiarism occurs when busy students take notes

TEXTCONNEX

Learning More about Plagiarism, Copyright and Fair Use, and Intellectual Property

- **Plagiarism:** For the Council of Writing Program Administrators' "Defining and Avoiding Plagiarism: The WPA Statement on Best Practices," see <www.wpacouncil.org/positions/index.html>. Educators at Indiana University offer tips on avoiding plagiarism at <www.Indiana.edu/~wts/wts/plagiarism.html>. Georgetown University's Honor Council offers an example of a campus honor code pertaining to plagiarism and academic ethics at <www.georgetown.edu/honor/plagiarism.html>.

- **Copyright and fair use:** For information on and discussion of fair use, see *Copyright and Fair Use* at <fairuse.stanford.edu>, and the U.S. Copyright Office at <www.loc.gov/copyright>. The University of Texas posts guidelines for fair use and multimedia projects at <www.utsystem.edu/OGC/IntellectualProperty/ccmcguide.htm>.

- **Intellectual property:** For information about what constitutes intellectual property and related issues, see the World Intellectual Property Organization Web site at <www.wipo.int/>. For a legal perspective, the American Intellectual Property Law Association offers information on and overviews of recent cases at <www.aipla.org/>.

carelessly, forgetting to jot down the source of a paraphrase or accidentally inserting material downloaded from a Web site into a paper. Deliberate plagiarism occurs when students wait until the last minute and then "borrow" a paper from a friend or cut and paste large portions of an online article into their own work. No matter how tired or pressured you may be, there is no justification for plagiarism.

To avoid plagiarism, adhere to these guidelines:

- Do not rely too much on one source, or you may slip into using that person's thoughts as your own.

- Keep accurate records while doing research and taking notes. If you do not know where you got an idea or a piece of information, do not use it in your paper until you find out.

- When you take notes, be sure to put quotation marks around words, phrases, or sentences taken verbatim from a source. If you use any of those words, phrases, or sentences when summarizing or paraphrasing the source, put them in quotation marks.

Changing a word here and there while keeping a source's sentence structure or phrasing constitutes plagiarism even if you credit the source for the ideas. (*See p. 200 for an example.*)

- In your research notebook, record your ideas in one color of ink and those of others in a different color.

- Cite the source of all ideas, opinions, facts, and statistics that are not common knowledge.

- Choose an appropriate documentation style, and use it consistently and properly. (*See Parts 4 and 5 for information about the most common documentation styles for academic writing.*)

www.mhhe.com/
bmhh

For information
on material that
does not need
citing, go to

Research >
Avoiding
Plagiarism >
Common
Knowledge

18b
plag

When working with information on the Web, it's important to take notes, just as you do with print sources, and to acknowledge that information—by paraphrasing, summarizing, and citing—just as you do with print sources. (*For more on taking notes, paraphrasing, and summarizing, see Chapter 19, pp. 196–204. For more on citations, see Parts 4 and 5.*) The Web can provide you with documents that are otherwise available to only a select few—for instance, the original manuscript of a famous poem from the eighteenth century—as well as valuable data that is up-to-the-minute, such as current temperature data from the Arctic illustrating trends in climate change. It's important to document that information so that others can find it.

While it's easy to "copy and paste" from the Internet into an individual text without providing citation, it's ill-advised, not least because

Tips LEARNING in COLLEGE

Determining What Is "Common Knowledge"

Information that an audience could be expected to know about from a wide range of sources is considered common knowledge. For example, the structure of DNA and the process of photosynthesis are considered common knowledge among biologists. However, a recent scientific discovery about genetics would not be common knowledge, and so you would need to cite the source of this information.

Maps, charts, graphs, and other visual displays of information are not considered common knowledge. Even though everyone knows that Paris is the capital of France, a reproduction of a map of France in your paper should be credited to the map's creator. (*For more information on properly citing visual and numerical resources in MLA style, see pp. 220–21, 235, and 244–45.*)

Tips | **LEARNING in COLLEGE**

Avoiding Inadvertent Plagiarism: Some Questions to Ask Yourself

- Is your thesis your own idea, or did you find it in one of your sources?
- Did you rely extensively on only one or two sources, instead of a variety of sources?
- Did you use uncommon terms, distinctive phrases, or quotations from a source but fail to enclose them in quotation marks?
- Did you include any words, phrases, or ideas that you don't really understand or explain?
- Did you indicate your source for all quotations, paraphrases, and summaries, either within the text or in a parenthetical citation?
- Did you include page numbers as required for all quotations, paraphrases, and summaries?
- Does every in-text citation have a corresponding entry in the list of works cited or references?

it's just as easy to detect such plagiarism by taking that copied text and using a search engine to locate the original online.

When working with electronic sources, keep in mind the following guidelines:

- Print or download any online source you consult, note the date on which you viewed it, and be sure to keep the complete URL of the site.
- If you cut and paste a passage from a Web site into a word-processing file, use a different font to identify that material as well as the URL and the date on which you visited the site.
- Acknowledge all sites you use as sources, including those you access via links on another site.
- As a courtesy, request the author's permission before quoting from blogs, newsgroup postings, or e-mails.
- Acknowledge any audio, video, or illustrated material that has informed your research.

Posting material on a publicly accessible Web site is usually considered the legal equivalent of publishing it in print format. (Password-protected sites generally are exempt.) When writing a composition to be posted online and accessible to the general public, you must seek copyright permission from all your sources. If your material links to other sites and resources, you must ask permission to do so of the rights holders. (*See the guidelines for fair use on pp. 193–94 and the box on p. 190.*)

www.mhhe.com/
bmhh

For more
information
and interactive
exercises, go to

Research >
Avoiding
Plagiarism >
Using Copyrighted
Materials

18c   Using copyrighted materials fairly

All written materials, including student papers, letters, and e-mail, are covered by copyright even if they do not bear an official copyright symbol. A copyright grants its owner exclusive rights to the use of a protected work, including reproducing, distributing, and displaying the work. The popularity of the Web has led to increased concerns about the fair use of copyrighted material. Before you post your paper on the Web or produce a multimedia presentation that includes audio, video, and graphic elements copied from a Web site, make sure that you have used copyrighted material fairly by considering the following four questions:

**18c
plag**

- **What is the purpose of the use?** Educational, nonprofit, and personal uses are more likely to be considered fair than is commercial use.

- **What is the nature of the work being used?** In most cases, imaginative and unpublished materials can be used only if you have the permission of the copyright holder.

- **How much of the copyrighted work is being used?** The use of a small portion of a text for academic purposes is more likely

Tip for Multilingual Students
Cultural Assumptions and Misunderstandings about Plagiarism

Respect for ownership of ideas is a core value of Western society. Your culture may consider the knowledge in classic texts a national heritage and, therefore, common property. As a result, you may have been encouraged to incorporate words and information from those texts into your writing without citing their source. American academic culture, however, requires you to identify any use you make of someone else's original work and to cite the work properly in an appropriate documentation style (*see Parts 4 and 5*). You must similarly credit the source of ideas that are not considered common knowledge. You should accept these rules as nonnegotiable and apply them conscientiously to avoid plagiarism and its serious consequences. When in doubt about citation rules, ask your instructor.

to be considered fair than the use of a whole work for commercial purposes.

- **What effect would this use have on the market for the original?** The use of a work is usually considered unfair if it would hurt sales of the original.

When in doubt, always ask permission.

19 Working with Sources and Avoiding Plagiarism

Once you have a research question to answer, an idea about what the library and Internet have to offer, and some sense of the kinds of materials you need, you are ready to begin selecting and using sources.

www.mhhe.com/
bmhh

For help with
creating a
bibliography,
go to

Research >
Bibliomaker

19a Maintaining a working bibliography

As you research, compile a **working bibliography**—a list of those books, articles, pamphlets, Web sites, and other sources that seem most likely to help you answer your research question. Maintain an accurate and complete record of all sources you consult. For each source, record the following information:

- Call number of the book, reference work, or other print source; the URL of each Web site
- All authors, editors, and translators
- Title of the chapter, article, or Web page
- Title of the book, periodical, or Web site in which the chapter, article, or page appears
- For books, the date of publication, place, and publisher as well as the edition or volume number, if applicable
- For periodical articles, the date and edition or volume number, issue, and page numbers if applicable
- For a Web source, the date you consulted it
- Medium (e.g., Print, Web)

(See the foldouts at the beginning of Chapters 21 and 26 for examples of these elements.)

You can record bibliographic information on note cards or in a word-processing file; you can print out bibliographic information obtained from online searches in databases and library catalogs; or you can record bibliographic information directly on photocopies of source material. You can also save most Web pages and other online sources to your own computer. Many professional researchers use bibliographic software such as *Endnote, ProCite,* and *Reference Manager* to help them keep track of sources and format bibliographic information. Ask your instructor before using any bibliographic software, and always review your citations carefully.

19a
plag

1. Using note cards
Before computers became widely available, most researchers used 3-by-5-inch note cards to compile the working bibliography, with each potential source getting a separate card. This method is still useful (*see Figure 19.1 on p. 196*). You can also use the cards to record brief quotations from or comments on those sources.

2. Printing the results of online searches
The results of searches in online indexes and databases usually include complete bibliographic information about the sources they list. You can print these results or save them to a disk. Be sure also to record the name of the database and the date of your search.

Caution: If you download the full text of an article from a database and refer to it in your paper, your citation must include information about the database as well as bibliographic information about the article itself.

You can similarly print out or save bibliographic information from the results of searches in online library catalogs. Some college libraries make it possible for you to send your list of sources to yourself by e-mail (*see Figure 19.2*).

BMCC Library ML419.A75 B47 1997

Bergreen, Laurence. Louis Armstrong:
An Extravagant Life. New York:
Broadway, 1997. Print.

Ostwald, David. "All That Jazz." Rev. of
Louis Armstrong: An Extravagant Life,
by Laurence Bergreen.
Commentary Nov. 1997: 68–72. Print.

"Louis Armstrong" New Orleans Online.
2007. New Orleans Tourism Marketing
Corporation, 2007. Web. 26 Feb. 2007.
<http://www.neworleansonline.com/
neworleans/music/musichistory/
musicgreats/satchmo.html>.

FIGURE 19.1 Three sample bibliography note cards. The cards are for a book (top), for a journal article (middle), and for a Web site (bottom).

3. Using photocopies and printouts from Web sites

If you photocopy articles, essays, or pages of reference works from a print or a microfilm source, take time to note the bibliographic information on the photocopy. Similarly, if you print out a source you found on a Web site or copy it to your computer, be sure to note the site's complete URL, name, sponsor, date of publication or last update, and the date you visited it.

19b Creating an annotated bibliography

An annotated bibliography can be very useful to you in your research. The bibliography includes full citation details, correctly formatted, which you will need for your paper. The annotation provides a summary of major points for each source, including your own reactions and ideas about where this material might fit in your paper (*see Figure 19.3 on p. 198*). As you conduct research, you will find that an annotated bibliography helps you remember what you have found in your search, as well as helping you organize your findings.

www.mhhe.com/
bmhh

For more
information
and interactive
exercises, go to

Research >
Research
Techniques

19c Taking notes on your sources

Take notes on your sources by annotating photocopies or printouts or by noting useful quotations and ideas on paper, on note cards, or in a computer file.

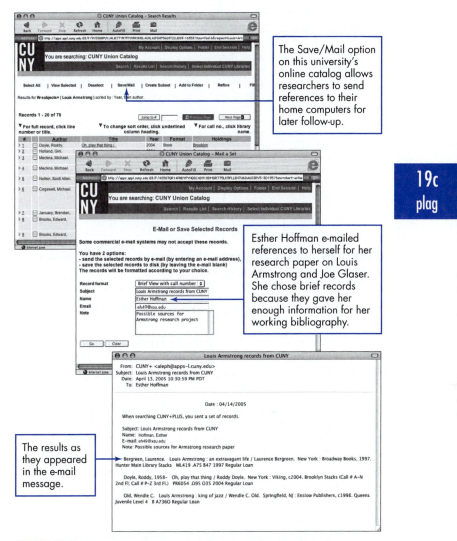

The Save/Mail option on this university's online catalog allows researchers to send references to their home computers for later follow-up.

Esther Hoffman e-mailed references to herself for her research paper on Louis Armstrong and Joe Glaser. She chose brief records because they gave her enough information for her working bibliography.

The results as they appeared in the e-mail message.

FIGURE 19.2 Three sample screens showing the results of an online search of a library database.

1. Annotating

One way to take notes is to annotate photocopied articles and printouts from online information services or Web sites. (*See Figure 19.4 on p. 199 for an annotated Web site printout.*) As you read, write the following notes directly on the page:

Bergreen, Laurence. *Louis Armstrong: An Extravagant Life.* New York: Broadway, 1997. Print.

Aimed at a popular audience, Bergreen's book provides a detailed history of Armstrong's life as well as its social context. Bergreen also presents Armstrong's relationship with manager Glaser throughout the years and Glaser's own colorful background. Essentially the partnership provided benefits to both performer and manager. (Ostwald notes a few errors.)

Collier, James Lincoln. *Louis Armstrong, an American Genius.* New York: Oxford UP, 1983. Print.

This scholarly study of Armstrong's life and work presents his formative influence on American music. Collier includes numerous telling details that support my ideas about Armstrong and Glaser's relationship, such as the fact that Glaser paid Armstrong's personal expenses while acting as his manager.

FIGURE 19.3 Sample annotated bibliography. A section of Esther Hoffman's annotated bibliography.

- On the first page, write down complete bibliographic information for the source.
- As you read, record questions, reactions, and ideas in the margins.
- Comment in the margins on ideas that agree with or differ from those you have already learned about.
- Put important and difficult passages into your own words by paraphrasing or summarizing them in the margins. (*For help with paraphrasing and summarizing, see pp. 200–04.*)
- Use a highlighter to mark statements that you may want to quote because they are key to your readers' understanding of the issue or are especially well expressed.

2. Taking notes

If you do not have photocopies or printouts to annotate, take notes on paper, index cards, or a computer. Use a separate page or card for each idea. Be sure to record the source's bibliographic information as well as the specific page number for each idea.

Enclose in quotation marks any exact words from a source. Label the passage a "quote," as Hoffman did in the following excerpt from her research notebook:

> Notes on Dan Morgenstern. "Louis Armstrong and the
> Development and Diffusion of Jazz." Louis Armstrong: A Cultural

Louis Armstrong / Satchmo   http://www.neworleansonline.com/neworleans/music/musichistory/m...

New Orleans Tourism Marketing Corporation, 2007. Web. 26 Feb. 2007. <http://www.new orleansonline.com/ neworleans/music/ musichistory/ musicgreats/ satchmo.html >.

Louis Armstrong

"Satchmo" — as he was affectionately called by his legions of friends — never boasted like his fellow New Orleanian, jazzman Jelly Roll Morton, that he invented jazz, or for that matter that he was one of its better players. But everyone who heard him play or hears his inimitable style today can only agree that Daniel Louis "Satchmo" Armstrong was perhaps the best there has ever been.

The worldwide popularity of jazz can be directly attributed to the infectious style of performance that "Satchmo" gave and the unselfishness that characterized his persona.

'Satchmo' worked at various unskilled jobs much of his youth. He sold coal and had a youthful propensity for mischief. On a dare from a friend, he fired a pistol on South Rampart Street. For firing a weapon in a public place, he received an 18-month sentence at the Colored Waif's Home where he eventually came under the influence of "Captain" Peter Davis. Sensing that young Armstrong possessed a burning desire to learn, Davis provided the basic musical training on the cornet to young Louis. With that kindly gesture the history of popular music was undoubtedly rewritten.

By 1922, young Satchmo was ready to join his idol, Joe "King" Oliver's Creole Jazz Band in Chicago. By the time of his arrival in the Windy City he had become an accomplished musician. Part of the influence that Armstrong brought to Chicago had been an incredible street training in the back alleys and clubs of Black Storyville, the area surrounding Liberty and Perdido Streets, the current site of New Orleans city government.

Armstrong wrote in his autobiography, "Satchmo," "There were all kinds of thrills for me in Storyville. On every corner I could hear music. And such good music...And that man Joe Oliver! My, my, that man kept me spellbound with that horn of his."

In the early '30s, Armstrong's popularity had reached such epic proportions that he and his band toured Europe, a major milestone for a performer, and especially a young black performer.

As the years passed, Armstrong's persona and star appeal continued to grow. Satchmo's popularity never waned during his entire life. He played for presidents, European royalty, the kings and queens of his beloved Africa. He frequently toured internationally as a special envoy for the U.S. State Department and represented his country and New Orleans with human quality, dignity, charm and excellence. At every stop he made over a half century of performing, he always promoted his love for New Orleans and an avowed passion for red beans and rice. But of all the accolades, the greatest was being s...

History & Heritage
Restaurants & Cuisine
Music
Festivals
Museums & The Arts
Tours
Attractions
Shopping
Nightlife & Harrah's
Architecture
Sports and Recreation
French Quarter
Mardi Gras
Holiday Happenin's
Romantic New Orleans
Family
Multicultural
Gay & Lesbian Travel
Voluntourism

Early influence follow up?

Check my e-mail for this link!

Annotate, highlight, and underline on a Web page printout just as you would any other print resource.

If you are working at a library computer, see if you can e-mail a Web page to yourself so you can save it on your own computer. That way, you will have both a print and an electronic record of the source.

19c
plag

FIGURE 19.4 **An annotated Web page printout.**

Legacy. Ed. Marc H. Miller. Seattle: U of Washington P and Queens Museum of Art, 1994. 95–145. Print.
■ Armstrong having trouble with managers. Fires Johnny Collins in London, 1933. Collins blocks Armstrong from playing with Chick Webb's band (pp. 124–5).

■ Armstrong turned to Glaser, an old Chicago acquaintance.
Quote: "Joe Glaser . . . proved to be the right man at the right
time" (p. 128).

Unless you think you might use a particular quotation in your paper,
express the author's ideas in your own words by using a paraphrase or
a summary.

www.mhhe.com/
bmhh

For more
information
and interactive
exercises, go to

Research >
Avoiding
Plagiarism >
Summarize/
Paraphrase

3. Paraphrasing

When you **paraphrase,** you put someone else's statements into your
words. A paraphrase is not a word-for-word translation. Even though
you express the source's ideas *in your own way,* you must still give
credit for the ideas to the original writer by citing his or her work
properly. If your paraphrase includes any exact phrasing from the
source, put quotation marks around those phrases.

In the first unacceptable paraphrase that follows, the writer has
done a word-for-word translation, using synonyms for some terms but
retaining phrases from the original and failing to enclose them in quotation marks ("nonsense syllables," "free invention of rhythm, melody,
and syllables"). The borrowed phrases are highlighted. Notice also how
close the sentence structures in the first faulty paraphrase are to the
original.

SOURCE

Scat singing. A technique of jazz singing in which onomato-
poeic or nonsense syllables are sung to improvised melodies.
Some writers have traced scat singing back to the practice, common in West African musics, of translating percussion patterns
into vocal lines by assigning syllables to characteristic rhythms.
However, since this allows little scope for melodic improvisation
and the earliest recorded examples of jazz scat singing involved
the free invention of rhythm, melody, and syllables, it is more
likely that the technique began in the USA as singers imitated
the sounds of jazz instrumentalists.

—J. BRADFORD ROBINSON,
The New Grove Dictionary of Jazz

UNACCEPTABLE PARAPHRASE: PLAGIARISM

Scat is a way of singing that uses nonsense syllables and extemporaneous melodies. Some people think that scat goes back to
the custom in West African music of turning drum rhythms into
vocal lines. But that doesn't explain the free invention of rhythm,
melody, and syllables of the first recorded instances of scat singing.
It is more likely that scat was started in the U.S. by singers imitating the way instrumental jazz sounded (Robinson 515).

To make this passage acceptable, the writer could add quotation marks around the borrowed words: "But that doesn't explain the 'free invention of rhythm, melody, and syllables' of the first recorded instances of scat singing (Robinson 515)."

However, merely substituting synonyms for borrowed words does *not* make the passage acceptable, because it relies on the sentence structure of the original.

UNACCEPTABLE PARAPHRASE (SENTENCE STRUCTURE OF SOURCE): PLAGIARISM

Scat is a way of singing that uses meaningless vocalization and extemporaneous melodies. One theory is that scat originated from the West African custom of turning drum rhythms into singing. But that doesn't explain the loose improvisation of pulse, pitch, and sound of the first recorded instances of scat singing. Scat more probably was started in the United States by singers imitating the way instrumental jazz sounded (Robinson 515).

19c
plag

Even if the writer changes the sentence structure but uses some of the original words without quotation marks (highlighted below), the result is plagiarism.

UNACCEPTABLE PARAPHRASE (WORDING FROM SOURCE): PLAGIARISM

"Scat, a highly inventive type of jazz singing, combines onomatopoetic or nonsense syllables with improvised melodies" (Robinson 515).

By contrast, the acceptable paraphrase expresses all ideas from the original more concisely. Although it quotes a few words from the source, the writer has used quotation marks and expressed the definition in a new and different way.

ACCEPTABLE PARAPHRASE

Scat, a highly inventive type of jazz singing, combines "nonsense syllables [with] improvised melodies." Although syllabic singing of drum rhythms occurs in West Africa, scat probably owes more to the early attempts of American singers to mimic both the sound and the inventive musical style of instrumental jazz (Robinson 515).

Note that the acceptable paraphrase still requires a citation (and would need one even without the direct quotation).

Exercise 19.1 Paraphrasing

Read the following passage, annotating as necessary. Write a paraphrase of the passage, and then compare your paraphrase with those of your classmates. What are the similarities and differences among your paraphrases? How can you tell if a paraphrase is acceptable or unacceptable?

SOURCE

The origins of jazz, an urban music, stemmed from the countryside of the South as well as the streets of America's cities. It resulted from two distinct musical traditions, those of West Africa and Europe. West Africa gave jazz its incessant rhythmic drive, the need to move and the emotional urgency that has served the music so well. The European ingredients had more to do with classical qualities pertaining to harmony and melody.

www.mhhe.com/
bmhh

For more
information
and interactive
exercises, go to

Research >
Avoiding
Plagiarism >
Summarize/
Paraphrase

4. Summarizing

When you **summarize,** you state the main point of a piece, condensing a few paragraphs into one sentence or a few pages into one paragraph. (*For specific guidelines on writing summaries, see Chapter 1, p. 6.*)

Here is a passage by John Ephland followed by two summaries. The unacceptable first summary is simply a restatement of Ephland's thesis, using much of his phrasing (highlighted). The second, acceptable summary states Ephland's main point in the writer's own words.

SOURCE

The origins of jazz, an urban music, stemmed from the countryside of the South as well as the streets of America's cities. It resulted from two distinct musical traditions, those of West Africa and Europe. West Africa gave jazz its incessant rhythmic drive, the need to move and the emotional urgency that has served the music so well. The European ingredients had more to do with classical qualities pertaining to harmony and melody.

The blending of these two traditions resulted in a music that played around with meter and reinterpreted the use of

Tips LEARNING in COLLEGE

What Must Be Acknowledged?

You *do not* have to document common knowledge (*see the box on p. 193*) or your own independent thinking.

You *must* acknowledge any concepts you learned from a source, whether or not you copy the source's language.

notes in new combinations, creating blue notes that expressed feelings both sad and joyous. The field hollers of Southern share-cropping slaves combined with the more urban, stylized sounds of musicians from New Orleans, creating a new music. Gospel music from the church melded with what became known in the 20th century as the blues offered a vocal ingredient that translated well to instruments.

—JOHN EPHLAND, "Down Beat's Jazz 101:
The Very Beginning"

UNACCEPTABLE SUMMARY: PLAGIARISM

The origins of jazz are two distinct musical traditions, those of West Africa and Europe. New meters and new note combinations capable of expressing both sad and joyous feelings resulted from the blending of these two traditions.

19c
plag

ACCEPTABLE SUMMARY

Jazz has its roots in the musical traditions of both West Africa and Europe. It combines rhythmic, harmonic, and melodic features of both traditions in new and emotionally expressive ways (Ephland).

Note that the acceptable summary still requires a citation.

Exercise 19.2 Summarizing

Read the following passage and write a summary of it. Compare your summary with those of your classmates. What are the similarities and differences among your summaries? How does writing a paraphrase compare with writing a summary? Which task was more difficult, and why?

SOURCE

Male musicians dominated the jazz scene when the music first surfaced, making it difficult for women to enter their ranks. The fraternity of jazzmen also frowned upon women wind instrumentalists. However, some African American women, in the late 19th century, played the instruments that were barred from the "opposite sex." . . . Many of their names have been lost in history, but a few have survived. For example, Mattie Simpson, a cornetist, performed "on principal and prominent streets of each city" (10) in Indianapolis, in 1895; Nettie Goff, a trombonist, was a member of The Mahara Minstrels; and Mrs.

Laurie Johnson, a trumpeter, had a career that spanned 30 years. They all broke instrumental taboos.

—Mario A. Charles, "The Age of a Jazzwoman: Valaida Snow, 1900–1956"

www.mhhe.com/
bmhh

For more information and interactive exercises, go to

Research >
Avoiding
Plagiarism > Using
Quotations

5. Quoting directly

Sometimes the writer of a source will say something so eloquently and perceptively that you will want to include that writer's words as a **direct quotation.** In general, you will want to quote directly from writers who are themselves primary sources. For example, in a research paper about Louis Armstrong, a direct quotation from Armstrong himself (or a direct quotation from someone who worked with him) would add nuance and texture to the paper. To avoid inadvertent plagiarism, indicate that the content is a direct quotation when you copy it onto your note cards, and place quotation marks around it. You might copy quotations in a different color, or deliberately make quotation marks oversized. (*For more information on using long quotations in block format, see Chapter 53, pp. 474–75.*)

> **Note:** Beware of writing a paper that consists of a string of quotations, one after another. If you notice that you have used more than one quotation every two or three paragraphs, convert most of the quotations into paraphrases (*see pp. 200–01*).

19d Taking stock of and synthesizing what you have learned

Assess the research you have done and synthesize what you have learned. Your credibility depends on the relevance and reliability of your sources as well as the scope and depth of your reading and observation.

As the context and kind of writing change, so too do the requirements for types and numbers of sources. As a general rule, you should consult more than two sources and use only sources that are both reliable and respected by people working in the field. Ask yourself the following questions about the sources you have consulted:

■ Are your sources trustworthy? (*See Chapter 16, pp. 179–85, for more on evaluating sources.*)

■ If you have started to develop a tentative answer to your research question, have your sources provided you with a sufficient number of facts, examples, and ideas to support that answer?

- Have you used sources that examine the issues from several different perspectives?

Think about how the sources you have read relate to one another. Ask yourself when, how, and why your sources agree or disagree, and consider where you stand on the issues they raise. Such questions can help you clarify what you have learned from your sources.

19e Integrating quotations, paraphrases, and summaries without plagiarizing

To support and develop your ideas, use paraphrased, summarized, or quoted material from sources. Here are some guidelines for doing so properly and effectively.

19e

plag

www.mhhe.com/
bmhh

For more
information
and interactive
exercises, go to

Research >
Avoiding
Plagiarism >
Using Sources
Accurately

1. Integrating quotations

Quotations should be short, enclosed in quotation marks, and well integrated into your sentence structure, as in the following example from Esther Hoffman's paper on Louis Armstrong and Joe Glaser:

> In his dedication to the unpublished manuscript "Louis Armstrong and the Jewish Family in New Orleans," Armstrong calls Glaser "the best friend that I ever had," while in a letter to Max Jones, he writes, "I did not get really happy until I got with my man—my dearest friend—Joe Glaser" (qtd. in Jones and Chilton 16).

When you are integrating someone else's words into your writing, use a **signal phrase** that indicates whom you are quoting. The signal phrases "Armstrong calls Glaser" and "he writes" identify Armstrong as the source of the two quotations in the preceding passage. The box on page 206 lists common signal phrases.

Brackets within quotations   Sentences that include quotations must make sense grammatically. Sometimes you may have to adjust a quotation to make it fit your sentence. Use brackets to indicate any such minor adjustments. For example, *my* has been changed to *his* to make the quotation fit in the following sentence:

> Armstrong confided to a friend that Glaser's death "broke [his] heart" (Bergreen 490).

Ellipses within quotations   Use **ellipses** (. . .) to indicate that words have been omitted from the body of a quotation, but be sure that what you omit does not significantly alter the source's meaning.

As Morgenstern put it, "Joe Glaser . . . proved to be the right man at the right time" (128).

Quotations in block format   Quotations longer than four lines should be used rarely because they tend to break up your text and make readers impatient. If you include a longer quotation, put it in block format (*see Chapter 53)* and be careful to integrate it into your paper. Tell your readers why you want them to read the block quotation, and afterwards, comment on it.

2. Integrating paraphrases and summaries

The principles for integrating paraphrases and summaries into your text are similar to those for including direct quotations. Provide a smooth transition between a source's point and your own voice, and give credit to the source. Use signal phrases to introduce ideas you have borrowed from your sources. Besides crediting others for their work, signal phrases make ideas more interesting by giving them a human face. Here are some examples:

Tips

LEARNING in COLLEGE

Varying Signal Phrases

When a writer relies on the same signal phrase throughout a paper, readers quickly become bored. Vary your signal phrases. Instead of using the verbs *says* and *writes* again and again, consider including some of the following:

acknowledges	denies	points out
adds	describes	proposes
admits	emphasizes	proves
argues	explains	refutes
asks	expresses	rejects
asserts	finds	remarks
charges	holds	reports
claims	implies	responds
comments	insists	shows
complains	interprets	speculates
concedes	maintains	states
concludes	notes	suggests
considers	observes	warns
contends		

> As Bergreen points out, Armstrong easily reached difficult high
> notes, the F's and G's that stymied other trumpeters (248).

In this passage, Hoffman uses the signal phrase "As Bergreen points
out" to identify Bergreen as the source of the paraphrased information
about Louis Armstrong's extraordinary technical abilities.

> A 1960 letter from Glaser to Lucille Armstrong corroborates
> Gold's account; it shows that Glaser assumed responsibility for
> buying the musician and his wife a new car as well as for filing
> the paperwork needed to retain the old license plate number.

In this passage, Hoffman uses "corroborates" to signal her paraphrase
of an original letter she found in the Louis Armstrong archives. She
names the source (the author of the letter), so she does not need additional parenthetical documentation. Remember that all summaries
and paraphrases must be acknowledged.

20a

20 Writing the Paper

You have chosen a research question and
have located, read, and evaluated a variety
of sources. Now you need a thesis that will
allow you to share what you have learned
as well as your perspective on the issue.

20a Planning and drafting your paper

Whether your paper is primarily informative, interpretive, or argumentative, keep your purpose and context in mind as you decide on
your thesis.

1. Gathering and evaluating your information

Your note-taking strategies will determine how you collect and organize your information. If you have taken notes on index cards, group
them according to topic and subtopic. For example, Esther Hoffman
could have used the following categories to organize her notes:

Biography – Armstrong
Biography – Glaser
Glaser as manager
Conflict – A & G
Armstrong – media image
Jazz – general info

Sorting index cards into stacks that match up topics and subtopics allows you to see what you have gathered. A small stack of cards for a particular subtopic might mean that the subtopic is not as important as you originally thought—or that you need to do additional research focused on that specific subtopic.

If your notes are primarily on your computer, you can create a new folder or page for each topic and subtopic, and then cut and paste to move information to the appropriate category.

www.mhhe.com/
bmhh

For help with
developing a
thesis, go to

Writing >
Paragraph/Essay
Development >
Thesis/Central
Idea

2. Deciding on a thesis

Consider the question that originally guided your research as well as the new questions provoked by what you have learned. Revise the wording of your question to make it intriguing as well as suitable (*see Chapter 13, pp. 154–55*). Compose an answer that you can use as your working thesis, as in the following example:

HOFFMAN'S FOCAL QUESTION

What kind of relationship did Louis Armstrong and Joe Glaser actually have?

HOFFMAN'S WORKING THESIS

Armstrong and Glaser enjoyed not only a successful business partnership but also a complex friendship based on mutual respect and caring.

(*For more on devising a thesis, see Chapter 2, pp. 23–26.*)

www.mhhe.com/
bmhh

For interactive
help with outlines,
go to

Writing >
Outlining Tutor

3. Outlining a plan for supporting and developing your thesis

Guided by your tentative thesis, outline a plan that uses your sources in a purposeful way. Decide on the kind of structure you will use—explanatory, exploratory, or argumentative—and choose facts, examples, and ideas drawn from a variety of sources to support your thesis. (*See Chapters 6–8 for more on these structures.*)

For her interpretive paper on Armstrong and Glaser, Hoffman decided on an exploratory structure, an approach organized around raising and answering a central question:

- Introduce Armstrong as a great musician who was once a poor waif.

- Introduce Glaser, Armstrong's manager for thirty-four years.

- State the question: What kind of relationship did these two actually have? Did Glaser dominate Armstrong?

- Discuss Glaser as Armstrong's business manager—support for the idea that it was Glaser who made Armstrong a star.

- Discuss Armstrong's resistance to being controlled by Glaser.

- Conclude: Armstrong and Glaser worked well together as friends who respected and cared for each other.

To develop this outline, Hoffman needed to list supporting facts, examples, or ideas for each point.

4. Writing a draft that you can revise, share, and edit

When you have a tentative thesis and a plan, you are ready to write a draft. As you write beyond the introduction, be prepared to reexamine and refine your thesis. When drawing on ideas from your sources, be sure to quote and paraphrase properly. (*For advice on quoting and paraphrasing, see Chapter 19, pp. 200–07.*)

Often, writers will come up with fresh ideas for their introduction, body paragraphs, or conclusion as they revise and edit their first draft—one reason it is important to spend time revising and editing your paper. (*For more on revising, see Chapter 4, pp. 52–73.*)

5. Integrating visuals

Well-chosen visuals can help illustrate your argument. Figure numbers and captions are tools for integrating visuals into your paper.

- **Figure numbers:** Both MLA and APA style require writers to number each image in a research paper. In MLA style, the word "figure" is abbreviated to "Fig." In APA style, the full word "Figure" is written out.

- **Captions:** Each visual that you include in your paper must be followed by a caption that includes the title of the visual (if given; otherwise, a brief description will do) and its source. In MLA style, each caption begins with the figure number and a period after the number (Fig. 1.); in APA style, use italics for the figure number (*Figure 1*) and no periods.

20b

www.mhhe.com/
bmhh

For more
information
and interactive
exercises, go to

Writing >
Paragraph/Essay
Development >
Drafting and
Revising

20b Revising your draft

You may prefer to revise a hard copy of your draft by hand, or you might find it easier to use the "Track Changes" feature in your word-processing program. Either way, be sure to keep previous versions of your drafts.

Tips | LEARNING in COLLEGE

Guidelines for Revising Your Research Paper

Consider these questions as you read your draft and gather feedback from your instructor and peers:

- Is your thesis clear and engaging? Where in your draft do you most clearly state your thesis?
- Does each paragraph include a topic sentence? Are the transitions between paragraphs clear and logical?
- Have you provided an adequate in-text citation for each source?
- Do you have enough evidence to support each point you make? Where should you include additional research?
- Does your introduction give a specific and interesting overview of your topic and thesis? Does your conclusion provide a compelling synthesis of your research and clearly sum up the support for your thesis?
- Have you integrated quotations, summaries, and paraphrases smoothly and used a variety of signal phrases?
- Do all of your illustrations have complete and accurate captions?
- Do all of your in-text citations match your Works Cited or References page? Is there anything on your Works Cited or References page that is not in the text of your paper?

---

www.mhhe.com/bmhh

For help with documenting sources, go to

Research > Avoiding Plagiarism > Citing Sources

20c Documenting your sources

Whenever you use information, ideas, or words from someone else's work, you must acknowledge that person. The only exception to this principle is when you use information that is common knowledge, such as the chemical composition of water or the names of the thirteen original states.

How sources are documented varies by field and discipline. Choose a documentation style that is appropriate for the particular course you are taking, and use it properly and consistently.

For her paper on Louis Armstrong and Joe Glaser, Esther Hoffman used the MLA documentation style. (*The final draft of the paper appears in Chapter 25, pp. 251–62.*)

CHARTING the TERRITORY

Documentation Styles Covered in This Text

TYPE OF COURSE	DOCUMENTATION STYLE MOST COMMONLY USED	WHERE TO FIND THIS STYLE IN THE HANDBOOK
Humanities (English, religion, music, art, philosophy)	MLA (Modern Language Association)	*Pages 213–62*
Social sciences (anthropology, psychology, sociology, education, business)	APA (American Psychological Association)	*Pages 263–96*

20c

PART

4

Next to the originator of a good sentence is

the first quoter of it.

—RALPH WALDO EMERSON

MLA
Documentation
Style

4 MLA Documentation Style

MLA style requires writers to provide bibliographic information about their sources in a works-cited list at the end of a paper. In order to format works-cited entries correctly, it is important to know first of all what kind of source you are citing. The directory on pages 224–25 will help you find the appropriate sample to use as your model. As an alternative, you can use the charts on the foldout pages that follow to help you locate the right example. Answering the questions provided will usually lead you to the sample entry you need. If you cannot find what you are looking for after consulting the appropriate directory or chart, ask your instructor for help.

WRITING OUTCOMES

Conventions

This section will help you learn to do the following:

- Integrate in-text citations and generate lists of works cited using MLA style **(21–22)**
- Apply MLA citation format to print, electronic, verbal, and visual sources **(21–22)**

Documentation allows others to see the path you have taken in researching and writing your paper. (*For more on what to document, see Chapter 20, pp. 210–11.*)

The documentation style developed by the Modern Language Association (MLA) is used by many researchers in the arts and humanities, especially language and literature. The guidelines presented here are based on the seventh edition of the *MLA Handbook for Writers of Research Papers* (New York: MLA, 2009).

MLA documentation style has three parts:

- In-text citations
- List of works cited
- Explanatory notes

In-text citations and a list of works cited are mandatory; explanatory notes are optional.

www.mhhe.com/
bmhh

For links to Web sites for documentation styles used in various disciplines, go to

Research > Links to Documentation Sites

**21
MLA**

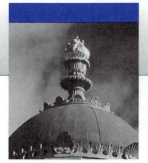

21 MLA Style: In-Text Citations

In-text citations let readers know that they can find full information about the source of a quotation or an idea you have paraphrased or summarized in the works-cited list at the end of your paper.

MLA IN-TEXT CITATIONS: DIRECTORY to SAMPLE TYPES

MLA IN-TEXT CITATIONS: DIRECTORY to SAMPLE TYPES *(continued)*

1. Author named in sentence   You can use the last name only, unless two or more of your sources have the same last name.

> signal phrase
> As Thomas J. Hennessey explains, record deals were usually negotiated
> by "white middlemen" (127).

Note that the parenthetical page citation comes after the closing quotation mark but before the period.

2. Author named in parentheses   If you do not name the source's author in your sentence, then you must provide the name in the parentheses.

> Armstrong easily reached difficult high notes, the F's and G's that
> no punctuation within parentheses
> stymied other trumpeters (Bergreen 248).

Note that there is no comma between the author's name and the page number. If you cite two or more distinct pages, however, separate the numbers with a comma: (Bergreen 450, 457).

GENERAL GUIDELINES
for MLA IN-TEXT CITATIONS

- Name the author, either in a signal phrase such as "Bergreen maintains" or in a parenthetical citation.
- Include a page reference in parentheses. No "p." precedes the page number, and if the author is named in the parentheses, there is no punctuation between the author's name and the page number.
- Place the citation as close to the material being cited as possible and before any punctuation marks that divide or end the sentence, such as commas, semicolons, or periods—except in a block quotation, where the citation comes after the period or other closing punctuation mark.
- Italicize titles of books, magazines, and plays, and place quotation marks around the titles of articles and short poems.
- For Internet sources, follow the same general guidelines as for print sources. Provide enough information for readers to find the full citation in your works-cited list.

21
MLA

3. Two or more works by the same author   You must identify which work you are citing, either in your sentence or in an abbreviated form in parentheses.

title italicized

In *Louis Armstrong: An American Genius,* Collier reports that Glaser

paid Armstrong's mortgage, taxes, and basic living expenses (330).

During those years, Glaser paid Armstrong's mortgage, taxes, and basic

living expenses (Collier, *Louis Armstrong* 330).

4. Two or three authors of the same work   If a source has up to three authors, you should name them all either in your text, as shown below, or in parentheses: (Jones and Chilton 160, 220).

According to Jones and Chilton, Glaser's responsibilities included

booking appearances, making travel arrangements, and paying the

band members' salaries (160, 220).

5. More than three authors   If the source has more than three authors, either list all the authors or give the first author's last name followed by *et al.,* the abbreviation for the Latin phrase meaning "and others." Do the same in your works-cited list.

> Changes in social regulations are bound to produce new forms of
> subjectivity (Henriques et al. 275).

6. Authors with the same last name   If two or more of your sources have the same last name, include the first initial of the author you are citing; if the first initial is also shared, use the full first name, as shown below.

> In the late nineteenth century, the sale of sheet music spread rapidly
> in a Manhattan area along Broadway known as Tin Pan Alley
> (Richard Campbell 63).

7. Organization as author   To cite works by organized groups, government agencies, associations, or corporations, treat the organization as the author. If the name is long, put it in a signal phrase.

> The Centre for Contemporary Cultural Studies claims that
> "there is nothing inherently concrete about historiography" (10).

8. Unknown author   When no author is given, cite a work by its title, using either the full title in a signal phrase or an abbreviated version in parentheses. Be sure to abbreviate in a way that points clearly to the corresponding entry in your list of works cited.

title of article

> "Squaresville, U.S.A. vs. Beatsville" makes the Midwestern small-town
> home seem boring compared with the West Coast artist's "pad" (31).

> The Midwestern small-town home seems boring compared with the
> West Coast artist's "pad" ("Squaresville" 31).

9. Entire work   When you want to acknowledge an entire work, such as a film or a book, do so in your text, not in a parenthetical citation. Be sure to include the work in your list of works cited.

Sidney J. Furie's film *Lady Sings the Blues* presents Billie Holiday as a beautiful woman in pain rather than as the great jazz artist she was.

10. Paraphrased or summarized source   If you include the author's name in your paraphrase or summary, include only the page number or numbers in your parenthetical citation. Signal phrases clarify that you are paraphrasing or summarizing.

signal phrase

Bergreen recounts how in southern states, where blacks were prohibited from entering many stores, Glaser sometimes had to shop for the band's food and other supplies (378, 381).

11. Source of a long quotation   For a poetry quotation of four or more typed lines or a prose quotation of five or more lines, do not use quotation marks. Instead, indent the material to be quoted by one inch. Allow one space before the parenthetical information after the final punctuation mark of the quotation. (*See also Chapter 53, pp. 474–75.*)

Glaser managed the Sunset Café, a club where Armstrong often performed:

> There was a pronounced gangster element at the Sunset, but Louis, accustomed to being employed and protected by mobsters, didn't think twice about that. Mr. Capone's men ensured the flow of alcohol, and their presence reassured many whites. (Bergreen 279)

12. Source of a short quotation   Close the quotation before the parenthetical citation. If the quotation concludes with an exclamation point or a question mark, include that punctuation mark before the closing quotation mark, and place the sentence period after the parenthetical citation.

His innovative singing style also featured "scat," a technique that

brackets enclose word that substitutes for omitted text

combines "nonsense syllables [with] improvised melodies"

(Robinson 515).

13. One-page source   You need not include a page number in the parenthetical citation for a one-page printed source.

NO PAGE NUMBER

Knittle notes that a benefit of deep breathing and relaxation is the "circulation of lymph throughout the body, a process that removes toxins from tissues and organs."

14. Government publication   To avoid an overly long parenthetical citation, give the name of the government agency that published the source within your text.

According to a report issued by the Bureau of National Affairs, many employers in 1964 needed guidance to apply new workplace rules that ensured fairness and complied with the Civil Rights Act of 1964 (32).

The President's Council on Bioethics documents the disturbing trend towards using genetic engineering to "enhance" lifestyles rather than cure disease (*Beyond Therapy*).

15. Photograph, map, graph, chart, or other visual
Visual included within the text of your paper

An aerial photograph of Manhattan (fig. 3), taken by the United States Geographical Survey, demonstrates how creative city planning can introduce parks and green spaces within even the most densely populated urban areas.

The caption you write for the image should include citation information.

Visual not included within the text of your paper

An aerial photograph of Manhattan taken by the United States Geographical Survey demonstrates how creative city planning can introduce parks and green spaces within even the most densely

populated urban areas (*TerraServer-USA*).

Because you are not including the image, you need to provide a parenthetical citation that directs your reader to your works-cited list and further information about the image, such as the site where it can be viewed, if you found it on a Web site (*see no. 16*).

16. Web site or other online electronic source

For online sources such as Web sites, the MLA recommends using the guidelines already established for print sources. If you cannot find the author of an online source, then identify the source by title, either in your text or in a parenthetical citation. Because most online sources do not have set page, section, or paragraph numbers, they must usually be cited as entire works.

In the 1920s, many young black musicians from New Orleans migrated

north to Chicago, hoping for a chance to perform with the best

("Chicago").

17. Work with numbered paragraphs or screens instead of pages

Give the paragraph or screen number(s) after the author's name and a comma. To distinguish them from page numbers, use the abbreviation *par(s).* or the type of division, such as *section(s).*

Rothstein suggests that many German Romantic musical techniques

may have originated in Italian opera (par. 9).

18. Work with no page or paragraph numbers

When citing an online or print source without page, paragraph, or other reference numbers, try to work the author's name into your text instead of putting it in a parenthetical citation.

author's name

Crouch argues that Armstrong remains a driving force in present-day

music, from country and western music to the chanted doggerel of rap.

19. Multivolume work

When citing more than one volume, include the volume number, followed by a colon, a space, and the page number.

Schuller argues that even though jazz's traditional framework appears

European, its musical essence is African (1: 62).

If you consult only one volume of a multivolume work, it is unnecessary to cite the volume number in the parenthetical reference. You should include it as part of the works-cited entry (*see p. 230*).

20. Literary work

Novels and literary nonfiction books   Include the relevant page number, followed by a semicolon, a space, and the chapter number.

> Louis Armstrong figures throughout Ellison's *Invisible Man,* including
>
> in the narrator's penultimate decision to become a "yes" man who
>
> "undermine[s] them with grins" (384; ch. 23).

If the author is not named in your sentence, add the name in front of the page number: (Ellison 384; ch. 23).

Poems   Use line numbers, not page numbers.

> In "Trumpet Player," Hughes says that the music "Is honey / Mixed with
>
> liquid fire" (lines 19-20). This image returns at the end, when Hughes
>
> concludes that "Trouble / Mellows to a golden note" (43-44).

Note that the word *lines* (not *l.* or *ll.*) is used in the first citation to establish what the numbers in parentheses refer to; subsequent citations need not use the word *lines.* (*See pp. 474–75 and 488 for more information about quoting poetry.*)

Plays and long, multisection poems   Use division (act, scene, canto, book, part) and lines, not page numbers. In the following example, notice that arabic numerals are used for act and scene divisions as well as for line numbers: (*Ham.* 2.3.22-27). The same is true for canto, verse, and lines in the following citation of Byron's *Don Juan:* (*DJ* 1.37.4-8). (The MLA Handbook lists abbreviations for titles of certain literary works.)

21. Religious text   Cite material in the Bible, Upanishads, or Koran (Qu'ran) by book, chapter, and verse, using an appropriate abbreviation when the name of the book is in parentheses rather than in your sentence. Name the edition from which you are citing.

> As the Bible says, "There is nothing new under the Sun" (*Holy Bible, Rev.*
>
> *Stand. Vers.,* Eccles. 1.9).

Note that titles of biblical books are not italicized.

22. Historical document   Cite familiar documents such as the Constitution and the Declaration of Independence in your text, providing the name and the numbers of the parts you are citing.

> Judges are allowed to remain in office "during good Behaviour," a vague
>
> standard that has had various interpretations (US Const., art. 3, sec. 1).

23. Indirect source   When you quote or paraphrase a quotation you found in someone else's work, put *qtd. in* (meaning "quoted in") before the name of your source.

> Armstrong confided to a friend that Glaser's death "broke [his] heart"
>
> (qtd. in Bergreen 490).

In your list of works cited, list only the work you consulted, in this case the indirect source by Bergreen.

24. Two or more sources in one citation   When you credit two or more sources, use a semicolon to separate the citations.

> Giving up his other business ventures, Glaser now became Armstrong's exclusive
>
> agent (Bergreen 376-78; Collier 273-76; Morgenstern 124-28).

25. Two or more sources in one sentence   Include a parenthetical reference after each idea or quotation you have borrowed.

> Americans lavish more money each year on their pets than they spend
>
> on children's toys (Merkin 21), but the feral cat population--consisting
>
> of abandoned pets and their offspring--is at an estimated 70 million
>
> and growing (Mott).

26. Work in an anthology   Give the name of the specific work's author, not the name of the editor of the whole collection.

> When Dexter Gordon threatened to quit, Armstrong offered him
>
> a raise--without consulting with Glaser (Morgenstern 132).

Here, Morgenstern is cited as the source even though his work appears in a collection edited by Marc Miller. Note that the list of works cited must include an entry for Morgenstern (*see p. 227*).

27. E-mail, letter, or personal interview   Cite by name the person you communicated with, using either a signal phrase or parentheses.

> Much to Glaser's surprise, both "Hello, Dolly" and "What a Wonderful World" became big hits after the rights had been sold (Jacobs).

In the works-cited list, you will need to identify the kind of communication and its date (*see pp. 236, 244, and 247*).

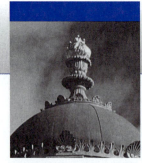

22 MLA Style: List of Works Cited

Besides in-text citations, MLA documentation style requires a works-cited page, where readers can find full bibliographic information about the sources you used. The list of works cited should appear at the end of your paper, beginning on a new page titled "Works Cited." Include only those sources you cite in your paper, unless your instructor tells you to prepare a works-consulted list.

MLA WORKS-CITED ENTRIES: DIRECTORY to SAMPLE TYPES

(*See pp. 215–24 for examples of in-text citations.*)

MLA WORKS-CITED ENTRIES: DIRECTORY to SAMPLE TYPES (*continued*)

22
MLA

MLA WORKS-CITED ENTRIES: DIRECTORY to SAMPLE TYPES *(continued)*

BOOKS

1. Book with one author   Italicize the book's title. Only the city, not the state, is included in the publication data. Conclude with the medium (Print). Notice that in the example the publisher's name, *Wayne State University Press,* is abbreviated to *Wayne State UP.*

> Hennessey, Thomas J. *From Jazz to Swing: African-Americans and Their*
>
> *Music 1890-1935.* Detroit: Wayne State UP, 1984. Print.

2. Two or more works by the same author(s)   When you list more than one work by the same author, give the author's name in the first entry only. For subsequent works authored by that person, replace the name with three hyphens and a period. Multiple works by one author are alphabetized by title.

> Collier, James Lincoln. *Jazz: The American Theme Song.* New York: Oxford
>
> UP, 1993. Print.

> ---. *Louis Armstrong, An American Genius.* New York: Oxford UP, 1983. Print.

3. Book with two or more authors   Name the two or three authors in the order in which they appear on the title page, putting the last name first for the first author only. When a work has more than three authors, you may list them all or use the abbreviation *et al.* (meaning "and others") to replace the names of all authors except the first.

> Davis, Miles, and Quincy Troupe. *Miles: The Autobiography.* New York:
>
> Simon, 1989. Print.

> Henriques, Julian, et al. *Changing the Subject: Psychology, Social Regulation,*
>
> *and Subjectivity.* New York: Methuen, 1984. Print.

4. Organization as author   Consider as an organization any group, commission, association, or corporation whose members are not identified on the title page.

> Centre for Contemporary Cultural Studies. *Making Histories: Studies*
>
> *in History Writing and Politics.* London: Hutchinson, 1982. Print.

5. Book by an editor or editors   If the title page lists an editor instead of an author, treat the editor as an author but put the abbreviation *ed.* after the name. Use *eds.* when more than one editor is listed. Only the first editor's name should appear in reverse order.

> Miller, Paul Eduard, ed. *Esquire's Jazz Book.* New York: Smith, 1944. Print.

6. Book with an author and an editor   Put the author and title first, followed by *Ed.* (meaning "edited by") and the name of the editor. However, if you cited something written by the editor rather than the author, see no. 14.

editor's name not in reverse order

> Armstrong, Louis. *Louis Armstrong: A Self-Portrait.* Ed. Richard Meryman.
>
> New York: Eakins, 1971. Print.

7. Work in an anthology or chapter in an edited book   List the author and title of the selection, followed by the title of the anthology, the abbreviation *Ed.* for "edited by," the editor's name, publication data, page numbers, and medium.

> Smith, Hale. "Here I Stand." *Readings in Black American Music.*
>
> Ed. Eileen Southern. New York: Norton, 1971. 286-89. Print.

GENERAL GUIDELINES
for the MLA WORKS-CITED LIST

- Begin on a new page.
- Begin with the centered title "Works Cited."
- Include an entry for every in-text citation.
- Include author, title, publication data, and medium (Print, Web, Radio, etc.) for each entry, if available. Use a period to set off each of these elements from the others. Leave one space after the periods.
- Do not number the entries.
- Put entries in alphabetical order by author's or editor's last name. (If the author is unknown, use the first word of the title, excluding the articles *a, an,* or *the*). If the work has more than one author, see no. 3.
- Italicize titles of books, periodicals, long poems, and plays. Put quotation marks around titles of articles, short stories, and short poems.
- Capitalize the first and last and all important words in all titles and subtitles. Do not capitalize articles, prepositions, coordinating conjunctions, and the *to* in infinitives.
- In the publication data, abbreviate publishers' names and months (*Oxford UP* instead of *Oxford University Press; Dec.* rather than *December*), and include the name of the city in which the publisher is located but not the state (unless the city is obscure or ambiguous): *Danbury: Grolier.* Use *n.p.* in place of publisher or location information if none is available. If a source does not give the date of publication, give the approximate date, enclosed in brackets: [c. 1975]. If you cannot approximate the date, write *n.d.* for "no date."
- Do not use *p., pp.,* or *page(s).* When page spans over 100 have the same first digit, use only the last two digits of the second number: 243-47. Use *n. pag.* if the source lacks page or paragraph numbers or other divisions.
- Abbreviate all months except *May, June,* and *July.*
- For articles and other print sources that skip pages, provide the page number for the beginning of the article followed by a plus (+) sign.
- Use a hanging indent: Start the first line of each entry at the left margin, and indent all subsequent lines of the entry five spaces (or one-half inch on the computer).
- Double-space within entries and between them.

8. Two or more items from one anthology   Include a complete entry for the anthology. Each selection from the anthology that you are citing should have its own entry in the alphabetical list that includes only the author, title of the selection, editor, and page numbers.

entry for a selection from the anthology
Johnson, Hall. "Notes on the Negro Spiritual." Southern 268-75.

entry for the anthology
Southern, Eileen, ed. *Readings in Black American Music.* New York:

Norton, 1971. Print.

entry for a selection from the anthology
Still, William Grant. "The Structure of Music." Southern 276-79.

9. Signed article in a reference work
Cite the author's name, title of the reference work (italicized), publication information, and medium. If entries appear in alphabetical order, omit page numbers.

Robinson, J. Bradford. "Scat Singing." *The New Grove Dictionary of Jazz.*

Ed. Barry Kernfeld. Vol. 3. London: Macmillan, 2002. Print.

22
MLA

10. Unsigned entry in a reference work
Start the entry with the title. For well-known reference works such as general-interest encyclopedias and dictionaries, the city and publisher can be omitted.

"Scat." *Merriam-Webster's Collegiate Dictionary.* 11th ed. 2003. Print.

11. Article from a collection of reprinted articles

Prager, Joshua Harris. "The Longest Replay." *Wall Street Journal* July
abbreviation for "reprinted"
1998. Rpt. in *Floating off the Page: The Best Stories from* The Wall

Street Journal's *"Middle Column."* Ed. Ken Wells. New York: Wall

Street Journal-Simon, 2002. 149-53. Print.

12. Anthology

Eggers, Dave, ed. *The Best American Nonrequired Reading 2003.*

Boston: Houghton, 2003. Print.

13. Publisher's imprint
For books published by a division within a publishing company, known as an "imprint," put a hyphen between the imprint and publisher.

Wells, Ken, ed. *Floating off the Page: The Best Stories from* The Wall Street

Journal's *"Middle Column."* New York: Wall Street Journal-Simon,

2002. Print.

14. Preface, foreword, introduction, or afterword   When the writer of the part is different from the author of the book, use the word *By* after the book's title and cite the author's full name. If the book's sole author wrote the part and the book also has an editor, use only the author's last name after *By.* If there is no editor, cite the entire book.

name of part of book

Crawford, Richard. Foreword. *The Jazz Tradition.* By Martin Williams.

New York: Oxford UP, 1993. v-xiii. Print.

15. Translation   Cite the work under the author's name, not the translator's. The translator's name goes after the title, with the abbreviation *Trans.* (meaning "translated by").

Goffin, Robert. *Horn of Plenty: The Story of Louis Armstrong.* Trans. James

F. Bezov. New York: Da Capo, 1977. Print.

16. Edition other than the first   Include the number of the edition: *2nd ed., 3rd ed.,* and so on. Place the number after the title, or if there is an editor, after that person's name.

Panassie, Hugues. *Louis Armstrong.* 2nd ed. New York: Da Capo, 1980.

Print.

17. Religious texts   Give the version, underlined; the editor's or translator's name (if any); and the publication information.

New American Standard Bible. La Habra: Lockman Foundation, 1995. Print.

The Upanishads. Trans. Eknath Easwaran. Tomales: Nilgiri, 1987. Print.

18. Multivolume work   Your citation should indicate whether you used more than one volume of a multivolume work. The first example indicates that the researcher used more than one volume; the second shows that only the second volume of the work was used.

Lissauer, Robert. *Lissauer's Encyclopedia of Popular Music in America.*

3 vols. New York: Facts on File, 1996. Print.

Lissauer, Robert. *Lissauer's Encyclopedia of Popular Music in America.*

Vol. 2. New York: Facts on File, 1996. Print.

19. Book in a series   After the medium, put the name of the series and, if available on the title page, the number of the work.

> Floyd, Samuel A., Jr., ed. *Black Music in the Harlem Renaissance.*
>   Name of series not italicized
>   New York: Greenwood, 1990. Print. Contributions in Afro-
>
>   American and African Studies 128.

20. Republished book   Put the original date of publication, followed by a period, before the current publication data. In the following example, the writer cites a 1974 republication of a book that originally appeared in 1936.

> Cuney-Hare, Maud. *Negro Musicians and Their Music.* 1936. New York:
>   Da Capo, 1974. Print.

21. Title in a title   When a book's title contains the title of another book, do not italicize the second title. In the following example, the novel *Invisible Man* is not italicized.

> O'Meally, Robert, ed. *New Essays on* Invisible Man. Cambridge:
>   Cambridge UP, 1988. Print.

22. Unknown author   The citation begins with the title. In the list of works cited, alphabetize the citation by the first important word, not by articles like *A, An,* or *The.*

> *Webster's College Dictionary.* New York: Random; New York:
>   McGraw, 1991. Print.

Note that this entry includes both of the publishers listed on the dictionary's title page; they are separated by a semicolon.

PERIODICALS

Periodicals are published at set intervals, usually four times a year for scholarly journals, monthly or weekly for magazines, and daily or weekly for newspapers. Between the author and the publication data are two titles: the title of the article, in quotation marks, and the title of the periodical, underlined. (*For online versions of print periodicals and periodicals published only online, see pp. 240–42.*)

23. Article in a journal paginated by volume
Put the volume number after the journal title. Place a period after the volume number, and follow it with the issue number. In the example, the volume is 27 and the issue is 2. Give the year of publication in parentheses, followed by a colon, a space, the page numbers of the article, and the medium.

> Tirro, Frank. "Constructive Elements in Jazz Improvisation." *Journal of the American Musicological Society* 27.2 (1974): 285-305. Print.

24. Article in a journal paginated by issue
Cite scholarly journals paginated by issue as you would those paginated by volume.

> Aguiar, Sarah Appleton. "'Everywhere and Nowhere': Beloved's 'Wild' Legacy in Toni Morrison's *Jazz*." *Notes on Contemporary Literature* 25.4 (1995): 11-12. Print.

25. Article in a monthly magazine
Provide the month and year, abbreviating the names of all months except *May, June,* and *July.*

> Walker, Malcolm. "Discography: Bill Evans." *Jazz Monthly* June 1965: 20-22. Print.

26. Article in a weekly magazine
Include the complete date of publication: day, month, and year.

> Taylor, J. R. "Jazz History: The Incompleted Past." *Village Voice* 3 July 1978: 65-67. Print.

27. Article in a newspaper
Provide the day, month, and year. If an edition is named on the top of the first page, specify the edition (*natl. ed.* or *late ed.,* for example) after the date. If the section letter is part of the page number, see the first example. Give the title of an unnumbered section with *sec.* If the article appears on nonconsecutive pages, put a plus sign (+) after the first page number.

> Blumenthal, Ralph. "Satchmo with His Tape Recorder Running." *New York Times* 3 Aug. 1999: E1+. Print.

> Just, Julie. "Children's Bookshelf." *New York Times* 15 Mar. 2009, natl. ed., Book Review sec.:13. Print.

28. Unsigned article   The citation begins with the title and is alphabetized by the first word other than an article like *A, An,* or *The.*

> "Squaresville, USA vs. Beatsville." *Life* 21 Sept. 1959: 31. Print.

29. Review   Begin with the name of the reviewer and, if there is one, the title of the review. Add *Rev. of* (meaning "review of") and the title as well as the author or performer of the work being reviewed. Notice that the word *by* precedes the author's name.

> Ostwald, David. "All That Jazz." Rev. of *Louis Armstrong:*
>
>   *An Extravagant Life,* by Laurence Bergreen. *Commentary*
>
>   Nov. 1997: 68-72. Print.

30. Editorial   Treat editorials as articles, but add the word *Editorial* after the title. If the editorial is unsigned, begin with the title.

> Shaw, Theodore M. "The Debate over Race Needs Minority Students'
>
>   Voices." Editorial. *Chronicle of Higher Education* 25 Feb. 2000: A72.
>
>   Print.

31. Abstract of a journal article   Collections of abstracts can be found at your library. Include the publication information for the original article, followed by the title of the publication that provides the abstract, the volume and issue, the year in parentheses, the item or the page number, and the medium.

> Theiler, Anne M., and Louise G. Lippman. "Effects of Mental Practice
>
>   and Modeling on Guitar and Vocal Performance." *Journal of General*
>
>   *Psychology* 122.4 (1995): 329-43. *Psychological Abstracts* 83.1 (1996):
>
>   item 30039. Print.

32. Letter to the editor

> Tyler, Steve. Letter. *National Geographic Adventure* Apr. 2004: 11. Print.

OTHER PRINT SOURCES

33. Government document   Either the name of the government and agency or the document's author's name comes first. If the government and agency names come first, follow the title of the document with the word *By* for a writer, *Ed.* for an editor, or *Comp.* for a compiler (if any). Publication information and medium come last.

> United States. Bureau of National Affairs. *The Civil Rights Act of 1964:*
>
> *Text, Analysis, Legislative History; What It Means to Employers,*
>
> *Businessmen, Unions, Employees, Minority Groups.* Washington: BNA,
>
> 1964. Print.

For the format to use when citing the *Congressional Record,* whether in print or online, see no. 62.

34. Pamphlet   Treat as you would a book. If the pamphlet has an author, list his or her name first; otherwise, begin with the title.

> *All Music Guide to Jazz.* 2nd ed. San Francisco: Miller Freeman, 1996. Print.

35. Conference proceedings   Cite as you would a book, but include information about the conference if it is not in the title.

> Mendel, Arthur, Gustave Reese, and Gilbert Chase, eds. *Papers Read*
>
> *at the International Congress of Musicology Held at New York September*
>
> *11th to 16th, 1939.* New York: Music Educators' National Conference
>
> for the Amer. Musicological Soc., 1944. Print.

36. Published dissertation   Cite as you would a book. After the title, add *Diss.* for "dissertation," the name of the institution, the year the dissertation was written, and the medium.

> Fraser, Wilmot Alfred. *Jazzology: A Study of the Tradition in Which Jazz*
>
> *Musicians Learn to Improvise.* Diss. U of Pennsylvania, 1983.
>
> Ann Arbor: UMI, 1987. Print.

37. Unpublished dissertation or essay   For a dissertation, begin with the author's name, followed by the title in quotation marks, the abbreviation *Diss.,* the name of the institution, the year the dissertation was written, and the medium.

> Reyes-Schramm, Adelaida. "The Role of Music in the Interaction of
>
> Black Americans and Hispanos in New York City's East Harlem."
>
> Diss. Columbia U, 1975. Print.

For an unpublished essay, see no. 45.

38. Abstract of a dissertation   Use the format for an unpublished dissertation. After the dissertation date, give the abbreviation *DA* or *DAI* (for *Dissertation Abstracts* or *Dissertation Abstracts International*), then the volume number, issue number, date of publication, page number, and medium.

> Quinn, Richard Allen. "Playing Together: Improvisation in Postwar
>
> American Literature and Culture." Diss. U of Iowa, 2000.
>
> *DAI* 61 (2001): 2305A. Print.

39. Published interview   Name the person interviewed and give the title of the interview or the descriptive term *Interview,* the name of the interviewer (if known and relevant), the publication information, and the medium.

> Armstrong, Louis. Interview by Richard Meryman. "Authentic American
>
> Genius." *Life* 15 Apr. 1966: 92-102. Print.

40. Map or chart   Cite as you would a book with an unknown author. Italicize the title of the map or chart, and add the word *Map* or *Chart* following the title.

> *Let's Go Map Guide to New Orleans.* Map. New York: St. Martin's,
>
> 1997. Print.

41. Cartoon   Include the cartoonist's name, the title of the cartoon (if any) in quotation marks, the word *Cartoon,* the publication information, and the medium.

> Myller, Jorgen. "Louis Armstrong's First Lesson." Cartoon.
>
> *Melody Maker* Mar. 1931: 12. Print.

42. Advertisement   Name the thing being advertised, include the word *Advertisement,* and indicate where the ad appeared.

> Hartwick College Summer Music Festival and Institute. Advertisement.
>
> *New York Times Magazine* 3 Jan. 1999: 54. Print.

43. Published letter   Treat like a work in an anthology, but include the date. Include the number, if one was assigned. If you use more than one letter from a published collection, follow the instructions for cross-referencing in no. 8.

> Hughes, Langston. "To Arna Bontemps." 17 Jan. 1938. *Arna*
>
> > *Bontemps--Langston Hughes Letters 1925-1967*. Ed. Charles H.
> >
> > Nichols. New York: Dodd, 1980. 27-28. Print.

44. Personal letter   To cite a letter you received, start with the writer's name, followed by the descriptive phrase *Letter to the author,* the date, and the medium.

> Cogswell, Michael. Letter to the author. 15 Mar. 1998. MS.

To cite someone else's unpublished personal letter, see the guidelines in no. 45.

45. Manuscripts, typescripts, and material in archives   Give the author, a title or description (*Notebook*), the form (*MS.* if manuscript, *TS.* if typescript), the name and location of the institution housing the material, and the medium.

> Glaser, Joe. Letter to Lucille Armstrong. 28 Sept. 1960. MS. Box 3. Louis
>
> > Armstrong Archives. Queens College City U of New York, Flushing.
>
> Pollack, Bracha. "A Man ahead of His Time." 1997. TS.

46. Legal source   To cite a specific act, give its name, Public Law number, its Statutes at Large number, pages, the date it was enacted, and medium.

> Microenterprise Results and Accountability Act of 2004. Pub. L.
>
> > 108-484. 3922. Stat. 23 Dec. 2004. Print.

To cite a law case, provide the names of the plaintiff and defendant, the case number, the court that decided the case, the date of the decision, and the medium. If possible, include publication information.

> Ashcroft v. the Free Speech Coalition. 535 US 234-152. Supreme Court
>
> > of the US. 2002. Print.

For more information about citing legal documents or case law, MLA recommends consulting *The Bluebook: A Uniform System of Citation,* published by the Harvard Law Review Association.

47. Microfiche/microform/microfilm   Cite as you would the print version. Provide the microfilm name and any fiche and grid numbers.

48. Publication in more than one medium   If you are citing a publication that consists of several different media, list all of the media you consulted. Follow the citation model of the medium you used primarily (below, a print book).

> Kamien, Roger. *Music: An Appreciation.* 8th ed. New York: McGraw,
>
> 2000. CD-ROM, print, Web.

ELECTRONIC SOURCES

The examples that follow are based on the guidelines for the citation of electronic sources in the seventh edition of the *MLA Handbook for Writers of Research Papers* (2009).

Note: The Internet address for an electronic source is its uniform resource locator, or URL. Only include a URL in a citation if the reader may not be able to find the source without it.

---

49. Online scholarly project

Entire Web site   Begin with the name of the editor, author, or compiler, followed by the title of the site and the electronic publication data, which includes, if relevant, the version number, the publisher or sponsor (or *n.p.*), the date of publication or update, and the medium. End with the date you used the project.

> Raeburn, Bruce Boyd, ed. *William Ransom Hogan Archive of New Orleans*
>
> *Jazz.* 30 Tulane U. Oct. 2004. Web. 3 May 2008.

Part of a scholarly Web site   When citing one part, document, or page of a project, add the author (if known) and the title of the part

CITING ELECTRONIC SOURCES IN MLA STYLE

- Begin with the name of the writer, editor, compiler, translator, director, or performer.
- Put the title of a short work in quotation marks.
- If there is no title, use a descriptive term such as *editorial* or *comment* (not italicized).
- Italicize the name of the publication or Web site. The online versions of some print magazines and newspapers have different titles than the print versions.
- Cite the date of publication or last update.
- For an online magazine or newspaper article or a Web original source, give the source (in quotation marks), the site title (italicized), version (if any), publisher or sponsor, date of publication, medium (Web), and access date.
- You may cite online sources that also appear in another medium with information about the other version. Do not cite online versions of print newspapers and magazines in this way.
- For a journal article, include the article title (in quotation marks), periodical title (italicized), volume and issue numbers, and inclusive page numbers or *n. pag.* Conclude with the medium (Web) and access date.
- To cite a periodical article from an online database, provide the print publication information, the database title (italicized), the medium, and your access date.
- If the source is not divided into sections or pages, include *n. pag.* (no pagination).
- Give the medium (Web). Include your most recent date of access to the specific source (not the general site).
- Conclude the citation with a URL only if readers may have difficulty finding the source without it.

Tips LEARNING in COLLEGE

URL Addresses

Include the URL (Web address) of an online source in a citation only if your reader would be unable to find the source without it. Place a URL at the end of your citation in angle brackets and end with a period.

> Raeburn, Bruce Boyd, ed. *William Ransom Hogan Archive of New Orleans Jazz.*
>
> Tulane U, 13 Apr. 2006. Web. 11 May 2008. <http://www.tulane.edu/
>
> ~lmiller/JazzHome.html>.

If you need to divide a URL between lines, do so after a slash and do not insert a hyphen. If the URL is long (more than one line of your text), give the URL of the site's search page. Do not make the URL a hyperlink.

22
MLA

in quotation marks. If the author is unknown, start with the title of the part in quotation marks.

> Raeburn, Bruce Boyd. "An Introduction to New Orleans Jazz." *William*
>
> *Ransom Hogan Archive of New Orleans Jazz.* Ed. Bruce Boyd Raeburn.
>
> Tulane U, 30 Oct. 2004. Web. 3 May 2008.

> "Armstrong Biography." *Satchmo.Net: The Official Site for the Louis*
>
> *Armstrong House and Archives.* Queens College City U of New York,
>
> 2003. Web. 3 May 2008.

50. Professional or personal Web site   Name the person responsible for the site, the title of the site (italicized), the publisher or sponsor (if none, list *n.p.*), the date of publication or update, the medium, and the date of access. If no title is available, use a descriptive term such as *Home page* (without italics or quotation marks).

> Henson, Keith. *The Keith Henson Jazzpage.* N.p. 1996. Web. 3 May 2008.

> Wildman, Joan. *The World of Jazz Improvisation.* U of Wisconsin, Madison,
>
> n.d. Web. 3 May 2008.

51. Home page for a course   After the instructor's name, list the course title; if there is no course title on the home page, use the title from the school's catalog, if available, or the course number. Include the department and school names.

Marshall, S. A. *Insects in Relation to Wildlife*. Dept. of Environmental

Biology, U of Guelph, Jan. 2005. Web. 18 Apr. 2008.

52. Site authored by a person using a pseudonym   Provide the name given on the Web site, even if it is obviously not the author's real name. You may provide the real name in brackets. (*See also no. 64.*)

Instapundit [Glenn Reynolds]. "More News on the Automotive

X-Prize." *Instapundit.com*. N.p., 16 May 2008. Web. 16 May 2008.

53. Online book

Entire book   Cite as for print books, including author; title (italicized); editor, translator, or compiler (if any); and publication data for the print version. Add the name of the database or project, medium, and date of access.

database italicized

Sandburg, Carl. *Chicago Poems*. New York: Holt, 1916. *Bartleby.com*.

Web. 3 May 2008.

Work in an online book   Add the title of the work after the author and put it in quotation marks, unless the part cited is an introduction, foreword, preface, or afterword.

Sandburg, Carl. "Chicago." *Chicago Poems*. New York: Holt,
no pagination
1916. N. pag. *Bartleby.com*. Web. 3 May 2008.

54. Article in an online scholarly journal, published only online
Any legitimate journal, whether published in print or online, will have a volume and/or an issue number, as is true for print journals (*see nos. 23 and 24*). Include these after the journal's name, with the year of publication in parentheses. Follow this information with the medium and access information. Give inclusive page numbers or *n. pag.*

Schmalfeldt, Janet. "On Keeping the Score." *Music Theory*

Online 4.2 (1998): n. pag. Web. 3 May 2008.

55. Article in an online scholarly journal that is also published in print   List the same information as in no. 54, including the volume number, issue number, publication year, and page numbers, before listing medium and access date.

> Parla, Jale. "The Wounded Tongue: Turkey's Language Reform and
>
>   the Canonicity of the Novel." *PMLA* 123.1 (2008): 27-40. Web.
>
>   7 May 2008.

56. Article in an online version of a print magazine or periodical   Provide the publication date—day, month, and year, or month and year—rather than the volume and issue numbers.

> Web site for the *Atlantic* magazine
>
> Davis, Francis. "Jazz--Religious and Circus." *TheAtlantic.com.* Atlantic
>
>   Monthly Group, Feb. 2000. Web. 3 Apr. 2008.

57. Article in a periodical that appears only online

> Ross, Michael E. "The New Sultans of Swing." *Salon.* Salon, 18 Apr.
>
>   1996. Web. 3 May 2008.

58. Article in an online newspaper   Follow the format used for an article in an online magazine.

> "Bulletin Board: Louis Armstrong Centenary." *New York Times.* New
>
>   York Times, 7 Nov. 2001. Web. 3 May 2008.

59. Editorial in an online newspaper   Include the word *Editorial* after the published title of the editorial.

> "A New Pope's Old Message." Editorial. *SFGate.* San Francisco
>
>   Chronicle, 20 Apr. 2005. Web. 20 Apr. 2008.

60. Letter to the editor in an online newspaper   Include the name of the letter writer, as well as the word *Letter*.

> Hughan, Wade C. Letter. *SFGate.* San Francisco Chronicle, 20 Apr.
>
> 2005. Web. 20 Apr. 2008.

61. Online government publication except the *Congressional Record*   Begin with the name of the country, followed by the name of the sponsoring department, the title of the document, and the names (if listed) of the authors.

> United States. National Commission on Terrorist Attacks upon the
>
> United States. *The 9/11 Commission Report.* By Thomas H. Kean,
>
> et al. 5 Aug. 2004. Web. 30 Mar. 2008.

62. *Congressional Record* (online or in print)   Abbreviate the title and include the date and page numbers. Give the medium.

> *Cong. Rec.* 28 Apr. 2005: D419-D428. Web.

63. Online review

> Kot, Greg. "The Mekons Find Renewal in Their Loud, Punky Past."
>
> Rev. of *Punk Rock,* by the Mekons. *Chicago Tribune Online Edition.*
>
> Chicago Tribune, 26 Mar. 2004. Web. 2 Apr. 2008.

64. Weblog ("blog") posting   A Weblog, or "blog," is an online diary. (*For more on blogs, see Tab 3: Common Assignments, p. 178.*) Cite a blog entry as you would a work from a Web site.

> Sullivan, Andrew. "The Grim Task in Iraq." *Andrewsullivan.com: The Daily*
>
> *Dish.* Atlantic Monthly Group, 25 Nov. 2003. Web. 24 Feb. 2008.

65. CD-ROM or DVD   Works on CD-ROM are usually cited like books or parts of books, but the term *CD-ROM* and the name of the vendor, if different from the publisher, are added.

> "Armstrong, (Daniel) Louis 'Satchmo.'" *Microsoft Encarta Multimedia*
>
> *Encyclopedia.* Redmond: Microsoft, 1994. CD-ROM.

66. CD-ROM or DVD—Material with no print version

"Aristotle." *Encarta 2000.* CD-ROM. Redmond: Microsoft, 1999.

67. CD-ROM or DVD—Entire book

Jones, Owen. *The Grammar of Ornament.* Palo Alto: Octavo, 1998.

CD-ROM.

68. Work from a subscription service   For material that you accessed through a service such as *EBSCO* or *InfoTrac,* add the following to your citation: the name of the database, the medium, and the date of access. Do not include the service (e.g., *InfoTrac*) or the library system.

Journal article

Hardack, Richard. " 'A Music Seeking Its Words': Double-Timing

and Double Consciousness in Toni Morrison's *Jazz.*"

Callaloo 18.2 (1995): 451-72. *Expanded Academic ASAP.* Web.

3 May 2008.

Newspaper article

Wickham, DeWayne. "Prep Program Puts 'Student' Back in 'Student-

Athlete.' " *USA Today* 27 Mar. 2007, natl. ed.: 21a. *Academic Search*

Premier. Web. 28 Mar. 2008.

Journal abstract

Porter, Christopher. "Space Is the Place: Jazz Artists Tap into the Power

of MySpace." *JazzTimes* 36.10 (2006): 48. *RILM Abstracts of Music*

Literature. Web. 28 Mar. 2008.

In the past, America Online offered personal database subscriptions. However, it has stopped doing so, and most subscription databases can be accessed at the library.

69. Posting to a news group   Treat as a Web site. Begin with the author and (in quotation marks) the title or subject line. End with the posting date, the site name, the medium (Web), and the date of access.

> Pomeroy, Leslie K., Jr. "Racing with the Moon." *rec.music.bluenote*.
>
>   N.p., 4 May 2008. Web. 6 May 2008.

70. Synchronous communication   Cite the online transcript of a synchronous discussion as you would a work from a Web site. If relevant, the speaker's name can begin the citation.

> Curran, Stuart, and Harry Rusche. "Discussion: Plenary Log 6. Third
>
>   Annual Graduate Student Conference in Romanticism." *Prometheus*
>
>   *Unplugged: Emory MOO*. Emory U, 20 Apr. 1996. Web. 4 Jan. 1999.

71. E-mail   Include the author, the subject line (if any) in quotation marks, the descriptive term *Message to* plus the name of the recipient, the date of the message, and the medium.

> Hoffman, Esther. "Re: My Louis Armstrong Paper." Message to J. Peritz.
>
>   5 May 2008. E-mail.

72. Online graphic   If a non-Web version exists, base the form of your citation on the most appropriate model. Include the creator's name, the title or description of the source, information about the non-Web version, the title of the Web site or database (italicized), the medium, and the date of access. If the source exists only online, cite as a part of a Web site (see no. 49).

> Seurat, Georges-Pierre. *Evening, Honfleur*. 1886. Museum of Mod. Art,
>
>   New York. *MoMA.org*. Web. 8 May 2008.

73. Online audio or video file   Follow the guidelines in no. 72. Mention the form (audio or video) in your text.

Online film, cited as a film

> *Night of the Living Dead*. Dir. George A. Romero. Image Ten, 1968.
>> *Internet Archive*. Web. 12 May 2008.

Original video, cited as part of a Web site

> Wesch, Michael. "The machine is us/ing us." *Digital Ethnography*.
>> Kansas State U, 2007. Web. 12 May 2008.

74. Online cartoon

> Toles, Tom. "The Rubik's Food Pyramid." *Washingtonpost.com*.
>> Washington Post, 21 Apr. 2005. Web. 29 Apr. 2008.

75. Online map

> "New Orleans." *Lonely Planet*. Lonely Planet, n.d. Web. 2 May 2008.

76. Computer software   Include the title, version, publisher, and date in your text or in an explanatory note. Do not include an entry in your Works Cited list.

AUDIOVISUAL AND OTHER NONPRINT SOURCES

77. Film, videotape, or DVD   Begin with the title (italicized). For a film, cite the director and the lead actors or narrator (*Perf.* or *Narr.*), followed by the distributor and year. Conclude with the medium (*Film, videocassette,* or *DVD*).

> *Artists and Models*. Dir. Raoul Walsh. Perf. Jack Benny, Ida Lupino,
>> and Alan Townsend. Paramount, 1937. Film.

22
MLA

78. TV or radio program   Give the episode title (in quotation marks), the program title (italicized), the name of the series (if any), the name of the network, the city, the broadcast date, and the medium.

> "The Music of Charlie Parker." *Jazz Set*. WBGO-FM, New York,
>
> 2 Dec. 1998. Radio.

79. Broadcast interview   Give the name of the person interviewed, followed by the word *Interview* and the name of the interviewer if you know it. End with information about the broadcast.

> Knox, Shelby. Interview by David Brancaccio. *NOW*. PBS. WNET,
>
> New York, 17 June 2005. Television.

80. Sound recording   The entry starts with the composer, conductor, or performer, depending on your focus. Include the work's title (italicized); the artist(s), if not already mentioned; the manufacturer; the date of release; and the medium.

> Armstrong, Louis. *Town Hall Concert Plus*. RCA Victor, 1957. LP.

81. Musical composition   Include only the composer and title, unless you are referring to a published score. Published scores are treated like books except that the date of composition appears after the title. Note that the titles of instrumental pieces are italicized only when they are known by name, not just by form and number, or when the reference is to a published score.

> Ellington, Duke. *Satin Doll*.

> Haydn, Franz Josef. Symphony no. 94 in G Major.

> reference to published score
> Haydn, Franz Josef. *Symphony No. 94 in G Major*. 1791.
>
> Ed. H. C. Robbins Landon. Salzburg: Haydn-Mozart, 1965. Print.

82. Artwork   Provide the artist's name, the title of the artwork (italicized), the date, the medium, and the institution or private collection and city in which the artwork can be found.

> Leonard, Herman. *Louis Armstrong: Birdland 1949*. 1949. Photograph.
>
> Barbara Gillman Gallery, Miami.

If you used a photograph of a work of art from a book, treat it like a work in an anthology (*see no. 7*), but italicize the titles of both the work and the book, and include the institution or collection and city where the work can be found prior to information about the book.

83. Personal, telephone, or e-mail interview
Begin with the person interviewed, followed by *Personal interview, Telephone interview,* or *E-mail interview* and the date of the interview. (*See no. 39 for a published interview and no. 79 for a broadcast interview.*)

> Jacobs, Phoebe. Personal interview. 5 May 2008.

84. Lecture or speech
To cite an oral presentation, give the speaker's name, the title (in quotation marks), the name of the forum or sponsor, the location, and the date. Conclude with *Address* or *Lecture.*

> Taylor, Billy. "What Is Jazz?" John F. Kennedy Center for the Performing
>
> Arts, Washington. 14 Feb. 1995. Lecture.

85. Performance
To cite a play, opera, ballet, or concert, begin with the title; followed by the authors (*By*); pertinent information about the live performance, such as the director (*Dir.*) and major performers; the site; the city; the performance date; and *Performance.*

> *Ragtime.* By Terrence McNally, Lynn Athrens, and Stephen Flaherty.
>
> Dir. Frank Galati. Ford Performing Arts Center, New York.
>
> 11 Nov. 1998. Performance.

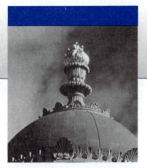

23 MLA Style: Explanatory Notes and Acknowledgments

Explanatory notes are used to cite multiple sources for borrowed material or to give readers supplemental information. Their purpose is to avoid distracting readers with an overly long parenthetical citation or an interesting but not directly relevant idea. You can also use explanatory notes to acknowledge people who helped you with research and writing. Acknowledgments are a courteous gesture in academic as well as workplace writing, even if you do not intend your paper for publication. If you acknowledge someone's assistance in your explanatory notes, be sure to send that person a copy of your paper. Because they contributed in some way to your work, they are likely to be very interested in your final product.

TEXT

One answer to these questions is suggested by a large (24-by-36-inch) painting discovered in Armstrong's house.[1]

NOTE

[1]I want to thank George Arevalo of the Louis Armstrong Archives for his help on this project. George showed me the two pictures I describe in this paper. Seeing those pictures helped me figure out what I wanted to say--and why I wanted to say it. For introducing me to archival research and to the art of Louis Armstrong, I also want to thank the head of the Louis Armstrong Archives, Michael Cogswell, and my English teacher, Professor Amy Tucker.

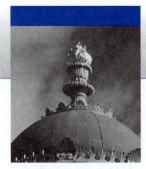

24 MLA Style: Paper Format

The following guidelines will help you prepare your research paper in the format recommended by the seventh edition of the *MLA Handbook for Writers of Research Papers*. For an example of a research paper that has been prepared using MLA style, see pages 251–62.

Materials

Before printing your paper, make sure that you have backed up your final draft. Use a high-quality printer and high-quality, white 8½-by-11-inch paper. Put the printed pages together with a paper clip, not a staple, and do not use a binder unless you have been told to do so by your instructor.

Heading and title

No separate title page is needed. In the upper left-hand corner of the first page, one inch from the top and side, type on separate, double-spaced lines your name, your instructor's name, the course number, and the date. Double-space between the date and the paper's title and the title and the first line of text, as well as throughout your paper. The title should be centered and properly capitalized (*see p. 251*). Do not underline the title or put it in quotation marks or bold type.

Margins and spacing

Use one-inch margins all around, except for the top right-hand corner, where the page number goes. Your right margin should be ragged (not "justified," or even).

Double-space lines throughout the paper, including quotations, notes, and the works-cited list. Indent the first word of each paragraph

24
MLA

TEXTCONNEX

Electronic Submission of Papers

If you are asked to submit your paper electronically, keep the following tips in mind:

- Confirm your instructor's e-mail address in advance of submitting the paper.
- Find out how your instructor would like you to submit documents. Some instructors prefer that shorter documents be cut and pasted into the body of an e-mail message. Others might prefer that you submit documents attached to e-mail messages. *Always ask permission before sending an attached document to anyone.*
- If you are asked to send a document as an attachment, confirm that the format of your document is compatible with the receiver's computer. Save your document as a "rich text format" (RTF) file, which simplifies the formatting of your document and makes it easier to share.
- As a courtesy, run a virus scan on the file you intend to submit electronically before sending it. You should also scan for viruses if you are submitting the document on a disk or CD-ROM.
- Send the submission to your own e-mail address as well so that you can make sure the paper has been transmitted successfully.

one-half inch (or five spaces) from the left margin. For block quotations, indent one inch (or ten spaces) from the left.

Page numbers

Put your last name and the page number in the upper right-hand corner of the page, one-half inch from the top and flush with the right margin.

Visuals

Place visuals (tables, charts, graphs, and images) close to the place in your text where you refer to them. Label and number tables consecutively (*Table 1, Table 2*), and give each one an explanatory caption; put this information above the table. The term *Figure* (abbreviated *Fig.*) is used to label all other kinds of visuals, except for musical illustrations, which are labeled *Example* (abbreviated *Ex.*). Place figure or example captions below the visual. Below all visuals, cite the source of the material and provide explanatory notes as needed. *(For more on using visuals effectively, see Chapter 2, pp. 36–46.)*

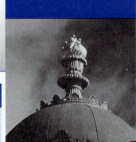

25 Student Paper in MLA Style

www.mhhe.com/
bmhh

For another
sample of a paper
in MLA style, go to

**Research >
Sample Research
Papers > MLA
Style**

As a first-year college student, Esther Hoffman wrote the following paper for her composition course. She knew little about Louis Armstrong and jazz before her instructor took the class to visit the Louis Armstrong Archives. She did archival research based on what she had learned from consulting online and print sources.

Esther Hoffman

Professor Tucker

English 120

16 May 2008

Louis Armstrong and Joe Glaser:

More Than Meets the Eye

Louis Armstrong's biography reads like a classic American success story. From humble beginnings Armstrong rose to become an international superstar, a so-called King of Jazz, and a familiar figure forty years after his death in 1971. Less well known is Joe Glaser, Armstrong's longtime manager. Yet Armstrong once credited his accomplishments to Glaser, saying, "Anything that I have done musically since I signed up with Joe Glaser at the Sunset, it was his suggestions" (qtd. in Jones and Chilton 175). Was Glaser really as central to Armstrong's work and life as this comment makes him seem? Did he dominate his famous client? On the contrary, the two appear to have enjoyed a remarkably equitable and successful partnership. However, to truly understand their relationship, it is necessary to consider the context of the jazz age and each man's background.

In the 1920s, jazz music was at its height in creativity and popularity. Chicago had become one of the jazz capitals of America, and its clubs showcased the premier talents of the time, performers like Jelly Roll Morton and Joe Oliver. Eager for fame and fortune, many young black musicians who had honed their craft in New Orleans "were drawn to Chicago, New York, Los Angeles, and other cities by the chance to make a career and hopefully a living" (James).

Among these émigrés was Louis Armstrong, a gifted artist who developed into "perhaps the best [jazz musician] that has ever been" ("Louis"). Armstrong played the trumpet and sang with

Hoffman 2

unusual improvisational ability as well as technical mastery. As

MLA in-text citation: author [Bergreen] named in signal phrase.
biographer Laurence Bergreen points out, Armstrong easily reached

difficult high notes, the F's and G's that stymied other trumpeters

(248). His innovative singing style also featured "scat," a technique

that "place[s] emphasis on the human voice as an additionally

MLA in-text citation: author named in parentheses.
important component in jazz music" (Anderson 329). According to

one popular anecdote, Armstrong invented scat during a recording

session; mid-song, he dropped his lyrics sheet and--not wanting to

disrupt a great take--began to improvise (Edwards 619). Eventually

Armstrong's innovations became the standard, as more and more

jazz musicians took their cue from his style.

Armstrong's beginnings give no hint of the greatness that

Development by narration (*see p. 38*).
he would achieve. In New Orleans, he was born into poverty and

received little formal education. As a youngster, Armstrong had

to take odd jobs like delivering coal and selling newspapers so that he

could earn money to help his family. At the age of twelve, Armstrong

was placed in the Colored Waifs' Home to serve an eighteen-month

sentence for firing a gun in a public place. There "Captain" Peter

Davis gave him "basic musical training on the cornet" ("Louis

Web source cited by title.
Armstrong"). Older, more established musicians soon noticed

Armstrong's talent and offered him opportunities to play with them.

In 1922, Joe Oliver invited Armstrong to join his band in Chicago,

and the twenty-one-year-old trumpeter headed north.

It was in Chicago that Armstrong met Joe Glaser. According

Focus introduced.
to Bergreen, Glaser had a reputation for being a tough but

trustworthy guy who could handle any situation. He was raised in

a middle-class home by parents who were Jewish immigrants from

Russia. As a young man, Glaser got caught up in the Chicago

Superscript number indicating explanatory note.
underworld and soon had a rap sheet that included indictments

for running a brothel as well as for statutory rape.[1] Glaser's mob

Hoffman 3

connections also led to his involvement in Chicago's club scene, a business almost completely controlled by gangsters like Al Capone. During the era of Prohibition, Glaser managed the Sunset Cafe, a club where Armstrong often performed:

> There was a pronounced gangster element at the Sunset, but Louis, accustomed to being employed and protected by mobsters, didn't think twice about that. Mr. Capone's men ensured the flow of alcohol, and their presence reassured many whites. (Bergreen 279)

By the early thirties, Armstrong had become one of the most popular musicians in the world. He attracted thousands of fans during his 1930 European tour, and his "Hot Five" and "Hot Seven" recordings were considered some of the best jazz ever played. Financially, Armstrong should have been doing very well, but instead he was having business difficulties. He owed money to Johnny Collins, his former manager, and Lil' Hardin, his ex-wife, was suing him for a share of the royalties on the song "Struttin' with Some Barbecue." At this point, Armstrong asked Glaser to be his business manager. Glaser quickly paid off Collins and settled with Lil' Hardin. Giving up his other business ventures, Glaser now became Armstrong's exclusive agent (Morgenstern 124-28; Collier 273-76; Bergreen 376-78). For the next thirty-four years, his responsibilities included booking appearances, organizing the bands, making travel arrangements, and paying the band members' salaries (Jones and Chilton 160, 220).

Some might posit that Glaser controlled all aspects of Armstrong's work and life. This view is suggested by a large (24-by-36-inch) oil painting discovered in Armstrong's house.[2] Joe Glaser is pictured in the middle of the canvas. Four black-and-white quadrants surround the central image of Glaser. One quadrant

Block quotation indented 10 spaces or 1".

Summary of material from a number of sources.

Citation of multiple sources.

Use of information from two separate pages in one source.

Hoffman 4

Development
by description
(*see p. 39*).

depicts a city scene, the scene in which Glaser thrived. The bottom two quadrants picture dogs, a reminder that Glaser raised show dogs. The remaining quadrant presents an image of Louis Armstrong. By placing Glaser in the center and Armstrong off in a corner, the unknown artist seems to suggest that even though Armstrong was the star, it was Glaser who made him one.

Presents a
claim plus
supporting
evidence.

In fact, Glaser did advance Armstrong's career in numerous important ways. In 1935, he negotiated the lucrative record contract with Decca that led to the production of hits like "I'm in the Mood for Love" and "You Are My Lucky Star" (Bergreen 380). Glaser also decided when to sell the rights to Armstrong's songs. Determined to make as much money as possible, he sometimes sold the rights to a song as soon as it was released, especially when he thought the song might not turn out to be a big hit. However, in at least two instances, this money-making strategy backfired: much to Glaser's surprise, both "Hello, Dolly" and "What a Wonderful World" became big hits after the rights had been sold (Jacobs).

Development
by illustration
(*see p. 36*).

To expand Armstrong's popularity, Glaser increased his exposure to white audiences in the United States. In 1935, articles on Armstrong appeared in *Vanity Fair* and *Esquire,* two magazines with a predominantly white readership (Bergreen 385). Glaser also promoted Armstrong's movie career. At a time when only a handful of black performers were accepted in Hollywood, Armstrong had roles in a number of films, including *Pennies from Heaven* (1936) with Bing Crosby. Moreover, "Jeepers Creepers," a song Armstrong sang in *Going Places* (1938), received an Academy Award nomination (Bogle 149, 157). Of course, more exposure sometimes meant more discomfort, if not danger, especially when

Note use of
transitional
expressions
(*see pp.
62–63*).

Armstrong and his band members were touring in the South. Bergreen recounts how in Southern states, where blacks were prohibited from entering many stores, Glaser sometimes had to shop for the band's food and other supplies (378, 381).

As Armstrong's manager, Glaser also exerted some control over the musician's personal finances and habits. According to Dave Gold, an accountant who worked for Associated Booking, it was Glaser who paid Armstrong's mortgage, taxes, and basic living expenses (Collier 330). A 1960 letter from Glaser to Lucille Armstrong corroborates Gold's account; it shows that Glaser assumed responsibility for buying the musician and his wife a new car as well as for filing the paperwork needed to retain the old license plate number. More personal were Glaser's attempts to control Armstrong's habitual use of marijuana. In 1931, Armstrong received a suspended sentence after his arrest for marijuana possession. He continued to use the drug, however, especially during performances, and told Glaser that he wanted to write a book about marijuana's positive effects. Glaser flatly rejected the book idea and, fearful of a scandal, also forbade Armstrong's smoking any marijuana while on tour in Europe (Pollack).

Clearly, Glaser was in a position to affect powerfully Armstrong's career and his life. However, Armstrong seemed to recognize that he gave Glaser whatever power over him the manager enjoyed. When he wanted to, Armstrong could and did resist Glaser's control, and that may be one reason why he liked and trusted Glaser as much as he did.

After Glaser became his manager, Armstrong no longer had to worry about the behind-the-scenes details of his career. He was free to concentrate on creating music and making the most of the

Support by expert opinion (*see p. 11*).

Support by key fact (*see p. 11*).

Support by anecdote (*see p. 11*).

Restatement of thesis.

opportunities his manager worked out for him. Glaser booked Armstrong into engagements with legendary performers like Benny Goodman, Ella Fitzgerald, and Duke Ellington. He also worked with the record companies to ensure that Armstrong would make the best and most profitable recordings possible (Bergreen 457). During the thirty-four years they worked together, both Armstrong and Glaser made lots of money. More important, their relationship freed Armstrong to make extraordinary music.

If Armstrong acquiesced to most of Glaser's business decisions, it may have been because he had no reason to resist them. However, when he deemed it necessary, Armstrong acted on his own. For example, in 1944 a talented band member named Dexter Gordon threatened to quit, so Armstrong offered him a raise--without consulting first with Glaser (Morgenstern 132). In 1957, when Armstrong wanted to put a stop to backstage crowding, he not only directed Glaser to make a sign prohibiting guests from going backstage but also told him exactly what to say on the sign (Armstrong, "Backstage Instructions"). As these incidents suggest, when Armstrong was displeased with the way his career was being handled, he acted to amend the situation.

Armstrong also knew how to resist Glaser's attempts to control the more personal aspects of his life. In a recent interview, Phoebe Jacobs, formerly one of Glaser's employees, sheds new light on the relationship between the manager and the musician. Armstrong's legendary generosity was tough on his pocketbook. It was well known that if someone needed money, Armstrong would readily hand over some bills. At one point, Glaser asked Jacobs to give Armstrong smaller denominations so that he would not give away so much money. The trumpeter soon figured out

Source cited: archival material.

Source cited: personal interview.

Hoffman 7

what was going on and admonished Jacobs for following Glaser's orders about money that belonged to him, not Glaser. On another occasion, Armstrong declined an invitation to join Glaser for dinner at a Chinese restaurant, saying, "I want to eat what I want to eat" (qtd. by Jacobs).

Even though he sometimes pushed Glaser away, Armstrong obviously loved and trusted his manager. In all the years of their association, the two men signed only one contract and, in the musician's words, "after that we didn't bother" (qtd. in Jones and Chilton 240). A picture of Joe Glaser in one of Armstrong's scrapbooks bears the following label in the star's handwriting: "the greatest." In his dedication to the unpublished manuscript "Louis Armstrong and the Jewish Family in New Orleans, the year of 1907," Armstrong calls Glaser "the best friend that I ever had," while in a letter to Max Jones, he writes, "I did not get really happy until I got with my man--my dearest friend--Joe Glaser" (qtd. in Jones and Chilton 16). In 1969, Joe Glaser died. Referring to him again as "the greatest," Armstrong confided to a friend that Glaser's death "broke [his] heart" (qtd. in Bergreen 490).

Although there are hints of a struggle for the upper hand, the relationship between Louis Armstrong and Joe Glaser seems to have been genuinely friendly and trusting. Armstrong gave Glaser a good deal of authority over his career, and Glaser used that authority to make Armstrong a musical and monetary success. Armstrong was happy to take the opportunities that Glaser provided for him, but he was not submissive. This equitable and friendly relationship is depicted by another picture found in Armstrong's house. The 25-by-21-inch picture, shown in fig. 1, is a caricature that may seem jarring to contemporary viewers, but

Authoritative quotation (*see p. 11*).

Memorable quotation (*see p. 204*).

Wording of quotation adjusted (*see pp. 205–06*).

Concludes with qualified version of thesis.

Memorable illustration.

Hoffman 8

Effective visual
(p. 51–52).

Fig. 1 An anonymous watercolor caricature of Armstrong with
his manager, Joe Glaser, c. 1950. Louis Armstrong Archives,
Queens College, City U of New York, Flushing.

when seen in its historical context it implies a mutual relationship
between Armstrong and Glaser. The pair stand side by side, and
Glaser has his hand on Armstrong's shoulder. Armstrong, who is

dressed for a performance, looks and smiles at us as if he were facing an audience. But Glaser looks only at Armstrong, the musician who was his main concern from 1935 to the day he died. In appearance alone, the men are clearly different. But seen in their longstanding partnership, the two make up a whole--one picture that offers us more than meets the eye.

Hoffman 10

Notes

New page, title centered.

¹Bergreen 372-76. Even though Ostwald points out a few mistakes in Bergreen's *Louis Armstrong: An Extravagant Life,* I think the book's new information about Glaser is useful and trustworthy.

Gives supplemental information about key source.

²I want to thank George Arevalo of the Louis Armstrong Archives for his help on this project. George showed me the two pictures I describe in this paper. Seeing those pictures helped me figure out what I wanted to say--and why I wanted to say it. For introducing me to archival research and to the art of Louis Armstrong, I also want to thank the head of the Louis Armstrong Archives, Michael Cogswell, and my English teacher, Professor Amy Tucker.

Indent first line 5 spaces or ½".

Acknowledges others who helped.

Works Cited

Anderson, T. J. "Body and Soul: Bob Kaufman's *Golden Sardine*."
   African American Review 34.2 (2000): 329-46. *Academic Search
   Complete*. Web. 11 Apr. 2008.

Armstrong, Louis. "Backstage Instructions to Glaser." Apr. 1957.
   MS. Accessions 1997-26. Louis Armstrong Archives. Queens
   College, City U of New York, Flushing.

---. "Louis Armstrong and the Jewish Family in New Orleans, the
   Year of 1907." 31 Mar. 1969. MS. Box 1. Louis Armstrong
   Archives. Queens College, City U of New York, Flushing.

Bergreen, Laurence. *Louis Armstrong: An Extravagant Life*. New York:
   Broadway, 1997. Print.

Bogle, Donald. "Louis Armstrong: The Films." Miller 147-79.

Collier, James Lincoln. *Louis Armstrong: An American Genius*. New
   York: Oxford UP, 1983. Print.

Edwards, Brent Hayes. "Louis Armstrong and the Syntax of Scat."
   Critical Inquiry 28.3 (2002): 618-49. Print.

Glaser, Joe. Letter to Lucille Armstrong. 28 Sept. 1960. MS. Box 3.
   Louis Armstrong Archives. Queens College, City U of New
   York, Flushing.

Jacobs, Phoebe. Personal interview. 5 May 2008.

James, Gregory N. *The Southern Diaspora: How the Great Migrations
   of Black and White Southerners Transformed America*. Chapel
   Hill: U of North Carolina P, 2007. *Blues, Jazz, and the Great
   Migration*. Web. 7 May 2008.

Jones, Max, and John Chilton. *Louis: The Louis Armstrong Story,
   1900-1971*. Boston: Little, 1971. Print.

"Louis Armstrong." *New Orleans Online*. New Orleans Tourism
   Marketing Corporation, 2008. Web. 7 May 2008.

New page,
title centered.

Source: journal
article from
database.

Source:
archival
material.

3 hyphens
used instead
of repeating
author's name.

Source:
whole book.

Source:
journal.

Hanging indent
5 spaces or 1/2".

Source:
personal
interview.

Entries in
alphabetical
order.

Miller, Marc, ed. *Louis Armstrong: A Cultural Legacy.* Seattle: U of
Washington P and Queens Museum of Art, 1994. Print.

Morgenstern, Dan. "Louis Armstrong and the Development and
Diffusion of Jazz." Miller 95-145.

Ostwald, David. "All That Jazz." Rev. of *Louis Armstrong: An
Extravagant Life,* by Laurence Bergreen. *Commentary* Nov. 1997:
68-72. Print.

Pollack, Bracha. "A Man ahead of His Time." 1997. TS.

Robinson, J. Bradford. "Scat Singing." *The New Grove Dictionary of
Jazz.* Ed. Barry Kernfeld. Vol. 3. London: Macmillan, 2002.
515-16. Print.

Source: work
in edited
book cross-
referenced
to Miller.

Source:
review in
a monthly
magazine.

This detail of a Mayan vase shows a scribe at work. Scribes—who documented the deeds of rulers—were esteemed in the great Mayan cities that flourished on the Yucatan Peninsula from around 100 to 900 CE.

Take the whole range of imaginative literature, and we are all wholesale borrowers. In every matter that relates to invention, to use, or beauty or form, we are borrowers.

—WENDELL PHILLIPS

APA
Documentation
Style

5 APA Documentation Style

APA style requires writers to provide bibliographic information about their sources in a list of references at the end of a paper. In order to format entries for the list of references correctly, it is important to know what kind of source you are citing. The directory on pages 271–72 will help you find the appropriate sample to use as a model. Alternatively, you can use the charts on the foldout pages that follow to help you locate the right example. Answering the questions in the charts will usually lead you to the sample entry you need. If you cannot find what you are looking for after consulting the appropriate directory or chart, ask your instructor for help.

WRITING OUTCOMES

Conventions

This section will help you learn to do the following:

- Integrate in-text citations and generate reference lists using APA style **(26–27)**

- Apply APA citation format to print, electronic, verbal, and visual sources **(26–27)**

- Acknowledge sources in a manner appropriate to a range of disciplines in the social sciences

❓ Is your source a complete book?

No　**Yes**
　　↓

	Go to this entry on page
Is it a complete book with one named author?	
Is it the only book by this author that you are citing?	1 (272)
Are you citing more than one book by this author?	4 (273)
Does it also have an editor or translator?	5, 7 (273)
Is it a complete book with more than one named author?	2 (272)
Is it a complete book without a named author or editor?	
Is the author an organization?	3 (273)
Is the author anonymous or unknown?	10 (274)
Is it a complete book with an editor or translator?	
Is there an editor instead of an author?	5 (273)
Is it a translation?	7 (273)
Is it an entire reference work?	9 (274)
Is it a complete book with a volume or an edition number?	
Is it part of a multivolume work (e.g., Volume 3)?	12 (274)
Does it have an edition number (e.g., Second Edition)?	11 (274)
Is it a republished work (e.g., a classic study)?	13 (274)

❓ Is your source part of a book?

No　**Yes**
　　↓

	Go to this entry on page
Is it a work from an anthology	
or a chapter in an edited book?	6 (273)
Is it an article in a reference work (e.g., an encyclopedia)?	8 (274)
Is it a published presentation from a conference?	25 (277)

Check the next panel or the directory on page 271 or consult your instructor.

The Elements of an APA References Entry: Online Journal Articles with DOI Assigned

Author, title, and other information about the print version of the article

Soares-Filho, B., Alencar, A., Nepstad, D., Cerqueira, G., del Carmen Vera Diaz, M., Rivero, S., et al. (2004). Simulating the response of land-cover changes to road paving and governance along a major Amazon highway: the Santarém-Cuiabá corridor. *Global Change Biology 10*(5), 745–764. doi:10.1111/j.1529-8817.2003.00769.x

DOI

Author, title, and other information about the print version of the article

DOI

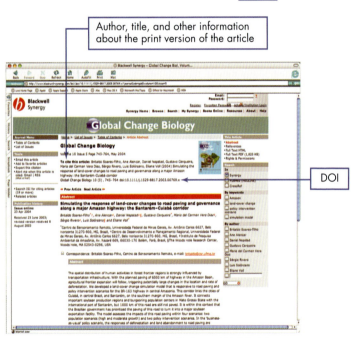

From Soares-Filho et al., *Global Change Biology, 10*(5), 745–764, May 2004, Blackwell Synergy. Reprinted with permission.

A citation for the final version of a journal article accessed online does not require a date of access. If the article has a DOI (Digital Object Identifier), the citation does not require a URL. Always include the journal's issue number. If you found the article via a database or subscription service, include database information only if the article is rare or available on just a few databases. This article lists the DOI on the top beneath the journal and citation information.

The Elements of an APA References Entry: Journal Articles

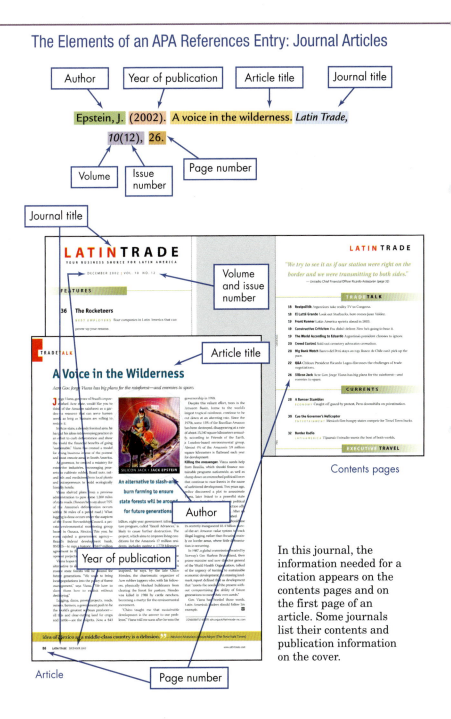

Author — Year of publication — Article title — Journal title

Epstein, J. (2002). A voice in the wilderness. *Latin Trade,*
10(12), 26.

Volume — Issue number — Page number

Journal title

Volume and issue number

Article title

Author

Year of publication

Page number

Contents pages

Article

In this journal, the information needed for a citation appears on the contents pages and on the first page of an article. Some journals list their contents and publication information on the cover.

? Is your source from an academic journal, a magazine, or a newspaper?

No   Yes
     ↓

Go to this entry on page

Is it from an academic journal?
Are the page numbers continued from one issue of the journal
to the next?   14 (275)
Do the page numbers in each issue of the journal start with 1? 15 (275)
Is it an abstract (a brief summary) of a journal article?   16 (275)
Is it a review (e.g., a review of a book)?   22 (276)
Is it a published presentation from a conference?   25 (277)

Is it from a monthly or weekly magazine?
Is it an article?   18 (276)
Is it a letter to the editor?   20 (276)
Is it a review (e.g., a review of a book)?   22 (276)

Is it from a newspaper?
Is it an article?   19 (276)
Is it an editorial or a letter to the editor?   20 (276)
Is it a review (e.g., a review of a book)?   22 (276)

Is the author unknown?   21 (276)

Are you citing two or more articles published in the same year
by the same author?   17 (275)

? Is it a print source but not a book, a part of a book, or an article
in an academic journal, a magazine, or a newspaper?

No   Yes
     ↓

Go to this entry on page

Is it published by the government or a
nongovernment organization?
Is it a government document?   23 (277)
Is it a report or a working paper?   24 (277)
Is it a brochure, pamphlet, or fact sheet?   27 (278)
Is it from the *Congressional Record*?   45 (282)

Is it an unpublished work?
Is it an unpublished conference presentation?   25 (277)
Is it an unpublished dissertation or a dissertation abstract? 26 (277)

Check the directory on page 271 or consult your instructor.

Entries in a List of References: ELECTRONIC OR OTHER NONPRINT SOURCES

? *Did you find your nonprint source online?*

No   Yes

? *Is your source a nonprint source that is not published online?*

No   Yes

Check the directory on page 271 or consult your instructor.

The Elements of an APA References Entry: Books

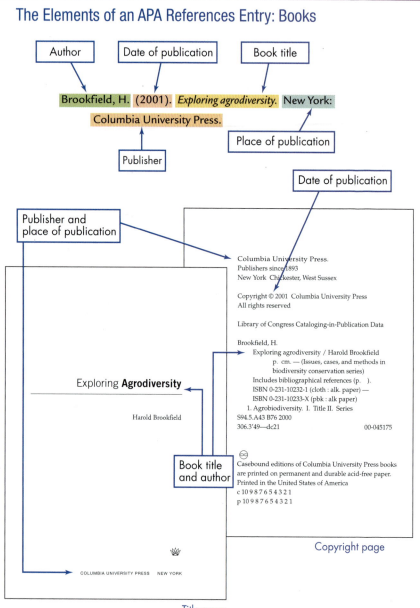

Author — Brookfield, H.

Date of publication — (2001).

Book title — *Exploring agrodiversity.*

Place of publication — New York:

Publisher — Columbia University Press.

Date of publication

Publisher and place of publication

Columbia University Press.
Publishers since 1893
New York Chichester, West Sussex

Copyright © 2001 Columbia University Press
All rights reserved

Library of Congress Cataloging-in-Publication Data

Brookfield, H.
    Exploring agrodiversity / Harold Brookfield
        p. cm. — (Issues, cases, and methods in
        biodiversity conservation series)
    Includes bibliographical references (p.   ).
    ISBN 0-231-10232-1 (cloth : alk. paper) —
    ISBN 0-231-10233-X (pbk : alk paper)
    1. Agrobiodiversity. I. Title II. Series
S94.5.A43 B76 2000
306.3'49—dc21   00-045175

Casebound editions of Columbia University Press books
are printed on permanent and durable acid-free paper.
Printed in the United States of America
c 10 9 8 7 6 5 4 3 2 1
p 10 9 8 7 6 5 4 3 2 1

Book title and author

Exploring **Agrodiversity**

Harold Brookfield

COLUMBIA UNIVERSITY PRESS   NEW YORK

Title page

Copyright page

Information for a book citation can be found on the book's title and copyright pages.

Instructors of courses in psychology, sociology, political science, communications, education, and business usually prefer a documentation style that emphasizes the author and the year of publication, in part because the style makes it easy to tell if the sources cited are current.

Information in Chapters 26–29 is based on the fifth edition of the American Psychological Association's *Publication Manual* (Washington, DC: APA, 2001) and the *APA Style Guide to Electronic References* (2007). For updates, check the APA-sponsored Web site at <http://www.apastyle.org>.

APA documentation style has two mandatory parts:

- In-text citations
- List of references

www.mhhe.com/ bmhh

For links to Web sites for documentation styles used in various disciplines, go to

Research > Links to Documentation Sites

26 APA Style: In-Text Citations

26 APA

In-text citations let readers know that they can find full information about the source of an idea you have paraphrased or summarized, or the source of a quotation, in the list of references at the end of your paper.

APA IN-TEXT CITATIONS: DIRECTORY to SAMPLE TYPES

(See pp. 272–84 for examples of reference entries.)

1. Author named in your sentence Follow the author's name with the year of publication (in parentheses).

signal phrase

> According to Brookfield (2001), nearly 12% of the Amazonian rain
>
> forest in Brazil has been shaped or influenced by thousands of years
>
> of indigenous human culture.

2. Author named in parentheses If you do not name the source's author in your sentence, include the name in parentheses, followed by the date and, if you are giving a quotation or a specific piece of information, the page number. The name, date, and page number are separated by commas.

> The Organization of Indigenous Peoples of the Colombian Amazon
>
> attempted in 2001 to take legal action to ban such fumigation over
>
> indigenous lands. Their efforts were not supported by the Colombian
>
> ampersand used within parentheses
> government (Lloyd & Soltani, 2001, p. 5).

3. Two to five authors If a source has five or fewer authors, name all of them the first time you cite the source.

> As Kaimowitz, Mertens, Wunder, and Pacheco (2004) report in
>
> "Hamburger Connection Fuels Amazon Destruction," there are three
>
> key factors behind the burgeoning demand for Brazilian beef and the
>
> resulting burning of the Amazon rain forest for pasture land.

If you put the names of the authors in parentheses, use an ampersand (&) instead of *and*.

> There are three key factors behind the burgeoning demand for Brazilian
>
> beef and the resulting burning of the Amazon rain forest for pasture
>
> land (Kaimowitz, Mertens, Wunder, & Pacheco, 2004, p. 3).

After the first time you cite a work by three or more authors, use the first author's name plus *et al.* Always use both names when citing a work by two authors.

> Another key factor is concern over livestock diseases in other countries
>
> (Kaimowitz et al., 2004, p. 4).

GENERAL GUIDELINES for APA IN-TEXT CITATIONS

- Identify the author(s) of the source, either in the sentence or in a parenthetical citation. Use only the last name of the author(s).
- Indicate the year of publication of the source following the author's name, either in parentheses if the author's name is part of the sentence or, if the author is not named in the sentence, after the author's name and a comma in a parenthetical citation.
- Include a page reference for a quotation or a specific piece of information. Put a *p.* before the page number. If the author is named in the text, the page number appears in the parenthetical citation following the borrowed material. Page numbers are not necessary when you are summarizing the source as a whole or paraphrasing an idea found throughout a work. (*For more on summary, paraphrase, and quotation, see Chapter 19, pp. 200–04.*)
- If the source does not have page numbers (as with many online sources), do your best to direct readers toward the specific part of the text you are citing (for example, citing the section title of the online source). If the source has no page or paragraph numbering or easily identifiable headings, just use the source name and date.

26
APA

4. Six or more authors   For in-text citations of a work by six or more authors, always give the first author's name plus *et al.* In the reference list, however, list the first six authors' names, followed by *et al.*

As Barbre et al. (1989) have argued, using personal narratives enables researchers to connect the individual and the social.

5. Organization as author   Treat the organization as the author and spell out its name the first time the source is cited. If the organization is well known, you may use an abbreviation thereafter.

According to a report issued by the Inter-American Association for Environmental Defense (2004), a significant population of Colombia's indigenous peoples live within these protected parklands.

Public service announcements were used to inform parents of these findings (National Institute of Mental Health [NIMH], 1991).

In subsequent citations, only the abbreviation and the date need to be given: (*NIMH, 1991*).

6. Unknown author   When no author or editor is given, use the first one or two important words of the title. Use quotation marks for titles of articles or chapters and italics for titles of books or reports.

> The transformation of women's lives has been hailed as "the single most important change of the past 1,000 years" ("Reflections," 1999, p. 77).

7. Two or more authors with the same last name   If the authors of two or more sources have the same last name, always include their first initial, even if the year of publication differs.

> M. Smith (1988) showed how globalization has restructured both cities and states.

8. Two or more works by the same author in the same year
When citing more than one work published by the same author in the same year, add a letter to the year in the in-text citation and reference list.

> J. P. Agarwhal describes the relationship between trade and foreign direct investment (FDI) (1996b).

9. Two or more sources cited at one time   When you are indebted to two or more sources, cite the authors in the order in which they appear in the list of references, separated by a semicolon.

> Other years see greater destruction from economic initiatives such as ranching (Prugh, 2004; Barrett, 2001).

10. E-mail, letters, or conversations   To cite information received from unpublished forms of personal communication, give the source's initials and last name, and provide as precise a date as possible. Do not include personal communications in your reference list.

> According to ethnobotanist G. Freid (personal communication, May 4, 2007), the work of research scientists in the Brazilian Amazon has been

greatly impeded in the last 10 years because of the destruction of

potentially unrecorded plant species.

> **Note:** Because readers do not have access to them, you should not
> include personal communications—e-mail, notes, and letters—in
> your reference list.

11. Indirect source When referring to a source that you know only
from reading another source, use the phrase *as cited in,* followed by the
author of the source you actually read and its year of publication.

> According to the Center for International Forestry Research, an
>
> Indonesia-based NGO (as cited in Prugh, 2004), an area of land the
>
> size of Uruguay was deforested in the years 2002 and 2003 alone.

26
APA

> **Note:** The work by the Center for International Forestry
> Research would not be included in the reference list, but the
> work by Prugh would be included.

12. Electronic source Cite an electronic source the same way you
would a print source, with the author's last name and the publication
date. If the document is a PDF (portable document format) file with
stable page numbers, cite the page number as you would a print
source. If the source has paragraph numbers instead of page numbers,
use *para.* or ¶ instead of *p.* when citing a specific part of the source
(*see no. 13*).

> Applications of herbicides have caused widespread damage to
>
> biodiversity, livestock, and crops, and have caused "thousands"
>
> of peasants and indigenous peoples to flee these lands (Amazon
>
> Alliance, 2004).

> **Note:** If the specific part lacks any kind of page or paragraph numbering, cite the heading and the number of the paragraph under that heading where the information can be found. If you cannot find the name of the author, or if the author is an organization, follow the appropriate guidelines for print sources (*see nos. 5 and 6*). If you cannot determine the date, use the abbreviation "n.d." in its place: (*Wilson, n.d.*).

13. Two or more sources in one sentence   Include a parenthetical reference after each fact, idea, or quotation you have borrowed.

> By one estimate, nearly 12% of the Amazonian rain forest in Brazil has been shaped or influenced by thousands of years of indigenous human culture (Brookfield, 2001); the evidence is as basic as the *terra preta do Indio,* or "Indian black soil," for which the Brazilian region of Santarem is known (Rough Guides, para. 2).

14. Sacred or classical text   Cite these within your text only, and include the version you consulted as well as any book, part, or section numbers that are standard for all versions.

> The famous song sets forth a series of opposites, culminating in "a time to love, and a time to hate; a time of war, and a time of peace" (Eccles. 3:8, King James Bible).

27 APA Style: References

APA documentation style requires a list of references where readers can find complete bibliographical information about the sources referred to in your paper. The list of references should appear at the end of your paper, beginning on a new page titled "References."

APA REFERENCE ENTRIES: DIRECTORY to SAMPLE TYPES

(See pp. 266–70 for examples of in-text citations.)

27

APA

APA LIST OF REFERENCES

- Begin on a new page.
- Begin with the centered title "References."
- Include a reference for every in-text citation except personal communications (*see in-text citation entry 10 on p. 268*).
- Put references in alphabetical order by author's last name.
- Give the last name and first or first and second initials for each author. If the work has more than one author, see no. 2.
- Put the publication year in parentheses following the author's or authors' names.
- Capitalize only the first word and proper nouns in titles. Also capitalize the first word following the colon in a subtitle.
- Use italics for titles of books but not articles. Do not enclose titles of articles in quotation marks.
- Include the city and publisher for books. If the city is not well known, include the state, using its two-letter postal abbreviation.
- Include the periodical name and volume number (both in italics) as well as the page numbers for an article.
- Separate the author's or authors' names, date (in parentheses), title, and publication information with periods.
- Use a hanging indent: Begin the first line of each entry at the left margin, and indent all subsequent lines of an entry one-half inch (five spaces).
- Double-space within and between entries.
- See p. 000 for guidelines on electronic sources.

BOOKS

1. Book with one author

Brookfield, H. (2001). *Exploring agrodiversity*. New York: Columbia University Press.

2. Book with two or more authors

Goulding, M., Mahar, D., & Smith, N. (1996). *Floods of fortune: Ecology and economy along the Amazon*. New York: Columbia University Press.

3. Organization as author When the publisher is the same as the author, use *Author* instead of repeating the organization's name as the publisher.

> Deutsche Bank, Economics Department. (1991). *Rebuilding eastern*
>
> *Europe.* Frankfurt, Germany: Author.

4. Two or more works by the same author List the works in publication order, with the earliest one first.

> Wilson, S. (Ed.). (1997). *The indigenous people of the Caribbean.*
>
> Gainesville: University Press of Florida.

> Wilson, S. (1999). *The emperor's giraffe and other stories of cultures*
>
> *in contact.* Boulder, CO: Westview Press.

If the works were published in the same year, put them in alphabetical order by title and add a letter (*a, b, c*) to the year to distinguish each entry in your in-text citations (*see no. 17*).

5. Book with editor(s) Add (*Ed.*) or (*Eds.*) after the name. If a book lists an author and an editor, treat the editor like a translator (*see no. 7*).

> Lifton, K. (Ed.). (1998). *The greening of sovereignty in world politics.*
>
> Cambridge, MA: MIT Press.

6. Selection in an edited book or anthology The selection's author, year of publication, and title come first, followed by the word *In* and information about the edited book. The page numbers of the selection go in parentheses after the book's title.

> Wilmer, F. (1998). Taking indigenous critiques seriously: The enemy 'r'
>
> us. In K. Lifton (Ed.), *The greening of sovereignty in world politics* (pp.
>
> 55–60). Cambridge, MA: MIT Press.

7. Translation After the title of the translation, put the name(s) of the translator(s) in parentheses, followed by the abbreviation *Trans.*

> Dostoyevsky, F. (1950). *Crime and Punishment* (C. Garnett, Trans.).
>
> New York: Modern Library. (Original work published 1866)

27

APA

8. Article in a reference work   Begin with the author of the selection, if given. If no author is given, begin with the selection's title.

title of the selection

Arawak. (2000). In P. Lagasse (Ed.), *The Columbia encyclopedia* 6th ed.,

    (p. 2533). New York: Columbia University Press.

9. Entire dictionary or reference work   Unless an author or edition is indicated on the title page, list dictionaries by title, with the edition number in parentheses. (The in-text citation should include the title or a portion of the title.) *(See no. 8 for information on listing an article in a reference book and no. 10 on alphabetizing a work listed by title.)*

    The American Heritage dictionary of the English language (4th ed.). (2000).

        Boston: Houghton Mifflin.

    Hinson, M. (2004). *The pianist's dictionary.* Bloomington: Indiana

        University Press.

10. Unknown author or editor   Start with the title. When alphabetizing, use the first important word of the title (excluding articles such as *The, A,* or *An*).

    Give me liberty. (1960). New York: World.

11. Edition other than the first

    Smyser, W. R. (1993). *The German economy: Colossus at crossroads*

        (2nd ed.). New York: St. Martin's Press.

12. One volume of a multivolume work   If the volume has its own title, put it before the title of the whole work.

    Handl, G. (1990). The Mesoamerican Biodiversity Legal Project. In

        Yearbook of international environmental law (Vol. 4). London: Graham

        & Trotman.

13. Republished book   In-text citations should give both years: "As Le Bon (1895/1960) pointed out . . ."

    Le Bon, G. (1960). *The crowd: A study of the popular mind.* New York:

        Viking. (Original work published 1895)

PERIODICALS

14. Article in a journal paginated by volume
Do not use *pp.* before the page numbers. Italicize the title of the periodical and the volume number.

> da Cunha, M. C., & de Almeida, M. (2000). Indigenous people, traditional
>
> people and conservation in the Amazon. *Daedalus, 129,* 315.

15. Article in a journal paginated by issue
Include the issue number (in parentheses). The issue number is not italicized.

> Epstein, J. (2002). A voice in the wilderness. *Latin Trade, 10*(12), 26.

16. Abstract
For an abstract that appears in the original source, add the word *Abstract* in brackets. If the abstract appears in a secondary print source, include the publication information for the complete article and original publication, followed by the publication information for the source of the abstract. If the dates of the publications differ, cite them both, with a slash between them, in the in-text citation: *Murphy (2003/2004).*

> Burnby, J. G. L. (1985, June). Pharmaceutical connections: The Maw's
>
> family [Abstract]. *Pharmaceutical Historian, 15*(2), 9-11.

> Murphy, M. (2003). Getting carbon out of thin air. *Chemistry &*
>
> *Industry, 6,* 14-16. Abstract obtained from *Fuel and Energy Abstracts,*
>
> 2004, *45*(6), 389.

17. Two or more works in one year by the same author
Alphabetize by title, and attach a letter to each entry's year of publication, beginning with *a*. In-text citations must use the letter as well as the year.

> Agarwal, J. P. (1996a). *Does foreign direct investment contribute to*
>
> *unemployment in home countries?—An empirical survey* (Discussion
>
> Paper No. 765). Kiel, Germany: Institute of World Economics.

> Agarwal, J. P. (1996b). Impact of Europe agreements on FDI in
>
> developing countries. *International Journal of Social Economics,*
>
> *23*(10/11), 150–163.

27
APA

18. Article in a magazine After the year, add the month for magazines published monthly or the month and day for magazines published weekly. Note that the volume number is also included.

> Gross, P. (2001, February). Exorcising sociobiology.
>> *New Criterion, 19,* 24.

19. Article in a newspaper Use *p.* or *pp.* with the section and page number. List all page numbers, separated by commas, if the article appears on discontinuous pages: *pp. C1, C4, C6.* If there is no identified author, begin with the title of the article.

> Smith, T. (2003, October 8). Grass is green for Amazon farmers.
>> *The New York Times,* p. W1.

20. Editorial or letter to the editor

> Krugman, P. (2000, July 16). Who's acquiring whom? [Editorial].
>> *The New York Times,* Sec. 4, p. 15.

> Deren, C. (2005, May 5). The last days of LI potatoes? [Letter to
>> the editor]. *Newsday,* p. A49.

21. Unsigned article Begin the entry with the title, and alphabetize it by the first important word (excluding articles such as *The, A,* or *An*).

> The biggest anniversary; reflections on a thousand years. (1999,
>> April 18). *The New York Times Magazine,* 77.

22. Review If the review is untitled, use the bracketed description in place of a title.

> Kaimowitz, D. (2002). Amazon deforestation revisited [Review of the
>> book *Brazil, forests in the balance: Challenges of conservation with
>> development*]. *Latin American Research Review, 37,* 221-236.

> Scott, A. O. (2002, May 10). Kicking up cosmic dust [Review of the
>> motion picture *Star wars: Episode II--Attack of the clones*]. *The New
>> York Times,* p. B1.

OTHER PRINT AND AUDIOVISUAL SOURCES

23. Government document
When no author is listed, use the government agency as the author.

> U.S. Bureau of the Census. (1975). *Historical statistics of the United States:*
> *Colonial times to 1970.* Washington, DC: U.S. Government Printing
> Office.

For an enacted resolution or piece of legislation, see no. 45.

24. Report or working paper
If the issuing agency numbered the report, include that number in parentheses after the title.

> Agarwal, J. P. (1996a). *Does foreign direct investment contribute to*
> *unemployment in home countries?—An empirical survey* (Discussion
> Paper No. 765). Kiel, Germany: Institute of World Economics.

For reports from a deposit service like the Educational Resources Information Center (ERIC), put the document number in parentheses at the end of the entry.

25. Conference presentation
Treat published conference presentations as a selection in a book (*no. 6*), as a periodical article (*no. 14 or 15*), or as a report (*no. 24*), whichever applies. For unpublished conference presentations, provide the author, the year and month of the conference, the title of the presentation, and the presentation's form, forum, and place.

> Markusen, J. (1998, June). *The role of multinationals in global economic*
> *analysis.* Paper presented at the First Annual Conference in
> Global Economic Analysis, West Lafayette, IN.

> Desantis, R. (1998, June). *Optimal export taxes, welfare, industry*
> *concentration and firm size: A general equilibrium analysis.* Poster
> session presented at the First Annual Conference in Global
> Economic Analysis, West Lafayette, IN.

26. Unpublished dissertation or dissertation abstract

> Weinbaum, A. E. (1998). Genealogies of "race" and reproduction in
> transatlantic modern thought (Doctoral dissertation, Columbia
> University, 1998). *Dissertation Abstracts International, 58,* 229.

27
APA

If you used the abstract but not the actual dissertation, treat the entry like a periodical article, with *Dissertation Abstracts International* as the periodical.

> Weinbaum, A. E. (1998). Genealogies of "race" and reproduction in
>
> transatlantic modern thought. *Dissertation Abstracts International,*
>
> *58,* 229.

27. Brochure, pamphlet, fact sheet
If there is no date of publication, put *n.d.* in place of the date. If the publisher is an organization, list it first, and name the publisher as *Author.*

> United States Postal Service. (1995, January). *A consumer's guide to*
>
> *postal services and products* [Brochure]. Washington, DC: Author.

> Union College. (n.d.). *The Nott Memorial: A national historic landmark at*
>
> *Union College* [Pamphlet]. Schenectady, NY: Author.

28. Film, DVD, videotape
Begin with the cited person's name and a parenthetical notation of his or her role. After the title, identify the medium in brackets, followed by the country and name of the distributor. (For online video, see no. 53.)

> Rowling, J. K., Goldenberg, M. (Writers), Yates, D. (Director), & Barron,
>
> D. (Producer). (2007). *Harry Potter and the order of the phoenix* [DVD].
>
> United States: Warner Home Video. (Original release date 2007)

For films and videos that might be hard to find, add the name and address of the distributor in parentheses after the bracketed medium.

29. CD, audio recording
For an audio podcast, see no. 51.

> Corigliano, J. (2007). Red violin concerto [Recorded by J. Bell]. *Red*
>
> *violin concerto* [CD]. New York: Sony Classics.

30. Radio broadcast
For an audio podcast, see no. 51.

> Adamski, G., & Conti, K. (Hosts). (2007, January 16). *Legally speaking*
>
> [Radio program]. Chicago: WGN Radio.

31. Television program For a single episode, treat the writer as the author and the producer as the editor of the series. For an entire series or specific news broadcast, treat the producer as author.

> Burns, E., Simon, D. (Writers), & Johnson, C. (Director). (2003). The
>
> target [Television series episode]. In D. Simon & N. K. Noble
>
> (Producers), *The wire*. New York: HBO.

> Simon, D., & Noble, N. K. (Producers). (2002). *The wire* [Television
>
> series]. New York: HBO.

32. Image, photograph, work of art, graph, chart If you have reproduced a graph, chart, map, or image, give the source information following the figure *(for an example, see p. 289)*. See no. 41 for images found online.

> Smith, W. E. (1950). *Guardia civil, Spain* [Photograph]. Minneapolis,
>
> MN: Minneapolis Institute of Arts.

ELECTRONIC SOURCES

33. Online journal article with DOI If your source has a DOI (Digital Object Identifier), include it at the end of the entry; an access date is not needed when a DOI is listed. Always include the issue number.

> Ray, R., Wilhelm, F., & Gross, J. (2008). All in the mind's eye? Anger
>
> rumination and reappraisal. *Journal of Personality and Social*
>
> *Psychology, 94*(1), 133–145. doi:10.1037/0022-3514.94.1.133

34. Online journal article without DOI Include the complete URL unless the source is only available via subscription or search, in which case include the home page URL. If your source is not likely to change (such as the final form of a print article), no access date is needed. Always include the issue number, followed by page numbers if available.

> Chan, L. (2004, November 3). Supporting and enhancing scholarship in
>
> the digital age: The role of open access institutional repository.
>
> *Canadian Journal of Communication, 29*(3). Retrieved from
>
> http://www.cjc-online.ca/viewarticle.php?id=850

27
APA

APA ELECTRONIC REFERENCES (from *APA Style Guide to Electronic References* (2007))

Cite online works as you would the same works in another medium, apart from the following considerations:

- Many online journal articles have a Digital Object Identifier (DOI), a unique alphanumeric string. Citations of online documents with DOIs do not require the URL or retrieval date.
- Only include a retrieval date for items that lack a publication date, items that probably will change (such as an in-press article), and reference sources (such as an encyclopedia article).
- Do not include the name of a database or library subscription service in the citation unless the work is only in a few databases or difficult to find in print. If you include the name, omit the URL.
- For online journal articles, always include the issue number.
- Include the URL of the home page for items that require a subscription, appear in reference works, or appear in frames.
- Include the full URL for all other items, except those with a DOI.

35. Article from an online, subscription, or library database

Do not include database information other than URL (for items without a DOI) in your citation unless the source is found only in a few databases. If you do include the database name, omit the URL. If there is no DOI and the source is only available via subscription or search, give the URL of the database's home page.

Epstein, J. (2002). A voice in the wilderness. *Latin Trade, 10*(12), 26. Retrieved from http://www.ebsco.com

Gore, W. C. (1916). Memory, concept, judgment, logic (theory). *Psychological Bulletin, 13*(9), 355–358. Retrieved from PsycARTICLES database.

36. Abstract as original source

Welsh, W. (2003). *Evaluation of prison-based therapeutic community drug treatment programs in Pennsylvania* (NCJ No. 221276) [Abstract].

Retrieved from National Criminal Justice Reference Service abstracts database.

37. Article in an online newspaper
Include the home page URL if the article is only available via search, subscription, or fee.

Rohter, L. (2004, December 12). South America seeks to fill the world's table. *The New York Times.* Retrieved from http://www .nytimes.com

38. Article in an online magazine
Include the volume number after the title if available.

Biello, D. (2007, December 5). Thunder, hail, fire: What does climate change mean for the U.S.? *Scientific American.* Retrieved from http://www.sciam.com

39. Online magazine content not in print edition

Francis, A. (2006, March 24). Fighting for the rainforest [Online exclusive]. *Newsweek International.* Retrieved from http:// www.newsweek.com/id/47178

40. Document on a Web site
If the document is an entire article or report, include the basic information for an online document.

Lloyd, J., & Soltani, A. (2001, December). *Report on: Plan Columbia and indigenous peoples.* Retrieved from http://www.amazonwatch .orgamazon/CO/uwa/reports/plancol_march02.pdf

41. Visual on a Web site
If you have used a graph, chart, map, or image, give the source information following the figure caption (*for an example, see p. 289*).

42. Section of an Internet document

U.S. Bureau of Oceans and International Environmental and Scientific Affairs. (2007, July 27). Projected greenhouse gas emissions. In

27
APA

Fourth U.S. climate action report—2006 (chap. 5). Retrieved from
http://www.state.gov/documents/organization/89652.pdf

43. Online book   Give information about the online source if the
book only exists in electronic format or is difficult to locate in print.

Münsterberg, H. (1913). *Psychology and industrial efficiency.* Retrieved
from http://www.gutenberg.org/etext/15154

44. Online government document except the *Congressional Record*

National Commission on Terrorist Attacks upon the United States.
(2004, August 5). *The 9/11 Commission report.* Retrieved from
http://www.gpoaccess.gov/911/pdf/fullreport.pdf

National Security Council. (2006, September). *9/11 five years later:
successes and challenges.* Retrieved from http://www.whitehouse
.gov/nsc/waronterror/2006/waronterror0906.pdf

45. *Congressional Record* (online or in print)   For enacted reso-
lutions or legislation, give the number of the congress after the number
of the resolution or legislation, the volume number for the *Congressional
Record,* the page number(s), and the year, followed by *(enacted).*

H. Res. 2408, 108th Cong., 150 Cong. Rec. 1331-1332 (2004)
(enacted).

Give the full name of the resolution or legislation when citing it within
your sentence, but abbreviate it when it appears in a parenthetical
in-text citation: *(H. Res. 2408, 2004).*

46. Online document lacking either date or author   Prefer
sources with author and date information. Use the abbreviation *n.d.*
(no date) for any undated document and give the access date. Begin
the entry with the document's title if no author is given.

Center for Science in the Public Interest. (n.d.). *Food additives to avoid.*

Retrieved March 4, 2008, from http://www.mindfully.org/Food/

Food-Additives-Avoid.htm

47. Published dissertation from a database   Include the dissertation file number (AAT) at the end of the entry, if available.

Gorski, A. (2007). *The environmental aesthetic appreciation of cultural*

landscapes. Retrieved from ProQuest Digital Dissertations.

(AAT 1443335)

48. Article in online reference work   Begin with the author's name if given. If no author is given, begin with the title. Include the date you accessed the article and the home page URL.

Special Olympics. (2008). In *Encyclopaedia Britannica online.* Retrieved

February 15, 2008, from http://www.britannica.com

49. Post to an electronic mailing list or newsgroup   Provide the message's author, its date, and its subject line as the title. After the phrase *Message posted to,* give the name of the mailing list or newsgroup, followed by the address of the archived message.

Glick, D. (2007, February 10). Bio-char sequestration in terrestrial

ecosystems—a review. Message posted to Terra Preta electronic

mailing lists archived at http://bioenergylists.org/pipermail

/terrapreta_bioenergylists.org/2007-February/000023.html

Jones, D. (2001, February 3). California solar power [Msg 1]. Message

posted to http://yarchive.net/space/politics/california_power.html

50. Blog posting

Sullivan, A. (2008, February 29). Rethinking the terror war. Message

posted to http://www.andrewsullivan.theatlantic.com/the

_daily_dish/2008/week9/index.html

27
APA

51. Audio podcast

McDonald, J. (Host). (2008, March 5). *Worldview.* Podcast retrieved

from http://www.npr.org/rss/podcast/podcast_detail.php?

siteId=14537681

52. E-mail or instant message (IM)   E-mail, instant messages, or other nonarchived personal communication should be cited in the body of your paper but not listed in the References (*see in-text citations, no. 10, on p. 268*).

53. Online video

Wesch, M. (2007). The machine is us/ing us [Video file]. Video posted

to http://mediatedcultures.net/ksudigg/?p=84

54. Computer software   Only cite specialized software. For down-loadable software, omit city and publisher; add "Available from" and the URL.

Buscemi, S. (2003). AllWrite! with online handbook (Version 2.1)

[Software]. New York: McGraw-Hill.

28 APA Style: Paper Format

The following guidelines are recommended by the *Publication Manual of the American Psychological Association,* fifth edition. For an example of a research paper that has been prepared using APA style, see pages 287–96.

Materials   Before printing your paper, make sure that you have backed up your final draft. Use a high-quality printer and high-quality, white 8½-by-11-inch paper. Do not justify your text or hyphenate words at the right margin; it should be ragged right.

Title page   The first page of your paper should be a title page. Center the title between the left and right margins in the upper half of the page, and put your name a few lines below the title. Most instructors will also want you to include the course number and title, the instructor's name, and the date. (*See p. 287 for an example.*)

Margins and spacing   Use one-inch margins all around, except for the top right-hand corner, where the page number goes.

Double-space lines throughout the paper, including in the abstract, within any notes, and in the list of references. Indent the first word of each paragraph one-half inch (or five spaces).

For quotations of more than forty words, use block format and indent five spaces from the left margin. Double-space the quoted lines.

Page numbers and abbreviated titles   All pages, including the title page, should have a number preceded by a short (one- or two-word) version of your title. Put this information in the upper right-hand corner of each page, about one-half inch from the top.

Abstract   Instructors sometimes require an abstract—a 75- to 120-word summary of your paper's thesis, major points or lines of development, and conclusions. The abstract appears on its own numbered page, titled "Abstract," and is placed right after the title page.

Headings   The primary headings should be centered, and all keywords in the heading should be capitalized.

Secondary headings should be italicized and should appear flush against the left-hand margin. Do not use a heading for your introduction, however.

Visuals   Place visuals (tables, charts, graphs, and images) close to the place in your text where you refer to them. Label each visual as a table or a figure, and number each kind consecutively (*Table 1, Table 2*). Provide an informative caption for each visual. Cite the source of the material, preceded by the word *Note* and a period, and provide explanatory notes as needed.

29 Student Paper in APA Style

www.mhhe.com/
bmhh

For another sample of a paper in APA style, go to

**Research >
Sample Research
Papers > APA
Style**

Audrey Galeano researched and wrote a report on the indigenous peoples of the Amazon for her anthropology course Indigenous Peoples and Globalization. Her sources included books, journal articles, and Web sites.

Saving the Amazon:

Globalization and Deforestation

Audrey Galeano

Anthropology 314: Indigenous Peoples and Globalization

Professor Mura

May 3, 2008

Abstract

The impact of globalization on fragile ecosystems is a complex problem. In the Amazon river basin, globalization has led to massive deforestation as multinational corporations exploit the rain forest's natural resources. In particular, large-scale industrial agriculture has caused significant damage to the local environment. In an effort to resist the loss of this ecosystem, indigenous peoples in the Amazon basin are reaching out to each other, to nongovernmental organizations (NGOs), and to other interest groups to combat industrial agriculture and promote sustainable regional agriculture. Although these efforts have had mixed success, it is hoped that the native peoples of this region can continue to live on their homelands without feeling intense pressure to acquiesce to industrialization or to relocate.

Annotations (right margin):

All pages: short title and page number.

Full title, centered.

Title appears on separate page, centered, with course information, and date.

Abstract appears on new page after title page. First line is not indented.

Objective stance used, with no reference to essay. Essay concisely summarized—key points included, but not details or statistics.

Paragraph should be no longer than 120 words.

Saving the Amazon:

Globalization and Deforestation

For thousands of years, the indigenous peoples of the Amazon river basin have practiced forms of sustainable agriculture. These peoples developed ways of farming and hunting that enabled them to provide food and trade goods for their communities with minimal impact on the environment. These methods have endured despite colonization and industrialization. Today, the greatest threat to indigenous peoples in the Amazon river basin is posed by the massive deforestation caused by industrial-scale farming and ranching, as revealed in satellite images taken by Brazil's National Institute of Space Research since 1988. (See graph in Figure 1.)

Because of the injury to ecosystems and native ways of life, indigenous peoples and antiglobalization activists have joined forces to promote sustainable agriculture and the rights of native peoples throughout the Amazon river basin.

Sustainable Lifeways, Endangered Lives

Recent work in historical ecology has altered our understanding of how humans have shaped what is romantically called "virgin forest." As anthropologist Anna Roosevelt (as cited in Society for California Archaeology, 2000) observes, "People adapt to environments but they also change them. There are no virgin environments on earth in areas where people lived." By one estimate, nearly 12 percent of the Amazonian rain forest in Brazil has been shaped or influenced by thousands of years of indigenous human culture (Brookfield, 2001); the evidence is as basic as the *terra preta do Indio,* or "Indian black soil," for which the Brazilian region of Santarem is known (Rough Guides, para. 2).

Saving the Amazon   4

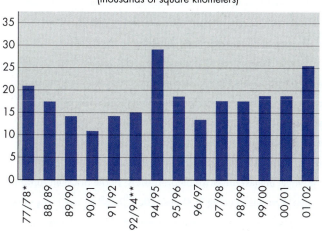

Annual Deforestation Rates in Brazilian Amazon
(thousands of square kilometers)

Graph presents statistics in visual form for readers.

Figure 1. Annual deforestation rates in the Brazilian Amazon, 1988-2002 (square kilometers). *Note.* From National Institute of Space Research. (2002). In D. Kaimowitz, B. Mertens, S. Wunder, & P. Pacheco, *Hamburger connection fuels Amazon destruction: Cattle ranching and deforestation in Brazil's Amazon.* Retrieved from http://www.cifor.cgiar.org/publications/pdf _files/media/Amazon.pdf

Informative caption and source note appear below figure.

The previous thousands of years of human influence on the Amazon is slight, however, compared to the modern-day destruction of rain forests around the globe, and in the Amazon river basin in particular. The sources of this destruction vary from country to country and year to year, with certain years affected more by climate change and other years seeing greater destruction from human initiatives, such as logging (Walker, Moran, & Anselin, 2000).

Support by key facts (see p. 11).

Saving the Amazon   5

According to the Center for International Forestry Research, an Indonesia-based NGO, an area of land the size of Uruguay was deforested in 2002-2003 alone. Nearly all of this land was cleared for industrial agriculture and cattle ranching (Prugh, 2004).

Globalization and Agricultural Destruction

Large-scale industrial agriculture seeks out the least expensive ways to produce the largest amounts of crops. Perhaps the largest cash crop of the late twentieth and early twenty-first centuries is soy, which has numerous uses and is among the least expensive crops to produce. According to Roberto Smeraldi, director of the environmental action group Friends of the Earth, "Soybeans are the single biggest driver for deforestation" in the Brazilian Amazon; in the 12 months ending in August 2003, 9,169 square miles of rain forest had been cleared by soy farmers, ranchers, and loggers in Brazil (as cited in Stewart, 2004, paras. 4-5). Although Brazilian officials have attempted to regulate the depredations of the rain forest by multinational soy producers, Stewart notes that, in 2003, soybean production brought nearly $8 billion to the Brazilian economy, forcing indigenous and small-scale farmers off their lands and damaging local climate.

An Associated Press (AP) report reprinted on the Organic Consumer's Association Web site describes the impact of soy production on Brazil's Xingu National Park, a protected rain forest reserve that is home to 14 indigenous tribes. "The soy is arriving very fast. Every time I leave the reservation I don't recognize anything anymore because the forest keeps disappearing," a director of the Xingu Indian Land Association is quoted as observing (AP, 2003, para. 11). Although the industrial soy farms have not crossed the borders of the Xingu National Park, they

---

Paragraph expands on introductory paragraph.

Discussion of details begun and linked to broader issue of globalization.

Abbreviation given at first mention of organization.

Abbreviation for organization used in parenthetical citation.

Saving the Amazon   6

surround the protected lands and have raised fears that chemical pesticides and deforestation will dry up rivers and kill fish. "Our Xingu is not just what's here. It's a very long thread, and when it rains the soy brings venom down the same river that passes by our door," says Capivara chief Jywapan Kayabi (para. 24).

First main cause of deforestation discussed.

Cattle ranching has also led to the deforestation of the Amazon. The cattle population of the Amazon nations increased from 26 million in 1990 to 57 million in 2002 (Prugh, 2004). Attention to the destruction caused by industrial cattle-ranching began in the late 1980s. Barrett (2001) points out that ranchers were following onto lands already depleted of fertility and biodiversity by logging, road building, and colonization of the Brazilian Amazon in the 1960s and 1970s. Ranching, Barrett observes, "doesn't require nutrient-rich soil" and therefore "took the place vacated by other activities, along with the blame for soil erosion and loss of biodiversity" (p. 1).

Second main cause of deforestation discussed.

Page number given for quotation.

Indigenous Peoples and Regional Activism

Depopulation of these lands as a result of colonization meant that traditional agricultural practices were no longer sustained. In recent years, antiglobalization NGOs, the international movement for indigenous peoples' rights, and increased understanding of the consequences of deforestation are helping native peoples reclaim lands and reestablish traditional agricultural practices. However, some kinds of alliances and interventions are not as productive as others.

Contributing factor in problem of deforestation shows complexity of situation.

Anthropologists da Cunha and de Almeida ask a provocative question: "Can traditional peoples be described as 'cultural conservationists'?" (2000, p. 315). Although as many as 50 indigenous groups in Amazonia still have no contact with the outside world, other indigenous peoples have secured their land rights through international efforts over the past 20 years. Some of these efforts, da Cunha and de Almeida argue, are influenced by romantic ideas about "noble savages" and fail to acknowledge the ways in which indigenous peoples in contemporary Brazil make a living from rain forest resources.

Local culture, history, and economics shown to be linked to global systems.

Barham and Coomes (1997) also note that a better understanding of how indigenous peoples live is necessary for the efforts of international groups such as Amazon Alliance to succeed. Indigenous peoples need to see some material benefit from conservationist practices. After all, as da Cunha and de Almeida write, "traditional peoples are neither outside the central economy nor any longer simply in the periphery of the world system" (2000).

Franke Wilmer (1998) suggests that "human action and its impact in the world are directed by a view that is dangerously out of touch with natural laws which, according to indigenous peoples, govern all life on this planet" (p. 57). For instance, although the Kayapo people of south central Amazonia have been devastated by colonization, they still "used their knowledge to manipulate ecosystems in remarkable ways . . . to maximize biological diversity" (Brookfield, 2001, p. 141). Among the Kayapo's sustainable practices are crop rotation, the use of ash to fertilize fields, and the transition of older fields back to secondary forest (Brookfield, 2001).

Ellipses indicate omission in quotation.

Some socially conscious global corporations have attempted to assist indigenous Amazonian farmers in developing sustainable, profitable crops. Two of the best-known efforts, described in a 2003 *New York Times* article by Tony Smith, provide a cautionary

Saving the Amazon   8

tale. In the 1990s, the British multinational "green" cosmetics company The Body Shop and American ice cream manufacturer Ben and Jerry's both developed "eco-friendly" products from the Amazon. Ben and Jerry's Rainforest Crunch ice cream used Brazil nuts that were harvested in a sustainable fashion by an Amazonian cooperative, and The Body Shop also used the oils from Brazil nuts in some of its cosmetics. But Rainforest Crunch proved so popular that the cooperative couldn't meet the demand, and Ben and Jerry's had to turn to other suppliers, "some notorious for their antilabor practices" (Smith, 2003, p. W1). The Body Shop wound up being sued by a chief of the Kayapo tribe, whose image was used in Body Shop advertising without permission (Smith).

Problems caused by one solution discussed.

The best solution might be for Brazilian business, developers, government officials, and indigenous peoples to work together. One new initiative described in the *Times* article is the cultivation of the sweet-scented native Amazon grass called priprioca, on which the Sao Paulo cosmetics company Natura is basing a new fragrance. Farmer Jose Mateus, who has grown watermelons and manioc on his small farm near the Amazon city of Belem, has agreed to grow priprioca instead--and he expects to get twice the price for the grass that he would for his usual crop (Smith, 2003). Eduardo Luppi, director of innovation for Natura, comments, "We do have the advantage that we are Brazilian and we are in Brazil. If you are in England or America and want to manage something like this in the Amazon by remote control, you can forget it" (as cited in Smith, 2003, p. W1).

Solutions described, backed up with experts' quotations, which come from secondary source.

Although indigenous peoples face extraordinary obstacles in their quest for environmental justice, some political officials support their struggles. In the Acre state of Brazil, Governor Jorge

Saving the Amazon   9

Viana was inspired by the example of martyred environmental activist Chico Mendes to secure financing from Brazil's federal development bank for sustainable development in his impoverished Amazonian state (Epstein, 2002). Viana, who holds a degree in forest engineering, told the journal *Latin Trade* that "we want to bring local populations into the policy of forest management. . . . We have to show them how to exploit without destroying" (as cited in Epstein, p. 26).

Conclusion

The social, economic, climate-related, and political pressures on the Amazonian ecosystem may prove insurmountable; report after report describes the enormous annual loss of rain forest habitat. The best hope for saving the rain forest is public pressure on multinational agricultural corporations to practice accountable, safe, and sustainable methods. In addition, it is important to encourage indigenous peoples to practice their age-old sustainable agriculture and land-management strategies while guaranteeing their rights and safety. Much in the Amazon has been ruined, but cooperative efforts like those discussed in this paper can nurture and sustain what remains for future generations.

Essay concludes on optimistic note, balancing writer's and sources' concerns.

Saving the Amazon   10

References

Associated Press. (2003, December 18). *Soybeans: The new threat to Brazilian rainforest.* Retrieved April 8, 2008, from http://www.organicconsumers.org/corp/soy121903.cfm

Barham, B. L., & Coomes, O. T. (1997). Rain forest extraction and conservation in Amazonia. *The Geographical Journal, 163*(2), 180–188.

Barrett, J. R. (2001). Livestock farming: Eating up the environment? *Environmental Health Perspectives, 109*(7), A312.

Brookfield, H. (2001). *Exploring agrodiversity.* New York: Columbia University Press.

da Cunha, M. C., & de Almeida, M. (2000). Indigenous people, traditional people and conservation in the Amazon. *Daedalus, 129,* 315.

Epstein, J. (2002). A voice in the wilderness. *Latin Trade, 10*(12), 26.

Glick, D. (2007, February 10). Bio-char sequestration in terrestrial ecosystems—a review. Message posted to Terra Preta electronic mailing list, archived at http://bioenergylists.org /pipermail/terrapreta_bioenergylists.org/2007-February /000023.html

Prugh, T. (2004). Ranching accelerates Amazon deforestation. *World Watch, 17*(4), 8.

Smith, T. (2003, October 8). Grass is green for Amazon farmers. *The New York Times,* p. W1.

Society for California Archaeology. (2000). *Interview with Dr. Anna Roosevelt.* Retrieved April 16, 2008, from http://www.society forcaliforniaarchaeology.org/about_california_archaeology .org/about_California_archaeology/2000_Roosevelt.html

New page, heading centered.

Entries in alphabetical order and double-spaced.

Hanging indent 5 spaces or ½".

Stewart, A. (2004, July 14). Brazil's soy success brings
environmental challenges. *Dow Jones.* Retrieved from
http://www.amazonia.org.br/English/noticias
/noticia.cfm?id=116059

Walker, R., Moran, E., & Anselin, L. (2000). Deforestation and
cattle ranching in the Brazilian Amazon: External capital and
household processes. *World Development 28*(4), 683-699.

Wilmer, F. (1998). Taking indigenous critiques seriously: The
enemy 'r' us. In K. Lifton (Ed.), *The greening of sovereignty in
world politics* (pp. 55-60). Cambridge, MA: MIT Press.

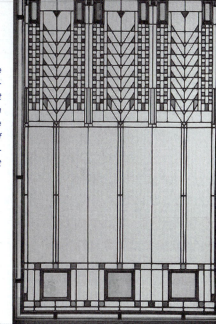

Frank Lloyd Wright's Robie House features 174 stained-glass windows. Sunlight brings out the clarity of each window's design; in turn, the designs—a variety of geometric, colorful patterns—transform the light

I . . . believe that words *can* help us move or keep

us paralyzed, and that our choices of language

and verbal tone have something—a great deal—

to do with how we live our lives and whom we

end up speaking with and hearing. . . .

—ADRIENNE RICH

Editing
for Clarity

6 Editing for Clarity

WRITING OUTCOMES

Processes and Conventions

This section will help you learn to do the following:

- Revise your sentences for clarity by using subordination appropriately **(36)**, choosing exact language **(40)**, and fixing problems such as wordiness **(30)**, mixed constructions **(31)**, and misplaced modifiers **(35)**

- Apply standard American English constructions to your writing **(32)**

- Use appropriate language that clearly expresses your intended meaning **(39–40)**

Test Yourself:

Take an online quiz at www.mhhe.com/bmhh to test your familiarity with the topics covered in chapters 30–41. As you read the following chapters, pay special attention to the sections that correspond to any questions you answer incorrectly.

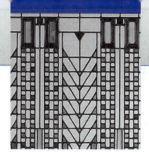

30 Avoiding Wordiness

A sentence does not have to be short and simple to be concise, but every word in it must count.

Wordiness and Grammar Checkers

Most computer grammar checkers recognize many wordy structures, but inconsistently so. One style checker flagged most passive verbs and some *it is* and *there are* (expletive) constructions, but not others. It also flagged the redundant expression *true fact* but missed *round circle* and the empty phrase *it is a fact that.*

30a Eliminating redundancies and unnecessary modifiers

www.mhhe.com/
bmhh

For information on and practice eliminating redundancies, go to

Editing >
Eliminating
Redundancies

Be on the lookout for redundancies such as *first and foremost, full and complete, past history,* and *blue in color.*

➤ Students living ~~in close proximity~~ in the dorms need

to cooperate ~~together if they want~~ to live in harmony.

Usually, modifiers such as *very, rather,* and *really* and intensifiers such as *absolutely, definitely,* and *incredibly* can be deleted.

30b

W

➤ The ending ~~definitely~~ shocked us ~~very much~~.

30b Replacing wordy phrases

Make your sentences more concise by replacing wordy phrases with appropriate alternatives.

Tests must now

➤ ~~It is necessary at this point in time that tests~~ be run

to measure

~~for the purposes of measuring~~ the switch's strength.

Wordy Phrases	Concise Alternatives
at that point in time	then
at this point in time	now
due to the fact that	because
for the reason that	because
in close proximity to	near
in order to	to
in spite of the fact that	although
in the event that	if
in the not-too-distant future	soon
is able to	can
is necessary that	must

Exercise 30.1 Identifying and editing wordy or empty phrases and unnecessary repetition

Eliminate wordy or empty phrases and unnecessary repetition to make the following sentences concise.

EXAMPLE

The
~~The truth is that the time of the~~ rainy season in Hawaii is

from ~~the month of~~ November to ~~the month of~~ March.

1. Charlotte Perkins Gilman was first and foremost known as a woman who was a champion of women's rights.
2. She was born on the date July 3, 1860, in the city of Hartford, which is in the state of Connecticut.
3. Gilman's "The Yellow Wallpaper," a novella about the holy matrimony of marriage and a state of madness, still speaks to contemporary readers in this present day and age.
4. The leading female heroine in Gilman's story is diagnosed by her physician husband as having an illness that is mental in origin.
5. Gilman wrote and published her book *Women and Economics* in the year 1898 and then published her book *Concerning Children* in the year 1900.

30c Editing roundabout sentences

Eliminate expletive constructions like *there is, there are,* and *it is,* replace the static verbs *be* and *have* with active verbs, and beware of overusing nouns derived from verbs.

➤ *The*
~~There are~~ stylistic similarities between "This Lime-Tree

indicate
Bower" and "Tintern Abbey/" ~~which are indications of the~~

influenced
~~influence~~ that Coleridge ~~had on~~ Wordsworth.

➤ The film *JFK*, ~~which was~~ directed by Oliver Stone, revived

interest in the conspiracy theory.

Often, you can reduce phrases to single words.

➤ Oliver Stone's film *JFK* revived interest in the conspiracy

theory.

You can combine short, repetitive sentences.

Because of a cold front from Canada, the meteorologist on Channel 7 is predicting a
➤ A major storm ~~is expected~~ in the western part of the state/,

~~A cold front is coming in from Canada. The meteorologist on~~

with
~~Channel 7 is predicting~~ high winds and heavy rain.

30c

W

Exercise 30.2 Writing straightforward sentences

Use the techniques described in this chapter to make each of the following passages into a single concise sentence.

EXAMPLE

The play opened on October 1. There were many reviews in which critics gave it a pan. The public loathed it too, which is why it closed after a run of less than two weeks.

The play opened on October 1, but critics panned it, the public loathed it, and it closed after a run of less than two weeks.

1. There are many concerns that environmentalists have about whether genetically modified food products are absolutely safe for the environment.

IDENTIFY AND EDIT
Wordy Sentences

W

To make your writing concise, ask yourself these questions
as you edit your writing:

❓ 1. *Do any sentences contain wordy or empty phrases such as at this point in time? Do any of them contain redundancies or other unnecessary repetitions?*

> More   now
> ■ ~~The fact is that at this point in time more~~ women than men
>   attend college.
>
> ■ Total college enrollments have increased steadily ~~upward~~
>   since the 1940s, but since the 1970s women have enrolled
>   in greater numbers than men ~~have~~.

❓ 2. *Can any clauses be reduced to phrases, or phrases to single words? Can any sentences be combined to reduce repetitive information?*

> College   report
> ■ ~~Reports that come from college~~ officials ~~indicate~~ that
>
>   applications from women exceed those from men/ ~~This~~
>   , indicating
>   ~~pattern indicates~~ that women will continue to outnumber
>
>   men in college.

❓ 3. *Do any sentences include* there is, *or* there are, *or* it is *expressions; weak verbs; or nouns derived from verbs?*

> men outnumbered women in college by
> ■ In 1970, ~~there were~~ more than 1.5 million. ~~more men in~~
>
>   ~~college than women.~~
>
>   reflects
> ■ This trend ~~is a reflection of~~ broad changes in gender roles
>
>   throughout American society.

---

2. Soybeans that are genetically engineered are very resistant to certain artificially made herbicides. These beans are also very resistant to certain artificially made insecticides.
3. These soybeans, which are resistant, permit the use of larger quantities of herbicides by farmers than before.
4. The herbicides kill surrounding plants. They also kill insects that are not considered pests, such as the Monarch butterfly.

5. There are also concerns from consumers about the handling of genetically modified soy crops. One of these concerns is that the genetically modified soy crops are not segregated from soy crops that have not been genetically modified.

Exercise 30.3   Chapter review: Revising wordy sentences

Use the techniques described in this chapter to make the following passage concise.

> In this day and age, people definitely should take preventive precautions to prevent identity theft from happening to them. Identity thieves have the ability to use someone else's personal information to commit fraud or theft, such as opening a fraudulent credit card account. Identity thieves also have the capacity to create counterfeit checks. This type of theft is often done in such a clever manner that often the victim of identity theft never realizes that his or her identity has been stolen. People whose identity has been stolen should first and foremost contact the Federal Trade Commission (FTC) for the purpose of disputing fraudulent charges. There is also the fact that people should learn how they can minimize the chance that they will face the risk of becoming a victim of this type of crime.

31a

miss

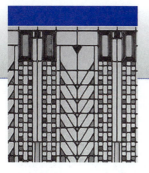

31 Adding Missing Words

Do not omit words the reader needs to understand your sentence.

31a   Adding needed words to compound structures

For conciseness, words can sometimes be omitted from compound structures: *His anger is extreme and his behavior* [*is*] *violent.* But do not leave out part of a compound structure unless both parts of the compound are the same.

> *with*
> ➤ The gang members neither cooperated‿nor listened to
>
> the authorities.

31b Adding the word *that*

Add the word *that* if doing so makes the sentence clearer.

> *that*
> ➤ The attorney argued‿men and women should receive equal
>
> pay for equal work.

31c Adding needed words in comparisons

To be clear, comparisons must be complete. Check comparisons to make sure your meaning is clear. In the following example, does the writer mean that she loved her grandmother more than her sister did—or more than she loved her sister? To clarify, add the missing words.

> *did*
> ➤ I loved my grandmother more than my sister‿.
>
> *I loved*
> ➤ I loved my grandmother more than‿my sister.

When you use *as* to compare people or things, be sure to use it twice.

> *as*
> ➤ Napoleon's temper was‿volatile as a volcano.

Include *other* or *else* to indicate that people or things belong to the group with which the subject is being compared.

> ➤ *Gone with the Wind* won more awards than any *other* film
>
> in Hollywood history.

> ➤ Professor Koonig wrote more books than anyone *else* in
>
> the department.

Complex comparisons may require more than one addition to be clear.

> *than Jones's book*
> **Smith's book is longer, but his account of the war is**
>   ^
>   *Jones's account.*
> **more interesting than ~~Jones's.~~**
>   ^

31d Adding the articles *a, an,* or *the*

Omitting an article usually sounds odd, unless the omission occurs in a series of nouns.

>   *the*
> **He gave me books he liked best.**
>   ^

> **He gave me books, CDs, and games.**

If the articles in a series are not the same, each one must be included.

> **I have a fish tank, birdcage, and rabbit hutch.**

>   *a*   *a*
> **I have *an* aquarium, birdcage, and rabbit hutch.**
>   ^   ^

(*For more information about the use of articles, multilingual writers should consult Chapter 48, pp. 426–28.*)

Exercise 31.1 Chapter review: Editing for missing words

Read the following paragraphs carefully, and supply any missing words.

31d
miss

Most early scientists thought the speed of light was infinite. The Italian scientist Galileo never agreed nor listened to arguments of his contemporaries. He set up experiment to measure the speed of light between two hills that were a known distance apart. Although its results were ambiguous, Galileo's experiment was more influential than any experiment of his day.

Almost one hundred years later, the Danish astronomer Olaus Roemer devised a sophisticated experiment to measure speed of light. Roemer hypothesized the farther away planet Jupiter is from Earth, the longer its light will take. Knowing Jupiter's distance from Earth at various times of the year, Roemer calculated the speed of light at 141,000 miles per second. Roemer's result was closer than that of any earlier scientist to the actual speed of light, which is now known to be 186,281.7 miles per second in a vacuum.

According to Albert Einstein's theory of relativity, the speed of light has never and will never be exceeded. The speed of light is variable, however. For instance, it travels about twenty-five percent slower through water.

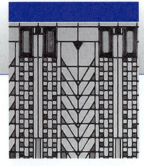

32 Unscrambling Mixed Constructions

Sentences that do not fit together grammatically or logically can be confusing and must be revised.

32a Untangling mixed-up grammar

A sentence should not start one way and then midway through change grammatical direction.

Family
➤ ~~For family~~ members who enjoy one another's company

often decide on a vacation spot together.

A prepositional phrase cannot be the subject of a sentence. Eliminating the preposition *for* makes it clear that *family members* is the subject of the verb *decide*.

can be
➤ In Mexican culture, ~~when~~ a Curanderos ~~is~~ consulted

for
~~can address~~ spiritual or physical illness.

The dependent clause *when a Curanderos is consulted* cannot serve as the subject of the sentence. Transforming the dependent clause into an independent clause with a subject and predicate fixes the problem.

> **Mixed Constructions and Grammar Checkers**
> Computer grammar checkers are unreliable at detecting mixed constructions. For example, a grammar checker failed to highlight the two examples of mixed-up sentences in section 32a.

32b   Repairing illogical predicates

A sentence's subject and verb must match both logically and grammatically. When they do not, the result is faulty predication.

> ~~The best kind of education for me would be a~~ *A* university with *would be best for me*
> both a school of music and a school of government.

A university is an institution, not a type of education, so the sentence needs revision.

The phrases *is when, is where,* and *the reason is . . . because* usually result in faulty predication.

> *the production of carbohydrates from the interaction of*
> Photosynthesis is ~~where~~ carbon dioxide, water, and
>
> chlorophyll. ~~interact in the presence of sunlight to form~~
>
> ~~carbohydrates.~~

Photosynthesis is a process, not a place.

> *that*
> The reason the joint did not hold is ~~because~~ the coupling
>
> bolt broke.

or

> The ~~reason the~~ joint did not hold ~~is~~ because the coupling
>
> bolt broke.

32b
mix

Exercise 32.1 Chapter review: Eliminating mixed constructions

Edit the following paragraph to eliminate mixed constructions. Some sentences may not need correction, and there may be several acceptable options for editing those that do need it.

Electrons spin around the nucleus of an atom according to definite rules. The single electron of a hydrogen atom occupies a kind of spherical shell around a single proton. According to the discoveries of quantum physics, states that we can never determine exactly where in this shell the electron is at a given time. The indeterminacy principle is a rule where we can only know the probability that the electron will be at a given point at a given moment. The set of places where the electron is most likely to be is called its orbital. By outlining a set of rules for the orbitals of electrons, the Austrian physicist Wolfgang Pauli developed the concept of the quantum state. Through using this concept permits scientists to describe the energy and behavior of any electron in a series of four numbers. The first of these, or principal quantum number, is where the average distance of the electron from the nucleus is specified. For the other quantum numbers describe the shape of the orbital and the "spin" of the electron. That no two electrons can ever be in exactly the same quantum state, according to Pauli's basic rule. The reason chemists use the four quantum numbers as a shorthand for each electron in an atom is because they can calculate the behavior of the atom as a whole.

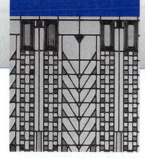

33 Fixing Confusing Shifts

Revise confusing shifts in point of view, tense, mood, or voice.

Confusing Shifts and Grammar Checkers

Computer grammar checkers rarely flag confusing shifts. Consider this blatant example:

➤ **The teacher entered the room and then roll is called.**

Although the sentence shifts confusingly from past to present tense and from active to passive voice, at least one grammar checker failed to highlight it.

33a Fixing shifts in point of view

A writer has three points of view to choose from: first person (*I* or *we*), second person (*you*), and third person (*he, she, it, one,* or *they*). Once you choose a point of view, use it consistently.

➤ **Students will have no trouble getting access to a computer**

    they
if ~~you~~ arrive at the lab before noon.

Note: When making a general statement about what people should or should not do, use the third person, not the second person.

    Do not switch from singular to plural or plural to singular without a reason for doing so. When correcting such shifts, choose the plural to avoid using *his or her* or introducing gender bias. (*See Chapter 39, pp. 342–44.*)

    People are
➤ **~~A person is~~ often assumed to be dumb if they are attractive**

and smart if they are unattractive.

33b Fixing shifts in tense

Verb tenses show the time of an action in relation to other actions. You should choose a time frame—present, past, or future—and use it consistently, changing tense only when the meaning of your text requires you to do so.

➤   **The wind was blowing a hundred miles an hour when**

was   *fell*
suddenly there ~~is~~ a big crash, and a tree ~~falls~~ into the

living room.

➤   **She has admired many strange buildings at the university**

thinks   *looks*
but ~~thought~~ that the new Science Center ~~looked~~ completely

out of place.

Exercise 33.1   Making point of view consistent

Edit the following sentences so that they are consistent in person and number.

EXAMPLE

they
When people vote, ~~you~~ participate in government.

or

you
When ~~people~~ vote, you participate in government.

1. On November 30, 1974, archeologists discovered the 3.5 million-year-old skeleton of an early hominid (or human ancestor) you call Lucy.
2. If you consider how long ago Lucy lived, one might be surprised so many of her bones remained intact.
3. When an early hominid like Lucy reached full height, they were about three and a half feet tall.
4. When these early hominids were born, she could expect to live about thirty years.
5. Lucy and the other hominids who lived with her in what is today Ethiopia, Africa, all walked upright and could manipulate a tool with their dextrous hands.

IDENTIFY AND EDIT
Confusing Shifts

shift

To avoid confusing shifts, ask yourself these questions as you edit your writing:

❓ 1. *Does the sentence shift from one point of view to another? For example, does it shift from third person to second?*

> - Over the centuries, millions of laborers helped build and
>   maintain the Great Wall of China, and ~~if you were one, you~~
>   _{most of them}
>   ~~probably~~ suffered great hardship as a result.

❓ 2. *Are the verbs in your sentence consistent in the following ways:*

> *In tense (past, present, or future)?*
> - Historians call the period before the unification of China the
>   _{ended}
>   Warring States period. It ~~ends~~ when the ruler of the Ch'in
>   state conquered the last of his independent neighbors.
>
> *In mood (statements vs. commands or hypothetical conditions)?*
> _{were}
> - If a similar wall ~~is~~ built today, it would cost untold amounts
>   of time and money.
>
> *In voice (active or passive)?*
> - The purpose of the wall was to protect against invasion, but
>   _{it also promoted}
>   commerce. ~~was promoted by it also.~~

33c
shift

33c Avoiding unnecessary shifts in mood and voice

Verbs have a mood and a voice. There are three basic moods: the **indicative,** used to state or question facts, acts, and opinions; the **imperative,** used to give commands or advice; and the **subjunctive,** used to express wishes, conjectures, and hypothetical conditions. Unnecessary shifts in mood can confuse and distract your readers.

_{could go}
➤ If he ~~goes~~ to night school, he would take a course in

accounting.

www.mhhe.com/
bmhh

For information
on shifts in verb
tense and voice,
go to

Editing > Verb
and Voice Shifts

Most verbs have two voices. In the **active voice,** the subject does the acting; in the **passive voice,** the subject is acted upon. Do not shift abruptly from one voice to the other.

They favored violet,

➤ The Impressionist painters hated black. ~~Violet,~~ green, blue,

pink, and red. ~~were favored by them.~~

Exercise 33.2 Keeping verbs consistent in tense, mood, and voice

Edit the following sentences so that the verbs are consistent in tense, mood, and voice unless meaning requires a shift. If a sentence is correct as is, circle its number.

EXAMPLE

The Silk Road, the famous trade route that linked Asia

followed

and Europe, ~~follows~~ the Great Wall of China for much

of its length.

1. Many visitors who have looked with amazement at the Great Wall of China did not know that its origins reached back to the seventh century BCE.
2. In 221 BCE, the ruler of the Ch'in state conquered the last of its independent neighbors and unifies China for the first time.
3. The Ch'in ruler ordered the walls the states had erected between themselves to be torn down, but the walls on the northern frontier were combined and reinforced.
4. Subsequent Chinese rulers extended and improved the wall until the seventeenth century CE, when it reached its present length of more than four thousand miles.
5. History shows that as a defense against invasion from the north, the wall was not always effective.
6. China was conquered by the Mongols in the thirteenth century, and the Manchus took control of the empire in the seventeenth century.
7. The wall, however, also served as a trade route and had helped open new regions to farming.
8. As a result, was it not for the wall, China's prosperity might have suffered.

33d Avoiding shifts between direct and indirect quotations and questions

Indirect quotations report what others wrote or said without repeating their words exactly. **Direct quotations** report the words of others exactly and should be enclosed in quotation marks. (*For more on punctuating quotations, see Chapter 53, pp. 477–78.*) Do not shift from one form of quotation to the other within a sentence.

➤ **In his inaugural speech, President Kennedy called on**

Americans not to ask what their country could do for them

   to   *they could*   *their*
but instead ⸢ask what ~~you can~~ do for ~~your~~ country.⸣

The writer could have included the quotation in its entirety: *In his inaugural speech, President Kennedy said, "My fellow Americans, ask not what your country can do for you; ask what you can do for your country."*

Similarly, do not shift from an indirect to a direct question.

                whether
➤ **The performance was so bad the audience wondered ~~had~~**

   had
the performers ever rehearsed.

As an alternative, the writer could ask the question directly: *Had the performers ever rehearsed? The performance was so bad the audience wasn't sure.*

**33d
shift**

Exercise 33.3   Chapter review: Eliminating confusing shifts

Edit the following passage, changing words as necessary to avoid confusing shifts.

  From about the first to the eighth century CE the Moche civilization dominated the north coast of what is now Peru. The people of this remarkable civilization, which flourished nearly a thousand years before the better-known Inca civilization, are sophisticated engineers and skilled artisans. They built enormous adobe pyramids and a vast system of irrigation canals was created and maintained. Moche smiths forged spectacular gold ornaments as well as copper tools and weapons. The Moche potter sculpted realistic-looking portraits and scenes of everyday life onto clay vessels; they also decorated vessels with intricate drawings of imposing and elaborately garbed figures involved in complex ceremonies. One such scene, which appeared on many Moche vessels, depicted a figure archeologists call the Warrior Priest engaged in a ceremony that involves the ritual sacrifice of bound prisoners.

A question is what do these drawings represent. You wonder whether they depict Moche gods and mythological events, or do they represent actual figures from Moche society conducting actual Moche rituals? A dramatic discovery in 1987 provided an answer to these questions. In that year, archeologists have uncovered a group of intact Moche tombs at a site called Sipán. In one of the tombs were the remains of a man who had been buried clothed in stunningly rich regalia. As this outfit was carefully removed by the archeologists, they realized that it corresponded to the outfit worn by the Warrior Priest depicted on Moche pottery. If the warrior priest was just a mythological figure, then this tomb should not exist, but it did. In other words, the archeologists realized, the man in the tomb was an actual Moche Warrior Priest. The archeologists who excavated the tomb explain that the art "enabled us to . . . identify the status, rank and wealth of the principal individual buried in the tomb, as well as the role that he played in the ceremonial life of his people" (Alva and Donnan, 1993, p. 141).

—Alva, W. & Donnan, C. B. (1993). *Royal Tombs of Sipán.* Los Angeles: Fowler Museum of Cultural History

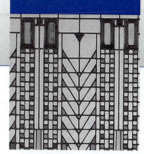

34 Using Parallel Constructions

Parallel constructions present equally important ideas in the same grammatical form.

➤ **At Gettysburg in 1863, Lincoln said that the Civil War was being fought to make sure that government *of the people, by the people,* and *for the people* might not perish from the earth.**

Correct items in a series or paired ideas that do not have the same grammatical form by making them parallel. Put items at the same level in an outline or items in a list in parallel form.

34a Making items in a series parallel

A list or series of equally important items should be parallel in grammatical structure.

➤ **The Census Bureau classifies people as employed if they receive payment for any kind of labor, are temporarily absent from their jobs, or ~~working~~ <u>work</u> at least fifteen hours as unpaid laborers in a family business.**

Parallel construction can make a sentence more forceful and memorable.

➤ **My sister obviously thought that I was too young, ~~too~~ ignorant, and ~~a troublemaker.~~ <u>too troublesome.</u>**

www.mhhe.com/
bmhh

For information
and exercises on
parallelism, go to

**Editing >
Coordination and
Subordination**

34a
//

Exercise 34.1 Identifying effective parallelism

Underline the parallel elements in the following passage.

I believe this government cannot endure permanently half slave and half free. I do not expect the Union to be dissolved—I do not expect the house to fall—but I do expect it will cease to be divided. It will become all one thing, or all the other. Either the opponents of slavery will arrest the further spread of it, and place it where the public mind shall rest in the belief that it is in the course of ultimate extinction; or its advocates will push it forward till it shall become alike lawful in all the states, old as well as new, North as well as South.

—ABRAHAM LINCOLN, speech at the
Republican State Convention,
Springfield, Illinois, June 16, 1858

34b   Making paired ideas parallel

Paired ideas connected with a coordinating conjunction (*and, but, or, nor, for, so, yet*), a correlative conjunction (*not only . . . but also, both . . . and, either . . . or, neither . . . nor*), or a comparative expression (*as much as, more than, less than*) must have parallel grammatical form.

➤ Successful teachers must ^both^ inspire ~~students~~ and ~~challenging~~ ^challenge their students.^

~~them is also important.~~

➤ I dreamed not only of getting the girl but also of ^winning^ the gold medal.

➤ The junta preferred to fight rather than ~~compromising.~~ ^to compromise.^

Exercise 34.2   Correcting faulty parallelism

Revise the following sentences to eliminate any faulty parallelism.

EXAMPLE

Newlywed couples need to learn to communicate effectively and budget in a wise manner.

Newlywed couples need to learn to communicate effectively and budget wisely.

1. Impressionism is a term that applies primarily to an art movement of the late nineteenth century, but the music of some composers of the era is also considered impressionist.

IDENTIFY AND EDIT
Faulty Parallelism

To avoid faulty parallelism, ask yourself these questions as
you edit your writing:

1. Are the items in a series in parallel form?

> ■ The senator stepped to the podium, ~~an angry glance shooting~~
> *glanced angrily at*
> ~~toward~~ her challenger, and began to refute his charges.

2. Are paired items in parallel form?

> ■ She claimed that her challenger ~~had~~ not only accused her
> *had*
> falsely of accepting illegal campaign contributions, but ~~his~~
> *also*
> ~~contributions were from illegal sources also.~~
> *had himself accepted illegal contributions.*

3. Are the items in outlines and lists in parallel form?

> FAULTY
> PARALLELISM
> She listed four reasons for voters to send her back
> to Washington:
> 1. Ability to protect the state's interests
> 2. Her seniority on important committees
> 3. Works with members of both parties to get
>   things done
> 4. Has a close working relationship with the
>   President
>
> REVISED
> She listed four reasons for voters to send her back
> to Washington:
> 1. *Her ability* to protect the state's interests
> 2. *Her seniority* on important committees
> 3. *Her ability* to work with members of both parties
>   to get things done
> 4. *Her* close working *relationship* with the
>   President

34b
//

---

2. The early impressionists include Edouard Manet, Claude Monet,
   and Mary Cassatt, and also among them are Edgar Degas and
   Camille Pissarro.
3. Impressionist composers include Claude Debussy, and Maurice
   Ravel is considered an impressionist also.
4. Just as impressionism in art challenged accepted conventions of
   color and line, in music the challenge from impressionism was to
   accepted conventions of form and harmony.

5. Critics at first condemned both impressionist artists and impressionist music.
6. Women impressionist painters included Mary Cassatt from the United States and Berthe Morisot, who was French.
7. Among Monet's goals were to observe the changing effects of light and color on a landscape and record his observations quickly.
8. To accomplish these goals he would often create not just one but a series of paintings of a subject over the course of a day.

34c Repeating function words as needed

Function words such as prepositions (*to, for, by*) and subordinating conjunctions (*although, that*) give information about a word or indicate the relationships among words in a sentence. Although they can sometimes be omitted, include them whenever they signal a parallel structure that might be missed by readers.

> ➤ **The project has three goals: to survey the valley for**
>   *to*
> **Inca-period sites, ‸excavate a test trench at each site,**
>   *to*
> **and ‸excavate one of those sites completely.**
>
> The writer added *to* to make it clear where one goal ends and the next begins.

Exercise 34.3   Chapter review: Correcting faulty parallelism

Edit the following passage so that parallel ideas are presented in parallel structures.

People can be classified as either Type A or Type B personalities depending on their competitiveness, how perfectionistic they are, and ability to relax. Type A people are often workaholics who not only drive themselves hard but also are driving others hard. In the workplace, employers often like Type A personalities because they tend to work quickly, punctually, and are efficient. However, because Type A people can characteristically also be impatient, verbally aggressive, or show hostility, they tend not to rise to top management positions as often as Type B people. Type A people also tend to be acutely aware of time, talking quickly, they interrupt when others are speaking, and try to complete other people's sentences. A Type

B person in contrast takes the world in stride, walking and talking more slowly, and listens attentively. Type B people are better at dealing with stress and keep things in perspective, rather than being worried the way Type A people do.

People with traits that put them clearly on either end of the continuum between Type A and Type B should try to adopt characteristics of the opposite type. For example, to moderate some of their characteristic behaviors and reduce their risk of high blood pressure and heart disease, Type A people can use exercise, relaxation techniques, diet, and meditate. Understanding one's personality is half the battle, but implementing change takes time, discipline, and patience is needed.

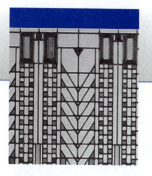

35 Fixing Misplaced and Dangling Modifiers

For a sentence to make sense, its parts must be arranged appropriately. When a modifying word, phrase, or clause is misplaced or dangling, readers get confused.

35a

mm

35a Fixing misplaced modifiers

Modifiers should come immediately before or after the words they modify. In the following sentence, the clause *after the police arrested them* modifies *protesters,* not *property.*

www.mhhe.com/
bmhh

For information
and exercises
on misplaced
modifiers, go to

**Editing >
Misplaced
Modifiers**

➤ *After the police arrested them, the*
~~The~~ protesters were charged with destroying college

property. ~~after the police arrested them.~~

Prepositional phrases used as adverbs are easy to misplace.

➤ *From the cabin's porch, the*
~~The~~ hikers watched the storm gathering force. ~~from the~~

~~cabin's porch.~~

> **Misplaced Modifiers and Grammar Checkers**
>
> Some grammar checkers will reliably highlight split infinitives (*see 35d*) but only occasionally highlight other types of misplaced modifier. One grammar checker, for example, missed the misplaced modifier *with a loud crash* in this sentence.
>
> ➤ **The valuable vase *with a loud crash* fell to the floor and broke into hundreds of pieces.**

35b Clarifying ambiguous modifiers

Adverbs can modify what precedes or follows them. Make sure that the adverbs you use are not ambiguously placed. In the following sentence, what is vehement, the objection or the argument? Changing the position of *vehemently* eliminates this ambiguity.

vehemently
➤ **Historians who object to this account ~~vehemently~~ argue**

that the presidency was never endangered.

Problems occur with limiting modifiers such as *only, even, almost, nearly,* and *just*. Check every sentence that includes one of these modifiers.

AMBIGUOUS   The restaurant *only offers* vegetarian dishes for dinner.

REVISED   The restaurant *offers only* vegetarian dishes for dinner.

or

The restaurant *offers* vegetarian dishes *only* at dinner.

35c Moving disruptive modifiers

Separating grammatical elements that belong together, such as a subject and verb, with a lengthy modifying phrase or clause disrupts the connection between the two sentence elements.

Despite their similar conceptions of the self,
➤ **Descartes and Hume, ~~despite their similar conceptions of the self,~~ deal with the issue of personal identity in different ways.**

IDENTIFY AND EDIT
Misplaced Modifiers

mm

To avoid misplaced modifiers, ask yourself these questions as you edit your writing:

❓ 1. Are all the modifiers close to the expressions they modify?

- *At the beginning of the Great Depression, people*
  ~~People~~ panicked and all tried to get their money out of the banks at the same time, forcing many banks to close. ~~at the beginning of the Great Depression.~~

❓ 2. Are any modifiers placed in such a way that they modify more than one expression? Pay particular attention to limiting modifiers such as only, even, and just.

- President Roosevelt *quickly* declared a bank holiday, ~~quickly~~ helping to restore confidence in the nation's financial system.

- Congress enacted many programs to combat the Depression *only* ~~only~~ within the first one hundred days of Roosevelt's presidency.

❓ 3. Do any modifiers disrupt the relationships among the grammatical elements of the sentence?

- *Given how entrenched segregation was at the time, the*
  ~~The~~ president's wife, Eleanor, was a surprisingly strong, ~~given how entrenched segregation was at the time,~~ advocate for racial justice in Roosevelt's administration.

35d
mm

35d Avoiding split infinitives

An **infinitive** couples the word *to* with the base form of a verb. In a **split infinitive,** one or more words intervene between *to* and the verb form. Avoid splitting infinitives with a modifier unless keeping them together results in an awkward or ambiguous construction.

In the example on the next page, the modifier *successfully* should be moved. The modifier *carefully* should probably stay where it is, however, even though it splits the infinitive *to assess.*

> *successfully,*
> ➤ **To** ~~successfully~~ **complete this assignment students have to**
>
> **carefully assess projected benefits in relation to potential**
>
> **problems.**

Exercise 35.1   Repositioning misplaced modifiers

Edit the following sentences to correct any misplaced modifiers. If a sentence is acceptable as written, circle its number.

EXAMPLE

Although
~~Global warming has received, although~~ **long a cause for**
global warming has received
concern among scientists and environmentalists, scant

attention from some governments.

1. R. Buckminster Fuller developed during his career as an architect and engineer some of the most important design innovations of the twentieth century.
2. Fuller, a weak student, was expelled from Harvard.
3. Fuller resolved to dedicate his life to improving people's lives after suffering from a period of severe depression at the age of 32.
4. Fuller intended his efficient designs to not waste precious resources.
5. Those who doubted Fuller often were proved wrong.
6. Fuller is known as the inventor of the geodesic dome to most people today.
7. The geodesic dome is a spherical structure that is both lightweight and economical, which Fuller developed in the late 1940s.
8. Today there are more than 300,000 domes around the world based on Fuller's designs.
9. His contention that wind generators on high-voltage transmission towers could supply much of the electricity the United States needs, policy makers have largely ignored.
10. His twenty-eight books have sold more than a million copies, in which he wrote about a range of social, political, cultural, and economic issues.

35e Fixing dangling modifiers

www.mhhe.com/
bmhh

For information
and exercises
on dangling
modifiers, go to

Editing > Dangling
Modifiers

A **dangling modifier** is a descriptive phrase that implies an actor different from the sentence's subject. When readers try to connect the modifying phrase with the subject, the result may be humorous as well as confusing.

DANGLING MODIFIER	*Swimming toward the boat on the horizon,* the crowded beach felt as if it were miles away.

To fix a dangling modifier, name its implied actor explicitly, either as the subject of the sentence or in the modifier itself.

REVISED	Swimming toward the boat on the horizon, *I* felt as if the crowded beach were miles away.
	or
	As *I swam* toward the boat on the horizon, the crowded beach seemed miles away.

Dangling Modifiers and Grammar Checkers

Computer grammar checkers cannot distinguish a descriptive phrase that properly modifies the subject of the sentence from one that implies a different actor. As a result, they do not flag dangling modifiers, and writers must rely on their own judgment to identify and correct them.

**35e
mm**

Simply moving a dangling modifier won't fix the problem. To make the meaning clear, you must make the implied actor in the modifying phrase explicit.

DANGLING MODIFIER	*After struggling for weeks in the wilderness,* the town pleased them mightily.

Moving the dangling modifier to the end of the sentence won't change its unintended meaning.

REVISED	After struggling for weeks in the wilderness, *they* were pleased to come upon the town.
	or
	After *they had struggled* for weeks in the wilderness, the town was a pleasing sight.

IDENTIFY AND EDIT
Dangling Modifiers

dm

To avoid dangling modifiers, ask yourself these questions when you see a descriptive phrase at the beginning of a sentence:

 1. *What is the subject of the sentence?*

> • Snorkeling in Hawaii, ancient sea turtles were an amazing sight.
>
> The subject of the sentence is *sea turtles.*

 2. *Could the phrase at the beginning of the sentence possibly describe this subject?*

> ?
>
> • Snorkeling in Hawaii, ancient sea turtles were an amazing sight.
>
> No, sea turtles do not snorkel in Hawaii or anywhere else.

 3. *Who or what is the phrase really describing? Either make that person or thing the subject of the main clause, or add a subject to the modifier.*

> *we saw*
> • Snorkeling in Hawaii, ancient sea turtles, ~~were~~ an amazing sight.
>
> *While we were snorkeling   amazed us.*
> • ~~Snorkeling~~ in Hawaii, ancient sea turtles ~~were an amazing sight.~~

Exercise 35.2   Correcting dangling modifiers

Edit the following sentences to correct any dangling modifiers. If a sentence is acceptable as is, circle its number.

EXAMPLE

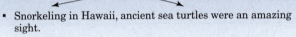

> *Passengers   that was entering the station*
> ~~Entering the station, passengers~~ waited to board the train.

1. Admired by many women artists as a pioneer in the mostly male art world, Georgia O'Keeffe lived and worked without regard to social conventions or artistic trends.
2. One of the most admired American artists of the twentieth century, her color-saturated images of cactus flowers, bleached bones, and pale skies are widely reproduced.
3. Growing up in Wisconsin, art was always important to her.
4. Defending her gifted student to the principal, one of her teachers said, "When the spirit moves Georgia, she can do more in a day than you or I can do in a week."
5. Without informing her, some of O'Keeffe's drawings were exhibited by Alfred Steiglitz at his 291 Gallery.
6. Marrying in 1924, O'Keeffe and Steiglitz enjoyed one of the most fruitful collaborations of the modernist era.
7. Despite critical and financial success in the 1920s, New York City did not provide suitable subject matter for her paintings.
8. Vacationing with a friend in the summer of 1929, O'Keeffe discovered the stark natural beauty of Taos, New Mexico.

Exercise 35.3   Chapter review: Editing for misplaced and dangling modifiers

Edit the following passage to eliminate any misplaced or dangling modifiers.

Henri Matisse and Pablo Picasso are considered often to have been the formative artists of the twentieth century. Although rivals for most of their careers, a traveling exhibit called "Matisse Picasso" exhibited their work side by side in museums in London, Paris, and New York.

Picasso's work may in comparison to Matisse's be more disturbing, and some say it is, in addition, more daring and experimental. Yet Matisse too, with his use of vivid colors and distorted shapes, was a daring innovator.

Looking for similarities, the works of both artists suggest an underlying anxiety. Yet each in different ways responded to this anxiety. Matisse painted tranquil yet often emotionally charged domestic scenes, whereas Picasso fought his inner fears with often jarringly disquieting images, by contrast.

35e
mm

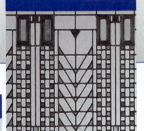

36 Using Coordination and Subordination Effectively

www.mhhe.com/
bmhh

For information
and exercises on
coordination and
subordination,
go to

Editing >
**Coordination and
Subordination**

Coordination and subordination allow you to combine and develop ideas in ways that readers can follow and understand.

Coordination gives two or more ideas equal weight. To coordinate parts within a sentence, join them with a coordinating conjunction (*and, but, or, for, nor, yet,* or *so*). To coordinate two or more sentences, use a comma plus a coordinating conjunction, or insert a semicolon.

➤ The auditorium was huge, *and* the acoustics were terrible.

➤ The tenor bellowed loudly, *but* no one in the back could hear him.

➤ Jones did not agree with her position on health care; *nevertheless,* he supported her campaign for office.

Note: When a semicolon is used to coordinate two sentences, it is often followed by a conjunctive adverb such as *moreover, nevertheless, however, therefore,* or *subsequently.*

Subordination makes one idea depend on another. Less important ideas belong in subordinate clauses. Subordinate clauses start with a relative pronoun (*who, whom, that, which, whoever, whomever, whose*) or a subordinating conjunction such as *after, although, because, if, since, when,* or *where.*

➤ The blue liquid, *which will be added to the beaker later,* must be kept at room temperature.

➤ Christopher Columbus discovered the New World in 1492, *although he never understood just what he had found.*

➤ *After writing the opening four sections,* Wordsworth put the work aside for two years.

Note: Commas often set off subordinate ideas, especially when the subordinate clause or phrase opens the sentence. (*For more on using commas, see Chapter 49, pp. 447–61.*)

If you do not fix the following problems with coordination and subordination, your readers will have difficulty following your train of thought.

36a Avoiding coordination for ideas of unequal importance

Coordination should be used only when two or more ideas deserve equal emphasis: *Smith supports bilingual education, but Johnson does not.* Subordination, not coordination, should be used to indicate information of secondary importance and to show its logical relation to the main idea.

➤ *When the*
~~The~~ police arrived, ~~and~~ the burglars ran away.

36b Keeping major ideas in main clauses

Major ideas belong in main clauses, not in subordinate clauses or phrases. The writer revised the following sentence because the subject of the paper was definitions of literacy, not those who value literacy.

➤ *Highly valued by businesspeople as well as academics, literacy*
~~Literacy, which~~ has been defined as the ability to talk

intelligently about many topics/. ~~is highly valued by~~

~~businesspeople as well as academics.~~

36c Avoiding excessive subordination

When a sentence seems overloaded, separate it into two or more sentences.

➤ Big-city mayors, ~~who are supported by public funds,~~ should

be cautious about spending taxpayers' money for personal

needs, ~~such as home furnishings,~~ especially when municipal

budget shortfalls have caused extensive job layoffs/.

They risk   *by using public funds for home furnishings.*
angering city workers and the general public/

36c
coord/sub

Exercise 36.1 Using coordination and subordination

Combine the following sets of sentences, using coordination, subordination, or both to clarify the relationships among ideas.

EXAMPLE

France was a major player in Europe's late-nineteenth-century imperial expansion. It began the conquest of Vietnam in 1858. By 1883 it controlled the entire country.

France, a major player in Europe's late-nineteenth-century imperial expansion, began its conquest of Vietnam in 1858 and controlled the entire country by 1883.

1. France divided Vietnam into three administrative regions. This was before World War II.
2. Most Vietnamese opposed French rule. Many groups formed to regain the country's independence.
3. Vietnam remained a French-administered colony during World War II. It was under Japanese control, however, from 1940 to 1945.
4. By the end of the war, a communist group called the Viet Minh had emerged as Vietnam's dominant nationalist organization. Ho Chi Minh (1890–1969) was the leader of the Viet Minh.
5. In 1945, the Viet Minh declared independence. They took control of northern Vietnam. The French, however, regained control of the south. The British helped the French.
6. The French reached an agreement with Ho Chi Minh in 1946. The agreement would have made Vietnam an autonomous country tied to France.
7. The agreement broke down. War started. The French wanted to reassert colonial control over all of Vietnam. Ho Chi Minh wanted total independence.
8. The United States supported the French. Russia and China supported the Viet Minh.
9. The French suffered a major defeat at Dien Bien Phu in 1954. After that they realized they could not defeat the Viet Minh.
10. An agreement reached in Geneva left Vietnam divided into two regions. One region was the communist-controlled north. The other region was the noncommunist south.

Exercise 36.2 Avoiding inappropriate or excessive coordination and subordination

Rewrite the numbered passages that follow to eliminate inappropriate or excessive coordination or subordination. Do not hesitate to break up long strings of clauses into two or more sentences when it seems appropriate to do so.

EXAMPLE

The Industrial Revolution triggered economic and social upheavals, including changes in family structure, patterns of work, and the distribution of wealth, and in 1848, in the wake of these upheavals, the governments of France, Italy,

and several central European countries were all threatened with revolution.

The Industrial Revolution triggered economic and social upheavals, including changes in family structure, patterns of work, and the distribution of wealth. In 1848, in the wake of these upheavals, the governments of France, Italy, and several central European countries were all threatened with revolution.

1. During the early years of the Industrial Revolution, the many thousands of people who had left the countryside to move to Europe's fast-growing cities in search of work encountered poverty, disease, lack of sanitation, and exhausting, dangerous factory jobs, making cities breeding grounds for insurrection, and this threat of unrest increased after an international financial crisis in 1848 and the epidemic of bankruptcies and unemployment that followed it.

2. France's King Louis-Phillipe, hopelessly unpopular, abdicated the throne in February and the country was thrown into a revolution in which citizens set up barricades in the narrow streets of Paris, restricting the movement of government troops.

3. Revolutionary fervor also took hold in Vienna, the capital of the Austrian Empire, and at the same time, nationalist forces gained strength in Hungary and other regions of the empire, prompting Hungarian nationalists to demand autonomy from Vienna and radicals in Prague to demand greater autonomy for the empire's Slavic peoples.

4. By the middle of 1848, however, events had begun to turn against the revolutionaries, and the rulers of the Austrian Empire used divisions among the revolutionaries to reassert their power, and the Empire provided supplies and encouragement to Romanian nationalists who feared persecution in an independent Hungary.

**36c
coord/sub**

Exercise 36.3 Chapter review: Editing for coordination and subordination

Edit the following passage to correct faulty coordination and subordination, and to eliminate choppy sentences and excessive coordination and subordination.

Germany and Italy were not always unified nations. For centuries they were divided into many city-states. They were also divided into many kingdoms, dukedoms, fiefdoms, and principalities. These city-states, kingdoms, dukedoms, fiefdoms, and principalities had maintained their autonomy for centuries.

Largely responsible for the unifications of Italy and Germany were two men. These men were Camillo di Cavour and Otto von Bismarck. Cavour became prime minister of the republic of Piedmont in 1852. Bismarck became chancellor of Prussia in 1862. Cavour was a practitioner of *realpolitik,* and *realpolitik* is a political policy based on the ruthless advancement of national interests. Bismarck was also a practitioner of *realpolitik.*

Cavour hoped to govern Piedmont in a way that would inspire other Italian states to join it to form a unified nation. Increasing the power of parliament, modernizing agriculture and industry, and building a railroad that encouraged trade with the rest of Europe, he also modernized the port of Genoa, updated the court system and installed a king, Victor Emmanuel, all of which made hopes for nationhood center on Piedmont. With the help of Napoleon III, Cavour engaged in a crafty political maneuver. Napoleon III was the emperor of France. Cavour induced Austria to attack Piedmont and then with French help defeated the Austrian armies, thus inspiring Modena and Tuscany to join Piedmont.

Bismarck used similar tactics in pursuit of unification as he prearranged French neutrality, and then he attacked and destroyed the Austrian army at Sadowa, and he eliminated Austrian influence in Prussia, and he paved the way for Prussian control of a large north German federation by 1867. Both men continued to use these tactics until they succeeded with the unification of Germany in 1871 and of Italy in 1879.

37 Varying Your Sentences

Enliven your prose by using a variety of sentence patterns.

www.mhhe.com/
bmhh

For information
and exercises on
sentence variety,
go to

Editing >
Sentence Variety

Sentence Variety and Grammar Checkers

A computer grammar checker might flag a very long sentence, but it cannot decide whether the sentence is too long.

37a Varying sentence openings

When all the sentences in a passage begin with the subject, you risk losing your readers' attention. Vary your sentences by moving a modifier to the beginning. The modifier may be a single word, a phrase, or a clause.

Eventually,
➤ ^Armstrong's innovations ~~eventually~~ became the standard.

In at least two instances, this
➤ ~~This~~ money-making strategy backfired. ~~in at least two~~

~~instances.~~

After Glaser became his manager,
➤ ^Armstrong no longer had to worry about business. ~~after~~

~~Glaser became his manager.~~

A **participial phrase** begins with an *-ing* verb (*driving*) or a past participle (*moved, driven*) and is used as a modifier. You can often move it to the beginning of a sentence for variety, but make sure that the phrase describes the explicit subject of the sentence, or you will end up with a dangling modifier (*see pp. 323–24*).

Pushing the other children aside,
➤ ^Joseph,~~ pushing the other children aside,~~ demanded that the

teacher give him a cookie first.

Stunned by the stock market crash, many
➤ ~~Many~~ brokers,~~ stunned by the stock market crash,~~

committed suicide.

37a
vary

37b   Varying sentence length and structure

Short, simple sentences will keep your readers alert if they occur in a context that also includes longer, complex sentences. Do not overuse one kind of sentence structure. Are most of your sentences short and simple? While appropriate in some scientific writing, a series of short sentences can make prose so choppy that meaning gets lost.

> **CHOPPY**   My cousin Jim is not an accountant. But he does my taxes every year. He suggests various deductions. These deductions reduce my tax bill considerably.

You can use subordination to combine a series of short, choppy sentences and form a longer, more meaningful sentence. Put the idea you want to emphasize in the main clause.

> **REVISED**   Even though he is not an accountant, my cousin Jim does my taxes every year, suggesting various deductions that reduce my tax bill considerably.

If a series of short sentences includes two major ideas of equal importance, use coordination for the two major ideas and subordinate the secondary information.

> **CHOPPY**   Bilingual education is designed for children. The native language of these children is not English. Smith supports expanding bilingual education. Johnson does not support expanding bilingual education.

> **REVISED**   Smith supports bilingual education for children whose native language is not English; Johnson, however, does not support bilingual education.

If most of your sentences are long and complex, put at least one of your ideas into a short, simple sentence. Your goal is to achieve a good mix.

> **DRAFT**   I dived quickly into the sea. I peered through my mask at the watery world. It turned darker. A school of fish went by. The distant light glittered on their bodies, and I stopped swimming. I waited to see if the fish might be chased by a shark. I was satisfied that there was no shark and continued down.

> **REVISED**   I dived quickly into the sea, peering through my mask at a watery world that turned darker as I descended. A school of fish went by, the distant light glittering on their bodies. I stopped swim-

ming and waited. Perhaps the fish were being chased by a shark? Satisfied that there was no shark, I continued down.

(For more on coordination and subordination, see pp. 326–30.)

| **Exercise 37.1** | Varying sentence openings |

Rewrite each sentence so that it does not begin with the subject.

> **EXAMPLE**   **He would ask her to marry him in his own good time.**
>
> *In his own good time, he would ask her to marry him.*

1. Germany entered World War II better prepared than the Allies, as it had in World War I.
2. The Germans, gambling on a quick victory, struck suddenly in both 1914 and 1939.
3. The United States entered World War II in 1941.
4. World War II, fought with highly mobile armies, never developed into the kind of prolonged stalemate that had characterized World War I.
5. The productive power of the United States, swinging into gear by the spring of 1943, contributed to the Allied victory.

37c Including a few cumulative and periodic sentences

37c
vary

Cumulative sentences, which add a series of descriptive participial or absolute phrases to the basic subject-plus-verb pattern, make writing more forceful. They work best in personal essays and the humanities.

➤ **The motorcycle spun out of control,** *plunging down the ravine, crashing through the fence,* **and** *coming to rest on its side.*

Cumulative sentences can also add details.

➤ **Wollstonecraft headed for France,** *her soul determined to be free, her mind committed to reason, her heart longing for love.*

Another way to increase the force of your writing is to use a few periodic sentences. In a **periodic sentence,** the key word, phrase, or idea appears at the end.

➤ **In 1946 and 1947, young people turned away from the horrors of World War II and fell in love—with the jukebox.**

Exercise 37.2   Constructing cumulative sentences

Combine the sentences in each numbered item that follows to create cumulative sentences.

> **EXAMPLE**
>
> **Europe suffered greatly in the fourteenth century. The Hundred Years War consumed France and England. Schism weakened Europe's strongest unifying institution, the Church. The Black Death swept away one third of the population.**
>
> *Europe suffered greatly in the fourteenth century, with the Hundred Years War consuming France and England; schism weakening the Church, Europe's strongest unifying institution; and the Black Death sweeping away one third of the population.*

1. The Black Death started in China around 1333. It spread to Europe over trade routes. It killed one third of the population in two years. It proved to be one of the worst natural disasters in history.
2. It was a horrible time. Dead bodies were abandoned on the streets. People were terrified of one another. Cattle and livestock were left to roam the countryside.
3. It was everyone for themselves. Friends deserted friends. Husbands left wives. Parents even abandoned children.

Exercise 37.3   Constructing periodic sentences

Rewrite the sentences that follow so that the keywords (underlined) appear at the end.

> **EXAMPLE**
>
> **Prince Gautama achieved enlightenment while sitting in deep meditation under a Bo-tree after a long spiritual quest.**
>
> *Sitting in deep meditation under a Bo-tree after a long spiritual quest, Prince Gautama achieved enlightenment.*

1. The Indus River in Pakistan was home to one of the earliest civilizations in the world, as were the Nile River in Egypt, the Tigris and Euphrates rivers in Iraq, and the Yellow River in China.
2. In 1921, archeologists discovered the remains of Harappa, one of the two great cities of the Indus civilization, which until then was unknown to modern scholars.
3. The Indus civilization, which flourished from about 2500 to 1700 BCE, had two main centers, Harappa and another city, Mohenjo-Daro.

37d Trying an occasional inversion, a rhetorical question, or an exclamation

Most sentences are declarative and follow the normal sentence pattern of subject plus verb plus object. Occasionally, though, you might try using an inverted sentence pattern or another sentence type, such as a rhetorical question or an exclamation.

You can create an **inversion** by putting the verb before the subject.

➤ **Characteristic of Smith's work are bold design and original thinking.**

Because many inversions sound odd, they should be used infrequently and carefully.

To get your readers to participate more actively, ask a question. Because you do not expect your audience to answer, this kind of question is called a **rhetorical question.**

➤ **Players injured at an early age too often find themselves without a job, without a college degree, and without physical health. Is it any wonder that a few turn to drugs and alcohol, become homeless, or end up in a morgue long before their time?**

Rhetorical questions work best in the middle or at the end of a long, complicated passage. Sometimes they can help make a transition from one topic to another. Avoid using them more than a few times in a paper, and avoid using them to begin an essay.

In academic writing, **exclamations** are rare. If you decide to use one, be sure that you want to express strong emotion and can do so without losing credibility.

➤ **Wordsworth completed the thirteen-book *Prelude* in 1805, after seven years of hard work. Instead of publishing his masterpiece, however, he devoted himself to revising it—for 45 years! The poem, in a fourteen-book version, was finally published in 1850, after he had died.**

37d

vary

Exercise 37.4   Chapter review: Revising for sentence variety

Revise the following passage for variety and emphasis using the strategies presented in this chapter.

The United Nations was established in 1945. It was intended to prevent another world war. It began with twenty-one members. Nearly every nation in the world belongs to the United Nations today.

The United Nations has four purposes, according to its charter. One purpose is to maintain international peace and security. Another is to develop friendly relations among nations. Another is to promote cooperation among nations in solving international problems and in promoting respect for human rights. Last is to provide a forum for harmonizing the actions of nations.

All of the members of the United Nations have a seat in the General Assembly. The General Assembly considers numerous topics. These topics include globalization, AIDS, and pollution. Every member has a vote in the General Assembly.

A smaller group within the United Nations has the primary responsibility for maintaining international peace and security. This group is called the Security Council. The Security Council has five permanent members. They are China, France, the Russian Federation, the United Kingdom, and the United States. The Security Council also has ten elected members. The General Assembly elects the members of the Security Council. The elected members serve for two-year terms.

38 Choosing Active Verbs

Active verbs such as *run, shout, write,* and *think* are more direct and forceful than forms of the *be* verb (*am, are, is, was, were, been, being*) or passive-voice constructions. The more active verbs you use, the clearer your writing will be.

Active Verbs and Grammar Checkers

Computer grammar checkers generally do not flag weak uses of the *be* verb. A grammar checker did not flag the sentence *The paper was an argument for a stronger police presence* because it is grammatically correct. The writer would need to notice the weak *be* verb and change the sentence to *The paper argued. . . .*

Some grammar checkers do flag most passive-voice sentences (*see section 38b*), but their suggestions for revising them can sometimes make the sentence worse.

38a Considering alternatives to *be* verbs

Be does a lot of work in English.

BE AS A LINKING VERB

Germany *is* relatively poor in natural resources.

BE AS HELPING VERB

Macbeth *was* returning from battle when he met the three witches.

Be verbs are so useful that they get overworked. Watch for weak, roundabout sentences with *be* verbs, and consider replacing those verbs with active verbs.

> **The mayor's refusal to meet with our representatives**
> *demonstrates*
> ~~is a demonstration of~~ **his lack of respect for us.**

Exercise 38.1 Editing for overuse of *be* verbs

In the following sentences, replace the *be* verbs with active verbs.

EXAMPLE

puzzled
The contradictory clues ~~were a puzzle to~~ the detective.

1. Historians are generally in agreement that the Egyptians were the inventors of sailing around 3000 BCE.
2. Many years passed before mariners were to understand that boats could sail upwind.
3. The invention of the keel was an improvement in sailboat navigation.
4. Steamships and transcontinental railroads were contributing factors in the disappearance of commercial sailing ships.
5. Today, either diesel or steam engines are the source of power for most ships.

38b
act

38b Preferring the active voice

Verbs can be in the active or passive voice. In the **active voice,** the subject of the sentence acts; in the **passive voice,** the subject is acted upon.

ACTIVE	The Senate finally passed the bill.
PASSIVE	The bill was finally passed by the Senate.

www.mhhe.com/
bmhh

For information
and exercises on
the active and
passive voices,
go to

Editing > Verbs
and Verbals

The passive voice downplays the actors as well as the action, so much so that the actors are often left out of the sentence.

> **PASSIVE** The bill was finally passed.

The active voice is more forceful, and readers usually want to know who or what does the acting.

> **PASSIVE** Polluting chemicals were dumped into the river.

> **ACTIVE** Industrial Products Corporation dumped polluting chemicals into the river.

However, when the recipient of the action is more important than the doer of the action, the passive voice is appropriate.

➤ **After her heart attack, my mother was taken to the hospital.**

Mother and the fact that she was taken to the hospital are more important than who took her to the hospital.

CHARTING the TERRITORY

Passive Voice

The passive voice is often used in scientific reports to keep the focus on the experiment and its results rather than on the experimenters.

➤ **After the bacteria were isolated, they were treated carefully with nicotine and were observed to stop reproducing.**

Exercise 38.2 Editing to avoid the passive voice

Change the verbs in the following sentences from passive to active voice. In some cases, you may have to give an identity to an otherwise unidentified actor. Circle the number of any sentence that is already in the active voice or that is better left in its passive-voice form.

> **EXAMPLE** **The milk was spilled.**
>
> *Someone spilled the milk.*

1. The remote islands of Oceania were settled by Polynesian sailors beginning in the early first millennium CE.
2. Around 500, Hawaii was reached.
3. By about 900, settlers had reached Easter Island, the most remote island in Polynesia.

4. New Zealand, the largest Polynesian island, was also the last to be settled.
5. These immensely long voyages were probably made by families of settlers in open, double-hulled sailing canoes.

Exercise 38.3   Chapter review: Using active verbs

Minimize the use of the passive voice and the *be* verbs in the following paragraph.

The idea of a lighter-than-air balloon was first conceived by inventors in the Middle Ages. Not until October 15, 1783, however, was Pilatre de Rosier successful in ascending in a hot-air balloon. Five weeks later, he and a companion were makers of history again, accomplishing the world's first aerial journey with a five-mile trip across the city of Paris. For the next century, lighter-than-air balloons were considered the future of human flight. Balloonists were able to reach heights of up to three miles and made long, cross-country journeys. In 1859, for instance, a balloonist was carried from St. Louis to Henderson, New York. Balloonists were unable, however, to control the movement of their craft. To overcome this deficiency, efforts were made to use hand-cranked propellers and even giant oars. The invention of the internal-combustion engine was what finally made it possible to create controllable, self-propelled balloons, which are known as airships. Hot air was replaced by hydrogen in the earliest airships. Hydrogen gas catches fire easily, however, and this was the doom of the airship as a major means of travel. In 1937, the German airship *Hindenburg* exploded as it was landing in New Jersey, a tragedy that was described by a radio announcer in a live broadcast. As a result, helium has replaced hydrogen in today's airships.

38b

act

39 Using Appropriate Language

Language is appropriate when it fits your topic, purpose, and audience. You can develop a sense of audience through reading how other writers in the field handle your topic.

39a Avoiding slang, regional expressions, and nonstandard English

In college papers, slang terms and the tone that goes with them should be avoided.

SLANG   In *Heart of Darkness,* we hear a lot about a *dude* named Kurtz, but we don't see the *guy* much.

REVISED   In *Heart of Darkness,* Marlow, the narrator, talks continually about Kurtz, but we meet Kurtz himself only at the end.

Like slang, regional and nonstandard expressions such as *y'all, hisself,* and *don't be doing that* work fine in conversation but not in college writing.

39b Using an appropriate level of formality

College writing assignments usually call for a style that avoids the extremes of the stuffy and the casual, the pretentious and the chatty. Revise passages that veer toward one extreme or the other.

PRETENTIOUS   Romantic lovers are characterized by a pre-occupation with a deliberately restricted set of qualities in the love object that are viewed as means to some ideal end.

REVISED   People in love see what they want to see, usually by idealizing the beloved.

39c Avoiding jargon

When specialists communicate with each other, they often use technical language. **Jargon** is the inappropriate use of specialized or technical language. You should not use language that is appropriate for specialists when you are writing for a general audience.

JARGON	An *opposition education theory* holds that children learn Spanish best *under strict discipline conditions*.
REVISED	An *alternative theory of education* holds that children learn Spanish best *when strict discipline is enforced*.

www.mhhe.com/
bmhh

For information
and exercises on
avoiding jargon,
euphemisms, and
doublespeak,
go to

Editing > Clichés,
Slang, Jargon . . .

If you need to use technical terms when writing for nonspecialists, be sure to define them.

➤ **Armstrong's innovative singing style featured "scat,"
a technique that combines "nonsense syllables [with]
improvised melodies" (Robinson 515).**

39d Avoiding euphemisms and doublespeak

Euphemisms and doublespeak have one goal: to cover up the truth.
Euphemisms substitute nice-sounding words like *correctional facility* and *passing away* for such harsh realities as *prison* and *death*.
Doublespeak is used to obscure facts and evade responsibility.

DOUBLESPEAK	Pursuant to the environmental protection regulations enforcement policy of the Bureau of Natural Resources, special management area land use permit issuance procedures have been instituted.

Avoid using words that evade or deceive.

39d
d

Exercise 39.1 Editing for informal language, pretentious language, jargon, and euphemisms

Edit the following sentences so that they are suitable for college writing.

1. With the invention of really cool steel engraving and mechanical printing presses in the nineteenth century, publishers could make tons of books like practically overnight.
2. France was the womb of nineteenth-century realism, a fecund literary land that gave birth to those behemoths of realism Stendhal, Balzac, and Flaubert.
3. Flaubert really hated the bourgeoisie because he thought they never thought about anything but cash, stuff, and looking good in front of others.
4. Flaubert's *Madame Bovary* is the story of this really bored provincial chick who dreams of being a fancy lady, cheats on her husband, and then does herself in.

5. Intense class antagonisms, combined with complex currents of historical determinism, extending back into the ancient traditions of serfdom and the czar, may precisely index the factors constitutive of the precipitant flowering of the Russian novel in the nineteenth century.

6. The present writer's former belief that nineteenth-century literature is incomprehensible is no longer operational.

**www.mhhe.com/
bmhh**

39e Avoiding biased or sexist language

For information and exercises on avoiding biased or sexist language, go to

Editing >
Word Choice

1. Biased language

Always review your writing to see if it is unintentionally biased. Be on the lookout for stereotypes that demean, ignore, or patronize people on the basis of gender, race, religion, national origin, ethnicity, physical ability, sexual orientation, occupation, or any other human condition. Revise for inclusiveness.

For example, do not assume that Irish Catholics have large families.

➤ Although the Browns are *The* Irish ~~Catholics, there are only~~ *an* ~~two *Catholic family with*~~ children. ~~in the family.~~

In addition, remember that a positive stereotype is still a stereotype.

➤ ~~Because Asian students are whizzes at math, we~~ all wanted *We* ~~them~~ in our study group. *math whizzes*

CHARTING the TERRITORY

Biased Language

The American Psychological Association recommends this test: Substitute your own group for the group you are discussing. If you are offended by the resulting statement, revise your phrasing to eliminate bias.

2. The generic use of *he* or *man*

Traditionally, the pronoun *he* and the noun *man* have been used to represent either gender. Today, however, the use of *he* or *man* or any other masculine noun to represent people in general is considered offensive.

BIASED	Everybody had his way.
REVISED	We all had our way.

BIASED	It's every man for himself.
REVISED	All of us have to save ourselves.

Follow these simple principles to avoid gender bias in your writing:

■ Replace terms that indicate gender with their genderless equivalents:

No	**Yes**
chairman	chair, chairperson
congressman	representative, member of Congress
forefathers	ancestors
man, mankind	people, humans
man-made	artificial
policeman	police officer
spokesman	spokesperson

■ Refer to men and women in parallel ways: *ladies and gentlemen, men and women, husband and wife.*

BIASED	D. H. Lawrence and Mrs. Woolf met each other, but Lawrence did not like the Bloomsbury circle that revolved around Virginia.
REVISED	D. H. Lawrence and Virginia Woolf met each other, but Lawrence did not like the Bloomsbury circle that revolved around Woolf.

39e
d

■ Replace the masculine pronouns *he, him, his,* and *himself* when they are being used generically to refer to both women and men. One way to replace masculine pronouns is to use the plural.

➤ ~~Each senator~~ *Senators* returned to ~~his district~~ *their districts* during the break.

➤ ~~A lawyer needs~~ *Lawyers need* to be frank with ~~his~~ *their* clients.

Some writers alternate *he* and *she,* and *him* and *her.* This strategy is effective but distracting. The constructions *his or her* and *he or she* are acceptable as long as they are not used excessively or more than once in a sentence.

➤ **Each student in the psychology class was to choose**

it

a book, ~~according to his or her interests,~~ to read ~~the~~

~~book~~ overnight, ~~to~~ do without ~~his or her normal~~ sleep, ~~to~~

the book the next morning,
write a short summary of ~~what he or she had read,~~ and

then ~~to~~ see if he or she dreamed about the book the

following night.

The constructions *his/her* and *s/he* are not acceptable.

Note: Using the neuter impersonal pronoun *one* can sometimes help you avoid masculine pronouns, but it can make your writing sound stuffy.

STUFFY	The American creed holds that if *one* works hard, *one* will succeed in life.
REVISED	The American creed holds that those who work hard will succeed in life.

(*For more on editing to avoid the generic use of* he, him, his, *or* himself, *see Chapter 46, pp. 404–05.*)

3. Sexist language

Avoid language that demeans or stereotypes women and men. Women are usually the explicit targets. For example, many labels and clichés imply that women are not as able or mature as men. Consider the meaning of words and phrases like *the fair sex, acting like a girl, poetess,* and *coed.*

Exercise 39.2 Editing to eliminate biased language

Identify the biased language in each of the following sentences, and rewrite each sentence using the suggestions in section 39e.

EXAMPLE

flight attendants
Because ~~stewardesses~~ travel so much, child care is an issue

for them.

1. Man is fast approaching a population crisis.
2. Each of us must do his part to reduce the production of green-house gases.
3. Every housewife should encourage her children to make re-cycling a habit, and every corporate chief executive officer should encourage his employees to carpool or take mass transit when-ever possible.
4. Congressmen should make conservation and environmental protection legislative priorities.
5. If he tried, the average motorist could help reduce our depen-dence on oil.

Exercise 39.3   Chapter review: Editing for appropriate language

Edit the following passage to make the language appropriate for a col-lege paper.

The writer of novels Henry James had many illustrious forefathers. His grandfather William traversed the Atlantic in 1789 with little more than a Latin grammar book and a desire to see the battlefields of the Revolutionary War. When William James met his maker in 1832, he left an estate worth $3 mil-lion, or about $100 million in today's cash. This little something was to be divided among eleven children and his better half, Catherine Barber James. William's fourth kid, Henry, who is often referred to as the elder Henry James so's that he is not confused with the novelist, became a lecturer and writer on metaphysics. His big thing was the doctrines of the Swedish mystic Emanuel Swedenborg. Although some thought the elder Henry James a few plates short of a picnic, his work was very well known and influential during his lifetime.

39e
d

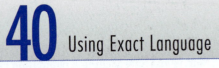

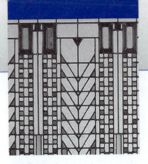

40 Using Exact Language

To convey your meaning clearly, you need to choose the right words. Is your choice of words as precise as it should be?

40a Choosing words with suitable connotations

Words have denotations and connotations. **Denotations** are the primary meanings of the word. **Connotations** are the feelings and images associated with a word.

As you revise, replace any word whose connotation does not fit what you want to say.

> *demand*
> **The players' union should ~~request~~ that the NFL amend**
>
> **its pension plan.**

If you cannot think of a more suitable word, consult a print or an online thesaurus for **synonyms**—words with similar meanings. Keep in mind, however, that most words have connotations that allow them to work in some contexts but not in others. To find out more about a synonym's connotations, look the word up in a dictionary. (*For help using the dictionary, see pp. 351–53.*)

Exercise 40.1 Choosing words with suitable connotations

Use a dictionary or thesaurus to list as many synonyms as you can for each of the underlined words in the passages that follow. Discuss why you think the authors chose the underlined words.

1. Space and time capture the imagination like no other scientific subject. . . . They form the arena of reality, the very fabric of the cosmos. Our entire existence—everything we do, think, and experience—takes place in some region of space during some interval of time. Yet science is still struggling to understand what space and time actually are.
   —BRIAN GREENE, *The Fabric of the Cosmos*

2. On Waverly Street, everybody knew everybody else. It was only one short block, after all—a narrow strip of patched and re-patched pavement, bracketed between a high stone cemetery wall at one end and the commercial clutter of Govans Road at the

other. The trees were <u>elderly</u> maples with lumpy, <u>bulbous</u> trunks. The <u>squat</u> clapboard houses seemed mostly front <u>porch</u>.

—ANNE TYLER, *Saint Maybe*

40b Including specific and concrete words

Specific words name particular kinds of things or items, such as *pines* or *college sophomores*.

Concrete words name things we can sense by touch, taste, smell, hearing, and sight, such as *velvet* or *sweater*.

By creating images that appeal to the senses, specific and concrete words make writing more precise.

VAGUE	The trees were affected by the bad weather.
PRECISE	The tall pines shook in the gale.

As you edit, develop specific and concrete details. Also check for overused, vague terms—such as *factor, thing, good, nice,* and *interesting*—and replace them with more specific and concrete words.

➤ The protesters were charged with ~~things~~ they never ~~did.~~
                                  crimes   *committed.*

Exercise 40.2 Including specific and concrete words

Draw on your own knowledge, experience, and imagination to rewrite the following paragraph with invented details described in specific and concrete language.

40b
d

EXAMPLE

Niagara Falls is an awe-inspiring sight.

The waters of the Niagara River flow over the edge of the half-mile-wide, crescent-shaped Horseshoe Falls and plunge with a roar to the bottom of the cataract two hundred feet below.

    Last summer I worked as an intern at a company in a field that interests me. The work was hard and the hours were long, but I gained a lot of experience. At first I was assigned only routine office work. As I learned more about the business, however, my employers began to give me more interesting tasks. By the end of the summer I was helping out on several high-priority projects. My employers liked my work and offered me another internship for the following summer.

40c   Using standard idioms

Idioms are customary forms of expression. They are not always logical and are hard to translate. Often they involve selecting the right preposition. If you are not sure which preposition to use, look up the main word in a dictionary.

Some verbs, called **phrasal verbs,** include a preposition to make their idiomatic meaning complete:

➤   **Henry *made up* with Gloria.**

➤   **Henry *made off* with Gloria.**

➤   **Henry *made out* with Gloria.**

(For a list of common idiomatic expressions, see Chapter 48, pp. 439–40. For more help with phrasal verbs and idiomatic expressions, see Chapter 48, pp. 437–40.)

40d   Avoiding clichés

A **cliché** is an overworked expression that no longer creates a vivid picture in a reader's imagination. Rephrase clichés in plain language.

made some good observations.

➤   **The speaker at our conference** ~~hit the nail on the head.~~
                                                         ^

The list that follows gives some clichés to avoid.

Examples of Clichés

agony of suspense	deep, dark secret	pretty as a picture
beat a hasty retreat	depths of despair	quick as a flash
beyond the shadow of a doubt	few and far between	rise to the occasion
blind as a bat	flat as a pancake	sadder but wiser
calm, cool, and collected	give 110 percent	sink or swim
cold, hard facts	green with envy	smart as a whip
cool as a cucumber	heave a sigh of relief	sneaking suspicion
crazy as a loon	hit the nail on the head	straight and narrow
dead as a doornail	last but not least	tired but happy
	the other side of the coin	tried and true
	pale as a ghost	ugly as sin
	pass the buck	untimely death
		white as a sheet
		worth its weight in gold

40e Using suitable figures of speech

Figures of speech make writing vivid by supplementing the literal meaning of words. A **simile** is a comparison that contains the word *like* or *as*.

➤ **His smile was like the sun peeking through after a rainstorm.**

A **metaphor** is an implied comparison. It treats one thing or action as if it were something else.

➤ **The critic's slash-and-burn review devastated the cast.**

Because it is compressed, a metaphor is often more forceful than a simile.

Only compatible comparisons make prose vivid. Be careful not to mix metaphors.

MIXED	His presentation of the plan was so *crystal clear* that in a *burst of speed* we decided *to come aboard*.
REVISED	His clear presentation immediately convinced us to support the plan.

40e
d

Exercise 40.3 Recognizing figures of speech

Identify and explain the figures of speech (simile or metaphor) in the following passages.

EXAMPLE

A miss is as good as a mile.

This expression is a simile suggesting that an error is an error, whether small ("a miss") or large ("a mile").

1. Her voice is full of money.
   —F. Scott Fitzgerald, *The Great Gatsby*

2. America is woven of many strands; I would recognize them and let it so remain. . . . Our fate is to become one, and yet many.
   —Ralph Ellison, *Invisible Man*

3. Our military forces are one team—in the game to win regardless of who carries the ball.

   —OMAR BRADLEY, testimony to the Committee on Armed Services, House of Representatives, October 19, 1949

4.   We are such stuff
   As dreams are made on, and our little life
   Is rounded with a sleep.
   —SHAKESPEARE, *The Tempest,* IV, i, 149

40f   Avoiding the misuse of words

Avoid mistakes in your use of new terms and unfamiliar words. Consult a dictionary whenever you include an unfamiliar word in your writing.

            exhibited
➤ **The aristocracy exuded numerous vices, including greed**

    licentiousness.
and license.

Exercise 40.4   Avoiding the misuse of words

In the following sentences, replace any of the underlined words that are misused with a word with an appropriate denotation, and circle those that are properly used. For help, consult a dictionary or the Glossary of Usage (*pp. 353–62*).

EXAMPLE

                               complement
Computer software and computer hardware compliment
    each other.
one another.

1. The nineteenth-century Englishman Charles Babbage was probably the first person to conceive of a general-purpose computing machine, but the ability to build one <u>alluded</u> him.
2. Because she was able to <u>imply</u> the kinds of instructions that would work with Babbage's machine, some historians <u>cite</u> Ada Lovelace, daughter of the poet Byron, as the first computer programmer.

3. Incredulous as it may seem, the first general-purpose digital electronic computer was 100 feet long and 10 feet high but had less computing power than one of today's inexpensive laptop computers.

4. The U.S. government was the principle source of funding for some of the most important advances in computing after World War II.

5. Without the invention of the transistor, today's small, powerful computing devices would not have been plausible.

40g Using the dictionary

A standard desk dictionary—such as the *Random House Webster's College Dictionary, Webster's New World Dictionary,* or the *American Heritage College Dictionary*—provides definitions of words as well as information about usage, the correct spellings of important place names, the official names of countries with their areas and populations, the names of capital cities, biographical entries, lists of abbreviations and symbols, names and locations of colleges and universities, titles and correct forms of address, and conversion tables for weights and measures. (*For ESL dictionaries, see Chapter 48, p. 425.*)

An entry from the *Random House Webster's College Dictionary* follows. The labels point to the kinds of information discussed in the following sections.

**40g
d**

Phonetic symbols showing pronunciation.

Word endings and grammatical abbreviations.

Dictionary entry.

com•pare (kəmpâr´), *v.,* **-pared, -par • ing,** *n.* —*v.t.* **1.** to examine (two or more objects, ideas, people, etc.) in order to note similarities and differences. **2.** to consider or describe as similar; liken: *"Shall I compare thee to a summer's day?"* **3.** to form or display the degrees of comparison of (an adjective or adverb). —*v.i.* **4.** to be worthy of comparison: *Whose plays can compare with Shakespeare's?* **5.** to be in similar standing; be alike: *This recital compares with the one he gave last year.* **6.** to appear in quality, progress, etc., as specified: *Their development compares poorly with that of neighbor nations.* **7.** to make comparisons. —*n.* **8.** comparison: *a beauty beyond compare.* —**Idiom. 9. compare notes,** to exchange views, ideas, or impressions. [1375–1425; late ME < OF *comperer* < L *comparāre* to place together, match, v. der. of *compar* alike, matching (see COM-, PAR)] —**com•par´er,** *n.* —**Usage.** A traditional rule states that COMPARE should be followed by *to* when it points out likenesses between unlike persons or things: *she compared his handwriting to knotted string.* It should be followed by *with,* the rule says, when it examines two entities of the same general class for similarities or differences: *She compared his handwriting with mine.* This rule, though sensible, is not always followed, even in formal speech and writing. Common practice is to use *to* for likeness between members of different classes: *to compare a language to a living organism.* Between members of the same category, both *to* and *with* are used: *Compare the Chicago of today with* (or *to*) *the Chicago of the 1890s.* After the past participle COMPARED, either *to* or *with* is used regardless of the type of comparison.

Definitions as transitive verb (*v.t.*).

Definitions as intransitive verb (*v.i.*).

Definition as noun (*n.*).

Etymology.

Special meaning.

Usage note.

CHARTING the TERRITORY

Dictionaries

In the library's reference section, you can find specialized dictionaries such as biographical and geographical dictionaries; foreign language dictionaries; dictionaries of first lines of poems and of famous quotations; dictionaries of legal and medical terms; and dictionaries of philosophy, sociology, engineering, and other disciplines.

1. Spelling, word division, and pronunciation

Entries in a dictionary are listed in alphabetical order according to their standard spelling. In the *Random House Webster's College Dictionary,* the verb *compare* is entered as **com•pare.** The dot separates the word into its two syllables. If you had to divide the word *compare* at the end of a line, you would place a hyphen where the dot appears.

Phonetic symbols in parentheses following the entry show its correct pronunciation. The second syllable of *compare* receives the greater stress when you pronounce the word correctly: you say "comPARE." In this dictionary, an accent mark (´) appears after the syllable that receives the primary stress.

Plurals of nouns are usually not given if they are formed by adding an *s,* unless the word is foreign (*gondolas, dashikis*). Irregular plurals—such as *children* for *child*—are noted.

> **Note:**
>
> Some dictionaries list alternate spellings, always giving the preferred spelling first or placing the full entry under the preferred spelling only.

2. Word endings and grammatical labels

The abbreviation *v.* immediately after the pronunciation tells you that *compare* is most frequently used as a verb. The next abbreviation, *n.,* indicates that *compare* can sometimes function as a noun, as in the phrase *beyond compare.*

Here is a list of common abbreviations for grammatical terms:

adj.	adjective	*prep.*	preposition
adv.	adverb	*pron.*	pronoun
conj.	conjunction	*sing.*	singular
interj.	interjection	*v.*	verb
n.	noun	*v.i.*	intransitive verb
pl.	plural	*v.t.*	transitive verb
poss.	possessive		

The *-pared* shows the simple past and past participle form of the verb; the present participle form, *-paring,* follows, indicating that *compare* drops the final *e* when *-ing* is added.

3. Definitions and word origins

In the sample entry on page 351, the definitions begin after the abbreviation *v.t.,* which indicates that the first three meanings relate to *compare* as a transitive verb. A little further down in the entry, *v.i.* introduces definitions of *compare* as an intransitive verb. Next, after *n.,* comes the definition of *compare* as a noun. Finally, the word *Idiom* signals a special meaning not included in the previous definitions.

Included in most dictionary entries is an **etymology**—a brief history of the word's origins—set off in brackets. There we see the date of the first known use of the word in English together with the earlier words from which it is derived. *Compare* came into English between 1375 and 1425 and was derived from the Old French word *comperer,* which came from Latin.

4. Usage

Some main entries in the dictionary conclude with examples of and comments about the common usage of the word.

41 Glossary of Usage

41 usage

The following words and expressions are often confused, misused, or considered nonstandard. This list will help you use these words precisely.

www.mhhe.com/
bmhh

For an online glossary of usage, go to

**Editing >
Word Choice**

a, an   Use *a* with a word that begins with a consonant sound: *a cat, a dog, a one-sided argument, a house.* Use *an* with a word that begins with a vowel sound: *an apple, an X-ray, an honor.*

accept, except   *Accept* is a verb meaning "to receive willingly": *Please accept my apologies. Except* is a preposition meaning "but": *Everyone except Julie saw the film.*

adapt, adopt   *Adapt* means "to adjust or become accustomed to": *They adapted to the customs of their new country. Adopt* means "to take as one's own": *We adopted a puppy.*

advice, advise   *Advice* is a noun; *advise* is a verb: *I took his advice and deeply regretted it. I advise you to disregard it, too.*

affect, effect   As a verb, *affect* means "to influence": *Inflation affects our sense of security.* As a noun, *affect* means "a feeling or an emotion": *To study affect, psychologists probe the unconscious.* As a noun, *effect* means "result": *Inflation is one of the many effects of war.* As a verb, *effect* means "to make or accomplish": *Inflation has effected many changes in the way we spend money.*

agree to, agree with   *Agree to* means "consent to"; *agree with* means "be in accord with": *They will agree to a peace treaty, even though they do not agree with each other on all points.*

ain't   A slang contraction for *is not, am not,* or *are not, ain't* should not be used in formal writing or speech.

all/all of, more/more of, some/some of   Except before some pronouns, the "of" in these constructions can usually be eliminated: *All France rejoiced. Some students cut class.* But: *All of us wish you well.*

all ready, already   *All ready* means "fully prepared"; *already* means "previously": *We were all ready to go out when we discovered that Jack had already ordered a pizza.*

all right, alright   The spelling *alright* is an alternate, but many educated readers still think it is incorrect in standard written English: *He told me it was all right to miss class tomorrow.*

all together, altogether   *All together* expresses unity or common location; *altogether* means "completely," often in a tone of ironic understatement: *At the NRA convention, it was altogether startling to see so many guns set out all together in one place.*

allude, elude, refer to   *Allude* means "to refer indirectly": *He alluded to his miserable adolescence. Elude* means "to avoid" or "to escape from": *She eluded the police for nearly two days.* Do not use *allude* to mean "to refer directly": *The teacher referred* [not *alluded*] *to page 468 in the text.*

almost, most   *Almost* means "nearly." *Most* means "the greater part of." Do not use *most* when you mean *almost: He wrote to me about almost* [not *most*] *everything he did. He told his mother about most things he did.*

a lot   *A lot* is always two words. Do not use *alot.*

A.M., AM, a.m.   These abbreviations mean "before noon" when used with numbers: *6 A.M., 6 a.m.* Be consistent, and do not use the abbreviations as a synonym for *morning: In the morning* [not *a.m.*], *the train is full.*

among, between   Generally, use *among* with three or more nouns, and *between* with two: *The distance between Boston and Knoxville is a thousand miles. The desire to quit smoking is common among those who have smoked for a long time.*

amoral, immoral   *Amoral* means "neither moral nor immoral" and "not caring about moral judgments"; *immoral* means "morally wrong": *Unlike such amoral natural disasters as earthquakes and hurricanes, war is intentionally violent and therefore immoral.*

amount, number   Use *amount* for quantities you cannot count; use *number* for quantities you can count: *The amount of oil left underground in the world is a matter of dispute, but the number of countries that profit from oil is well known.*

an   *See* a, an.

anxious, eager   *Anxious* means "fearful": *I am anxious before a test. Eager* signals strong interest or desire: *I am eager to be done with that exam.*

anymore, any more   *Anymore* means "no longer." *Any more* means "no more." Both are used in negative contexts: *I do not enjoy dancing anymore. I do not want any more peanut butter.*

anyone/any one, anybody/any body, everyone/every one, every-body/every body   *Anyone, anybody, everyone,* and *everybody* are indefinite pronouns: *Anybody can make a mistake.* When the pronoun *one* or the noun *body* is modified by the adjective *any* or *every,* the words should be separated by a space: *A good mystery writer accounts for every body that turns up in the story.*

as   Do not use *as* as a synonym for *since, when,* or *because: I told him he should visit Alcatraz since* [not *as*] *he was going to San Francisco. When* [not *as*] *I complained about the meal, the cook said he did not like to eat there himself. Because* [not *as*] *we asked her nicely, our teacher decided to cancel the exam.*

as, like   In formal writing, avoid the use of *like* as a conjunction: *He sneezed as if* [not *like*] *he had a cold. Like* is perfectly acceptable as a preposition that introduces a comparison: *She handled the reins like an expert.*

at   Avoid the use of *at* to complete the notion of *where:* not *Where is Michael at?* but *Where is Michael?*

awful, awfully   Use *awful* and *awfully* to convey the emotion of terror or wonder (awe-full): *The vampire flew out the window with an awful shriek.* In writing, do not use *awful* to mean "bad" or *awfully* to mean "very" or "extremely."

awhile, a while   *Awhile* is an adverb: *Stay awhile with me. A while* is an article and a noun. Always use *a while* after a preposition: *Many authors are unable to write anything else for a while after they publish their first novel.*

41

usage

being as, being that   Do not use *being as* or *being that* as synonyms for *since* or *because: Because* [not *being as*] *the mountain was there, we had to climb it.*

belief, believe   *Belief* is a noun meaning "conviction"; *believe* is a verb meaning "to have confidence in the truth of": *Her belief that lying was often justified made it hard for us to believe her story.*

beside, besides   *Beside* is a preposition meaning "next to" or "apart from": *The ski slope was beside the lodge. She was beside herself with joy. Besides* is both a preposition and an adverb meaning "in addition to" or "except for": *Besides a bicycle, he will need a tent and a pack.*

better   Avoid using *better* in expressions of quantity: *Crossing the continent by train took more than* [not *better than*] *four days.*

between   *See* among, between.

bring, take   Use *bring* when an object is being moved toward you, and *take* when it is being moved away: *Please bring me a new disk and take the old one home with you.*

but that, but what   In expressions of doubt, avoid writing *but that* or *but what* when you mean *that: I have no doubt that* [not *but that*] *you can learn to write well.*

can, may   *Can* refers to ability; *may* refers to possibility or permission: *I see that you can skateboard without crashing into people; nevertheless, you may not skateboard on the promenade.*

can't hardly   This double negative is ungrammatical and self-contradictory: *I can* [not *can't*] *hardly understand algebra. I can't understand algebra.*

capital, capitol   *Capital* refers to a city; *capitol* refers to a building where lawmakers meet: *Protesters traveled to the state capital to converge on the capitol steps. Capital* also refers to wealth or resources.

censor, censure   *Censor* means "to remove or suppress material"; *censure* means "to reprimand formally": *The Chinese government has been censured by the U.S. Congress for censoring newspapers.*

cite, sight, site   The verb *cite* means "to quote or mention": *Be sure to cite all your sources in your bibliography.* As a noun, the word *sight* means "view": *It was love at first sight. Site* is a noun meaning "a particular place"; locations on the Internet are referred to as *sites.*

compare to, compare with   Use *compare to* to point out similarities between two unlike things: *She compared his singing to the croaking of a wounded frog.* Use *compare with* for differences or likenesses between two similar things: *Compare Shakespeare's* Antony and Cleopatra *with Dryden's* All for Love.

complement, compliment   *Complement* means "to go well with": *I consider sauerkraut the perfect complement to sausages. Compliment* means "praise": *She received many compliments on her thesis.*

conscience, conscious   The noun *conscience* means "a sense of right and wrong": *His conscience bothered him.* The adjective *conscious* means "awake" or "aware": *I was conscious of a presence in the room.*

continual, continuous   *Continual* means "repeated regularly and frequently": *She continually checked her computer for new e-mail. Continuous* means "extended or prolonged without interruption": *The car alarm made a continuous wail in the night.*

could of, should of, would of   Avoid these ungrammatical forms of *could have, should have,* and *would have.*

criteria, criterion   *Criteria* is the plural form of the Latin word *criterion,* meaning "standard of judgment": *The criteria are not very strict. The most important criterion is whether you can do the work.*

data   *Data* is the plural form of the Latin word *datum,* meaning "fact." Although *data* is often used informally as a singular noun, in writing, treat *data* as a plural noun: *The data indicate that recycling has gained popularity.*

differ from, differ with   *Differ from* expresses a lack of similarity; *differ with* expresses disagreement: *The ancient Greeks differed less from the Persians than we often think. Aristotle differed with Plato on some important issues.*

different from, different than   The correct idiom is *different from*. Avoid *different than*: *The east coast of Florida is very different from the west coast.*

discreet, discrete   *Discreet* means "tactful" or "prudent"; *discrete* means "separate" or "distinct": *What's a discreet way of telling them that these are two discrete issues?*

disinterested, uninterested   *Disinterested* means "impartial": *We expect members of a jury to be disinterested. Uninterested* means "indifferent" or "unconcerned": *Most people today are uninterested in alchemy.*

don't, doesn't   *Don't* is the contraction for *do not* and is used with *I, you, we, they,* and plural nouns; *doesn't* is the contraction for *does not* and is used with *he, she, it,* and singular nouns: *You don't know what you're talking about. He doesn't know what you're talking about either.*

due to   *Due to* is an overworked and often confusing expression when it is used for *because of.* Use *due to* only in expressions of time in infinitive constructions or in other contexts where the meaning is "scheduled": *The plane is due to arrive in one hour. He is due to receive a promotion this year.*

each and every   Use one of these words or the other but not both: *Every cow came in at feeding time. Each one had to be watered.*

each other, one another   Use *each other* in sentences involving two subjects and *one another* in sentences involving more than two: *Husbands and wives should help each other. Classmates should share ideas with one another.*

eager   *See* anxious, eager.

effect   *See* affect, effect.

e.g., i.e.   The abbreviation *e.g.* stands for the Latin words meaning "for example"; the abbreviation *i.e.* stands for the Latin for "that is": *Come as soon as you can, i.e., today or tomorrow. Bring fruit with you, e.g., apples and peaches.* In formal writing, replace the abbreviations with the English words: *Keats wrote many different kinds of lyrics—for example, odes, sonnets, and songs.*

either, neither   Both *either* and *neither* are singular: *Neither of the two boys has played the game. Either of the two girls is willing to show you the way home. Either* has an intensive use that *neither* does not, and when it is used as an intensive, *either* is always negative: *She told him she would not go either.* (*For* [either . . . or] *and* [neither . . . nor] *constructions, see p. 385.*)

elicit, illicit   The verb *elicit* means "to draw out"; the adjective *illicit* means "unlawful": *The detective was unable to elicit any information about other illicit activity.*

elude   *See* allude, elude, refer to.

emigrate, immigrate   *Emigrate* means "to move away from one's country": *My grandfather emigrated from Greece in 1905. Immigrate* means "to move to another country and settle there": *Grandpa immigrated to the United States.*

41

usage

eminent, imminent, immanent *Eminent* means "celebrated" or "well known": *Many eminent Victorians were melancholy and disturbed. Imminent* means "about to happen" or "about to come": *In August 1939, many Europeans sensed that war was imminent. Immanent* refers to something invisible but dwelling throughout the world: *Medieval Christians believed that God's power was immanent through the universe.*

etc. The abbreviation *etc.* stands for the Latin *et cetera,* meaning "and others" or "and other things." Because *and* is included in the abbreviation, do not write *and etc.* In a series, a comma comes before *etc.,* just as it would before the coordinating conjunction that closes a series: *He brought string, wax, paper, etc.* In most college writing, it is better to end a series of examples with a final example or the words *and so on.*

everybody/every body, everyone/every one *See* anyone/any one . . .

except *See* accept, except.

expect, suppose *Expect* means "to hope" or "to anticipate": *I expect a good grade on my final paper. Suppose* means "to presume": *I suppose you did not win the lottery on Saturday.*

explicit, implicit *Explicit* means "stated outright"; *implicit* means "implied, unstated": *Her explicit instructions were to go to the party without her, but the implicit message she conveyed was disapproval.*

farther, further *Farther* describes geographical distances: *Ten miles farther on is a hotel. Further* means "in addition" when geography is not involved: *He said further that he didn't like my attitude.*

fewer, less *Fewer* refers to items that can be counted individually; *less* refers to general amounts: *Fewer people signed up for indoor soccer this year than last. Your argument has less substance than you think.*

firstly *Firstly* is common in British English but not in the United States. *First, second, third,* and so on are the accepted forms.

flaunt, flout *Flaunt* means "to wave" or "to show publicly" with a delight tinged with pride and even arrogance: *He flaunted his wealth by wearing overalls lined with mink. Flout* means "to scorn" or "to defy," especially in a public way, seemingly without concern for the consequences: *She flouted the traffic laws by running through red lights.*

former, latter *Former* refers to the first and *latter* to the second of two things mentioned previously: *Mario and Alice are both good cooks; the former is fonder of Chinese cooking, the latter of Mexican.*

further *See* farther, further.

get In formal writing, avoid colloquial uses of *get,* as in *get with it, get it all together, get-up-and-go, get it,* and *that gets me.*

good, well *Good* is an adjective and should not be used in place of the adverb *well: He felt good about doing well on the exam.*

half, a half, half a Write *half, a half,* or *half a* but not *half of, a half a,* or *a half of: Half the clerical staff went out on strike. I want a half-dozen eggs to throw at the actors. Half a loaf is better than none, unless you are on a diet.*

hanged, hung   People are *hanged* by the neck until dead. Pictures and all other things that can be suspended are *hung*.

hopefully   *Hopefully* means "with hope." It is often misused to mean "it is hoped": *We waited hopefully for our ship to come in* [not *Hopefully, our ship will come in*].

i.e.   *See* e.g., i.e.

if . . . then   Avoid using these words in tandem. Redundant: *If I get my license, then I can drive a cab.* Better: *If I get my license, I can drive a cab. Once I get my license, I can drive a cab.*

illicit   *See* elicit, illicit.

immigrate   *See* emigrate, immigrate.

imminent   *See* eminent, imminent, immanent.

immoral   *See* amoral, immoral.

implicit   *See* explicit, implicit.

imply, infer   *Imply* means "to suggest something without stating it directly": *By putting his fingers in his ears, he implied that she should stop singing. Infer* means "to draw a conclusion from evidence": *When she dozed off in the middle of his declaration of eternal love, he inferred that she did not feel the same way about him.*

in, in to, into   *In* refers to a location inside something: *Charles kept a snake in his room. In to* refers to motion with a purpose: *The resident manager came in to capture it. Into* refers to movement from outside to inside or from separation to contact: *The snake escaped by crawling into a drain. The manager ran into the wall, and Charles got into big trouble.*

incredible, incredulous   The *incredible* cannot be believed; the *incredulous* do not believe. Stories and events may be *incredible;* people are *incredulous: Nancy told an incredible story of being abducted by a UFO over the weekend. We were all incredulous.*

infer   *See* imply, infer.

inside of, outside of   The "of" is unnecessary in these phrases: *He was outside the house.*

ironically   *Ironically* means "contrary to what was or might have been expected." It should not be confused with *surprisingly,* which means "unexpected," or with *coincidentally,* which means "occurring at the same time or place." *Ironically, his fastball lost speed after his arm healed.*

irregardless   This construction is a double negative because both the prefix *ir-* and the suffix *-less* are negatives. Use *regardless* instead.

it's, its   *It's* is a contraction, usually for *it is* but sometimes for *it has: It's often been said that English is a difficult language to learn. Its* is a possessive pronoun: *The dog sat down and scratched its fleas.*

kind(s)   *Kind* is singular: *This kind of house is easy to build. Kinds* is plural and should be used only to indicate more than one kind: *These three kinds of toys are better than those two kinds.*

41

usage

lay, lie *Lay* means "to place." Its main forms are *lay, laid,* and *laid.* It generally has a direct object, specifying what has been placed: *She laid her book on the steps and left it there. Lie* means "to recline" and does not take a direct object. Its main forms are *lie, lay,* and *lain: She often lies awake at night.*

less *See* fewer, less.

like *See* as, like.

literally *Literally* means "actually" or "exactly as written": *Literally thousands gathered along the parade route.* Do not use *literally* as an intensive adverb when it can be misleading or even ridiculous, as here: *His blood literally boiled.*

loose, lose *Loose* is an adjective that means "not securely attached"; *lose* is a verb that means "to misplace": *Better tighten that loose screw before you lose the whole structure.*

may *See* can, may.

maybe, may be *Maybe* is an adverb meaning "perhaps": *Maybe he can get a summer job as a lifeguard. May be* is a verb phrase meaning "is possible": *It may be that I can get a job as a lifeguard, too.*

moral, morale *Moral* means "lesson," especially a lesson about standards of behavior or the nature of life: *The moral of the story is do not drink and drive. Morale* means "attitude" or "mental condition": *Office morale dropped sharply after the dean was arrested.*

more/more of *See* all/all of . . .

more important, more importantly The correct idiom is *more important,* not *more importantly.*

most *See* almost, most.

myself (himself, herself, etc.) Pronouns ending with *-self* refer to or intensify other words: *Jack hurt himself. Standing in the doorway was the man himself.* When you are unsure whether to use *I* or *me, she* or *her,* or *he* or *him* in a compound subject or object, you may be tempted to substitute one of the *-self* pronouns. Don't do it: *The quarrel was between her and me* [not *myself*]. (*For more on pronouns, see Part 7, starting on p. 403.*)

neither *See* either, neither.

nohow, nowheres These words are nonstandard for *anyway, in no way, in any way, in any place,* and *in no place.* Do not use them in formal writing.

number *See* amount, number.

off of Omit the *of: She took the painting off the wall.*

one another *See* each other, one another.

outside of *See* inside of, outside of.

plus Avoid using *plus* as a substitute for *and: He had to walk the dog, do the dishes, empty the garbage, and* [not *plus*] *write a term paper.*

practicable, practical *Practicable* is an adjective applied to things that can be done: *A space program that would land human beings on Mars is now practicable. Practical* means "sensible": *Many people do not think such a journey is practical.*

precede, proceed *Precede* means "come before"; *proceed* means "go forward": *Despite the heavy snows that preceded us, we managed to proceed up the hiking trail.*

previous to, prior to Avoid these wordy and somewhat pompous substitutions for *before.*

principal, principle *Principal* is an adjective meaning "most important" or a noun meaning "the head of an organization" or "a sum of money": *Our principal objections to the school's principal are that he is a liar and a cheat. Principle* is a noun meaning "a basic standard or law": *We believe in the principles of honesty and fair play.*

proceed *See* precede, proceed.

raise, rise *Raise* means "to lift or cause to move upward." It takes a direct object—someone raises something: *I raised the windows in the classroom. Rise* means "to go upward." It does not take a direct object—something rises by itself: *We watched the balloon rise to the ceiling.*

real, really Do not use the words *real* or *really* when you mean *very*: *The cake was very* [not *real* or *really*] *good.*

reason . . . is because This is a redundant expression. Use either *the reason is that* or *because*: *The reason he fell on the ice is that he cannot skate. He fell on the ice because he cannot skate.*

refer to *See* allude, elude, refer to.

relation, relationship *Relation* describes a connection between things: *There is a relation between smoking and lung cancer. Relationship* describes a connection between people: *The brothers have always had a close relationship.*

respectfully, respectively *Respectfully* means "with respect": *Treat your partners respectfully. Respectively* means "in the given order": *The three Williams she referred to were Shakespeare, Wordsworth, and Yeats, respectively.*

rise *See* raise, rise.

set, sit *Set* is usually a transitive verb meaning "to establish" or "to place." It takes a direct object, and its principal parts are *set, set,* and *set: DiMaggio set the standard of excellence in fielding. She set the box down in the corner. Sit* is usually intransitive, meaning "to place oneself in a sitting position." Its principal parts are *sit, sat,* and *sat: The dog sat on command.*

41

usage

shall, will *Shall* was once the standard first-person future form of the verb *to be* when a simple statement of fact was intended: *I shall be twenty-one on my next birthday.* Today, most writers use *will* in the ordinary future tense for the first person: *I will celebrate my birthday by throwing a big party. Shall* is still used in questions. *Shall we dance?*

should of *See* could of, should of, would of.

site *See* cite, sight, site.

some Avoid using the adjective *some* in place of the adverb *somewhat: He felt somewhat* [not *some*] *better after a good night's sleep.*

some of *See* all/all of . . .

somewheres Use *somewhere* or *someplace* instead.

suppose *See* expect, suppose.

sure Avoid confusing the adjective *sure* with the adverb *surely: The dress she wore to the party was surely bizarre.*

sure and *Sure and* is often used colloquially. In formal writing, *sure to* is preferred: *Be sure to* [not *be sure and*] *get to the wedding on time.*

take *See* bring, take.

that, which Many writers use *that* for restrictive (i.e., essential) clauses and *which* for nonrestrictive (i.e., nonessential) clauses: *The bull that escaped from the ring ran through my china shop, which was located in the square.* (*Also see Chapter 49, pp. 451–55.*)

their, there, they're *Their* is a possessive pronoun: *They gave their lives. There* is an adverb of place: *She was standing there. They're* is a contraction of *they are: They're reading more poetry this semester.*

this here, these here, that there, them there When writing, avoid these nonstandard forms.

to, too, two *To* is a preposition; *too* is an adverb; *two* is a number: *The two of us got lost too many times on our way to his house.*

try and *Try to* is the standard form: *Try to* [not *try and*] *understand.*

uninterested *See* disinterested, uninterested.

use, utilize *Utilize* seldom says more than *use,* and the simpler term is almost always better: *We must learn how to use the computer's zip drive.*

verbally, orally To say something *orally* is to say it aloud: *We agreed orally to share credit for the work, but when I asked her to confirm it in writing, she refused.* To say something *verbally* is to use words: *His eyes flashed anger, but he did not express his feelings verbally.*

wait for, wait on People *wait for* those who are late; they *wait on* tables.

weather, whether The noun *weather* refers to the atmosphere: *She worried that the weather would not clear up in time for the victory celebration. Whether* is a conjunction referring to a choice between alternatives: *I can't decide whether to go now or next week.*

well *See* good, well.

whether *See* weather, whether.

which, who, whose *Which* is used for things, and *who* and *whose* for people: *My fountain pen, which I had lost last week, was found by a child who had never seen one before, whose whole life had been spent with ballpoints.*

who, whom Use *who* with subjects and their complements. Use *whom* with objects (of verbs). *The person who will fill the post is John, whom you met last week.* (Also see Chapter 46, pp. 415–16.)

will *See* shall, will.

would of *See* could of, should of, would of.

your, you're *Your* is a possessive pronoun: *Is that your new car? You're* is a contraction of *you are: You're a lucky guy.*

Like musical compositions, grammatical writing follows specific conventions that create a harmonious and meaningful whole.

There is a core simplicity to the
English language and its American
variant, but it's a slippery core.

—STEPHEN KING

Editing
for Grammar
Conventions

7 Editing for Grammar Conventions

WRITING OUTCOMES

Conventions

This section will help you learn to do the following:

- Recognize the rules of standard American English grammar
- Correctly use verbs **(45)**, pronouns **(46)**, adjectives **(47)**, adverbs **(47)**, and other parts of speech
- Avoid grammatical errors commonly made by multilingual writers **(48)**

Test Yourself:

Take an online quiz at www.mhhe.com/bmhh to test your familiarity with the topics covered in chapters 42–48. As you read the following chapters, pay special attention to the sections that correspond to any questions you answer incorrectly.

42 Fixing Sentence Fragments

A word group that begins with a capital letter and ends with a period may not be a complete sentence. A complete sentence meets all three of the following requirements:

www.mhhe.com/ bmhh

For information and exercises on sentence fragments, go to

Editing > Sentence Fragments

- **A sentence names a *subject,*** the who or what that the sentence addresses.

- **A sentence has a complete *verb* that indicates tense, person, and number.**

- **A sentence includes at least one independent *clause.***
  An independent clause has a subject and a complete verb and does not begin with a subordinating word such as *although, because, since, that, unless, which,* or *while.*

In the following example, the first word group meets all three requirements and is a complete sentence. Although the second word group has a subject and a complete verb, they are part of a dependent clause that begins with the subordinating word *that.* Because the second word group does not have an independent clause with a subject and a complete verb, it is not a complete sentence.

POSSIBLE FRAGMENT   Pool hustlers deceive their opponents in many ways. For example, deliberately putting so much spin on the ball that it jumps out of the intended pocket.

You can fix fragments in one of two ways: Either transform them into sentences or attach them to a nearby independent clause.

➤ **Pool hustlers deceive their opponents in many ways. For**

  they
  example, deliberately putting so much spin on the ball that

  it jumps out of the intended pocket.

➤ **Pool hustlers deceive their opponents in many ways/,**

  for example, by
  For example, deliberately putting so much spin on the

  ball that it jumps out of the intended pocket.

42 frag

365

Fragments and Grammar Checkers

Grammar checkers identify some fragments, but they will not tell you what the fragment is missing or how to edit it. Grammar checkers can also miss fragments without subjects that could be interpreted as commands. Consider the following fragment from a passage about the mathematical achievements of the ancient Maya: *Develop the concept of zero, for example.*

42a Repairing dependent-clause fragments

Fragments often begin with a subordinating word such as *although, because, even though, since, so that, whenever,* or *whereas.* Usually, a fragment that begins with a subordinating word can be attached to a nearby independent clause.

➤ **None of the thirty-three subjects indicated any concern**

about the amount or kind of fruit the institution served/,

even
~~Even~~ though all of them identified diet as an important issue.

Sometimes it is better to transform such a fragment into a complete sentence by deleting the subordinating word.

➤ **The solidarity of our group was undermined in two ways.**

Participants
~~When participants~~ either disagreed about priorities or

advocated significantly different political strategies.

CHARTING the TERRITORY

Intentional Fragments

Advertisers often use attention-getting fragments: "Nothing but Net." "Because you're worth it." Occasionally, you may want to use a sentence fragment for stylistic reasons. Keep in mind, however, that advertising and college writing have different contexts and purposes. In formal writing, use deliberate sentence fragments sparingly.

IDENTIFY AND EDIT
Fragments

frag

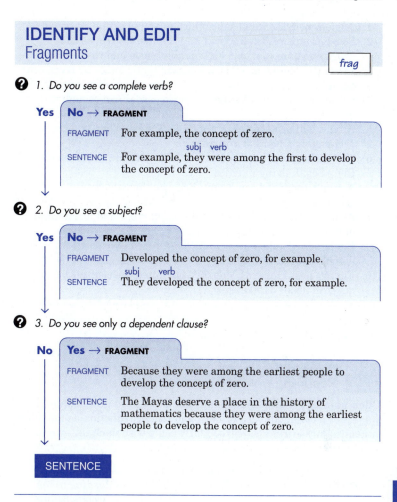

❷ 1. *Do you see a complete verb?*

Yes | **No →** **FRAGMENT**

FRAGMENT   For example, the concept of zero.

SENTENCE   For example, they were among the first to develop
the concept of zero.

❷ 2. *Do you see a subject?*

Yes | **No →** **FRAGMENT**

FRAGMENT   Developed the concept of zero, for example.

SENTENCE   They developed the concept of zero, for example.

❷ 3. *Do you see only a dependent clause?*

No | **Yes →** **FRAGMENT**

FRAGMENT   Because they were among the earliest people to
develop the concept of zero.

SENTENCE   The Mayas deserve a place in the history of
mathematics because they were among the earliest
people to develop the concept of zero.

SENTENCE

42a
frag

Exercise 42.1   Editing to repair dependent-clause fragments

Correct the dependent-clause fragments in the following items by attaching them to a sentence or by eliminating or replacing the subordinating word.

EXAMPLE

The most commonly traded stone in Mesopotamia was
                              which
obsidian/, ~~Which~~ is black, volcanic, and glasslike.

1. Ancient people traded salt. Which is an important nutrient.
2. Some groups resorted to war and conquest. Because they wanted to gain control over valuable goods and resources.
3. When they could, people transported large stones by river. Since doing so required less effort than other means of moving them.
4. Obsidian is hard and makes a sharp edge. Even though it is brittle.
5. After a while, a type of currency developed. When traders began exchanging silver bars or rings.
6. The earliest writing appeared in Mesopotamia. After people there began living in cities.
7. Agriculture thrived in Egypt. Because the Nile flooded regularly.
8. Although the Egyptians had abundant crops and large supplies of limestone. They imported many goods.
9. Egypt added gold objects to its lengthy list of exports. After its artisans began to work the precious metal in about 4000 BCE.
10. Egypt's first king was Menes. Who united the country by conquest in about 3150 BCE.

42b Repairing phrase fragments

Often unintentional fragments are **phrases,** word groups that lack a subject or a complete verb or both and usually function as modifiers or nouns. Phrase fragments frequently begin with **verbals**—words derived from verbs, such as *putting* or *to put.*

FRAGMENT	That summer, we had the time of our lives. *Fishing in the early morning, splashing in the lake after lunch, exploring the woods before dinner, and playing Scrabble until bedtime.*

One way to fix this fragment is to transform it into an independent clause with its own subject and verb:

➤ That summer, we had the time of our lives. ~~Fishing~~ *We fished* in the early morning, ~~splashing~~ *splashed* in the lake after lunch, ~~exploring~~ *explored* the woods before dinner, and ~~playing~~ *played* Scrabble until bedtime.

Another way to fix the problem is to attach the fragment to the part of the previous sentence that it modifies (in this case, *the time of our lives*).

➤ **That summer, we had the time of our lives/, ~~Fishing~~** *fishing* **in the**

    early morning, splashing in the lake after lunch, exploring

    the woods before dinner, and playing Scrabble until bedtime.

Phrase fragments can also begin with one-word prepositions such as *as, at, by, for, from, in, of, on,* or *to*. To correct these, it is usually easiest to attach them to a nearby sentence.

➤ **Impressionist painters often depicted their subjects in**

    everyday situations/, ~~At~~ *at* **a restaurant, perhaps, or by the**

    seashore.

Exercise 42.2 Identifying fragments

Underline the fragments in the following passage, and identify each as either a phrase (without a subject or verb) or a dependent clause.

> **EXAMPLE**   **I am headed to the library tonight.**
>   *dependent clause*
>   **Because I have a paper due.**

42b
frag

    Pool hustlers deceive their opponents in many ways. Sometimes appearing unfamiliar with the rules of the game. They may try acting as if they are drunk. Or pretend to be inept. For example, they will put so much spin on the ball that it jumps out of the intended pocket. So their opponents will be tricked into betting. Some other ways to cheat. When their opponents are not looking, pool hustlers may remove their own balls from the table. Then change the position of the balls on the table. Because today's pool balls have metallic cores. Hustlers can use electromagnets to affect the path of the balls. Be aware of these tricks!

Exercise 42.3 Editing to repair phrase fragments

Repair the phrase fragments in the items that follow by attaching them to a sentence or adding words to turn them into sentences.

EXAMPLE

such

Film music can create a mood/ ~~Such~~ as romantic,

lighthearted, or mysterious.

1. The ominous music prepares us for a shocking scene. And confuses us when the shock does not come.
2. Filmmakers may try to evoke nostalgic feelings. By choosing songs from a particular era.
3. The musical producer used a mix of traditional songs and new compositions. In the Civil War drama *Cold Mountain*.
4. Usually, filmmakers edit the images first and add music later. To be sure that the music supports the visual elements.
5. Music can provide transitions between scenes. Marking the passage of time, signaling a change of place, or foreshadowing a shift in mood.
6. Exactly matching the rhythms of the music to the movement on screen is known as "Mickey Mousing." After the animated classic.
7. To create atmosphere, filmmakers sometimes use sounds from nature. Such as crashing waves, bird calls, and moaning winds.
8. Do not underestimate the effect of a short "dead track," the complete absence of sound. Forcing us to look intently at the image.

42c Repairing other types of fragments

Word groups that start with transitions or with words that introduce examples, appositives, lists, and compound predicates can also cause problems.

1. Word groups that start with transitions

Some fragments start with two- or three-word prepositions that function as transitions, such as *as well as, as compared with, except for, in addition to, in contrast with, in spite of,* or *instead of.*

➤ **For sixty-five years, the growth in consumer spending has**

as

been both steep and steady/, ~~As~~ compared with the growth

in gross domestic product (GDP), which has fluctuated

significantly.

2. Words and phrases that introduce examples

It is always a good idea to check word groups beginning with *for example, like, specifically,* or *such as.*

➤ Elizabeth I of England faced many dangers as a princess.

       she fell
For example, ~~falling~~ out of favor with her sister, Queen Mary,

  was
and ~~being~~ imprisoned in the Tower of London.

3. Appositives

An **appositive** is a noun or noun phrase that renames a noun or pronoun.

➤ In 1965, Lyndon Johnson increased the number of troops in

     a
Vietnam/, ⋀ former French colony in southeast Asia.

4. Lists

Usually, you can connect a list to the preceding sentence using a colon. If you want to emphasize the list, consider using a dash instead.

➤ In the 1930s, three great band leaders helped popularize

jazz/: Louis Armstrong, Benny Goodman, and Duke Ellington.

5. Compound predicates

A **compound predicate** is made up of at least two verbs as well as their objects and modifiers, connected by a coordinating conjunction such as *and, but,* or *or.* The parts of a compound predicate have the same subject and should be together in one sentence.

➤ The group gathered at dawn at the base of the mountain/

  and
~~And~~ assembled their gear in preparation for the morning's

climb.

42c
frag

Exercise 42.4	Chapter review: Editing for sentence fragments

Edit the following passage to repair fragments.

According to the United States Constitution, which was ratified in 1788, the president and vice president of the United States were not to be elected directly by the people in a popular election. But elected indirectly by an "electoral college," made up of "electors." Who were at first often chosen by the state legislatures. In the early nineteenth century, the population of the United States grew rapidly and electors were increasingly chosen by statewide popular vote. Gradually making the electoral college system more democratic. Nonetheless, in the elections of 1824, 1876, 1888, and 2000, the elected candidate won the vote in the electoral college. But not a majority of the popular vote.

43 Repairing Comma Splices and Run-on Sentences

A **comma splice** is a sentence with at least two independent clauses joined by only a comma.

COMMA SPLICE   Dogs that compete in the annual Westminster Dog Show are already champions, they have each won at least one dog show before arriving at Madison Square Garden.

A **run-on sentence,** sometimes called a **fused sentence,** does not even have a comma between the independent clauses, making it difficult for readers to tell where one clause ends and the next begins.

RUN-ON   From time to time, new breeds enter the ring the Border collie is a recent addition to the show.

www.mhhe.com/
bmhh

For information and exercises on comma splices and run-on sentences, go to

Editing > Comma Splices or Editing > Run-on Sentences

Comma splices and run-ons often occur when clauses are linked with a transitional expression such as *as a result, for example, in addition, in other words,* or *on the contrary* or a conjunctive adverb such as *however, consequently, moreover,* or *nevertheless.* (*See p. 375 for a list of familiar conjunctive adverbs and transitional expressions.*)

COMMA SPLICE	Rare books can be extremely valuable, for example, an original edition of Audubon's Birds of America is worth thousands of dollars.

RUN-ON	Most students complied with the new policy however a few refused to do so.

Run-ons may also occur when a sentence's second clause either specifies or explains its first clause.

RUN-ON	The economy changed in 1991 corporate bankruptcies increased by 40 percent.

Comma Splices, Run-on Sentences, and Grammar Checkers

Computer grammar checkers are unreliable at distinguishing between properly and improperly joined independent clauses. One grammar checker, for example, correctly flagged this sentence for incorrect comma usage: *Many history textbooks are clear, some are hard to follow.* It failed, however, to flag this longer alternative: *Many history textbooks are clear and easy to read, some are dense and hard to follow.*

You can repair comma splices and run-on sentences in one of five ways:

- Join the two clauses with a comma and a coordinating conjunction (*and, but, or, nor, for, so, yet*).
- Join the two clauses with a semicolon.
- Separate the clauses into two sentences.
- Turn one of the independent clauses into a dependent clause.
- Transform the two clauses into a single independent clause.

43
cs/run-on

Exercise 43.1 Identifying comma splices and run-on sentences

Bracket the comma splices and run-on sentences in the following passage. For each error, note if it is a comma splice (CS) or a run-on sentence (RO).

EXAMPLE	[**The Gutenberg Bible is one of the first printed**
	CS
	books, copies are extremely rare.]

Rare books can be extremely valuable. Most books have to be in good shape to fetch high prices nevertheless some remain valuable no matter what. A first edition of Audubon's *Birds of America* can be worth more than a million dollars however it must be in good condition. On the other hand, even without a cover, an early edition of Cotton Mather's *An Ecclesiastical History of New England* will be worth at least three thousand dollars. Generally speaking, the newer a book is the more important its condition, even a book from the 1940s will have to be in excellent condition to be worth three figures. There are other factors that determine a book's value, certainly whether the author has signed it is important. Even students can collect books for instance they can search for bargains and great "finds" at yard and garage sales. In addition, used-book and author sites on the Internet offer opportunities for beginning collectors.

43a   Joining two clauses with a comma and a coordinating conjunction such as *and* or *but*

Be sure to choose the coordinating conjunction that most clearly expresses the logical relationship between the clauses.

➤ John is a very stubborn person, so I had a hard time

convincing him to let me take the wheel.

43b   Joining two clauses with a semicolon

A semicolon tells readers that two clauses are logically connected. However, a semicolon does not spell out the logic of the connection.

➤ Most students complied with the new policy; a few

refused to do so.

To show the logic of the connection, you can add a conjunctive adverb or transitional expression.

                                                ; however,
➤ Most students complied with the new policy, a few refused.

Familiar Conjunctive Adverbs and Transitional Expressions

also	incidentally	now
as a result	indeed	nonetheless
besides	in fact	of course
certainly	in other words	on the contrary
consequently	instead	otherwise
finally	in the meantime	similarly
for example	likewise	still
for instance	meanwhile	then
furthermore	moreover	therefore
however	nevertheless	thus
in addition	next	undoubtedly

The conjunctive adverb or transitional expression is followed by a comma when it appears at the beginning of the second clause. It can also appear in the middle of a clause, set off by two commas, or at the end, preceded by a comma.

➤ Most students complied with the new policy/; a few refused.
, however,

➤ Most students complied with the new policy/; a few refused.
, however

When the first independent clause introduces or expands on the second one, you can use a colon instead of a semicolon.

➤ Professor Johnson then revealed his most important point:

the paper would count for half my grade.

Exercise 43.2   Editing to repair comma splices and run-on sentences

43b
cs/run-on

Some of the sentences below contain comma splices, and some are run-ons. Circle the number of each sentence that is correct. Edit those that are not correct using either (1) a semicolon and, if appropriate, a conjunctive adverb or transitional expression or (2) a comma with a co-ordinating conjunction.

EXAMPLE   Slavery has always been an oppressive
but
institution, its severity has varied from society

to society throughout history.

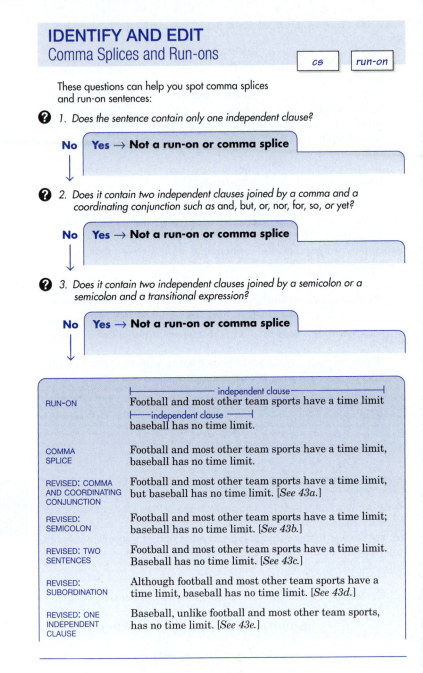

IDENTIFY AND EDIT
Comma Splices and Run-ons

| cs | run-on |

These questions can help you spot comma splices and run-on sentences:

? 1. *Does the sentence contain only one independent clause?*

No ↓ | **Yes →** Not a run-on or comma splice

? 2. *Does it contain two independent clauses joined by a comma and a coordinating conjunction such as* and, but, or, nor, for, so, *or* yet?

No ↓ | **Yes →** Not a run-on or comma splice

? 3. *Does it contain two independent clauses joined by a semicolon or a semicolon and a transitional expression?*

No ↓ | **Yes →** Not a run-on or comma splice

RUN-ON	├─────── independent clause ───────┤ Football and most other team sports have a time limit ├── independent clause ──┤ baseball has no time limit.
COMMA SPLICE	Football and most other team sports have a time limit, baseball has no time limit.
REVISED: COMMA AND COORDINATING CONJUNCTION	Football and most other team sports have a time limit, but baseball has no time limit. [*See 43a.*]
REVISED: SEMICOLON	Football and most other team sports have a time limit; baseball has no time limit. [*See 43b.*]
REVISED: TWO SENTENCES	Football and most other team sports have a time limit. Baseball has no time limit. [*See 43c.*]
REVISED: SUBORDINATION	Although football and most other team sports have a time limit, baseball has no time limit. [*See 43d.*]
REVISED: ONE INDEPENDENT CLAUSE	Baseball, unlike football and most other team sports, has no time limit. [*See 43e.*]

1. The earliest large societies probably did not depend on slave labor, but that does not mean the people in them were free to work where and how they pleased.
2. All early civilizations were autocratic in a sense all people in them were slaves.
3. No one knows when slavery began, it was common in many ancient agricultural civilizations.
4. The ancient Egyptians enslaved thousands of people from Nubia and other parts of Africa, some of these people were then sent to Mesopotamia.
5. Egypt's kings also used slaves to build some of the country's most famous monuments, for example, the pyramids were almost entirely the work of slaves.
6. Some stones in the Great Pyramid at Giza weigh nearly one hundred tons they could never have been set in place without the effort of thousands of workers.
7. In ancient Mesopotamia, slavery was not necessarily a lifelong condition, in fact slaves could sometimes work their way to freedom.
8. In both Egypt and Mesopotamia, slaves could sometimes own property.

43c Separating clauses into two sentences

The simplest way to correct comma splices and run-on sentences is to turn the clauses into separate sentences.

➤ I realized that it was time to choose/ ~~either~~ I had to learn *. Either*

how to drive, or I had to move back to the city.

When the two independent clauses are part of a quotation, with a phrase such as *he said* or *she noted* between them, each clause should be a separate sentence.

➤ "This was the longest day of my life," she said/.

"~~unfortunately,~~ it's not over yet." *"Unfortunately,*

43d Turning one of the independent clauses into a dependent clause

Remember that readers will expect subsequent sentences to tell them more about the subject of the main clause.

43d
cs/run-on

> *Although most*
> ~~Most~~ students complied with the new policy, ~~however~~ a few
> ^   ^
>
> refused to do so.

43e Transforming two clauses into one independent clause

Transforming two clauses into one clear and correct independent clause is often worth the work.

> I realized that it was time ~~to choose./~~ either ~~I had~~ to learn
>
> how to drive or ~~I had~~ to move back to the city.

Sometimes you can change one of the clauses to a phrase and place it next to the word it modifies.

> *, first printed in the nineteenth century,*
> Baseball cards are an obsession among some collectors~~/. the~~
> ^
>
> ~~cards were first printed in the nineteenth century.~~

Exercise 43.3 Editing to repair comma splices and run-on sentences

Some of the sentences below contain comma splices, and some are run-ons. Circle the number of each sentence that is correct. Edit those that are not correct by (1) separating the clauses into two sentences, (2) changing one clause into a dependent clause introduced by a subordinating word, or (3) combining the clauses into one independent clause.

EXAMPLE

The human population of the world, ~~was~~ no more than about
^
10 million at the beginning of the agricultural revolution

10,000 years ago, ~~it~~ had increased to about 800 million by the

beginning of the industrial revolution in the eighteenth

century.

1. Globally, population has increased steadily particular regions have suffered sometimes drastic declines.
2. For example, Europe lost about one-third of its population when the bubonic plague struck for the first time in the fourteenth century.
3. The plague was not the only catastrophe to strike Europe in the fourteenth century, a devastating famine also slowed population growth at the beginning of the century.
4. Images of death and destruction pervade the art of the time these images reflect the demoralizing effect of the plague.
5. The native population of Mexico collapsed in the wake of European conquest and colonization in the sixteenth century, it dropped from perhaps as many as 25 million in 1500 to little more than 1 million by 1600.
6. Hernando Cortés used diplomacy and superior military technology—horses and cannons—to conquer the Aztecs, whose forces vastly outnumbered his.
7. These were not the only reasons for Spanish success, however, at least as important was the impact of a smallpox epidemic on Aztec population and morale.
8. The population decline had many causes, these included the conquerors' efforts to destroy native culture and exploit native labor as well as the devastating effect of disease.

Exercise 43.4   Chapter review: Editing for comma splices and run-ons

Turn back to Exercise 43.1 (*p. 373*). Edit the paragraph to eliminate comma splices and run-ons using the methods described in this chapter.

Exercise 43.5   Chapter review: Editing for comma splices and run-ons

Edit the passage that follows to eliminate comma splices and run-on sentences.

> The economy of the United States has always been turbulent. Many people think that the Great Depression of the 1930s was the only economic cataclysm this country has suffered the United States has had a long history of financial panics and upheavals. The early years of the nation were no exception.

43e

cs/run-on

Before the Revolution, the American economy was closely linked with Britain's, during the war and for many years after it, Britain barred the import of American goods. Americans, however, continued to import British goods with the loss of British markets the new country's trade deficit ballooned. Eventually, this deficit triggered a severe depression social unrest followed. The economy began to recover at the end of the 1780s with the establishment of a stable government, the opening of new markets to American shipping, and the adoption of new forms of industry. Exports grew steadily throughout the 1790s, indeed the United States soon found itself in direct competition with both England and France.

The American economy suffered a new setback beginning in 1803 England declared war on France. France and England each threatened to impound any American ships engaged in trade with the other. President Thomas Jefferson sought to change the policies of France and England with the Embargo Act of 1807, it prohibited all trade between the United States and the warring countries. Jefferson hoped to bring France and England to the negotiating table, the ploy failed. The economies of France and England suffered little from the loss of trade with the United States, meanwhile the United States' shipping industry came almost to a halt.

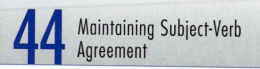

44 Maintaining Subject-Verb Agreement

Verbs must agree with their subjects in **person** (first, second, or third—*I, we; you; he, she, it, they*) and **number** (singular or plural). For regular verbs, the present tense *-s* or *-es* ending is added to the verb if its subject is third-person singular; otherwise, the verb has no ending.

Present Tense Forms of a Regular Verb: *Read*

	SINGULAR	PLURAL
FIRST PERSON	I *read.*	We *read.*
SECOND PERSON	You *read.*	You *read.*
THIRD PERSON	He, she, it *reads.*	They *read.*

Note, however, that the verb *be* has irregular forms in both the present and the past tense.

Present Tense and Past Tense Forms of the Irregular Verb *Be*

	SINGULAR	PLURAL
FIRST PERSON	I *am/was* here.	We *are/were* here.
SECOND PERSON	You *are/were* here.	You *are/were* here.
THIRD PERSON	He, she, it *is/was* here.	They *are/were* here.

www.mhhe.com/
bmhh

For information and exercises on subject-verb agreement, go to

**Editing >
Subject-Verb
Agreement**

The verbs *have* and *do* have the following forms in the present tense.

Present Tense Forms of the Verb *Have*

	SINGULAR	PLURAL
FIRST PERSON	I *have.*	We *have.*
SECOND PERSON	You *have.*	You *have.*
THIRD PERSON	He, she, it *has.*	They *have.*

**44
sv agr**

Present Tense Forms of the Verb *Do* and Its Negative *Don't*

	SINGULAR	PLURAL
FIRST PERSON	I *do/don't.*	We *do/don't.*
SECOND PERSON	You *do/don't.*	You *do/don't.*
THIRD PERSON	He, she, it *does/doesn't.*	They *do/don't.*

Exercise 44.1 Identifying subject-verb agreement

In each sentence, underline the subject, and circle the verb that goes with it.

> **EXAMPLE** Graphic design <u>studios</u> ((require)/requires) their
>
> designers to be trained in the use of design
>
> software.

1. Nowadays, computers (gives/give) graphic designers a great deal of freedom.
2. Before computers, a design (was/were) produced mostly by hand.
3. Alternative designs (is/are) produced much faster on the computer than by hand.
4. With computers, a designer (is/are) able to reduce or enlarge text in seconds.
5. Page layout programs (takes/take) some of the drudgery out of combining images with text.
6. Designers (has/have) the option of removing blemishes and other imperfections from photographs.
7. They (doesn't/don't) have to make special prints to show their work to others.
8. Designs (is/are) e-mailed as attachments all the time.
9. Still, the design professional (doesn't/don't) feel that the computer is anything more than just another tool.
10. Nonetheless, to be a graphic designer today, you (needs/need) to be ready to spend a lot of time staring at a screen.

44a When a word group separates the subject from the verb

To locate the subject of a sentence, find the verb and then ask the *who* or *what* question about it ("Who is?" "What is?"). Does that subject match the verb in number?

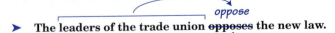

> ➤ The leaders of the trade union ~~opposes~~ the new law.

> The answer to the question "Who opposes?" is *leaders,* a plural noun, so the verb should be in the plural form: *oppose.*

IDENTIFY AND EDIT
Problems with Subject-Verb Agreement

agr

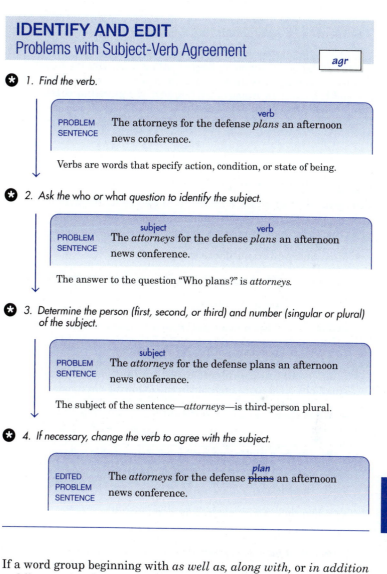

✪ 1. *Find the verb.*

> | PROBLEM SENTENCE | verb
The attorneys for the defense *plans* an afternoon news conference. |
>
> Verbs are words that specify action, condition, or state of being.

✪ 2. *Ask the* who or what *question to identify the subject.*

> | PROBLEM SENTENCE | subject   verb
The *attorneys* for the defense *plans* an afternoon news conference. |
>
> The answer to the question "Who plans?" is *attorneys.*

✪ 3. *Determine the person (first, second, or third) and number (singular or plural) of the subject.*

> | PROBLEM SENTENCE | subject
The *attorneys* for the defense plans an afternoon news conference. |
>
> The subject of the sentence—*attorneys*—is third-person plural.

✪ 4. *If necessary, change the verb to agree with the subject.*

> | EDITED PROBLEM SENTENCE | plan
The *attorneys* for the defense ~~plans~~ an afternoon news conference. |

44a

sv agr

If a word group beginning with *as well as, along with,* or *in addition to* follows a singular subject, the subject does not become plural.

➤   *opposes*
 My teacher, as well as other faculty members, ~~oppose~~ the

 new school policy.

Subject-Verb Agreement and Grammar Checkers

A grammar checker failed to flag this sentence for correction: *The candidate's position on foreign policy issues trouble some voters.* The subject is the singular noun *position,* so the verb should be *troubles.* Apparently, however, the grammar checker interpreted the word *issues* as the subject.

44b Compound subjects

Compound subjects are made up of two or more parts joined by either a coordinating conjunction (*and, or, nor*) or a correlative conjunction (*both . . . and, either . . . or, neither . . . nor*).

- **Most compound subjects are plural.**

   PLURAL   *The king and his advisers were* shocked by this turn of events.

   PLURAL   This poem's *first line and last word have* a powerful effect on the reader.

- **Some compound subjects are singular.** Compound subjects should be treated as singular in the following circumstances:

   - When they refer to the same entity:

      ➤ *My best girlfriend and most dependable advisor is* my mother.

   - When they are considered as a single unit:

      ➤ In some ways, *forty acres and a mule continues* to be what is needed.

   - When they are preceded by the word *each* or *every:*

      ➤ *Each* man, woman, and child *deserves* respect.

▪ **Some compound subjects can be either plural or singular.**
Compound subjects connected by *or, nor, either . . . or,* or *neither . . .
nor* can take either a singular or a plural verb, depending on the
subject that is closest to the verb.

SINGULAR   **Either the children or *their mother is***

            to blame.

PLURAL   **Neither the experimenter nor *her subjects were***

            aware of the takeover.

44c   Collective subjects

A **collective noun** names a unit made up of many persons or things,
treating it as an entity, such as *audience, family, group,* and *team.*

▪ **Most often, collective nouns are singular.** Words such as
news, physics, and *measles* are usually singular as well, despite
their *-s* ending. Units of measurement used collectively, such as
six inches or *20%,* are also treated as singular.

➤ The *audience is* restless.

➤ That *news leaves* me speechless.

➤ *One-fourth* of the liquid *was* poured into test tube 1.

▪ **Some collective subjects are plural.** When the members of a
group are acting as individuals, the collective subject can be considered plural.

➤ The *group were* passing around a bottle of beer.

You may want to add a modifying phrase that contains a plural
noun to make the sentence clearer and avoid awkwardness.

➤ The *group of troublemakers were* passing around

     a bottle of beer.

When units of measurement refer to people or things, they are
plural.

44c
sv agr

> ➤ *One-fourth* of the students in the class *are* failing

the course.

44d Indefinite subjects

Indefinite pronouns do not refer to a specific person or item.

■ **Most indefinite pronouns are singular.** The following indefinite pronouns are always singular: *anybody, anyone, anything, each, either, everybody, everyone, everything, neither, nobody, no one, none, nothing, one, somebody, someone,* and *something.*

> ➤ *Everyone* in my hiking club *is* an experienced climber.

None and *neither* are always singular.

> ➤ In the movie, five men set out on an expedition,

but *none returns.*

> ➤ *Neither sees* a way out of this predicament.

■ **Some indefinite pronouns are always plural.** A handful of indefinite pronouns that mean more than one by definition (*both, few, many, several*) are always plural.

> ➤ *Both* of us *want* to go to the rally for the environment.

■ **Some indefinite pronouns can be either plural or singular.** Some indefinite pronouns (*some, any, all, most*) may be either plural or singular depending on whether they refer to a plural or singular noun in the context of the sentence.

> ➤ *Some* of the *book is* missing, but *all* of the *papers are*

here.

Exercise 44.2 Editing for subject-verb agreement

Underline the simple subjects and verbs in each of the following sentences, and then check for subject-verb agreement. Circle the number of each correct sentence. Repair the other sentences by changing the verb form.

> **EXAMPLE** The <u>audience</u> for new productions of
> *appears*
> Shakespeare's plays ~~appear~~ to be growing.

1. Designers since the invention of printing has sought to create attractive, readable type.
2. A layout shows the general design of a book or magazine.
3. Half of all ad pages contains lots of white space.
4. The size of the page, width of the margins, and style of type is some of the things that concern a designer.
5. China and Japan were centers for the development of the art of calligraphy.
6. Neither a standard style of lettering nor a uniform alphabet were prevalent in the early days of the printing press.
7. A pioneering type designer and graphic artist were Albrecht Dürer.
8. A number of contemporary typefaces show the influence of Dürer's designs.
9. A design committee approve any changes to the look of a publication.
10. Each letter and punctuation mark are designed for maximum readability.

44e   When the subject comes after the verb

➤ **Out back behind the lean-to *stand an old oak tree and a***

weeping willow.

In sentences that begin with *there is* or *there are,* the subject always follows the verb.

➤ **There *is* a worn wooden *bench* in the shade of the two trees.**

44f   Subject complement

A **subject complement** renames and specifies the sentence's subject. It follows a **linking verb** that joins the subject to its description or definition. In the sentence on the next page, the verb has been changed to agree with *gift,* the subject, instead of *books,* the subject complement.

44f

sv agr

is

➤ One gift that gives her pleasure ~~are~~ books.
^

(*For more information on linking verbs and subject complements, see Chapter 61, p. 523, and Chapter 62, p. 530.*)

44g Relative pronouns

When a relative pronoun such as *who, which,* or *that* is the subject of a dependent clause, it is taking the place of a noun that appears earlier in the sentence—its **antecedent.** The verb that goes with *who, which,* or *that* needs to agree with this antecedent.

➤ Measles is a childhood *disease that has* dangerous

side effects.

The phrase *one of the* implies more than one and is, therefore, plural. *Only one of the* implies just one, however, and is singular.

PLURAL   Tuberculosis is *one of the* diseases *that have*

long, tragic histories in many parts of the world.

SINGULAR   Barbara is the *only one of the* scientists *who has*

a degree in physics.

Exercise 44.3 Editing for subject-verb agreement problems

In some of the sentences below, the verb does not agree with the subject. Circle the number of each sentence in which subject and verb agree. In the others, change verbs as needed to bring subjects and verbs into agreement.

is

EXAMPLE   The best part of the play ~~are~~ her soliloquies.
^

1. The Guerilla Girls are a group of women who acts on behalf of female artists.
2. One of their main concerns are to combat the underrepresentation of women artists in museum shows.
3. No one knows how many Guerilla Girls there are, and none of them have ever revealed her true identity.
4. The Guerilla Girls maintain their anonymity by appearing only in gorilla masks.
5. Some people claim that a few famous artists is members of the Guerilla Girls.

6. Their story begin in 1985, when the Museum of Modern Art in New York exhibited a major survey of contemporary art.
7. Fewer than ten percent of the artists represented was women.
8. Not everyone is amused by the protests of the Guerilla Girls.
9. They often shows up in costume at exhibits dominated by the work of male artists.
10. Several of the Guerilla Girls have coauthored a book.

44h Phrases beginning with *-ing* verbs

A **gerund phrase** is an *-ing* verb form followed by objects, complements, or modifiers. When a gerund phrase is the subject in a sentence, it is singular.

➤ *Experimenting with drugs is* **a dangerous rave practice.**

44i Titles of works, names of companies, or words representing themselves

➤ **Ernest Hemingway's** *For Whom the Bell Tolls is* **arguably**

his darkest work.

➤ *China Airlines is* **based in Taiwan.**

➤ **The phrase** *dog days designates* **the hottest part of the summer.**

44i
sv agr

Exercise 44.4 Chapter review: Editing for subject-verb agreement

Edit the passage to correct subject-verb agreement errors.

The end of the nineteenth century saw the rise of a new kind of architecture. Originating in response to the development of new building materials, this so-called modern architecture characterizes most of the buildings we sees around us today.

Iron and reinforced concrete makes the modern building possible. Previously, the structural characteristics of wood and stone limited the dimensions of a building. Wood-frame structures becomes unstable above a certain height. Stone can bear great weight, but architects building in stone confronts severe limits on the height of a structure in relation to the width of its base. The principal advantage of iron and steel are that they reduce those limits, permitting much greater height than stone.

At first the new materials was used for decoration. However, architects like Hermann Muthesius and Walter Gropius began to use iron and steel as structural elements within their buildings. The designs of Frank Lloyd Wright also shows how the development of iron and steel technology revolutionized building interiors. When every wall do not have to bear weight from the floors above, open floor plans is possible.

45 Recognizing Problems with Verbs

Verbs report action and show time. They change form to indicate person and number, voice and mood.

www.mhhe.com/
bmhh

For information and exercises on verb forms and tenses, go to

Editing > Verbs and Verbals

45a Learning the forms of regular and irregular verbs

English verbs have five main forms, except for the verb *be,* which has eight.

- The **base form** is the form you find if you look up the verb in a dictionary. (*For irregular verbs, other forms are given as well. See pp. 391–93 for a list.*)

- The **present tense** form is used to indicate an action occurring at the moment or habitually, as well as to introduce quotations, literary events, and scientific facts (*pp. 397–99 and pp. 399–400*).

- The **past tense** is used to indicate an action completed at a specific time in the past (*pp. 397–99*).

- The **past participle** is used with *have, has,* or *had* to form the perfect tenses (*pp. 397–99*); with a form of the *be* verb to form the passive voice (*Chapter 38, pp. 337–39*); and as an adjective (the *polished* silver).

- The **present participle** is used with a form of the *be* verb to form the progressive tenses (*pp. 397–99*). It can also be used as a noun (the *writing* is finished) and as an adjective (the *smiling* man).

Regular verbs always add *-d* or *-ed* to the base verb to form the past tense and past participle. **Irregular verbs,** by contrast, do not form the past tense or past participle in a consistent way. Here are the five principal forms of the regular verb *walk* and the irregular verb *begin* as well as the eight forms of the verb *be*.

Principal Forms of *Walk* and *Begin*

BASE	PRESENT TENSE (THIRD PERSON)	PAST TENSE	PAST PARTICIPLE	PRESENT PARTICIPLE
walk	walks	walked	walked	walking
begin	begins	began	begun	beginning

Principal Forms of *Be*

BASE	PRESENT TENSE	PAST TENSE	PAST PARTICIPLE	PRESENT PARTICIPLE
be	I *am*. He, she, it *is*. We, you, they *are*.	I *was*. He, she, it *was*. We, you, they *were*.	I have *been*.	I am *being*.

1. A list of common irregular verbs

You can also find the past tense and past participle forms of irregular verbs by looking up the base form in a standard dictionary.

**45a
vb**

Forms of Common Irregular Verbs

BASE	PAST TENSE	PAST PARTICIPLE
arise	arose	arisen
awake	awoke	awoke/awakened
be	was/were	been
beat	beat	beaten
become	became	become
begin	began	begun
blow	blew	blown

BASE	PAST TENSE	PAST PARTICIPLE
break	broke	broken
bring	brought	brought
buy	bought	bought
catch	caught	caught
choose	chose	chosen
cling	clung	clung
come	came	come
do	did	done
draw	drew	drawn
drink	drank	drunk
drive	drove	driven
eat	ate	eaten
fall	fell	fallen
fight	fought	fought
fly	flew	flown
forget	forgot	forgotten/forgot
forgive	forgave	forgiven
freeze	froze	frozen
get	got	gotten/got
give	gave	given
go	went	gone
grow	grew	grown
hang	hung	hung (for things)
hang	hanged	hanged (for people)
have	had	had
hear	heard	heard
know	knew	known
lose	lost	lost
pay	paid	paid
raise	raised	raised
ride	rode	ridden
ring	rang	rung
rise	rose	risen
say	said	said
see	saw	seen
set	set	set
shake	shook	shaken
sit	sat	sat
spin	spun	spun
steal	stole	stolen
spend	spent	spent
strive	strove/strived	striven/strived
swear	swore	sworn

BASE	PAST TENSE	PAST PARTICIPLE
swim	swam	swum
swing	swung	swung
take	took	taken
tear	tore	torn
tread	trod	trod/trodden
wear	wore	worn
weave	wove	woven
wring	wrung	wrung
write	wrote	written

2. *Went* and *gone, saw* and *seen*

Went and *saw* are the past tense forms of the irregular verbs *go* and *see*. *Gone* and *seen* are the past participle forms. These verb forms are sometimes confused.

➤ I had ~~went~~ there yesterday.
   gone

➤ We ~~seen~~ the rabid dog and called for help.
   saw

3. Irregular verbs such as *drink* (*drank/drunk*)

For a few irregular verbs, such as *swim* (*swam / swum*), *drink* (*drank / drunk*), and *ring* (*rang / rung*), the difference between the past tense form and the past participle is only one letter. Be careful not to mix up these forms in your writing.

➤ I had ~~drank~~ more than eight bottles of water that day.
   drunk

➤ The church bell had ~~rang~~ five times before she heard it.
   rung

45a
vb

| **Exercise 45.1** | Using irregular verb forms |

Use the past participle or past tense form of the verb in parentheses, whichever is appropriate, to fill in the blanks in the following sentences.

EXAMPLE Today, a woman's right to vote is _taken_ for granted. (take)

1. Elizabeth Cady Stanton and Lucretia Mott _____ two of the founders of the women's rights movement in the United States. (be)

2. The movement had _____ out of the abolitionist movement. (grow)
3. Stanton and Mott hoped to address the inequalities between men and women that they _____ in American society. (see)
4. In 1848, hundreds of people, both men and women, _____ to Seneca Falls in upstate New York for the first convention on women's rights. (go)
5. Many of the words in the convention's Declaration of Sentiments were _____ directly from the Declaration of Independence. (draw)
6. With the Declaration of Sentiments' demand for a woman's right to vote, the women's suffrage movement had _____ . (begin)

45b Distinguishing between *lay* and *lie*, *sit* and *set*, and *rise* and *raise*

Even experienced writers confuse the verbs *lay* and *lie*, *sit* and *set*, and *rise* and *raise*. The correct forms are given below.

Often-Confused Verb Pairs and Their Principal Forms

BASE	PAST	PAST PARTICIPLE	PRESENT PARTICIPLE
lay (to place)	laid	laid	laying
lie (to recline)	lay	lain	lying
sit (to be seated)	sat	sat	sitting
set (to put on a surface)	set	set	setting
rise (to go/get up)	rose	risen	rising
raise (to lift up)	raised	raised	raising

One verb in each of these pairs (*lay, set, raise*) is **transitive,** which means that an object receives the action of the verb. The other verb (*lie, sit, rise*) is **intransitive** and cannot take an object. You should use a form of *lay, set,* or *raise* if you can replace the verb with *place* or *put.*

direct object

➤ The dog *lays a bone* at your feet, then *lies* down and closes

his eyes.

Lay and *lie* are also confusing because the past tense of the irregular verb *lie* is *lay* (*lie, lay, lain*). To avoid using the wrong form, always double-check the verb *lay* when it appears in your writing.

➤ He washed the dishes carefully, then ~~lay~~ *laid* them on a

clean towel.

Exercise 45.2 Distinguishing commonly confused verbs

Some of the sentences that follow have the wrong choice of verb. Edit
the incorrect sentences, and circle the number of each sentence that
is already correct.

EXAMPLE She was ~~laying~~ *lying* down after nearly fainting.

1. Humans, like many other animals, usually lay down to sleep.
2. We found the manuscript lying on the desk where he left it.
3. The restless students had been setting at their desks all morning.
4. The actor sat the prop on the wrong table.
5. The archeologists rose the lid of the tomb.
6. The Wright brothers' contraption rose above the sands of
   Kitty Hawk.

45c Adding an -*s* or -*es* ending

In the present tense, almost all verbs add an -*s* or -*es* ending if the subject is third-person singular. (*See Chapter 44, pp. 381–90, for more on
standard subject-verb combinations.*) Third-person singular subjects
can be nouns (*woman, Benjamin, desk*), pronouns (*he, she, it*), or indefinite pronouns (*everyone*).

➤ The stock market ~~rise~~ *rises* when economic news is good.

If the subject is in the first person (*I*), the second person (*you*),
or the third-person plural (*people, they*), the verb does *not* add an -*s* or
-*es* ending.

➤ You invests your money wisely.

➤ People needs to learn about companies before buying

their stock.

45c
vb

Verb Forms and Grammar and Spelling Checkers

Grammar checkers will sometimes highlight an incorrect verb form, but they will miss more than they catch. For example, a grammar checker flagged the incorrect form in this sentence: *She had chose to go to the state college.* It also suggested the correct form: *chosen.* However, the checker missed the misuse of *set* in this sentence: *I am going to set down for a while.*

Similarly, spelling checkers will point out misspelled verbs, but they will not highlight a verb form that is used incorrectly in a sentence.

45d   Adding a *-d* or an *-ed* ending

These endings should be included on all regular verbs in the past tense and all past participles of regular verbs.

> The driving instructor ~~ask~~ *asked* the student driver to pull over
>
> to the curb.

> After we had ~~mix~~ *mixed* the formula, we let it cool.

Also check for missing *-d* or *-ed* endings on past participles used as adjectives.

> The ~~concern~~ *concerned* parents met with the school board.

Exercise 45.3   Editing for verb form

Underline the verbs in each sentence. Then check to ensure that the correct verb forms are used, using the advice in sections 45a–e. Circle the number of each correct sentence. Edit the remaining sentences.

EXAMPLE   The dentist has ~~forgave~~ *forgiven* Maya for biting his finger.

1. Humans are tremendously adaptable creatures.
2. Desert peoples have learn that loose, light garments protects them from the heat.
3. They have long drank from deep wells that they digged for water.
4. Arctic peoples have developed cultural practices that keeps them alive in a region where the temperature rarely rise above zero for months at a time.

5. Many people in mountainous areas have long builded terraces on steep slopes to create more land for farming.
6. Anthropologists and archeologists have argued about whether all cultural practices have an adaptive purpose.
7. Some practices may have went from adaptive to destructive.
8. For example, in ancient times, irrigation canals increased food production in arid areas.
9. After many centuries passed, however, the canals had deposit so much salt on the irrigated fields that the fields had became unfarmable.
10. By then, much of the population had fleed.

45e Using tenses accurately

Tenses show the time of a verb's action. English has three basic time frames—present, past, and future—and each tense has simple, perfect, and progressive verb forms to indicate the time span of the actions that are taking place. (*For a review of the present tense forms of a typical verb and of the verbs* be, have, *and* do, *see p. 381; for a review of the principal forms of regular and irregular verbs, which are used to form tenses, see pp. 391–93.*)

1. The simple present and past tenses

The **simple present tense** is used for actions occurring at the moment or habitually. The **simple past tense** is used for actions completed at a specific time in the past.

SIMPLE PRESENT

Every May, she *plans* next year's marketing strategy.

SIMPLE PAST

In the early morning hours before the office opened, she *planned* her marketing strategy.

2. The simple future tense

The **simple future tense,** used for actions that have not yet begun, takes *will* plus the verb.

SIMPLE FUTURE

In May, I *will plan* next year's marketing strategy.

3. The perfect tenses

The **perfect tenses,** used to indicate actions that were or will be completed by the time of another action or a specific time, take a form of *have* (*has, had*) plus the past participle.

PRESENT PERFECT

She *has* already *planned* next year's marketing strategy.

PAST PERFECT

By the time she resigned, Mary *had* already *planned* next year's marketing strategy.

FUTURE PERFECT

By the end of May, she *will have planned* next year's marketing strategy.

When the verb in the past perfect is irregular, be sure to use the proper form of the past participle.

➤ **By the time the week was over, both plants had** ~~grew~~ *grown*

five inches.

4. Progressive tenses

The progressive forms of the simple and perfect tenses, used to indicate ongoing action, take a form of *be* (*am, are, were*) plus the present participle.

PRESENT PROGRESSIVE

She *is planning* next year's marketing strategy now.

PAST PROGRESSIVE

She *was planning* next year's marketing strategy when she started to look for another job.

FUTURE PROGRESSIVE

During the month of May, she *will be planning* next year's marketing strategy.

5. Perfect progressive tenses

Perfect progressive tenses, used to indicate an action that takes place over a specific period of time, take *have* plus *be* plus the verb. The present perfect progressive tense is used for actions that start in the past and continue to the present; the past and future perfect progressive tenses are used for actions that ended or will end at a specified time or before another action.

PRESENT PERFECT PROGRESSIVE

She *has been planning* next year's marketing strategy since the beginning of May.

PAST PERFECT PROGRESSIVE

She *had been planning* next year's marketing strategy when she was offered another job.

FUTURE PERFECT PROGRESSIVE

By May 18, she *will have been planning* next year's marketing strategy for more than two weeks.

45f   Using the past perfect tense

When a past event was ongoing but ended before a particular time or another past event, use the past perfect rather than the simple past.

➤ **Before the Johnstown Flood occurred in 1889, people in the**

had

area expressed their concern about the safety of the dam on

the Conemaugh River.

People expressed their concern before the flood occurred.

If two past events happened simultaneously, however, use the simple past, not the past perfect.

➤ **When the Conemaugh flooded, many people in the area** ~~had~~

lost their lives.

Research findings are thought of as having been collected at one time in the past. Use the past or present perfect tense to report the results of research:

responded

➤ **Three of the compounds (nos. 2, 3, and 6)** ~~respond~~ **positively**

by turning purple.

45g
vb

45g   Using the present tense

If the conventions of a discipline require you to state what your paper does, do so in the present, not the future, tense.

➤   **In this paper, I *describe* the effects of increasing NaCl concentrations on the germination of radish seeds.**

Here are some other special uses of the present tense.

- By convention, events in a novel, short story, poem, or other literary work are described in the present tense.

  ➤   **Even though Huck's journey down the river ~~was~~ *is* an escape from society, his relationship with Jim ~~was~~ *is* a form of community.**

- Like events in a literary work, scientific facts are considered to be perpetually present, even though they were discovered in the past.

  ➤   **Mendel discovered that genes ~~had~~ *have* different forms, or alleles.**

- The present tense is also used to introduce a quote, paraphrase, or summary of someone else's writing.

  ➤   **William Julius Wilson ~~wrote~~ *writes* that "the disappearance of work has become a characteristic feature of the inner-city ghetto" (31).**

Exercise 45.4   Using verb tenses

Underline the verb that best fits the sentence.

EXAMPLE   Marlow (<u>encounters</u>/encountered) Kurtz in the climax of Conrad's *Heart of Darkness.*

1. Newton showed that planetary motion (followed/follows) mathematical laws.

2. In *Principia Mathematica,* Newton (states/stated), "To every action there is always opposed an equal reaction."

3. Newton (publishes/published) the *Principia* in 1675.

4. With the *Principia,* Newton (had changed/changed) the course of science.

5. By the time of his death, Newton (had become/became) internationally famous.

6. Scientists and philosophers (were absorbing/absorbed) the implications of Newton's discoveries long after his death.

45h   Using complete verbs

With only a few exceptions, all English sentences must contain a main verb along with any helping verbs that are needed to express the tense (*see pp. 397–99*) or voice (*see pp. 337–38*). **Helping verbs** include forms of *be, have,* and *do* and the modal verbs *can, could, may, might, shall, should,* and *will.* Helping verbs can be part of contractions (*he's running, we'd better go*), but they cannot be left out of the sentence entirely.

will
➤   They ⌃ be going on a field trip next week.

A **linking verb,** often a form of *be,* connects the subject to a description or definition of it. Linking verbs can be part of contractions (*she's a student*), but they should not be left out entirely.

is
➤   Montreal ⌃ a major Canadian city.

Exercise 45.5   Editing for verb tense

Edit the following passage, replacing or deleting verb parts so that the tenses reflect the context of the passage.

EXAMPLE   Returning to the area, the survivors ~~had~~ found massive destruction.

For some time, anthropologists are being puzzled by the lack of a written language among the ancient Incas of South America. The Incas, who had conquered most of Andean South America by about 1500, had sophisticated architecture, advanced knowledge of engineering and astronomy, and sophisticated social and political structures. Why aren't they having a written language as well?

Ancient Egypt, Iraq, and China, as well as early Mexican civilizations such as the Aztec and Maya, had all been having written language. It is seeming strange that only the Incas will have lacked a written language.

45h
vb

Anthropologists now think that the Incas have possessed a kind of written language after all. Scholars will believe that the Incas used knots in multicolored strings as the medium for their "writing." The Incas called these strings *khipu.*

45i Using the subjunctive mood

The **mood** of a verb indicates the writer's attitude. Use the **indicative mood** to state or to question facts, acts, and opinions (*Our collection is on display. Did you see it?*). Use the **imperative mood** for commands, directions, and entreaties. The subject of an imperative sentence is always *you,* but the *you* is usually understood, not written out (*Shut the door!*). Use the **subjunctive mood** to express a wish, a demand, a request, or a recommendation, or to make a statement contrary to fact (*I wish I were a millionaire*). The mood that writers have the most trouble with is the subjunctive.

Present tense subjunctive verbs do not change form to signal person or number. The only form used is the verb's base form: *find* or *be,* not *finds* or *am, are, is.* The verb *be* has only one past tense form in the subjunctive mood: *were.*

WISH

If only I *were* more prepared for this test.

Words such as *ask, insist, recommend, request,* and *suggest* indicate the subjunctive mood; the verb in the *that* clause that follows should be in the subjunctive.

DEMAND

I insist that all applicants *find* their seats by 8:00 a.m.

CONTRARY-TO-FACT STATEMENT

He would not be so irresponsible if his father *were* [not *was*] still alive.

Note: Some common expressions of conjecture are in the subjunctive mood, including *as it were, come rain or shine, far be it from me,* and *be that as it may.*

Exercise 45.6   Using the subjunctive

Fill in each blank with the correct form of the base verb in parentheses. Some of the sentences are in the subjunctive; others are in the indicative or imperative mood.

EXAMPLE   We ask that everyone _bring_ pencils to the exam. (bring)

1. The stockholders wish the company _____ run more profitably. (be)
2. The board demanded that the CEO _____. (resign)
3. "If I _____ you," said the board chairperson, "I would take a long vacation." (be)
4. Judging from the stock's recent rise, the management change _____ investors. (please)
5. _____ share value or face the consequences! (increase)

(*For more on the use of speculation and the subjunctive, see Chapter 48, pp. 442–43.*)

46 Fixing Problems with Pronouns

A **pronoun** (*he / him, it / its, they / their*) takes the place of a noun. The noun that the pronoun replaces is called its **antecedent.** In the following sentence, *snow* is the antecedent of the pronoun *it*.

➤ The *snow* fell all day long, and by nightfall *it* was three

feet deep.

Like nouns, pronouns are singular or plural.

46

pn agr

SINGULAR

The *house* was dark and gloomy, and *it* sat in a grove of tall cedars.

PLURAL

The *cars* swept by on the highway, all of *them* doing more than sixty-five miles per hour.

A pronoun needs an antecedent to refer to and agree with, and a pronoun must match its antecedent in number (plural/singular) and **gender** (*he / his, she / her, it / its*). A pronoun must also be in a form, or case, that matches its function in the sentence.

Pronoun Problems and Grammar Checkers

Do not rely on grammar checkers to alert you to problems in
pronoun-antecedent agreement or pronoun reference. Some computer grammar checkers do reliably flag many errors in pronoun
case, but by no means all. One grammar checker, for example,
missed the case error in the following sentence: *Ford's son Edsel,
who [should be whom] the auto magnate treated very cruelly, was
a brilliant automotive designer. (See pp. 415–16 for a discussion
of the proper use of who and whom.)*

46a Making pronouns agree with their antecedents

Problems with pronoun-antecedent agreement tend to occur when a
pronoun's antecedent is an indefinite pronoun, a collective noun, or
a compound noun. Problems may also occur when writers are trying
to avoid the generic use of *he.*

1. Indefinite pronouns

Indefinite pronouns such as *someone, anybody,* and *nothing* refer to
nonspecific people or things. They sometimes function as antecedents
for other pronouns. Most indefinite pronouns are singular (*anybody,
anyone, anything, each, either, everybody, everyone, everything, much,
neither, nobody, none, no one, nothing, one, somebody, something*).

> **ALWAYS SINGULAR** Did *either* of the boys lose *his* bicycle?

A few indefinite pronouns—*both, few, many,* and *several*—are plural.

> **ALWAYS PLURAL** *Both* of the boys lost *their* bicycles.

The indefinite pronouns *all, any, more, most,* and *some* can be
either singular or plural depending on the noun to which the pronoun
refers.

> **PLURAL** The students debated, *some* arguing that *their*
> assumptions about the issue were more
> credible than the teacher's.

> **SINGULAR** The bread is on the counter, but *some* of *it*
> has already been eaten.

Problems arise when writers attempt to make indefinite pronouns
agree with their antecedents without introducing gender bias. There
are three ways to avoid gender bias when correcting a pronoun agreement problem such as the following.

FAULTY   **None of the great Romantic writers believed that their achievements equaled their aspirations.**

- If possible, change a singular indefinite pronoun to a plural pronoun, editing the sentence as necessary.

  All
➤ ~~None~~ of the great Romantic writers believed that their

  fell short of
achievements ~~equaled~~ their aspirations.

- Reword the sentence to eliminate the indefinite pronoun.

  The
➤ ~~None of the~~ great Romantic writers believed that their

  did not equal
achievements ~~equaled~~ their aspirations.

- Substitute *he or she* or *his or her* (but never *his/her*) for the singular pronoun. Change the sentence as necessary to avoid using this construction more than once.

➤ **None of the great Romantic writers believed that**

  his or her   *had been realized*
~~their achievements equaled their~~ **aspirations.**

2. Generic nouns

A **generic noun** represents anyone and everyone in a group—a typical doctor, the average voter. Because most groups consist of both males and females, using male pronouns to refer to generic nouns is usually sexist. To fix agreement problems with generic nouns, use one of the three options suggested above.

College students   *s*
➤ **A ~~college student~~ should have a mind of their own.**

          an independent point of view.
➤ **A college student should have a ~~mind of their own.~~**

          his or her
➤ **A college student should have a mind of ~~their~~ own.**

46a
pn agr

IDENTIFY AND EDIT
Problems with Gender Bias
and Pronoun-Antecedent Agreement

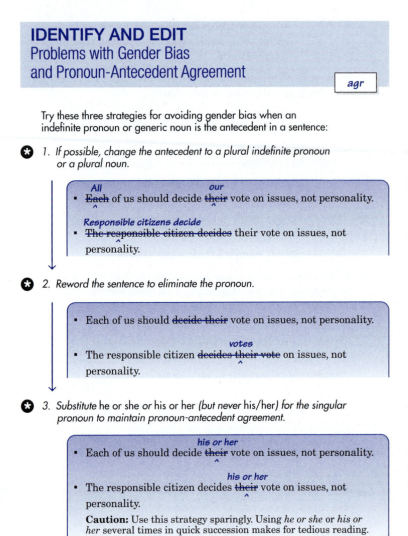

agr

Try these three strategies for avoiding gender bias when an indefinite pronoun or generic noun is the antecedent in a sentence:

✱ *1. If possible, change the antecedent to a plural indefinite pronoun or a plural noun.*

> *All*
> • ~~Each~~ of us should decide ~~their~~ *our* vote on issues, not personality.
>
> *Responsible citizens decide*
> • ~~The responsible citizen decides~~ their vote on issues, not personality.

✱ *2. Reword the sentence to eliminate the pronoun.*

> • Each of us should ~~decide their~~ vote on issues, not personality.
>
> *votes*
> • The responsible citizen ~~decides their vote~~ on issues, not personality.

✱ *3. Substitute he or she or his or her (but never his/her) for the singular pronoun to maintain pronoun-antecedent agreement.*

> *his or her*
> • Each of us should decide ~~their~~ vote on issues, not personality.
>
> *his or her*
> • The responsible citizen decides ~~their~~ vote on issues, not personality.
>
> **Caution:** Use this strategy sparingly. Using *he or she* or *his or her* several times in quick succession makes for tedious reading.

3. Collective nouns

Collective nouns such as *team, family, jury, committee,* and *crowd* are singular unless the people in the group are acting as individuals.

➤ All together, the crowd surged through the palace gates,

its
trampling over everything in ~~their~~ path.

➤ **The committee left the conference room and returned to**

    their
    ~~its~~ **offices.**
      ^

If you are using a collective noun that has a plural meaning, consider adding a plural noun to clarify the meaning: *The committee members . . . returned to their offices.*

4. Compound antecedent

Compound antecedents joined by *and* are almost always plural.

➤ **To remove all traces of the crime, James put the book and**

               their
the magnifying glass back in ~~its~~ place.
                   ^

When a compound antecedent is joined by *or* or *nor,* the pronoun should agree with the closest part of the compound antecedent. If one part is singular and the other is plural, the sentence will be smoother and more effective if the plural antecedent is closest to the pronoun.

    PLURAL   Neither *the child nor the parents* shared *their* food.

When the two parts of the compound antecedent refer to the same person, or when the word *each* or *every* precedes the compound antecedent, use a singular pronoun.

    SINGULAR   Being *a teacher and a mother* keeps *her* busy.

    SINGULAR   *Every* poem and letter by Keats has *its* own
                          special power.

Exercise 46.1	Editing for pronoun-antecedent agreement

46a

pn agr

Some of the sentences that follow contain errors in pronoun-antecedent agreement. Circle the number of each correct sentence, and edit the others so that the pronouns agree with their antecedents. Rewrite sentences as necessary to avoid gender bias; you may eliminate pronouns or change words. There will be several possible answers for rewritten sentences.

                                               their
    EXAMPLE   **Neither the dog nor the cats ate ~~its~~ chow.**
                                            ^

1. Everybody at the displaced-persons camp had to submit his medical records before boarding the ships to the United States.

2. Many were forbidden to board because they had histories of tuberculosis and other illnesses.
3. This was always devastating news because no one wanted to be separated from their family.
4. Some immigrants resorted to forging his medical records.
5. After all, a mother could not be separated from their children, and the family had to get to America.
6. Immigrants had heard that a doctor in America takes good care of their patients and felt they had a chance for a better life there.
7. Even so, was it fair to expose others to illness just to bring parents and a child to its new surroundings?
8. Every difficulty and ethical dilemma presented its own challenge for displaced persons trying to find a home with a future after World War II.

46b Making pronoun references clear

If a pronoun does not clearly refer to a specific antecedent, readers can become confused.

1. Ambiguous references

If a pronoun can refer to more than one noun in a sentence, the reference is ambiguous. To clear up the ambiguity, eliminate the pronoun and use the appropriate noun.

> **The friendly banter between Hamlet and Horatio eventually**
>
> *Hamlet*
> **provokes ~~him~~ to declare that his world view has changed.**

Sometimes the ambiguous reference can be cleared up by rewriting the sentence.

> *When*   *was in London, she*   *with Cassandra.*
> **Jane Austen ~~and Cassandra~~ corresponded regularly ~~when~~**
>
> ~~she was in London.~~

2. Implied references

The antecedent that a pronoun refers to must be present in the sentence, and it must be a noun or another pronoun, not a word that modifies a noun. Possessives and verbs cannot be antecedents.

> _his_
> In ~~Wilson's~~ essay "When Work Disappears," ~~he~~ _Wilson_ proposes a
> four-point plan for the revitalization of blighted inner-city
> communities.

> Every weekday afternoon, my brothers skateboard home
> _their skateboards_
> from school, and then they leave ~~them~~ in the driveway.

3. _This, that,_ and _which_

The pronouns _this, that,_ and _which_ are often used to refer to ideas expressed in preceding sentences. To make the sentence containing the pronoun clearer, either change the pronoun to a specific noun or add a specific antecedent or clarifying noun.

> As government funding for higher education decreases,
> _these higher costs_
> tuition increases. Are we students supposed to accept ~~this~~
> without protest?

> As government funding for higher education decreases,
> tuition increases. Are we students supposed to accept
> _situation_
> this without protest?

4. _You, they,_ and _it_

The pronouns _you, they,_ and _it_ should refer to definite, explicitly stated antecedents. If their antecedents are unclear, they should be replaced with appropriately specific nouns, or the sentence should be rewritten to eliminate the pronoun.

> _the government pays_
> In some countries such as Canada, ~~they pay~~ for such medical
> procedures.

46b

pn agr

students

➤ According to college policy, ~~you~~ must have a permit to park
   ^

a car on campus.

The

➤ ~~In the~~ textbook/ ~~it~~ states that borrowing to fund the purchase
   ^

of financial assets results in a double-counting of debt.

Exercise 46.2   Editing to clarify pronoun reference

Rewrite each sentence to eliminate unclear pronoun references. Some
sentences have several possible correct answers.

> **EXAMPLE**   **You are not allowed to drive if you are a woman
> in Saudi Arabia.**
>
> *Women in Saudi Arabia are not allowed to drive.*

1. The tight race between presidential candidates John Kerry and
   George W. Bush in 2004 compelled him to campaign intensively
   in many states.
2. The candidates debated three times, answering them thoughtfully.
3. During one debate, Kerry told Bush that he had an inadequate
   plan of action.
4. After Bush's election, he promised to return money to some
   taxpayers.
5. When Kerry challenged the numbers behind Bush's proposed
   tax cuts, Bush accused Kerry of being "wishy-washy." This stuck
   throughout the campaign.
6. With Kerry as president, they would work on strengthening the
   economy with more jobs and higher incomes.
7. Even after all the campaigning, debating, and polling, you were
   still left wondering who would win the election on Tuesday,
   November 2, 2004.

46c   Choosing the correct pronoun case: for example, *I* vs. *me*

When a pronoun's form, or **case,** does not match its function in a sentence, readers will feel that something is wrong. Most problems with
pronoun case involve the subjective and objective forms.

- Pronouns in the subjective case are used as subjects or subject complements in sentences: *I, you, he, she, it, we, they, who, whoever.*

- Pronouns in the objective case are used as objects of verbs or prepositions: *me, you, him, her, it, us, them, whom, whomever.*

1. Pronouns in compound structures

Compound structures (words or phrases joined by *and, or,* or *nor*) can appear as subjects or objects. If you are not sure which form of a pronoun to use in a compound structure, treat the pronoun as the only subject or object, and note how the sentence sounds.

> **SUBJECT**   **Angela and *I* [not *me*] were cleaning up the kitchen.**

Me [was] cleaning up the kitchen is clearly wrong. The correct form is the subjective pronoun *I.*

> **OBJECT**   **My parents waited for an explanation from John and *me* [not *I*].**

My parents waited for an explanation from I is clearly wrong. The correct form is the objective pronoun *me.*

2. Subject complements

A **subject complement** renames and specifies the sentence's subject. It follows a **linking verb.**

> **SUBJECT COMPLEMENT**   **Mark's best friends are Jane and *I* [not *me*].**

You can also switch the order to make the pronoun into the subject: *Jane and I are Mark's best friends.*

3. Appositives

Appositives are nouns or noun phrases that rename nouns or pronouns. They appear right after the word they rename and have the same function in the sentence that the word has.

> **SUBJECTIVE**   **The two weary travelers, Ramon and *I* [not *me*], found shelter in an old cabin.**

> **OBJECTIVE**   **The police arrested two protesters, Jane and *me* [not *I*].**

46c

pn agr

IDENTIFY AND EDIT
Problems with Pronoun Case

case

Follow these steps to decide on the proper form of pronouns in compound structures:

✸ *1. Identify the compound structure (a pronoun and a noun or other pronoun joined by* and, but, or, *or* nor*) in the problem sentence.*

> PROBLEM
> SENTENCE
>
> compound structure
> [Her or her roommate] should call the campus technical support office and sign up for the broadband Internet service.
>
> PROBLEM
> SENTENCE
>
> compound structure
> The director gave the leading roles to [my brother and I].

✸ *2. Isolate the pronoun that you are unsure about, then read the sentence to yourself without the rest of the compound structure. If the result sounds wrong, change the case of the pronoun, and read the sentence again.*

> PROBLEM
> SENTENCE
>
> [Her ~~or her roommate~~] should call the campus technical support office and sign up for the broadband Internet service.
>
> *Her should call the campus technical support office* sounds wrong. The pronoun should be in the subjective case: *she.*
>
> PROBLEM
> SENTENCE
>
> The director gave the leading roles to [~~my brother and~~ I].
>
> *The director gave the leading roles to I* sounds wrong. The pronoun should be in the objective case: *me.*

✸ *3. If necessary, correct the original sentence.*

> *She*
> - ~~Her~~ or her roommate should call the campus technical support office and sign up for broadband Internet service.
>   ^
>
>   *me*
> - The director gave the leading roles to my brother and ~~I~~.
>   ^

4. *We* or *us*

When *we* or *us* comes before a noun, it has the same function in the sentence as the noun it precedes.

SUBJECTIVE   *We* [not *Us*] **students never get to decide such**

                things.

We renames the subject: *students.*

OBJECTIVE   **Things were looking desperate for *us* [not *we*]**

                campers.

Us renames the object of the preposition *for: campers.*

5. Comparisons with *than* or *as*

In comparisons, words are often left out of the sentence because the reader can guess what they would be. When a pronoun follows *than* or *as,* make sure you are using the correct form by mentally adding the missing word or words.

➤   **Meg is quicker than she [is].**

➤   **We find ourselves remembering Maria as often as [we remember] her.**

If a sentence with a comparison sounds too awkward or formal, add the missing words: *Meg is quicker than she is.*

6. Pronouns as the subject or the object of an infinitive

An **infinitive** is *to* plus the base verb (*to breathe*). A pronoun that functions as the subject or object of an infinitive should be in the objective case.

infinitive   infinitive
subject   object

➤   **We wanted our lawyer and *her* to defend *us* against this unfair charge.**

7. Pronouns in front of an *-ing* noun (a gerund)

When a noun or pronoun appears before a **gerund** (an *-ing* verb form functioning as a noun), it should usually be treated as a possessive.

       animals'
➤   **The ~~animals~~ fighting disturbed the entire neighborhood.**

          their
➤   **Because of ~~them~~ screeching, no one could get any sleep.**

46c

pn agr

Exercise 46.3   Choosing pronoun case

Underline the pronoun in parentheses that is appropriate to the sentence.

> EXAMPLE   **Michael and (I/me) grew up in Philadelphia.**

1. The first person to receive a diploma was (I/me). Matt and Lara followed behind me.
2. Throughout the ceremony, I joked with Lara and (he/him), enjoying my last official college event with them.
3. Lara joked that the people least likely to succeed after college were Matt and (her/she).
4. That outcome is highly unlikely, however, because Lara and (he/him) were tied for valedictorian.
5. Graduation was a bittersweet day for my friends and (I/me).

Exercise 46.4   Choosing pronoun case with appositives

Underline the pronoun in parentheses that is appropriate to the sentence.

> EXAMPLE   **(We/Us) players are ready to hit the field.**

1. (We/Us) Americans live in a cultural melting pot.
2. My parents, for example, have passed on Finnish and Spanish cultural traditions to their children, my two brothers and (I/me).
3. Our grandparents have told fascinating stories about our ancestors to (we/us) grandchildren.
4. On New Year's Eve, the younger family members, my brothers and (I/me), tell fortunes according to a Finnish custom, and then, following a Spanish tradition, the whole family eats grapes.
5. My grandmother gave her oldest grandchild, (I/me), a journal with her observations of our family's varied cultural traditions—our own melting pot.

Exercise 46.5   Choosing pronoun case with comparisons, infinitives, and gerunds

Underline the pronoun in parentheses that is appropriate to the sentence.

> EXAMPLE   **Troy is a better driver than (she/her).**

1. Robert Browning, an admirer of Elizabeth Barrett, started to court (she/her) in 1844, thus beginning one of the most famous romances in history.
2. Barrett's parents did not want Browning and (she/her) to marry, but the couple wed secretly in 1846.

3. (Their/Them) moving to Italy from England helped Barrett improve her poor health.
4. Even though Browning also had great talent, Barrett was recognized as a poet earlier than (he/him).
5. Today, however, he is considered as prominent a poet as (she/her).

Exercise 46.6 Editing for pronoun case

Edit the following passage, substituting the correct form of the pronoun for any pronoun in the wrong case.

me

EXAMPLE **The winning points were scored by Hatcher and I.**
^

   Sociolinguists investigate the relationship between linguistic variations and culture. They spend a lot of time in the field to gather data for analysis. For instance, them might compare the speech patterns of people who live in a city with those of people who reside in the suburbs. Sociolinguists might discover differences in pronunciation or word choice. Their researching helps us understand both language and culture.

   Us laypeople might confuse sociolinguistics with sociology. Sociolinguists do a more specialized type of research than do most sociologists, who study broad patterns within societies. Being concerned with such particulars as the pronunciation of a single vowel, sociolinguists work at a finer level of detail than them.

46d Choosing between *who* and *whom*

The relative pronouns *who, whom, whoever,* and *whomever* are used to introduce dependent clauses and in questions. Their case depends on their function in the dependent clause or question.

46d
pn agr

- **Subjective:** *who, whoever*
- **Objective:** *whom, whomever*

1. Pronouns in dependent clauses

If the pronoun is functioning as a subject and is performing an action, use *who* or *whoever.* If the pronoun is the object of a verb or preposition, use *whom* or *whomever.*

SUBJECT   **Henry Ford, *who* started the Ford Motor Company, was autocratic and stubborn.**

OBJECT
    Ford's son Edsel, *whom* the auto magnate treated cruelly, was a brilliant automobile designer.

2. Pronouns in questions

To choose the correct form for the pronoun, answer the question with a personal pronoun.

SUBJECT
    ***Who* founded the General Motors Corporation?**

The answer could be *He founded it. He* is in the subjective case, so *who* is correct.

OBJECT
    ***Whom* did the Chrysler Corporation turn to for leadership in the 1980s?**

The answer could be *It turned to him. Him* is in the objective case, so *whom* is correct.

Exercise 46.7   Choosing between *who* and *whom*

Underline the pronoun that is appropriate to the sentence.

EXAMPLE
    Arlia is the one (<u>who</u>/whom) people say will have the top sales results.

1. (Who/Whom) invented the light bulb? Thomas Edison did.
2. He was a scientist and inventor (who/whom) also invented the phonograph and improved the telegraph, telephone, and motion picture technology.
3. Edison, (who/whom) patented 1,093 inventions in his lifetime, was nicknamed the "Wizard of Menlo Park."
4. The hardworking Edison, (who/whom) everyone greatly admired, believed that "genius is one percent inspiration and ninety-nine percent perspiration."
5. (Who/Whom) should we remember the next time we switch on the light? Thomas Edison.

Exercise 46.8   Chapter review: Fixing problems with pronouns

Edit the following passage so that all pronouns have clear antecedents, agree with their antecedents, and are in the appropriate case.

Margaret Mead was probably the best-known anthropologist of the twentieth century. It was she whom wrote *Coming of Age in Samoa,* a book well known in the 1930s and still in print today. It was her who gave us the idea that Melanesian natives grow up free of the strictures and repressions that can characterize adolescence in our society. Her writings found an audience just as the work of Sigmund Freud was becoming widely known in the United States.

In his work, he argued for "an incomparably freer sexual life," saying that rigid attitudes toward sexuality contributed to mental illness among we Westerners. Her accessible and gracefully written account of life among the Samoans showed them to be both relatively free of pathology and relaxed about sexual matters. Their work both provoked and contributed to a debate over theories about the best way to raise children.

47 Recognizing Problems with Adjectives and Adverbs

Adjectives and **adverbs** are words that qualify—or modify—the meanings of other words. Adjectives modify nouns and pronouns. Adverbs modify verbs, adjectives, and other adverbs.

47a Using adverbs correctly

Adverbs modify verbs, adjectives, other adverbs, and even whole clauses. They tell where, when, why, how, how often, how much, or to what degree.

➤ The authenticity of the document is *hotly* contested.

➤ The water was *brilliant* blue and *icy* cold.

47a
ad

www.mhhe.com/
bmhh

For information
and exercises on
adjectives and
adverbs, go to

Editing >
Adjectives
and Adverbs

➤ Dickens mixed humor and pathos *better* than any other

English writer after Shakespeare.

➤ *Consequently,* Dickens is still read by millions.

Do not substitute an adjective for an adverb. Watch especially for the adjectives *bad, good,* and *real,* which sometimes substitute for the adverbs *badly, well,* and *really* in casual speech.

badly
➤ He plays the role so ~~bad~~ that it is an insult to Shakespeare.

really
➤ At times, he gets ~~real~~ close to the edge of the stage.

well
➤ I've seen other actors play the role ~~good~~, but they were

classically trained.

Adjectives, Adverbs, and Grammar Checkers

Computer grammar checkers are sensitive to some problems with adjectives and adverbs but miss far more than they catch. A grammar checker failed to flag the errors in the following sentences: *The price took a suddenly plunge* [should be *sudden*], and *the price plunged sudden* [should be *suddenly*].

47b Using adjectives correctly

Adjectives modify nouns and pronouns; they do not modify any other kind of word. Adjectives tell what kind or how many. They may come before or after the noun or pronoun they modify.

➤ The *looming* clouds, *ominous* and *gray,* frightened the

children.

Some proper nouns have adjective forms. Proper adjectives, like the proper nouns they are derived from, are capitalized: *America / American.*

In some cases, a noun is used as an adjective without a change in form.

➤ *Cigarette* **smoking harms the lungs and is banned in offices.**

Occasionally, descriptive adjectives function as if they were nouns.

➤ **The *unemployed* should not be equated with the *lazy*.**

■ Do not use an adjective when an adverb is needed.

really well.
➤ **He hit that ball** ~~real good.~~

certainly
➤ **She** ~~sure~~ **made me work hard for my grade.**

■ Use adjectives after linking verbs to describe the subject. Descriptive adjectives that modify a sentence's subject but appear after a linking verb are called **subject complements.**

➤ **During the winter, both Emily and Anne *were sick*.**

Linking verbs are related to states of being and the five senses: *appear, become, feel, grow, look, smell, sound,* and *taste.* Verbs related to the senses can be either linking or action verbs, depending on the meaning of the sentence.

LINKING   **The dog smelled *bad* [adjective].**

ACTION   **The dog smelled *badly* [adverb].**

■ Be aware of adjectives and adverbs that are spelled alike. In most instances, *-ly* endings indicate adverbs; however, words with *-ly* endings can sometimes be adjectives (*the lovely girl*). In standard English, many adverbs do not require the *-ly* ending, and some words are both adjectives and adverbs: *fast, only, hard, right,* and *straight.* Note that *right* also has an *-ly* form as an adverb: *rightly.* When in doubt, consult a dictionary.

47b
ad

Exercise 47.1   Identifying adjectives and adverbs

In the sentences that follow on the next page, underline and label all adjectives (adj), nouns used as adjectives (n), and adverbs (adv). Then draw an arrow from each modifier to the word or words it modifies.

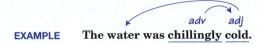

EXAMPLE   The water was <u>chillingly</u> <u>cold</u>.

1. The spread of destructive viruses to computers around the world is a serious problem with potentially deadly consequences.
2. Carried by infected e-mails, the viruses spread fast, moving from computer to computer at the click of a mouse.
3. Viruses have hit businesses badly in the past, disrupting railroads, delaying flights, and closing stores and offices.
4. Because viruses are so harmful, computer users should install antivirus software and update it regularly.
5. Other precautions include maintaining a good firewall and screening e-mail well to avoid opening suspicious messages.

Exercise 47.2   Editing adjectives and adverbs

Edit the sentences that follow so that adjectives are not used where adverbs belong and adverbs are not used where adjectives belong. Circle the number of any sentence that is already correct.

EXAMPLE   She hid the money so ~~good~~ that she could not

find it when she needed it.

1. Sociology, the scholarly study of human society, is well and thriving today.
2. The discipline's intellectual roots reach real far back, to the eighteenth century.
3. Auguste Comte (1798–1857) invented the word *sociology,* and mostly sociologists would probable agree that he founded the discipline.
4. According to Comte, scientific laws control human social behavior as sure as they control the motion of planets around the sun.
5. Comte believed his scientific approach was good because it would further human progress.
6. Emile Durkheim (1858–1917) helped place modern sociology on a well foundation.
7. Durkheim argued that societies can be good understood only if analyzed on their own terms, apart from the individuals who constitute them.
8. He proposed that society shapes the individual more than the other way around, and that the individual fares bad without a sense of social belonging.

47c Using positive, comparative, and superlative adjectives and adverbs

Most adjectives and adverbs have three forms: positive (*dumb*), comparative (*dumber*), and superlative (*dumbest*). The simplest form of the adjective is the positive form.

1. Comparatives and superlatives

Use the comparative form to compare two things and the superlative form to compare three or more things.

➤ In total area, New York is a *larger* state than Pennsylvania.

➤ Texas is the *largest* state in the Southwest.

2. -er/-est endings and *more/most*

To form comparatives and superlatives of short adjectives, add the suffixes *-er* and *-est* (*brighter*/*brightest*). With longer adjectives (three or more syllables), use *more* or *less* and *most* or *least* (*more dangerous*/*most dangerous*).

➤ Mercury is the ~~most near~~ planet to the sun.
   nearest

A few short adverbs have *-er* and *-est* endings in their comparative and superlative forms (*harder*/*hardest*). Most adverbs, however, including all adverbs that end in *-ly,* use *more* or *less* and *most* or *least* in their comparative and superlative forms.

➤ She sings *more loudly* than we expected.

Two common adjectives—*good* and *bad*—form the comparative and superlative in an irregular way: *good, better, best* and *bad, worse, worst.*

➤ He felt ~~badder~~ as his illness progressed.
   worse

3. Double comparatives and superlatives

Use either an *-er* or an *-est* ending or *more*/*most* to form the comparative or superlative, as appropriate; do not use both.

➤ Since World War II, Britain has been the ~~most~~ closest ally

   of the United States.

47c
ad

4. Concepts that cannot be compared

Do not use comparative or superlative forms with *absolute* adjectives such as *unique, infinite,* and *impossible.* If something is unique, for example, it is the only one of its kind, making comparison impossible.

➤ You will never find ~~a more unique~~ restaurant ~~than~~ this one.

        another   *like*

47d   Avoiding double negatives

The words *no, not,* and *never* can modify the meaning of nouns and pronouns as well as other sentence elements.

NOUN	You are *no* friend of mine.
ADJECTIVE	The red house was *not* large.
VERB	He *never* ran in a marathon.

When two negatives are used together, though, they cancel each other out, resulting in a positive meaning. Unless you want your sentence to have a positive meaning *(I am not unaware of your feelings in this matter),* edit by changing or eliminating one of the negative words.

           any

➤ They don't have ~~no~~ reason to go there.

    can

➤ He ~~can't~~ hardly do that assignment.

Exercise 47.3   Editing comparisons

Edit the sentences that follow so that adjectives and adverbs are used correctly in comparisons. Some of the sentences are already correct; circle their numbers.

                worse

  EXAMPLE   He felt ~~badder~~ as his illness progressed.

1. Biotechnology, perhaps the controversialest application of science in recent decades, is the basis of genetic engineering, cloning, and gene therapy.
2. Some of these fields are more popular than others.
3. Ethicists find it more easy to defend the genetic engineering of plants than the cloning of animals.
4. Gene therapy is often a last resort for people suffering from the worser types of cancer.

5. Gene therapy, one of the more newer forms of biotechnology, involves introducing cells containing specialized genetic material into the patient's body.

6. Cloning, a way of creating an exact duplicate of an organism, is probably more hard to justify than any other biotechnological procedure.

7. A female lamb cloned in Scotland in 1997 seemed no different from others of her breed.

8. Despite the successes that have been achieved with animal cloning, most people do not want no humans to be cloned.

9. The Raelians, a fringe group, claimed they had cloned a human infant.

10. Many people cannot hardly believe that the Raelians really cloned an infant.

Exercise 47.4 Fixing problems with adjectives and adverbs

Edit the following passage to correct any problems with adjectives and adverbs.

Although there are many approaches to sociology, the two most commonest ones are functionalism and conflict theory. The functionalist view, usual associated with Harvard sociologist Talcott Parsons, sees society as a whole that tries to maintain equilibrium, or stasis. No ancestor of conflict theory is most famous than Karl Marx, who invented the concept of class warfare. Promoted here in the United States by the African-American sociologist W. E. B. Du Bois, conflict theory sees society as made up of groups that cannot hardly avoid being in conflict or competition with one another.

For a functionalist like Parsons, societies are best understood according to how good they maintain stability. On the other hand, for a conflict theorist like Du Bois, a society is more better analyzed in terms of how its parts compete for power.

Other sociological theories, such as interactionist and feminist theory, have sure made major contributions to the field. However, each of these can be seen most best as examples of functionalist or conflict theory. Relating small-scale behavior such as gestures and facial expressions to the larger context of a group or society, interactionist theory is really a development of the functionalist view. Similarly, feminist sociological theory understands society in terms of gender inequality—a view most perfectly recognizable as a subtype of conflict theory.

47d
ad

48 Special Editing Topics for Multilingual Writers

Your native language or even the language of your ancestors may influence the way you use English. The following sections will help you with some common problems encountered by writers whose first language is not English. These sections might help native speakers as well.

www.mhhe.com/
bmhh

For information
and exercises on
problem areas
for multilingual
writers, go to

Editing >
Multilingual
ESL Writers

48a Learning in English as a second language

To some extent, college presents everyone with an unfamiliar culture and its languages. The language of anthropology, for example, probably sounds strange to most students, including those who have been speaking English all their lives. If you spoke another language before learning English, you already have experience trying to feel at home in a new culture and working to acquire a new language.

1. Becoming aware of cultural differences in communication

Because you are familiar with at least two languages and cultures, you already know that there is more than one way to interact politely and effectively with other people. In fact, you may wonder about the way people communicate in college classrooms in the United States. Your classmates may pride themselves on being direct; you may think that they sound almost impolite in their enthusiasm to make a point. They may strive to be precise; you may wonder why they are explaining things that attentive people should be able to figure out for themselves.

Colleges in the United States encourage students to openly exchange views, clearly state opinions, and support judgments with examples, observations, and reasons. You may be reluctant to participate because you are concerned about an "accent" or about the fine points of grammar or pronunciation. Communication is your first priority, so gather up your confidence and join the conversation:

- Participate actively in small-group discussions.
- Ask and answer questions during class discussions.
- Approach instructors and fellow students outside class when you need additional help.

2. Using writing to learn more about English

To develop fluency in English, get into the habit of writing in English every day.

- **Write a personal journal.** Explore your thoughts and feelings about your studies and college life.

- **Keep a writer's notebook.** Write down a quotation from something you have read, and then either comment on it or put the idea into your own words. Write down bits of dialogue you overhear. Make lists of words and phrases that are new to you. Go over these lists with your writing group, a friend, or a tutor in the writing center.
- **Write letters and e-mail in English.** Letters and e-mail are a good way to practice the informal style used in conversation.

3. Using learning tools that are available for multilingual students

The following kinds of reference books can help you as you write papers for your college courses.

www.mhhe.com/
bmhh

For access to online dictionaries, go to

Dictionaries and Thesauri

ESL dictionary   A good dictionary designed especially for ESL students can be a useful source of information about word meanings. Ordinary dictionaries frequently define difficult words with other difficult words. In the *American Heritage Dictionary,* for example, the word *haze* is defined as "Atmospheric moisture, dust, smoke, and vapor suspended to form a partially opaque condition." An ESL dictionary defines it more simply as "A light mist or smoke."

Do not confuse ESL dictionaries with bilingual or "translation" dictionaries. Translation dictionaries frequently oversimplify word meanings, as do abridged dictionaries, because they do not indicate shades of meaning.

Like all standard English dictionaries, an ESL dictionary includes instructions that explain the abbreviations used in the entries. They also list the special notations used for words classified as *slang, vulgar, informal, nonstandard,* or another category worthy of special attention. In the ESL/Learner's Edition of the *Random House Webster's Dictionary of American English* (1997), you will find "pig out" as the sixth entry under the word *pig:*

Pig out (no obj) Slang. to eat too much food: *We pigged out on pizza last night.*

The entry tells you that "pig out" does not take a direct object ("no obj") and that its use is very informal ("Slang"), appropriate in talking with classmates but not in writing papers.

The dictionary will help you with spelling, syllabication, pronunciation, definitions, word origins, and usage (*see Chapter 40, pp. 351–53*).

48a
ESL

Dictionary of American idioms   An idiom is an expression that is peculiar to a particular language and cannot be understood by looking at the individual words. "To catch a bus" is an idiom.

Desk encyclopedia In the reference section of your college library, you will find one-volume encyclopedias on every subject from U.S. history to classical or biblical allusions. Look up people, places, and events that are new to you for a quick identification.

COUNT AND NONCOUNT NOUNS

A common noun that refers to something specific that can be counted is a **count noun.** Count nouns can be singular or plural, like *cup* or *suggestion* (*four cups, several suggestions*). **Noncount nouns** are nonspecific; these common nouns refer to categories of people, places, or things and cannot be counted. They do not have a plural form (*the pottery is beautiful, his advice was useful*).

Count Nouns	Noncount Nouns
cars	transportation
computers	Internet
facts	information
clouds	rain
stars	sunshine
tools	equipment
machines	machinery
suggestions	advice
earrings	jewelry
tables	furniture
smiles	happiness

Following is a list of some quantifiers (words that tell how much or how many) for count nouns and for noncount nouns, as well as a few quantifiers that can be used with both.

- **With count nouns only:** *several, many, a couple of, a number of, a few, few*
- **With noncount nouns only:** *a great deal of, much, not much, little, a little, less,* a word that indicates a unit (*a bag of sugar*)
- **With either count or noncount nouns:** *all, any, some, a lot of*

48b Using articles (*a, an,* and *the*) appropriately

Some languages do not use articles at all, and most languages do not use articles in the same way as English. Therefore, articles often cause problems for multilingual writers. In English, there are only three articles: *a, an,* and *the.*

1. Using *a* or *an*

A or *an* refers to one nonspecific person, place, or thing. *A* is used before words that begin with consonant sounds, whether or not the first letter is a vowel (*a European vacation, a country*), and *an* is used before words that begin with vowel sounds, whether or not the first letter is a consonant (*an hour, an opener*).

Count nouns that are singular and refer to a nonspecific person, place, or thing take *a* or *an*. Noncount nouns and plural nouns do not take *a* or *an*. For a list of count and noncount nouns, see the box on page 426.

an
➤ The manager needs to hire ^assistant.

➤ We needed to buy ~~a~~ furniture for our apartment.

2. Using *the*

The refers to a specific person, place, or thing and can be used with singular or plural nouns. A person, place, or thing is specific if it has already been referred to in a preceding sentence, if it is specified within the sentence itself, or if it is commonly known.

The problem
➤ We are trying to solve a difficult problem. ~~Problem~~ started

when we planned two meetings for the same day.

The girl
➤ ~~Girl~~ you have been waiting for is here.

The moon
➤ ~~Moon~~ is shining brightly this evening.

Exception: When a noun represents all examples of something, *the* should be omitted.

Dogs
➤ ~~The dogs~~ were first domesticated long before recorded

history.

Common nouns that refer to a specific person, place, or thing take *the*. Most proper nouns do not use articles unless they are plural, in which case they take the article *the*. There are some exceptions, however:

48b
ESL

- Proper nouns that include a common noun and *of* as part of the title: *the Museum of Modern Art, the Fourth of July, the Statue of Liberty*

- Names of highways: *the Santa Monica Freeway*

- Landmark buildings: *the Eiffel Tower*

- Hotels: *the Marriott Hotel*

- Cultural and political institutions: *the Metropolitan Opera, the Pentagon*

- Parts of the globe, names of oceans and seas, deserts, land and water formations: *the West, the Equator, the North Pole, the Mediterranean, the Sahara, the Bering Strait*

- Countries with more than one word in their names: *the Dominican Republic*

Exercise 48.1   Using articles in context

Correct the errors in article use in the following passage.

In his book *Travels with Charley,* John Steinbeck describes the journey he took that helped him discover his country. The Hurricane Donna struck New York state and delayed the beginning of the long-planned trip. While author was traveling in the New England, weather became cold, and leaves turned their fall colors. On his way, he met farmer who had a Yankee face and the Yankee accent. Steinbeck discovered that the best way to learn about local population was to visit local bar or church. He also saw many people fleeing New England to escape winter. Many shops were closed, and some had signs saying they would be closed until following summer. As he traveled through states, he noticed the changes in the language. These differences were apparent in road signs. A trouble arose when he was not allowed to cross Canadian border because he did not have vaccination certificate for his dog, Charley. Steinbeck and his companion were later able to resume their trip without the further problems.

48c   Using helping verbs with main verbs

Verbs change form to indicate person, number, tense, voice, and mood. (*For a detailed discussion of verbs, see Chapter 45.*) To do all this, a **main verb** is often accompanied by one or more **helping verbs** in a **verb phrase.** Helping verbs include forms of *do, have,* and *be* as well as the modal verbs such as *may, must, should,* and *would.*

1. *Do, Does, Did*

The helping verb *do* and its forms *does* and *did* combine with the base form of a verb to ask a question or to emphasize something. It can also combine with the word *not* to create an emphatic negative statement.

QUESTION	*Do* you hear those dogs barking?
EMPHATIC STATEMENT	I *do* hear them barking.
EMPHATIC NEGATIVE	I *do not* want to have to call the police about those dogs.

2. *Have, Has, Had*

The helping verb *have* and its forms *has* and *had* combine with a past participle (usually ending in *-d, -t,* or *-n*) to form the *perfect tenses.* Do not confuse the simple past tense with the present perfect tense (formed with *have* or *has*), which is distinct from the simple past because the action can continue in the present. (*For a review of perfect tense forms, see Chapter 45, pp. 397–98.*)

SIMPLE PAST	Those dogs *barked* all day.
PRESENT PERFECT	Those dogs *have barked* all day.
PAST PERFECT	Those dogs *had barked* all day.

3. *Be*

Forms of *be* combine with a present participle (ending in *-ing*) to form the **progressive tenses,** which express continuing action. Do not confuse the simple present tense or the present perfect with these progressive forms. Unlike the simple present, which indicates an action that occurs frequently and might include the present moment, the present progressive form indicates an action that is going on right now. In its past form, the progressive tense indicates actions that are going on simultaneously. (*For a review of progressive tense forms, see Chapter 45, pp. 398–99.*)

48c
ESL

SIMPLE PRESENT	Those dogs *bark* all the time.
PRESENT PROGRESSIVE	Those dogs *are barking* all the time.
PAST PROGRESSIVE	Those dogs *were barking* all day while I *was trying* to study.

Note: A number of verbs that are related to thoughts, preferences, and ownership are seldom used in the progressive tense in English. These include *appear, believe, know, like, need, own, seem, understand,* and *want.*

Forms of *be* combine with the past participle (which usually ends in *-d, -t,* or *-n*) to form the passive voice, which is often used to express a state of being instead of an action.

BE + PAST PARTICIPLE

PASSIVE   The dogs *were scolded* by their owner.

PASSIVE   I *was satisfied* by her answer.

Intransitive verbs such as *happen* and *occur* cannot appear in the passive voice because they do not take direct objects.

➤ **The accident ~~was~~ happened after he returned from his trip.**

4. Modals

Other helping verbs, called **modals,** signify the manner, or mode, of an action. Unlike *be, have,* and *do,* one-word modals such as *may, must,* and *will* are almost never used alone as main verbs, nor do they change form to show person or number. Modals do not add *-s* endings, two modals are never used together (such as *might could*), and modals are always followed by the base form of the verb without *to* (*he could be nicer*).

The one-word modals are *can, could, may, might, will, would, shall, should,* and *must.*

               hv   mv

➤ **Contrary to press reports, she *will* not *run* for political office.**

Note that a negative word such as *not* may come between the helping and the main verb.

Phrasal modals, however, do change form to show time, person, and number. Here are some phrasal modals: *have to, have got to, used to, be supposed to, be going to, be allowed to, be able to.*

           hv   mv

➤ **Yesterday, I *was going to study* for three hours.**

          hv   mv

➤ **Next week, I *am going to study* three hours a day.**

Exercise 48.2   Using modals and other helping verbs

Correct any errors in the use of modals and other helping verbs in the following sentences.

EXAMPLE

had

We been hoping that we could ~~to~~ visit California before

we graduated.

1. Do you know where you and Erica will to go on vacation this summer?
2. You should to look online. You can to find great deals there.
3. I have been looking all over the Internet, but I not found any cheap hotels.
4. Have you thought about camping? My sister did able to save a lot of money by camping when she traveling around Europe last summer.
5. That is a great idea! Are there any campsites she can suggests in Spain and Portugal?
6. I am not sure if she went to Portugal, but she must been to Spain. Let me ask her.
7. That is excellent. I just hope I will not have buy too much camping gear.
8. I have a lot of gear, and I am sure Erica coulds borrow some of my sister's things.

48d Using verbs followed by gerunds or infinitives

Verbs in English differ as to whether they can be followed by a gerund, an infinitive, or either. Some verbs, like *avoid,* can be followed by a gerund but not an infinitive.

climbing

➤ We avoided ~~to climb~~ the mountain during the storm.

Other verbs, like *attempt,* can be followed by an infinitive but not a gerund.

to reach

➤ We attempted ~~reaching~~ the summit when the weather

cleared.

Others can be followed by either a gerund or an infinitive with no change in meaning.

➤ We began climbing.

➤ We began to climb.

**48d
ESL**

Still others have a different meaning when followed by a gerund than they do when followed by an infinitive. Compare these examples:

➤ **She stopped eating.**

She was eating but she stopped.

➤ **She stopped to eat.**

She stopped what she was doing before in order to eat.

The following lists provide common examples of each type of verb.

Some Verbs That Take Only an Infinitive

afford	hurry	promise
appear	intend	refuse
attempt	learn	request
choose	manage	seem
claim	mean	tend
decide	need	threaten
expect	offer	want
fail	plan	wish
hope	prepare	would like

Some Verbs That Take Only a Gerund

admit	finish	recommend
advise	forgive	regret
avoid	imagine	resist
consider	look forward to	risk
defend	mention	suggest
deny	mind	support
discuss	practice	tolerate
enjoy	propose	understand
feel like	quit	urge

Some Verbs That Can Take Either a Gerund or an Infinitive

An asterisk (*) indicates those verbs for which the choice of gerund or infinitive affects meaning.

begin	love	start
continue	prefer	*stop
hate	*remember	*try
like		

Note: For some verbs, such as *allow, cause, encourage, have, persuade, remind,* and *tell,* a noun or pronoun must precede the infinitive: *I reminded my sister to return my sweater.* For a few verbs, such as *ask, expect, need,* and *want,* the noun may either precede or follow the infinitive, depending on the meaning you want to express: *I want to return my sweater to my sister. I want my sister to return my sweater.*

Make, let, and *have* are followed by a noun or pronoun plus the base form without *to: Make that boy come home on time.*

Exercise 48.3   Using gerunds versus infinitives after verbs

Underline the correct choice—gerund or infinitive—in each pair in parentheses.

EXAMPLE

Most people hope (<u>to work</u>/working) in rewarding jobs.

1. In the past, people were expected (to stay/staying) at the same job for a long time, ideally for their whole career.
2. Today, people tend (to change/changing) careers several times before retiring.
3. People who are not happy with their careers attempt (to find/finding) other jobs that interest them more.
4. Others, who regret (not to get/not getting) undergraduate or graduate degrees when they were younger, go back to school.
5. Some people even look forward to (to change/changing) jobs every few years to avoid boredom.
6. So, if you do not like your job, stop (to complain/complaining) and do something about it.

48e Using complete subjects and verbs

48e
ESL

1. Using a complete subject
Every clause in English has a subject, even if it is only a stand-in subject like *there* or *it.* Check your clauses to make sure that each one has a subject.

                                     it

➤ **No one thought the party could end, but ^ ended abruptly**

   when the stock market crashed.

➤   *There is*
   ~~Is~~ general agreement that the crash helped bring on the
   _∧

Great Depression.

2. Including a complete verb

Verb structure, as well as where the verb is placed within a sentence, varies dramatically across languages, but in English each sentence needs to include at least one complete verb. The verb cannot be an infinitive—the *to* form of the verb—or an *-ing* form without a helping verb.

NOT COMPLETE	The caterer *to bring* dinner.
COMPLETE VERBS	The caterer *brings* dinner.
	The caterer *will bring* dinner.
	The caterer *is bringing* dinner.
NOT COMPLETE	Children *running* in the park.
COMPLETE VERBS	Children *are running* in the park.
	Children *have been running* in the park.
	Children *will be running* in the park.

48f   Using only one subject or object

Watch out for repeated subjects in your clauses.

➤   The celebrity ~~he~~ signed my program.

Watch out as well for repeated objects in clauses that begin with relative pronouns (*that, which, who, whom, whose*) or relative adverbs (*where, when, how*).

➤   Our dog guards the house where we live ~~there.~~

Even if the relative pronoun does not appear in the sentence but is only implied, you should still omit repeated objects.

➤   He is the man I need to talk to ~~him.~~

The relative pronoun *whom* (he is the man *whom* I need to talk to) is implied, so *him* is not needed.

48g   Using adjectives correctly

English adjectives do not change form to agree with the form of the nouns they modify. They stay the same whatever the number or gender of the noun. (*For more on adjectives, see Chapter 47, pp. 417–23, and Chapter 61, pp. 522–23.*)

> **Juan is an *attentive* father. Alyssa is an *attentive* mother. They are *attentive* parents.**

Adjectives usually come before a noun, but they can also occur after a linking verb.

> **The food at the restaurant was *delicious*.**

The position of an adjective can affect its meaning, however. The phrase *my old friend,* for example, can refer to a long friendship (*a friend I have known for a long time*) or an elderly friend (*my friend who is eighty years old*). In the sentence *My friend is old,* by contrast, *old* has only one meaning—elderly.

1. Adjective order

When two or more adjectives modify a noun cumulatively, they follow a sequence—determined by their meaning—that is particular to English logic:

1. Adjectives of size and shape: *big, small, huge, tiny, tall, short, narrow, thick, round, square*
2. Adjectives that suggest subjective evaluation: *cozy, intelligent, outrageous, elegant, original*
3. Adjectives of color: *yellow, green, pale*
4. Adjectives of origin and type: *African, Czech, gothic*
5. Nouns used as adjectives: *brick, plastic, glass, stone*
6. NOUN

> **the tall, African, stone statues**

2. Present and past participles used as adjectives

Both the present and past participle forms of verbs can function as adjectives. To use them properly, keep the following in mind:

- Present participle adjectives usually modify nouns that are the agent of an action.
- Past participle adjectives usually modify nouns that are the recipient of an action.

> **This problem is *confusing*.**

The present participle *confusing* modifies *problem,* which is the agent, or cause of the confusion.

48g
ESL

➤ **The students are *confused* by the problem.**

The past participle *confused* modifies *students,* who are the
recipients of the confusion the problem is causing.

The following are some other present and past participle pairs that
often cause problems.

amazing/amazed   frightening/frightened
annoying/annoyed   interesting/interested
boring/bored   satisfying/satisfied
depressing/depressed   shocking/shocked
embarrassing/embarrassed   surprising/surprised
exciting/excited   tiring/tired
fascinating/fascinated

Exercise 48.4   Working with English adjectives

Correct any errors in adjective placement or agreement in the following sentences. Some of the sentences may be correct as written; circle
their numbers.

EXAMPLE

huge brick

The houses in the development were all ~~brick huge~~
mansions.

1. House hunting can be a time-consuming activity and frustrating.
2. Prospective home buyers are bombarded with images of spacious,
   elegant houses.
3. Multiple bedrooms, bathrooms fully equipped, and gardens
   landscaped are becoming standard features of suburban new
   properties.
4. The kitchens are filled with shiny surfaces and hi-tech numerous
   gadgets.
5. Many American young families cannot afford those expensives
   properties.

Exercise 48.5   Choosing the correct participle

Underline the correct participle from each pair in parentheses.

EXAMPLE

The (tiring/<u>tired</u>) students celebrated the end of final exams.

1. The review material for the art history final is very (boring/bored).
2. The term paper I am writing for the class is on a (challenging/challenged) topic: twentieth-century painting.
3. The paintings of Picasso are especially (interesting/interested).
4. Most students have already submitted their (completing/completed) papers.
5. After a week of studying, I am (prepared/preparing) for the exam.

48h Putting adverbs in the correct place

Although adverbs can appear in almost any position within a sentence, they should not separate a verb from its direct object. (*For more on adverbs, see Chapter 47, pp. 417–23, and Chapter 61, pp. 523–25.*)

> *quickly*
> ➤ Juan found ~~quickly~~ his cat.

The negative word *not* usually precedes the main verb and follows the first helping verb in a verb phrase.

> *not*
> ➤ I have been ~~not~~ sick lately.

48i Using prepositions

Every language uses prepositions idiomatically in ways that do not match their literal meaning, which is why prepositional phrases can be difficult for multilingual writers. In English, prepositions combine with other words in such a variety of ways that the combinations can only be learned with repetition and over time (*see Chapter 61, pp. 525–26*). (*For a list of common prepositions, see p. 525.*)

1. Idiomatic uses of prepositions indicating time and location

The prepositions that indicate time and location are often the most idiosyncratic in a language. The following are some common ways in which the prepositions *at, by, in,* and *on* are used.

48i
ESL

TIME

AT The wedding ceremony starts *at two o'clock.* [a specific clock time]

BY Our honeymoon plans should be ready *by next week.* [a particular time]

IN The reception will start *in the evening.* [a portion of the day]

ON The wedding will take place *on May 1*. The rehearsal is *on Tuesday*. [a particular date or day of the week]

LOCATION

AT I will meet you *at the zoo*. [a particular place]

You need to turn right *at the light*. [a corner or an intersection]

We took a seat *at the table*. [near a piece of furniture]

BY Meet me *by the fountain*. [a familiar place]

IN Park your car *in the parking lot* and give the money to the attendant *in the booth*. [on a space of some kind or inside a structure]

I enjoyed the bratwurst *in Chicago*. [a city, state, or other geographic location]

I found that article *in this book*. [a print medium]

ON An excellent restaurant is located *on Mulberry Street*. [a street, avenue, or other thoroughfare]

I spilled milk *on the floor*. [a surface]

I watched the report *on television*. [an electronic medium]

2. Prepositions plus gerunds (-*ing*)

A gerund is the -*ing* form of a verb acting as a noun. A gerund can occur after a preposition (*thanks for coming*), but when the preposition is *to,* be careful not to confuse it with the infinitive form of a verb.

> I look forward to ~~win~~ at Jeopardy. *(winning)*

Following is a list of common idiomatic expressions in English. These often cause problems for multilingual writers, who must study and memorize them.

COMMON IDIOMATIC EXPRESSIONS in ENGLISH

COMMON ADJECTIVE + PREPOSITION COMBINATIONS

afraid of: fearing someone or something

anxious about: worried

ashamed of: embarrassed by someone or something

aware of: know about

content with: having no complaints about; happy about

fond of: having positive feelings for

full of: filled with

grateful to (someone) (for something): thankful; appreciative

interested in: curious; wanting to know more about

jealous of: feeling envy toward

proud/suspicious of: pleased about/distrustful of

tired of: had enough of; bored with

responsible to (someone) (for something): accountable; in charge

satisfied with: having no complaints about

COMMON VERB + PREPOSITION COMBINATIONS

apologize to: express regret for actions

arrive in (a place): come to a city/country (*I arrived in Paris.*)

arrive at (an event at a specific location): come to a building or a house
    (*I arrived at the Louvre at ten.*)

blame for: hold responsible; accuse

complain about: find fault; criticize

concentrate on: focus; pay attention

consist of: contain; be made of

congratulate on: offer good wishes for success

depend on: trust

explain to: make something clear to someone

insist on: be firm

laugh at: express amusement

rely on: trust

smile at: act friendly toward

take care of: look after; tend

thank for: express appreciation

throw to: toss something to someone to catch

48j
ESL

(continued)

COMMON IDIOMATIC EXPRESSIONS in ENGLISH *(continued)*

COMMON VERB + PREPOSITION COMBINATIONS *(continued)*

throw at: toss an object toward someone or something

throw (something) away: discard

throw (something) out: discard; present an idea for consideration

worry about: feel concern; fear for someone's safety or well-being

COMMON PARTICIPLES

Verb + preposition combinations that create **verb phrasals,** expressions with meanings that are different from the meaning of the verb itself. An asterisk (*) indicates a separable participle.

break down: stop functioning

*call off: cancel

*fill out: complete

*find out: discover

get over: recover

*give up: surrender; stop work on

*leave out: omit

look forward to: anticipate

look into: research

*look up: check a fact

look up to: admire

put up with: endure

run across: meet unexpectedly

run out: use up

stand up for: defend

turn down: reject

48j   Using direct objects with two-word verbs

If a two-word verb has a direct object, the preposition (particle) may be either separable (*I filled the form out*) or inseparable (*I got over the shock*). If the verb is separable, the direct object can also follow the preposition if it is a noun (*I filled out the form*). If the direct object is a pronoun, however, it must appear between the verb and preposition.

➤   I filled out ~~it~~.
         it

48k Using coordination and subordination appropriately

Do not use both subordination and coordination together to combine the same two clauses, even if the subordinating and coordinating words are similar in meaning. Some examples include *although* or *even though* with *but* and *because* with *therefore*.

➤ Although I came early, ~~but~~ the tickets were already sold out.

or

➤ ~~Although~~ I came early, but the tickets were already sold out.

(For more on coordination and subordination, see Chapter 36, pp. 326–30.)

48l Putting sentence parts in the correct order for English

In some languages (such as Spanish), it is acceptable to omit subjects. In others (such as Arabic), it is acceptable to omit certain kinds of verbs. Other languages (such as Japanese) place verbs last, and still others (such as Hebrew) allow verbs to precede the subject. English, however, has its own distinct order for sentence parts. (*See also Chapter 62, pp. 530–33.*)

MODIFIERS + SUBJECT → VERB + OBJECTS, COMPLEMENTS, MODIFIERS

    mod   subj   verb   mod   obj   obj comp
➤ The playful kitten batted the crystal glasses on the shelf.

Changing a **direct quotation** (someone else's exact words) to an **indirect quotation** (a report on what the person said or wrote) often requires changing many sentence elements. When the quotation is a declarative sentence, however, the subject-before-verb word order does not change.

DIRECT QUOTATION	The instructor said, "You have only one more week to finish your papers."
INDIRECT QUOTATION	The instructor told the students that they had only one more week to finish their papers.

Note: In the indirect quotation, the verb tense changes from present to past.

Changing a direct question to an indirect question, however, does require a word order change—from the verb-subject pattern of a question to the subject-verb pattern of a declarative sentence.

48l
ESL

DIRECT QUESTION	The instructor always asks, "Are you ready to begin?"
INDIRECT QUESTION	The instructor always asks [*us*] if we are ready to begin.

In an indirect quotation of a command, a pronoun or noun takes the place of the command's omitted subject, *you,* and is followed by the infinitive (*to*) form of the verb.

DIRECT QUOTATION: COMMAND	The instructor always says "[*you*] Write down the assignment before you leave."
INDIRECT QUOTATION: COMMAND	The instructor always tells *us* to write down the assignment before we leave.

Exercise 48.6   Using English word order

Find and correct the errors in the following sentences. Some sentences have more than one error.

EXAMPLE

Because they worry about food so much, ~~therefore~~ Americans may have more eating-related problems than people in other developed countries.

1. As Michael Pollan in the *New York Times Magazine* writes, Americans have become the world's most anxious eaters.
2. Researchers have found that Americans they worry more about what they eat than people do in other developed countries.
3. Therefore, tend to enjoy their food less and associate a good meal with guilty pleasure.
4. Paradoxically, this worrying does not stop regularly many Americans from overeating.
5. The report also tells to readers that it is not uncommon for people to visit the gym after overeating.
6. The people of many other nations take pleasure in eating and turn often a meal into a festive occasion.
7. Although they relish their meals, but they are less prone to obesity or eating disorders than Americans.
8. Some scientists speculate that the people of these nations therefore are less obese because they cook with more healthful ingredients than Americans.
9. The question arises, however, whether might people's attitude toward eating be as important to good health as what they eat?

48m Understanding the purposes and constructions of *if* clauses

If clauses (also called **conditional clauses**) state facts, make predictions, and speculate about unlikely or impossible events. These conditional constructions most often employ *if,* but *when, unless,* or other words can introduce conditional constructions as well.

- Use the present tense for facts. When the relationship you are describing is usually true, the verbs in both clauses should be in the same tense.

STATES FACTS

If people *practice* doing good consistently, they *have* a sense of satisfaction.

When Meg *found* a new cause, she always *talked* about it incessantly.

- In a sentence that predicts, use the present tense in the *if* clause. The verb in the independent clause is a modal plus the base form of the verb.

PREDICTS POSSIBILITIES

If you *practice* doing good through politics, you *will have* a greater effect on your community.

- If you are speculating about something that is unlikely to happen, use the past tense in the *if* clause and *could, should,* or *would* plus the base verb in the independent clause.

SPECULATES ON THE UNLIKELY

If you *were* a better person, you *would practice* doing good every day.

- Use the past perfect tense in the *if* clause if you are speculating about an event that did not happen. In the independent clause, use *could have, might have,* or *would have* plus the past participle.

SPECULATES ON SOMETHING THAT DID NOT HAPPEN

If you *had practiced* doing good when you were young, you *would have been* a different person today.

- Use *were* in the *if* clause and *could, might,* or *would* plus the base form in the main clause if you are speculating about something that could never happen.

SPECULATES ABOUT THE IMPOSSIBLE

If Lincoln *were* alive today, he *would fight* for equal protection under the law.

48m
ESL

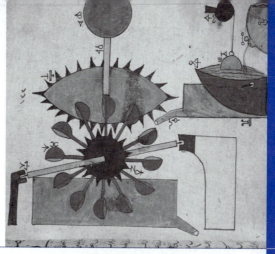

The great twelfth-century inventor al-Jazari designed many innovative mechanical devices. This plan for a water-operated automaton documents the engineering behind one invention's design; each working part relies on the precise placement of others.

It wasn't a matter of rewriting but simply

of tightening up all the bolts.

—MARGUERITE YOURCENAR

Editing
for Correctness

Punctuation, Mechanics, and Spelling

8 Editing for Correctness

WRITING OUTCOMES

Conventions

This section will help you learn to do the following:

- Recognize and correct common mistakes in punctuation **(49–54)** and spelling **(60)**
- Understand appropriate use of abbreviations **(56)**, numerals **(57)**, capitalization **(55)**, and italics **(58)**

Test Yourself:

Go to www.mhhe.com/bmhh and take online quizzes in Sentence Punctuation (chapters 49–54) and Mechanics and Spelling (chapters 55–60) to test your familiarity with these topics. As you read the following chapters, pay special attention to the sections that correspond to any questions you answer incorrectly.

49 Commas

You may have been told that commas are used to mark pauses, but that is not an accurate general principle. To clarify meaning, commas are used in the following situations:

- Following introductory elements (*pp. 447–48*)
- After each item in a series and between coordinate adjectives (*pp. 448 and 450*)
- Between coordinated independent clauses (*pp. 449–50*)
- To set off interruptions or nonessential information (*pp. 451–55*)
- To set off direct quotations (*p. 457*)
- In dates, addresses, people's titles, and numbers (*p. 458*)
- To replace an omitted word or phrase or to prevent misreading (*pp. 458–59*)

www.mhhe.com/
bmhh
For information
and exercises on
commas, go to
Editing > Commas

49a   Using a comma after an introductory word group

A comma both attaches an introductory word, phrase, or clause to and distinguishes it from the rest of the sentence.

➤ **Finally, the car careened to the right, endangering passers-by.**

➤ **Reflecting on her life experiences, Washburn attributed her successes to her own efforts.**

➤ **Until he noticed the handprint on the wall, the detective was frustrated by the lack of clues.**

Do not add a comma after a word group that functions as the subject of the sentence, however.

➤ **Persuading his or her constituents/ is one of a politician's most important tasks.**

When the introductory phrase is less than five words long and there is no danger of confusion without a comma, the comma can be omitted.

➤ **For several hours we rode on in silence.**

49a
∧
,

447

> **Commas and Grammar Checkers**
>
> Computer grammar checkers usually will not highlight missing commas following introductory elements or between independent clauses joined by a coordinating conjunction such as *and,* and they cannot decide whether a sentence element is essential or nonessential.

Exercise 49.1   Using commas with introductory word groups

Edit the following sentences, adding commas as needed after introductory word groups. Some sentences may be correct; circle their numbers.

> EXAMPLE   **During the early Middle Ages, Western Europeans**
>   ^
>
> **remained fairly cut off from the East.**

1. After the year 1000 CE Europeans became less isolated.
2. To the Holy Lands traveled Western pilgrims and merchants in a steady stream.
3. Increasingly aware of the rich civilizations beyond their borders Europeans began to enter into business relationships with the cities and countries in the East.
4. Establishing contact with the principal ports of the eastern Mediterranean and Black seas allowed merchants to develop a vigorous trade.
5. As this trade expanded across the Mediterranean world Western Europeans were able to enjoy spices and other exotic products.
6. In the thirteenth and fourteenth centuries European missionaries and merchants traveled to China, India, and the Near East.

49b   Using commas between items in a series

A comma should appear after each item in a series.

> ➤   **Three industries that have been important to New England**
>
> **are shipbuilding, tourism, and commercial fishing.**
>   ^

Commas clarify which items are part of the series.

> CONFUSING   For the hiking trip, we needed to pack lunch, chocolate and trail mix.
>
> CLEAR   For the hiking trip, we needed to pack lunch, chocolate, and trail mix.

CHARTING the TERRITORY

Commas in Journalism

If you are writing for a journalism course, you may be required to leave out the final comma that precedes *and* in a series, just as magazines and newspapers usually do. Follow the convention that your instructor prefers.

49c Using a comma in front of a coordinating conjunction joining independent clauses

When a coordinating conjunction (*and, but, for, nor, or, so,* or *yet*) is used to join clauses that could each stand alone as a sentence, put a comma before the coordinating conjunction.

➤ **Injuries were so frequent that he began to worry‸, and his**

   style of play became more cautious.

If the word groups you are joining are not independent clauses, do not add a comma (*see p. 459*).

Exception: If you are joining two short clauses, you may leave out the comma unless it is needed for clarity.

➤ **The running back caught the ball and the fans cheered.**

Exercise 49.2 Combining sentences with commas and coordinating conjunctions

Use a comma and a coordinating conjunction to combine each set of sentences into one sentence. Vary your choice of conjunctions.

> EXAMPLE   The experiment did not support our
>   *, yet we*
>   hypothesis.‸ ~~We~~ considered it a success.

1. Asperger's syndrome and autism, although they are both classified as autism spectrum disorders, are not the same. Asperger's syndrome is often confused with autism.
2. People with Asperger's syndrome have normal IQs. They experience difficulty interacting with others in a social setting.

49c

‸
,

3. Children with this disorder often engage in solitary, repetitive routines. In school they may have difficulty working in groups.
4. People with Asperger's syndrome also have a difficult time with nonverbal communication. They may be unable to read other people's body language.
5. The public has only recently become aware of Asperger's syndrome. Drugs that can cure this neurobiological disorder have yet to be developed.

49d Adding a comma between coordinate adjectives

A comma is used between **coordinate adjectives** because these adjectives modify the noun independently.

> ➤ **This brave, intelligent, persistent woman was the first**
>
> **female to earn a Ph.D. in psychology.**

If you cannot add *and* between the adjectives or change their order, they are **cumulative adjectives** and should not be separated with a comma or commas (*see p. 460*).

Exercise 49.3 Using commas with series of nouns and adjectives

Edit the following sentences, adding commas as needed to separate items in a series and coordinate adjectives. Some sentences may be correct; circle their numbers.

> **EXAMPLE** **One part of the wall was covered with pictures**
>
> **of leaping, prancing animals.**

1. Scholars have studied prehistoric cave paintings for almost a century.
2. Paintings have been found in North America Europe Africa and Australia.
3. Paintings found in southeastern France contain images of animals birds and fish.
4. Some scholars believe that the cave painter may have been a rapturous entranced shaman.
5. We can picture the flickering dazzling torchlight that guided the painter's way through dank dark passageways.
6. Mixing colors with their saliva and blowing the paint onto the wall with their breath must have given the cave painters feelings of creative power supernatural control and expressive glory.

IDENTIFY AND EDIT
Commas with Coordinate Adjectives

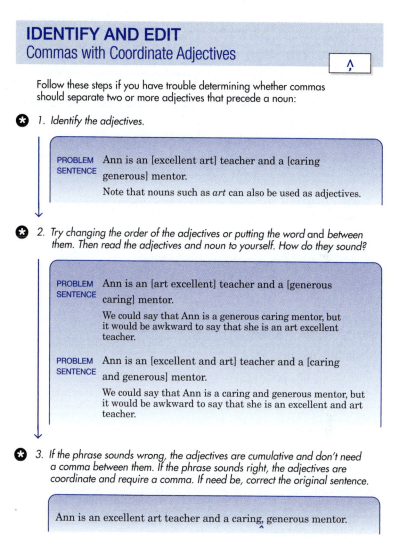

Follow these steps if you have trouble determining whether commas should separate two or more adjectives that precede a noun:

❋ 1. Identify the adjectives.

> PROBLEM
> SENTENCE
> Ann is an [excellent art] teacher and a [caring generous] mentor.
>
> Note that nouns such as *art* can also be used as adjectives.

❋ 2. Try changing the order of the adjectives or putting the word and between them. Then read the adjectives and noun to yourself. How do they sound?

> PROBLEM
> SENTENCE
> Ann is an [art excellent] teacher and a [generous caring] mentor.
>
> We could say that Ann is a generous caring mentor, but it would be awkward to say that she is an art excellent teacher.
>
> PROBLEM
> SENTENCE
> Ann is an [excellent and art] teacher and a [caring and generous] mentor.
>
> We could say that Ann is a caring and generous mentor, but it would be awkward to say that she is an excellent and art teacher.

❋ 3. If the phrase sounds wrong, the adjectives are cumulative and don't need a comma between them. If the phrase sounds right, the adjectives are coordinate and require a comma. If need be, correct the original sentence.

> Ann is an excellent art teacher and a caring, generous mentor.

49e
∧
,

49e Using commas to set off nonessential elements

Nonessential, or **nonrestrictive,** words, phrases, and clauses add information to a sentence but are not required for its basic meaning to be understood. Nonrestrictive additions are set off with commas.

➤ **Mary Shelley's best-known novel, *Frankenstein or the***

Modern Prometheus, was first published in 1818.

The sentence would have the same basic meaning without the title.

Restrictive words, phrases, and clauses are essential to a sentence because they identify exactly who or what the writer is talking about. Restrictive additions are not set off with commas.

➤ **Mary Shelley's novel *Frankenstein or the Modern Prometheus***

was first published in 1818.

Without the title, the reader would not know which novel the sentence is referring to.

Three types of additions to sentences often cause problems: adjective clauses, adjective phrases, and appositives.

1. Adjective clauses

Adjective clauses begin with a relative pronoun or an adverb—*who, whom, whose, which, that, where,* or *when*—and modify a noun or pronoun within the sentence.

NONRESTRICTIVE

With his tale of Odysseus, *whose journey can be traced on modern maps,* Homer brought accounts of alien and strange creatures to the ancient Greeks.

RESTRICTIVE

The contestant *whom he most wanted to beat* was his father.

Note: Use *that* only with restrictive clauses. *Which* can introduce either restrictive or nonrestrictive clauses. Some writers prefer to use *which* only with nonrestrictive clauses.

2. Adjective phrases

Like an adjective clause, an adjective phrase also modifies a noun or pronoun in a sentence. Adjective phrases begin with a preposition (for example, *with, by, at,* or *for*) or a verbal (a word formed from a verb). Adjective phrases can be either restrictive or nonrestrictive.

NONRESTRICTIVE

Some people, *by their faith in human nature or their general good will,* bring out the best in others.

The phrase is nonessential because it does not specify which people are being discussed.

RESTRICTIVE

People *fighting passionately for their rights* can inspire others to join a cause.

The phrase indicates which people the writer is talking about.

3. Appositives

Appositives are nouns or noun phrases that rename nouns or pronouns and appear right after the word they rename.

NONRESTRICTIVE

One researcher, *the widely respected R. S. Smith,* has shown that a child's performance on IQ tests can be very inconsistent.

Because *one researcher* already refers to the person at issue, the researcher's name is supplementary but not essential information.

RESTRICTIVE

The researcher *R. S. Smith* has shown that a child's performance on IQ tests is not reliable.

The name *R. S. Smith* tells readers which researcher is meant.

Exercise 49.4   Using commas with nonrestrictive elements

Edit the following sentences, adding commas as needed to set off nonrestrictive clauses, adjective phrases, and appositives. Some sentences may be correct; circle their numbers.

EXAMPLE   **The brain, connected by nerves to all the other**

parts of the body, seems to be the seat of the mind, an

abstract term for the workings of the brain.

1. The mind-body problem under debate for centuries concerns the relationship between the mind and the body.
2. Prehistoric peoples must have observed that when a person died the body remained and the mind departed.
3. Since the time of the ancient Greeks the prevailing opinion has been that the mind and the body are separate entities.
4. Plato the Greek philosopher is often credited with originating the concept of mind-body dualism.

49e

IDENTIFY AND EDIT
Commas with Nonrestrictive Words
and Word Groups

⌄

Follow these steps if you have trouble determining whether a
word or word group should be set off with a comma or commas:

❋ 1. *Identify the word or word group that may need to be set off with commas.*
   Pay special attention to words that appear between the subject and verb.

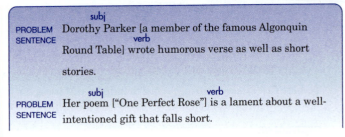

> PROBLEM   subj
> SENTENCE Dorothy Parker [a member of the famous Algonquin
>   verb
>   Round Table] wrote humorous verse as well as short
>
>   stories.
>
> PROBLEM   subj   verb
> SENTENCE Her poem ["One Perfect Rose"] is a lament about a well-
>   intentioned gift that falls short.

❋ 2. *Read the sentence to yourself without the word or word group. Does the*
   basic meaning stay the same, or does it change? Can you tell what person,
   place, or thing the sentence is about?

> SENTENCE   Dorothy Parker wrote humorous verse as well as
> WITHOUT   short stories.
> THE WORD
> GROUP   The subject of the sentence is identified by name, and the
>   basic meaning of the sentence does not change.
>
> SENTENCE   Her poem is a lament about a well-intentioned gift
> WITHOUT   that falls short.
> THE WORD
> GROUP   Without the words "One Perfect Rose," we cannot tell what
>   poem the sentence is describing.

❋ 3. *If the meaning of the sentence stays the same without the word or word*
   group, set it off with commas. If the meaning changes, the word or word
   group should not be set off with commas.

> ▪ Dorothy Parker, a member of the famous Algonquin Round
>   Table, wrote humorous verse as well as short stories.
>
> ▪ Her poem "One Perfect Rose" is a lament about a well-intentioned
>   gift that falls short.
>
> The sentence is correct. Commas are not needed to enclose "One
> Perfect Rose."

5. The French philosopher René Descartes described the mind and the body as independent.
6. Descartes's influential theories helped lay the foundation for scientific rationalism which views nature as a vast machine.

49f Using a comma or commas with transitional and parenthetical expressions, contrasting comments, and absolute phrases

1. Transitional expressions

Conjunctive adverbs (*however, therefore, moreover*) and other transitional phrases (*for example, on the other hand*) are usually set off by commas. (*For a list of transitional expressions, see Chapter 43, p. 375.*)

➤ **Brian Wilson, for example, was unable to cope with the pressures of touring with the Beach Boys.**

When a transitional expression connects two independent clauses, use a semicolon before and a comma after it.

➤ **The Beatles were a phenomenon when they toured the United States in 1964; subsequently, they became the most successful rock band of all time.**

Short expressions such as *also, at least, certainly, instead, of course, then, perhaps,* and *therefore* do not always need to be set off with commas.

➤ **I found my notes and *also* got my story in on time.**

2. Parenthetical expressions

The information that parenthetical expressions provide is relatively insignificant and could easily be left out. Therefore, they are set off with a comma or commas.

➤ **Human cloning, so they say, will be possible within a decade.**

3. Contrasting comments

Contrasting comments beginning with words such as *not, unlike,* or *in contrast to* should be set off with commas.

➤ **Adam Sandler is talented as a comedian, not a tragedian.**

49f
,

4. Absolute phrases

Absolute phrases usually include a noun (*sunlight*) followed by a participle (*shining*) and are used to modify whole sentences.

➤ **The snake slithered through the tall grass, the sunlight**

  shining now and then on its green skin.

49g   Using a comma or commas to set off words of direct address, *yes* and *no,* mild interjections, and tag questions

➤ **We have finished this project, Mr. Smith, without any help**

  from your foundation.

➤ **Yes, I will meet you at noon.**

➤ **Of course, if you think that's what we should do, then**

  we'll do it.

➤ **We can do better, don't you think?**

Exercise 49.5   Using commas to set off other nonessential
sentence elements

Edit the following sentences, adding commas where they are needed to set off nonessential elements.

EXAMPLE   **Yes, I will go with you to dinner; however, I must**

  leave by ten, not a minute later.

1. Millions of viewers watch reality-based television shows. Cultural critics however argue that shows such as *Survivor, American Idol,* and *The Bachelor* exploit human greed and the desire for fame.
2. These shows so the critics say take advantage of our insecurities.
3. The participants who appear on these shows are average, everyday people not actors.
4. *American Idol* follows its contestants singers hoping to beat out their competitors by singing and performing in front of judges and home audiences.
5. The message is always the same: You too can be rich and famous Average Jane or Joe.
6. Yes many of these shows hold the promise that anyone can win a million dollars or gain instant celebrity.

7. These shows of course are extremely enjoyable.
8. Their entertainment value explains why we watch them don't you think?

49h Using a comma or commas to separate a direct quotation from the rest of the sentence

➤ Irving Howe declares, "Whitman is quite realistic about the

place of the self in an urban world" (261).

➤ "Whitman is quite realistic about the place of the self in an

urban world," declares Irving Howe (261).

If the quoted sentence is interrupted, use commas to set off the interrupting words.

➤ "I don't understand," she said, "why you would think that."

A comma is not needed to separate an indirect quotation or a paraphrase from the words that identify its source.

➤ Irving Howe notes/ that Whitman realistically depicts the

urban self as free to wander (261).

(*For more on using quotations, see Chapter 53, pp. 473–81.*)

Exercise 49.6 Using commas to set off direct quotations

Edit the following sentences to correct problems with the use of commas. Some sentences may be correct; circle their numbers.

> EXAMPLE "Nothing I studied was on the test," she moaned
>
> to her friends.

1. Professor Bartman entered the room and proclaimed "Today we will examine Erikson's eight stages of human development."
2. "Who may I ask has read the assignment" he queried.
3. "Patricia" he hissed "please enlighten the rest of the class."
4. "What would you like to know?" she asked.
5. Now smiling, he replied "Begin by telling us what the eight stages are."
6. She explained that the first stage occurs when infants must learn to trust that their needs will be met.

49h
∧
,

49i Using commas with dates, addresses, titles and numbers

∎ **Dates.** Use paired commas in dates when the month, day, and year are included. Do not use commas when the day of the month is omitted or when the day appears before the month.

➤ **On March 4, 1931, she traveled to New York.**

➤ **She traveled to New York in March 1931.**

➤ **She traveled to New York on 4 March 1931.**

∎ **Addresses.** Use commas to set off the parts of an address or the name of a state, but do not use a comma preceding a zip code.

➤ **Here is my address for the summer: 63 Oceanside Drive, Apt. 2A, Surf City, New Jersey 06106.**

∎ **People's titles or degrees.** Put a comma between the person's name and the title or degree when it comes after the name, followed by another comma.

➤ **Luis Mendez, MD, gave her the green light to resume her exercise regimen.**

∎ **Numbers.** When a number has more than four digits, use commas to mark off the numerals by hundreds—that is, by groups of three beginning at the right.

➤ **Andrew Jackson received 647,276 votes in the 1828 presidential election.**

If the number is four digits long, the comma is not required.

➤ **The survey had 1856 [or 1,856] respondents.**

Exceptions: Street numbers, zip codes, telephone numbers, page numbers (p. 2304), and years (1828) do not include commas.

49j Using a comma to take the place of an omitted word or phrase or to prevent misreading

When a writer omits one or more words from a sentence to create an effect, a comma is often needed to make the meaning of the sentence clear for readers.

➤ **Under the tree he found his puppy, and under the car, his cat.**

Commas are also used to keep readers from misunderstanding a writer's meaning when words are repeated or might be misread.

➤ **Many birds that sing, sing first thing in the morning.**

49k Common errors in using commas

A comma used incorrectly can confuse readers. Commas should *not* be used in the following situations.

■ To separate major elements in an independent clause:

➤ **Reflecting on one's life/ is necessary for emotional growth.**

The subject, *reflecting,* should not be separated from the verb, *is.*

➤ **Washburn decided/ that her own efforts were responsible for her successes.**

The verb *decided* should not be separated from its direct object, the subordinate clause *that her own efforts were responsible for her successes.*

■ Before the first or after the final item in a series:

➤ **Americans work longer hours than/ German, French, or British workers/ are expected to work.**

Note: Commas should never be used after *such as* or *like* (see p. 460).

■ To separate compound word groups that are not independent clauses:

➤ **Injuries were so frequent that he became worried/ and started to play more cautiously.**

■ To set off restrictive elements:

➤ **The applicants/ who had studied for the admissions test/ were restless and eager for the exam to begin.**

➤ **The director/ Michael Curtiz/ was responsible for many great films in the 1930s and 1940s, including *Casablanca*.**

Adverb clauses beginning with *after, as soon as, before, because, if, since, unless, until,* or *when* are usually essential to a sentence's meaning and therefore are not usually set off with commas when they appear at the end of a sentence.

49k

RESTRICTIVE   I am eager to test the children's IQ
               again *because significant variations in
               a child's test score indicate that the test
               itself may be flawed.*

Clauses beginning with *although, even though, though,* or
whereas present a contrasting thought and are usually
nonrestrictive.

NONRESTRICTIVE   IQ tests can be useful indicators of a
                  child's abilities, *although they should
                  not be taken as the definitive measure of
                  a child's intelligence.*

■ Between cumulative adjectives (*see p. 450*):

➤ **Three/ well-known/ American writers visited the artist's
studio.**

■ Between adjectives and nouns:

➤ **An art review by a celebrated, powerful/ writer would be
guaranteed publication.**

■ Between adverbs and adjectives:

➤ **The studio was a delightfully/ chaotic environment,
with canvases everywhere and paints spilled out in a
fiesta of color.**

■ After coordinating conjunctions (*and, but, or, nor, for, so, yet*):

➤ **The *duomo* in Siena was begun in the thirteenth century,
and/ it was used as a model for other Italian cathedrals.**

■ After *although, such as,* or *like:*

➤ **Stage designers can achieve many unusual effects, such
as/ the helicopter that landed in *Miss Saigon.***

■ Before a parenthesis:

➤ **When they occupy an office cubicle/ (a relatively recent
invention), workers need to be especially considerate of
their neighbors.**

■ With a question mark or an exclamation point:

➤ **"Where are my glasses?/" she asked in a panic.**

Exercise 49.7   Chapter review: Editing for comma use

Edit the following passage, adding and deleting commas as needed.

Every society has families but the structure of the family varies from, society to society. Over time the function of the family, has changed so that in today's postindustrial society for instance the primary function of the family is to provide "emotional gratification" according to Professor Paula Stein noted sociologist of Stonehall University New Hampshire. In a recent interview Stein also said "Images of the family tend to be based on ideals not realities." To back up this claim Stein pointed to, a new as yet unpublished survey of more than 10000 married American couples, that she and her staff conducted. Expected to be released in the October 17 2003 edition of the *Weekly Sociologist,* the survey indicates that the biggest change has been the increase in the variety of family arrangements including singles single parents and childless, couples. Most Americans marry for love they say, but research portrays courtship as an analysis of costs benefits assets and liabilities, not unlike a business deal.

Virtually all children, are upset by divorce, but most recover in a few years while others suffer lasting serious, problems. Despite the high rate of divorce which reached its height in 1979, Americans still believe in the institution of marriage as indicated by the high rate of remarriages that form *blended families.* "Yes some see the breakup of the family as a social problem or the cause of other problems but, others see changes in the family as adaptations to changing social conditions as I do" concluded the professor.

50 Semicolons

Semicolons are used to join ideas that are closely related and grammatically equivalent.

Semicolons and Grammar Checkers

Grammar checker programs will catch some comma splices that can be corrected by adding a semicolon between the two clauses. They will also catch some incorrect uses of the semicolon. They will not tell you when a semicolon could be used for clarity, however, nor will they tell you if the semicolon is the best choice.

---

www.mhhe.com/
bmhh

For information
and exercises on
semicolons, go to

**Editing >
Semicolons**

50a Using a semicolon to join independent clauses

A semicolon should be used to join two related independent clauses when they are not joined by a comma and a coordinating conjunction (*and, but, or, nor, for, so, yet*). If readers are able to see the relationship between the two without the help of a coordinating conjunction, a semicolon is effective.

➤ **Before 8000 BC wheat was not the luxuriant plant it is today; it was merely one of many wild grasses that spread throughout the Middle East.**

Sometimes, the close relationship is a contrast.

➤ **Philip had completed the assignment; Lucy had not.**

Note: If a comma is used between two clauses without a coordinating conjunction, the sentence is a comma splice, a serious error. If no punctuation appears between the two clauses, the sentence is a run-on. One way to correct a comma splice or a run-on is with a semicolon. (*For more on comma splices and run-on sentences, see Chapter 43, pp. 372–80.*)

50b Using semicolons with transitional expressions that connect independent clauses

Transitional expressions, including transitional phrases (*after all, even so, for example*) and conjunctive adverbs (*consequently, however*), indicate the way that two clauses are related to each other. When a transitional expression appears between two clauses, it is preceded by a semicolon and usually followed by a comma. (*For a list of transitional expressions, see Chapter 43, p. 375.*)

➤ **Sheila had to wait until the plumber arrived; consequently, she was late for the exam.**

The semicolon always appears between the two clauses, even when the transitional expression appears in another position within the second clause. Wherever it appears, the transitional expression is usually set off with a comma or commas.

➤ **My friends are all taking golf lessons; my roommate and I,**

however, are more interested in tennis.

50c Using a semicolon to separate items or clauses in a series when the items or clauses contain commas

Because the following sentence contains so many elements, the semicolons are needed for clarity.

➤ **The committee included Dr. Curtis Youngblood, the county**

medical examiner; Roberta Collingwood, the director of the

bureau's criminal division; and Darcy Coolidge, the chief

of police.

A comma is the correct punctuation before a coordinating conjunction (*and, but, for, nor, or, so, yet*) that joins independent clauses: *Forsythia blooms in the early spring, but azaleas bloom later.* However, if the independent clauses already contain internal commas, a semicolon can help readers locate the point where the clauses are separated.

➤ **The closing scenes return to the English countryside,**

recalling the opening; but these scenes are bathed in a

different, cooler light, suggesting that memories of her

marriage still haunt her.

Exercise 50.1 Editing using semicolons

Use semicolons to correct any comma splices and run-on sentences in the following items. (*See Chapter 43 for a detailed discussion of comma splices and run-ons.*) Also add semicolons in place of commas in sentences that contain a series with internal commas.

EXAMPLE **The witness took the stand/; the defendant,**

meanwhile, never looked up from her notepad.

50c

;

1. The Pop Art movement flourished in the United States and in Britain in the 1960s it was a reaction to the abstract art that had dominated the art scene during the 1950s.
2. Pop artists were inspired by popular culture and consumerism, for example, they painted advertisements, comic strips, supermarket products, and even dollar bills!
3. The artists' goal was to transform ordinary daily experiences into art, they also wanted to comment on the modern world of mass production.
4. Pop artist Andy Warhol used silkscreening techniques to create identical, mass-produced images on canvas, so the result was repeated images of Campbell's soup cans and Coca-Cola bottles, as well as famous people like Marilyn Monroe, Elvis Presley, and Jacqueline Kennedy.
5. Other pop artists include Roy Lichtenstein, who is best known for his depiction of cartoons, Richard Hamilton, who is famous for his collages of commercial art, and David Hockney, whose trademark theme is swimming pools.
6. These artists all attained great fame in the art world however, many people did not accept their work as real art.

50d Common errors in using semicolons

Watch out for and correct common errors in using the semicolon.

- To join a dependent clause to an independent clause:

  ➤ **Professional writers need to devote time every day to their writing⁄ because otherwise they can lose momentum.**

  ➤ **Although housecats seem tame and lovable⁄, they can be fierce hunters.**

- To join independent clauses linked by a coordinating conjunction (*and, but, or, nor, for, so,* or *yet*):

  ➤ **Nineteenth-century women wore colorful clothes⁄, but their clothes often look drab in the black-and-white photographs of the era.**

▪ To introduce a series or an explanation:

➤ **My day was planned/: a morning walk, an afternoon in the library, dinner with friends, and a great horror movie.**

➤ **The doctor finally diagnosed the problem/: a severe sinus infection.**

Exercise 50.2   Combining sentences with semicolons

Use a semicolon to combine each set of sentences into one sentence. Add, remove, or change words as necessary. Use a semicolon and a transitional expression between clauses for at least two of your revised sentences. More than one answer is possible for each item.

EXAMPLE   **A recent *New York Times* article discusses new**

discoveries/ ~~These discoveries are~~ about personality in
                    the
animals/; ~~Some~~ scientists ~~are~~ quoted in the article. ~~The~~

~~scientists~~ are studying personality traits in hyenas and

wild birds.

1. Some scientists are studying a European bird related to the chickadee. The scientists are at the Netherlands Institute of Ecology. They are conducting experiments with this bird.
2. Another scientist has studied hyena populations. His name is Dr. Samuel Gosling. Dr. Gosling asked handlers to rate the hyenas using a questionnaire. He adapted a version of a questionnaire used for humans.
3. These studies and others indicate that animals display personality traits. These traits include boldness and shyness. Bold birds quickly investigate new items in their environment. Shy birds take more time.
4. Bold birds have an advantage over shy birds in some situations. They do not have an advantage in other situations.
5. Some experts on human personality are skeptical. They doubt that animals have the same personality traits that humans do. Scientists who study personality in animals need to be careful to avoid anthropomorphism. That is the tendency to attribute human characteristics to animals.

50d

;

51 | Colons

A colon draws attention to what it is introducing. It also has other conventional uses.

Colons and Grammar Checkers

A grammar checker may point out when you have used a colon incorrectly, but since colons are usually optional, most of the time you will need to decide whether a colon is your best choice in a sentence.

---

www.mhhe.com/
bmhh

For information and exercises on colons, go to
Editing > Colons

51a Using colons to introduce lists, appositives, or quotations

Colons are almost always preceded by complete sentences (independent clauses).

LIST	**The novel deals with three kinds of futility: pervasive poverty, unrequited love, and inescapable aging.**
APPOSITIVE	**In October 1954, the Northeast was devastated by a ferocious storm: Hurricane Hazel.**
QUOTATION	**He took my hand and said the words I had been dreading: "I really want us to be just friends."**

51b Using a colon when a second independent clause elaborates on the first one

The colon can be used to link independent clauses when the second clause restates or elaborates on the first. Use it when you want to emphasize the second clause.

➤ **I can predict tonight's sequence of events: My brother will arrive late, talk loudly, and eat too much.**

Note: When a complete sentence follows a colon, the first word may begin with either a capital or a lowercase letter. Whatever you decide to do, though, you should use the same style throughout your document.

51c Using colons in business letters, to indicate ratios, to indicate times of day, to cite city and publisher citations in bibliographies, and to separate titles and subtitles

➤ **Dear Mr. Worth:**

➤ **The ratio of armed to unarmed members of the gang was 3:1.**

➤ **He woke up at 6:30 in the morning.**

➤ **New York: McGraw-Hill, 2008**

➤ *Possible Lives: The Promise of Public Education in America*

Note: Colons are often used to separate biblical chapters and verses (John 3:16), but the Modern Language Association (MLA) recommends using a period instead (John 3.16).

51d Common errors in using the colon

■ Between a verb and its object or complement:

➤ **The critical elements in a good smoothie are: yogurt, fresh fruit, and honey.**

■ Between a preposition and its object or objects:

➤ **The novel deals with: pervasive poverty.**

➤ **Many feel that cancer can be prevented by a diet of: fruit, nuts, and vegetables.**

■ After *such as, for example,* or *including:*

➤ **I am ready for a change, such as: a trip to the Bahamas or a move to another town.**

Exercise 51.1 Chapter review: Editing for colons

Edit the following passage by adding or deleting colons.

EXAMPLE **The director of the soup kitchen is considering ways to raise funds, for example: a bake sale, car wash, or readathon.**

51d
:

Ciguatera is a form of food poisoning, humans are poisoned when they consume reef fish that contain toxic substances called ciguatoxins. These toxins accumulate at the end of the food chain: large carnivorous fish prey on smaller herbivorous fish. These smaller fish feed on ciguatoxins, which are produced by microorganisms that grow on the surface of marine algae. Ciguatoxins are found in certain marine fish, snapper, mackerel, barracuda, and grouper. People should avoid eating fish from reef waters, including: the tropical and subtropical waters of the Pacific and Indian oceans and the Caribbean Sea.

Some people think that ciguatera can be destroyed by: cooking or freezing the fish. People who consume reef fish should avoid eating: the head, internal organs, or eggs. People who eat contaminated fish experience gastrointestinal and neurological problems: vomiting, diarrhea, numbness, and muscle pains. Most physicians offer the same advice, "Eat fish only from reputable restaurants and dealers."

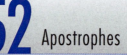

52 Apostrophes

Apostrophes show possession and indicate omitted letters in contractions. Apostrophes are used in such a variety of ways that they can be confusing. The most common confusion is between plurals and possessives.

Apostrophes and Grammar Checkers

A spelling checker will sometimes highlight *its* used incorrectly (instead of *it's*) or an error in a possessive (for example, *Englands' glory*), but this identification is not trustworthy or consistent. Spelling and grammar checkers will miss many apostrophe errors, so you should double-check all words that end in *-s* in your work.

52a Using apostrophes to indicate possession

www.mhhe.com/
bmhh

For information
and exercises on
apostrophes, go to

**Editing >
Apostrophes**

For a noun to be possessive, two elements are usually required: some-one or something is the possessor, and someone, something, or some attribute or quality is possessed.

Note: If you are wondering whether a particular noun should be in the possessive form, reword the sentence using the word *of* (*the bone of the dog*) to make sure that the noun is not plural.

1. Forming possessives with -'s

To form the possessive of all singular nouns, as well as plural nouns that do not end in -*s,* add an apostrophe plus -*s* to the noun.

NOUN/PRONOUN	NUMBER	AS A POSSESSIVE
baby	singular	a *baby's* smile
hour	singular	an *hour's* time
men	plural	the *men's* club
children	plural	the *children's* papers

Even singular nouns that end in -*s* form the possessive by adding -*'s.*

➤ **James's adventure, Ross's flag, Elvis's songs**

If a singular noun with more than two syllables ends in -*s,* and adding -*'s* would make the word sound awkward, it is acceptable to use only an apostrophe to form the possessive.

➤ **Socrates' students remained loyal to him.**

2. Forming possessives with only an apostrophe

Plural nouns that end in -*s* take only an apostrophe to form the possessive.

NOUN/PRONOUN	NUMBER	AS A POSSESSIVE
babies	plural	the *babies'* smiles
companies	plural	the *companies'* employees
robbers	plural	the *robbers'* clever plan

52a
ⱽ

3. Showing joint possession

To express joint ownership by two or more people, use the possessive form for the last name only; to express individual ownership, use the possessive form for each name.

➤ **Felicia and Elias's report**

➤ **The city's and the state's finances**

4. Forming the possessive of compound nouns

For compound words, add an apostrophe plus -*s* to the last word in the compound to form the possessive.

➤ **My father-in-law's job**

52b Using an apostrophe and -s with indefinite pronouns

Indefinite pronouns such as *no one, everyone, everything,* and *something* do not refer to a specific person or a specific item. Use -'*s* to form the possessive.

➤ **Well, it is anybody's guess.**

Exercise 52.1 Using apostrophes to form the possessive

Write the possessive form of each word. The first one has been done for you.

Word(s)	Possessive
the press	*the press's*
nobody	
newspapers	
Monday and Tuesday classes (individual ownership)	
deer	
women	
someone	
Edward	
trade-off	
well-worn footpath	
United States	
this year and last year combined population (joint ownership)	

52c Using apostrophes to mark contractions

In a contraction, the apostrophe serves as a substitute for omitted letters.

it's	for *it is* or *it has*
weren't	for *were not*

Apostrophes can also substitute for omitted numbers in a year (*the class of '08*).

52d Forming plural letters, words used as words, numbers, and abbreviations

An apostrophe plus *-s* (*'s*) can be used to show the plural of a letter. Underline or italicize single letters but not the apostrophe or the *-s*.

➤ *Committee* **has two** *m***'s, two** *t***'s, and two** *e***'s.**

If a word is used as a word rather than as a symbol of the meaning it conveys, it can be made plural by adding an apostrophe plus *-s*. The word should be italicized or underlined but not the *-s*.

➤ **There are twelve** *no***'s in the first paragraph.**

MLA and APA style now recommend against using an apostrophe to form plurals of numbers and abbreviations.

➤ **He makes his 2s look like 5s.**

➤ **Professor Morris has two PhDs.**

52e Common errors in using apostrophes

Do not use an apostrophe in the following situations.

- **With a plural noun.** Most often, writers misuse the apostrophe by adding it to a plural noun that is not possessive. The plurals of most nouns are formed by adding *-s: boy / boys, girl / girls, teacher / teachers*. Possessives are formed by adding an apostrophe plus *-s* (*'s*): *boy / boy's, girl / girl's, teacher / teacher's*. The possessive form and the plural form are not interchangeable.

  ➤ **The** ~~teacher's~~ *teachers* **asked the** ~~girl's~~ *girls* **and** ~~boy's~~ *boys* **for their attention.**

52e
∨

- **With possessive pronouns and contractions.** Be careful not to use a contraction when a possessive is called for, and vice versa. Personal pronouns and the relative pronoun *who* have special possessive forms, which never require apostrophes (*my/mine, your/yours, his, her/hers, it/its, our/ours, their/theirs,* and *whose*). When an apostrophe appears with a pronoun, the apostrophe usually marks omissions in a contraction, unless the pronoun is indefinite (*see p. 470*).

its
➤ The dog sat down and scratched ~~it's~~ fleas.

Its is a possessive pronoun. *It's* is a contraction for *it is* or *it has: It's [It + is] too hot.*

their
➤ They gave ~~they're~~ lives.

Their is a possessive pronoun; *they're* is a contraction of *they are*. Both are also confused with the adverb *there: She was standing there.*

Exercise 52.2 Distinguishing between contractions and pronouns

Underline the correct word choice in each sentence.

> **EXAMPLE** **Transcendentalists have had a strong influence on American thought; (there/<u>they're</u>/their) important figures in our literary history.**

1. In the essay "The Over-soul," Ralph Waldo Emerson describes the unity of nature by cataloging (it's/its) divine, yet earthly, expressions, such as waterfalls and well-worn footpaths.
2. Emerson states that you must have faith to believe in something that supersedes or contradicts (your/you're) real-life experiences.
3. (Who's/Whose) the author of the poem at the beginning of Emerson's "Self-Reliance"?
4. Emerson believes that (there/they're/their) are ways to live within a society without having to give in to its pressures.
5. According to Emerson, people should occasionally silence the noise of (there/they're/their) inner voices and learn to listen to the world's unconscious voice.
6. Emerson also believes that, in the end, (it's/its) the individual—and the individual alone—who must decide his or her own fate.

Exercise 52.3 Chapter review: Editing for apostrophes

Edit the following passage by adding and deleting apostrophes and correcting any incorrect word choices.

Transcendentalism was a movement of thought in the mid-to-late 1800s that was originated by Ralph Waldo Emerson, Henry David Thoreau, and several other's who's scholarship helped to shape the democratic ideals of their day and usher America into it's modern age. Emerson, a member of New Englands' elite, was particularly interested in spreading Transcendentalist notion's of self-reliance; he is probably best known for his essay "Self-Reliance," which is still widely read in todays' universities. Most people remember Thoreau, however, not only for what he wrote but also for how he lived: its well known that—for a while, at least—he chose to live a simple life in a cabin on Walden Pond. Altogether, one could say that Emerson's and Thoreau's main accomplishment was to expand the influence of literature and philosophy over the development of the average Americans' identity. With a new national literature forming, people's interest in they're self-development quickly increased as they began to read more and more about what it meant to be American. In fact, one could even say (perhaps half-jokingly) that, today, the success of home makeovers on TV and the popularity of self-help books might have a lot to do with Emerson's and Thoreau's ideas about self-sufficiency and living simply—idea's that took root in this nation more than a hundred years ago.

53 Quotation Marks

Quotation marks are used to enclose words, phrases, and sentences that are quoted directly; titles of short works such as poems, articles, songs, and short stories; and words and phrases used in a special sense.

53
" "

Note: Citations in this chapter follow MLA style. See Part 5 for examples of APA style.

Quotation Marks and Grammar Checkers

A grammar checker cannot determine where a quotation should begin and end, but it can alert you to the lack of an opening or closing quotation mark. Grammar checkers may not point out errors in the use of quotation marks with other marks of punctuation, however. For example, a grammar checker did not highlight the error in the placement of the period at the end of the following sentence.

➤ **Barbara Ehrenreich observes, "There are no Palm Pilots, cable channels, or Web sites to advise the low-wage job seeker".**

---

www.mhhe.com/
bmhh

For information
and exercises on
quotation marks,
go to

Editing >
Quotation Marks

53a Using quotation marks to indicate direct quotations

Direct quotations from written material may include whole sentences or only a few words or phrases.

➤ **In *Angela's Ashes*, Frank McCourt writes, "Worse than the ordinary miserable childhood is the miserable Irish childhood" (11).**

➤ **Frank McCourt believes that being Irish worsens what is all too "ordinary"—a "miserable childhood" (11).**

Use quotation marks to enclose everything a speaker says in written dialogue. If the quoted sentence is interrupted by a phrase like *he said,* enclose the rest of the quotation in quotation marks.

Do not use quotation marks to set off an indirect quotation, which reports what a speaker said but does not use the exact words.

➤ **He said that ⁒he didn't know what I was talking about.⁒**

Exception: If you are using a quotation that is longer than four typed lines, set it off from the text as a **block quotation.** A block quotation is *not* surrounded by quotation marks.

> *Note:* The following long quotes follow MLA style. For examples of APA style, see Part 5.

As Carl Schorske points out, the young Freud was passionately

interested in classical archeology:

> He cultivated a new friendship in the Viennese professional
>
> elite—especially rare in those days of withdrawal—with

Emanuel Loewy, a professor of archeology. "He keeps me up till three o'clock in the morning," Freud wrote appreciatively to Fliess. "He tells me about Rome." (273)

Longer verse quotations (four lines or more) are indented block style, like long prose quotations. If you cannot fit an entire line of poetry on a single line of your typescript, you may indent the turned line an extra quarter inch (three spaces).

In the following lines from "Crossing Brooklyn Ferry," Walt Whitman celebrates the beauty of the Manhattan skyline and his love for that city:

> Ah, what can ever be more stately and
> > admirable to me than mast-hemm'd
> > Manhattan?
> River and sunset and scallop-edg'd waves of
> > flood-tide?
> The sea-gulls oscillating their bodies, the
> > hay-boat in the twilight, and the belated lighter?
> What gods can exceed these that clasp me by
> > the hand, and with voices I love call me
> > promptly and loudly by my nighest name as
> I approach? (lines 92-95)

Use single quotation marks to set off a quotation within a quotation.

➤ **When the press demanded better players and a successful football season, the president of the university said, "I know you're saying to me, 'We want a winning football team.' But I'm telling you this: 'I want an honest football team.' "**

53b Using quotation marks to enclose titles of short works

The titles of long works, such as books, are usually underlined or put in italics (*see Chapter 58, p. 501*). The titles of book chapters, essays, most poems, and other short works are usually put in quotation marks. Quotation marks are also used for titles of unpublished works, including student papers, theses, and dissertations.

➤ **"The Girl in Conflict" is Chapter 11 of *Coming of Age in Samoa*.**

Note: If quotation marks are needed within the title of a short work, use single quotation marks: "The 'Animal Rights' War on Medicine."

53b
" "

53c Using quotation marks to indicate that a word or phrase is being used in a special way

Put quotation marks around a word or phrase that someone else has used in a way that you or your readers may not agree with. Quotation marks used in this way function the same way that raised eyebrows do in conversation and should be used sparingly.

> ➤ **The "worker's paradise" of Stalinist Russia included slave-labor camps.**

Words cited as words can also be put in quotation marks, although the more common practice is to italicize them.

> ➤ **The words "compliment" and "complement" sound alike but have different meanings.**

Exercise 53.1 Using double and single quotation marks

Below is a passage from the Seneca Falls Declaration (1848) by Elizabeth Cady Stanton, followed by a series of quotations from this passage. Add, delete, or replace quotation marks to quote from the passage accurately. Some sentences may be correct; circle their numbers.

The history of mankind is a history of repeated injuries and usurpations on the part of man toward woman, having in direct object the establishment of an absolute tyranny over her. To prove this, let facts be submitted to a candid world.

WHEREAS, The great precept of nature is conceded to be that "man shall pursue his own true and substantial happiness." Blackstone in his *Commentaries* remarks that this law of Nature being coeval with mankind, and dictated by God himself, is of course superior in obligation to any other. It is binding over all the globe, in all countries and at all times; no human laws are of any validity if contrary to this, and such of them as are valid, derive all their force, and all their validity, and all their authority, mediately and immediately, from this original; therefore,

RESOLVED, That such laws as conflict, in any way, with the true and substantial happiness of woman, are contrary to the great precept of nature and of no validity, for this is "superior in obligation to any other."

EXAMPLE   As Elizabeth Cady Stanton points out, "The great precept of nature is conceded to be that ^man shall pursue his own true and substantial happiness." "

1. "The history of mankind is a history of repeated injuries and usurpations on the part of man toward woman," Elizabeth Cady Stanton asserts, "having in direct object the establishment of an absolute tyranny over her."
2. To prove this, writes Stanton, let facts be submitted to a candid world.
3. Stanton argues that men have oppressed women throughout history.
4. Stanton contends "that all laws are subject to natural laws."
5. Stanton resolves "that such laws as conflict, in any way, with the true and substantial happiness of woman, are contrary to the great precept of nature and of no validity, for this is "superior in obligation to any other." "

53d Other punctuation with quotation marks

As you edit, check all closing quotation marks and the marks of punctuation that appear next to them to make sure that you have placed them in the right order.

1. Periods and commas

Place the period or comma before the final quotation mark even when the quotation is only one or two words long.

➤ **Elizabeth Cady Stanton presents her case for women's rights to a "candid world."**

Exception: A parenthetical citation in either MLA or APA style always appears between the closing quotation mark and the period: *"Squaresville, U.S.A. vs. Beatsville" makes the Midwestern small-town home seem boring compared with the West Coast artist's "pad" (31).*

2. Colons and semicolons

Place colons and semicolons after the final quotation mark.

➤ **Dean Wilcox cited the items he called his "daily delights": a free parking space for his scooter at the faculty club, a special table in the club itself, and friends to laugh with after a day's work.**

53d
" "

3. Question marks and exclamation points

Place a question mark or an exclamation point after the final quotation mark unless the quoted material is itself a question or an exclamation.

➤ **Why did she name her car "Buck"?**

➤ **He had many questions, such as "Can you really do unto others as you would have them do unto you?"**

4. Dashes

Place a dash outside either an opening or a closing quotation mark, or both, if it precedes or follows the quotation or if two dashes are used to set off the quotation.

➤ **One phrase—"time is running out"—haunted me throughout my dream.**

Place a dash inside either an opening or a closing quotation mark if it is part of the quotation.

➤ **"Where is the—" she called. "Oh, here it is. Never mind."**

Exercise 53.2   Using quotation marks with other punctuation

Edit the following sentences to correct problems with the use of quotation marks with other punctuation. Some sentences may be correct; circle their numbers.

> **EXAMPLE**   **In June 1776, Richard Henry Lee proposed that the Continental Congress adopt a resolution that "these united Colonies are, and of right ought to be, free and independent States."/**

1. "We hold these truths to be self-evident", wrote Thomas Jefferson in 1776.
2. Most Americans can recite their "unalienable rights:" "life, liberty, and the pursuit of happiness."
3. According to the Declaration of Independence, "whenever any form of government becomes destructive to these ends, it is the right of the people to alter or to abolish it."!
4. The signers of the Declaration of Independence contended that the "history of the present King of Great Britain is a history of repeated injuries and usurpations, all having in direct object the establishment of an absolute tyranny over these states."

5. What did the creators of this document mean by a "candid world?"
6. Feminists and civil rights advocates have challenged the Declaration's most famous phrase "—all men are created equal"—on the grounds that these "unalienable rights" were originally extended only to white men who owned property.

53e Integrating quotations into your sentences

If you introduce a quotation with a complete sentence, you can use a colon before it.

➤ **He was better than anyone else at the job, but he didn't want it: "I don't know what to do," he said.**

If you introduce a direct quotation with *he said, she noted,* or a similar expression, use a comma.

➤ **He said, "She believed I could do it."**

➤ **"She believed I could do it," he said.**

Do not use a comma after expressions such as *he said* or *the researchers note* if an indirect quotation or a paraphrase follows.

➤ **He said/ that he believed he could do it.**

When a quotation is integrated into a sentence's structure, treat the quotation as you would any other sentence element, adding a comma or not as appropriate.

➤ **Telling me that she wanted to "play hooky from her life," she set off on a three-week vacation.**

➤ **He said he had his "special reasons."**

If your quotation begins a sentence, capitalize the first letter after the quotation mark even if the first word does not begin a sentence in the original source. If you change a lowercase letter to a capital letter, enclose it in brackets (*see Chapter 55, p. 493*).

➤ **"[A]ll men are created equal," asserts the Declaration of Independence.**

If the sentence you are quoting is interrupted by an expression such as *she said,* begin the sentence with a quotation mark and a capital letter, end the first part of the quotation with a comma and a quotation mark, insert the interrupting words followed by another comma, and then resume the quotation with a lowercase letter.

53e
" "

➤ **"The first thing that strikes one about Plath's journals," writes Katha Pollitt in the *Atlantic*, "is what they leave out."**

If you end one quoted sentence and insert an expression such as *he said* before beginning the next quoted sentence, place a comma at the end of the first quoted sentence and a period after the interruption.

➤ **"There are at least four kinds of doublespeak," William Lutz observes. "The first is the euphemism, an inoffensive or positive word or phrase used to avoid a harsh, unpleasant, or distasteful reality."**

53f Common errors in using quotation marks

Watch out for and correct common errors in using quotation marks.

- **To distance yourself from slang, clichés, or trite expressions.** It is best to avoid overused or slang expressions altogether in college writing. If your writing situation permits slang, however, do not enclose it in quotation marks.

WEAK	Californians are so "laid back."
REVISED	Many Californians have a carefree style.

- **For indirect quotations.** Do not use quotation marks for indirect quotations. Watch out for errors in pronoun reference as well. (*See Chapter 46, pp. 408–10.*)

INCORRECT	He wanted to tell his boss that "he needed a vacation."
CORRECT	He told his boss that his boss needed a vacation.
CORRECT	He said to his boss, "You need a vacation."

- **In quotations that end with a question.** Only the question mark that ends the quoted sentence is needed, even when the entire sentence that includes the quotation is also a question.

  ➤ **What did Juliet mean when she cried, "O Romeo, Romeo! Wherefore art thou Romeo?"~~?~~**

- **To enclose the title of your own paper.** Do not use quotation marks around the title of your own essay at the beginning of your paper.

  ➤ **~~"~~Edgar Allan Poe and the Paradox of the Gothic~~"~~**

Exercise 53.3 Chapter review: Editing for quotation marks

Edit the following passage to correct problems with the use of quotation marks.

On August 28, 1963, Dr. Martin Luther King Jr. delivered his famous 'I Have a Dream' speech at the nation's Lincoln Memorial. According to King, "When the architects of our republic wrote the magnificent words of the Constitution and the Declaration of Independence, they were signing a promissory note to which every American was to fall heir". King declared that "this note was a promise that all men, yes, black men as well as white men, would be guaranteed the unalienable rights of life, liberty, and the pursuit of happiness." This promissory note, however, came back "marked "insufficient funds."" King's speech, therefore, was designed to rally his supporters to "make justice a reality."

Unlike the more militant civil rights leaders of the 1950s, King advocated nonviolence. This stance is why King said that the 'Negro community' should not drink "from the cup of bitterness and hatred" and that they should not use physical violence.

King's dream was uniquely American: "I have a dream that one day this nation will rise up and live out the true meaning of its creed: 'We hold these truths to be self-evident: that all men are created equal.'" King challenged all Americans to fully embrace racial equality. Nearly fifty years later, we must ask ourselves if King's dream has in fact become a reality. Are "all of God's children, black men and white men, Jews and Gentiles, Protestants and Catholics . . . able to join hands and sing in the words of the old Negro spiritual, "Free at last! free at last! thank God Almighty, we are free at last!?""

53f
" "

54 Other Punctuation Marks

Punctuation and Grammar Checkers

Your grammar checker might highlight a period used instead of a question mark at the end of a question. However, grammar checkers will not tell you when you might use a pair of dashes or parentheses to set material off in a sentence, or when you need a second dash or parenthesis to enclose parenthetical material.

www.mhhe.com/
bmhh

For information and exercises on end punctuation, go to

Editing > End Punctuation

54a The period

Use a period to end all sentences except direct questions or exclamations. Statements that ask questions indirectly end in a period.

➤ **She asked me where I had gone to college.**

A period is conventionally used with the following common abbreviations, which end in lowercase letters.

Mr.	Mrs.	i.e.	Mass.
Ms.	Dr.	e.g.	Jan.

If the abbreviation is made up of capital letters, however, the periods are optional.

RN (or R.N.) BA (or B.A.)
MD (or M.D.) PhD (or Ph.D.)

Periods are omitted in abbreviations for organizations, famous people, states in mailing addresses, and acronyms (words made up of initials).

FBI	JFK	MA	NATO
CIA	LBJ	TX	NAFTA

When in doubt, consult a dictionary.

54b The question mark

Use a question mark after a direct question.

➤ **Who wrote *The Old Man and the Sea*?**

Occasionally, a question mark changes a statement into a question.

➤ **You expect me to believe a story like that?**

482

Do not use a question mark after an indirect quotation, even if the words being indirectly quoted were originally a question.

➤ **He asked her if she would be at home later?.**

54c   The exclamation point

Use exclamation points sparingly to convey shock, surprise, or some other strong emotion.

➤ **Stolen! The money was stolen! Right before our eyes, somebody snatched my purse and ran off with it.**

Using numerous exclamation points throughout a document actually weakens their force. As much as possible, try to convey emotion with your choice of words and your sentence structure instead of with an exclamation point.

➤ **Jefferson and Adams both died on the same day in 1826, exactly fifty years after the signing of the Declaration of Independence!.**

> The fact that the sentence reports is surprising enough without the addition of an exclamation point.

Exercise 54.1   Chapter review: Editing for end punctuation

Insert periods, question marks, and exclamation points in the following passage. Delete any unnecessary commas.

Do you realize that there is a volcano larger than Mt St Helens Mt Vesuvius Mt Etna Mauna Loa is the largest volcano on Earth, covering at least half the island of Hawaii The summit of Mauna Loa stands 56,000 feet above its base This is why Native Hawaiians named this volcano, the "Long Mountain" Mauna Loa is also one of the most active volcanoes on the planet, having erupted thirty-three times since 1843 (most people do not think of a volcano as dormant) Its last eruption occurred in 1984 Most people associate a volcanic eruption with red lava spewing from the volcano's crater, but few people realize that the lava flow, and volcanic gases are also extremely hazardous Tourists like to follow the lava to where it meets the sea, but this practice is dangerous because of the steam produced when the lava meets the water So, the next time you visit an active volcano, beware

54c

www.mhhe.com/ bmhh

For information and exercises on dashes, go to

Editing > Dashes

54d Dashes

Use a dash or dashes to set off words, phrases, or clauses that deserve special attention. A typeset dash, sometimes called an *em dash,* is a single, unbroken line about as wide as a capital *M*. Most word-processing programs provide the em dash as a special character. Otherwise, the dash can be made on the keyboard with two hyphens in a row. Do not put a space before or after the dash.

1. To set off parenthetical material, a series, or an explanation

➤ **All finite creations—including humans—are incomplete and contradictory.**

➤ **Coca-Cola, potato chips, and brevity—these are the marks of a good study session in the dorm.**

➤ **A surprising number of people have taken up birdwatching— a peaceful, relatively inexpensive hobby.**

Sometimes, a dash is used to set off an independent clause within a sentence. In such sentences, the set-off clause provides interesting information but is not essential to the main assertion.

➤ **The first rotary gasoline engine—it was made by Mazda— burned 15% more fuel than conventional engines.**

2. To indicate a sudden change in tone or idea

➤ **Breathing heavily, the archaeologist opened the old chest in wild anticipation and found—an old pair of socks and an empty soda can.**

Note: Used sparingly, the dash can be an effective mark of punctuation, but if it is overused, it can make your writing disjointed.

Exercise 54.2 Using dashes

Insert or correct dashes where needed in the following sentences.

EXAMPLE **Women once shut out of electoral office**

altogether have made great progress in recent

decades.

1. Patsy Mink, Geraldine Ferraro, Antonia Novello, and Madeleine Albright all are political pioneers in the history of the United States.
2. Patsy Mink the first Asian-American woman elected to the U.S. Congress served for twenty-four years in the U.S. House of Representatives.
3. Geraldine Ferraro congresswoman from Queens, New York became the first female vice presidential candidate when she was nominated by the Democratic Party in 1984.
4. Antonia Novello—former U.S. surgeon general—was the first woman—and the first Hispanic—to hold this position.
5. Madeleine Albright, the first female secretary of state, has observed, "To understand Europe, you have to be a genius-or French."

www.mhhe.com/
bmhh

For information
and exercises on
parentheses, go to

**Editing >
Parentheses**

54e Parentheses

Parentheses should be used infrequently and only to set off supplementary information, a digression, or a comment that interrupts the flow of thought within a sentence or paragraph.

> **The tickets (ranging in price from $10 to $50) go on sale Monday morning.**

When parentheses enclose a whole sentence by itself, the sentence begins with a capital letter and ends with a period before the final parenthesis. A sentence that appears inside parentheses *within a sentence* should neither begin with a capital letter nor end with a period.

> **Folktales and urban legends often reflect the concerns of a particular era. (The familiar tale of a cat accidentally caught in a microwave oven is an example of this phenomenon.)**

> **John Henry (he was the man with the forty-pound hammer) was a hero to miners fearing the loss of their jobs to machines.**

If the material in parentheses is at the end of an introductory or nonessential word group that is followed by a comma, the comma should be placed after the closing parenthesis. A comma should never appear before the opening parenthesis.

> **As he walked past/ (dressed, as always, in his Sunday best), I got ready to throw the spitball.**

54e

Parentheses are used to enclose numbers or letters that label items in a list.

➤ **He says the argument is nonsense because (1) university presidents don't work as well as machines, (2) university presidents don't do any real work at all, and (3) universities would be better off if they were run by faculty committees.**

Parentheses also enclose in-text citations in many systems of documenting sources. (*For more on documenting sources, see Parts 4 and 5.*)

Note: Too many parentheses are distracting to readers. If you find that you have used a large number of parentheses in a draft, go over it carefully to see if any of the material within parentheses really deserves more emphasis.

Exercise 54.3   Using parentheses

Insert parentheses where needed in the following sentences, and correct any errors in their use.

> **EXAMPLE**   **During leap year, February has twenty-nine**
> **( )**
> **˄29˄ days.**

1. German meteorologist Alfred Wegener he was also a geophysicist proposed the first comprehensive theory of continental drift.
2. According to this geological theory, 1 the earth originally contained a single large continent, 2 this land mass eventually separated into six continents, and 3 these continents gradually drifted apart.
3. Wegener contended that continents will continue to drift. They are not rigidly fixed. The evidence indicates that his predictions are accurate.
4. The continents are moving at a rate of one yard .09144 meters per century.
5. The movement of the continents, (slow though this movement may be), occasionally causes earthquakes along fault lines such as the famous San Andreas Fault in California.

54f   Brackets

Brackets set off information you add to a quotation that is not part of the quotation itself.

➤ **Samuel Eliot Morison has written, "This passage has attracted a good deal of scorn to the Florentine mariner [Verrazzano], but without justice."**

Morison's sentence does not include the name of the "Florentine mariner," so the writer places the name in brackets.

Brackets may be used to enclose the word *sic* (Latin for "thus") after a word in a quotation that was incorrect in the original.

➤ **The critic noted that "the battle scenes in *The Patriot* are realistic, but the rest of the film is historically inacurate [sic] and overly melodramatic."**

54g Ellipses

Use three spaced periods, called ellipses or an ellipsis mark, to show readers that you have omitted words from a passage you are quoting.

FULL QUOTATION FROM A WORK BY WILKINS

In the nineteenth century, railroads, lacing their way across continents, reaching into the heart of every major city in Europe and America, and bringing a new romance to travel, added to the unity of nations and fueled the nationalist fires already set burning by the French Revolution and the wars of Napoleon.

EDITED QUOTATION

In his account of nineteenth-century society, Wilkins argues that "railroads . . . added to the unity of nations and fueled the nationalist fires already set burning by the French Revolution and the wars of Napoleon."

If you are omitting the end of a quoted sentence, the three ellipsis points are preceded by a period to end the sentence.

EDITED QUOTATION

In describing the growth of railroads, Wilkins pictures them "lacing their way across continents, reaching into the heart of every major city in Europe and America. . . ."

When you need to add a parenthetical reference after the ellipses at the end of a sentence, place it after the quotation mark but before the final period: . . ." (253).

Ellipses are usually not needed before or after a word or phrase being quoted.

➤ **Railroads brought "a new romance to travel," according to Wilkins.**

To indicate the omission of an entire line or more from the middle of a poem, insert a line of spaced periods.

54g

Note: Ellipses should be used only as a means of shortening a quotation, never as a device for changing its fundamental meaning or for creating emphasis where none exists in the original.

54h Slashes

Use the slash to show divisions between lines of poetry when you quote more than one line of a poem as part of a sentence. Add a space on either side of the slash. When you are quoting four or more lines of poetry, use a block quotation instead (*see pp. 474–75*).

➤ **In "The Tower," Yeats makes his peace with "All those things whereof / Man makes a superhuman / Mirror-resembling dream" (163–165).**

The slash is sometimes used between two words that represent choices or combinations. Do not add a space on either side of the slash when it is used in this way.

➤ **The college offers three credit/noncredit courses.**

Some writers use the slash as a marker between the words *and* and *or* or between *he* and *she* or *his* and *her* to avoid sexism. Most writers, however, consider such usage awkward. It is usually better to rephrase the sentence.

Exercise 54.4 Using brackets, ellipses, and slashes

Insert brackets, ellipses, and slashes where needed in the following sentences, and correct any errors in their use. Refer to the following excerpts from a poem and an essay.

> The lights begin to twinkle from the rocks;
> The long day wanes; the slow moon climbs, the deep
> Moans round with many voices. Come, my friends.
> 'T is not too late to seek a newer world. (54–57)
>
> —ALFRED, LORD TENNYSON, *Ulysses*

> Now when I had mastered the language of this water and had come to know every trifling feature that bordered the great river as familiarly as I knew the letters of the alphabet, I had made a valuable acquisition. But I had lost something, too. I had lost something which could never be restored to me while I lived. All the grace, the beauty, the poetry had gone out of the majestic river!
>
> —MARK TWAIN, "Two Views of the Mississippi"

EXAMPLE   The speaker in the poem *Ulysses* longs to

seek "*/ / /* a newer world" (57).

1. Ulysses is tempted as he looks toward the sea: "The lights begin to twinkle from the rocks; The long day wanes . . ." (54–55).
2. In "Two Views of the Mississippi," Mark Twain writes that "I had mastered the language of this water. I had made a valuable acquisition."
3. Twain regrets that he "has lost something"—his sense of the beauty of the river.
4. In Tennyson's poem, "the deep the ocean / moans round with many voices" (55–56).
5. In *Ulysses* the ocean beckons with possibilities; in "Two Views of the Mississippi," the river has become too familiar: "All the grace had gone out of the majestic river!"

Exercise 54.5   Chapter review: Editing for dashes, parentheses, and other punctuation marks

Edit the following passage by adding or deleting dashes, parentheses, brackets, ellipses, and slashes. Make any other additions, deletions, or changes that are necessary for correctness and sense. Refer to the following excerpt as necessary.

> This is a book about that most admirable of human virtues—courage.
> . . . .
>
> Some of my colleagues who are criticized today for lack of forthright principles—or who are looked upon with scornful eyes as compromising "politicians"—are simply engaged in the fine art of conciliating, balancing and interpreting the forces and factions of public opinion, an art essential to keeping our nation united and enabling our Government to function.
>
> —JOHN F. KENNEDY, *Profiles in Courage,* pp. 1, 5

John Fitzgerald Kennedy—the youngest man to be elected U.S. president—he was also the youngest president to be assassinated. He was born on May 29, 1917, in Brookline, Massachusetts. Kennedy was born into a family with a tradition of public service; his father, Joseph Kennedy, served as ambassador to Great Britain. (his maternal grandfather, John Frances Fitzgerald, served as the mayor of Boston.)

54h

Caroline, John Fitzgerald Jr., and Patrick B. (Who died in infancy) are the children of the late John F. Kennedy. Kennedy's background, a Harvard education, military service as a lieutenant in the navy, and public service as Massachusetts senator—helped provide John F. Kennedy with the experience, insight, and recognition needed to defeat Richard Nixon in 1960.

Even before being elected U.S. president, Kennedy received the Pulitzer Prize for his book *Profiles in Courage* 1957. According to Kennedy, "This *Profiles in Courage* is a book about that most admirable of human virtues—courage" 1. "Some of my colleagues," Kennedy continues, "who are criticized today for lack of forthright principles / are simply engaged in the fine art of conciliating . . ." 5.

During Kennedy's presidency, Americans witnessed 1 the Cuban missile crisis, 2 the Bay of Pigs invasion, and 3 the Berlin crisis. Most Americans—we hope—are able to recognize Kennedy's famous words—which were first delivered during his Inaugural Address: "Ask not what your country can do for you—ask what you can do for your country."

55 Capitalization

Many rules for the use of capital letters have been fixed by custom, such as the convention of beginning each sentence with a capital letter, but the rules change all the time. A recent dictionary is a good guide to capitalization.

www.mhhe.com/
bmhh

For information
and exercises on
capitalization,
go to

Editing >
Capitalization

55a   Proper nouns

Proper nouns are the names of specific people, places, or things, names that set off the individual from the group, such as the name *Jane* instead of the common noun *person*. Capitalize proper nouns, words derived from proper nouns, brand names, abbreviations of capitalized words, and call letters at radio and television stations.

Ronald Reagan
Reaganomics
Apple computer
FBI (government agency)
WNBC (television station)

Note: Although holidays and the names of months and days of the week are capitalized, seasons, such as *summer,* are not. Neither are the days of the month when they are spelled out (*the seventh of March*).

TYPES and EXAMPLES of PROPER NOUNS

- **People:** John F. Kennedy, Ruth Bader Ginsburg, Albert Einstein
- **Nationalities, ethnic groups, and languages:** English, Swiss, African Americans, Arabs, Chinese, Turkish
- **Places:** the United States of America, Tennessee, the Irunia Restaurant, the Great Lakes
- **Organizations and institutions:** Phi Beta Kappa, Republican Party (Republicans), Department of Defense, Cumberland College, the North Carolina Tarheels
- **Religious bodies, books, and figures:** Jews, Christians, Baptists, Hindus, Roman Catholic Church, the Bible, the Koran or Qur'an, the Torah, God, Holy Spirit, Allah
- **The genus in scientific names:** *Homo sapiens, H. sapiens, Acer rubrum, A. rubrum*
- **Days and months:** Monday, Veterans Day, August, the Fourth of July
- **Historical events, movements, and periods:** World War II, Impressionism, the Renaissance, the Jazz Age

Capitalization and Grammar Checkers

Grammar checkers will flag words that should be capitalized or lowercase by convention, but they won't flag proper nouns unless the noun is stored in the program's dictionary, and they won't necessarily point out a noun that can be either proper or common, depending on the context. For example, a grammar checker flagged the capitalization error in the first sentence but not the second:

➤ **Maria is going to study the mammals of north America.**

➤ **The Darwin Martin House, designed by Frank Lloyd Wright, is located in buffalo, New York.**

55a
cap

55b Personal titles

Capitalize titles when they come before a proper name, but do not capitalize them when they appear alone or after the name.

➤ Every Sunday, *Aunt Lou* tells fantastic stories.

➤ My *aunt* is arriving this afternoon.

➤ The most likely candidate for the Democratic nomination was Grover Cleveland, *governor* of New York.

Exceptions: If the name for a family relationship is used alone (without a possessive such as *my* before it), it should be capitalized.

➤ I saw *Father* infrequently during the summer months.

President of the United States or the *President* (meaning the chief executive of the United States) is frequently but not always capitalized. Most writers do not capitalize the title *president* unless they are referring to the President of the United States.

55c Titles of creative works

Capitalize the important words in titles and subtitles. Do not capitalize articles (*a, an, the*), the *to* in infinitives, or prepositions and conjunctions unless they begin or end the title or subtitle. Capitalize both words in a hyphenated word. Capitalize the first word after a colon or semicolon in a title.

- **Book:** *Two Years before the Mast*
- **Play:** *The Taming of the Shrew*
- **Building:** the Eiffel Tower
- **Ship or aircraft:** the *Titanic* or the *Concorde*
- **Painting:** the *Mona Lisa*
- **Article or essay:** "On Old Age"
- **Poem:** "Ode on a Grecian Urn"
- **Music:** "The Star-Spangled Banner"
- **Document:** the Bill of Rights
- **Course:** Economics 206: Macro-Economic Analysis

55d Names of areas and regions

Names of geographical regions are generally capitalized if they are well established, like *the Midwest* and *Central Europe.* Names of directions, as in the sentence *Turn south,* are not capitalized.

CORRECT	*East* meets *West* at the summit.
CORRECT	You will need to go *west* on Sunset.

The word *western,* when used as a general direction or the name of a genre, is not capitalized. It is capitalized when it is part of the name of a specific region.

➤ The ~~Western~~ *High Noon* is one of my favorite movies.
       western

➤ I visited ~~western~~ Europe last year.
       Western

55e Names of races, ethnic groups, and sacred things

The words *black* and *white* are usually not capitalized when they are used to refer to members of racial groups because they are adjectives that substitute for the implied common nouns *black person* and *white person.* However, names of ethnic groups and races are capitalized: *African Americans, Italians, Asians, Caucasians.*

Note: In accordance with current APA guidelines, most social scientists capitalize the terms *Black* and *White,* treating them as proper nouns.

Many religious terms, such as *sacrament, altar,* and *rabbi,* are not capitalized. The word *Bible* is capitalized (though *biblical* is not), but it is never capitalized when it is used as a metaphor for an essential book.

➤ His book *Winning at Stud Poker* used to be the *bible* of gamblers.

55f First word of a sentence or quoted sentence

A capital letter is used to signal the beginning of a new sentence. Capitalize the first word of a quoted sentence but not the first word of a quoted phrase.

➤ Jim, the narrator of *My Ántonia,* concludes, "Whatever we had missed, we possessed together the precious, the incommunicable past" (324).

➤ Jim took comfort in sharing with Ántonia "the precious, the incommunicable past" (324).

If you need to change the first letter of a quotation to fit your sentence, enclose the letter in brackets.

➤ The lawyer noted that "[t]he man seen leaving the area after the blast was not the same height as the defendant."

55f
cap

If you interrupt the sentence you are quoting with an expression such as *he said,* the first word of the rest of the quotation should not be capitalized.

➤ **"When I come home an hour later," she explained, "the trains are usually less crowded."**

55g First word after a colon

If the word group that follows a colon is not a complete sentence, do not capitalize it. If it is a complete sentence, you can capitalize it or not, but be consistent throughout your document.

➤ **The question is serious: do you think this peace will last?**

or

➤ **The question is serious: Do you think this peace will last?**

Exercise 55.1 Chapter review: Editing for capitalization

Edit the following passage, changing letters to capital or lowercase as necessary.

Perhaps the most notable writer of the 1920s is F. Scott Fitzgerald. He was born on September 24, 1896, in St. Paul, Minnesota, to Edward Fitzgerald and Mary "mollie" McQuillan, who were both members of the catholic church. After attending Princeton university and embarking on a career as a writer, Fitzgerald married southern belle Zelda Sayre from Montgomery, Alabama. Together, he and his Wife lived the celebrated life of the roaring twenties and the jazz age. Fitzgerald wrote numerous short stories as well as four novels: *This Side of Paradise, The Beautiful and Damned, The Great Gatsby,* and *Tender is the night. The Great Gatsby,* which he finished in the Winter of 1924 and published in 1925, is considered Fitzgerald's most brilliant and critically acclaimed work. readers who have read this novel will remember the opening words spoken by Nick Carraway, the narrator in the story: "in my younger and more vulnerable years my father gave me some advice that i've been turning over in my mind ever since. 'Whenever you feel like criticizing anyone,' he told me, 'Just remember that all the people in this world haven't had the advantages that you've had.'"

56 Abbreviations and Symbols

Unless you are writing a scientific or technical report, spell out most terms and titles, except in the following cases.

56a Titles that always precede or follow a person's name

www.mhhe.com/
bmhh

For information
and exercises on
abbreviations,
go to

Editing >
Abbreviations

Some abbreviations appear before a person's name (*Mr., Mrs., Dr.*) and some follow a proper name (*Jr., Sr., MD, Esq., PhD*). When an abbreviation follows a person's name, a comma is placed between the name and the abbreviation.

> Mrs. Jean Bascom
> Elaine Less, CPA, LL.D.

Do not use two abbreviations that represent the same thing: *Dr. Peter Joyce, MD.* Use either *Dr. Peter Joyce* or *Peter Joyce, MD.*
Spell out titles used without proper names.

doctor.
➤ **Mr. Carew asked if she had seen the dr.**

56b Familiar abbreviations

If you use a technical term or the name of an organization in a report, you may abbreviate it as long as your readers are likely to be familiar with the abbreviation. Abbreviations of three or more capital letters generally do not use periods.

FAMILIAR ABBREVIATION   The *EPA* has had a lasting impact on the air quality in this country.

UNFAMILIAR ABBREVIATION   After you have completed them, take these forms to the *Human Resources and Education Center* [not *HREC*].

Write out an unfamiliar term or name the first time you use it, and give the abbreviation in parentheses.

➤ **The Student Nonviolent Coordinating Committee (SNCC) was far to the left of other civil rights organizations, and its leaders often mocked the "conservatism" of Dr. Martin Luther King, Jr. However, SNCC quickly burned itself out and disappeared.**

56b
abbr

Abbreviations or symbols associated with numbers should be used only when accompanying a number: *3 p.m.*, not *in the p.m.; $500,* not

How many $ do you have? The abbreviation *B.C.* ("Before Christ") follows a date; *A.D.* ("in the year of our Lord") precedes the date. The alternative abbreviations *B.C.E.* ("Before the Common Era") and *C.E.* ("Common Era") can be used instead of *B.C.* or *A.D.*, respectively.

> 6:00 p.m. or 6:00 P.M. or 6:00 PM
> 9:45 a.m. or 9:45 A.M. or 9:45 AM
> 498 B.C. or 498 B.C.E. or 498 BC or 498 BCE or 498 BCE
> A.D. 275 or 275 C.E. or AD 275 or 275 CE or 275 CE
> 6,000 rpm
> 271 cm

Note: Be consistent. If you use *A.M.* in one sentence, do not switch to *A.M.* in the next sentence. If an abbreviation is made up of capital letters, the periods are optional: *B.C. or BC.* (*For more on using periods with abbreviations, see Chapter 54, p. 482.*)

CHARTING the TERRITORY

Abbreviations and Symbols

Some abbreviations and symbols may be acceptable in certain contexts, as long as readers will know what they stand for. For example, a medical writer might use *PT* (*physical therapy*) in a medical report or professional newsletter.

In charts and graphs, abbreviations and symbols such as = for *equals, in.* for *inches, %* for *percent,* and $ with numbers are acceptable because they save space.

CHARTING the TERRITORY

Scientific Abbreviations

Most abbreviations used in scientific or technical writing, such as those related to measurement, should be given without periods: *mph, lb, dc, rpm.* If an abbreviation looks like an actual word, however, you can use a period to prevent confusion: *in., Fig.*

56c Latin abbreviations

Latin abbreviations can be used in notes or works-cited lists, but in formal writing, it is usually a good idea to avoid even common Latin abbreviations (*e.g., et al., etc.,* and *i.e.*). Instead of *e.g.,* use *such as* or *for example*. Reword or omit constructions that use *etc.*

cf.	compare (*confer*)
e.g.	for example, such as (*exempli gratia*)
et al.	and others (*et alia*)
etc.	and so forth, and so on (*et cetera*)
i.e.	that is (*id est*)
N.B.	note well (*nota bene*)
viz.	namely (*videlicet*)

Abbreviations and Grammar Checkers

Computer grammar or spelling checkers may flag an abbreviation, but they generally will not tell you if your use of it is acceptable or consistent within a piece of writing.

56d Inappropriate abbreviations and symbols

Days of the week (*Sat.*), places (*TX* or *Tex.*), the word *company* (*Co.*), people's names (*Wm.*), disciplines and professions (*econ.*), parts of speech (*v.*), parts of written works (*ch., p.*), symbols (@), and units of measurement (*lb.*) are all spelled out in formal writing.

➤ The *environmental* [not *env.*] **engineers from the Paramus Water *Company* [not *Co.*] are arriving in *New York City* [not *NYC*] this *Thursday* [not *Thurs.*] to correct the problems in the *physical education* [not *phys. ed.*] building in time for *Christmas* [not *Xmas*].**

Exceptions: If an abbreviation such as *Inc., Co.,* or *Corp.* is part of a company's official name, then it can be included in formal writing: *Time Inc. announced these changes in late December.* The ampersand symbol (&) can also be used but only if it is part of an official name: *Church & Dwight.*

Exercise 56.1 Chapter review: Editing for abbreviations and symbols

Spell out any inappropriate abbreviations in this passage of nontechnical writing.

In today's digital-savvy world, a person who has never used a computer with access to the WWW and a Motion Pictures Experts Group Layer 3 (MP3) player would be surprised to find that anyone can download and groove to the sounds of

56d
abbr

"Nights in White Satin" by the 1960s rock band the Moody Blues at 3 AM without ever having to have spent $ for the album *Days of Future Past*. However, such file sharing, commonly known as "file swapping," is illegal and surrounded by controversy. The Recording Industry Association of America (RIAA), which represents the U.S. recording industry, has taken aggressive legal action against such acts of online piracy. E.g., in a landmark case in 2004, U.S. District Judge Denny Chin ruled that ISPs must identify those subscribers who share music online, at least in the states of NY, NJ, and CT. As the nature of music recordings changes with the proliferation of digital music services & file formats, this controversy is far from being resolved. In recent yrs companies such as Apple & Microsoft as well as celluar phone carriers have set up online music stores. Consumers can buy downloadable music files for very little $.

57 Numbers

www.mhhe.com/
bmhh

For information
and exercises on
numbers, go to

Editing > Numbers

57a Numbers versus words

In nontechnical writing, spell out numbers up to one hundred and round numbers greater than one hundred.

➤ Approximately *twenty-five* students failed the exam, but more than *two hundred and fifty* passed.

When you are using a great many numbers or when a spelled-out number would require more than three or four words, use numerals.

➤ This regulation affects nearly *10,500* taxpayers, substantially more than the *200* originally projected. Of those affected, *2,325* filled out the papers incorrectly and another *743* called the office for help.

Round numbers larger than one million are expressed in numerals and words: *8 million, 2.4 trillion.*

Use all numerals rather than mixing numerals and spelled-out words for the same type of item in a passage.

➤ **We wrote to 132 people but only 16 responded.**

Exception: When two numbers appear together, spell out one and use numerals for the other: *two 20-pound bags*.

Punctuation tip: Use a hyphen with two-word numbers from twenty-one through ninety-nine, whether they appear alone or within a larger number: *fifty-six, one hundred twenty-eight*. A hyphen also appears in two-word fractions (*one-third, five-eighths*) and in compound words made up of a spelled-out number or numeral and another word (*forty-hour work week, 5-page paper*).

In technical and business writing, use numerals for exact measurements and all numbers greater than ten.

➤ **The endosperm halves were placed in each of 14 small glass test tubes.**

➤ **With its $1.9 trillion economy, Germany has an important trade role to play.**

57b Numbers that begin sentences

If a number begins a sentence, reword the sentence or spell out the numeral.

➤ *Twenty-five* **children are in each elementary class.**

57c Conventional uses of numerals

- **Dates:** October 9, 2002; A.D. 1066 (*or* AD 1066)
- **Time of day:** 6 A.M. (*or* AM *or* a.m.), a quarter past eight in the evening, three o'clock in the morning
- **Addresses:** 21 Meadow Road, Apt. 6J
- **Percentages:** 73 percent, 73%
- **Fractions and decimals:** 21.84, 6½
- **Measurements:** 100 mph, 9 kg
- **Volume, page, chapter:** volume 4, chapter 8, page 44
- **Scenes in a play:** *Hamlet,* act 2, scene 1
- **Scores and statistics:** 3 to 0, 98–92, an average age of 35
- **Amounts of money:** $125, $2.25, $2.8 million

57c
num

| Exercise 57.1 | Chapter review: Editing for numbers |

Edit the sentences that follow to correct errors in the use of numbers. Some sentences are correct; circle their numbers.

$546

EXAMPLE   I have ~~five hundred forty-six dollars~~ in my

bank account.

1. The soccer team raised one thousand sixty seven dollars by selling entertainment booklets filled with coupons, discounts, and special promotions.
2. 55% of the participants in the sociology student's survey reported that they would lie to a professor in order to have a late assignment accepted.
3. In one year alone, 115 employees at the company objected to their performance appraisals, but only twenty-four filed formal complaints.
4. When preparing a professional letter, set the margins at 1 inch.
5. Eighty-five applicants hoped to win the four-year scholarship, but only one person was awarded full tuition and living expenses.
6. Four out of 5 children who enter preschool in Upper East County already know the alphabet.
7. The motorcycle accident occurred at a half past 4 in the morning on the interstate highway, but paramedics did not arrive until six thirty AM.
8. The horticulturist at the nursery raises more than 200 varieties of orchids.

58 Italics (Underlining)

Italics, a typeface in which the characters slant to the right, are used to set off certain words and phrases. If italics are not available, you can underline words that would be typeset in italics. MLA style requires italics.

58a Titles of works or separate publications

www.mhhe.com/
bmhh

For information
and exercises on
italics, go to
Editing > Italics

Italicize (or underline) titles of books, magazines, journals, newspapers, comic strips, plays, films, musical compositions, choreographic works, artworks, Web sites, software, long poems, pamphlets, and other long works. In titles of lengthy works, *a, an,* or *the* is capitalized and italicized (underlined) if it is the first word, but *the* is not generally treated as part of the title in names of newspapers and periodicals: the *New York Times.*

➤ Picasso's *Guernica* captures the anguish and despair of violence.

➤ Plays by Shakespeare provide details and story lines for Verdi's opera *Falstaff,* Cole Porter's musical comedy *Kiss Me, Kate,* and Baz Luhrmann's film *Romeo and Juliet.*

Court cases may also be italicized or underlined.

➤ In *Brown v. Board of Education of Topeka* (1954), the U.S. Supreme Court ruled that segregation in public schools is unconstitutional.

Exception: Do not use italics or underlining when referring to the Bible and other sacred books.

Quotation marks are used for the titles of short works—essays, newspaper and magazine articles and columns, short stories, individual episodes of television and radio programs, short poems, songs, and chapters or other book subdivisions. Quotation marks are also used for titles of unpublished works, including student papers, theses, and dissertations. (*See Chapter 53, pp. 475–76, for more on quotation marks with titles.*)

58b Names of ships, trains, aircraft, and spaceships

➤ The commentators were stunned into silence when the space shuttle *Challenger* exploded.

58c Foreign terms

**58c
ital**

➤ In the Paris airport, we recognized the familiar no smoking sign: *Défense de fumer.*

Foreign words that have become so common in English that everyone accepts them as part of the language require no italics or underlining: rigor mortis, pasta, and sombrero, for example.

58d   Scientific names

The scientific (Latin) names of organisms are always italicized.

➤ **Most chicks are infected with *Cryptosporidium baileyi*, a parasite typical of young animals.**

Note: Although the whole name is italicized, only the genus part of the name is capitalized.

58e   Words, letters, and numbers referred to as themselves

For clarity, italicize words or phrases used as words rather than for the meaning they convey. (You may also use quotation marks for this purpose.) Letters and numbers used alone should also be italicized.

➤ **The word *bookkeeper* has three sets of double letters: double *o*, double *k*, and double *e*.**

➤ **Add a *3* to that column.**

58f   For emphasis

An occasional word in italics helps you make a point. Too much emphasis, however, may mean no emphasis at all.

WEAK   You don't *mean* that your *teacher* told the whole *class* that *he* did not know the answer *himself*?

REVISED   Your teacher admitted that he did not know the answer? That is amazing.

If you add italics or underlining to a quotation, indicate the change in parentheses following the quotation.

➤ **Instead of promising that no harm will come to us, Blake only assures us that we "need not *fear* harm" (emphasis added).**

Exercise 58.1   Chapter review: Editing for italics

Edit the following passage, underlining the words that should be italicized and circling the italicized words that should be roman.

Today, thousands of people in the United States practice *yoga* for its physical, spiritual, and mental benefits. The word *yoga*, originating from the Sanskrit root yuj, means the union of the body, spirit, and mind. Although there are many styles of *yoga,* people who want a gentle introduction to *yoga* should practice Iyengar yoga, a style developed by B.K.S. Iyengar of India, which uses props such as blocks, belts, and pillows to help the body find alignment in asanas (poses) and pranayama (breathing). Those people who want to learn more about Iyengar yoga are encouraged to read the following books written by the master himself: *Light on Yoga, Light on Pranayama,* The *Art of Yoga,* The *Tree of Yoga,* and *Light on the Yoga Sutras of Patanjali.* Those who want to learn about the general benefits of *yoga* can find numerous articles, such as "*Yoga and Weight Loss,*" by doing a general online search. All forms of *yoga* promise the *diligent* and *faithful* practitioner increased *strength, flexibility,* and *balance.*

59 Hyphens

59a To form compound words

www.mhhe.com/
bmhh

For information
and exercises on
hyphens, go to
Editing > Hyphens

A hyphen joins two nouns to make one compound word. Scientists speak of a *kilogram-meter* as a measure of force, and professors of literature talk about the *scholar-poet.* The hyphen lets us know that the two nouns work together as one.

A dictionary is the best resource when you are unsure about whether to use a hyphen. If you cannot find a compound word in the dictionary, spell it as two separate words.

59b To create compound adjective or noun forms

A noun can also be linked with an adjective, an adverb, or another part of speech to form a compound adjective.

**59b
hyph**

accident-prone
quick-witted

Hyphens are also used in nouns designating family relationships and compounds of more than two words:

brother-in-law
stick-in-the-mud

Compound nouns with hyphens generally form plurals by adding -s or -es to the most important word.

attorney general/attorneys general
mother-in-law/mothers-in-law

Some proper nouns that are joined to make an adjective are hyphenated: the *Franco-Prussian war.*

Hyphens often help clarify adjectives that come before the word they modify. Modifiers that are hyphenated when they are placed *before* the word they modify are usually not hyphenated when they are placed *after* the word they modify.

➤ **It was a *bad-mannered* reply.**

➤ **The reply was *bad mannered*.**

Do not use a hyphen to connect -*ly* adverbs to the words they modify.

➤ **They explored the *newly/discovered* territories.**

In a pair or series of compound nouns or adjectives, add suspended hyphens after the first word of each item.

➤ **The child care center accepted three-, four-, and five-year-olds.**

59c To spell out fractions and compound numbers

Use a hyphen when writing out fractions or compound numbers from twenty-one to ninety-nine.

three-fourths of a gallon
thirty-two

Note: In MLA style, use a hyphen to show inclusive numbers: *pages 100-40.*

59d To attach some prefixes and suffixes

Use a hyphen to join a prefix and a capitalized word.

➤ **Skipping the parade on the Fourth of July is positively *un-American!***

A hyphen is sometimes used to join a capital letter and a word: *T-shirt, V-six engine.*

The prefixes *ex-, self-,* and *all-* and the suffixes -*elect* and -*odd* (or -*something*) generally take hyphens. However, most prefixes are not attached by hyphens, unless a hyphen is needed to show pronunciation or to reveal a special meaning that distinguishes the word from the same word without a hyphen: *recreate* versus *re-create.* Check a dictionary to be certain you are using the standard spelling.

➤ Because he was an *ex-convict,* he was a *nonjudgmental coworker.*

➤ They were *self-sufficient, antisocial* neighbors.

59e To divide words at the ends of lines

When you must divide words, do so between syllables. However, pronunciation alone cannot always tell you where to divide a word. If you are unsure about how to break a word into syllables, consult your dictionary.

➤ My writing group had a very fruitful *collaboration* [not *colla-boration*].

Note: Never leave just one or two letters on a line.

Exercise 59.1 Chapter review: Editing for hyphens

Edit the following passage, adding and deleting hyphens as necessary.

We need only to turn on the television or pick up a recent issue of a popular fashion or fitness magazine to see evidence of modern society's obsession with images of thinness. Few actors, models, or celebrities fail to flaunt their thinly-trimmed waist-lines, regardless of their gender. Not surpri-singly, more than ten million females and almost one million males in the United States are currently battling eating disorders such as anorexia nervosa and bulimia nervosa. A person who is anorexic fears gaining weight, and thus en-gages in self star-vation and excessive weight loss. A person who is bulimic binges and then engages in self-induced purging in order to lose weight. Although we are often quick to assume that those with eating disorders suffer from low self-esteem and have a history of family or peer problems, we cannot ignore the role of the media in encouraging eating disorders, particularly when thinness is equated with physical attractiveness, health and fitness, and success over-all. We need to remember the threat of these eating disorders the next time we hear a ten year old girl tell her mommy that she "can't afford" to eat more than one half of her peanut butter and jelly sandwich.

**59e
hyph**

60 Spelling

www.mhhe.com/
bmhh

For information
and exercises on
spelling, go to

Editing > Spelling

Proofread your writing carefully. Misspellings creep into the prose of even the best writers. Use the following strategies to help you improve your spelling.

- Become familiar with major spelling rules and commonly misspelled words.
- Use your dictionary whenever you are unsure about the spelling of a specific word.

Spelling Checkers

Computer spell checkers are helpful tools. Remember, however, that a spell checker cannot tell how you are using a particular word. If you write *their* but mean *there,* a spell checker cannot point out your mistake.

60a Basic spelling rules

1. *i* before *e*

Use *i* before *e* except after *c* or when sounded like *a,* as in *neighbor* and *weigh.*

- ***i* before *e*:** believe, relieve, chief, grief, wield, yield
- **Except after *c*:** receive, deceive, ceiling, conceit
- **Exceptions:** seize, caffeine, codeine, weird, height

2. Adding suffixes

- **Final silent *e*:** When adding a suffix that begins with a vowel, drop the final silent *e* from the root word. Keep the final *e* if the suffix begins with a consonant.

  force/forcing   remove/removable
  surprise/surprising   care/careful

  Exceptions: argue/argument, true/truly, change/changeable, judge/judgment, acknowledge/acknowledgment

  Exception: Keep the silent *e* if it is needed to clarify the pronunciation or if the word would be confused with another word without the *e*.

  dye/dyeing (to avoid confusion with *dying*)
  hoe/hoeing (to avoid mispronunciation)

- **Final y:** When adding the suffix *-ing* to a word ending in *y*, retain the *y*.

    enjoy/enjoying   cry/crying

    Change the *y* to *i* or *ie* when the final *y* follows a consonant, but not when it follows a vowel.

    happy/happier   defray/defrayed

- **Final consonants:** When adding a suffix to a word that ends in a consonant preceded by a vowel, double the final consonant if the root word has only one syllable or an accent on the last syllable.

    grip/gripping   refer/referred

    Exceptions: bus/busing, focus/focused

3. Forming plurals

Most plurals are formed by adding *s*. Some are formed by adding *es*.

When to Form the Plural with *es*

SINGULAR ENDING	PLURAL ENDING
s, sh, x, z, "soft" ch bus, bush, fox, buzz, peach	**es** buses, bushes, foxes, buzzes, peaches
consonant + o hero, tomato	**es** heroes, tomatoes
Exception: solo/solos	
consonant + y beauty, city	**change y to i and add es** beauties, cities
Exception: a person's name—Kirby, the Kirbys	
f, fe leaf, knife, wife	**change f to v and add s or es** leaves, knives, wives

Exception: Words that end in *ff* and some other words that end in *f* (*staff, roof*) form the plural by adding only an *s* (*staffs, roofs*).

60a

sp

Most plurals follow standard rules, but some have irregular forms (*child/children, tooth/teeth*), and some words with foreign roots create plurals in the pattern of the language they come from, as do these words.

analysis/analyses	medium/media
crisis/crises	stimulus/stimuli
datum/data	thesis/theses

Some nouns with foreign roots have regular and irregular plural forms (*appendix / appendices / appendixes*). Be consistent in the spelling you choose.

> *Note:* Some writers now treat *data* as though it were singular, but the preferred practice is still to recognize that *data* is plural and takes a plural verb: *The data are clear on this point: the pass / fail course has become outdated by events.*

Compound nouns with hyphens generally form plurals by adding *s* or *es* to the most important word.

attorney general/attorneys general
mother-in-law/mothers-in-law

For some compound words that appear as one word, the same rule applies (*passersby*); for others, it does not (*cupfuls*).

If both words in the compound are equally important, add *s* to the second word: *singer-songwriters*.

A few words such as *fish* and *sheep* have the same forms for singular and plural.

Tip for Multilingual Writers: *American and British Spelling*

Standard British spelling differs from American spelling for some words—among them *color / colour, canceled / cancelled, theater / theatre, realize / realise,* and *judgment / judgement.*

Exercise 60.1   Practicing spelling

Write the correct plural form for each of the following words. Consult the preceding rules or a dictionary, as needed.

Bentley	hoof	trophy
president-elect	potato	index
life	fungus	Sidney
box	brother-in-law	self
appendix	stereo	nucleus

Exercise 60.2	Practicing spelling

Some words in the following list are misspelled. Circle each of the misspelled words, and write the correct spelling next to it.

either	boxxing	hopping
hygiene	supplyed	nieghbor
dealer	neither	worried
buying	divorced	tring
exced	managable	receipt

60b Words pronounced alike but spelled differently

Homonyms sound alike but have different meanings and different spellings. The following is a list of common homonyms as well as words that are almost homonyms.

COMMON HOMONYMS and NEAR HOMONYMS

accept: "to take willingly"
except: "to leave out" (verb); "but for" (preposition)

affect: "to influence" (verb); "a feeling or an emotion" (noun)
effect: "to make or accomplish" (verb); "result" (noun)

all ready: "prepared"
already: "by this time"

discreet: "tactful" or "prudent"
discrete: "separate" or "distinct"

cite: "to quote or refer to"
sight: "spectacle, sense"
site: "place"

desert: "dry, sandy place" (noun); "to leave" (verb)
dessert: "after-dinner course"

hear: "perceive by listening"
here: "at this place"

it's: contraction for *it is* or *it has*
its: possessive pronoun

loose: "not tight"
lose: "to misplace"

passed: past tense of *pass*
past: "former time"

peace: "quiet, harmony"
piece: "part of "

plain: "simple"
plane: "aircraft" or "tool for leveling wood"

precede: "to come before"
proceed: "to go forward"

principal: "most important" (adjective); "the head of an organization" or "a sum of money" (noun)
principle: "a basic standard or law" (noun)

(continued)

60b
sp

COMMON HOMONYMS and NEAR HOMONYMS (continued)

their: possessive pronoun
there: adverb of place
they're: contraction for
 they are

to: indicating movement
too: "also"
two: number

weather: "atmospheric
 condition"
whether: "if it is or was true"

who's: contraction for *who is*
whose: possessive of *who*

your: possessive pronoun
you're: contraction for *you are*

COMMONLY MISSPELLED WORDS

A
absence
accessible
accidentally
accommodate
achieve
address
amateur
analysis
analyze
apparent
appearance
appropriate
argument
athlete
average

B
basically
beginning
believe
beneficial
business

C
calendar
cemetery
certain

changing
chief
column
commitment
committee
competition
conceive
consistency
continuous
convenient
criticism
curiosity
curious
curriculum

D
decision
definitely
descendant
desirable
desperate
discipline
discussion
disease
dissatisfied

E
ecstasy

efficient
eighth
embarrass
emphasize
entirely
environment
especially
exaggerate
exercise
existence

F
familiar
fascinate
February
foreign
fulfill

G
gauge
government
grammar
guarantee
guard
guidance

H
harass

COMMONLY MISSPELLED WORDS

height
heroes
humorous

I
imaginary
immediately
incredible
independence
individual
influential
intelligence
interest
irrelevant
irresistible

J
judgment

K
knowledge

L
laboratory
license
luxury
lying

M
maintenance
manageable
marriage
meant
medicine
mischievous
misspelled
mortgage
muscle

N
necessary
neighbor

nuclear
nuisance
numerous

O
occasion
occur
official
opponent
opportunity

P
parallel
parliament
particularly
performance
permanent
permissible
persuade
pitiful
playwright
possession
practically
preference
prejudice
prevalent
privilege
professor
pronunciation

Q
questionnaire
quizzes

R
receive
recommend
referred
remembrance
reminisce
repetition
restaurant

rhyme
rhythm
ridiculous

S
sacrifice
schedule
secretary
seize
separate
similar
sincerely
sophomore
succeed
summary
surprise

T
technique
tendency
thorough
together
tomorrow
tragedy
twelfth

U
unanimous
unconscious
unnecessary
usually

V
vacuum
vengeance
villain

W
weird
wholly
writing

60b

sp

Exercise 60.3 Fixing commonly misspelled words

Highlight the words in the preceding list that give you trouble. In a list or spelling log, write down other words you often misspell. Try to group your errors. Do they fall into patterns—errors with suffixes or plurals, for example? Errors with silent letters or doubled consonants?

Leucaena leucocephala, or white leadtree, is widely used in reforestation, land reclamation, and erosion prevention programs. It enriches the soil as well. Just as trees require soil to grow, language is "rooted" in basic grammar.

PART
9

Grammar and rhetoric are complementary....

Grammar maps out the possible;

rhetoric narrows the possible down to the

desirable or effective.

—Francis Christensen

Basic
Grammar

9 Basic Grammar

WRITING OUTCOMES

Conventions

This section will help you learn to do the following:

- Become familiar with the basic parts of speech **(61)**
- Identify simple and complete subjects and predicates **(62)**
- Understand how phrases and dependent clauses function in sentences **(63)**
- Recognize common sentence structures and purposes **(64)**

Test Yourself:

Take an online quiz at www.mhhe.com/bmhh to test your familiarity with the topics covered in chapters 61–64. As you read the following chapters, pay special attention to the sections that correspond to any questions you answer incorrectly.

Written language, although based on the grammar of spoken language, has a logic and rules of its own. The chapters that follow explain the basic rules of standard written English. (*Non-native speakers of standard American English should see Chapter 48 as well.*)

61 Parts of Speech

English has eight primary **parts of speech:** verbs, nouns, pronouns, adjectives, adverbs, prepositions, conjunctions, and interjections. All English words belong to one or more of these categories. Particular words can belong to different categories, depending on the role they play in a sentence. For example, the word *button* can be a noun (*the button on a coat*) or a verb (*he will button his jacket now*).

www.mhhe.com/ bmhh

For information and exercises on parts of speech, go to

Editing > Parts of Speech

61a   Verbs

Verbs report action (*run, write*), condition (*bloom, sit*), or state of being (*be, seem*). Verbs also change form to indicate person, number, tense, voice, and mood. To do all this, a **main verb** is often preceded by one or more **helping verbs,** thereby becoming a **verb phrase.**

>   mv
> The play *begins* at eight.

> hv   mv   hv   mv
> I *may change* seats after the play *has begun.*

1. Main verbs
Main verbs change form (**tense**) to indicate when something has happened. If a word does not indicate tense, it is not a main verb. All main verbs have five forms, except for *be*, which has eight.

PRESENT TENSE THIRD PERSON SINGULAR (OR -S FORM)	Usually, he/she/it (*talks, sings*).
BASE FORM	(*talk, sing*)
PAST TENSE	Yesterday I (*talked, sang*).
PAST PARTICIPLE	In the past, I have (*talked, sung*).
PRESENT PARTICIPLE	Right now I am (*talking, singing*).

61a
gram

515

(For more on subject-verb agreement and verb tense, see Chapter 45, pp. 390–403, and Chapter 44, pp. 381–390, as well as the list of common irregular verbs on pp. 391–93. For information on using verbs followed by infinitives or gerunds, see Chapter 48, pp. 431–33.)

2. Helping verbs that show time

Some helping verbs—mostly forms of *be, have,* and *do*—function to signify time (*will have been playing, has played*) or emphasis (*does play*). Forms of *do* are also used to ask questions (*Do you play?*). Here is a fuller list of such helping (**auxiliary**) verbs.

be, am, is	being, been	do, does, did
are, was, were	have, has, had	

(For information on matching helping verbs with the appropriate tense of the main verb, see Chapter 48, pp. 428–30.)

3. Modals

Other helping verbs, called **modals,** express an attitude toward the action or circumstance of a sentence:

can	ought to	will
could	shall	would
may	should	must
might		

Modal verbs share several characteristics:

- They do not change form to indicate person or number.
- They do not change form to indicate tense.
- They are followed directly by the base form of the verb without *to.*

➤   **We must ~~to~~ study now.**

Some verbal expressions ending in *to* also function as modals, including *have to, be able to,* and *be supposed to.* These **phrasal modals** behave more like ordinary verbs than true modals, changing form to indicate tense and agree with the subject.

Exercise 61.1   Identifying verbs

Underline the main verb in each sentence, and circle any helping verbs.

    EXAMPLE   **Government of the people, by the people, for the people (shall) not <u>perish</u> from the earth.**

1. An increasing number of Americans, both men and women, undergo cosmetic surgery for aesthetic rather than medical reasons.
2. A decade ago, the average American believed that only Hollywood celebrities underwent face-lifts and tummy tucks.
3. Do you think that you need to improve your physical appearance?
4. Men, often in their mid-forties, are choosing a variety of surgical procedures, including hair replacement and chin augmentation.
5. For a lean, flat abdomen, a cosmetic surgeon may suggest both abdominoplasty and liposuction.
6. People are now able to achieve their ideal body image, not through exercise and diet, but through elective cosmetic surgery.

61b Nouns

Nouns name people (*Shakespeare, actors, Englishman*), places (*Manhattan, city, island*), things (*Kleenex, handkerchief, sneeze, cats*), and ideas (*Marxism, justice, democracy, clarity*).

➤ *Shakespeare* **lived in** *England* **and wrote** *plays* **about the human** *condition.*

1. Proper and common nouns

Proper nouns name specific people, places, and things and are always capitalized: *Aretha Franklin, Hinduism, Albany, Microsoft.* All other nouns are **common nouns:** *singer, religion, capital, corporation.*

2. Count and noncount nouns

A common noun that refers to something specific that can be counted is a **count noun.** Count nouns can be singular or plural, like *cup* or *suggestion* (*four cups, several suggestions*). **Noncount nouns** are nonspecific; these common nouns refer to categories of people, places, or things and cannot be counted. They do not have a plural form (*the pottery is beautiful; his advice was useful*). (*For use of articles and quantifiers with count and noncount nouns, see Chapter 48, pp. 426–28.*)

3. Concrete and abstract nouns

Nouns that name things that can be perceived by the senses are called **concrete nouns:** *boy, wind, book, song.* **Abstract nouns** name qualities and concepts that do not have physical properties: *charity, patience, beauty, hope.* (*For more on using concrete and abstract nouns, see Chapter 40, p. 347*)

61b
gram

4. Singular and plural nouns

Most nouns name things that can be counted and are singular or plural. Singular nouns typically become plural by adding *s* or *es: boy/boys, ocean/oceans, church/churches, agency/agencies.* Some have irregular plurals, such as *man/men, child/children,* and *tooth/teeth.* Noncount nouns like *intelligence* and *electricity* do not form plurals. (*See Chapter 60, pp 507–08, for help forming plurals.*)

5. Collective nouns

Collective nouns such as *team, family, herd,* and *orchestra* are treated as singular. They are not noncount nouns, however, because collective nouns can be counted and can be made plural: *teams, families.* (*Also see Chapter 44, p. 385 and 405–07.*)

6. Possessive nouns

When nouns are used in the **possessive case** to indicate ownership, they change their form. To form the possessive case, singular nouns add an apostrophe plus *s* ('*s*), whereas plural nouns ending in -*s* just add an apostrophe ('). (*Also see Chapter 52, pp. 468–71.*)

SINGULAR	insect	insect's sting
PLURAL	neighbors	neighbors' car

61c Pronouns

A **pronoun** takes the place of a noun. The noun that the pronoun replaces is called its **antecedent.** (*For more on pronoun-antecedent agreement, see Chapter 46, pp. 403–07.*)

➤ The **snow** fell all day long, and by nightfall *it* was three feet deep.

The box on pages 520–21 summarizes the different kinds of pronouns.

1. Personal pronouns

The **personal pronouns** *I, me, you, he, his, she, her, it, we, us, they,* and *them* refer to specific people or things and vary in form to indicate person, number, gender, and case. (*For more on pronoun reference and case, see Chapter 46, pp. 408–16.*)

➤ *You* told *us* that *he* gave Jane a lock of *his* hair.

2. Possessive pronouns

Like possessive nouns, **possessive pronouns** indicate ownership. However, unlike possessive nouns, possessive pronouns do not add apostrophes: *my/mine, your/yours, her/hers, his, its, our/ours, their/theirs.*

➤ Brunch is at *her* place this Saturday.

3. Reflexive and intensive pronouns

Pronouns ending in *-self* or *-selves* are either reflexive or intensive. **Reflexive pronouns** refer back to the subject and are necessary for sentence sense.

➤ Many of the women blamed *themselves* for the problem.

Intensive pronouns add emphasis to the nouns or pronouns they follow and are grammatically optional.

➤ President Harding *himself* drank whiskey during Prohibition.

4. Relative pronouns

The **relative pronouns** *who, whom, whose, that,* and *which* relate a dependent clause—a word group containing a subject and verb and a subordinating word—to an antecedent noun or pronoun in the sentence.

dependent clause

➤ In Kipling's story, Dravot is the man *who* would be king.

The form of a relative pronoun varies according to its **case**—the grammatical role it plays in the sentence. (*For more on pronoun case, see Chapter 46, pp. 410–16.*)

5. Demonstrative pronouns

The **demonstrative pronouns** *this, that, these,* and *those* point out nouns and pronouns that come later.

➤ *This* is the book literary critics have been waiting for.

Sometimes these pronouns function as adjectives: *This book won the Pulitzer.* Sometimes they are noun equivalents: *This is my book.*

6. Interrogative pronouns

Interrogative pronouns such as *who, whatever,* and *whom* are used to ask questions.

➤ *Whatever* happened to you?

61c

gram

PRONOUNS

PERSONAL (INCLUDING POSSESSIVE)

SINGULAR	PLURAL
I, me, my, mine	we, us, our, ours
you, your, yours	you, your, yours
he, him, his	they, them, their, theirs
she, her, hers	
it, its	

REFLEXIVE AND INTENSIVE

SINGULAR	PLURAL
myself	ourselves
yourself	yourselves
himself, herself, itself	themselves
oneself	

RELATIVE

who	whoever	what	whatever	that
whom	whomever	whose	whichever	which

DEMONSTRATIVE

this, that, these, those

The form of the interrogative pronouns *who, whom, whoever,* and *whomever* indicates the grammatical role they play in a sentence. (*See Chapter 46, pp. 415–16.*)

7. Indefinite pronouns
Indefinite pronouns such as *someone, anybody, nothing,* and *few* refer to a nonspecific person or thing and do not change form to indicate person, number, or gender.

➤ *Anybody* **who cares enough to come and help may take** *some* **home.**

INTERROGATIVE

who	what	which
whoever	whatever	whichever
whom	whomever	whose

INDEFINITE

SINGULAR		PLURAL	SINGULAR/PLURAL
anybody	nobody	both	all
anyone	no one	few	any
anything	none	many	either
each	nothing	several	more
everybody	one		most
everyone	somebody		some
everything	someone		
much	something		
neither			

RECIPROCAL

each other, any other

Most indefinite pronouns are always singular (*anybody, everyone*). Some are always plural (*many, few*), and a handful can be singular or plural (*any, most*). (*See Chapter 44, p. 386 and Chapter 46, pp. 404–05.*)

8. Reciprocal pronouns

Reciprocal pronouns such as *each other* and *one another* refer to the separate parts of their plural antecedent.

➤ **My sister and I are close because we live near *each other*.**

Exercise 61.2   Identifying nouns and pronouns

Underline the nouns and circle the pronouns in each sentence.

EXAMPLE   We have nothing to fear but fear itself.

61c

gram

1. Following World War I, the nation witnessed an unprecedented explosion of African-American fiction, poetry, drama, music, art, social commentary, and political activism.
2. Many African-American intellectuals, artists, cultural critics, and political leaders during the 1920s and 1930s were drawn to Harlem, a vibrant section of upper Manhattan in New York City.
3. Sociologist and intellectual Alain Locke, author of *The New Negro,* is best known as the New Negro Movement's founder.
4. W. E. B. Du Bois was the author of *The Souls of Black Folk,* and he was also a cofounder of the National Association for the Advancement of Colored People (NAACP), a preeminent civil rights organization.
5. These intellectuals of the Harlem Renaissance profoundly influenced each other.
6. They spoke about the effect of marginality and alienation on themselves and on the shaping of their consciousness as African Americans.
7. Zora Neal Hurston was herself a cultural anthropologist who studied the folklore of the rural South, which is reflected in her novel *Their Eyes Were Watching God.*
8. Nella Larson, author of *Quicksand* and *Passing,* was awarded a Guggenheim fellowship for her creative writing in 1929.
9. Who among the visual artists during the Harlem Renaissance did not use Africa as a source of inspiration?

Exercise 61.3   Identifying types of nouns and pronouns

On a separate sheet of paper, list each noun and pronoun that you identified in Exercise 61.2. For each noun, label it proper or common, count or noncount, concrete or abstract, and singular or plural. Also identify the one collective noun and the one possessive noun. For each pronoun, label it personal, possessive, reflexive, intensive, relative, demonstrative, interrogative, indefinite, or reciprocal. Note if the pronoun is singular or plural.

61d   Adjectives

Adjectives modify nouns and pronouns by answering questions like *Which one? What kind? How many? What size? What color? What condition?* and *Whose?* They can describe, enumerate, identify, define, and limit (*one person, that person*). When articles (*a, an, the*) identify nouns, they function as adjectives.

Sometimes proper nouns are treated as adjectives; the proper adjectives that result are capitalized: *Britain/British.* Pronouns can also function as adjectives (*his green car*), and adjectives often have forms that allow you to make comparisons (*great, greater, greatest*).

➤ The *decisive* and *diligent* king regularly attended meetings of the council. [What kind of king?]

➤ *These four artistic* qualities affect how an advertisement is received. [Which, how many, what kind of qualities?]

➤ *My little blue* Volkswagen died *one icy winter* morning. [Whose, what size, what color car? Which, what kind of morning?]

Like all modifiers, adjectives should be close to the words they modify. Most often, adjectives appear before the noun they modify, but **descriptive adjectives**—adjectives that designate qualities or attributes—may come before or after the noun or pronoun they modify for stylistic reasons. Adjectives that describe the subject and follow linking verbs (*be, am, is, are, was, being, been, appear, become, feel, grow, look, make, prove, taste*) are called **subject complements.**

BEFORE SUBJECT

The *sick* and *destitute* poet no longer believed that love would save him.

AFTER SUBJECT

The poet, *sick* and *destitute,* no longer believed that love would save him.

AFTER LINKING VERB

No longer believing that love would save him, the poet was *sick* and *destitute.*

(*For more on adjectives, see Chapter 47. For common problems multilingual writers have with adjectives, see Chapter 48, pp. 434–36.*)

61e Adverbs

Adverbs often end in *-ly* (*beautifully, gracefully, quietly*) and usually answer such questions as *When? Where? How? How often? How much? To what degree?* and *Why?*

➤ The authenticity of the document is *hotly* contested. [How is it contested?]

Adverbs modify verbs, other adverbs, and adjectives. Like adjectives, adverbs can be used to compare (*less, lesser, least*). In addition to

61e
gram

modifying individual words, they can be used to modify whole clauses. Adverbs can be placed at the beginning or end of a sentence or before the verb they modify, but they usually should not be placed between the verb and its direct object.

➤ The water was *brilliant* blue and *icy* cold. [The adverbs intensify the adjectives *blue* and *cold.*]

➤ Dickens mixed humor and pathos *better* than any other English writer after Shakespeare. [The adverb compares Dickens with other writers.]

➤ *Consequently,* he is still read by millions.

Consequently is a conjunctive adverb that modifies the independent clause that follows it and shows how the sentence is related to the preceding sentence. (*For more on conjunctive adverbs, see the material on conjunctions, pp. 526–27. For issues muiltilingual writers have with adverbs, see Chapter 48, p. 434, p. 437.*)

No, not, and *never* are among the most common adverbs.

| **Exercise 61.4** | Identifying adjectives and adverbs |

Underline the adjectives and circle the adverbs in each sentence.

EXAMPLE   Peter Piper (patiently) picked a peck of pickled peppers.

1. A growing number of Americans are overweight or clinically obese.
2. Obesity increases a person's risk for type 2 diabetes, heart disease, high blood pressure, stroke, liver damage, cancer, and premature death.
3. Fad diets promise Americans rapid but temporary weight loss, not weight management.
4. Robert C. Atkins, M.D., author of *Dr. Atkins' New Diet Revolution,* best explains a low-carbohydrate, high-protein diet.
5. Other fad diets, such as the Sugar Busters diet, work on the premise that high glycemic carbohydrates are primarily responsible for weight gain.
6. In the best seller *Eat Right for Your Type,* naturopath Peter J. D'Adamo argues that certain foods should be avoided based on a person's blood type.
7. Many other fad diets, such as the grapefruit diet and the cabbage diet, promise quick weight loss.
8. Many fad diets inevitably drive dieters to carbohydrate cravings and binge eating.

9. Few fad diets emphasize the need for dieters to increase their metabolic rate significantly with regular aerobic exercise.

61f Prepositions

Prepositions (*on, in, at, by*) usually appear as part of a **prepositional phrase.** Their main function is to allow the noun or pronoun in the phrase to modify another word in the sentence. Prepositional phrases always begin with a preposition and end with a noun, pronoun, or other word group that functions as the **object of the preposition** (in *time,* on the *table*).

A preposition can be one word (*about, despite, on*) or a word group (*according to, as well as, in spite of*). Place prepositional phrases as close as possible to the words they modify. Adjectival prepositional phrases usually appear right after the noun or pronoun they modify and answer questions like *Which one?* and *What kind of?* Adverbial phrases answer questions like *When? Where? How?* and *Why?*

AS ADJECTIVE	Many species *of birds* nest there.
AS ADVERB	The younger children stared *out the window.*

COMMON PREPOSITIONS AND PREPOSITIONAL PHRASES

about	before	from	over
above	behind	in	since
according to	below	in addition to	through
across	beside	including	to
after	between	in front of	toward
against	beyond	in regard to	under
along	by	inside	until
along with	by means of	instead of	up
among	down	into	upon
apart from	during	like	up to
as	except	near	via
as to	except for	of	with
as well as	excluding	on	within
at	following	on account of	without
because of			

Multilingual writers often have difficulty with the idiomatic use of prepositions (*see Chapter 48, pp. 437–40*).

61f

gram

61g Conjunctions

Conjunctions join words, phrases, or clauses and indicate their relation to each other.

1. Coordinating conjunctions

The common **coordinating conjunctions** (or **coordinators**) are *and, but, or, for, nor, yet,* and *so.* Coordinating conjunctions join elements of equal weight or function.

➤ She was strong *and* healthy.

➤ The war was short *but* devastating.

➤ They must have been tired, *for* they had been climbing all day long.

2. Correlative conjunctions

The **correlative conjunctions** also link sentence elements of equal value, but they always come in pairs: *both ... and, either ... or, neither ... nor,* and *not only ... but also.*

➤ *Neither* the doctor *nor* the police believe his story.

3. Subordinating conjunctions

Common **subordinating conjunctions** (or **subordinators**) link sentence elements that are not of equal importance. They include the following words and phrases:

Subordinating Words

after	once	until
although	since	when
as	that	whenever
because	though	where
before	till	wherever
if	unless	while

Subordinating Phrases

as if	even though	in that
as soon as	even when	rather than
as though	for as much as	sooner than
even after	in order that	so that
even if	in order to	

Because subordinating conjunctions join unequal sentence parts, they are used to introduce dependent, or subordinate, clauses in a sentence.

➤ **The software will not run properly *if* the computer lacks sufficient memory.**

(For help in punctuating sentences with conjunctions, see p. 449 and pp. 459–60. Help for multilingual writers appears in Chapter 48, p. 371 and pp. 440–41.)

4. Conjunctive adverbs

Conjunctive adverbs indicate the relation between two clauses, but unlike conjunctions (*and, but*), they are not grammatically strong enough on their own to hold the clauses together. A period or semicolon is also needed.

➤ **Swimming is an excellent exercise for the heart and for the muscles; *however,* swimming does not help a person control weight as well as jogging does.**

Common Conjunctive Adverbs

accordingly	however	now
also	incidentally	otherwise
anyway	indeed	similarly
as a result	instead	specifically
besides	likewise	still
certainly	meanwhile	subsequently
consequently	moreover	suddenly
finally	nevertheless	then
furthermore	next	therefore
hence	nonetheless	thus

61h Interjections

Interjections are forceful expressions. They are not often used in academic and business writing except in quotations of dialogue.

➤ **"*Wow!*" Davis said. "Are you telling me that there's a former presidential adviser who hasn't written a book?"**

Exercise 61.5 Chapter review: Identifying parts of speech

In the following sentences, label each word according to its part of speech: verb (v), noun (n), pronoun (pn), adjective (adj), adverb (adv), preposition (prep), conjunction (conj), or interjection (interj).

EXAMPLE   Tell-all books are, alas, the biggest sellers.
           adj   n   v   interj adj   adj   n

61h

gram

1. Cancer begins when your body's cells divide abnormally and form a malignant growth or tumor.
2. Many types of cancer, alas, can attack parts of your body imperceptibly, including your body's skin, organs, and blood.
3. One of the most commonly diagnosed types of cancer in the United States, however, is skin cancer.
4. People who are fair-skinned and freckled are more prone to develop skin cancer if they are exposed often to ultraviolet radiation.
5. Many people are relieved to discover that most skin cancers can usually be treated successfully if detected early.

62 Parts of Sentences

Every complete sentence contains at least one **subject** (a noun and its modifiers) and one **predicate** (a verb and its objects, complements, and modifiers) that together make a statement, ask a question, or give a command.

       subj   pred

➤ The *children solved* the puzzle.

62a Subjects

The **simple subject** is the word or words that name the topic of the sentence; it is always a noun or pronoun. To find the subject, ask who or what the sentence is about. The **complete subject** is the simple subject plus its modifiers.

           simple subj

➤ Did *Sir Walter Raleigh* give Queen Elizabeth I the requisite obedience? [Who gave the queen obedience?]

         complete subj
               simple subj

➤ *Three 6-year-old children* solved the puzzle in less than five minutes. [Who solved the puzzle?]

A **compound subject** contains two or more simple subjects connected with a conjunction such as *and, but, or,* or *neither . . . nor.*

compound
simple   simple
➤ *Original thinking* and *bold design* **characterize her work.**

In **imperative sentences,** which give directions or commands, the subject *you* is usually implied, not stated. A helping verb is needed to transform an imperative sentence into a question.

➤ **[*You*] Keep this advice in mind.**

➤ ***Would* you keep this advice in mind?**

In sentences beginning with *there* or *here* followed by some form of *be,* the subject comes after the verb.

simple subj
➤ **Here are the *remnants* of an infamous empire.**

For more on subjects, multilingual writers should see Chapter 48, pp. 433–34.

62b Verbs and their objects or complements

In a sentence, the **predicate** says something about the subject. The verb constitutes the **simple predicate.** The verb plus its object or complement make up the **complete predicate.**

Exercise 62.1 Identifying the subject and predicate

Place one line under the complete subject and two lines under the complete predicate in each sentence. Circle the simple subject and simple predicate. If the subject is implied, write "implied subject" instead.

EXAMPLE Little (Jack Horner) (sat) in a corner.

1. Did Gene Roddenberry, the creator and producer of *Star Trek,* anticipate that his science fiction television series would be watched by people of all ages for more than thirty years?
2. Both Captain James T. Kirk from *Star Trek: The Original Series* and Captain Jean-Luc Picard from *Star Trek: The Next Generation* command a ship called the *Enterprise.*
3. Do not forget that the captain in *Star Trek: Voyager* is a woman, Kathryn Janeway.
4. There are six *Star Trek* series: *The Original Series, The Next Generation, Deep Space Nine, Voyager, Enterprise,* and *The Animated Adventures.*

62b
gram

5. Captain Benjamin Sisko commanded Starfleet's Deep Space
   Nine station and served as the emissary for the Bajoran people.

---

1. Understanding verb functions in sentences

Based on how they function in sentences, verbs are linking, transitive,
or intransitive. The kind of verb determines what elements the complete predicate must include and therefore determines the correct
order of sentence parts. Most meaningful English sentences use one
of five basic sentence patterns:

- **SUBJECT + LINKING VERB + SUBJECT COMPLEMENT**
  New Yorkers are busy people.

- **SUBJECT + TRANSITIVE VERB + DIRECT OBJECT**
  The police officer caught the jaywalker.

- **SUBJECT + TRANSITIVE VERB + INDIRECT OBJECT + DIRECT OBJECT**
  The officer gave the jaywalker a ticket.

- **SUBJECT + TRANSITIVE VERB + DIRECT OBJECT + OBJECT
  COMPLEMENT**
  The ticket made the jaywalker unhappy.

- **SUBJECT + INTRANSITIVE VERB**
  She sighed.

Questions and commands have different word orders (*see p. 533*). (*To
learn how word order changes from direct to indirect quotations, see
Chapter 48, pp. 441–42.*)

Linking verbs and subject complements   A **linking** verb joins a
subject to information about the subject that follows the verb. That
information is called the **subject complement.** The subject complement may be a noun, a pronoun, or an adjective.

>   subj   lv   comp
> ➤ **Ann Yearsley was** *a milkmaid.*

The most frequently used linking verb is the *be* verb (*is, are, was,
were*), but verbs such as *seem, look, appear, feel, become, smell, sound,*
and *taste* can substitute for *be* verbs in these constructions, linking a
sentence's subject to its complement.

>   subj   lv   comp
> ➤ **That new hairstyle** *looks* **beautiful.**

Transitive verbs and direct objects   A **transitive verb** identifies
an action that the subject performs or does to somebody or something

else—the receiver of the action, or **direct object.** To complete its meaning, a transitive verb needs a direct object, usually a noun, pronoun, or word group that acts like a noun or pronoun.

NOUN   I threw *the ball.*

PRONOUN   I threw *it* over a fence.

WORD GROUP   I put *what I needed* into my backpack.

Most often, the subject is doing the action, the direct object is being acted upon, and the transitive verb is in the **active voice.**

ACTIVE   *Parents* sometimes *consider* their *children* unreasonable.

If the verb in a sentence is transitive, it can be in the **passive voice.** In the following revised sentence, the direct object (*children*) has become the subject; the original subject (*parents*) is introduced with the preposition *by* and is now part of a prepositional phrase.

PASSIVE   Children are considered unreasonable by their parents.

(*For more on the active and passive voices, see Chapter 38, pp. 336–39.*)

Exercise 62.2   Using active and passive voice

Rewrite each sentence, changing the verb from the passive to the active voice.

EXAMPLE

A new nation was brought forth on this continent by our fathers four score and seven years ago.

Four score and seven years ago our fathers brought forth on this continent a new nation.

1. The first national convention on women's rights was organized by Lucretia Mott and Elizabeth Cady Stanton.
2. The convention was held by them in 1848 at Seneca Falls, a town in upstate New York.
3. The Declaration of Sentiments, which included a demand that women be granted the right to vote, was issued by the convention.
4. The Declaration of Sentiments was modeled by the leaders who drafted it on the Declaration of Independence.

62b
gram

Transitive verbs, indirect objects, and direct objects **Indirect objects** name to whom an action was done or for whom it was completed and are most commonly used with verbs such as *give, ask, tell, sing,* and *write.*

> subj　　　v　　ind obj　　　　　　dir obj
> ➤ **Coleridge wrote *Sara* a heartrending letter.**

Note that indirect objects appear after the verb but before the direct object.

Transitive verbs, direct objects, and object complements In addition to a direct object and an indirect object, a transitive verb can take another element in its predicate: an **object complement.** An object complement describes or renames the direct object it follows.

> 　　　　　　　　　　　　　　　　　dir obj　　　obj comp
> ➤ **His investment in a plantation made Johnson *a rich man.***

Intransitive verbs An **intransitive verb** describes an action by a subject that is not done directly to anything or anyone else. Therefore, an intransitive verb cannot take an object or a complement. However, adverbs and adverb phrases often appear in predicates built around intransitive verbs. In the sentence that follows, the complete predicate is in italics and the intransitive verb is underlined.

> ➤ **As a recruit, I *<u>complied</u> with the order mandating short hair.***

Some verbs, such as *cooperate, assent, disappear,* and *insist,* are always intransitive. Others, such as *increase, grow, roll,* and *work,* can be either transitive or intransitive.

> **TRANSITIVE**　　　I *grow* carrots and celery in my victory garden.
>
> **INTRANSITIVE**　　My son *grows* taller every week.

Tips LEARNING in COLLEGE

Using the Dictionary to Determine Prepositions and Transitive and Intransitive Verbs

Your dictionary will note if a verb is intransitive (*v.i*), transitive (*v.t.*), or both. It will also tell you—or show by example—the appropriate preposition to use when you are modifying an intransitive verb with an adverbial phrase. For example, we may *accede to* a rule, but if and when we *comply,* it has to be *with* something or someone.

2. Understanding word order in questions

In most questions, the verb, or part of it, precedes the subject.

▪ For simple forms of the verb *be,* put the subject before the verb.

She *was* on time for the meeting.	*Was* she on time for the meeting?

▪ For other simple verbs, begin the question with a form of *do* followed by the subject and then the main verb.

You *noticed* the change in the report.	*Did* you *notice* the change in the report?

▪ For verbs consisting of a main verb with one or more helping verbs, put the subject after the first (or only) helping verb.

He *is pleased* with the results.	*Is* he *pleased* with the results?

▪ For questions that begin with question words like *how, what, who, when, where,* or *why,* follow the same patterns.

When did the guests *arrive*?

Where have you *been* hiding?

▪ When the question word is the subject, however, the question follows the S-V word order of a declarative sentence.

What happened last night?

3. Understanding word order in commands

In commands, or imperative sentences, the subject, which is always *you,* is omitted.

➤ **[You] Read the instructions before using this machine.**

➤ **[You] Do not enter.**

➤ **[You] Do not touch this chemical—it is hazardous.**

Exercise 62.3   Identifying objects and complements of verbs

Underline the verb in each sentence, and label it transitive (trans), intransitive (intrans), or linking (link). If the verb is transitive, circle and label the direct object (DO) and label any indirect object (IO) or object complement (OC). If the verb is linking, circle and label the subject complement (SC).

EXAMPLE   The ancient Mayas <u>deserve</u> a ⟨place⟩ in the history
trans   DO

of mathematics.

62b

gram

1. Hybrid cars produce low tailpipe emissions.
2. Automakers promise consumers affordable gasoline-electric cars.
3. Hybrid cars are desirable alternatives to gasoline-powered vehicles.
4. Their two sources of power make hybrid cars fuel efficient.
5. Consumers agree that automakers should design and manufacture more hybrid models.

63 Phrases and Dependent Clauses

www.mhhe.com/ bmhh

For information and exercises on phrases and clauses, go to

Editing > Phrases and Clauses

A **phrase** is a group of related words that lacks either a subject or a predicate or both. Phrases function within sentences but not on their own. A **dependent clause** has a subject and a predicate but cannot function as a complete sentence because it begins with a subordinating word.

63a Noun phrases

A **noun phrase** consists of a noun or noun substitute plus all of its modifiers. Noun phrases can function as a sentence's subject, object, or subject complement.

SUBJECT	*The old, dark, ramshackle house* collapsed.
OBJECT	Greg cooked *an authentic, delicious haggis* for the Robert Burns dinner.
SUBJECT COMPLEMENT	Tom became *an accomplished and well-known cook.*

63b Verb phrases and verbals

A **verb phrase** is a verb plus its helping verbs. It functions as the predicate in a sentence: *Mary should have photographed me.* **Verbals** are words derived from verbs. They function as nouns, adjectives, or adverbs, not as verbs.

VERBAL AS NOUN	*Crawling* comes before walking.
VERBAL AS ADJECTIVE	Chris tripped over the *crawling* child.
VERBAL AS ADVERB	The child began *to crawl.*

Verbals may take modifiers, objects, and complements to form **verbal phrases.** There are three kinds of verbal phrases: participial, gerund, and infinitive.

1. Participial phrases

A **participial phrase** begins with either a present participle (the *-ing* form of a verb) or a past participle (the *-ed* or *-en* form of a verb). Participial phrases always function as adjectives.

➤ ***Working in groups,*** **the children solved the problem.**

➤ ***Insulted by his remark,*** **Elizabeth refused to dance.**

➤ **His pitching arm,** ***broken in two places by the fall,*** **would never be the same again.**

2. Gerund phrases

A **gerund phrase** uses the *-ing* form of the verb, just as some participial phrases do. But gerund phrases always function as nouns, not adjectives.

➤ *subj*
Walking one hour a day **will keep you fit.**

➤ *dir obj*
The instructor praised ***my acting in both scenes.***

3. Infinitive phrases

An **infinitive phrase** is formed using the infinitive, or *to* form, of a verb: *to be, to do, to live.* It can function as an adverb, an adjective, or a noun and can be the subject, subject or object complement, or direct object in a sentence.

➤ *noun/subj*
To finish his novel **was his greatest ambition.**

➤ *adj/obj comp*
He made many efforts ***to finish his novel*** **for his publisher.**

➤ *adv/dir obj*
He needed ***to finish his novel.***

63b
gram

63c Appositive phrases

Appositives rename nouns or pronouns and appear right after the word they rename.

noun	appositive

➤ **One researcher, *the widely respected R. S. Smith,* has shown that a child's performance on such tests can be very consistent.**

63d Absolute phrases

Absolute phrases modify an entire sentence. They include a noun or pronoun, a participle, and their related modifiers, objects, or complements.

➤ **The sheriff and the outlaw both having entered the bar, a showdown was sure to follow.**

Exercise 63.1 Identifying phrases

For the underlined words in the sentences below, identify what kind of phrase each is and how it functions in the sentence.

> **EXAMPLE** **Raking leaves is a seasonal chore for many American teenagers.** [*verbal phrase, gerund, functioning as the subject of the sentence*]

1. The earliest of the little-known ancient <u>civilizations of the Andes</u> emerged more than four thousand years ago.
2. The Chavin culture, <u>the earliest Andean culture with widespread influence</u>, dates to between 800 and 200 BCE.
3. The distinctive art style of the Chavin culture probably reflects a compelling and <u>influential religious movement</u>.
4. The Paracas and Nazca cultures <u>appear to have been</u> the regional successors to the Chavin culture on Peru's south coast.
5. The Moche culture, <u>encompassing most of Peru's north coast</u>, flourished from about CE 200 to 700.
6. The primary function of Moche warfare was probably <u>to secure captives for sacrifice</u>.
7. <u>Interpreting the silent remnants of past cultures</u> is the archeologist's challenge.
8. To see the <u>magnificent objects</u> buried with the Moche lord at Sipan is an awe-inspiring experience.

9. Hiram Bingham, <u>an American archeologist</u>, set out for Peru in 1911.

10. Bingham discovered the spectacular ruins of the Inca city of Machu Picchu, <u>securing for himself an enduring place in the history of Andean archeology</u>.

63e Dependent clauses

Although **dependent clauses** (also known as **subordinate clauses**) have a subject and predicate, they cannot stand alone as complete sentences. They are introduced by subordinators—either a subordinating conjunction such as *after, in order to,* or *since (for a more complete listing, see p. 526)* or a relative pronoun such as *who, which,* or *that (for more, see the box on p. 520)*. They function in sentences as adjectives, adverbs, or nouns.

1. Adjective clauses

An **adjective clause** modifies a noun or pronoun. Relative pronouns (*who, whom, whose, which, that*) or relative adverbs (*where, when*) are used to connect adjective clauses to the nouns or pronouns they modify. The relative pronoun usually follows the word that is being modified and also points back to the noun or pronoun. (*For help with punctuating restrictive and nonrestrictive clauses, see Chapter 49, pp. 451–53 and 459–60.*)

➤ Odysseus's journey, *which can be traced on modern maps,* has inspired many works of literature.

In adjective clauses, the direct object sometimes comes before rather than after the verb.

dir obj subj   v

➤ The contestant *whom he most wanted to beat* was his father.

2. Adverb clauses

An **adverb clause** modifies a verb, an adjective, or an adverb and answers the same questions adverbs answer: *When? Where? What? Why?* and *How?* Adverb clauses are often introduced by subordinators (*after, when, before, because, although, if, though, whenever, where, wherever*).

➤ *After we had talked for an hour,* he began to get nervous.

➤ He reacted *as if he already knew.*

63e
gram

3. Noun clauses

A **noun clause** is a dependent clause that functions as a noun. In a sentence, a noun clause may serve as the subject, object, or complement and is usually introduced by a relative pronoun (*who, which, that*) or a relative adverb (*how, what, where, when, why*).

SUBJECT *What he saw* shocked him.

OBJECT The instructor found out *who had skipped class.*

COMPLEMENT The book was *where I had left it.*

As in an adjective clause, in a noun clause the direct object or subject complement can come first, violating the typical sentence order.

dir obj subj

➤ **The doctor wondered *to whom he* should send the bill.**

Exercise 63.2 Identifying dependent clauses

Underline any dependent clauses in the sentences below. Identify each one as an adjective, adverb, or noun clause.

EXAMPLE **Because they were among the first to develop the concept of zero, the ancient Mayas deserve a prominent place in the history of mathematics.** [*adverb clause*]

1. During the 1970s and 1980s, Asian-American writers, who often drew upon their immigrant experiences, gained a wide readership.
2. Because these writers wrote about their struggles and the struggles of their ancestors, readers were able to learn about the Chinese Exclusion Act of 1892 and the internment of Japanese Americans during World War II.
3. Many readers know Amy Tan as the Chinese-American novelist who wrote *The Joy Luck Club,* which was adapted into a feature film, but are unfamiliar with most of her other novels, such as *The Kitchen God's Wife, The Hundred Secret Senses,* and *The Bonesetter's Daughter.*
4. During the 1990s, Asian-American novelists, poets, and playwrights wrote about how their experiences related to those of other immigrant groups.

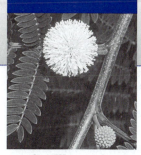

64 Types of Sentences

Classifying by how many clauses they contain and how those clauses are joined, we can categorize sentences into four types: simple, compound, complex, and compound-complex. We can also classify sentences by purpose: declarative, interrogative, imperative, and exclamatory.

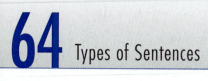

www.mhhe.com/
bmhh

For information
and exercises on
types of sentences,
go to

Editing > Sentence
Types

64a   Sentence structures

A clause is a group of related words that includes a subject and a predicate. **Independent clauses** can stand on their own as complete sentences. **Dependent, or subordinate, clauses** cannot stand alone. They function in sentences as adjectives, adverbs, or nouns. The presence of one or both of these two types of clauses, and their relation to each other, determines whether the sentence is simple, compound, complex, or compound-complex.

1. Simple sentences

A simple sentence has only one independent clause. Simple does not necessarily mean short, however. Although a simple sentence does not include any dependent clauses, it may have several embedded phrases, a compound subject, and a compound predicate.

> **INDEPENDENT CLAUSE**
>
> The bloodhound is the oldest known breed of dog.

> **INDEPENDENT CLAUSE: COMPOUND SUBJ + COMPOUND PRED**
>
> Historians, novelists, short-story writers, and playwrights write about characters, design plots, and usually seek the dramatic resolution of a problem.

2. Compound sentences

A compound sentence contains two or more independent clauses but no dependent clause. The independent clauses may be joined by a comma and a coordinating conjunction or by a semicolon with or without a conjunctive adverb.

➤ **The police arrested him for drunk driving, *so* he lost his car.**

➤ **The sun blasted the earth; *therefore,* the plants withered and died.**

3. Complex sentences

A complex sentence contains one independent clause and one or more dependent clauses.

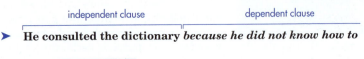

> He consulted the dictionary *because he did not know how to*
>
> *pronounce the word.*

4. Compound-complex sentences

A compound-complex sentence contains two or more coordinated independent clauses and at least one dependent clause (italicized in the example).

> **She discovered a new world of international finance, but she worked so hard investing other people's money *that she had no time to invest any of her own.***

| **Exercise 64.1** | Classifying sentences |

Identify each sentence as simple, compound, complex, or compound-complex.

> **EXAMPLE**   **Biotechnology promises great benefits for humanity, but it also raises many difficult ethical issues. [*compound*]**

1. Rock and roll originated in the 1950s.
2. Chuck Berry, Jerry Lee Lewis, and Elvis Presley were early rock-and-roll greats.
3. Teenagers loved the new music, but it disturbed many parents.
4. As much as the music itself, it was the sexually suggestive body language of the performers that worried the older generation.
5. The social turmoil that marked the 1960s influenced many performers, and some began to use their music as a vehicle for protest.

64b   Sentence purposes

When you write a sentence, your purpose helps you decide which sentence type to use. If you want to provide information, you usually use a declarative sentence. If you want to ask a question, you usually use an interrogative sentence. To make a request or give an order (a command), you use the imperative. An exclamatory sentence emphasizes a point or expresses strong emotion.

DECLARATIVE   He watches *Seinfeld* reruns.

INTERROGATIVE   Does he watch *Seinfeld* reruns?

IMPERATIVE   Do not watch reruns of *Seinfeld*.

EXCLAMATORY   I'm really looking forward to watching *Seinfeld* reruns with you!

64b
gram

Timeline of World History

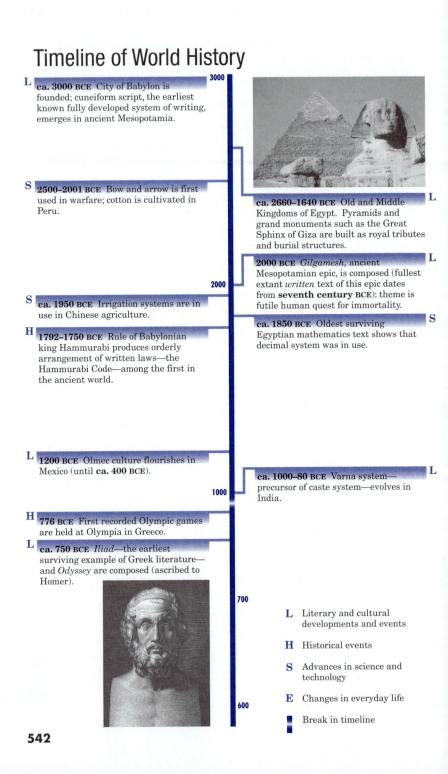

L **ca. 3000 BCE** City of Babylon is founded; cuneiform script, the earliest known fully developed system of writing, emerges in ancient Mesopotamia.

3000

S **2500–2001 BCE** Bow and arrow is first used in warfare; cotton is cultivated in Peru.

L **ca. 2660–1640 BCE** Old and Middle Kingdoms of Egypt. Pyramids and grand monuments such as the Great Sphinx of Giza are built as royal tributes and burial structures.

L **2000 BCE** *Gilgamesh,* ancient Mesopotamian epic, is composed (fullest extant *written* text of this epic dates from **seventh century BCE**): theme is futile human quest for immortality.

2000

S **ca. 1950 BCE** Irrigation systems are in use in Chinese agriculture.

S **ca. 1850 BCE** Oldest surviving Egyptian mathematics text shows that decimal system was in use.

H **1792–1750 BCE** Rule of Babylonian king Hammurabi produces orderly arrangement of written laws—the Hammurabi Code—among the first in the ancient world.

L **1200 BCE** Olmec culture flourishes in Mexico (until **ca. 400 BCE**).

L **ca. 1000–80 BCE** Varna system— precursor of caste system—evolves in India.

1000

H **776 BCE** First recorded Olympic games are held at Olympia in Greece.

L **ca. 750 BCE** *Iliad*—the earliest surviving example of Greek literature— and *Odyssey* are composed (ascribed to Homer).

700

L Literary and cultural developments and events

H Historical events

S Advances in science and technology

E Changes in everyday life

▮ Break in timeline

600

L **551–479 BCE** Life of Confucius, China's greatest philosopher.

L **ca. 560–480 BCE** Life of Buddha (Siddhartha), founder of Buddhism.

H **508 BCE** Athens becomes world's first democracy.

L **ca. 500 BCE** Many Old Testament books are transcribed.

S **ca. 500 BCE** Greeks adopt Ptolemaic model of cosmos, in which the sun revolves around the earth.

L **461–429 BCE** Reign of Pericles ushers in flowering of Athenian culture: Aeschylus, *Oresteia* (**458 BCE**); Sophocles, *Antigone* (**ca. 442–441 BCE**) and *Oedipus the King* (**ca. 429 BCE**); Euripides, *Medea* (**431 BCE**); Aristophanes, *Lysistrata* (**411 BCE**); Plato, *Republic* (**ca. 406 BCE**).

H **399 BCE** Greek philosopher Socrates is tried and executed for corruption of youth.

H **404 BCE** Golden age of Periclean Athens ends with fall of Athens to Sparta.

L **387 BCE** Greek philosopher Plato founds the Academy.

L **350 BCE** Aristotle, student of Plato, writes *Poetics*, founds rival school, Lyceum; earliest portion of *Mahabharata* (Sanskrit heroic epic) is composed midcentury.

H **356–323 BCE** Life of Alexander the Great, king of Macedonia, who conquers the Persian Empire

S **ca. 300 BCE** Euclid writes *Elements*, seminal work of elementary geometry.

S **ca. 250 BCE** Archimedes, founder of mathematical physics, writes *Measurement of the Circle* (includes concept of π).

L **ca. 250 BCE** *Ramayana* (Sanskrit heroic epic) is composed midcentury.

H **215 BCE** Construction of Great Wall of China begins.

H **ca. 200–500 BCE** Roman Empire encompasses entire Mediterranean region.

L **23–13 BCE** Roman poet Horace composes *Odes*.

L **27–19 BCE** Roman poet Virgil composes epic poem *Aeneid*.

L **8** Ovid composes *Metamorphoses*, a 15-volume poem based on Greek and Roman myths.

H **30** Jesus is crucified by the Romans in Jerusalem.

500

400

300

200

100

0

ca. 65–85 New Testament Gospels are composed. **L**

ca. 300 Large towns exist in inland Niger Delta, later to develop into Empire of Ghana in West Africa. **L**

300

400

L **413–26** St. Augustine writes *City of God,* interpreting history in light of Christianity.

410 Visigoths sack Rome. **H**

L **478** First Shinto shrine is built in Japan.

500

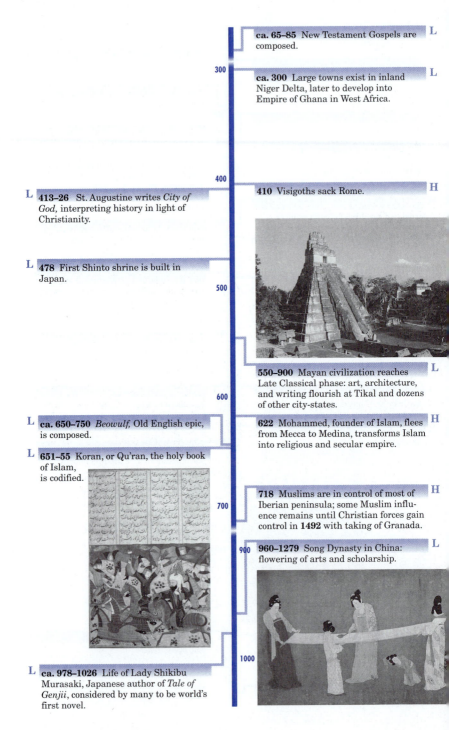

550–900 Mayan civilization reaches Late Classical phase: art, architecture, and writing flourish at Tikal and dozens of other city-states. **L**

600

L **ca. 650–750** *Beowulf,* Old English epic, is composed.

622 Mohammed, founder of Islam, flees from Mecca to Medina, transforms Islam into religious and secular empire. **H**

L **651–55** Koran, or Qu'ran, the holy book of Islam, is codified.

700

718 Muslims are in control of most of Iberian peninsula; some Muslim influence remains until Christian forces gain control in **1492** with taking of Granada. **H**

960–1279 Song Dynasty in China: flowering of arts and scholarship. **L**

900

1000

L **ca. 978–1026** Life of Lady Shikibu Murasaki, Japanese author of *Tale of Genjii*, considered by many to be world's first novel.

L **ca. 1100** *Song of Roland,* French epic poem, is composed.

H **1096–1291** The Crusades, nine military expeditions in which European Christians attempted to reconquer the Holy Land (Palestine) from the Muslims, take place.

1100

L **ca. 1200** Zen Buddhism travels from China to Japan, becomes influential in Japanese politics, painting, landscape, and culture, especially in the tea ceremony.

1200

H **ca. 1290–1918** Ottoman Empire, Muslim Turkish state comprising Anatolia, modern southeastern Europe, and the Arab Middle East and North Africa, is established.

1300

L **ca. 1300–1650** Renaissance in Europe: "rebirth" of arts and culture.

L **1307–21** Dante Alighieri composes *La Divina Commedia,* an epic poem describing his imaginary journey through heaven and hell.

H **1312–27** Empire of Mali in West Africa reaches its height under Mansa Musa, builder of Great Mosque at Timbuktu.

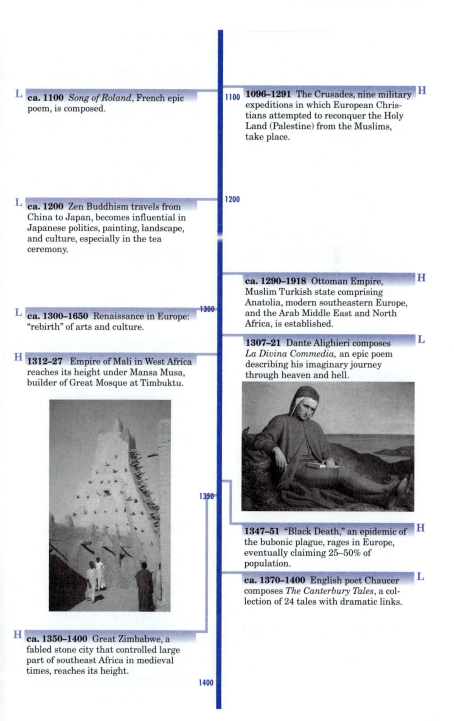

1350

H **1347–51** "Black Death," an epidemic of the bubonic plague, rages in Europe, eventually claiming 25–50% of population.

L **ca. 1370–1400** English poet Chaucer composes *The Canterbury Tales,* a collection of 24 tales with dramatic links.

H **ca. 1350–1400** Great Zimbabwe, a fabled stone city that controlled large part of southeast Africa in medieval times, reaches its height.

1400

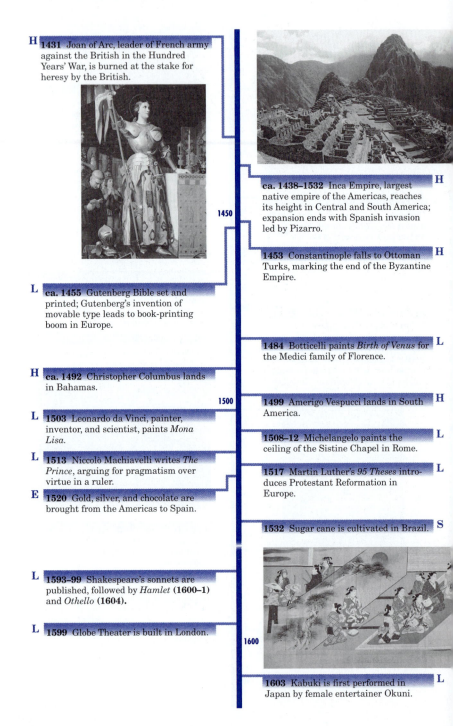

H **1431** Joan of Arc, leader of French army against the British in the Hundred Years' War, is burned at the stake for heresy by the British.

ca. 1438–1532 Inca Empire, largest native empire of the Americas, reaches its height in Central and South America; expansion ends with Spanish invasion led by Pizarro. **H**

1450

1453 Constantinople falls to Ottoman Turks, marking the end of the Byzantine Empire. **H**

L **ca. 1455** Gutenberg Bible set and printed; Gutenberg's invention of movable type leads to book-printing boom in Europe.

1484 Botticelli paints *Birth of Venus* for the Medici family of Florence. **L**

H **ca. 1492** Christopher Columbus lands in Bahamas.

1500

1499 Amerigo Vespucci lands in South America. **H**

L **1503** Leonardo da Vinci, painter, inventor, and scientist, paints *Mona Lisa*.

1508–12 Michelangelo paints the ceiling of the Sistine Chapel in Rome. **L**

L **1513** Niccolò Machiavelli writes *The Prince*, arguing for pragmatism over virtue in a ruler.

1517 Martin Luther's *95 Theses* introduces Protestant Reformation in Europe. **L**

E **1520** Gold, silver, and chocolate are brought from the Americas to Spain.

1532 Sugar cane is cultivated in Brazil. **S**

L **1593–99** Shakespeare's sonnets are published, followed by *Hamlet* (1600–1) and *Othello* (1604).

L **1599** Globe Theater is built in London.

1600

1603 Kabuki is first performed in Japan by female entertainer Okuni. **L**

L **1605** Miguel de Cervantes Saavedra writes his masterpiece *Don Quixote.*

E **1609** Tea is first shipped to Europe from China.

L **1611** King James Bible is published, becomes most popular version for more than three centuries.

H **1619** African captives are brought to Jamestown, Virginia to be servants; slave system develops over next 80 years.

L **1631–48** Taj Mahal, premier example of Mogul architecture, is built in Agra, India.

L **1637** René Descartes, called by some the founder of modern philosophy, writes *Discourse on Method* (from which comes *"Cogito, ergo sum"*: "I think; therefore, I am").

L **1651** Thomas Hobbes writes *Leviathan,* portraying humans in a state of nature as "nasty, brutish, and short" and offering as a remedy a social contract in which the ruler's power—for the sake of expediency—is absolute.

S **1608** Galileo Galilei invents astronomical telescope, provides evidence to support Nicolaus Copernicus's theory that the earth and planets revolve around the sun.

H **1614** Pocahontas, Native American princess, marries tobacco planter John Rolfe.

H **1620** Pilgrims sail for America and found Plymouth Colony.

L **1632** Rembrandt van Rijn, prolific Dutch painter, paints his first major portrait, *The Anatomy Lesson of Dr. Tulp.*

H **1642–1648** English Civil War pits Parliamentary forces under Oliver Cromwell against Charles I; Charles I is defeated and beheaded in **1649.**

L **1667** John Milton writes *Paradise Lost,* an epic poem describing man's "first disobedience" and the promise of his redemption.

1625

1650

1675

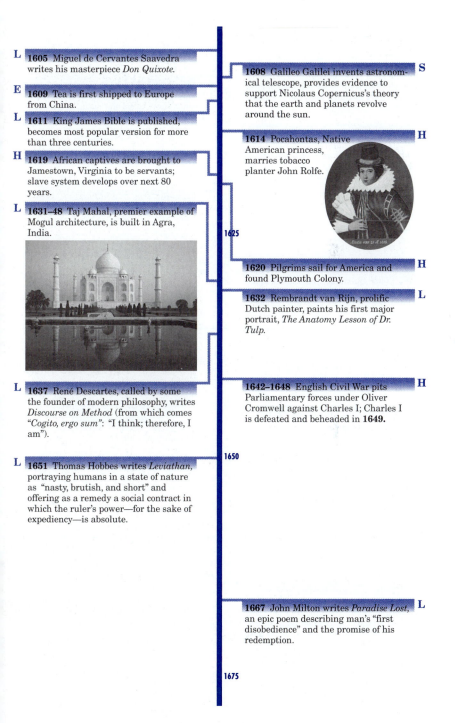

S **1687** Isaac Newton publishes *Principia,* in which he codifies laws of motion and gravity not modified until the twentieth century.

ca. 1688–1790 The Enlightenment, an intellectual movement committed to secular views based on reason, takes hold in Europe. **L**

L **1690** John Locke publishes *Essay Concerning Human Understanding,* in which he espouses an empiricist view of philosophy (limiting true knowledge to what can be perceived through the senses or through introspection).

1700

ca. 1701 Peter the Great begins westernization of Russia. **H**

1740

L **ca. 1740s** Culmination of the Baroque era in music: Vivaldi, *The Four Seasons;* Bach, *Brandenberg Concertos;* Handel, *Messiah.*

1750

L **1755–73** Samuel Johnson publishes *Dictionary of the English Language.*

Johann Sebastian Bach

1760

L **1767–87** *Sturm und Drang* (Storm and Stress), a literary and intellectual movement in Germany that prefigures Romanticism (**ca. 1789–1825** in England).

1761 Jean-Jacques Rousseau publishes *The Social Contract,* in which he praises the natural goodness of human beings but insists on the need for society to attain true happiness. **L**

S **1769** James Watt patents steam engine.

1770

ca. 1770 Industrial Revolution begins, fueled by steam power: first steam-driven cotton factory (**1789**) and first steam-powered rolling mill open in England (**1790**). **S**

H **1775–81** American Revolution: hostilities begin at Lexington and Concord, Massachusetts, in 1775, although the Continental Congress will not officially vote for independence until July 2, 1776.

1776 "Declaration of Independence" is approved by the Continental Congress on July 4. **H**

1780

Adam Smith publishes *Causes of the Wealth of Nations,* advocates regulation of markets through supply and demand and competition. **L**

L **1781** Immanuel Kant publishes *Critique of Pure Reason,* an attempt at reconciling empiricism and rationalism, and for many the single most important work of modern philosophy.

L **1780s–90s** Height of the Classical era in music: Mozart writes the opera *Don Giovanni* (**1787**); Haydn establishes the form of the symphony with *The Clock Symphony* (**1794**).

H **1788** Bread riots occur in France.

L **1789** William Blake's *Songs of Innocence,* followed by *Marriage of Heaven and Hell* (**1790**) and *Songs of Experience* (**1794**), usher in early Romanticism in England; Olaudah Equiano's *The Interesting Narrative of the Life of Olaudah Equiano, or Gustaus Vassa, the African,* one of the first slave narratives, is published.

1790

H **1789–99** French Revolution transforms France from a monarchy to a modern state.

H **1793** Queen Marie Antoinette and King Louis XVI of France are guillotined.

L **1792** Mary Wollstonecraft publishes *A Vindication of the Rights of Woman,* an early work of feminism.

L **ca. 1795–1825** English Romantic poetry flourishes with the work of William Wordsworth (**1770–1850**), Lord Byron (**1788–1824**), Percy Bysshe Shelley (**1792–1822**), and John Keats (**1795–1821**).

S **1798** Thomas Malthus's *An Essay on the Principle of Population* stirs interest in birth control and concerns about overpopulation.

S **1799** Rosetta Stone is found in Egypt, makes deciphering hieroglyphics possible; perfectly preserved mammoth is found in Siberia.

1800

S **1800** Alessandro Volta produces first battery of zinc and copper plates.

L **1803** Beethoven composes *Third Symphony (Eroica),* marking the start of his dramatic middle period.

H **1804–6** Lewis and Clark Expedition from St. Louis to the Pacific fuels westward expansion in the USA.

H **1804** Napoleon becomes emperor of France.

L **1807** Hegel publishes *Phenomenology of Spirit,* which introduces the concept of "master-slave" dialectic.

L **1808** Goethe publishes *Part 1* of *Faust,* a drama about a man who sells his soul for knowledge and power.

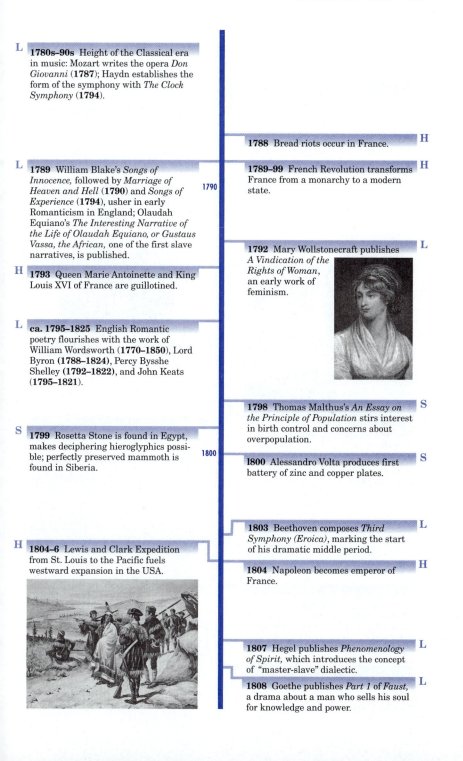

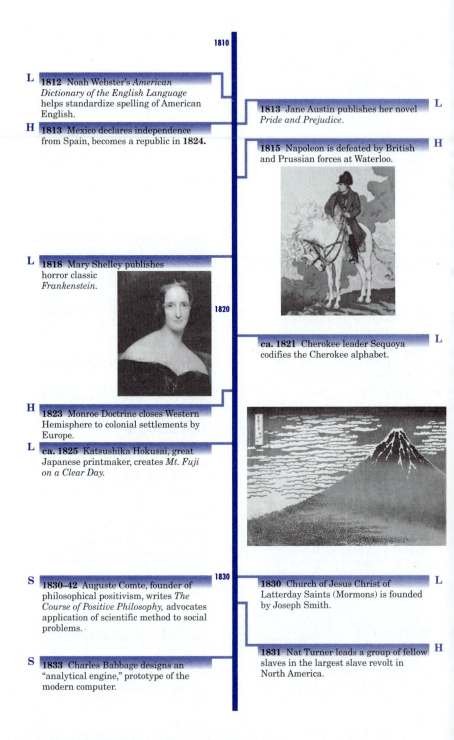

1810

L **1812** Noah Webster's *American Dictionary of the English Language* helps standardize spelling of American English.

H **1813** Mexico declares independence from Spain, becomes a republic in **1824**.

L **1813** Jane Austin publishes her novel *Pride and Prejudice*.

H **1815** Napoleon is defeated by British and Prussian forces at Waterloo.

L **1818** Mary Shelley publishes horror classic *Frankenstein*.

1820

L **ca. 1821** Cherokee leader Sequoya codifies the Cherokee alphabet.

H **1823** Monroe Doctrine closes Western Hemisphere to colonial settlements by Europe.

L **ca. 1825** Katsushika Hokusai, great Japanese printmaker, creates *Mt. Fuji on a Clear Day.*

1830

S **1830–42** Auguste Comte, founder of philosophical positivism, writes *The Course of Positive Philosophy,* advocates application of scientific method to social problems.

L **1830** Church of Jesus Christ of Latterday Saints (Mormons) is founded by Joseph Smith.

H **1831** Nat Turner leads a group of fellow slaves in the largest slave revolt in North America.

S **1833** Charles Babbage designs an "analytical engine," prototype of the modern computer.

1836 Samuel Colt puts his revolver into **S** mass production, revolutionizes manufacture of small arms.

L **1837** Ralph Waldo Emerson, American transcendentalist, delivers "The American Scholar," an address expressing American literary independence.

1837–1901 Queen Victoria reigns in **H** England, Ireland, and India.

1838 Charles Dickens publishes *Oliver* **L** *Twist,* the first of many novels that sharply criticize abuses brought on by the Industrial Revolution in England.

S **1839** Daguerreotypes, forerunners of modern photographs, are developed by L. M. Daguerre and J. N. Niepce in France.

1840

1840s Rise of Romantic movement in **L** France, Germany, and Italy.

H **1841** First university degrees granted to women in USA.

L **1843** Søren Kierkegaard, Christian existentialist philosopher, publishes *Either/Or.*

1843 Richard Wagner composes *The* **L** *Flying Dutchman,* an opera expressing his ideal of the *Gesamtkunstwerk* (total work of art).

S **1844** Samuel Morse invents telegraph.

L **1847** Charlotte Brontë publishes *Jane Eyre;* Emily Brontë publishes *Wuthering Heights;* Anne Brontë publishes *Agnes Grey.*

1850

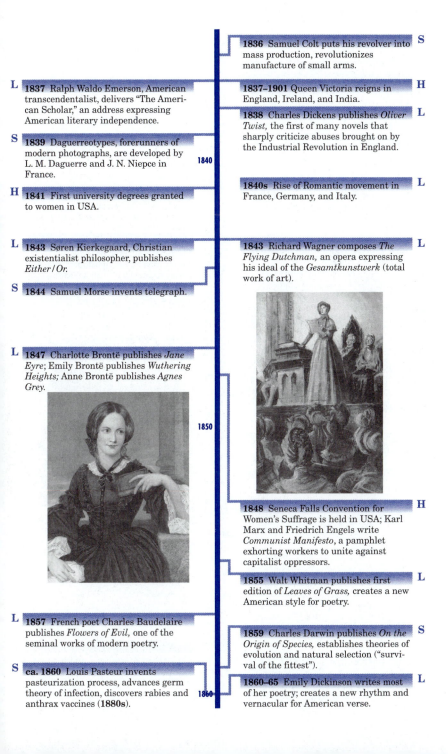

1848 Seneca Falls Convention for **H** Women's Suffrage is held in USA; Karl Marx and Friedrich Engels write *Communist Manifesto*, a pamphlet exhorting workers to unite against capitalist oppressors.

1855 Walt Whitman publishes first **L** edition of *Leaves of Grass,* creates a new American style for poetry.

L **1857** French poet Charles Baudelaire publishes *Flowers of Evil,* one of the seminal works of modern poetry.

1859 Charles Darwin publishes *On the* **S** *Origin of Species,* establishes theories of evolution and natural selection ("survival of the fittest").

S **ca. 1860** Louis Pasteur invents pasteurization process, advances germ theory of infection, discovers rabies and anthrax vaccines (**1880s**).

1860

1860–65 Emily Dickinson writes most **L** of her poetry; creates a new rhythm and vernacular for American verse.

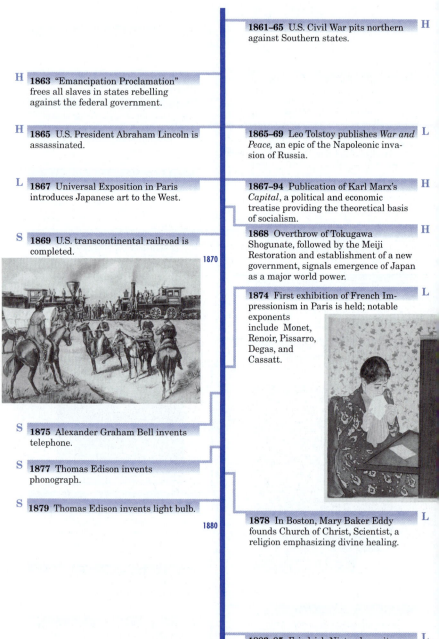

H **1861–65** U.S. Civil War pits northern against Southern states.

H **1863** "Emancipation Proclamation" frees all slaves in states rebelling against the federal government.

H **1865** U.S. President Abraham Lincoln is assassinated.

L **1865–69** Leo Tolstoy publishes *War and Peace,* an epic of the Napoleonic invasion of Russia.

L **1867** Universal Exposition in Paris introduces Japanese art to the West.

H **1867–94** Publication of Karl Marx's *Capital*, a political and economic treatise providing the theoretical basis of socialism.

S **1869** U.S. transcontinental railroad is completed.

H **1868** Overthrow of Tokugawa Shogunate, followed by the Meiji Restoration and establishment of a new government, signals emergence of Japan as a major world power.

1870

L **1874** First exhibition of French Impressionism in Paris is held; notable exponents include Monet, Renoir, Pissarro, Degas, and Cassatt.

S **1875** Alexander Graham Bell invents telephone.

S **1877** Thomas Edison invents phonograph.

S **1879** Thomas Edison invents light bulb.

1880

L **1878** In Boston, Mary Baker Eddy founds Church of Christ, Scientist, a religion emphasizing divine healing.

L **1883–85** Friedrich Nietzsche writes *Thus Spake Zarathustra*, which expounds on the concept of *Übermensch* (superman).

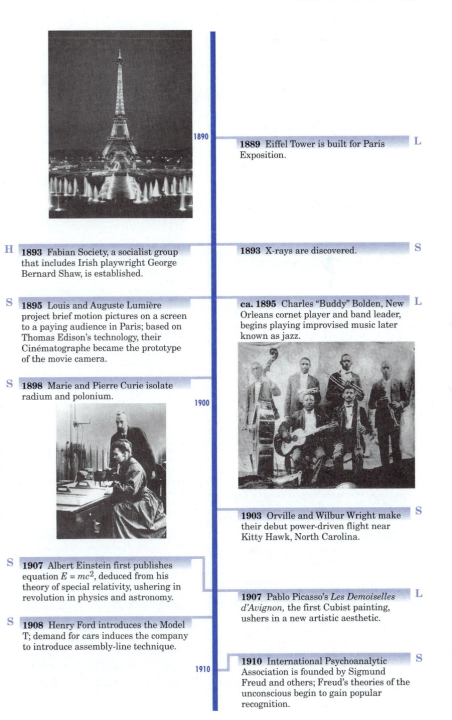

1890

1889 Eiffel Tower is built for Paris Exposition. **L**

H **1893** Fabian Society, a socialist group that includes Irish playwright George Bernard Shaw, is established.

1893 X-rays are discovered. **S**

S **1895** Louis and Auguste Lumière project brief motion pictures on a screen to a paying audience in Paris; based on Thomas Edison's technology, their Cinématographe became the prototype of the movie camera.

ca. 1895 Charles "Buddy" Bolden, New Orleans cornet player and band leader, begins playing improvised music later known as jazz. **L**

S **1898** Marie and Pierre Curie isolate radium and polonium.

1900

1903 Orville and Wilbur Wright make their debut power-driven flight near Kitty Hawk, North Carolina. **S**

S **1907** Albert Einstein first publishes equation $E = mc^2$, deduced from his theory of special relativity, ushering in revolution in physics and astronomy.

1907 Pablo Picasso's *Les Demoiselles d'Avignon*, the first Cubist painting, ushers in a new artistic aesthetic. **L**

S **1908** Henry Ford introduces the Model T; demand for cars induces the company to introduce assembly-line technique.

1910

1910 International Psychoanalytic Association is founded by Sigmund Freud and others; Freud's theories of the unconscious begin to gain popular recognition. **S**

L **1913** *The Rite of Spring,* a ballet with groundbreaking music by Igor Stravinsky and choreography by Vaslav Nijinsky, is first performed.

L **1914–21** James Joyce writes *Ulysses,* a masterpiece of modernist literature; publication in USA is delayed until **1933** because of obscenity charges.

H **1914** Serbian nationalist assassinates heir to the Austro-Hungarian Empire in Sarajevo, sparking World War I.

E **1915** Margaret Sanger opens the first birth control clinic in USA.

H **1915** British passenger ship *Lusitania* is sunk by German submarine, fueling American sympathy for war efforts of Britain, France, and Russia.

H **1917** USA enters World War I; Russian Revolution: Bolsheviks led by Vladimir Lenin seize power.

L **1918** Romanian poet Tristan Tzara writes manifesto for Dada, an avant-garde artistic movement established in part in reaction to the senseless slaughter of World War I.

H **1918** Treaty of Versailles ends World War I; death toll approaches 15 million worldwide; race riots rock major U.S. cities.

1920

E **1918–19** Influenza epidemic kills 22 million worldwide.

H **1920** Nineteenth Amendment to the U.S. Constitution grants women suffrage.

L **ca. 1920** Arnold Schoenberg invents 12-tone system of musical composition.

H **1922** First fascist government formed by Benito Mussolini in Italy.

L **1920s** Harlem Renaissance: flowering of African-American literature and the arts, particularly jazz, centered in New York City.

H **1924** Joseph Stalin succeeds Lenin as head of Soviet Union.

L **1927** Martin Heidegger publishes *Being and Time,* a founding work of existentialist philosophy; Martha Graham, pioneer of modern dance, opens a dance studio in New York.

S **1927** Charles Lindbergh makes first solo, nonstop transatlantic flight; Werner Heisenberg develops Uncertainty Principle, which, together with Theory of Relativity, becomes basis of quantum physics; first successful transmission of an image via "television" occurs.

L **1929** Virginia Woolf, central to the Bloomsbury literary group, publishes feminist work *A Room of One's Own.*

1930

H **1930s** The Great Depression, precipitated by a stock market crash in **1929,** begins in USA and spreads abroad; in response, President Roosevelt introduces "New Deal" measures based on Keynesian economics.

S **1931** Incompleteness Theorem is developed by the mathematician and philosopher Kurt Gödel.

H **1933** Adolf Hitler becomes chancellor of Germany, gradually assumes dictatorial power.

H **1936–39** Spanish Civil War.

L **1935** African American Jesse Owens wins four gold medals in track at the Berlin Olympics.

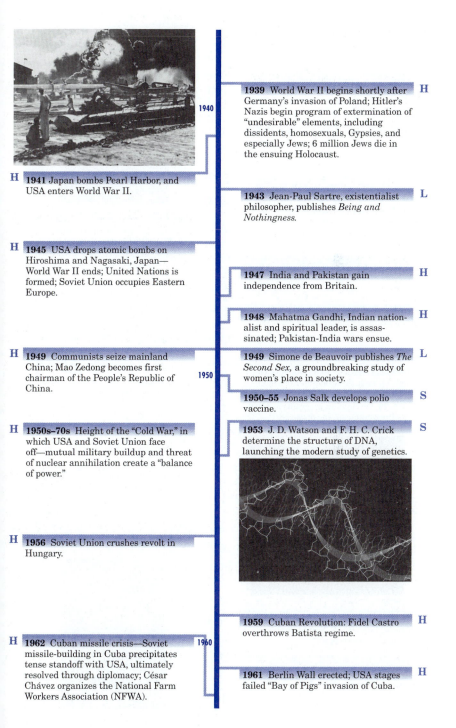

1940

1939 World War II begins shortly after Germany's invasion of Poland; Hitler's Nazis begin program of extermination of "undesirable" elements, including dissidents, homosexuals, Gypsies, and especially Jews; 6 million Jews die in the ensuing Holocaust. **H**

H **1941** Japan bombs Pearl Harbor, and USA enters World War II.

1943 Jean-Paul Sartre, existentialist philosopher, publishes *Being and Nothingness*. **L**

H **1945** USA drops atomic bombs on Hiroshima and Nagasaki, Japan—World War II ends; United Nations is formed; Soviet Union occupies Eastern Europe.

1947 India and Pakistan gain independence from Britain. **H**

1948 Mahatma Gandhi, Indian nationalist and spiritual leader, is assassinated; Pakistan-India wars ensue. **H**

H **1949** Communists seize mainland China; Mao Zedong becomes first chairman of the People's Republic of China.

1950

1949 Simone de Beauvoir publishes *The Second Sex*, a groundbreaking study of women's place in society. **L**

1950–55 Jonas Salk develops polio vaccine. **S**

H **1950s–70s** Height of the "Cold War," in which USA and Soviet Union face off—mutual military buildup and threat of nuclear annihilation create a "balance of power."

1953 J. D. Watson and F. H. C. Crick determine the structure of DNA, launching the modern study of genetics. **S**

H **1956** Soviet Union crushes revolt in Hungary.

1959 Cuban Revolution: Fidel Castro overthrows Batista regime. **H**

H **1962** Cuban missile crisis—Soviet missile-building in Cuba precipitates tense standoff with USA, ultimately resolved through diplomacy; César Chávez organizes the National Farm Workers Association (NFWA).

1960

1961 Berlin Wall erected; USA stages failed "Bay of Pigs" invasion of Cuba. **H**

H **1964** U.S. involvement in Vietnam War escalates with Tonkin Gulf Resolution; Malcolm X is assassinated in New York; Watts riots roil Los Angeles.

H **1966** Mao Zedong's Cultural Revolution begins, aiming to revitalize communist zeal; Black Panther Party is founded in Oakland, California.

H **1968** Martin Luther King, Jr. is assassinated in Memphis, Tennessee.

S **1969** American astronaut Neil Armstrong becomes first man to walk on the moon.

1970

1963 Martin Luther King, Jr., delivers "I Have a Dream" speech to crowd of 250,000 at the Lincoln Memorial; **L**

President John F. Kennedy is assassinated in Dallas. **H**

H **1971** East Pakistan (now Bangladesh) declares independence from West Pakistan.

H **1974** President Richard Nixon resigns as a result of the Watergate scandal.

1973 *Gulag Archipelego* by Alexander Solzhenitsyn is published in Paris, it is a massive study of the Soviet penal system based on the author's firsthand experience. **L**

S **1975** Bill Gates and Paul Allen build and sell their first computer product, creating Microsoft.

1975–79 Vaccination programs against smallpox eradicate the disease worldwide.

1975 Wave of former colonies— Mozambique, Surinam, Papua New Guinea—gain independence. **H**

1979 Islamic revolution in Iran: Shah flees, Khomeini comes to power. **H**

1980

1981 First cases of acquired immune deficiency syndrome (AIDS) in USA are reported in New York and California. **H**

S **1982** Benoit Mandelbrot publishes *The Fractal Geometry of Nature,* contributing to chaos theory.

H **1986** Chernobyl nuclear power plant disaster spreads fallout over Soviet Union and parts of Europe.

1989 Prodemocracy protests in Tiananmen Square, China, are quashed by government crackdown; Berlin Wall is demolished; Eastern Europe is democratized. H

1990

1991 Soviet Union is dissolved, making way for looser confederation of republics. H

1995 Internet boom hits—the number of people online grows exponentially. E

2000 Initial sequencing of human genome completed. S

2000

2001 Hijacked planes fly into 110-story World Trade Center Towers in New York City and the Pentagon in Washington, D.C. —thousands die; USA invades Afghanistan and later Iraq in "war on terrorism." H

2004 Massive Indian Ocean tsunami devastates coastal communities from Indonesia to Somalia. H

2005 Voters in France and Holland reject the proposed constitution for the European Union. H

2005 Hurricane Katrina overwhelms U.S. Gulf coast and forces evacuation of New Orleans. H

Answers
to Tutorials and Selected Exercises

Note to instructors: answers to all exercises appear in the Instructor's Manual on the instructor version of **www.mhhe.com/bmhh.**

Answers to Tutorial A, page x

1. Students today face many pressures that can lead to plagiarism.
2. If students paraphrase another writer's work too closely without giving the source, they have plagiarized. *Or* If a student paraphrases another writer's work too closely without giving the source, he or she has plagiarized.
3. Although many students do not realize it, they can plagiarize by using their own words in another writer's sentence structure.
4. Colleges deal with plagiarism in different ways. Some expel students caught plagiarizing; others give warnings first. *Or* Colleges deal with plagiarism in different ways. Some expel students caught plagiarizing, while others give warnings first.
5. The Internet has made a variety of sources available to students.
6. No error.
7. Plagiarism-detection software (can *or* may) be helpful to teachers.

Answers to Tutorial B, page xi

1. Look up *the reason . . . is because* and go to section 32b (Illogical Predicates). You'll see that *because* is incorrect. *The reason* is a noun and can't take *is because* as its predicate. (*A student is because . . .* doesn't make sense, does it?) Corrected sentence: The reason some students plagiarize is that they feel pressured to keep a high GPA.
2. Find *none* and go to section 44d to find that indefinite subjects such as *none, every,* and *each* are always singular. *Have* should be *has.*
3. In the index, the entry for *it* directs you to section 46b (Pronoun reference). In this case, *it* does not refer clearly to an antecedent, so the sentence must be changed. Corrected sentence: Our honor code says students must report others who plagiarize.
4. Look up *his/her* and go to section 39e (Biased or sexist language). Although *his/her* avoids the sexism of using *his* to refer to both men and women, it is considered clunky and unacceptable in academic writing. Instead, make the subject plural and use *their.* Corrected sentence:

Students who let other students turn in their work for a paper are guilty of plagiarism.

5. The entry for *I vs. me* leads you to section 46c (Pronoun case), which tells you *my friend and me* is correct. You wouldn't say *A teacher accused I*. Corrected sentence: A teacher once accused my friend and me of copying material from Wikipedia.

6. The entry for *different from, different than* leads you to the Glossary of Usage (41), which tells you to avoid *different than*. Corrected sentence: Turning in someone else's writing as your own is no different from any other type of cheating.

7. Look up *except* and you will find a reference to the Glossary of Usage (41), which tells you *accepts* (*receives willingly* or *tolerates*) should be used in this sentence. Corrected sentence: Many students do not understand plagiarism because our society accepts many forms of borrowing, such as music samples and Web site mashups.

Answers to Tutorial C, page xi

1. The *number* of prominent authors accused of plagiarism has increased recently.

2. Instructors must ensure that *every one* of their students knows how to use sources appropriately.

3. Schools should *adopt* a program of educational seminars about integrating and documenting sources.

4. Students who *flout* school policy by failing to document sources must be *censured* [*censured* is correct].

5. Even when unintentional, plagiarism has a negative *effect* on the academic community.

6. When writing research papers, students have to *cite* their sources.

Answers to Tutorial D, page xii

Hulbert, Ann. "How Kaavya Got Packaged and Got into Trouble." Slate. 27 Apr. 2006. 15 Mar. 2007 <http://www.slate.com/id/2140683/>.

Lathrop, Ann and Kathleen Foss. Student Cheating and Plagiarism in the Internet Era: A Wake-Up Call. Englewood, CO: Libraries Unlimited, 2000.

Read, Brock. "Are Professors to Blame for Plagiarism?" Weblog posting. The Wired Campus. 18 Oct. 2006. 5 Mar. 2007 <http://chronicle.com/wiredcampus/index.php?id=1644>.

Answers to Tutorial E, page xii

1. Section 5c (Thinking intentionally about design) recommends using a common font such as Courier, Times New Roman, or Bookman, in an 11- or 12-point size.

2. Section 3d (Integrating visuals) states that line graphs effectively demonstrate change over time.

3. Scan the detailed Contents inside the back cover to find the listing for section 11c (Creating a hypertext essay). Internal links connect to other places in the same document, while external links connect to files outside the document (such as audio or video files).

4. Turn to Chapter 14, Finding and Managing Print and Online Sources. The title of section 14g (Using your library's online catalog or card catalog to find books), answers this question.

5. Section 15c (Questioning Internet sources) indicates that a Web site that ends in .com and sells a product probably has a strong bias. Joe should be skeptical of any claims made by this site, particularly those not supported by evidence.

Answers to Exercise 1.5, page 12

Answers will vary.

1. Possible warrant: College students can decide for themselves what constitutes a good education.

2. Possible warrant: Those who are eligible to vote and to serve in the military should be able to decide for themselves whether to consume alcohol.

3. Possible warrant: The strongest country in the world has an obligation to set an example.

Answers to Exercise 2.5, page 34

1. Pie chart
2. Bar graph
3. Line graph

Answers to Exercise 4.2, page 63

Answers will vary.

1. *Original*

   Vivaldi was famous and influential as a virtuoso violinist and composer. Vivaldi died in poverty, having lost popularity in the last years before his death. He had been acclaimed during his lifetime and forgotten for two hundred years after his death. Many composers suffer that fate. The baroque revival of the 1950s brought his music back to the public's attention.

   Revised

   During his prime, Vivaldi was an acclaimed violin virtuoso and an influential composer. As has happened to many famous musicians, however, his popularity eventually waned, and he died in poverty and obscurity. He remained forgotten for two hundred years until the baroque revival of the 1950s brought his music back to the public's attention.

2. *Original*

   People who want to adopt an exotic pet need to be aware of the consequences. Baby snakes and reptiles can seem fairly easy to manage. Adult snakes and reptiles can grow large. Many species of reptiles and snakes require carefully controlled environments. Lion and tiger cubs are playful and friendly. They can seem as harmless as kittens. Domestic cats can revert to a wild state quite easily. Big cats can escape. An escaped lion or tiger is a danger to itself and to others. Most exotic animals need professional care. This kind of care is available in zoos and wild-animal parks. The best environment for an exotic animal is the wild.

   Revised

   People thinking about adopting an exotic pet should know the consequences of doing so—and think again. Baby snakes and reptiles, for example, may seem easy to manage, but many require carefully controlled environments, and some of them can grow very large. Similarly, lion and tiger cubs may seem as playful, friendly, and harmless as kittens, but once full grown, they can revert to a wild state quite easily. They can also escape, posing a danger to themselves and others. Most exotic animals need the kind of professional care that is available in zoos and wild-animal parks, not in people's homes. The best environment for an exotic animal, however, is in the wild.

Answers to Exercise 4.5, page 69

Answers will vary.

Answers to Exercise 30.1, page 300

Answers may vary.

1. Charlotte Perkins Gilman was a champion of women's rights.
2. She was born on July 3, 1860, in Hartford, Connecticut.
3. Gilman's "The Yellow Wallpaper," a novella about marriage and madness, still speaks to readers.

Answers to Exercise 30.2, page 301

Answers may vary.

1. Environmentalists worry about the environmental safety of genetically modified food products.
2. Genetically engineered soybeans resist certain herbicides and insecticides.
3. These genetically altered soybeans encourage farmers to use larger quantities of herbicides.

Answer to Exercise 30.3, page 303

Responses may vary.

People today should take measures to prevent identity theft. Identity thieves use someone else's personal information to commit fraud or theft, such as opening a fraudulent credit card account or creating counterfeit checks. Often the victim of identify theft never realizes that his or her identity has been cleverly stolen. Victims of identity theft should contact the Federal Trade Commission (FTC) to dispute fraudulent charges. People should also learn how to minimize their risk of falling victim to this type of crime.

Answer to Exercise 31.1, page 305

Most early scientists thought that the speed of light was infinite. The Italian scientist Galileo never agreed with or listened to the arguments of his contemporaries. He set up an experiment to measure the speed of light between two hills that were a known distance apart. Although its results were ambiguous, Galileo's experiment was more influential than any other experiment of his day.

Almost one hundred years later, the Danish astronomer Olaus Roemer devised a sophisticated experiment to measure the speed of light. Roemer hypothesized that the farther away the planet Jupiter is from Earth, the longer its light will take to reach Earth. Knowing

Jupiter's distance from Earth at various times of the year, Roemer calculated the speed of light to be 141,000 miles per second. Roemer's result was closer than any earlier scientist's to the actual speed of light, which is now known to be 186,281.7 miles per second in a vacuum.

According to Albert Einstein's theory of relativity, the speed of light has never been and will never be exceeded. The speed of light is variable, however. For instance, it travels about 25 percent slower through water than through a vacuum.

Answer to Exercise 32.1, page 308

Responses may vary.

Electrons spin around the nucleus of an atom according to definite rules. The single electron of a hydrogen atom occupies a kind of spherical shell around a single proton. According to the discoveries of quantum physics, we can never determine exactly where in this shell the electron is at a given time. The Indeterminacy Principle states that we can only know the probability that the electron will be at a given point at a given moment. The set of places where the electron is most likely to be is called its orbital. By outlining a set of rules for the orbitals of electrons, the Austrian physicist Wolfgang Pauli developed the concept of the quantum state. Using this concept, scientists can describe the energy and behavior of any electron in a series of four numbers. The first of these, or principal quantum number, specifies the average distance of the electron from the nucleus. The other quantum numbers describe the shape of the orbital and the "spin" of the electron. According to Pauli's basic rule, no two electrons can ever be in exactly the same quantum state. Using the four quantum numbers as a shorthand for each electron in an atom, chemists can calculate the behavior of the atom as a whole.

Answers to Exercise 33.1, page 310

1. On November 30th, 1974, archeologists discovered the 3.5-million-year-old skeleton of an early hominid (or human ancestor) they call Lucy.
2. If you consider how long ago Lucy lived, you might be surprised so many of her bones remained intact. *Or* Considering how long ago Lucy lived, one might be surprised so many of her bones remained intact.
3. When early hominids like Lucy reached full height, they were about three and a half feet tall.

Answers to Exercise 33.2, page 312

1. Many visitors who have looked with amazement at the Great Wall of China do not know that its origins reach back to the seventh century BCE.
2. In 221 BCE, the ruler of the Ch'in state conquered the last of its independent neighbors and unified China for the first time.
3. The Ch'in ruler ordered the walls the states had erected between themselves to be torn down, but ordered the walls on the northern frontier to be combined and reinforced.

Answer to Exercise 33.3, page 313

Responses will vary.

 From about the first to the eighth century CE the Moche civilization dominated the north coast of what is now Peru. The people of this remarkable civilization, which flourished nearly a thousand years before the better-known Inca civilization, were sophisticated engineers and skilled artisans. They built enormous adobe pyramids and created and maintained a vast system of irrigation canals. Moche smiths forged spectacular gold ornaments as well as copper tools and weapons. Moche potters sculpted realistic-looking portraits and scenes of everyday life onto clay vessels; they also decorated vessels with intricate drawings of imposing and elaborately garbed figures involved in complex ceremonies. One such scene, which appears on many Moche vessels, depicts a figure archeologists call the Warrior Priest engaged in a ceremony that involves the ritual sacrifice of bound prisoners.

 What do these drawings represent? Do they depict Moche gods and mythological events, or do they depict actual figures from Moche society conducting actual Moche rituals? A dramatic discovery in 1987 provided an answer to these questions. In that year, archeologists uncovered a group of intact Moche tombs at a site called Sipán. In one of the tombs were the remains of a man who had been buried clothed in stunningly rich regalia. As archeologists carefully removed the parts of this outfit, they realized that it corresponded to the outfit worn by the Warrior Priest depicted on Moche pottery. If the Warrior Priest were just a mythological figure, then this tomb should not exist, but it did. In other words, the archeologists realized, the man in the tomb was an actual Moche Warrior Priest. The archeologists who excavated the tomb explain that the art "enabled us to . . . identify the status, rank and wealth of the principal individual buried in the tomb, as well as the role that he played in the ceremonial life of his people" (Alva and Donnan, 1993, p. 141).

Answer to Exercise 34.1, page 315

I believe this government cannot endure permanently <u>half slave</u> and <u>half free</u>. <u>I do not expect</u> the Union to be dissolved—<u>I do not expect</u> the house to fall—but <u>I do expect</u> it will cease to be divided. It will become <u>all one thing</u>, or <u>all the other</u>. <u>Either the opponents of slavery will arrest the further spread of it</u>, and place it where the public mind shall rest in the belief that it is in the course of ultimate extinction; <u>or its advocates will push it forward</u> till it shall become alike lawful in all the states, <u>old</u> as well as <u>new</u>, <u>North</u> as well as <u>South</u>.

Answers to Exercise 34.2, page 316

1. Impressionism, a term that applies primarily to an art movement of the late nineteenth century, also applies to the music of some composers of the era.
2. The early impressionists include Edouard Manet, Claude Monet, Mary Cassat, Edgar Degas, and Camille Pissarro. *Or* The early impressionists include Edouard Manet, Claude Monet, and Mary Cassat, as well as Edgar Degas and Camille Pissarro.
3. Impressionist composers include both Claude Debussy and Maurice Ravel.

Answer to Exercise 34.3, page 318

Responses will vary.

People can be classified as either Type A or Type B personalities depending on their level of competitiveness, degree of perfectionism, and ability to relax. Type A people are often workaholics who not only drive themselves hard but also drive others hard. In the workplace, employers often like Type A personalities because they tend to be punctual and to work quickly and efficiently. However, because Type A people also tend to be impatient, verbally aggressive, or hostile, they do not rise to top management positions as often as Type B people. Type A people also tend to be acutely aware of time, to talk quickly, and either to interrupt others or to complete their sentences for them. Type B people, in contrast, take the world in stride, walk and talk more slowly, and listen attentively. Type B people are better at dealing with stress and keeping things in perspective than Type A people, who, in contrast, tend to worry more than Type B people.

People with traits that put them clearly on either end of the continuum between Type A and Type B should try to adopt characteristics of the opposite type. For example, to moderate some of their characteristic behaviors and reduce their risk of high blood pressure and heart disease, Type A people can use exercise, relaxation techniques, diet, and meditation. Understanding one's personality is half the battle, but implementing change takes time, discipline, and patience.

Answers to Exercise 35.1, page 322

1. R. Buckminster Fuller, during his career as an architect and engineer, developed some of the most important design innovations of the twentieth century.
2. Correct
3. After suffering from a period of severe depression at the age of 32, Fuller resolved to dedicate his life to improving people's lives.

Answers to Exercise 35.2, page 324

Answers may vary.
1. Correct
2. O'Keefe is one of the most admired American artists of the twentieth century, and her color-saturated images of cactus flowers, bleached bones, and pale skies are widely reproduced.
3. Art was always important to O'Keefe while she was growing up in Wisconsin.

Answer to Exercise 35.3, page 325

Responses may vary.

Henri Matisse and Pablo Picasso, often considered to have been the formative artists of the twentieth century, were also rivals for most of their careers. Both artists were the subject of a travelling exhibit called "Matisse Picasso," which exhibited their works side by side in museums in London, Paris, and New York.

Picasso's work may be more disturbing than Matisse's, and some say it is also more daring and experimental. Yet Matisse too, with his vivid colors and distorted shapes, was a daring innovator.

Looking for similarities, viewers can see that the works of both artists suggest an underlying anxiety. Yet each artist responded differently from the other to this anxiety. Matisse painted tranquil yet often emotionally charged domestic scenes, whereas Picasso fought his inner fears with often jarringly disquieting images.

Answers to Exercise 36.1, page 327

Answers may vary.

1. Before World War II, France divided Vietnam into three administrative regions.
2. Many Vietnamese opposed French rule, and many groups formed to regain the country's independence.
3. Although it was under Japanese control from 1940 to 1945, Vietnam remained a French-administered colony during World War II.

Answers to Exercise 36.2, page 328

Answers may vary.

1. During the early years of the Industrial Revolution, many thousands of people left the countryside in search of work in Europe's fast-growing cities. There they encountered poverty, disease, lack of sanitation, and exhausting, dangerous, factory jobs. These conditions made the cities breeding grounds for insurrection. After an international financial crisis in 1848 and the epidemic of bankruptcies and unemployment that followed it, the threat of unrest increased.
2. Louis-Philippe, France's hopelessly unpopular king, abdicated in February, throwing the country into revolution. Citizens set up barricades in the narrow streets of Paris, restricting the movement of government troops.
3. Revolutionary fervor also took hold in Vienna, the capital of the Austrian Empire. At the same time, nationalist forces gained strength in Hungary and other regions of the empire. Hungarian nationalists demanded autonomy from Vienna and radicals in Prague demanded autonomy for the empire's Slavic peoples.

Answer to Exercise 36.3, page 329

Responses will vary.

Germany and Italy were not always unified nations. On the contrary, they were divided for centuries into many city-states, kingdoms, dukedoms, fiefdoms, and principalities, all of them intent on maintaining their autonomy.

Two men, Camillo di Cavour in Italy and Otto von Bismarck in Germany, were largely responsible for the unification of each country. Cavour, who became prime minister of the republic of Piedmont in 1852, and Bismarck, who was named chancellor of Prussia in 1862, were both practitioners of *realpolitik,* a political policy based on the ruthless advancement of national interests.

Cavour hoped to govern Piedmont in a way that would make it the focus of national aspirations throughout Italy and inspire other Italian states to join it to form a unified nation. He increased the power of Piedmont's parliament, modernized its agriculture and industry, built a railroad that opened the country to trade with the rest of Europe, and installed Victor Emmanuel as king. Modena and Tuscany joined Piedmont after Piedmont, with the help of Napoleon III of France, defeated an Austrian invasion that Cavour had craftily provoked.

Bismarck used similar tactics in pursuit of Germany's unification. For example, after arranging for French neutrality, he attacked and destroyed the Austrian army at Sadowa, eliminating Austrian influence in Prussia and paving the way for Prussian control of a large north German federation by 1867. Both men continued to use these tactics until they succeeded with the unification of Germany in 1871 and of Italy in 1879.

Answers to Exercise 37.1, page 333

Answers may vary.

1. As it had in World War I, Germany entered World War II better prepared than the Allies.
2. Gambling on a quick victory, the Germans struck suddenly in both 1914 and 1939.
3. In 1941, the United States entered World War II.

Answers to Exercise 37.2, page 334

Answers may vary.

1. The Black Death, one of the worst natural disasters in history, started in China around 1333, spread to Europe over trade routes, and killed one third of Europe's population in two years.
2. It was a horrible time, with dead bodies abandoned on the streets, people terrified of one another, and cattle and livestock left to roam the countryside.
3. It was all for themselves, friends deserting friends, husbands leaving wives, parents even abandoning children.

Answers to Exercise 37.3, page 334

1. As were the Nile River in Egypt, the Tigris and Euphrates Rivers in Iraq, and the Yellow River in China, the Indus River in Pakistan was home to one of the earliest civilizations in the world.

2. The Indus civilization was unknown to modern scholars until 1921, when archeologists discovered the remains of one of its two great cities, <u>Harappa</u>.

3. Harappa and another city, Mohenjo-Daro, were the two main centers of <u>the Indus civilization, which flourished from about 2500 to 1700 BCE.</u>

Answer to Exercise 37.4, page 335

Responses will vary.

    Established in 1945, the United Nations was intended to prevent another world war. Only twenty-one nations belonged to the United Nations when it began, but today nearly every nation in the world is a member.

    According to its charter, the United Nations has four purposes: to maintain international peace and security, to develop friendly relations among nations, to promote cooperation among nations for the solution of international problems and the protection of human rights, and to provide a forum for coordinating international action.

    All members of the United Nations have a seat and a vote in the General Assembly, which considers a variety of topics such as globalization, AIDS, and pollution. Primary responsibility for maintaining international peace and security, however, rests with the Security Council, a much smaller body within the United Nations. The Security Council has fifteen members. Five of them—China, France, Russia, the United Kingdom, and the United States—are permanent. The other ten are elected by the General Assembly for two-year terms.

Answers to Exercise 38.1, page 337

1. Historians generally agree that the Egyptians invented sailing around 3000 BCE.

2. Many years passed before mariners learned to sail upwind.

3. The invention of the keel improved sailboat navigation.

Answers to Exercise 38.2, page 338

1. Polynesian sailors settled the remote islands of Oceania beginning in the early first millennium CE.

2. Polynesian settlers reached Hawaii around 500 CE.

3. By about 900, settlers had reached Easter Island, the most remote island in Polynesia. [already in active voice]

Answer to Exercise 38.3, page 339

Responses will vary.

Inventors first conceived of the idea of a lighter-than-air balloon in the Middle Ages. However, not until October 15, 1783 did Pilatre de Rosier successfully ascend in a hot-air balloon. Five weeks later, he and a companion made history again, accomplishing the world's first aerial journey with a five-mile trip across the city of Paris. For the next century, many people considered lighter-than-air balloons the future of human flight. Balloonists reached heights of up to three miles and made long, cross-country journeys. In 1859, for instance, the wind carried a balloonist from St. Louis to Henderson, New York. Balloonists couldn't, however, control the movement of their craft. Some tried to use hand-cranked propellers and even giant oars to overcome this deficiency. The invention of the internal-combustion engine finally made possible controllable, self-propelled balloons, which are known as airships. Hydrogen gas replaced hot air in the earliest airships. Hydrogen gas catches fire easily, however, a fact that doomed the airship as a major means of travel. In 1937, the German airship *Hindenburg* exploded as it was landing in New Jersey, a tragedy that an announcer described in a live radio broadcast. As a result, helium has replaced hydrogen in today's airships.

Answers to Exercise 39.1, page 341

Answers will vary.

1. With the invention of steel engraving and mechanical printing presses in the nineteenth century, publishers could print books in far greater quantity than before.
2. Nineteenth-century realism began in France, which produced such notable realists as Stendhal, Balzac, and Flaubert.
3. Flaubert thought the bourgeoisie were materialistic and vain.

Answers to Exercise 39.2, page 344

1. Humanity is fast approaching a population crisis.
2. We must all do our part to reduce the production of greenhouse gasses.
3. Families should make recycling a habit, and employers should encourage commuters to carpool or take mass transit whenever possible.

Answer to Exercise 39.3, page 344

Responses may vary.

Novelist Henry James had many famous ancestors. His grandfather William crossed the Atlantic in 1789 with little more than a Latin grammar book and a desire to see the battlefields of the Revolutionary War. When William James died in 1832, he left an estate of $3 million, equivalent to about $100 million today. This amount was to be divided among eleven children and his wife, Catherine Barber James. Henry, William's fourth child, often referred to as the elder Henry James to distinguish him from the novelist, became a lecturer and writer on metaphysics. He was interested in the doctrines of the Swedish mystic Emanuel Swedenborg. Although some thought the older Henry James an eccentric, his work was well known and influential during his lifetime.

Answers to Exercise 40.1, page 346

Answers will vary.

Answers to Exercise 40.2, page 347

Answers will vary.

Answers to Exercise 40.3, page 349

1. Metaphor
2. Metaphor
3. Metaphor

Answers to Exercise 40.4, page 350

1. eluded
2. infer; cite is correct
3. incredible

Answers to Exercise 42.1, page 367

1. Ancient people traded salt, which is an important nutrient.
2. Some groups resorted to war and conquest because they wanted to gain control over valuable goods and resources.
3. When they could, people transported large stones by river since doing so required less effort than other means of moving them.

Answer to Exercise 42.2, page 369

Pool hustlers deceive their opponents in many ways. <u>Sometimes appearing unfamiliar with the rules of the game</u> (phrase). They may try acting as if they are drunk. <u>Or pretend to be inept</u> (phrase). For example, they will put so much spin on the ball that it jumps out of the intended pocket. <u>So their opponents will be tricked into betting</u> (dep. clause). <u>Some other ways to cheat</u> (phrase). When their opponents are not looking, pool hustlers may remove their own balls from the table. <u>Then change the position of the balls on the table</u> (phrase). <u>Because today's pool balls have metallic cores</u> (dep. clause). Hustlers can use electromagnets to affect the path of balls. Be aware of these tricks!

Answers to Exercise 42.3, page 370

1. The ominous music prepares us for a shocking scene and confuses us when the shock does not come.
2. Filmmakers may try to evoke nostalgic feelings by choosing songs from a particular era.
3. The musical producer used a mix of traditional songs and new compositions in the Civil War drama *Cold Mountain*.

Answer to Exercise 42.4, page 372

Responses may vary.

According to the United States Constitution, which was ratified in 1788, the president and vice president of the United States were not to be elected directly by the people in a popular election. Instead they were to be elected indirectly by an "electoral college," made up of "electors" who at first were often chosen by the state legislatures. In the early nineteenth century, the population of the United States grew rapidly and electors were increasingly chosen by statewide popular vote, gradually making the electoral college system more democratic. Nonetheless, in the elections of 1824, 1876, 1888, and 2000, the elected candidate won the vote in the electoral college but not a majority of the popular vote.

Answer to Exercise 43.1, page 373

Rare books can be extremely valuable. [Most books have to be in good shape to fetch high prices nevertheless some remain valuable no matter what] (RO). [A first edition of Audubon's *Birds of America* can be worth more than a million dollars however it must be in good condition] (RO). On the other hand, even without a cover, an early edition of Cotton Mather's *An Ecclesiastical History of New England* will be worth at least three thousand dollars. [Generally speaking, the newer a book is the more important its condition, even a book from the 1940s will have to be in excellent condition to be worth three figures] (CS). [There are other factors that determine a book's value, certainly whether the author has signed it is important] (CS). [Even students can collect books for instance they can search for bargains and great "finds" at yard and garage sales] (RO). In addition, used-book and author sites on the Internet offer opportunities for beginning collectors.

Answers to Exercise 43.2, page 375

Answers may vary.
1. Correct
2. All early civilizations were autocratic; in a sense, all people in them were slaves.
3. No one knows when slavery began, but it was common in many ancient agricultural civilizations.

Answers to Exercise 43.3, page 378

Answers may vary.
1. Although globally population has increased steadily, particular regions have suffered sometimes drastic declines.
2. Correct
3. The plague was not the only catastrophe to strike Europe in the fourteenth century. A devastating famine also slowed population growth at the beginning of the century.

Answer to Exercise 43.4, page 379

Responses will vary.

Rare books can be extremely valuable. Although most books have to be in good shape to fetch high prices, some remain valuable no matter what. For example, a first edition of Audubon's *Birds of America* can be worth more than a million dollars, but it must be in good condition. On the other hand, even without a cover, an early edition of Cotton Mather's *An Ecclesiastical History of New England* will be worth at least three thousand dollars. Generally speaking, the newer a book is the more important its condition; even a book from the 1940s will have to be in excellent condition to be worth three figures. Other important factors that determine a book's value include, certainly, whether the author has signed it. Even students can collect books, for instance by searching for bargains and great "finds" at yard and garage sales. In addition, used-book and author sites on the Internet offer opportunities for beginning collectors.

Answer to Exercise 43.5, page 380

Responses will vary.

The economy of the United States has always been turbulent. Many people think that the Great Depression of the 1930s was the only economic cataclysm this country has suffered, but the United States has had a long history of financial panics and upheavals. The early years of the nation were no exception.

Before the Revolution, the American economy was closely linked with Britain's, but during the war and for many years after it, Britain barred the import of American goods. Americans, however, continued to import British goods, but with the loss of British markets the new country's trade deficit ballooned. Eventually, this deficit triggered a severe depression, and social unrest followed. The economy began to recover at the end of the 1780s with the establishment of a stable government, the opening of new markets to American shipping, and the adoption of new forms of industry. Exports grew steadily throughout the 1790s; indeed the United States soon found itself in direct competition with both England and France.

Beginning in 1803, when England declared war on France, the American economy suffered a new setback. France and England each threatened to impound any American ships engaged in trade with the other. President Thomas Jefferson sought to change the policies of France and England with the Embargo Act of 1807, which prohibited all trade between the United States and the warring countries. Jefferson hoped to bring France and England to the negotiating table, but the ploy failed. The economies of France and England suffered little from the loss of trade with the United States; the United States' shipping industry, however, came almost to a halt.

Answers to Exercise 44.1, page 382

1. Nowadays, <u>computers</u> (gives/give) graphic designers a great deal of freedom.
2. Before computers, a <u>design</u> (was/were) produced mostly by hand.
3. Alternative <u>designs</u> (is/are) produced much faster on the computer than by hand.

Answers to Exercise 44.2, page 386

1. <u>Designers</u> since the invention of printing <u>have</u> sought to create attractive, readable type.
2. Correct; subject is <u>layout</u>, verb is <u>shows</u>.
3. Correct; subject is <u>half</u>, verb is <u>contains</u>.

Answers to Exercise 44.3, page 388

1. The Guerilla Girls is a group of women who act on behalf of female artists.
2. One of their main concerns is to combat the underrepresentation of women artists in museum shows.
3. No one knows how many Guerilla Girls there are, and none of them has ever revealed her true identity.

Answer to Exercise 44.4, page 389

The end of the nineteenth century saw the rise of a new kind of architecture. Originating in response to the development of new building materials, this so-called modern architecture characterizes most of the buildings we see around us today.

Iron and reinforced concrete make the modern building possible. Previously, the structural characteristics of wood and stone limited the dimensions of a building. Wood-frame structures become unstable above a certain height. Stone can bear great weight, but architects building in stone confront severe limits on the height of a structure in relation to the width of its base. The principal advantage of iron and steel is that they reduce those limits, permitting much greater height than stone.

At first the new materials were used for decoration. However, architects like Hermann Muthesius and Walter Gropius began to use iron and steel as structural elements within their buildings. The designs of Frank

Lloyd Wright also show how the development of iron and steel technology revolutionized building interiors. When every wall does not have to bear weight from the floors above, open floor plans are possible.

Answers to Exercise 45.1, page 393

1. were
2. grown
3. saw

Answers to Exercise 45.2, page 395

1. Humans, like many other mammals, usually lie down to sleep.
2. Correct
3. The restless students had been sitting at their desks all morning.

Answers to Exercise 45.3, page 396

1. Correct
2. Desert peoples have learned that loose, light garments protect them from the heat.
3. They have long drunk from deep wells that they dug for water.

Answers to Exercise 45.4, page 400

1. follows
2. states
3. published

Answer to Exercise 45.5, page 401

For some time, anthropologists were puzzled by the lack of a written language among the ancient Incas of South America. The Incas, who had conquered most of Andean South America by about 1500, had sophisticated architecture, advanced knowledge of engineering and astronomy, and sophisticated social and political structures. Why didn't they have a written language as well?

Ancient Egypt, Iraq, and China, as well as early Mexican civilizations such as the Aztec and Maya, all had written language. It seems strange that only the Incas lacked a written language.

Anthropologists now think that the Incas possessed a kind of written language after all. Scholars believe that the Incas used knots in multicolored strings as the medium for their "writing." The Incas called these knotted strings *khipu.*

Answers to Exercise 45.6, page 402

1. were
2. resign
3. were

Answers to Exercise 46.1, page 407

Answers may vary.
1. All the people at the displaced-persons camp had to submit their medical records before boarding the ships to the United States.
2. Correct
3. This was always devastating news because families wanted to stay together.

Answers to Exercise 46.2, page 410

Answers may vary.
1. The tight race between presidential candidates John Kerry and George W. Bush in 2004 compelled Kerry to campaign intensively in many states.
2. The candidates debated three times, with both men answering all questions thoughtfully.
3. During one debate, Kerry said that Bush had an inadequate plan of action.

Answers to Exercise 46.3, page 413

1. I
2. him
3. she

Answers to Exercise 46.4, page 414

1. We
2. me
3. us

Answers to Exercise 46.5, page 414

1. her
2. her
3. Their

Answer to Exercise 46.6, page 415

Sociolinguists investigate the relationship between linguistic variations and culture. They spend a lot of time in the field to gather data for analysis. For instance, they might compare the speech patterns of people who live in a city with those of people who reside in the suburbs. Sociolinguists might discover differences in pronunciation or word choice. Their researching helps us understand both language and culture.

We laypeople might confuse sociolinguistics with sociology. Sociolinguists do a more specialized type of research than do most sociologists, who study broad patterns within societies. Being concerned with such particulars as the pronunciation of a single vowel, sociolinguists work at a finer level of detail than they.

Answers to Exercise 46.7, page 416

1. Who
2. who
3. who

Answer to Exercise 46.8, page 416

Responses may vary.

Margaret Mead was probably the best-known anthropologist of the twentieth century. It was she who wrote *Coming of Age in Samoa,* a book well known in the 1930s and still in print today. It was she who gave us the idea that Melanesian natives grow up free of the strictures and repression that can characterize adolescence in our society. Her writings found an audience just as the work of Sigmund Freud was becoming widely known in the United States.

In his work, Freud argued for "an incomparably freer sexual life," saying that rigid attitudes toward sexuality contributed to mental illness among us Westerners. Mead's accessible and gracefully written account of life among the Samoans showed them to be both relatively free of pathology and relaxed about sexual matters. The work of both Mead and Freud provoked and contributed to a debate over theories about the best way to raise children.

Answers to Exercise 47.1, page 419

1. The spread of destructive (adj) viruses to computers around the world is a serious (adj) problem with potentially (adv) deadly (adj) consequences.

2. Carried by infected (adj) e-mails, the viruses spread fast (adv), moving from computer to computer at the click of a mouse.

3. Viruses have hit businesses badly (adv) in the past, disrupting railroads, delaying flights, and closing stores and offices.

Answers to Exercise 47.2, page 420

1. Correct
2. The discipline's intellectual roots reach really far back, to the eighteenth century. (*Very* is preferable.)
3. Auguste Comte (1798–1857) invented the word *sociology,* and most sociologists would probably agree that he founded the discipline.

Answers to Exercise 47.3, page 422

1. Biotechnology, perhaps the most controversial application of science in recent decades, is the basis of genetic engineering, cloning, and gene therapy.
2. Correct
3. Ethicists find it easier to defend the genetic engineering of plants than the cloning of animals.

Answer to Exercise 47.4, page 423

Although there are many approaches to sociology, the two most common are functionalism and conflict theory. The functionalist view, usually associated with Harvard sociologist Talcott Parsons, sees society as a whole that tries to maintain equilibrium, or stasis. No ancestor of conflict theory is more famous than Karl Marx, who invented the concept of class warfare. Promoted here in the United States by the African-American sociologist W. E. B. Du Bois, conflict theory sees society as made up of groups that cannot avoid being in conflict or competition with one another.

For a functionalist like Parsons, societies are best understood according to how well they maintain stability. On the other hand, for a conflict theorist like Du Bois, a society is best analyzed in terms of how its parts compete for power.

Other sociological theories, such as interactionist and feminist theory, have certainly made major contributions to the field. However, each of these can best be seen as examples of functionalist or conflict theory. Relating small-scale behavior such as gestures and facial expressions to the larger context of a group or society, interactionist theory is really a development of the functionalist view. Similarly, feminist sociological theory understands society in terms of gender inequality—a view recognizable as a subtype of conflict theory.

Answer to Exercise 48.1, page 428

In his book *Travels with Charley,* John Steinbeck describes a journey he took that helped him discover his country. Hurricane Donna struck New York State and delayed the beginning of the long-planned trip. While the author was traveling in New England, the weather became cold and leaves turned their fall colors. On his way, he met a farmer who had a Yankee face and Yankee accent. Steinbeck discovered that the best way to learn about the local population was to visit a local bar or a church. He also saw many people fleeing New England to escape the winter. Many shops were closed, and some had signs saying they would be closed until the following summer. As he traveled through the states, he noticed changes in the language. These differences were apparent in road signs. Trouble arose when he was not allowed to cross the Canadian border because he did not have a vaccination certificate for his dog, Charley. Steinbeck and his companion were later able to resume their trip without further problems.

Answers to Exercise 48.2, page 430

1. Do you know where you and Erica will go on vacation this summer?
2. You should look online. You can find great deals there.
3. I have been looking all over the Internet, but I have not found any cheap hotels.

Answers to Exercise 48.3, page 433

1. In the past, people were expected (to stay/staying) at the same job for a long time, ideally for their whole career.

2. Today, people tend (<u>to change</u>/changing) careers several times before retiring.
3. People who are not happy with their careers attempt (<u>to find</u>/finding) other jobs that interest them more.

Answers to Exercise 48.4, page 436

1. House hunting can be a time-consuming and frustrating activity.
2. Prospective home buyers are bombarded with images of elegant, spacious houses.
3. Multiple bedrooms, fully equipped bathrooms, and landscaped gardens are becoming standard features of new suburban properties.

Answers to Exercise 48.5, page 436

1. The review material for the art history final is very (<u>boring</u>/bored).
2. The term paper I am writing for the class is on a (<u>challenging</u>/challenged) topic: twentieth-century painting.
3. The paintings of Picasso are especially (<u>interesting</u>/interested).

Answers to Exercise 48.6, page 442

1. As Michael Pollan writes in the *New York Times Magazine,* Americans have become the world's most anxious eaters.
2. Researchers have found that Americans worry more about what they eat than people in other developed countries do.
3. Therefore, they tend to enjoy their food less and associate a good meal with guilty pleasure.

Answers to Exercise 49.1, page 448

1. After the year 1000 CE, Europeans became less isolated.
2. Correct
3. Increasingly aware of the rich civilizations beyond their borders, Europeans began to enter into business relationships with the cities and countries in the East.

Answers to Exercise 49.2, page 449

1. Asperger's syndrome is a developmental disorder, yet Asperger's syndrome is often confused with autism.

2. People with Asperger's syndrome have normal IQs, but they have difficulty interacting with others in a social setting.
3. In school, students afflicted with this disorder may have difficulty working in groups, for they prefer solitary, repetitive routines.

Answers to Exercise 49.3, page 450

1. Correct
2. Paintings have been found in North America, Europe, Africa, and Australia.
3. Paintings found in southeastern France contain images of animals, birds, and fish.

Answers to Exercise 49.4, page 453

1. The mind-body problem, under debate for centuries, concerns the relationship between the mind and the body.
2. Correct
3. Since the time of the ancient Greeks, the prevailing opinion has been that the mind and body are separate entities.

Answers to Exercise 49.5, page 456

1. Millions of viewers watch reality-based television shows. Cultural critics, however, argue that shows such as *Survivor, American Idol,* and *The Bachelor* exploit human greed and the desire for fame.
2. These shows, so the critics say, take advantage of our insecurities.
3. The participants who appear on these shows are average, everyday people, not actors.

Answers to Exercise 49.6, page 457

1. Professor Bartman entered the room and proclaimed, "Today we will examine Erikson's eight stages of human development."
2. "Who may I ask has read the assignment?" he queried.
3. "Patricia," he hissed, "please enlighten the rest of the class."

Answer to Exercise 49.7, page 461

Every society has families, but the structure of the family varies from society to society. Over time the function of the family has changed so that in today's postindustrial society, for instance, the primary function of the family is to provide "emotional gratification," according to Professor Paula Stein, noted sociologist of Stonehall University, New Hampshire. In a recent interview, Stein [or In a recent interview Stein . . .] also said, "Images of the family tend to be based on ideals, not realities." To back up this claim, Stein pointed to a new, as yet unpublished survey of more than 10,000 married American couples that she and her staff conducted. Expected to be released in the October 17, 2003, edition of the *Weekly Sociologist,* the survey indicates that the biggest change has been the increase in the variety of family arrangements, including singles, single parents, and childless couples. Most Americans marry for love, they say, but research portrays courtship as an analysis of costs, benefits, assets, and liabilities, not unlike a business deal.

Virtually all children are upset by divorce, but most recover in a few years while others suffer lasting, serious problems. Despite the high rate of divorce, which reached its height in 1979, Americans still believe in the institution of marriage, as indicated by the high rate of remarriages that form *blended families.* "Yes, some see the breakup of the family as a social problem or cause of other problems, but others see changes in the family as adaptations to changing social conditions, as I do," concluded the professor.

Answers to Exercise 50.1, page 463

1. The Pop Art movement flourished in the United States and in Britain in the 1960s; it was a reaction to the abstract art that had dominated the art scene during the 1950s.

2. Pop artists were inspired by popular culture and consumerism; for example, they painted advertisements, comic strips, supermarket products, and even dollar bills!

3. The artists' goal was to transform ordinary daily experiences into art; they also wanted to comment on the modern world of mass production.

Answers to Exercise 50.2, page 465

1. Some scientists are studying a European bird related to the chickadee; these scientists, at the Netherlands Institute of Ecology, are conducting experiments with this bird.

2. Another scientist, Dr. Samuel Gosling, has studied hyena populations; he asked handlers to rate the hyenas using a questionnaire that was adapted from a questionnaire used for humans.

3. These studies and others indicate that animals display personality traits like boldness and shyness; bold birds quickly investigate new items in their environment while shy birds take more time.

Answer to Exercise 51.1, page 467

Ciguatera is a form of food poisoning: humans are poisoned when they consume reef fish that contain toxic substances called ciguatoxins. These toxins accumulate at the end of the food chain: large carnivorous fish prey on smaller herbivorous fish. These smaller fish feed on ciguatoxins, which are produced by microorganisms that grow on the surface of marine algae. Ciguatoxins are found in certain marine fish: snapper, mackerel, barracuda, and grouper. People should avoid eating fish from reef waters, including the tropical and subtropical waters of the Pacific and Indian Oceans, and the Caribbean Sea.

Some people think that ciguatera can be destroyed by cooking or freezing the fish. People who consume reef fish should avoid eating the head, internal organs, or eggs. People who eat contaminated fish experience gastrointestinal and neurological problems: vomiting, diarrhea, numbness, and muscle pains. Most physicians offer the same advice: "Eat fish only from reputable restaurants and dealers."

Answers to Exercise 52.1, page 470

Word(s)	Possessive
the press	the press's
nobody	nobody's
newspapers	newspapers'

Answers to Exercise 52.2, page 472

1. In the essay "The Over-soul," Ralph Waldo Emerson describes the unity of nature by cataloging (it's/<u>its</u>) divine, yet earthly, expressions, such as waterfalls and well-worn footpaths.

2. Emerson states that you must have faith to believe in something that supersedes or contradicts (<u>your</u>/you're) real-life experiences.

3. (<u>Who's</u>/Whose) the author of the poem at the beginning of Emerson's "Self-Reliance"?

Answer to Exercise 52.3, page 472

Transcendentalism was a movement of thought in the mid-to-late 1800s that was originated by Ralph Waldo Emerson, Henry David Thoreau, and several others whose scholarship helped to shape the democratic ideals of their day and usher America into its modern age. Emerson, a member of New England's elite, was particularly interested in spreading Transcendentalist notions of self-reliance; he is probably best known for his essay "Self-Reliance," which is still widely read in today's universities. Most people remember Thoreau, however, not only for what he wrote but also for how he lived: it's well known that—for a while, at least—he chose to live a simple life in a cabin on Walden Pond. Altogether, one could say that Emerson and Thoreau's main accomplishment was to expand the influence of literature and philosophy over the development of the average American's identity. With a new national literature forming, people's interest in their self-development quickly increased as they began to read more and more about what it meant to be American. In fact, one could even say (perhaps half-jokingly) that, today, the success of home makeovers on TV and the popularity of self-help books might have a lot to do with Emerson's and Thoreau's ideas about self-sufficiency and living simply—ideas that took root in this nation more than a hundred years ago.

Answers to Exercise 53.1, page 476

1. Correct
2. "To prove this," writes Stanton, "let facts be submitted to a candid world."
3. Correct

Answers to Exercise 53.2, page 478

1. "We hold these truths to be self-evident," wrote Thomas Jefferson in 1776.
2. Most Americans can recite their "unalienable rights": "life, liberty, and the pursuit of happiness."
3. According to the Declaration of Independence, "whenever any form of government becomes destructive to these ends, it is the right of the people to alter or to abolish it."

Answer to Exercise 53.3, page 481

On August 28, 1963, Dr. Martin Luther King Jr., delivered his famous "I Have a Dream" speech at the nation's Lincoln Memorial. According to King, "When the architects of our republic wrote the magnificent words of the Constitution and the Declaration of Independence, they were signing a promissory note to which every American was to fall heir." King declared that "this note was a promise that all men, yes, black men as well as white men, would be guaranteed the unalienable rights of life, liberty, and the pursuit of happiness. This promissory note, however, came back marked 'insufficient funds.'" King's speech, therefore, was designed to rally his supporters to "make justice a reality."

Unlike the more militant civil rights leaders of the 1950s, King advocated nonviolence. This stance is why King said that the "Negro community" should not drink "from the cup of bitterness and hatred," and that they should not use physical violence.

King's dream was uniquely American: "I have a dream that one day this nation will rise up and live out the true meaning of its creed: 'We hold these truths to be self-evident: that all men are created equal.'" King challenged all Americans to fully embrace racial equality. Nearly fifty years later, we must ask ourselves if King's dream has in fact become a reality. Are "all of God's children, black men and white men, Jews and Gentiles, Protestants and Catholics . . . able to join hands and sing in the words of the old Negro spiritual, 'Free at last! Free at last! Thank God Almighty, we are free at last!'"?

Answer to Exercise 54.1, page 483

Do you realize that there is a volcano larger than Mt. St. Helens? Mt. Vesuvius? Mt. Etna? Mauna Loa is the largest volcano on Earth, covering at least half the island of Hawaii. The summit of Mauna Loa stands 56,000 feet above its base. This is why Native Hawaiians named this volcano the "Long Mountain." Mauna Loa is also one of the most active volcanoes on the planet, having erupted thirty-three times since 1843 (most people do not think of a volcano as dormant). Its last eruption occurred in 1984. Most people associate a volcanic eruption with red lava spewing from the volcano's crater, but few people realize that the lava flow and volcanic gases are also extremely hazardous. Tourists like to follow the lava to where it meets the sea, but this practice is dangerous because of the steam produced when the lava meets the water. So, the next time you visit an active volcano, beware!

Answers to Exercise 54.2, page 484

1. Patsy Mink, Geraldine Ferraro, Antonia Novello, and Madeline Albright—all are political pioneers in the history of the United States.
2. Patsy Mink—the first Asian-American woman elected to the U.S. Congress—served for twenty-four years in the U.S. House of Representatives.

3. Geraldine Ferraro—congresswoman from Queens, New York—became the first female vice presidential candidate when she was nominated by the Democratic Party in 1984.

Answers to Exercise 54.3, page 486

1. German meteorologist Alfred Wegener (he was also a geophysicist) proposed the first comprehensive theory of continental drift.
2. According to this geological theory, (1) the earth originally contained a single large continent, (2) this land mass eventually separated into six continents, and (3) these continents gradually drifted apart.
3. Wegener contended that continents will continue to drift (they are not rigidly fixed), and the evidence indicates that his predictions are accurate.

Answers to Exercise 54.4, page 488

1. Ulysses is tempted as he looks toward the sea: "The lights begin to twinkle from the rocks; / The long day wanes; ..." (54–55).
2. In "Two Views of the Mississippi," Mark Twain writes that "... I had mastered the language of this water. ... I had made a valuable acquisition."
3. Twain regrets that he "[has] lost something"—his sense of the beauty of the river.

Answer to Exercise 54.5, page 489

Responses will vary.

John Fitzgerald Kennedy—the youngest man to be elected U.S. President—was also the youngest President to be assassinated. He was born on May 29, 1917, in Brookline, Massachusetts. Kennedy was born into a family with a tradition of public service—his father, Joseph Kennedy, served as ambassador to Great Britain. (His maternal grandfather, John Frances Fitzgerald, served as the mayor of Boston.)

Caroline, John Fitzgerald Jr., and Patrick B. (who died in infancy) are the children of the late John F. Kennedy. Kennedy's background— a Harvard education, military service as a lieutenant in the navy, and public service as Massachusetts senator—helped provide him with the experience, insight, and recognition needed to defeat Richard Nixon in 1960.

Even before being elected U.S. President, Kennedy received the Pulitzer Prize for his book *Profiles in Courage* (1957). According to

Kennedy, "This [*Profiles in Courage*] is a book about that most admirable of human virtues—courage" (1). "Some of my colleagues,"
Kennedy continues, "who are criticized today for lack of forthright
principles . . . are simply engaged in the fine art of conciliating . . ." (5).

During Kennedy's presidency, Americans witnessed (1) the Cuban
Missile Crisis, (2) the Bay of Pigs Invasion, and (3) the Berlin Crisis.
Most Americans, we hope, are able to recognize Kennedy's famous words,
which were first delivered during his Inaugural Address: "Ask not what
your country can do for you—ask what you can do for your country."

Answer to Exercise 55.1, page 494

Perhaps the most notable writer of the 1920s is F. Scott Fitzgerald.
He was born on September 24, 1896, in St. Paul, Minnesota, to Edward
Fitzgerald and Mary "Mollie" McQuillan, who were both members of the
Catholic Church. After attending Princeton University and embarking
on a career as a writer, Fitzgerald married southern belle Zelda Sayre
from Montgomery, Alabama. Together, he and his wife lived the celebrated life of the Roaring Twenties and the Jazz Age. Fitzgerald wrote
numerous short stories as well as four novels: *This Side of Paradise, The
Beautiful and Damned, The Great Gatsby,* and *Tender Is the Night. The
Great Gatsby,* which he finished in the winter of 1924 and published in
1925, is considered Fitzgerald's most brilliant and critically acclaimed
work. Readers who have read this novel will remember these opening
words spoken by Nick Carraway, the narrator in the story: "In my
younger and more vulnerable years my father gave me some advice that
I've been turning over in my mind ever since. 'Whenever you feel like
criticizing anyone,' he told me, 'just remember that all the people in this
world haven't had the advantages that you've had.'"

Answer to Exercise 56.1, page 497

In today's digital-savvy world, a person who has never used a computer with access to the World Wide Web (WWW) and a Motion Pictures Experts Group Layer 3 (MP3) player would be surprised to find
that anyone can download and groove to the sounds of "Nights in White
Satin" by the 1960s rock band the Moody Blues at 3 AM without ever
having to have spent money for the album *Days of Future Past.* However, such file sharing, commonly known as "file swapping," is illegal
and surrounded by controversy. The Recording Industry Association
of America (RIAA), which represents the U.S. recording industry, has
taken aggressive legal action against such acts of online piracy. For
example, in a landmark case in 2004, U.S. District Judge Denny Chin
ruled that Internet service providers must identify those subscribers

who share music online, at least in the states of New York, New Jersey, and Connecticut. As the nature of music recordings changes with the proliferation of digital music services and file formats, this controversy is far from being resolved. In recent years, companies such as Apple and Microsoft as well as cellular phone carriers have set up online music stores. Consumers can buy downloadable music files for very little money.

Answers to Exercise 57.1, page 500

1. The soccer team raised $1,067 by selling entertainment booklets filled with coupons, discounts, and special promotions.
2. Fifty-five percent of the participants in the sociology student's survey reported that they would lie to a professor in order to have a late assignment accepted.
3. In one year alone, 115 employees at the company objected to their performance appraisals, but only 24 filed formal complaints.

Answer to Exercise 58.1, page 502

Today, thousands of people in the United States practice yoga for its physical, spiritual, and mental benefits. The word *yoga,* originating from the Sanskrit root *yuj,* means the union of the body, spirit, and mind. Although there are many styles of yoga, people who want a gentle introduction to yoga should practice Iyengar Yoga, a style developed by B.K.S. Iyengar of India, which uses props such as blocks, belts, and pillows to help the body find alignment in *asanas* (poses) and *pranayana* (breathing). Those people who want to learn more about Iyengar Yoga are encouraged to read the following books written by the master himself: *Light on Yoga, Light on Pranayama, The Art of Yoga, The Tree of Yoga,* and *Light on the Yoga Sutras of Patanjali.* Those who want to learn about the general benefits of yoga can find numerous articles such as "Yoga and Weight Loss" by doing a general online search. All forms of yoga promise the diligent and faithful practitioner increased strength, flexibility, and balance.

Answer to Exercise 59.1, page 505

We need only to turn on the television or pick up a recent issue of a popular fashion or fitness magazine to see evidence of modern society's obsession with images of thinness. Few actors, models, or celebrities fail to flaunt their thinly trimmed waistlines, regardless of their gender. Not surprisingly, more than ten million females and almost one million males in the United States are currently battling eating disorders such as anorexia nervosa and bulimia nervosa. A person who is anorexic fears gaining weight and thus engages in self-starvation with excessive weight loss. A person who is bulimic binges and then engages in self-induced purging in order to lose weight. Although we are often quick to assume that those with eating disorders suffer from low self-esteem and have a history of family or peer problems, we cannot ignore the role of the media in encouraging eating disorders, particularly when thinness is equated with physical attractiveness, health and fitness, and success overall. We need to remember the threat of these eating disorders the next time we hear a ten-year-old girl tell her mommy that she "can't afford" to eat more than one-half of her peanut-butter-and-jelly sandwich.

Answers to Exercise 60.1, page 508

Bentleys
presidents elect
lives

Answers to Exercise 60.2, page 509

either (correct)
hygiene (correct)
dealer (correct)

Answers to Exercise 60.3, page 512

Answers will vary.

Answers to Exercise 61.1, page 516

1. undergo (mv)
2. believed (mv)
3. think (mv)

Answers to Exercise 61.2 and Exercise 61.3, pages 521 and 522

1. Following World War I, the nation witnessed an unprecedented explosion of African-American fiction, poetry, drama, music, art, social commentary, and political activism.

Nouns:
World War I—proper, concrete, singular (count/noncount not applicable)
nation—common, count, concrete, singular
explosion—common, count, concrete, singular
fiction—common, noncount, concrete, singular
poetry—common, noncount, concrete, singular
drama—common, noncount, concrete, singular
music—common, noncount, concrete, singular
art—common, noncount, concrete, singular
commentary—common, count, concrete, singular
activism—common, noncount, concrete, singular

2. Many African-American intellectuals, artists, cultural critics, and
political leaders during the 1920s and 1930s were drawn to Harlem,
a vibrant section of upper Manhattan in New York City.

Nouns:
intellectuals—common, count, concrete, plural
artists—common, count, concrete, plural
critics—common, count, concrete, plural
leaders—common, count, concrete, plural
1920s—either common or proper could be correct, count, concrete, plural
1930s—either common or proper could be correct, count, concrete, plural
Harlem—proper, concrete, singular (count/noncount not applicable)
section—common, count, concrete, singular
Manhattan—proper, concrete, singular (count/noncount not applicable)
New York City—proper, concrete, singular (count/noncount not applicable)

3. Sociologist and intellectual Alain Locke, author of *The New Negro,* is
best known as the New Negro Movement's founder.

Nouns:
Sociologist—common, count, concrete, singular
intellectual—common, count, concrete, singular
Alain Locke—proper, concrete, singular (count/noncount not applicable)
author—common, count, concrete, singular
The New Negro—proper, concrete, singular (count/noncount not
   applicable)
New Negro Movement's (as a whole)—possessive proper noun,
   concrete, singular (count/noncount not applicable)
founder—common, count, concrete, singular

Answers to Exercise 61.4, page 524

1. Adj: growing, overweight, obese; adv: clinically
2. Adj: person's, Type 2, heart, high, blood, liver, premature
3. Adj: fad, rapid, temporary, weight, weight

Answers to Exercise 61.5, page 527

1. Cancer (n) begins (v) when (conj) your (pron/adj) body's (noun/adj) cells (n) divide (v) abnormally (adv) and (conj) form (v) a (adj) malignant (adj) growth (n) or (conj) tumor (n).
2. Many (adj) types (n) of (prep) cancer (n) alas (interj) can (v) attack (v) parts (n) of (conj) your (pron/adj) body (n) imperceptibly (adv), including (prep) your (pron/adj) body's (n/adj) skin (n), organs (n), and (conj) blood (n).
3. One (n) of (prep) the (adj) most (adv) commonly (adv) diagnosed (adj) types (n) of (prep) cancer (n) in (prep) the (adj) United States (n), however (adv), is (v) skin (n/adj) cancer (n).

Answers to Exercise 62.1, page 529

1. Did Gene Roddenberry, the creator and producer of *Star Trek,* anticipate that his science fiction television series would be watched by people of all ages for more than thirty years?
2. Both Captain James T. Kirk from *Star Trek: The Original Series* and Captain Jean-Luc Picard from *Star Trek: The Next Generation* command a ship called the *Enterprise.*
3. Do not forget that the captain in *Star Trek: Voyager* is a woman, Kathryn Janeway. [implied subject]

Answers to Exercise 62.2, page 531

1. Lucretia Mott and Elizabeth Cady Stanton organized the first national convention on women's rights.
2. They held the convention in 1848 at Seneca Falls, a town in upstate New York.
3. The convention issued the Declaration of Sentiments, which included a demand that women be granted the right to vote.

Answers to Exercise 62.3, page 533

1. Hybrid cars produce (trans) low tailpipe emissions (DO).
2. Automakers promise (trans) consumers (IO) affordable gasoline-electric cars (DO).
3. Hybrid cars are (link) desirable alternatives (SC) to gasoline-powered vehicles.

Answers to Exercise 63.1, page 536

1. Noun phrase functioning as the subject of the sentence
2. Noun phrase, appositive
3. Noun phrase functioning as the object of the sentence

Answers to Exercise 63.2, page 538

1. During the 1970s and 1980s, Asian-American writers, <u>who often drew upon their immigrant experiences</u>, gained a wide readership. [adj. clause]

2. <u>Because these writers wrote about their struggles and the struggles of their ancestors</u>, readers were able to learn about the Chinese Exclusion Act of 1892 and the internment of Japanese Americans during World War II. [adv. clause]

3. Many readers know Amy Tan as the Chinese-American novelist <u>who wrote *The Joy Luck Club*,</u> <u>which was adapted into a feature film</u>, but are unfamiliar with most of her other novels, such as *The Kitchen God's Wife, The Hundred Secret Senses,* and *The Bonesetter's Daughter.* [two adj. clauses, the first modifying "Amy Tan," the second modifying "*The Joy Luck Club*"]

Answers to Exercise 64.1, page 540

1. Simple
2. Simple
3. Compound

Quick Reference for

Helpful information for multilingual writers also appears in Chapter 48 (pp. 424-443) and in *Tips for Multilingual Writers* boxes that appear throughout this book.

Nouns and Pronouns

Count and Noncount Nouns

Count nouns name persons, places, or things that can be counted. Count nouns can be singular or plural.

Noncount nouns name a class of things. Usually, noncount nouns have only a singular form.

COUNT	NONCOUNT	COUNT	NONCOUNT
cars	information	child	humanity
table	furniture	book	advice

Pronouns

Common Problem: Personal pronoun restates subject.

INCORRECT   My sister, *she* works in the city.

CORRECT   My sister works in the city.

Pronouns replace nouns. They stand for persons, places, or things and can be singular or plural.

Personal pronouns act as subjects, objects, or words that show possession.

Subject pronouns: I, we, you, he, she, it, one, they, who

Object pronouns: me, us, you, him, her, it, one, them, whom

Possessive pronouns: my, mine, our, ours, your, yours, his, her, hers, its, their, theirs, whose

Relative pronouns introduce dependent clauses.

Relative pronouns: that, whatever, which, whichever, who, whoever, whom, whomever, whose

EXAMPLE   His sister, *who* lives in Canada, came to visit.

Sentence Structure

Subjects and Verbs

English requires both a subject and a verb in every sentence or clause.

    S   V   S   V
    She slept.   He ate.

Direct and Indirect Objects

Verbs may be followed by *direct* or *indirect objects*. A *direct object* receives the action of the verb.

    S   V   DO
    He drove the car.

An *indirect object* is the person or thing to which something is done.

    S   V   IO   DO
    She gave her sister a birthday gift.

Friday 4:30 a.m.

Tehran, Iran
Kabul, Afghanistan

Friday 8:00 a.m.

Shanghai, China
Manila, Philippines
Singapore

Friday 9:00 a.m.

Tokyo, Japan

Friday 10:00 a.m.

Sydney, Australia

ARCTIC

GREENLAND

ICELAND

Nuuk ★

Reykjavik ★

60°N

NORWAY
SWEDEN
FINLAND
Helsinki
EST.
Stockholm
LAT.
Moscow
DEN.
RUSS.
LITH.
UNITED
KINGDOM
NETH.
BELARUS
Dublin
London
BELG.
Berlin
POLAND
IRELAND
GER.
UKRAINE
LUX.
CZECH.
Paris
FRANCE
AUST.
SLOVK.
MOLDOVA
KAZAKHSTAN
SWITZ.
SLOVN.
HUNG.
ROM.
GEORGIA
ITALY
CRO.
BOS.
UZBEKISTAN
Madrid
Rome
SERB.
BULG.
ARMENIA
TURKMENISTAN
PORTUGAL
SPAIN
MONT.
GREECE
TURKEY
AZERBAIJAN
Lisbon
ALB.
Tehran
CYPRUS
LEBANON
SYRIA
IRAQ
Kat.
AFGHAN.
TUNISIA
ISRAEL
Baghdad
IRAN
MOROCCO
Jerusalem
JORDAN
Cairo
KUWAIT
ALGERIA
LIBYA
EGYPT
BAHRAIN
QATAR
U.A.E.
WESTERN
SAHARA
Riyadh ★
SAUDI ARABIA
OMAN
MAURITANIA
MALI
NIGER
CHAD
SUDAN
ERITREA
YEMEN
Dakar ★
SENEGAL
DJIBOUTI
GAMBIA
BURKINA
FASO
Addis
GUINEA BISSAU
GUINEA
BENIN
NIGERIA
CENTRAL AFRICAN
Ababa
IVORY
GHANA
REPUBLIC
ETHIOPIA
SIERRA LEONE
COAST
TOGO
CAMEROON
SOMALIA
LIBERIA
EQUATORIAL GUINEA
UGANDA
KENYA
SAO TOME & PRINCIPE
GABON
CONGO
RWANDA
Nairobi
DEMOCRATIC
BURUNDI
REPUBLIC
Kinshasa
OF THE CONGO
TANZANIA
ANGOLA
COMOROS
ZAMBIA
Rio De Janeiro
ZIMBABWE
MALAWI
MAURITIUS
São Paulo
NAMIBIA
BOTSWANA
MOZAMBIQUE
MADAGASCAR
SOUTH
ARGENTINA
SWAZILAND
AFRICA
LESOTHO
URUGUAY
30°S
Cape Town ★
Buenos Aires

ATLANTIC

OCEAN

0°

60°E

30°N

Canary Islands

30°W

Montreal

ew York
ngton D. C.

uda

EP.

Puerto Rico
ST. KITTS AND NEVIS
ANTIGUA AND BARBUDA
DOMINICA
BARBADOS
CIA
ST. VINCENT AND
THE GRENADINES
DA
aracas
TRINIDAD AND TOBAGO
SURINAME
UELA
FRENCH GUIANA
GUYANA

BRAZIL

OLIVIA

PARAGUAY

60°W

FALKLAND ISLANDS

SOUTH GEORGIA ISLAND

60°S

75°S

ANTARCTICA

30°E

<table>
<tr><td>**Friday 1:00 a.m.**</td><td>**Friday 2:00 a.m.**</td><td>**Friday 3:00 a.m.**</td><td>**Friday 4:00 a.m.**</td></tr>
<tr><td>Dublin, Ireland</td><td>Stockholm, Sweden</td><td>Cairo, Egypt</td><td>Moscow, Russia</td></tr>
<tr><td>Lisbon, Portugal</td><td>Berlin, Germany</td><td></td><td>Baghdad, Iraq</td></tr>
<tr><td></td><td>Rome, Italy</td><td></td><td></td></tr>
<tr><td></td><td>Cape Town, South Africa</td><td></td><td></td></tr>
</table>

Multilingual Writers

Articles

Common Problem: Article is omitted.

INCORRECT   Water is cold. I bought watch.

CORRECT   *The* water is cold. I bought *a* watch.

Using Articles with Count and Noncount Nouns

Definite article (*the*): used for specific reference with all types of nouns.

The car I bought is red. [*singular count noun*]

The dogs howled at the moon. [*plural count noun*]

The furniture makes the room appear cluttered. [*noncount noun*]

Do not use *the* before most singular proper nouns, such as names of people, cities, languages, and so on.

~~The~~ Dallas is a beautiful city.

Indefinite articles (*a, an*): used with singular count nouns only.

Use *a* before a word that begins with a consonant sound.

     a pencil

     a sports car

     a tropical rain forest

Use *an* before a word that begins with a vowel sound.

     an orange

     an hour

     an instrument

Do not use an indefinite article with a noncount noun.

     Water

~~A water~~ is leaking from the faucet.

No article: Plural count nouns and noncount nouns do not require *indefinite* articles. Plural count nouns and noncount nouns do not need *definite* articles when they refer to all of the items in a group.

Plural count nouns and noncount nouns

Every night I hear ~~a~~ dogs barking.

I needed to find ~~an~~ information in the library.

Plural count nouns

SPECIFIC ITEM   *The* dogs next door never stop barking.

ALL ITEMS IN A GROUP   Dogs make good pets.

Noncount nouns

SPECIFIC ITEM   *The* jewelry she wore to the party was beautiful.

ALL ITEMS IN A GROUP   Jewelry is expensive.

Verbs

Common Problem: *be* **verb is left out.**

INCORRECT   He sleeping now. She happy.

CORRECT   He *is* sleeping now. She *is* happy.

Verb Tenses

Tense refers to the time of action expressed by a verb.

Present tense (**base form or form with -s ending**): action taking place now. I *sleep* here. She *sleeps*. We *sleep* late every weekend.

Past tense (**-d or -ed ending**): past action. I *laughed*. He *laughed*. They *laughed* together.

Future tense (***will* + base form**): action that is going to take place. I *will go* to the movie. He *will run* in the marathon. You *will write* the paper.

Present perfect tense (***have* or *has* + past participle**): past action that was or will be completed. I *have spoken*. He *has washed* the floor. We *have made* lunch.

Past perfect tense (***had* + past participle**): past action completed before another past action. I *had spoken*. She *has been* busy. They *had noticed* a slight error.

Future perfect tense (***will* + *have* + past participle**): action that will begin and end in the future before another action happens. I *will have eaten*. She *will have danced* in the recital by then. You *will have taken* the train.

Present progressive tense (***am, are,* or *is* + present participle**): continuing action. I *am writing* a novel. He *is working* on a new project. They *are studying* for the test.

Past progressive tense (***was* or *were* + present participle**): past continuing action. I *was cleaning* the house. She *was working* in the yard. You *were making* dinner.

Future progressive tense (***will* + *be* + present participle**): future continuing action. I *will be traveling* to Europe. She *will be sightseeing* in New York. They *will be eating* together tonight.

Present perfect progressive tense (***have* or *has* + *been* + present participle**): past action that continues in the present. I *have been practicing*. He *has been sleeping* all morning. They *have been coming* every weekend.

Past perfect progressive tense (***had* + *been* + present participle**): continuous action completed before another past action. I *had been driving* for six hours. She *had been reading* when I arrived. They *had been singing*.

Future perfect progressive tense (***will* + *have* + *been* + present participle**): action that will begin, continue, and end in the future. I *will have been driving* for ten hours. He *will have been living* there for three years. You *will have been studying* for the test all afternoon.

ARCTIC OCEAN

CANADA

Anchorage

Seattle

Ottawa

UNITED STATES
Denver   Chicago
San Francisco   Was

Los Angeles   Atlanta   Ber
                Dallas

                    Miami
                        Havana   THE BAHAMA
MEXICO   DOM
Honolulu   CUBA
Mexico City   JAMAICA
PACIFIC   BELIZE   HAITI
                    HONDURAS
            GUATEMALA   NICARAGUA   ST.
            EL SALVADOR   PANAMA   GRE
            COSTA RICA
                    Bogotá   VENE
                        COLOMBIA
150°W   120°W   90°W
                    ECUADOR

                        PERU
OCEAN
                    Lima

                            CHILE

                        Santiago

Thursday 5:00 p.m.	Thursday 7:00 p.m.	Thursday 8:00 p.m.	Thursday 9:00 p.m
San Francisco, USA	Chicago, USA	Montreal, Canada	Sao Paulo, Brazil
	Mexico City, Mexico	New York, USA	Buenos Aires, Argen
		Havana, Cuba	
		Santiago, Chile	

Credits

Text Credits

Preface for Instructors: WPA Outcome Statements for First-Year Composition, from http://www.wpacouncil.org/positions/outcomes.html. Reprinted with permission of the Council of Writing Program Administrators. **Introduction:** Adapted from Robert S. Feldman, *P.O.W.E.R. Learning Strategies for Success in College and Life,* 2nd ed., New York: McGraw-Hill, 2003. Copyright © 2003 The McGraw-Hill Companies. Reproduced with permission of The McGraw-Hill Companies. **p. 6:** From Hentoff, Nat, "Misguided Multiculturalism," *The Village Voice,* July 19–25, 2000, pp. 29–30. Copyright © 2000 Village Voice Media. Reprinted with the permission of the *Village Voice.* **Fig. 2.3:** Reprinted by permission of Gary Klass, Illinois State University. **Fig. 2.6:** From Clarke & Cornish, "Modeling Offenders' Decisions," in *Crime and Justice,* Vol. 6, Tonry & Morris, eds., p. 169. University of Chicago Press, 1985. Reprinted by permission of the University of Chicago Press. **p. 40:** Excerpt from Robert Reich, "The Future of Work," as found in *Harper's Magazine,* 1989. Reprinted by permission of the author. **Fig. 3.1:** *China: Population Density, 2000.* Copyright © 2005 Center for International Earth Science Information Network (CIESIN), Columbia University; and Centro Internacional de Agricultura Tropical (CIAT). Gridded Population of the World Version 3 (GPWv3). Palisades, NY: Socioeconomic Data and Applications Center (SEDAC), CIESIN, Columbia University. Available at: http://sedac.ciesin.columbia.edu/gdw **Fig. 3.4:** From Galle, *Business Communication: A Technology-Based Approach,* 1st ed., 1996, Fig. 8.4, p. 240. Copyright © 1996 The McGraw-Hill Companies. Reproduced with permission of The McGraw-Hill Companies. **Fig. 3.6:** From Lahey, *Psychology: An Introduction,* 9th ed., 2007, Fig. 12.2, p. 466. Copyright © 2007 The McGraw-Hill Companies. Reproduced with permission of The McGraw-Hill Companies. **Fig. 3.7:** From Schaefer, *Sociology,* 10th ed., 2007, Fig. 2.1, p. 29. Copyright © 2007 The McGraw-Hill Companies. Reproduced with permission of The McGraw-Hill Companies. **Fig. 3.8:** Graph showing heat-related deaths in Chicago, 1995, from URL: http://www.usgcrp.gov/usgcrp/Library/nationalassessment/overviewhealth.htm#Temperature-related%20Illnesses%20and%20Deaths **Fig. 3.9:** Reprinted with permission from *State of the News Media* report by the Project for Excellent in Journalism: www.stateofthemedia.com. Based on Nielsen Media Research data. http://www.stateofthemedia.org/2007/chartland.asp?id=215&ct=line&dir=&sort=&col1_box=1 Nielsen data reprinted with permission from Nielsen Media Research. **p. 47:** From Jonathan Fast, 2003, "After Columbine: How People Mourn in Sudden Death," *Social Work,* October 2003, 48(4), 484–491. Copyright © 2003 National Association of Social Workers, Inc. *Social Work.* **p. 48:** Excerpt from Damian Robinson, 2004, "Riding into the Afterlife," *Archaeology,* March/April, 57(2), 10–11. Copyright © 2004 Archaeological Institute of America. **p. 48:** Excerpt from Jill Suitor, Rebecca Powers & Rachel Brown, "Avenues to Prestige Among Adolescents in Public and Religiously Affiliated High Schools," *Adolescence,* 39(154), 229–241. Reprinted by permission of Libra Publishers. **p. 49:** Excerpt from Mark Chapell, Diane Casey, Carmen De la Cruz, Jennifer Ferrell, Jennifer Forman, Randi Lipkin, Megan Newsham, Michael Sterling & Suzanne Whittaker, 2004, "Bullying in College by Students and Teachers," *Adolescence,* 39(153), 53–64. Reprinted by permission of Libra Publishers. **p. 49:** Excerpt from Robert Faust, 2004, "Integrated Pest Management Programs Strive to Solve Agricultural Problems," *Agricultural Research,* 52(11), 2-2. U.S. Department of Agriculture. **p. 49:** Excerpt from Yang Guorong, 2002, "Transforming Knowledge Into Wisdom," *Philosophy East and West,* 52(4), 441–458. Reprinted by permission of University of Hawaii Press. **Fig. 4.1:** Microsoft Word® screen shot reprinted with permission from Microsoft Corporation. **Fig. 4.3:** From William Collins, *Mathematics: Applications and Connections,* Course 2. Glencoe-McGraw-Hill, 1998. Copyright © 1998 The McGraw-Hill Companies. Reproduced with permission of The McGraw-Hill Companies. **Fig. 4.2:** Microsoft Word® screen shot reprinted with permission from Microsoft Corporation. **Fig. 5.1:** Microsoft Word® toolbar reprinted with permission from Microsoft Corporation. **p. 113:** Excerpt from Gloria Ladson Billings, *The Dreamkeepers: Successful Teachers of African-American Children,* San Francisco, CA: Jossey-Bass, 1994, pp. 35–36. Reprinted with permission of John Wiley & Sons, Inc. **Fig. 11.3:** Copyright © 1993, Vietnam Woman's Memorial Foundation, Inc., Glenna Goodacre, sculptor. 1735 Connecticut Avenue, NW, Third Floor, Washington, DC 20009. Reprinted by permission.: Microsoft Internet Explorer® screen shot reprinted with permission from Microsoft Corporation. **Fig. 11.4:** Screen shot of University of Alaska web site reprinted with permission. Microsoft Internet Explorer® screen shot reprinted with permission from Microsoft Corporation. **Fig. 11.5:** Screen shot of Library of Congress web site http://www.loc.gov Microsoft Internet Explorer® screen shot reprinted with permission from Microsoft Corporation. **Fig. 11.6:** Screen shot of Cedar Mesa Music: http:ccedarmesa.blogspot.com. Used by permission of Cedar Mesa Music. Microsoft Internet Explorer® screen shot reprinted with permission from Microsoft Corporation. **Fig. 14.1:** Screen shot of Fletcher Library web site at ASU: http://library.west.asu.edu/refguides/quick/index.html. Reprinted by permission of Fletcher Library, Arizona State University. Microsoft Internet Explorer® screen shot reprinted with permission from Microsoft Corporation. **Fig. 14.2:** Image published with permission of ProQuest. Further reproduction is prohibited without permission. Microsoft Internet Explorer® screen shot reprinted with permission from Microsoft Corporation. **Fig. 14.3:** Google search results © Google, Inc. Used with permission. Microsoft Internet Explorer® screen shot reprinted with permission from Microsoft Corporation. **Fig. 14.4:** Screen shot reprinted by permission of The City University of New York. Microsoft Internet Explorer® screen shot reprinted with permission from Microsoft Corporation. **Fig. 14.5:** Screen shot reprinted by permission of The City University of New York. Microsoft Internet Explorer® screen shot reprinted with permission from Microsoft Corporation. **Fig. 15.1:** Microsoft Excel® screen shot reprinted with permission from Microsoft Corporation. **Fig. 15.2:** Image courtesy of SkeetobiteWeather.com. **Fig. 15.3:** Deceptive hurricane map from the National Oceanic and Atmospheric Administration. **Fig. 16.1:** Screen shot from The Valley of the Shadow home page: http://valley.vcdh.virginia.edu. Reprinted with permission. Microsoft Internet Explorer® screen shot reprinted with permission from Microsoft Corporation. **Fig. 16.2:** Screen shot from CivilWarTraveler.com reprinted with permission from Page One Publications. Microsoft Internet Explorer® screen shot reprinted with permission from Microsoft Corporation. **Fig. 19.2:** Screen shot reprinted by permission of The City University of New York. Microsoft Internet Explorer® screen shot reprinted with permission from Microsoft Corporation. **Fig. 19.4:** Screen shot of New Orleans Online URL: http://www.neworleansonline.com/neworleans/music/satchmobio.html. Reprinted by permission of NewOrleansOnline.com (New Orleans Tourism Marketing Corporation). Microsoft Internet Explorer® screen shot reprinted with permission from Microsoft Corporation; Photos from New Orleans Online web site courtesy of the Louis Armstrong House Museum, Queens College, City University of New York, Flushing, New York. **p. 200:** Definition of "scat singing." Copyright © 2000 by Houghton Mifflin Company. Reproduced by permission from *The American Heritage Dictionary of the English Language,* Fourth Edition. **pp. 202–203:** Excerpt from *Down Beat Jazz 101: The Very Beginning* http://www.downbeat.com/default.asp?sect=education&subsect=jazz_02. Reprinted with permission from the Down Beat archives. **MLA Foldout:** Excerpt from copyright page from Laurence Bergreen, *Louis Armstrong: An Extravagant Life,* New York: Broadway, 1997. Reprinted by permission of Random House, Inc.; Journal contents page and first page of the article: Brent Hayes Edwards, "Louis Armstrong and the Syntax of Scat," *Critical Inquiry,* 28, 618–649 (2002). Reprinted by permission of the University of Chicago Press, via RightsLink; ProQuest search results published with permission of ProQuest. Further reproduction is prohibited without permission. **p. 258:** Watercolor caricature of Louis Armstrong and Joe Glaser. Courtesy of the Louis Armstrong House Museum, Queens College, City University of New York, Flushing, New York. **APA Foldout:** Title and copyright pages from *Exploring Agrodiversity,* by H. Brookfield. Copyright © 2001 Columbia University Press. Reprinted with permission of the publisher; Table of contents and article excerpt from Epstein, J. (2002). A voice in the wilderness. *Latin Trade,* 10(12), 26. Reprinted with permission of Latin Trade; Search results reprinted with permission from EBSCO. Screen shot of Microsoft® Internet Explorer used by permission of Microsoft Corporation. **p. 289, Fig. 1:** From D. Kaimowitz, B. Mertens, S. Wunder & P. Pacheco, 2002, *Hamburger Connection Fuels Amazon Destruction: Cattle Ranching and Deforestation in Brazil's Amazon.* Reprinted with permission. URL: http://www.cifor.cgiar.org/publications/pdf_files/media/Amazon. **pp. 313–314:** From W. Alva & C.B. Donnan, 1993, *Royal Tombs of Sipan,* p. 141. Los Angeles: Fowler Museum of Cultural History. Reprinted by permission. **p. 351:** Definition of "compare" from *Random House Webster's College Dictionary.* **p. 425:** Definition of "pig out." *ESL Learner's Edition of Random House Webster's Dictionary of American English,* Random House, 1997. **p. 425:** Definition of "haze." Copyright © 2000 by Houghton Mifflin Company. Reproduced by permission from *The American Heritage Dictionary of the English Language,* Fourth Edition. **p. 488:** Reprinted with the permission of Scribner, an imprint of Simon & Schuster Adult Publishing Group, from *The Complete Works of W. B. Yeats, Volume I: The Poems, Revised,* edited by Richard J. Finneran. Copyright © 1928 by The Macmillan Company; copyright renewed © 1956 by Georgie Yeats. All rights reserved.

Photo Credits

Preface: ix © 2007 Frank Lloyd Wright Foundation, Scottsdale, AZ/Artists Rights Society (ARS), NY; **p. xxxiii** © Visual Language. **Part 1: pp. 1, 3, 16, 35, 52, 73:** © Design Firm: Pentagram Design, NCY. Art Directors: John Klotnia and Woody Pirtle. Graphic Designers: Seung il Choi, John Klotnia, and Ivette Montes de Oca. Illustrators: Lori Anzalone, Dugald Stermer, and Kevin Torline. Printer: Sandy Alexander, Inc. Paper: Mohawk Vellum, 60 # Text Recycled. Client: National Audubon Society. © Pentagram; **pp. 4, 7:** Courtesy, ACLU; **p. 37:** © David Leeson/Dallas Morning News/Corbis; **p. 38:** © Frank Micelotta/Getty Images; **p. 40:** © Bettmann/Corbis **Part 2: pp. 85, 87, 94, 101, 112, 119, 124, 136:** © Philadelphia Museum of Art/Corbis; **p. 107:** © Reuters/Corbis; **p. 117:** © PPA/Topham/The Image Works; **p. 118:** © Jacob Halaska/Jupiter Images; **p. 126:** © Walter Evans/Library of Congress. **Part 3: pp. 151, 153, 158, 173, 179, 186, 189, 194, 207:** NASA and The Hubble Heritage Team (STSCi/AURA) **Part 4: pp. 213, 215, 224, 247, 248, 250:** © Mike Nevros/Folio, Inc.; **p. 258:** Courtesy of the Louis Armstrong House Museum Queens College. **Part 5: pp. 263, 265, 270, 285, 286:** Rollout Photograph K4010 © Justin Kerr. **Part 6: pp. 297, 299, 303, 306, 309, 315, 319, 326, 331, 336, 340, 346, 353:** © 2007 Frank Lloyd Wright Foundation, Scottsdale, AZ / Artists Rights Society (ARS), NY. **Part 7: pp. 363, 365, 372, 381, 390, 403, 417, 424:** © Royalty-Free/Corbis. **Part 8: pp. 445, 447, 461, 466, 468, 473, 482, 490, 495, 498, 500, 503, 506:** © Bridgeman-Giraudon/Art Resource, NY. **Part 9: pp. 513, 515, 528, 534, 539:** Agricultural Research Service, USDA. **Timeline: p. 542: (left)** © Bettmann/Corbis, **(right)** © Royalty-Free/Corbis; **p. 543:** © Royalty-Free/Corbis; **p. 544: (top)** © PNC/zefa/Corbis, **(bottom left)** © Corbis, **(bottom right)** © Burstein Collection/Corbis; **p. 545: (left)** © Nik Wheeler/Corbis, **(right)** Bildarchiv Preussischer Kulturbesitz/Art Resource, NY; **p. 546: (left)** © Bettmann/Corbis, **(right)** © Royalty-Free/Corbis, **(bottom)** © Burstein Collection/Corbis; **p. 547: (left)** © Royalty-Free/Corbis, **(right)** © Bettmann/Corbis; **p. 548:** © Corbis; **p. 549: (left)** © Bettmann/Corbis, **(right)** © Bettmann/Corbis; **p. 550: (left)** © Archivo Iconográfico, S.A./Corbis, **(top right)** © Fototeca Storica Nazionale/Getty Images, **(bottom right)** © Historical Picture Archive/Corbis; **p. 551: (left)** © Bettmann/Corbis, **(right)** © Bettmann/Corbis; **p. 552: (left)** © Bettmann/Corbis, **(right)** © Philadelphia Museum of Art/Corbis; **p. 553: (top left)** © Royalty-Free/Corbis, **(bottom left)** © Underwood & Underwood/ Corbis, **(right)** © Lebrecht Music & Arts; **p. 554:** © Bettmann/Corbis; **p. 555: (left)** © Corbis/Royalty Free, **(right)** © Will and Deni McIntyre/Photo Researchers, Inc.; **p. 556: (left)** © Photodisc/Getty Images, **(top)** © Bettmann/Corbis, **(bottom right)** © Jack Star/PhotoLink/Getty Images; **p. 557: (top left)** © Bettmann/Corbis, **(bottom left)** © Kyle Niemi/U.S. Coast Guard/Getty Images, **(right)** © Chad Baker/Ryan McVay/Getty Images

Index

Index for Multilingual Writers

Abbreviations and Symbols for Editing and Proofreading

abbr	Faulty abbreviation **56d**		*p*	Punctuation error
ad	Misused adjective or adverb **47**		⌃	Comma **49a–j**
agr	Problem with subject-verb or pronoun agreement **44, 46a**		*no ,*	Unnecessary comma **49k**
appr	Inappropriate word or phrase **39**		;	Semicolon **50**
			:	Colon **51**
art	Incorrect or missing article **48b**		⌄	Apostrophe **52**
awk	Awkward		" "	Quotation marks **53**
cap	Faulty capitalization **55**		*. ? !*	Period, question mark, exclamation point **54a–c**
case	Error in pronoun case **46c**		— ( ) [ ]	Dash, parentheses, **54d–e**
cliché	Overused expression **40d**		*. . . /*	brackets, ellipses, slash **54f–h**
coh	Problem with coherence **4f**		*para*	Problem with paraphrase **18b, 19c, e**
com	Incomplete comparison **31c**			
coord	Problem with coordination **36**		*pass*	Ineffective use of passive voice **38b**
cs	Comma splice **43**			
d	Diction problem **39, 40**		*pn agr*	Problem with pronoun agreement **46a**
dev	More development needed **3b, c**		*quote*	Problem with a quotation **19c**
dm	Dangling modifier **35e**		*ref*	Problem with pronoun reference **46b, 53a, e**
doc	Documentation problem			
	APA **26, 27**		*rep*	Unnecessary repetition **30a**
	MLA **21, 22**		*run-on*	Run-on (or fused) sentence **43**
emph	Problem with emphasis **36**		*sexist*	Sexist language **39e, 46a**
exact	Inexact word **40**		*shift*	Shift in point of view, tense, mood, or voice **33**
exam	Example needed **36**			
frag	Sentence fragment **42**		*sl*	Slang **39a**
fs	Fused (or run-on) sentence **43**		*sp*	Misspelled word **60**
hyph	Problem with hyphen **59**		*sub*	Problem with subordination **36**
inc	Incomplete construction **31**			
intro	Stronger introduction needed **3c**		*sv agr*	Problem with subject-verb agreement **44**
ital	Italics or underlining needed **58**		*t*	Verb tense error **45e**
			trans	Transition needed **4f**
jarg	Jargon **39c**		*usage*	See Glossary of Usage **41**
lc	Lowercase letter needed **55**		*var*	Vary your sentence structure **37**
mix	Mixed construction **32**			
mm	Misplaced modifier **35a–d**		*vb*	Verb problem **45**
mng	Meaning not clear		*w*	Wordy **30**
mood	Error in mood **45i**		*ww*	Wrong word **40**
ms	Error in manuscript form **5**		*//*	Parallelism needed **34**
	APA **28**		*#*	Add space
	MLA **24**		⌃	Insert
num	Error in number style **57**		⌒	Close up space
¶	Paragraph **3c**		*x*	Obvious error
			??	Unclear

Contents